UNDERSTANDING AND RESPONDING TO THE TERRORISM PHENOMENON

NATO Science for Peace and Security Series

This Series presents the results of scientific meetings supported under the NATO Programme: Science for Peace and Security (SPS).

The NATO SPS Programme supports meetings in the following Key Priority areas: (1) Defence Against Terrorism; (2) Countering other Threats to Security and (3) NATO, Partner and Mediterranean Dialogue Country Priorities. The types of meeting supported are generally "Advanced Study Institutes" and "Advanced Research Workshops". The NATO SPS Series collects together the results of these meetings. The meetings are co-organized by scientists from NATO countries and scientists from NATO's "Partner" or "Mediterranean Dialogue" countries. The observations and recommendations made at the meetings, as well as the contents of the volumes in the Series, reflect those of participants and contributors only; they should not necessarily be regarded as reflecting NATO views or policy.

Advanced Study Institutes (ASI) are high-level tutorial courses to convey the latest developments in a subject to an advanced-level audience.

Advanced Research Workshops (ARW) are expert meetings where an intense but informal exchange of views at the frontiers of a subject aims at identifying directions for future action.

Following a transformation of the programme in 2006 the Series has been re-named and re-organised. Recent volumes on topics not related to security, which result from meetings supported under the programme earlier, may be found in the NATO Science Series.

The Series is published by IOS Press, Amsterdam, and Springer Science and Business Media, Dordrecht, in conjunction with the NATO Public Diplomacy Division.

Sub-Series

A.	Chemistry and Biology	Springer Science and Business Media
B.	Physics and Biophysics	Springer Science and Business Media
C.	Environmental Security	Springer Science and Business Media
D.	Information and Communication Security	IOS Press
E.	Human and Societal Dynamics	IOS Press

http://www.nato.int/science
http://www.springer.com
http://www.iospress.nl

Understanding and Responding to the Terrorism Phenomenon

A Multi-Dimensional Perspective

Edited by

Ozgur Nikbay

Superintendent, Turkish National Police,
Virginia Commonwealth University, Virginia, USA

and

Suleyman Hancerli

Superintendent, Turkish National Police,
University of North Texas, Texas, USA

Amsterdam • Berlin • Oxford • Tokyo • Washington, DC

Published in cooperation with NATO Public Diplomacy Division

Proceedings of the NATO Advanced Research Workshop on Terrorist Operations
Washington, DC, USA
8–9 September 2006

ISBN 978-1-58603-750-5
Library of Congress Control Number: 2007928563

Publisher
IOS Press
Nieuwe Hemweg 6B
1013 BG Amsterdam
Netherlands
fax: +31 20 687 0019
e-mail: order@iospress.nl

Distributor in the UK and Ireland
Gazelle Books Services Ltd.
White Cross Mills
Hightown
Lancaster LA1 4XS
United Kingdom
fax: +44 1524 63232
e-mail: sales@gazellebooks.co.uk

Distributor in the USA and Canada
IOS Press, Inc.
4502 Rachael Manor Drive
Fairfax, VA 22032
USA
fax: +1 703 323 3668
e-mail: iosbooks@iospress.com

Understanding and Responding to the Terrorism Phenomenon
O. Nikbay and S. Hancerli (Eds.)
IOS Press, 2007

v

Preface

Suleyman Hancerli and Ozgur Nikbay, who are members of the Turkish National Police (TNP) and Turkish Institute for Police Studies (TIPS), have developed two new projects titled "Understanding and Responding to Terrorism Motivated Hostage and Kidnap Situations" and "Understanding and Responding to Suicide Attacks" and have submitted the proposals to NATO Headquarters in November, 2005. NATO has granted their two proposals and combined them under the Advanced Research Workshop (ARW) under the title "Terrorist Operations." In addition to NATO, this combined ARW was sponsored by the TNP, the University of North Texas, the Center on Terrorism at John Jay College, the Rutgers School of Criminal Justice, Michigan State University, Roger Williams University, the TIPS, and the Transnational Crime and Corruption Center at American University.

In addition to the ARW of the Terrorist Operations directed by Suleyman Hancerli and Ozgur Nikbay, NATO Headquarters funded two additional projects (1) "ARW of the Policing Responses to Terrorist Operations" directed by fellow TNP members Bilal Sevinc, Huseyin Durmaz, Ahmet S. Yayla, and Siddik Ekici, and (2) "ARW of the Sociological Approach to Terrorism" directed by TNP members Suleyman Ozeren and Ismail D. Gunes. The three projects together culminated in the convening the "Conference of Understanding and Responding to Terrorism: A Multi-dimensional Approach", which was held at the Capital Hilton Hotel in Washington, D.C., on September 08–09, 2006. This conference was the product of the remarkable efforts of the entire community of TIPS. This conference could not be accomplished without the TIPS members' outstanding amount of hard work. The executive directors of the conference created a website for the participants to visit and learn more about the conference. This website can be visited at http://tipsonline.org/nato/.

These three ARWs brought together well-known key speakers and participants from top universities, research study centers, and law enforcement agencies to understand the threat of terrorism, to promote cooperation between governments and agencies, and to look at practical ways to thwart and respond to terrorism within a multi-dimensional perspective. The number of the participants in this program was over 350. Approximately 200 key speakers out of the 350 participants made their presentations in the sessions throughout the program. The participants came to the conference from 17 different countries including but not limited to the USA, Turkey, Russia, Italy, France Azerbaijan, Kyrgyz Republic, Singapore, Georgia, Macedonia, Jordan, and Ukraine. The participants debated their ideas, thoughts, information, and knowledge about how to deal with the terrorism phenomenon and how to respond to the threat of terrorism in the 43 sessions throughout the program. All the representatives of the countries, law enforcement professionals, faculty members, public and civilian organizations had a chance to explore workable actions in combating terrorism, to respond to terrorism and advance the cooperation level against it. Given the strong scholarly record on terrorism by the participants, the executive directors of the ARWs invited the participants to submit their papers for publication by IOS Press.

The papers were collected and edited by Suleyman Hancerli and Ozgur Nikbay, the editors of this book. In fact, there are four parts and 34 chapters in this book. The first part (Understanding Terrorism) has six chapters; the second part (Suicide Attacks, Radical terrorism and Case Studies) has seven chapters; while the third part (Strategies and Tactics for Dealing with Terrorist Hostage Sieges, Hijackings and Kidnappings) has ten chapters; and the fourth part of the book (Counter-Terrorism Policies: Lessons for the Future) has eleven chapters. The editors selected as the title for the book *Understanding and Responding to the Terrorism Phenomenon*: *A Multi-Dimensional Perspective*. This title encapsulates the various themes of the 34 chapters of this book which highlight how to understand the terrorism phenomenon and analyze how to respond to terrorist operations and how to promote counter-terrorism policies on the part of the governments and law enforcement professionals.

March 2007

Suleyman Hancerli
Texas, US

Ozgur Nikbay
Virginia, US

Acknowledgments

We would like to state that this book is the product of the remarkable efforts of the entire community of the Turkish Institute for Police Studies, TIPS, in the United States. We, therefore, dedicate this book to all TIPS members who are all working hard to complete their graduate studies in the U.S.

We would first like to give special thanks to Gokhan Aydiner, the previous Commissioner of the Turkish National Police, Dr. Emile Sahliyeh, Dr. Herman Totten, Dr. Cindy J. Smith, Dr. Ami Pedahzur, Dr. Mohammed Al-Masri, Dr. Recep Gultekin, Samih Teymur, Selcuk Zengin, Ahmet Celik, Ali Ozdogan, Huseyin Durmaz, Lisa Hollinger, D.H. Shreve, and all TIPS members for their great guidance and support of this book.

We are also grateful to the Threats and Challenges Section of the Public Diplomacy Division in the NATO Headquarters and IOS Press for their support and guidance of this book. We would like to thank the authors of the chapters in this book for providing their well written and scholarly articles for this book. Lastly, we would also like to thank our families for their personal support.

About the Editors

Suleyman Hancerli is a Superintendent in the Turkish National Police, TNP. He, in fact, has been in the agency for 13 years. He used to work as an instructor in the Turkish National Police Academy between 1994 and 2000. He has been working as an instructor and head of the Tactical Training Unit at the Turkish International Academy against Drugs and Organized Crime, TADOC, since it was established by the TNP in cooperation with the office of the United Nations International Drug Control Program, UNDCP, in Ankara in 2000. He has a Bachelor's degree from the Police Academy in Turkey, a Master's degree in the Criminal Justice Department and has currently been doing Ph.D. studies in the Department of Information Science at the University of North Texas in the U.S. Suleyman Hancerli shared his information, knowledge, and experience about his policing experience with more than 20 Nations' law enforcement professionals during his teaching experience at Turkish National Police Academy, TADOC, and other police agencies abroad. He is specifically interested in researching terrorism, organized crimes, drugs, democratic policing, crisis management, and hostage holding situations.

Ozgur Nikbay is a Superintendent in the Turkish National Police, serving since 1995 and a Ph.D. candidate at the Center for Public Policy and Administration of Virginia Commonwealth University. He holds a B.A. degree from the Turkish National Police Academy, an M.A. degree from the Institute of Forensic Science at Istanbul University, and an M.S. degree from Criminal Justice Program at the University of Baltimore. He used to work as the chief supervisor in a newly established special motorcycle unit working for VIP escort and traffic services in Istanbul in 1995. He was deployed to the Intelligence Division for Counter-terrorism in Istanbul Police Department in 1997. He served there as an assistant supervisor of the Unit against a Revolutionary Left Wing terrorist group and later supervisor for the Bureau against Marxist-Leninist/separatist terrorist organizations. He has also international policing experience due to his service as a police officer for the United Nations Mission in Kosovo for one year. His academic interest is also the same as his professional area, which is counter-terrorism. He is specifically interested in researching suicide attacks, which is the topic he studied in both masters degrees and that he is currently working on for his dissertation.

List of Contributors

Ahmet Pek, Chief of Police
Head of Anti-Smuggling and Organized Crime Department, Ankara, Turkey

Agostino V. Hassell, Ph.D.
Repton Group LLC, NY, US

Ali Ozdogan, Ph.D. Candidate
American University, Department of Government, Washington DC, US

Aziz Ozmen, Ph.D. Candidate
Sam Houston State University, College of Criminal Justice, TX, US

Brian Forst, Ph.D.
American University, School of Public Affairs, Washington DC, US

Behsat Ekici, Ph.D. Student
University of Pittsburgh, Public and International Affairs, PA, US

Brian Richardson, Ph.D.
University of North Texas, Department of Communication Studies, TX, US

Cindy J. Smith, Ph.D.
University of Baltimore, Criminal Justice Graduate Program, MD, US

Charles B. Strozier, Ph.D.
John Jay College, Center on Terrorism at John Jay College, NY, US

Christopher T. Voss
Crisis Negotiation Unit, FBI Academy, Quantico, VA, US

Emrullah Uslu, Ph.D. Candidate
University of Utah, Middle East Center, UT, US

Ekrem Mus, Ph.D. Candidate
Virginia Commonwealth University, Centre for Public Policy, VA, US

Ferhat Goktepe, Ph.D. Candidate
Spalding University, College of Education, KY, US

Garry Noesner, FBI Retired
Senior Vice President, Control Risks Group, Washington DC, US

Graeme R. Newman, Ph.D.
The University at Albany, US

I-Shian Suen, Ph.D.
Virginia Commonwealth University, Public Policy and Administration, VA, US

Jeremy L. Jones
Crisis Negotiation Unit, FBI Academy, Quantico, VA, US

John Flood, FBI Chief Negotiator
Head of Crisis Negotiation Unit, FBI Academy, Quantico, VA, US

Kamil Yilmaz, Ph.D. Candidate
Columbia University, School of International and Public Affairs, NY, US

Keith Spence, Ph.D.
University of Leicester, Department of Criminology, Leicester, UK

Leonid Syukiyaynen, Ph.D.
Higher School of Academics, Moscow, Russia

Marie I. Chevrier, Ph.D.
University of Texas at Dallas, School of Social Sciences, TX, US

Morton Gulak, Ph.D.
Virginia Commonwealth University, School of Government, VA, US

Murat Gunbeyi, Ph.D. Candidate
Spalding University, College of Education, KY, US

Maki Haberfeld, Ph.D.
John Jay College of Criminal Justice, Law and Police Science, NY, USA

Murat Kocak, Ph.D. Student
Kent State University, Department of Political Science, OH, US

Mike Webster, Ph.D.
Centurion Consulting Services Ltd., BC, Canada

Niyazi Ekici, Ph.D. Candidate
Rutgers University, School of Criminal Justice, NJ, US

Onder Aytac, Ph.D.
Turkish National Police Academy (Bachelor Program), Ankara, Turkey

Robert J. Louden, Ph.D.
Georgian Court University, Department of Criminal Justice, NJ, US

Ronald V. Clarke, Ph.D.
Rutgers University, School of Criminal Justice, NJ, US

Ramazan Yalcinkaya, Ph.D.
University of North Texas, Department of Information Science, TX, US

Seda Demiralp, Ph.D. Student
American University, Department of Government, Washington DC, US

Serhan Ercikti, Ph.D. Candidate
University of Louisville, Education and Human Development, KY, US

Suleyman Demirci, Ph.D. (ABD)
Virginia Commonwealth University, Public Policy and Administration, VA, US

Steve Romano, FBI Retired
President of Consulting and Training of Romano & Associates, SC, US

Saliha Koday, Ph.D.
Ataturk University, Erzurum, Turkey

Tuncay Durna, Ph.D.
Police Training Adviser, OSCE Mission to Serbia

Thomas Mijares, Ph.D.
Southwest Texas State University, Criminal Justice Department, TX, US

Tom Strentz, Ph.D.
Retired FBI Chief Negotiator, LA, US

Ulvi Kun, Ph.D. Candidate
Virginia Commonwealth University, Centre for Public Policy, VA, US

Wayne Hanniman, Inspector
National Security Community Outreach Program, RCMP, Ontario, Canada

Yoram Schweitzer
Tel Aviv University, Jaffee Center for Strategic Studies, Israel

Zeki Koday, Ph.D.
Ataturk University, Erzurum, Turkey

Contents

Part I

Understanding Terrorism

Understanding and Responding to Terrorism

Suleyman HANCERLI [a1] and Ozgur NIKBAY [b2]
[a]*University of North Texas,* [b]*Virginia Commonwealth University*

Abstract. This study is the executive summary of the entire book consisting of four primary parts: (1) understanding the terrorism phenomenon; (2) suicide attacks, radical terrorism and case studies; (3) strategies and tactics for dealing with terrorist hostage sieges, hijackings, and kidnappings; and (4) counter-terrorism policies and lessons for the future. The 34 chapters in the 4 parts are summarized by the authors in this study for the readers to understand every aspect of the terrorism phenomenon carefully processed throughout this book.

Keywords. Terrorism, terrorist operations, suicide attacks, hijacking, kidnapping, hostage sieges, and counter-terrorism policies.

Introduction

Terrorism is as old as humanity itself. Very little has changed in the methods and reasons for these attacks. The threats of terrorism still terrify governments, public professionals, citizens, organizations, economies, and business industries. They also create a great deal of psychological distress within the general populations of affected areas. When a terrorist attack takes place in a country, everybody suffers either physically or psychologically from this attack. Terrorists ravage everyday life of populations by causing fear and anxiety in communities through their actions. They have used many tactics, such as suicide attacks, hijacking, kidnapping, and hostage sieges.

Terrorists take advantages of the media, internet, and other technologies to get information about their potential targets. They are well prepared and more organized than ever. They usually select figurative and/or political targets. That is why they attacked the twin towers on September 11, 2001. After this tragic event, many governments felt how vulnerable their citizens and lands were to terrorist attacks. Americans were feeling secure within their borders before 9/11. However, this tragedy changed everything and highlighted the governments' security deficiencies. Since terrorism as a global phenomenon required a global response, dealing with terrorist activities requires not only changes in law enforcement practices but also new governmental responses. Many governments, therefore, adapted new counter-terrorism policies and changed their response strategies to fight terrorism. All nations are

---

[1] Suleyman Hancerli is a Superintendent in the Turkish National Police. He has been in the agency for 13 years.
[2] Ozgur Nikbay is a Superintendent in the Turkish National Police. He has been in the agency for 12 years.

expected to have cooperation, solidarity, combined initiatives, and information sharing in combating terrorism because terrorist attacks are not limited within the borders of any nations. The governments today are keenly aware of the importance of cooperation and collaboration between law enforcement and military professionals in the war on terrorism.

However, there are some difficulties. One of them is to make a clear definition of terrorism because although a particular group might be considered a terrorist entity to one nation, they may be considered freedom fighters to another. Making a universal definition of terrorism might be very difficult, but almost every definition of terrorism contains the same general characteristics. A definition of terrorism quoted from the American Heritage Dictionary in the Fourth Edition [1] is as follow:

"The unlawful use or threatened use of force or violence by a person or an organized group against people or property with the intention of intimidating or coercing societies or governments, often for ideological or political reasons."[3]

There are four primary sections in this book: the first, "Understanding Terrorism" has six chapters; the second, "Suicide Attacks, Radical terrorism and Case Studies" has seven chapters; while the third, "Strategies and Tactics for Dealing with Terrorist Hostage Sieges, Hijackings and Kidnappings" has ten chapters; and the fourth section of the book "Counter-Terrorism Policies: Lessons for the Future" has eleven chapters. This book, "Understanding and Responding to the Terrorism Phenomenon: A Multi-Dimensional Perspective", encapsulates these various themes which highlighted how to understand the terrorism phenomenon and analyzed how to respond to terrorist operations and how to promote counter terrorism policies. This chapter is the executive summary of this book.

1. Part I:
Understanding Terrorism

There are six chapters in this part, and each chapter focuses on a different aspect of terrorism phenomenon. The six chapters also help the readers understand the different features of terrorist attacks.

Strentz [2] talks about the personality types of terrorists. He states that in order to more effectively deal with terrorist groups, law enforcement professionals must know those three distinct personality types in a terrorist group: (1) leader, (2) opportunist, and (3) follower/idealist. Being aware of these three characterizations of members in a terrorist organization will help counter terrorist professionals identify and infiltrate these groups through use of psychological profiling.

In his study, Strozier [3] explains how terrorists use the Internet to attack their targets. Strozier, in fact, states how the advent of the Internet has lent itself to the facilitation of terrorist activities. He talks about three main cases used to exemplify this problem. The first one is the March 11, 2004 attacks, which killed 191 people and wounded over 1,800 on the train system in Spain by Moroccan radicals. These terrorists had met in prison and were found to have kept in touch using the Internet. In addition to that, they apparently regularly visited several websites which had an effect on their actions. Secondly, the London suicide bombers of July 7, 2006 used the

---

[3] Available from: http://www.bartleby.com/61/26/T0122600.html [Retrieved on March 19, 2007]

internet to get all the necessary information for those attacks. Lastly, by reading information on the Internet, a couple of young people who participated in the planning of a terrorist attack in Australia in November of 2005 became radicalized to the point of desiring to be a part of the plan. It is clear that the age of communication and the vast amount of technology available has provided groups like Al-Qaeda with a breeding ground for hate and a site for recruitment. With technological advances, terrorists will have even more tools at their disposal, the next probably being live feeds from advanced cell phones.

Chevrier [4] focuses on the potential threat of bioterrorism in her study by starting with an explanation of what it is, what we know about it, and how it should be addressed. Bioterrorism is defined as the use of a biological agent or toxin by a group or individual with ties to a country's government or acting as an individual to harm another group or individual. It is not so much that actual incident that puts fear into people as the possibility of one. Because the destruction from a biological weapon can be so devastating, it behooves governments to maintain a protocol in the event of an incident as well as to provide preventative measures for the general public, for example, through vaccination or by having the antidote for such agents stockpiled. Some ways that governments can decrease the chances of a biological war are having close monitoring of their own biological agents and being open and honest about the goings on within the research departments working with these agents. Doing this will give justification for such activities and prevent other countries from building their own arsenals in the "what if" scenario. Since many governments are certainly doing research in this field, thereby not only providing expertise in the field for said country but also creating the opportunity for access to those who might want to use biological weapons illegally, strict regulations must be passed regarding the correct way to keep these agents secure. Through strengthening the Biological Weapons Convention, the goal of keeping all countries safe from illegal use of biological weapons may be met.

In his study on the supply and demand of terrorism, Forst [5] asserts that fear at a reasonable level can be beneficial in society to motivate us to protect ourselves. On the other hand, irrational fear, being bigger than the potential threat, is a burden that causes nations to overreact to perceived dangers. Forst uses the analogy of a market with both supply and demand to refer to terrorism. In this framework, the supply side, which receives all the attention, is made up of ideological causes. In contrast, the demand side, being based on fear, would be the nations that overreact to the fear of an attack and create more hatred among those that suffer under the sanctions. Forst suggests changing the way that Office of Homeland Security and affiliated agencies manage terrorist threats and also suggests that such organizations be aware of the public fear and work to manage it as well. Forst sums up by saying that we can rest assured and learn to cope with the fear if we work toward securing our primary targets from terrorists and use intelligence to discover and capture definite terrorists.

According to Ozsoy [6], the best defense against terrorism is education which not only teaches about Islam but also helps society understand the motives behind the terrorists' actions. Using the term 'Islamic terror' is not only an insult to all peace-loving Muslims but also a falsehood perpetuated in the world today. The acts of terrorism are no more concurrent with the rules of Islam than with the laws of Christianity or Judaism. Both murder and suicide are mortal sins according to the teachings of the Qur'an, which means that the people who condone terrorism are clearly extremists with a warped sense of Islam and in no way represent the true Muslim. Therefore, seeing the terrorist through an Islamic lens is counter-productive to fighting it. Only by identifying each different terrorist organization's rationale for its actions can terrorism be effectively combated. Moreover, Ozsoy coins the term 'man of society,' which is something that each person should strive to be. To become this person, one must learn to understand the needs of both his regional area and his role within the global community, including the interdependency among all nations at the same time recognizing the inherent value of the individual himself. Being able to balance between individual needs and global responsibilities is a trait that all people will need in the era of globalization.

2. Part II:
Suicide Attacks, Radical Terrorism and Case studies

There are seven chapters in this part, and each chapter focuses on a different aspect of suicide attacks, suicide bombings and/or terrorist groups in a case study approach.

Nikbay, Smith, and Mus [7] attempt to remedy the problem of not having enough data about suicide bombers by compiling previous research done by them with further research. By doing this, they hope to provide a database accessible to law enforcement on the profiles and characteristics of suicide bombers. This is an especially important area of research because suicide bombers present a serious threat to the public with their ability to easily target an area and inflict mass casualties. In order to accomplish the goal of providing this information, the authors investigate suicide attacks that were planned but not completed, attempted unsuccessfully, and carried out in Turkey from 1996 to 2006. Using Turkish National Police records, both quantitative and qualitative analysis was done since the record offered both statistical data and interviews with attackers. By examining and analyzing the data, some trends could be noticed. Changes could be found in three areas; in the groups that perpetrate suicide attacks (from mostly the PKK-KONGRA GEL to mostly Al-Qaeda), in the targets chosen, and in the common characteristics of bombers. Based on the discovery of these changes, the authors suggest that data be continually collected and records be regularly updated so that officials in Turkey can remain informed about the issues. Also, they assert that the suicide bombers' terrorist organization affiliation be taken into account because the reasons for carrying out such attacks varies based on the organization.

Using interviews with Palestinian suicide bombers who were dispatched from 1993 to 2006, Schweitzer [8] catalogs the history of Palestinian suicide bombings dividing the time spans into two periods of April 1993 to March 2000 and October 2000 to June 2006. The two time periods are significant in the fact that the first period was less intense with many of the attempts being poorly done and being less successful. However, in the second period, the successful suicide bombing rate more than tripled with more than 200 additional unsuccessful attacks. In this second period, the attacks became more sophisticated with less error in delivery.

Yilmaz [9] talks about radical Islamist movements in the former Soviet regions. Yilmaz, in fact, agrees with Ozsoy [6] that the term Islamic terror is problematic. He contends that in some former Soviet regions Islam is seen as a political movement with the agenda of separation from government and even with a motive to achieve anarchy in those regions. These beliefs lead to the government's rationale of approaching Islam as having a terrorist or antigovernment agenda, meaning that military and police action against Muslims is at minimum justified and possibly necessary. In fact, these former Soviet regions seem to think that they have the West's stamp of approval in being part of the war on terror. There is a need on the part of governments to turn this thinking around. These post-Soviet regimes should realize that the growth of Islam in their territories is not a threat but actually an asset to their countries. The following actions should be taken to rectify the situation: Governments must protect the rights and freedom of religion of all citizens within their borders. They also must join forces with people of true Islamic faith to tap into the strength of Islam in fighting extremists and separatists. They must provide education for Russian people about the background and history of true Islam. Finally, due to the fact that Islam has political clout in the world, they should continue to cultivate relationships with countries with large Muslim populations, like they have with Turkey, in which case both sides benefited economically, through tourism and in security.

Demiralp [10] discusses the phenomenon of how the fringe population (minority, politically powerless, poor) becomes less radicalized and more conforming to the rule of law when their chance to become part of the institution increases. Three examples are given from other countries: radical socialists in Latin America and Islamists in both Jordan and Egypt. In all three of these cases, the anarchist groups realized that they could further their cause through democratic means when opportunities for them opened up in the government. This realization led to them becoming more moderate and keeping their activities within the rule of law since they now had power in the law-making body. The current case discussed is the one of Turkey. Like the other countries, Turkey is experiencing a moderation of some of the previously radicalized populations. Having changed some policies to decentralize the government and get ready for acceptance into the EU, they have made it more possible for the people who before felt powerless and disenfranchised to come to the center and begin profiting through legal democratic processes. These cases prove that when you make political, economic, and cultural resources more accessible to all citizens of a country, there is less cause for discontent and less need for radicalization. These new developments in Turkey have caused leaders in the radical Islamist and separatist Kurdish parties to stop emphasizing their ethnic and religious distinctions from the majority in Turkey and start preaching acceptance of pluralist values that benefit the whole of the population. Advances like these, which are desired by governments to reduce violence within their borders, should be a sign for all countries to pay attention and include the minority populations in the running of the country so that they would have some stake in it.

The pro-PKK-KONGRA GEL activities have enjoyed the freedom to organize within some European countries, leading to frustration in efforts to implement effective countermeasures and ultimately frustration toward these other countries on the part of Turkey. This situation arises from the different perspectives held by such European countries and Turkey on international relations, the former having the opinion that international relations are based on interdependency theories and the latter having the opinion that the realist perspective shows the world as "anarchy." Turkey would like European countries to crack down on PKK-KONGRA GEL associations and stop the flow of financial support to them. Neither side appears to trust the other side, with Europe finding Turkey's record on human rights to be lacking and Turkey distrusting Europe due to historical and cultural differences. In sum, Europe and Turkey approach this situation from two competing viewpoints. Turkey's realist leaning tells it to solve the pro-PKK-KONGRA GEL activities through any means necessary, whereas some European countries' neo-liberal tendency in which non-governmental organizations have influence in governmental activities tells it to allow such organizations to exist in freedom to a point [11].

Pek and Ekici [12] argued that by getting involved in all aspects of the illegal drug trade in the 1990s and making liaisons with many Kurdish organized crime networks, the PKK-KONGRA GEL was able to facilitate the growth of its military and propaganda machine. Evidence was obtained by the KOMDB (Anti-Smuggling and Organized Crime Department in the Turkish National Police) that implicated the PKK-KONGRA GEL in numerous activities, including drug production, trafficking, delivery, and turf warfare. In addition to that, they used connections with financial institutions to launder the money from both their legal and illegal activities. These funds, in turn, were used for more propaganda, cultural associations and the organization formerly known as MED TV, now called MEDYA TV. Through the information collected from many sources both inside and outside the PKK-KONGRA GEL, law enforcement was able to ascertain that not only did the PKK-KONGRA GEL make use of Kurdish organized crime organizations, but also they exploited Kurdish refugees, especially children, for tasks like drug running. The PKK-KONGRA GEL accomplished their goals through many avenues: setting up customs check points along the borders of Turkey, Iran, and Iraq, using their highly trained military system for transporting drugs, and making use of a communication system based on the Kurdish language, which made surveillance and penetration by law enforcement difficult. The success of their organization is evidenced by the fact that numerous heroin markets in some EU countries were controlled by them.

Using Geographic Information Systems (GIS) and focusing on terrorist attacks perpetrated by PKK-KONGRA GEL from 2003 to 2004, Demirci and Suen [13] attempt to draw conclusions about the locations in which terror incidents commonly occur. They state that by becoming aware of these high frequency areas, law enforcement can focus its resources better and even become proactive in heading off possible attacks on the more predicted targets. Spatial methodologies should be used to exploit GIS, whose usage to now has been limited to street level crimes, in a way not done before. By doing this, new problem solving strategies, like Hotspot policing and Information Driven Policing, can be ascertained by intelligence agencies and law enforcement. GIS is able to offer a variety of uses. For example, it can be used to show, scrutinize, and disseminate spatial and non-spatial data, to combine many data sets, to give an analytical framework for solving problems, to advance good decision-making and resource assignment and distribution, to examine spatial dependency and pattern among specific juxtaposed cities, and to advance intelligence based on location. With all of these capabilities, law enforcement and intelligence agencies can derive a huge benefit from utilizing GIS.

3. Part III:
Strategies and Tactics for Dealing with Terrorist Hostage Sieges, Hijackings and Kidnappings

This part consists of ten chapters which focuses on a different aspect of terrorist attacks, including hostage sieges, hijackings, skyjackings, and/or kidnap situations. These chapters make huge contributions to the hostage negotiation practices and tactical team intervention strategies of law enforcement agencies in dealing with these particular terrorist attacks.

Using a perspective from research done by Louden in 1999, "The Structure and Procedures of Hostage/Crisis Negotiation Units in Police Organizations", Louden [14] examines the issues surrounding hostage negotiation and asserts that it should continue to be used as a strategy by law enforcement due to its effectiveness. After defining negotiation as communicating and coming to a compromise and defining hostage-taking as forcing another to remain against his/her will by coercion and threat of death and using this situation to get a third party to comply with some wish of the hostage taker, Louden goes on to discuss the history of hostage incidents from back when the tactical approach was the preferred method of dealing with these situations. He points out that this began to change after the 1972 kidnappings at the Munich Olympics and the aftermath of the dismal outcome from using a tactical assault. After that time, the police agencies in the U.S. along with the FBI began to implement and enhance their use of hostage negotiation and continued to do so up until the September 11 attacks. Those attacks called this practice into question, since it was clear that this strategy would not and did not work in these attacks. However, the author wants to emphasize that negotiation is still a very important strategy that must be honed and used by law enforcement. Lastly the author informs that, recently, the FBI and many police agencies have stopped using the term "hostage negotiation" and have preferred "crisis negotiation."

By analyzing the ITERATE dataset, Kocak [15] contends that in a hostage situation, the best way to increase the probability of survival of the hostages is by implementing the negotiation strategy. The same dataset shows that the shootout strategy results in higher fatalities whether carried out at the beginning of an incident or after negotiations have failed. Except in rare cases, such as when hostage takers intend to kill all hostages regardless of the negotiators action, negotiation is the option that increases the likelihood of a peaceful outcome. Considering this conclusion, it is vital that governments not only use the negotiation option before other options, but also that they maintain highly trained negotiation teams to deal with these situations. Another study by Hancerli [16] draws the same conclusions and goes on to point out that collective research studies would be useful in determining new guidelines for negotiation practices.

Noesner [17] acknowledges the fact that in addition to hijacking and suicide bombings, terrorists use tactics such as hostage taking. Because of this fact, he agrees with Hancerli [16] and others who have researched this topic that governments must have well trained negotiation teams with professionals who specialize in crisis management. He contends that it is through this method rather than through tactical responses that resolution can be brought to a hostage situation. In order to prepare for such an event, law enforcement must develop systematic procedures, well thought out policies, and training with hostage siege simulations on a regular basis. In addition, he also emphasizes that politicians must stand back and allow the trained professionals to deal with such situations, and they must be careful when talking to the media because the statements made by government officials during a hostage siege can influence the outcome for the worse. Since it is the law enforcement officers who are trained to resolve these types of incidents, it is they who must take the lead. In other words, even if politicians become worried about the elapsing of time in a hostage incident, they should refrain from talking to the media and give the negotiation team time to bring it to a peaceful conclusion. This process is helpful not only in achieving the ultimate goal, which is the safe release of the hostages, but also in collecting information from the hostage takers. A country that can effectively resolve a hostage situation will be viewed as a success.

Richardson [18] argues for using a systems perspective when implementing crisis negotiation. He uses the analogy of a body system wherein our different organs, muscles, veins, etc. not only work together, but depend on each other in a symbiotic way. If one part of our body system breaks down, it wreaks havoc on the other parts, ultimately causing the whole system to fail. Because all parts in a system work interdependently rather than independently, each affects the other. If this view is taken toward negotiation, it becomes clear that each part of a hostage situation, including the negotiation team, the tactical team, the hostage, the hostage taker, the media, and possibly others, are working interdependently. How any part of the system acts causes a reaction in another part of the system. Viewing crisis negotiation this way will help all parties involved understand the complex relationships that exist, hopefully improving the abilities of hostage negotiators to reach an acceptable outcome in hostage situations.

In his study, Webster [19] talks about kidnap situations and characterizes them into two distinct categories, which are instrumental kidnapping and expressive kidnapping. First, some examples of instrumentally motivated kidnapping are for monetary gain, to achieve an agenda of either causing some action or stopping some action, as part of a larger plan, or as a shield to protect the kidnappers themselves. Second, some examples of expressively motivated kidnappings are to have the person, like when a parent takes a child, to prove power or strength, to sexually assault, murder or both, as revenge, or for vigilantism. In the first type of kidnapping, the kidnapping is done in order to bring about some other result, but in the second type, the kidnapping itself was the goal of the kidnapper. The motivations for each are different, and these differences in motivation have brought about a change in the type of victim preferred by the kidnapper. Although in the past, specific people were chosen due to a high chance of monetary gain or political influence, nowadays even a common person can randomly become a target. In Iraq, most kidnappings begin as an instrumental motive, but when in the end the hostage takers cannot achieve their goals, it sometimes turns into an expressive motive. Therefore, in kidnapping situations, negotiation should be used as an effective means to overcome the inherent mistrust between hostage takers and hostage negotiators. Negotiators must come to a conclusion deemed fair by both sides for a resolution to be effective. It is clear that in order to achieve this, negotiators must be highly trained and able to plan and execute skillful negotiations.

Due to the economic damage caused to developing countries by rampant kidnapping within their borders, Richardson, Voss, Flood, and Jones [20] make a case for systematic approach, having two parts, to decrease the incidence of kidnapping. Obviously, kidnapping is done for economic reasons, so making it less lucrative should be part of the answer. Law makers and law enforcement professionals can raise the cost of such a crime by passing tough legislation regarding prosecution and conviction of kidnappers. At the same time, using crisis negotiation techniques will help secure the life of the hostage while gathering data for evidence in future court cases. Since it is surely a goal of all countries wanting to develop economically through investment and tourism to reduce the likelihood of kidnapping, this two pronged approach should be used as an effective deterrent to kidnappers due to the fact that the business of kidnapping becomes more difficult with a higher cost and less payoff.

Romano [21] approaches the topic of kidnapping from the perspective of international companies. He points out the idea that international companies may be especially vulnerable to kidnappings of employees. Romano uses the sole definition of kidnapping as the detention of an individual for the purpose of getting money. He goes on to say that even in cases of kidnapping by terrorist groups, like the FARC in Colombia or Abu Sayyaf Group in the Philippines, the goal is ultimately to get paid. Since payment secures the safe return of the hostage, the party that will pay the ransom has some negotiation power. In the case of international companies with employees abroad, especially Americans and people from other western countries, the possibility of dealing with a kidnapping situation increases. Therefore, it is necessary for such companies to have contingency plans in place for the protection of their employees. By having a well thought out plan of action in such an event with trained members of the corporation able to interface with law enforcement, governments, and the media, the odds of a successful outcome with the return of the victim will improve.

Yalcinkaya and Ozmen [22] discuss hijack situations and aviation securities. According to them, 9/11 attacks caused the aviation industry to reexamine its need for security. In their study, they emphasize how easily aviation can be targeted and how much destruction can be done in such a case. They point out that airplanes are often targeted by terrorists because of the potential for so much fear and destruction to be spread. In addition to that, it is an easily accessible area due to inherent difficulties in creating security around airports for several reasons, a lack of intelligence sharing or international security standards, vulnerability in computer databases, cargo areas and airplanes, and ease of forgery of travel documents to name a few. These issues have put fear into the minds of the public and have worried governments greatly. Since in the past, the airline industry was focused on customer satisfaction and decreasing costs to turn profits, they neglected security concerns. However, all that has changed as of 9/11, and efforts to make aviation even more secure should be pursued.

Mijares [23] focuses on critical incidents and discusses the important aspects of how they need to be dealt with. Mijares defines critical incidents as situations in which the urgent and serious nature of what transpires requires more training than a typical police officer has. As a matter of fact, his main point is that the officers who respond first to these situations need to be well trained because what happens in the beginning of dealing with it sets the course for either a failed or successful outcome. Mijares feels that the current training received by patrol officers is insufficient because they don't get a chance to practice the skills. He, therefore, recommends that training consist of simulations of critical incidents that are modeled after past incidents. Finally, he emphasizes that all responses to incidents must follow the letter of the law and be justifiable based on the traditions of the criminal justice system.

4. Part IV:
Counter Terrorism Policies and Lessons for the Future

There are eleven chapters in this part, and each chapter focuses on a different aspect of counter-terrorism policies and responding strategies of governments in the war on terrorism. These chapters make significant contributions to the counter-terrorism strategies of governments. The summaries of the chapters in this part help the readers understand the different features of counter-terrorism measurements of governments.

In their study, Clarke and Newman [24] talk about the perspective of situational crime prevention. They, in fact, remove the distinction between crime and terrorism and focus on using situational crime prevention to decrease the likelihood of terrorist attacks. They theorize that since both crime and terrorism depend on the ability of the criminal/terrorist to obtain the tools to achieve their plans, they can both be approached from a perspective of situational crime prevention. They further argue that to reduce terrorism, you must make it difficult or impossible for terrorists to get the tools they need to carry out their attacks. Those tools would be any device providing means of communication or transportation, money, false documents, and intelligence on targets. In their opinion, if we want to interrupt the ability to acquire these tools, we need to change them, making them harder to use illegally, reduce the supply, and keep records of who has obtained these tools. Finally, in order to decrease the benefit of committing terrorist acts and increase the risk to terrorists, we should make it harder to attain their goals by protecting targets attractive to them, strengthen controls on tools and weapons needed for their actions, take away the rewards of terrorism by using bomb and bullet proof materials when building important buildings, and avoid provoking terrorists with the use of violence. Following these guidelines will lead to situational crime prevention, which will be more likely to impact the incidence of terrorism.

Gulak, Kun, Koday and Koday [25] inquire about how we can protect our critical infrastructures, such as telecommunications, electric plants, and so on, from terrorist attacks. Their conclusion is that by using "crime prevention through environmental design (CPTED), we can strengthen these utilities and make them less vulnerable to attack. The three strategies for accomplishing the goal of producing desired behavioral effects are designing in "natural access control," providing opportunity for easy surveillance, and using emblems, flags, or other proprietary markers to show ownership. Following these strategies not only improve the sense of safety around the building but also causes crime to drop in frequency. These strategies should be used in conjunction with other programs meant to reduce crime, such as Neighborhood Watch Programs. In order to achieve the goals of CPTED, governmental grants should be provided by local, state, and federal branches and guidelines of all categories should be made available for proper implementation. These funds should also be used to train the operating officers in CPTED and security awareness. Lastly, all highly populated public spaces should use CPTED in their design. They point out that when our infrastructure is more secure, it can reduce the fear that the threat of terrorism brings.

By analyzing the response to terrorist threats that Canada enacted after the 9/11 attacks, Hanniman [26] proposes that a multi-faceted approach in a community to handling the threat of terror in the world since 2001 is the best way to prevent and react to terrorism and should be used as a model for other countries. Canada has been successful in improving national security by involving the public in addition to using law enforcement and increasing security measures. Through an in-depth case study it has become apparent that the policies implemented by Canada, such as improving the ability to investigate, obtaining cultural sensitivity training for investigators, developing new methods for increasing human resources, establishing community outreach programs, especially for youths, and enlisting leaders of many different ethnicities in the community to stand up against terror has been ultimately successful in battling terrorism. It is clear that through all these efforts rather than through only one or a couple of them the loftiest of goals can be reached.

According to Durna and Hancerli [27], even in countries which have declared a so called "war on terror," policies that go against the basic principles and standards of democracy should be avoided. Unfortunately, one of the goals of terrorists and one that is often achieved by them is to create such a fear in the government that less than democratic tactics are used by law enforcement against not only the terrorists but also the general public because any one of them could be part of a terrorist organization. These policies lead to mistrust of the government on the part of the citizens in the country, making them more easily targeted by terrorists for recruitment and setting the stage for an overthrow of the government. It becomes a vicious cycle where neither the public nor the government profits. In other words, terrorists, such as PKK-KONGRA GEL, may want governments to take action against them very harshly because the civilians in the community may also suffer from the counter actions of governments. Their aim is to get support from the citizens against the governments. Durna and Hancerli state that practicing democratic policing helps to promote faith and good relationships between the citizens and the police agencies. In fact, practicing democratic policing strengthens the core aspects of democracy in a community.

Durna and Hancerli [27] state that there are some recommendations for how governments can avoid stepping on the democratic rights of citizens, at the same time taking security measures that ensure their safety. For example, the paper asserts that any security measures be carried out in a legal way, suggests that policies be implemented in a way that minimizes the negative impact on the public, and warns that civil liberties must always be protected by law enforcement. If these recommendations are followed, the negative image of the government will be reduced and citizens will not be inclined to feel that their best interest lies with someone other than their own government.

Ekici, Ozkan, and Demir [28] point out that although the Turkish government and many in Turkey feel that the Kurds are treated democratically and fairly, receiving broadcasts in Kurdish dialects, having almost 25 percent representation in the Turkish Parliament, having the opportunity to learn in the Kurdish language, and even having Kurdish elected officials as high as president, such as Turgut Ozal, the 8th President of Turkey, and interior minister (currently), some Kurds in the community still feel oppressed and discriminated against by the majority population through the institutions set up by them. Due to these sentiments, the PKK-KONGRA GEL has aimed to fight against this oppression, destabilize Turkey, and work toward establishing a separate Kurdish state in the southeastern region of Turkey through the use of terrorism. Their terrorist acts include numerous violent acts, including but not limited to attacking anti-terrorism government facilities, kidnapping, and murder under the leadership of Abdullah Ocalan.

Ozdogan [29] urges countries to make policies for the security of their nations within the confines of the law and to keep civil liberties in mind. He points out that civil liberties have decreased since 9/11 in direct relationship to the power of the executive branch increasing. Specifically, the Patriot Act has caused our civil liberties to decline, which has caused certain scholars and civil rights advocates to complain. However, currently the American public doesn't appear to be worried about this issue. This fact causes the author to fear that without a public that demands the rights, freedoms, and liberties, countries could become places lacking in liberty. Therefore, he urges people to stand up and give voice to force the government to reenact the civil liberties that all citizens should enjoy.

Haberfeld and Von Hassel [30] talk about democratic policing as a response to terrorism. Their goal, in fact, is to make a case for proactive policing in response to terrorist attacks. They point out that police are generally in the practice of responding to crime but that they need instead to ready themselves for terrorist incidents so that they can prevent them and better respond to them when necessary. Since the police force is the first to arrive on the scene in case of a crime or terrorist incident, they must be well-trained to confront these situations. The authors make two recommendations, which are (1) training and (2) intelligence gathering. In the area of training, officers must know the history of terrorist groups just like they would learn about a specific criminal's history, have an understanding of how terrorist incidents came to be, and go through simulations of attacks to practice their response tactics. By looking at other countries who have been dealing with these problems for years, we can learn about what strategies are effective. Most importantly, being proactive by preparing and empowering police officers to fight against terrorism is one of the best methods.

According to Goktepe and Ercikti [31], the intelligence system of the United States appears to have failed terribly in the events leading up to September 11th. Since it is clear that intelligence is vital to a country's security, the authors investigate the role of intelligence in the case of terrorism in both the United States and Turkey by examining response models. By looking at the issue closely, the paper hopes to analyze the way that each country has reacted to and coped with terrorism. The conclusion that is reached is that the two countries, being leaders in the war on terrorism, ought to work together and share intelligence with not only each other but also other willing nations. Working together, they can put pressure on states that sponsor terrorism through offering terrorists places to hide, stay, and work to stop these allowances and to be willing to extradite criminals so that they may be brought to justice. The authors also recommend a departure from current intelligence strategies. Rather than collecting intelligence and keeping it on a national level, they insist that it must be a multi-national effort using highly trained, multi-lingual, computer specialists. They maintain that only these types of people can respond to the global demand of the current situation. Questions of sovereignty must be put aside so that intelligence agents can pursue criminals and gather data across borders. With this cooperative strategy, terrorists might find it harder to plan and execute their attacks or to get away with them.

Gunbeyi and Gundogdu [32] contend that defining terrorism and distinguishing it from freedom fighting is a difficult task. However, since both the U.S. (since the end of WW1) and Turkey (for the last 35 years), as well as other nations have suffered at the hands of terrorists, it is necessary to agree on the fact that terrorism in any form must be addressed through international cooperation. Without the vast resources of all countries in terms of money, military, intelligence sharing, and law enforcement, counter-terrorism goals can not be achieved. By creating a clear definition, we might help other nations see that this is a global problem that affects every nation and must be dealt with by all.

Sykiainen [33] advocate that the perceived role of Islam in the international community changed from one that supports terrorism and radicalization to one that fights against extremism arm in arm with the West. He argues that although many believe that Islam is responsible for the spread of terrorism, actually Islam abhors it and in no way has a place for the murder of innocents. As proof of this fact, he gives numerous examples, such as Saudi Arabia breaking off ties with the Taliban, The Grand Mufti of Saudi Arabia condemning the 9/11 attacks as being anti-Islamic, and the Al-Azhar Academy of Islamic Research saying that Islam is based on principles of cultural tolerance, law, and cooperation as well as pointing out the Jihad is supposed to be something that strives for justice through legal ways, not an excuse for murder. Unfortunately, the interpretation of the Shari'a as something that allows these horrific acts of terrorism is still strong in some parts of the Muslim world. If Muslim countries begin to fight terrorism side by side with Western countries, the world can begin to see that true Islamic and Shari'a doctrine does not condone violence and has nothing to do with acts of terrorism. Not only can Muslim countries benefit from this partnership, but also Western countries can benefit. By working together all countries can increase their security and protect their national interests.

Spence [34] focuses on the role of globalization in the growth of security issues and brings up the question of whether or not a Human Security agenda can address this problem. He points to the use of private security and military companies, especially in Iraq and also in other countries as proof that there is an escalation of security concerns among nations and that a single nation can no longer be fully responsible for keeping the whole country secure in this day and age of multiple threats from terrorism. The Human Security agenda may be able to address the lack of security in a globalized environment by emphasizing the need for countries to work interdependently toward common goals of security. Although Human Security can't be the only answer or the complete answer, it can address the problem of instability and can develop innovative methods for dealing with terrorism from the perspective of global human interests rather than individual national ones. He insists that without cooperation among nations to work on this problem, there won't be progress, but if nations abandon conventional military strategies and embrace the concept of Human Security, progress may be made.

5. Concluding Remarks

Terrorist organizations terrify everybody in the community and give them fear and anxiety by using their tactics, including but not limited to suicide attacks, hijackings, kidnappings, and hostage holding situations. To carry out their attacks, they take advantage of every possible means, such as getting involved in illegal drug marketing, making liaisons with some other crime networks, using biological weapons, and using mass media, Internet, and other advanced technologies.

They usually select the most vulnerable targets as they did in New York (2001), Bali (2002), Istanbul (2003), Madrid (2004) suicide attacks, and London (2005) bombings. Although terrorists inflicted huge damages on the nations through these attacks, they have been confronted with bigger counter attacks and responses from the governments. Many nations, in fact, learned their lessons from previous terrorist events, and they are fully aware of the threat and know exactly how to cope with it. Nations now have cooperation, solidarity, combined initiatives, as well as information sharing in combating terrorism. By working together all nations increase their security and protect their national and international interests; in fact, without cooperation among nations based on not only paramilitary strategies but also concept of human security in the community to work on this problem, there won't be any progress. The governments today have numerous means and tools in implementing cooperation and collaboration on the part of their professionals. For instance, they take advantage of using democratic policing, community policing, proactive policing, problem oriented policing, situational crime prevention perspective, crime prevention through environmental design (CPTED), using geographic information systems (GIS), and community based programs, such as community outreach programs and neighborhood watch programs. During these practices, the civil liberties of the public in the community should not be decreased because the public always has its rights, freedoms, and liberties while the professionals use counter-terrorism measurements and response strategies toward terrorism. Terrorists want governments to take very harsh action against them because the general public may also suffer from the counter actions of the governments. Their aim is to get support from the citizens against the governments' measures and counter-terrorism policies.

In addition, in responding to terrorist attacks, not only governmental agencies but also civilian organizations and private companies should have plans in case of politically motivated crisis situations. For instances, all hostage holding situations should be less profitable and have more risks on the part of terrorists. The professionals should use the negotiation practice first before using other options in hostage holding situations. They have to maintain highly trained police negotiation teams to deal with the situations, such as hijackings, kidnappings, and hostage sieges. Advanced research studies also would be useful in determining new guidelines for these practices. Lastly, the employees of the private companies and civilian organizations should be aware of the survival strategies in case of being held as captives by terrorists.

Finally, one of the best defense strategies against radical terrorism is education which helps society understand the real motives behind the terrorist attacks. For instance, the governments can provide education for their citizens about what true Islam is because many still believe that Islam is responsible for the threat of terrorism. However, Islam abhors it and in no way has a place for the murder of innocents. The real Islam is based on principles of cultural tolerance, law, and cooperation. In this sense, making a pervasive and international definition of terrorism might be very beneficial for all nations to define who the real enemy is in the war on terrorism.

References

[1]   The American Heritage Dictionary of the English Language: Fourth Edition. 2000. [Online] Available from: URL: http://www.bartleby.com/61/26/T0122600.html [Retrieved on March 19, 2007]

[2]   T. Strentz, A terrorist operational profile: A psycho-social paradigm and plan for their destruction. In S. Hancerli, O. Nikbay, (Editors). *Understanding and responding to the terrorism phenomenon: A multi-dimensional perspective.* Amsterdam, the Netherlands: IOS Press (2007).

[3]   C. B. Strozier, Historical and psychological reflections on the emergence of the new terrorism. In S. Hancerli, O. Nikbay, (Editors). *Understanding and responding to the terrorism phenomenon: A multi-dimensional perspective.* Amsterdam, the Netherlands: IOS Press (2007).

[4]   M. I. Chevrier, Biological weapons, terrorism and transparency. In S. Hancerli, O. Nikbay, (Editors). *Understanding and responding to the terrorism phenomenon: A multi-dimensional perspective.* Amsterdam, the Netherlands: IOS Press (2007).

[5]   B. Forst, The demand side of terrorism: Fear. In S. Hancerli, O. Nikbay, (Editors). *Understanding and responding to the terrorism phenomenon: A multi-dimensional perspective.* Amsterdam, the Netherlands: IOS Press (2007).

[6]   I. Ozsoy, Terrorism: A socio-economic analysis. In S. Hancerli, O. Nikbay, (Editors). *Understanding and responding to the terrorism phenomenon: A multi-dimensional perspective.* Amsterdam, the Netherlands: IOS Press (2007).

[7]   O. Nikbay, C. J. Smith and E. Mus, Suicide attacks as a devastating terrorist modus operandi: An updated evaluation of Turkish cases. In S. Hancerli, O. Nikbay, (Editors). *Understanding and responding to the terrorism phenomenon: A multi-dimensional perspective.* Amsterdam, the Netherlands: IOS Press (2007).

[8]   Y. Schweitzer, Palestinian istishhadia campaign: A dynamic and practical tool. In S. Hancerli, O. Nikbay, (Editors). *Understanding and responding to the terrorism phenomenon: A multi-dimensional perspective.* Amsterdam, the Netherlands: IOS Press (2007).

[9]   K. Yilmaz, The rise of radical Islam in post-Soviet states: fiction or reality? In S. Hancerli, O. Nikbay, (Editors). *Understanding and responding to the terrorism phenomenon: A multi-dimensional perspective.* Amsterdam, the Netherlands: IOS Press (2007).

[10] S. Demiralp, The rise of the periphery and peripheralization of the center: moderation of Islamic and Kurdish extremism in Turkey. In S. Hancerli, O. Nikbay, (Editors). *Understanding and responding to the terrorism phenomenon: A multi-dimensional perspective.* Amsterdam, the Netherlands: IOS Press (2007).

[11] E. Uslu, O. Aytac, War of paradigms: PKK, Europe, and Turkey. In S. Hancerli, O. Nikbay, (Editors). *Understanding and responding to the terrorism phenomenon: A multi-dimensional perspective.* Amsterdam, the Netherlands: IOS Press (2007).

[12] A. Pek, B. Ekici, Narcoterrorism in Turkey: The financing of PKK-KONGRA GEL from illicit drug business. In S. Hancerli, O. Nikbay, (Editors). *Understanding and responding to the terrorism phenomenon: A multi-dimensional perspective.* Amsterdam, the Netherlands: IOS Press (2007).

[13] S. Demirci, I. Suen, Spatial pattern analysis of PKK-KONGRA GEL terror incidents in turkey: 2003-2004. In S. Hancerli, O. Nikbay, (Editors). *Understanding and responding to the terrorism phenomenon: A multi-dimensional perspective.* Amsterdam, the Netherlands: IOS Press (2007).

[14] R. J. Louden, Local law enforcement hostage/crisis negotiation: an essay on continued viability in the aftermath of the attacks of 9/11. In S. Hancerli, O. Nikbay, (Editors). *Understanding and responding to the terrorism phenomenon: A multi-dimensional perspective.* Amsterdam, the Netherlands: IOS Press (2007).

[15] M. Kocak, Probability of hostage fatality in hostage-taking terrorism: Negotiation option and characteristics of negotiators. In S. Hancerli, O. Nikbay, (Editors). *Understanding and responding to the terrorism phenomenon: A multi-dimensional perspective.* Amsterdam, the Netherlands: IOS Press (2007).

[16] S. Hancerli, T. Durna, Successful police negotiation strategies in terrorism motivated hostage situations. In S. Hancerli, O. Nikbay, (Editors). *Understanding and responding to the terrorism phenomenon: A multi-dimensional perspective.* Amsterdam, the Netherlands: IOS Press (2007).

[17] G. Noesner, Negotiating the terrorist hostage siege: Are nations prepared to respond and manage effectively? In S. Hancerli, O. Nikbay, (Editors). *Understanding and responding to the terrorism phenomenon: A multi-dimensional perspective.* Amsterdam, the Netherlands: IOS Press (2007).

[18] B. Richardson, Hostage negotiation: A systems perspective in a case study approach. In S. Hancerli, O. Nikbay, (Editors). *Understanding and responding to the terrorism phenomenon: A multi-dimensional perspective.* Amsterdam, the Netherlands: IOS Press (2007).

[19] M. Webster, Kidnapping: A brief psychological overview. In S. Hancerli, O. Nikbay, (Editors). *Understanding and responding to the terrorism phenomenon: A multi-dimensional perspective.* Amsterdam, the Netherlands: IOS Press (2007).

[20] J. Richardson, C. Voss, J. Flood and J. Jones, Disrupting the business of kidnapping: How kidnapping harms the world economy and how governments can thwart kidnapping organizations? In S. Hancerli, O. Nikbay, (Editors). *Understanding and responding to the terrorism phenomenon: A multi-dimensional perspective.* Amsterdam, the Netherlands: IOS Press (2007).

[21] S. Romano, International kidnap negotiations: Preparation, response and related issues. In S. Hancerli, O. Nikbay, (Editors). *Understanding and responding to the terrorism phenomenon: A multi-dimensional perspective.* Amsterdam, the Netherlands: IOS Press (2007).

[22] R. Yalcinkaya, A. Ozmen, Hijackings and aviation security. In S. Hancerli, O. Nikbay, (Editors). *Understanding and responding to the terrorism phenomenon: A multi-dimensional perspective.* Amsterdam, the Netherlands: IOS Press (2007).

[23] T. Mijares, Learning from the "lesser" acts: Suggestions for improving responses to critical incidents. In S. Hancerli, O. Nikbay, (Editors). *Understanding and responding to the terrorism phenomenon: A multi-dimensional perspective.* Amsterdam, the Netherlands: IOS Press (2007).

[24] R. V. Clarke, G. R. Newman, Situational crime prevention and the control of terrorism. In S. Hancerli, O. Nikbay, (Editors). *Understanding and responding to the terrorism phenomenon: A multi-dimensional perspective.* Amsterdam, the Netherlands: IOS Press (2007).

[25] M. Gulak, U. Kun, Z. Koday and S. Koday, Preventing terrorist attacks on critical infrastructures by use of crime prevention through environmental design, CPTED. In S. Hancerli, O. Nikbay, (Editors). *Understanding and responding to the terrorism phenomenon: A multi-dimensional perspective.* Amsterdam, the Netherlands: IOS Press (2007).

[26] W. Hanniman, A community-based multi-faceted response to the terrorist threat in Canada. In S. Hancerli, O. Nikbay, (Editors). *Understanding and responding to the terrorism phenomenon: A multi-dimensional perspective.* Amsterdam, the Netherlands: IOS Press (2007).

[27] T. Durna, S. Hancerli, Implementing democratic policing in the PKK terrorism torn areas of Turkey. In S. Hancerli, O. Nikbay, (Editors). *Understanding and responding to the terrorism phenomenon: A multi-dimensional perspective.* Amsterdam, the Netherlands: IOS Press (2007).

[28] N. Ekici, M. Ozkan and O. O. Demir, Turkish government policies and the rise of the PKK-KONGRA GEL. In S. Hancerli, O. Nikbay, (Editors). *Understanding and responding to the terrorism phenomenon: A multi-dimensional perspective.* Amsterdam, the Netherlands: IOS Press (2007).

[29] A. Ozdogan, Expansion of the executive power by the Patriot Act. In S. Hancerli, O. Nikbay, (Editors). *Understanding and responding to the terrorism phenomenon: A multi-dimensional perspective.* Amsterdam, the Netherlands: IOS Press (2007).

[30] M. M. Haberfeld, A. V. Hassell, Proper proactive training to terrorist presence and operations in friendly urban environments. In S. Hancerli, O. Nikbay, (Editors). *Understanding and responding to the terrorism phenomenon: A multi-dimensional perspective.* Amsterdam, the Netherlands: IOS Press (2007).

[31] F. Goktepe, S. Ercikti, Comparative analysis of the role of intelligence in counter-terrorism: Turkey and the United States. In S. Hancerli, O. Nikbay, (Editors). *Understanding and responding to the terrorism phenomenon: A multi-dimensional perspective.* Amsterdam, the Netherlands: IOS Press (2007).

[32] M. Gunbeyi, T. Gundogdu, The counter-terrorism issue in the U.S. and Turkey's policies. In S. Hancerli, O. Nikbay, (Editors). *Understanding and responding to the terrorism phenomenon: A multi-dimensional perspective.* Amsterdam, the Netherlands: IOS Press (2007).

[33] L. Sykiainen, Role of Islamic political and legal thought for responding to terrorism. In S. Hancerli, O. Nikbay, (Editors). *Understanding and responding to the terrorism phenomenon: A multi-dimensional perspective.* Amsterdam, the Netherlands: IOS Press (2007).

[34] K. Spence, Globalizing security, securing globalization: Privatization, commodification and the 'new' terrorist threat. In S. Hancerli, O. Nikbay, (Editors). *Understanding and responding to the terrorism phenomenon: A multi-dimensional perspective.* Amsterdam, the Netherlands: IOS Press (2007).

Understanding and Responding to the Terrorism Phenomenon
O. Nikbay and S. Hancerli (Eds.)
IOS Press, 2007

A Terrorist Operational Profile:
A Psycho-Social Paradigm and Plan for
Their Destruction

Thomas STRENTZ[*], Ph.D.
FBI Supervisory Special Agent - Retired

Abstract. Domestic terrorist groups that operate within and against democracies are not composed of people who are identically motivated or psychologically similar. Democracies, by their very nature, provide effective and legitimate channels for change and dissent. Therefore, when they are faced with internal terrorist threats it is axiomatic that those who are making the threats have motives other than promoting political, social, or economic change. Research has shown that most domestic groups include at least three types of personalities, a paranoid type, and antisocial type and an inadequate. Each has its strength and weakness. Each plays a role in the groups' ability to function. To more effectively engage and eliminate a terrorist group, it behooves law enforcement to more closely examine and categorize the group membership and approach the weak link using the methods suggested in this paper.

Keywords. Domestic terrorist profile, leader, opportunist, idealist, psychology, interview, interrogation, group dynamic.

Introduction and Problem Statement

The problem is the threat posed by domestic terrorist groups to our democratic way of life and institutions. Over the years democracies around the world have faced threats from within and without. The focus of this paper will be on the typical internal threat from domestic groups. The underlying assumption is that democracies have, by virtue of their being, established legitimate avenues of dissent. Therefore, when citizens choose violence over established methods of change, their actions strongly suggest some serious psychological pathology. This pathology can be and has been successfully used against these organizations. The case study method will provide examples of the problem and the psychological literature and experience of the researcher will suggest some solutions. The threats posed by foreign groups' lies beyond the bounds of this article.

---

[*] The researcher's background as a former USMC sergeant, Parole Agent with a Masters of Social Work degree that included an internship at the Atascadero State Hospital for the Sexual Psychopath and then a PhD in Government Policy, is particularly unique and well suited for this work. He served as a Special Agent and then a Supervisory Special Agent in the Federal Bureau of Investigation from 1968 until 1988. Most of the research was conducted when the researcher was a member of the Behavioral Science and then the Special Operations Unit at the FBI Academy. Therefore, the methods used in this article reflect the case study method and the personal work experience of the researcher.

1. Case Studies

1.1. The Bombing of the Capitol of the United States of America

On March 1, 1971, the Capitol of the United States was bombed by members of a radical left- wing group of college age citizens who called themselves "The Weather Underground." Late on that Sunday night they placed a large explosive device in a rest room on the Senate side of this grand edifice. It detonated early Monday morning and did some structural damage. Because of the early morning hour of the explosion, no one was killed or injured.

FBI and U.S. Army bomb technicians conducted a thorough crime scene investigation. In so doing, they determined the approximate size of the device. It was clear to them that the bomb was too large to be inconspicuously carried into the building. It was theorized that a transporting unit, like a wagon or baby carriage would have been required.

The Federal Bureau of Investigation (FBI) responded and conducted one of the largest and most thorough investigations in the history of the Washington Field Office, if not the entire Bureau. Other Special Agents and the researcher worked in fourteen hour shifts and interviewed thousands of people over more than a few weeks to solve this case.

Through informant information, the FBI discovered who did it. However, the FBI had to prove it in court. In this endeavor, the researcher identified Leslie Bacon, who in his judgment could as well have been named Loser Bacon, as the person who tested security around our Capitol. She pushed a baby carriage in and around the grand halls of this magnificent, and to many, sacred building on that Sunday afternoon.

Through the media and by reviewing the names of people who signed a guest register in our Capitol, the FBI and Capitol Police identified thousands of visitors who were potential witnesses. Among them were a U.S. Army Major and his wife who were interviewed by the researcher. They positively identified Ms. Bacon as having been on Capitol Hill with a baby carriage that Sunday afternoon.

They remembered her because they climbed the hundreds of stairs in their assent to the Capitol from the Washington Monument side of the mall. As they sat recovering from this climb they saw Ms. Bacon, who was clearly over-weight, pushing a baby carriage. They watched her as she pushed the carriage and walked around them. They stared, wondered, and discussed how she could have transported that carriage up all those stairs. As first time visitors to our Capitol, they did not know that the approach from the Library of Congress side is level.

Investigation conducted by the researcher and other FBI Special Agents revealed that Ms. Bacon was not married, did not have a baby, did not own a baby carriage or have any legitimate reason to be in possession of a baby carriage on the grounds of our Capitol that afternoon.

The Major, his wife and researcher, among others, testified before a grand jury and Ms. Bacon was indicted. Unfortunately, the trial strategy of the U.S. Department of Justice and the FBI was to treat Ms. Bacon like a criminal who, under pressure, would become a government witness against the makers and planters of the bomb. This did not work. In fact, the researcher, given his back ground in mental health, told them it would not work.

Ms. Bacon was not a common criminal. She, like so many others, was a follower who had failed at many tasks but now found acceptance and success as a lowly member of a large radical group. In the opinion of the researcher, anyone with a modicum of knowledge of psychology and group dynamics would understand that as a follower, Ms. Bacon needed acceptance, status and recognition. This was intentionally and deliberately provided by "The Weather Underground" and unwittingly by the FBI. In sum, the FBI treated her like the criminal with an Anti-Social Personality (ASP). Typically, among the traits of such a person is a lack of loyalty. He or she is at the ready to make a deal to benefit himself and forsake any and all associates.

In fact, Ms. Bacon was more like the person with an Inadequate Personality. As a person with an Inadequate Personality, Ms. Bacon is what Eric Hoffer would call "a true believer" [1]. She was not the type of person who made things happen. She let things happen and often wondered what happened. She was a follower. In exchange for the status and recognition provided by her peers in "The Weather Underground," she gave them loyalty. She would rather be a martyr and go to jail than turn on "her friends" who satisfied so many of her basic social and psychological needs. Sociologists call this Exchange Theory. She was not convicted and today the March 1, 1971 bombing of the U.S. Capitol remains officially unsolved.

1.2. The Symbionese Liberation Army

That was thirty years ago. Over the years with the Symbionese Liberation Army (SLA), the New World Liberation Front (NWLF) in California, and more recently in the terrorist group in Beslan, that took over the school and killed hundreds of innocent children in September of 2004, we have seen persons and groups of like structure.

When the infamous SLA was finally cornered on May 17, 1974 in Los Angeles, a shootout occurred in which all six on-scene members perished. This group had gained early notoriety by killing Dr. Marcos Foster, the Oakland, California Superintendent of Schools. Later they kidnapped Patricia Campbell Hearst, the daughter of the millionaire media mogul William Randolph Hearst, robbed banks and engaged the media and law enforcement in highly publicized events, public statements, and press releases that captured and held the headlines for two years.

Six of the nine members were killed in the Los Angeles shootout. Interestingly enough, five members, the loyal followers, were in the "crawl space" under the house shooting at law enforcement. Their Antisocial member, a convicted felon, FBI informant, and prison escapee, Donald David DeFreeze was shot and killed at the back door. The researcher interviewed police and FBI agents who were on the scene. It is their unanimous opinion that he was trying to use the confusion of the shooting as a diversion to assure his escape.

These groups can be disrupted and destroyed from within if we recognize what type of person we are dealing with and use the correct and proven approach to pit some members against each other while we recognize that there are those who cannot be so easily manipulated.

1.3. Solution

In this paradigm, the researcher is not suggesting that all members of terrorist groups are suffering from some psychological pathology. However, terrorist groups that operate in nations where legitimate and proven procedures to initiate change exist have more than their share of people with some pathology. When one is aware of three psychological "types," one will better understand the workings of many domestic terrorists groups and with this understanding be in a better position to turn members of the group against each other.

2. The Paradigm, a Theoretical Design of Typical Terrorist Groups

Again, it is not the intent of this paper to suggest that members of terrorist groups are mentally ill. However, within the democratic process there are proven, effective, and non-violent avenues available to one and all to alter the system. When people ignore the non-violent approach in favor of violence, one must consider the possibility that some other motivation, such as a personality disorder, may be the root cause.

1. *The Leader*, sometimes in name only, is a person of total dedication. He or she is a theoretician with a strong personality that may border on Paranoia.
2. *The Opportunist* or activist-operator is a person with an anti-social personality (ASP). He or she is an opportunist who is a member of the group because of personal and selfish motives. Typically, this person is a former felon.
3. *The Idealist* or follower is typically a naive person who has a life pattern of searching for the truth. In their search, they tend to drift from group to group. Within the diagnostic categories identified in second edition of Diagnostic and Statistical Manual of Mental Disorders, (DSM II), this person would be classified as having an Inadequate Personality. In the newer publication, DSM IV, they fit in the classification of Dependent or Avoidant.

2.1. The Leader

In Left-Wing groups the leader is frequently a female. Some examples include Nancy Ling Perry of the SLA, Ulrike Meinhof of the German Baader Meinhof gang [2] and Fusako Sigenobu of the Japanese Red Army [2, 3]. Again, the researcher does not mean to suggest this person is mentally ill. However, if one understands the dynamics and make up of the Paranoid Personality Disorder, one will more easily understand this person (DSM IV). Based on researchers and interviews with police officers from the former Soviet Union, Shamil Basayev, the leader of the Chechen terrorist group that attacked the school is Beslan, fits this profile.

This person is cynical, yet has a very high level of dedication to the goals of the group. Of the three typical terrorist group personality types, this element shows the least indication of self- interest. They are rigid, dedicated, overly suspicious and highly motivated. They tend to project personal faults and inadequacies onto others and ascribe evil motives to those who disagree with them. The leader is convinced of their righteousness and the underlying evil of those who oppose them. The development of the leader's thought pattern is gradual and culminates in an intricate, complex, and elaborate belief system. They see themselves as unique people who possess superior ability and knowledge. Simply stated, they seem very Paranoid.

Their primary defense mechanism is projection, and to a lesser extent denial and rationalization. Some experts suggest they use these defense mechanisms and other means to over-compensate for basic feelings of inadequacy. As a group, they tend to "specialize." They know a lot about very little. When conversing with this person they will attempt to steer the conversation into the area in which they feel comfortable. In this endeavor, and to a point, they control others' parts in the discussion. They tend to be perfectionists, because they are too insecure to tolerate error. They are very persuasive people and tend to be totally dedicated to molding the minds of others to their perspective. Again, they seem very paranoid.

2.1.1. The Leader's Psychological Development

The jury on the cause or causes of mental aberrations is still out on the basic issue of heredity versus environment. However, the authorities agree that Paranoia is a gradually developed delusional system sustained by perceptions of events that are interpreted, or perhaps more accurately mis-interpreted, to support their basic and irrational thought patterns and causal links that do not exist. Typically, the Paranoid person refuses to be confused by the facts or any other interpretation of actions, words, or events than their own. McNeil says it well in his quote: "Paranoia is a poison of suspicion that infuses and affects the total psychic life of its victim" [4 pg 103].

The Paranoid state begins early in life and is agitated, and in some cases strained, by the normal perils of living [5]. Normal people develop a basic trust in others and consider the world a safe place in which they can freely grow, develop and interact with their fellow man. The Paranoid person has an entirely different take on reality. For reasons still unclear, in everyday social activity they identify ulterior motives, evil plots, conspiracies, and sub-rosa efforts by many if not most around them.

Typically, the terrorist group leader is irrationally dedicated to a set of beliefs that are not generally supported or held by most members of their democracy. Although the evidence the leader may present to justify their beliefs may be inconclusive, they are unwilling to accept any other explanation. Arguments and logic are futile. They tend to be insulated from the belief system of others. In fact, any serious questioning of them that challenges the authenticity of their explanation of causal links and conspiracies tends to convenience them that their interrogators have sold out to the enemy. This type of reasoning is typical of the Paranoid person.

Frequently, the leaders develop their beliefs around a grain of truth. But their fallacious and perverted sense of logic brings them to invalid conclusions that no longer resemble an objective, accurate or logical perception of reality. In common parlance, they have gone off the deep end. Again, it is important to note that though the leader of a terrorist group operating in a democracy has personality traits most commonly associated with the Paranoid Personality Disorder, they may not be, in a clinical sense, mentally ill. Certainly, they are more dedicated, single-minded, intelligent and theoretically oriented than most people. They are more suspicious and, like the blindly prejudiced individual, inclined to selectively interpret events to fit their view of reality. They are, on the surface, self-confident and have all the answers to the problems of life. Because their thinking process so closely parallels that of the Paranoid Personality Disorder, knowledge of this disorder is crucial to the understanding and interrogating of this person.

2.1.2. The Leader's Role in the Group

Typically, they can read people well and appeal to their needs. They use their followers in comfortable, self-fulfilling roles. They allow them to have their fantasies. They understand, tolerate and satisfy their needs for recognition, achievement and self-fulfillment. The leader allows each follower to be complete within themselves. They allow the criminal element, the opportunists, to play out his fantasy of self-fulfillment, all to achieve the group goal and purpose.

2.1.3. The Leader and Law Enforcement

Police involvement with this person is infrequent because he or she typically works behind the scenes as the planner, policy maker and organizer. To law enforcement, they are the shadow figure who fades into the background. If apprehended, the leader is generally intelligent enough to maintain their silence. However, should he or she begin to talk, their general superior attitude and their self-assured discussion of their conspiracy theory of history and current events will begin to evolve. This is especially true if the leader thinks the interrogator is a possible convert. They are not an easy mark for the interrogator. The interview will probably deteriorate into a political, economic, social, religious and/or psychological lecture.

2.2. The Opportunist

Typically, this person is a male who has a history of criminal activity, offenses, and convictions. His criminal activity always predates his involvement in political, religious, or social causes or crusades. The researcher has named him "The Opportunist" because his involvement in the group is self serving. He views the group as providing a vehicle to satisfy his needs for excitement, control, and power. Psychologically, this person most closely approximates that of the Antisocial Personality (ASP). The acronym asp is particularly appropriate because an Asp is a poisonous snake. The opportunist is just that. Some examples include Donald David DeFreeze of the American SLA and Andreas Baader of the German Baader Meinholf Gang.

It is easy to recognize an Antisocial Personality Disorder (ASP) hostage-taker by his glibness, his narcissism, his seemingly stress-free voice and attitude, his high verbal skills, and his constant use of rationalization and projection to justify his situation.

When one compares his chronological to his emotional age, he appears to many to be an "adult adolescent." As a member of a terrorist group he is motivated by a very selfish, narcissistic orientation. He is a member of the group because it suits his personal, not political or religious, needs. He is a social pariah. He targets the society that law enforcement is sworn to protect. Typically he uses the group to suit his wants and fulfill his needs.

2.2.1. The Opportunist's Psychological Development

Like that of the leader, and most mental disorders, there are good theories to explain hereditary as well as environmental causes. Typically in early childhood they will exhibit the youthful predictors of enuresis, cruelty to animals and pyromania first identified by the Jesuits some five hundred years ago [6].

The best description of this disorder is in the excellent and well-titled text *Without Conscience*, by Dr. Robert D. Hare:

> "The Antisocial Personality, Psychopath, is a social predator who charms, manipulates, and ruthlessly plows his way through life, leaving a broad trail of broken hearts, shattered expectations, and empty wallets. Completely lacking in conscience and feeling for others, he selfishly takes what he wants and does as he pleases, violating social norms and expectations without the slightest sense of guilt or regret [7 pg 11]".

Like the leader, we can easily identify this type of person. However, the treatment and cure for this disorder remains beyond present day medical science.

2.2.2. The Opportunist's Role in the Group

This is the person who turns a political, social, religious, or economic protest group into a terrorist group. Because of their penchant for, and long history of, criminal activity that always predates their involvement in the group, they encourage the group to engage in criminal activity in the name of their cause. Simply stated, this person initiates, plans, and directs the robbery, kidnapping, bombing, and other criminal acts, all in the name of the group's goals. In fact, they take more than their share of the money from any robberies or ransoms. Many times these criminal acts, to include bombing, are designed by them to settle grudges against various people.

2.2.3. The Opportunist and Law Enforcement

His involvement in a group will be instrumental and very self-serving. Remember, "It's all about me!" His demeanor will remind you of criminal informants with whom you have been involved. When this person is removed from the group, they typically revert to rhetoric until and unless he is replaced by another ASP. When Paul Galanti was arrested by the Italian Police in co-operation with the FBI, he immediately told them was the American General, General James Dozier, who had been kidnapped by the Red Brigades, was being held. He knew this because his brother was a member of this terrorist group. Based on the information provided by Paul, his brother was arrested by the police but, Paul went free. Again, "It's all about me!"

When the SLA was surrounded by law enforcement in Los Angeles, most of them died shooting at police from under the house. Donald DeFreeze was killed at the back door, probably attempting an escape. Again, "It's all about me!"

When this person is removed from the group by law enforcement, the reward is for civilized society is double. Their absence tends to dramatically reduce the criminal activity of the group and, in their interest to do what is best for them, they are all too willing to tell the police about the group, it's members, their plans and anything else that might be of value to law enforcement and help them help themselves.

2.3. The Follower or Idealist

This person may be male or female. They share the political, economic, religious and/or social philosophy of the leader and are as dedicated as the leader. However, they are not psychologically strong individuals and tend to move from group to group as they seek their place in the world. One of the best characterizations of this person was completed and published by a self educated writer, Eric Hoffer, in his book *The True Believer* [1].

2.3.1. The Follower's Psychological Development

It is difficult, if not impossible, to state with any degree of statistical accuracy how many people in society could be classified as having an Inadequate Personality Disorder. It is equally difficult to point to a cause for this behavior pattern. As discussed above, there is evidence to suggest that some disorders may be congenital. No such evidence is available to identify the cause of the Inadequate Personality Disorder. Some speak of him as the product of a poorly functioning family. There are many anecdotal illustrations of heredity as well as environmental examples.

When the researcher served an internship at the Atascadero California State Hospital for the Sexual Psychopath, he encountered many patients who were labeled as having an Inadequate Personality Disorder. Most of them were exhibitionist or had engaged in arson. During many interviews with their families, the researcher encountered pathology in some and none in others.

Again, the jury is still out on the issue of heredity versus environment or nature versus nurture. Many may have come to expect authority figures in their life to be both critical and nurturing in such a way as to send the message that this person is incapable or unable to do things for them- selves. Typically, they get the message from their parents that though they are not capable, they are loved enough that authority figures, their parents, and later others, will do things for them [8].

There are many explanations for the development of this personality disorder. One is set forth in Midge Decter's book, *Liberal Parents, Radical Children*. She discusses a misdirected youthful idealism that seeks to achieve, yet falls short of the mark. These followers are taught from youth that everything that frustrates them is an injustice that must be altered [9]. Basically, an individual with a personality disorder is not psychotic or insane. They are not out of touch with reality. Typically, they have a long term pattern of maladaptive behavior that is usually recognized by the teenage years. In the opinion of the researcher, an observant teacher can spot this disorder in elementary school.

In the most recent edition of the American Psychiatric Association's reference text, entitled *Diagnostic and Statistical Manual of Mental Disorders, IV edition* [10] the traits of the Inadequate Personality Disorder are scattered among those with the current diagnosis of an Avoidant Personality Disorder as well as the person with a Dependent Personality Disorder.

Prior to the publishing of *DSM III* in May of 1987, this person was labeled The Inadequate Personality. However, the researchers many discussions with experienced negotiators have made it clear that there is a subset of hostage takers who frequently function inadequately [11, 8].

He or she was described in DSM II as:

"An individual whose behavior is characterized by inadequate responses to intellectual, emotional, social, and physical demands. They are neither physically nor mentally grossly deficient on examination, but they do show in-adaptability, ineptness, poor judgment, lack of physical and emotional stamina, and social incompatibility [12 pg 44]".

2.3.2. The Follower's Role in the Group

As a member of the group, they are just that, members, the foot soldiers, and the followers. They do what they are told and most commonly must be told when, where, and how to do it. This was the role of Leslie Bacon in the terrorist group that planted a bomb in the U.S. Capitol in 1971. Leslie was a loser as are others in this terrorist group role. In exchange for their membership and doing what they are told, they are rewarded by having many of their social and psychological needs for affiliation, recognition and socialization satisfied.

They are desperate, dependent and now delinquent youth who are seeking the truth and have fallen victim to the leader's rhetoric and the opportunist's deceit. They tend to be short lived group members who are inclined to drift from group to group as they continue their search for "the truth."

2.3.3. The Follower and Law Enforcement

It is not likely that law enforcement will have had any previous contact with this person. They are the university drop outs who typically cannot tolerate the discipline required to earn a degree. Of the three roles in the group, the follower is the most psychologically salvageable. Given time they may outgrow their revolutionary rationale, role and rhetoric. Some who have become disillusioned with terrorist groups have later come forward and fully cooperated with law enforcement. Therefore, the key to dealing this person is to create disillusionment. This may take the form of pointing out how the opportunist used the group for personal gain.

3. Recommendations and Conclusion

In this study, the three separate elements: leader, opportunist and follower/idealist, have been identified in current terrorist groups. These roles attract specific personality types who compliment each other. Terrorist groups are fluid, task-oriented gatherings of individuals. Individuals change, but roles remain. These three roles are seen in many terrorist groups that operate in democratic nations throughout the world. For instance, in a kidnap for ransom case, the victim is likely to encounter all three. The opportunist seizes him, he is interrogated by the leader and finally encounters the followers who guard and feed him. Knowledge of the roles of these three functionaries will not prevent terrorism. However, it does provide an excellent depiction of our adversaries. We can better judge their capacity for violence, better interview them when they are in our custody, and effectively defuse the group by knowing who the opportunist is and remembering that he is basically a criminal "It's all about me."

In this sense, the message for law enforcement is clear. Do not focus your efforts toward the arrest, incarceration and interrogation of the follower. They know little, and are reluctant to discuss the group. The group is their cherished family. The group has given their empty life meaning and purpose. The leader is equally reluctant to talk. However, the opportunist is the key. He is loyal only to himself and is seeking personal satisfaction and comfort. He is the friend of no man yet he appears to be the friend of all. He wants what is best for him and will provide information on anyone, to include family members, to ensure his personal safety and well being. Additionally, without his criminal expertise, the terrorist group is reduced to a hate group. If terrorism is a new form of warfare, then new police counter-strategies will be needed to effectively meet this threat. The terrorist operational profile is one such strategy for a better understanding of the group dynamics and it will help us defuse our adversaries' ability to disrupt our democracies.

References

[1] E. Hoffer, *The True Believer*, Harper and Rowe: New York; 1952.
[2] Newsweek Magazine, "Year of Terror," 1976, January pp. 27-28.
[3] S. Sloan, *Terrorism,* Berg: New York; 2006.
[4] E. McNeil, *The Quiet Furies*, Prentice Hall: Englewood Cliffs, New Jersey; 1967.
[5] E.B. McNeil, *The Psychoses*, Prentice Hall: Englewood Cliffs, New Jersey; 1970.
[6] T. Strentz, *Psychological Aspects of Crisis Negotiations*, CRC press: Boca Raton, Forida; 2005.
[7] R.D. Hare, *Without Conscience,* The Guilford Press: London; 1993.
[8] M. Mullins, W. McMains, *Crisis Negotiations*, 3rd Edition, Lexis Nexus: New York; 2006.
[9] M.Decter, *Liberal Parents, Radical Children,* Coward, McCann and Geoghegan: New York; 1975.
[10] American Psychiatric Association, *Diagnostic and Statistical Manual of Mental Disorders,* Fourth Edition, Washington, D.C.: 2000.
[11] L Shelton, Personal interview in Baton Rouge, LA and Vushtri/Kosovo; 2006.
[12] American Psychiatric Association, *Diagnostic and Statistical Manual of Mental Disorders,* Second Edition, Washington, D.C.: 1952.

Understanding and Responding to the Terrorism Phenomenon
O. Nikbay and S. Hancerli (Eds.)
IOS Press, 2007

Historical and Psychological Reflections on the Emergence of the New Terrorism

Charles B. STROZIER

John Jay College and the Graduate Center, City University of New York, USA

Abstract. The paper begins with developing the historical difference between the old and new forms of terrorism, emphasizing that the old, mostly left-wing terrorism was circumscribed in its violence because it was political. The new violence is right-wing and millennial, which lifts the restrictions on the violence. Then the changing form of Al-Qaeda is discussed, especially after the American attacks following 9/11, and its dispersal. That in turns leads into an analysis of the significance of the internet, including its psychological meanings, in fostering the organization, recruitment, and aspirations of jihadis everywhere. The importance of the American war in Iraq is noted as a training ground for future terrorists.

Keywords. Terrorism, Al-Qaeda, internet, Osama bin Laden, Iraq

Introduction

Terrorism after the French Revolution was for the most part a form of violence embraced by relatively small groups with concrete political objectives aimed at transformation of the state and the creation of greater social justice. From Russia in the middle of the 19th century, through German radicals in subsequent decades, and spreading to the United States in the period after the Civil War, what we would now call "left-wing" terrorism became a familiar part of the landscape. The objective was to kill kings, emperors, and other leaders of government, as well as their "complicit" functionaries such as police and tax collectors, who conspired to maintain the authoritarian state. At the more nihilistic and fanatical edge of terrorism, some anarchists talked loosely of vast destruction that would somehow cleanse social life and lead to a new kind of political redemption. For the most part, however, terrorism in its European form before the World War I targeted relatively few individuals. The social and political impact was often very significant, as in Russia after the assassination of Tsar Alexander II on March 1, 1881, but in retrospect, the relative insignificance of the social disarray caused by terrorism is its most striking historical fact.

In the first half of the twentieth century, terrorism faded from the political landscape. In 1914 the radicalism of socialists in general was called into question when most supported their national causes at the outset of World War I. After the war, any spirit of potential left-wing terrorism was absorbed in the social and economic chaos that spread all over Europe after about 1923. Radical dissenters, who did exist (the Communist Party in Germany regularly won about a third of the vote in the early

1930s until Hitler took over the government in 1933) struggled themselves with authoritarian regimes, especially the Soviet Union and Nazi Germany but also fascist Italy and Spain, all regimes ready to use extreme force against any trouble-makers. Then came the maelstrom of World War II and the Holocaust. The puny activities of radicals on the fringe of society paled in comparison with such mass violence.

After mid-century, however, and especially after the 1960s, Europe, the Middle East, and Latin America witnessed a decisive return of the form of terrorism that had prevailed in Europe between the French Revolution and World War I. The somewhat mystical dream of a socialist revolution reappeared with the Baader-Meinhof group in Germany. In Peru the Shining Path attempted to take over a whole country and turn it toward a Maoist form of government. And in Israel after 1967 the Palestinian Liberation Organization (PLO) under the leadership of Yassir Arafat sought to create a Palestinian state that was secular and socialist. The firm commitment of the PLO to terrorism became evident after the killing of the Israeli athletes at the Munich Olympics in 1972.

The noise of targeted assassinations and images of helpless civilians being thrown off ships, or blown out of the sky, understandably captured the imagination of many people in the 1970s and 1980s. The violent acts they committed - as in Northern Ireland for several decades after 1972 - were exceedingly brutal, however limited, and seemed for the most part like mere acts of criminality, even if politically motivated. What was seldom remarked on in these years, however, is how truly limited most of the violence was. In all the years of struggle in Northern Ireland, for example, fewer than 2,000 people perished. There were only accidental deaths in the first intifada in Israel in the late 1980s, and so on. It is clear, particularly in retrospect, that what constrained the scale of the violence was the political character of the terrorism that was dominant in the world. The PLO, the IRA, and the Shining Path, not to mention a proliferation of smaller and much less well-known groups, all had much more in common with their nineteenth century antecedents in Russia, Western Europe, and the United States, than anything that was to emerge suddenly after the end of the Cold War.

1. The New Terrorism and Al-Qaeda

The global terrorist movement of Al-Qaeda in the 1990s has been described quite well in scholarly work by Steve Coll [1], Jonathan Randal [2] Bruce Hoffman [3], Jessica Stern [4], and most authoritatively by Lawrence Wright in *The Looming Tower: Al-Qaeda and the Road to 9/11* [5]. Left relatively undisturbed and up to its own devices, Osama bin Laden, first in Sudan and then in Afghanistan, was able to create a remarkably vibrant and, by historical standards, gigantic terrorist organization. He built training camps throughout Afghanistan because he so totally dominated the Taliban. Many tens of thousands of people passed through these camps over the years. Elite training was provided for specially skilled and talented terrorists such as Mohamed Atta, visiting from Germany, or people such as Khalid Sheikh Mohammed.

The structure of Al-Qaeda roughly paralleled that of a global corporation. Osama bin Laden, with Imam Zawahiri at his side, played the role of CEO and religious leader. This mix of a bureaucratic structure, with a charismatic religious fanatic at its pinnacle, turned Al-Qaeda into a very special kind of entity with enormous power to carry out lethal attacks. The central role of Osama bin Laden cannot be overemphasized. All key figures took a personal oath of loyalty to him, and it was his vision that provided direction for the organization. Lawrence Wright [6] has also stressed the significance of Ayman al-Zawahiri, the Egyptian doctor, in shaping the global vision of bin Laden, shifting it from a somewhat parochial emphasis on its rage at Saudi Arabia and the other corrupt regimes of the Middle East into a recognition that the "far enemy," that is, the United States, represents, or should represent, the ultimate target in any kind of large-scale attack. The corrupt regimes of the Middle East are mere clients of America, and of course in this line of thinking there can be no Israel without United States backing.

Al-Qaeda had separate divisions for funding, training, recruitment, and other activities. Each was headed by a separate individual who reported to bin Laden himself. The usefulness of such a structure is that the separate divisions could operate relatively autonomously, as long as the overall vision for the organization was provided by bin Laden. Communication in a secret organization devoted to terrorism was limited but effective. In addition, such a structure allowed Al-Qaeda to continue if attacked from the outside and its members were disbursed.

1.1. Al-Qaeda after the War in Afghanistan

That dispersal, of course, came after 9/11 and the American attack on Afghanistan in the fall of 2001. In retrospect, it is not altogether clear that our safety was increased as a result of the change in Al-Qaeda from a rather tightly organized bureaucratic entity into a global jihadist movement dedicated to destruction and mass violence. Richard Clarke [7] has commented that Al-Qaeda now is a "many-headed hydra that is just as deadly and far harder to slay." The recent State Department report, "Patterns of Terrorism," for 2005 notes that there has been a significant increase in the number of terrorist attacks in the last few years, from 175 in 2003, to 655 in 2004, to some 2,500 in 2005 (though the politics of counting and the confusions over definition raises some suspicion about the legitimacy of these numbers). The State Department report on terrorism also notes three important general trends in terrorism that emerged with great clarity by 2005: the wide growth of microactors in the form of small autonomous cells throughout the world; a marked sophistication in the ability of terrorists from Indonesia to the Middle East, Chechnya, and elsewhere, to exploit the opportunities for global exchange of information, finance, and ideas; and the increasing overlap of terrorism with transnational crime, as, for example, with the PKK in Turkey.

Jessica Stern [4] has characterized the shift in Al-Qaeda after 9/11 as a move from a commanded-cadre organization to that of a virtual network. While generally accurate, what such a characterization fails to note is the completely serendipitous historical moment that occurred with the rapid growth and most of all sophistication of the internet just as Al-Qaeda was cast to the winds from its bases in Afghanistan. The technological revolution associated with the internet has been so rapid and all-consuming that it is easy to forget how relatively primitive it was as recently as a decade ago, while broadband and other means of access, not to mention the rapid spread of computers themselves, along with internet cafes throughout the world, has transformed the whole basis of communication in the world. The technological changes associated with the internet in the last four or five years furthermore has proven ideally suited for meeting the needs of a global terrorist organization such as Al-Qaeda.

On the internet a coder of modest talent and on a limited budget can draw on existing templates to create a web site of great sophistication. Colors may be striking, icons usefully deployed, and wild prose strewn about with emphases on certain passages highlighted, not to mention streaming video (as Abu Masad al-Zarqawi used to show beheadings in Iraq). The all-important chat rooms are easily configured as part of the website. And it is all smoke and mirrors if penetrated by the authorities, closed down quickly and moved to another site, rising again phoenix-like from the ashes.

The internet is thus ideally suited technologically to the special needs of the global jihad after losing its base in 2001. But the internet is also a powerful psychological tool in nourishing the goals of Al-Qaeda. The number and relative sophistication of the now thousands of web sites devoted to radical Islamist rhetoric lends the impression to its participants of a vast social movement that transcends the reality of Al-Qaeda and its jihad, which in fact is rather beleaguered in Iraq and the Middle East, on the retreat in Indonesia, and huddling in the tenements of Europe. But a website can seem majestic and awe-inspiring with its soaring rhetoric of hate. The anonymity serves useful purposes, for it connects the often lonely individual to a spiritual community that can feel powerfully vibrant and lend meaning to his life. And the very absence of Osama bin Laden enhances rather than diminishes his charisma. He presents himself to the world as the new Saladin, and for countless naïve young Moslems inspires dreams of fighting back against the "American and Zionist crusaders." He creates an image of himself as the sole creator of jihad. It is a powerful myth. In it he brought America to its knees. He has eluded capture ever since. He is magical. He speaks mysteriously and without warning and only on rare occasion to inspire his followers. The internet was made for Osama bin Laden. Nothing since the printing press more effectively fosters immanence.

The current State Department report on terrorism stresses, as part of the Republican Party line, the disruption of communication between the key leaders and their followers throughout the world since 2001. These hapless bureaucrats who must toe the line in the authoritarian Bush administration, however, are clutching at straws, clearly hoping that the new generation of extremists is acting on its own and without overall direction, thus making them less worrisome in terms of their capacity for wreaking havoc. The report suggests merely that individuals acting in cells are difficult to characterize and that they sometimes act like an insular "band of brothers."

But the State Department underestimates the dynamism of the new global jihad. Other scholars who have conducted empirical work on the global jihad - most notably Scott Atran[1], Marc Sageman [8], and Robert Pape [9] - have stressed, on the contrary, that the new Al-Qaeda in the post-9/11 world is remarkably self-adjusting and spreading dynamically around the world. Those who have observed it up close and on the ground have been struck by Al-Qaeda's ready access to huge numbers of radicalized young people. In fact, the problem seems to be, whether with Jemaah Islamiyah in Indonesia, Hamas in the West Bank, or Al-Qaeda in Mesopotamia in Iraq, to find ways of vetting the best recruits for suicide terrorism missions. Volunteers are lined up around the block. The same can be said for other dimensions of their activities, including funding and the willingness to take on almost anything. As Sageman and Atran especially have noted in their work, there is an intense sense of idealism and altruistic sacrifice in their

---

[1] For Atran's 26 recent publications about terrorism see his personal website that can be readily reached by Googling his name.

experience of what motivates them to carry out suicide missions. Those in the new movement of global jihad are also clearly older, more mature, many are married, many are relatively well educated (and some highly educated) and provide a large measure of vitality for the new global movement.

2. The War in Iraq and the Future of Terrorism

If the technical and serendipitous changes in the internet have proven advantageous for the new forms of Al-Qaeda in the world, a less accidental but equally significant development since 9/11 has been the American war in Iraq. The most significant loss for Osama bin Laden was no longer to have a client state where he could base his organization and provide advanced training for terrorists committed to carrying out acts of violence. The war in Iraq has provided the jihadis with exactly what they lost in Afghanistan. To fight against Americans in Iraq is to learn the trade. There is no substitute for such training, and it is clear that the 140,000 American troops on the ground in Iraq provides ideal target practice but most of all training for those who will probably become the next generation of terrorists as the war in Iraq dies down. It is often remarked that there has been no major attack in the United States since 9/11, as though our counterterrorism measures at the national, state, and city level have somehow proven effective in protecting us. Unfortunately, it would seem that a more accurate assessment is that the terrorists who will threaten the U.S. in future years are currently distracted by the task at hand, which is to attack the soldiers in Iraq and learn the trade of terrorism.

It is not surprising that well over 10,000 Al-Qaeda jihadi elements flocked to Iraq after the American invasion in order to join with the Sunni-based counterinsurgency. While these foreign elements in the war zone constitute only some 20-25% of the total numbers of those in the counterinsurgency, they have been particularly gruesome in their violence under the leader of Abu Musab al-Zarqawi and represent the future of terrorism both within and outside of the Middle East in future years. Zarqawi, in this regard, was a particularly important and interesting figure. He was astonishingly violent as well as clever in his use of the internet. He perfected the method of showing beheadings with streaming video, organized his followers to plant Improvised Explosive Devices (IED) throughout the country, and acted to foment civil war between Sunnis and Shiites. At times, these strategic goals put him in conflict with his Sunni counterinsurgent collaborators, not to mention with the Al-Qaeda leadership in hiding, especially Zawahiri and even Osama bin Laden, but the point of his activities was not mindless or hedonistic violence but had clear goals. On the one hand, Zarqawi aspired to create the caliphate of the seventh century, a wildly mystical and religious goal, but he also had practical and political aspirations of taking over Iraq after a civil war and making it a safe haven for terrorists in the same way that Afghanistan served the needs of Osama bin Laden in the 1990s.

3. An Apocalyptic Future?

These developments in Iraq and their enormous significance for future violence parallel some of bin Laden's apparent embrace of apocalyptic violence in the future. The remarkable story that Michael Scheuer revealed on November 14, 2004, on *Sixty Minutes*, has unfortunately not received the kind of attention it deserves. As Scheuer discussed, bin Laden in May of 2003 had sought out a fatwa that would authorize the use of weapons of mass destruction, including nuclear weapons, on behalf of the global jihad. The fatwa he sought and acquired in this regard was from Sheikh Nasir bin Hamid al Fahd, a radical Saudi cleric. It is not at all clear at this point what bin Laden will specifically do with such a fatwa, nor even whether he will be able to carry out any future acts of terrorism. Nevertheless, the fact of this fatwa legitimizing the use of nuclear weapons and other ultimate weapons carries fearsome meanings for the future.

It is worth mentioning a few terrorist attacks in the last couple of years to illustrate the protean character of the new forms of violence perpetrated by Al-Qaeda in the post-9/11 world. The group in Spain, for example, under the leadership of Abu Dahdah that carried out the attacks on the Spanish trains on March 11, 2004, killing 191 people and wounding about 1,800, was an action that grew out of a remarkably informal cell. Some six or seven Moroccan radicals ended up in Spanish prisons for minor drug charges. It was there they were radicalized and recruited to carry out their action. They remained in touch after they were released from prison and were planning their action and, as best one can tell from the ongoing Spanish investigation that has been widely reported, were deeply influenced by various websites, particularly one called The Global Islamic Media Front that has connections to Al-Qaeda. The attacks in Spain, of course, had some important political meanings for the Spanish national elections that were scheduled for a few days after the attacks, and in fact as a result of the bombings, the election was swung in favor of Jose Luis Rodriguez Zapatero of the Socialist Party. Nevertheless, these local motivations should not obscure that the Spanish train bombings were part of a larger movement to wreak havoc in Europe as an extension of the goals of the global jihad.

In the spring of 2006, it was also widely reported that the four London suicide terrorists who bombed the subways on July 7, 2005 were basically independent actors who were radicalized in their local mosque and who obtained all the information they needed to carry out their attacks on the internet. It was very much a grassroots group of young men who as a result of their interaction and general involvement in the rhetoric of violence conceived of and carried out their attacks purely on their own initiative.

A third example serves to underline the significance of the internet as a means of extending propaganda and providing communication between those drawn to the global jihad. In Australia in November of 2005, sixteen men were arrested by the police for plotting terrorist attacks. The group had apparently been followed for some time by the Australian police, who felt that the cell was moving toward action and it was time to carry out the arrests. One of those arrested was a cleric, Abdul Nacer Benbricka, while the others were young Muslims radicalized by reading what is readily available on the internet.

4. Conclusion

We are clearly in a new age of violence. Americans are keenly aware of how the world has changed since 9/11. New forms and new threats endanger our lives in ways that we are constantly reminded of. What is less often noted is how the accidental sophistication of modern means of communication, especially through the internet, have provided an ideal form of allowed Al-Qaeda to develop its operations with a whole new generation of terrorists. Nor has the technology stabilized. Its future changes will undoubtedly continue to disturb. The next phase, it seems to me, will probably be live feeds from more advanced cell phones. Disgruntled Palestinians will increasingly be able to show their oppression with technological sophistication that goes beyond Al-Jazeera. Sunni insurgents in Iraq will show American atrocities such as Haditha in real time. Images of scenes from places like the elementary school in Beslan, Russia, attacked by Chechnyans in 2004 will have unpredictable consequences. Torture scenes like those from Abu Ghraib will move even more rapidly into public consciousness. All of us need to attend carefully to these transformations as we prepare for long-term measures that will ensure our security.

References

[1]   S. Coll, Ghost Wars: The secret history of the CIA, Afghanistan, and bin Laden, from the Soviet invasion to September 10, 2001. New York: Penquin; 2001. 720 p.
[2]   J. Randal, Osama: The making of a terrorist. New York: Vintage Press, 2005.
[3]   B. Hoffman, *Inside terrorism*. Rev.ed. New York: Columbia University Press, 2006.
[4]   J. Stern, The protean enemy. *Foreign Affairs,* 2003 July/August.
[5]   L. Wright, *The looming tower: Al-Qaeda and the road to 9/11.* New York: Knopf; 2006. 480 p.
[6]   L. Wright, The man behind bin Laden. New York. *The New Yorker;* 2002, September 16. Available from:http:// www.newyorker.com/fact/content/articles/020916fa_ fact2a?020916fa_fact2a.
[7]   R. Clarke, *Against all enemies: Inside America's war on terror*. New York: The Free Press; 2004. 304 p.
[8]   M. Sageman, *Understanding terror networks*. Phildelphia: University of Pennsylvania Press; 2004. 236 p.
[9]   R. Pape, *Dying to win: The strategic logic of suicide terrorism*. New York: Random House; 2005. 368 p.

Understanding and Responding to the Terrorism Phenomenon
O. Nikbay and S. Hancerli (Eds.)
IOS Press, 2007

Biological Weapons Terrorism and Transparency

Marie Isabelle CHEVRIER[1], Ph.D.
University of Texas at Dallas, USA

Abstract: The prospect of large scale biological weapons terrorism is dreadful. Yet the empirical record of terrorists turning to disease is scant and its consequences have been modest compared to other terrorist incidents. This chapter describes the terrorist incidents that have taken place and the state biological weapons programs that have been in place in the past. It describes rapid advancements in biotechnology that could make the potential problem more severe. The author argues that secrecy in bioweapons defense as well as possibly hidden offensive programs exacerbate the problem and could lead to weapons development through misunderstandings or mistaken intelligence. She argues for greater transparency and strengthening of the international agreements that outlaw the possession and development of biological weapons.

Keywords: Biological weapons, transparency, secrecy, bioterrorism, and arms control.

Introduction

The prospect of biological terrorism has captured the imagination of novelists, filmmakers, and political leaders. The threat of catastrophic biological terrorism has been described as a major threat to the United States, and its NATO allies. Yet the paradox of biological terrorism is that despite its theoretical potential to cause mass destruction, bioterrorism has been extremely infrequent and its consequences—in terms of the number of fatalities and casualties—have been very small.

The purpose of this paper is to explore the threat of bioterrorism. It begins with a description of biological weapons and biological terrorism. It then seeks to answer a series of questions. What do we know about bioterrorism? What do we fear? What about biological weapons and bioterrorism is hidden? And finally, what should be done?

1. Biological Weapons and Bioterrorism

Biological weapons consist of a microbial or other biological agent or a toxin combined with a way to deliver that agent or toxin. Biological weapons can utilize agents that

---

[1] "The author, Marie Isabelle Chevrier, is Associate Professor of Public Policy and Political Economy at The University of Texas at Dallas. She is Chair of the Scientists Working Group on Chemical and Biological Weapons at the Center for Arms Control and Nonproliferation in Washington DC. She has published widely and is co-editor of the forthcoming book, *Incapacitating Biochemical Weapons*.

typically cause death, or that typically cause incapacitation. They may use agents or toxins that affect humans, animals, plants or the environment. The use of biological weapons has been deemed "repugnant to the conscience of mankind" (BWC) and the development and production of biological weapons is banned by international treaty— the 1972 Biological Weapons Convention (BWC), UN Security Council Resolution 1540 and customary international law.

A commonly agreed definition of terrorism, and hence bioterrorism, does not exist. Nevertheless, for the purposes of this paper, bioterrorism is the deliberate dissemination of biological agents or toxins to cause harm for the purpose of spreading fear or dread in a population, more widespread than the affected target, for a political purpose. This definition excludes the more common, criminal use of a biological agent or toxin to kill or harm a specific individual or group for other purposes such as revenge. Bioterrorism can be perpetrated by states or non state actors, by a group, or individual.

1.1. Bioterrorism: What Do We Know?

The modern empirical record of bioterrorist acts is scant indeed. Thus, any conclusions about bioterrorism based on this historical record are prone to unreliability. It is difficult to make any robust conclusions based on such a small number of incidents. Nevertheless, this is what we know.

In 1984 a religious group, the Rajneeshes, had a growing community in The Dalles, Oregon a small city close to Portland, the largest city in Oregon. The people in the surrounding city were not happy about the existence of this group, which they thought of as a cult and they sought to limit the size and influence of the group through legislation. In order to gain votes in an upcoming election members of the Rajneeshes hatched a plan. They would dispense the bacterium that causes food poisoning, Salmonella typhimurium, throughout the city to sicken people so that they would not vote on election day. That would allow the Rajneeshes to control, or at least affect the election.

In order to maximize the likelihood of success the group had at least one trial, which was unsuccessful, before election day. Ultimately, however, the group found a way to successfully contaminate salad bars in area restaurants. According to public health records, more than 750 people contracted food poisoning. Of these, 45 were sick enough to be hospitalized. The group did not intend to kill anyone and there were no deaths. At the time, health personnel believed the disease was naturally occurring. It was not until much later that a defector from the religious group went to authorities and revealed the plot [1, 2].

The second case of confirmed bioterrorism is well known. In late September 2001 a potent, powdered formulation containing spores that cause the disease anthrax was put into envelopes and mailed to several recipients including members of the US Senate and the news media. The envelopes that were recovered also contained curious notes warning the recipients to take antibiotics because the contents of the envelopes contained anthrax spores. Despite these warnings, twenty-two people contracted the disease and five people died, including workers at postal facilities where the letters were processed, unknowingly exposed to the bacterial spores. Many more people heeded the letters' warnings and took prophylactic antibiotics. The perpetrator or perpetrators of this crime have not been identified. The anthrax spores in the letters were all of the same type—a variant of the Ames strain. This strain has been available in laboratories, including biodefense labs, in the US, UK, Canada and one or more other countries [3, 1].

In addition to these two cases of confirmed bioterrorism, two other topics are worth discussing. The first topic concerns the attempts of Aum Shinrikyo, the Japanese group responsible for the chemical weapon attacks in the Tokyo subway in 1995. Before turning to chemical weapons the group attempted to produce and disseminate the agent causing anthrax in wet slurry with a sprayer. The attempts by the group were unsuccessful for at least two reasons. First, the strain of anthrax obtained by the cult was a vaccine strain that could not produce disease. Second, the method of dispersal was also ineffective. The sprayer became clogged, and in any event, the particle size of the mist produced by the sprayer would likely not have been able to penetrate the lungs and produce the disease. It is worthwhile to note that the Aum group had significant monetary resources and several personnel reasonably well-trained in biology and were unable to successfully implement their intentions [1].

The second topic concerns Al Qaeda and its interest in biological weapons. Documents captured 2001 indicate that Al Qaeda was interested in biological weapons but had neither obtained disease causing anthrax cultures, nor begun any laboratory work. Like Aum Shinrikyo, Al Qaeda demonstrated interest in biological weapons, but success was elusive [1].

In contrast to non-state actors, states have demonstrated interest in biological weapons and have the resources to implement that interest. In the 20th Century many states have had active, offensive biological weapons programs producing a variety of lethal and incapacitating agents and weapons. The agents included animal and plant pathogens as well as human pathogens. The list of countries that had offensive biological weapons programs or contributed to the offensive programs of other states prior to the 1972 treaty that banned their existence includes Canada, France, Germany, Japan, the United Kingdom and the United States. The Soviet Union, South Africa and Iraq all had offensive programs and produced biological agents for weapons purposes after the Convention entered into force. The United States and other countries continue to suspect that other countries maintain offensive programs in violation of their obligations under the BWC [4].

The existence of state programs raises the possibility that state-sponsored terrorist groups could obtain biological agents and/or weapons from state programs. Despite this possibility, there is no credible evidence, thus far, that any states have knowingly supplied terrorist groups with biological agents or delivery mechanisms. There are reasons why governments with offensive programs would be reluctant to supply terrorist groups with biological weapons including the risk that their own clandestine programs would be unveiled, and that governments would not want to cede decisions on how and when to use biological weapons to a group over which they do not exercise complete or sufficient control. Nevertheless, the most that we know is that with the exceptions noted above, terrorist groups have not used biological weapons and a link between suspected state programs and terrorist groups has not been established. Another possible link between state biological weapons programs and non-state groups is the potential for members of terrorist organizations to gain access to dangerous pathogens while working for a government and then smuggle them clandestinely out of government laboratories. Thus, government programs that deal with dangerous pathogens, even those that are ostensibly for defensive purposes are vulnerable to theft.

1.2. Past State Programs

Several states have had extensive offensive biological weapons programs prior to the entry into force of the BWC. Throughout the 20th Century states developed, produced and stockpiled lethal and non-lethal biological weapons directed at humans, animals and plants. After the BWC entered into force the former USSR maintained and expanded its offensive BW program in violation of the BWC [4].

State programs shared a number of characteristics. Nearly all the BW programs entailed a high level of secrecy even when the existence of the programs was not constrained by international law. This high level of secrecy meant that many programs did not receive the type of oversight that typically is characteristic of other weapon programs. Most of the offensive programs were justified by a real or perceived threat from another state. Consequently, the secrecy of programs raised suspicions among states regarding possible BW programs developed by their adversaries. The absence of an international treaty banning such programs prior to 1972 permitted states to initiate offensive programs whether or not such suspicions were justified. Another common characteristic of offensive programs was collaboration between friendly or allied states and the sharing of information among states. This characteristic meant that some states specialized in certain tasks in BW development or testing. In other instances such sharing of information may have contributed to more rapid proliferation.

Despite the existence of BW programs both before and after entry into force of the BWC there is no evidence that states have knowingly supplied terrorist groups or networks with pathogens or weapons. The Ames strain of anthrax contained in the 2001 letters in the United States is rumored to have originated from a US biodefense lab, but other sources of the strain are also possible. Despite fears and speculation, there also does not exist any credible, open-source, evidence that scientists who worked in the Soviet BW program are now working in illicit offensive BW programs in so-called rogue states or for terrorist organizations. Similarly, there has not been a documented case of smallpox since the world wide eradication of the disease. Although the virus is retained in the United States and what is now the Russian Federation, there is also no credible, open source evidence that the virus has been stolen or clandestinely smuggled out of any Russian or US laboratory.

2. What Do We Fear

In contrast to what is known about bioterrorism, the fear of epidemics deliberately initiated by terrorists is widespread. One of the fundamental responsibilities of governments is to protect their citizens from harm, including preventable disease. Because of the potential of dangerous pathogens or toxins to lead to widespread death, disease or poisoning, the fear of bioterrorism is extensive.

Focusing on the possible consequences of a bioterrorist event rather than the probability that such an event will occur contributes to the prevalence of such a fear. In addition to an epidemic killing people in the tens of thousands or more we also fear the catastrophic economic consequences of an attack, perhaps especially, an attack on crops or livestock. We also fear the widespread disruption that even a small outbreak of anthrax or other disease caused by terrorism would entail. The letters containing anthrax spores sent to members of the US Congress and others in 2001 demonstrate how an attack that caused disease and death on a small scale led to large scale consequences in other areas. Finally perhaps it is a universal human characteristic to fear the unknown. We fear what we do not know, and therefore cannot control. Our perceived helplessness in the face of a bioterrorist attack generates its own fear.

3. Scientific Potential

Against this background, advances in science have contributed both to the potential consequences of bioterrorist attacks and our fears of them. Two phenomena merit attention. The first is the rapid pace of advancement in the biological sciences. Commercial, government and academic laboratories continue to explore new lines of research that could lead to the discovery of new cures or treatment for disease. At the same time these lines of research have the potential to make the consequences of a biological attack more deadly or more difficult to control, or conversely easier to control and target groups that share certain genetic similarities.

The second phenomenon is the rapid spread of scientific knowledge throughout the world. The speed with which information travels electronically means that the news of scientific discoveries is almost instantaneous. The ability to build on advances in science occurs much more rapidly than in the past. Similarly, scientists do not need to be in physical proximity to work together on projects. All of this is both potentially extremely beneficial and at the same time is worrisome from the prospect of the potential of bioterrorism.

3.1 Reality and Potential

Given the discussion above, analysts face a conundrum. Why has the reality of bioterrorism not matched its potential? The truth of the matter is that we do not know for sure. One possibility is that it is difficult for non-state actors to assemble the very different kinds of expertise necessary to effectively assemble and test a biological weapon that has mass destruction potential. Expertise in biology is not sufficient. Barriers to the acquisition of the agents with the greatest weapons potential have been strengthened since the 2001 anthrax letters. Preparation of an agent, and the production and testing of dispersal mechanisms all require different kinds of training and experience.

Empirically, it remains true that states retain the ability to harness different types of expertise on a single team to produce biological weapons that could cause mass destruction—deaths in the tens of thousands or more, or widespread animal epidemics or plant disease. Biological weapons attacks that produce relatively few fatalities are within the ability of groups that have scientific expertise and even malevolent individuals. Even such small scale attacks, however, could have enormous economic consequences, as well as mass disruption of medical care delivery, transportation networks, or other public or private services.

3. 2. What is hidden?

By definition, we don't know what is hidden. We do have a window, however, on what has been hidden in the past. Secrecy has been used to shroud offensive biological weapons programs in most states that had such programs in the past, both before and after the 1975 Biological Weapons Convention, which bans the production, possession and transfer of biological weapons. But offensive activities by states are not the only aspect of biological weapons that have been hidden or secret. Many of the activities that have ostensibly been undertaken for defense against potential biological weapons have been hidden. The BWC allows states to possess biological agents and toxins of types and in quantities that are justified for a "prophylactic, protective, or other peaceful purpose" [5] Nevertheless, in practice few states describe their biological defense programs in detail, or justify their possession of agents and toxins for permitted purposes. Secrecy in biodefense activities fuels suspicions that some states may be crossing the line between offensive and defensive biological weapons development. Secrecy in biodefense also means that activities may not receive appropriate oversight or review to ensure all activities are in compliance with the BWC.

In the past, sales or transfers of equipment that could be used for offensive as well as legitimate purposes were not always carefully monitored. Although, equipment necessary for large-scale offensive programs is more carefully monitored in some parts of the world, it is not universal. Similarly, while the ability to purchase or transfer pathogens or toxins with weapons potential has been inhibited in recent years, many pathogens, like anthrax can be found naturally in many parts of the world, although its accurate identification, production, preparation, dispersal and testing are not trivial tasks. Some deadly toxins, such as botulinum toxin, are produced in large quantities for medical purposes and are therefore subject to diversion or theft if not closely and carefully monitored.

Finally, there is currently no way to easily and reliably track people with the expertise necessary to produce biological weapons. Many of the scientists and technicians who have worked in clandestine offensive weapons programs in Iraq, the former USSR or elsewhere are free to relocate and apply their knowledge in legitimate areas. However, they may also go underground or use their expertise for malevolent purposes, either alone or with others.

4. What Should Be Done?

A number of efforts addressing the threat of use of biological weapons from either states are non-state actors should be undertaken in tandem to lessen the probability of bioterrorism and to mitigate its consequences should it occur. A number of these activities are already underway. First, to address the threat of the state use of biological weapons, the States Parties participating 6th Review Conference of the BTWC which concluded in early December 2006 have taken a number of decisions. The Final Declaration of the Conference establishes a small Implementation Support Unit (ISU) of three people within the United Nations Department of Disarmament affairs. Second, the States Parties have agreed to hold annual meetings of experts and governmental representatives on a number of topics of relevance to the Convention. These annual meetings keep States Parties attention on the threat of biological weapons and provide a forum for technical experts, government officials, the media, and members of non-governmental and intergovernmental organizations to meet, discuss, plan, and exchange ideas and information on how best to address the threat [6].

In 1986 Parties to the BTWC inaugurated an information exchange on activities relevant to the Convention, and expanded the exchange in 1991. This exchange, frequently referred to as Confidence Building Measures (CBMs) has had a disappointing participation rate over the years. The 6th Review Conference took a number of decisions in regard to CMBs. One of the functions of the new ISU will be to promote greater participation in the CBM process and to facilitate electronic submissions of CBMs through the development of a secure website open to States Parties only [6].

The emphasis placed on CBMs by the 6th Review Conference implies that the States Parties place a high priority on the exchange of accurate information on, among other things, biodefense activities. Such transparency among States Parties is to be lauded. While the CBM website will be open to States Parties only, States should be encouraged to provide public access to the information contained in their CBM submissions. Such transparency measures are likely to reduce the uncertainty surrounding what would be secret activities of relevance to the Convention.

Strengthening the BWC through annual meetings, support staff, promotion of universality and greater participation in CBM exchanges addresses only part of the BW threat. In implementing the BWC States Parties must continue to control the access to dangerous pathogens. Governments have a special responsibility to establish strict and effective means to eliminate, to the extent possible, any theft, or inadvertent proliferation from their own laboratories. Governments need to monitor advances in the life sciences and assess their relevance to the Convention.

National legislation, to make sure that any violation of the provisions of the Convention by individuals or non-state groups is punishable through criminal prosecution, has been an area of concern for several years. The European Union has undertaken a joint action to promote the passage of appropriate national legislations in states that have not yet done so.

Governments must ensure that their own houses are in order. That means that they must establish strong oversight of their own biodefense activities including interagency and, as appropriate, legislative oversight, to ensure that zealousness in biodefense does not lead to activities of questionable compliance. Such "gray area" projects are likely to lead to other governments pursuing similarly suspect activities in response—all of which could diminish rather than strengthen the effectiveness of the treaty. Transparency in biodefense activities serves at least two essential purposes. First, to provide a protective, prophylactic or other peaceful purpose justification for its work with biological agents and toxins as stated in the BWC. Second, transparency will limit the likelihood that other States will pursue offensive development activities in the mistaken belief that secret activities undertaken in the name of biodefense have offensive potential and must be widely pursued.

5. Conclusion

Assessing the threat of bioterrorism is a complex undertaking because the empirical record of biological weapons attacks is so scant. Much of what we know about the bioterrorist threat is based on the potential to do harm rather than the likelihood that an attack will take place. At the same time the evidence of states activities in offensive biological weapons activities is extensive and widespread. Moreover, the two phenomenons are interrelated. State biological weapons programs provide an opportunity for scientists and technical experts to acquire expertise that could be used for malevolent purposes. Unless dangerous pathogens and toxins are very strictly controlled, they are vulnerable to theft. Secret biological activities, even when carried out under the auspices of biodefense can still engender suspicion by others. Thus states much coordinate their activities in addressing bioterrorism with simultaneous efforts to control biological weapons programs sponsored by states, principally through strengthening the Biological Weapons Convention.

References

[1] M. Leitenberg, *The problem of biological weapons*. Stockholm: The Swedish National Defence College; 2004.
[2] J. McDermott, *The killing winds: The menace of biological warfare*. New York: Arbor House; 1987.
[3] L.A. Cole, *The anthrax letters: A medical detective story*. Washington D.C.: The National Academies Press; 2003.
[4] M. Wheelis, L. Rozsa, M. Dando, Editors. *Deadly cultures: Biological weapons since 1945*. Cambridge, MA: Harvard University Press; 2006.
[5] BWC, Convention on the prohibition of the development, production and stockpiling of bacteriological (biological) and toxin weapons and on their destruction, Signed at Washington, London, and Moscow. 1972, April 10. [Online] Available from; URL: http://www.unog.ch/80256EE600585943/(httpPages) /04FBBDD6315AC 720C1257180004B1B2F?OpenDocument [2006, December 10].
[6] Final Document, Sixth review conference of the states parties to the convention on the prohibition of the development, production and stockpiling of bacteriological (biological) and toxin weapons and on their destruction. 2006, 8 December. [Online] Available from; URL: www.bwpp.org/documents/6thRev ConDraft FinalReport.pdf. [2006, December 12].

The Demand Side of Terrorism: Fear

Brian FORST, Ph.D.
School of Public Affairs, American University, USA

Abstract. This paper considers terrorism as a market, with a supply side that has received inordinate attention and a demand side that has received too little. The demand for terrorism is principally about fear: there would be little reason to produce terrorism if it did not bring attention to the causes of terrorists, and it brings attention primarily by way of fear. We consider here the nature and sources of the demand side of the terrorism market, starting with the truism that acts of terrorism serve the purposes of terrorists because of the public's fear. The paper then analyzes fear in terms of its relationship to actual risks, perceived risks, and internal and external stimuli that contribute to it, and it describes a model of fear management based on the Routine Activities Theory and the balancing of the social costs of fear. It considers the roles of media and politics as both stimuli and prospective tools for managing fear.

Keywords. Fear, terrorism, opportunity theory, Routine Activities Theory

Introduction

Terrorism is not a good in a moral sense, but in an economic sense there is today, clearly, a considerable market for it. Consider first the supply side of this market. The producers of terrorism are attracted to targets they perceive will serve their political agendas by drawing attention to those agendas in ways that are not otherwise readily attainable. Terrorists aim to generate interest in larger ideological causes through acts of martyrdom and aim to enlist others in those causes. Now consider the demand side response. The "War on Terrorism" launched by the consumers of terrorism immediately after al Qaeda's 9/11 attack on the United States served the principal goals of the terrorists, allowing them to characterize the U.S. response as a war on Islam and thus attract bystanders to terrorism and increase the number of acts of suicide terrorism. The war did accomplish some valuable short-term objectives for the U.S. as well, including the overthrow of the Taliban government of Afghanistan that harbored al Qaeda headquarters and training facilities, and the tightening up of security at airports, seaports, and formal border entry points. But its unintended consequences may have more than offset these achievements. It legitimized al Qaeda and other terrorist groups in the eyes of marginalized people throughout Islam, and it created strong incentives to find alternative ways of circumventing and defeating the enemy in this new war. In the name of defeating terrorism, the War on Terrorism increased the demand for terrorism, by all appearances attracting more terrorists.

The fuel that feeds this engine of escalation is fear, the core of the demand for terrorism. Unfortunately, the supply side of the terrorism market has received a disproportionate share of the attention to date. We see, hear, and read considerably more about terrorists - who they are, where they are from, what instruments of violence and devious schemes they employ, and so on - than we do about the demand side of terrorism. The media in Muslim cultures, by contrast, focus on the dark side of the War on Terrorism, depicting the al Qaeda as misguided souls, if not as martyrs, and describing the War as a matter that worsens *their* fears and justifies their sense of righteous wrath.

Prior to the 9/11 attack, people in the United States and other Western nations had relatively little fear of terrorism. Judging from the extent of media attention, fear had been reserved largely for rapists and pedophiles, sharks and cancer. The 9/11 attack and the shock it engendered produced an unprecedented level of fear in the United States. Within days, people throughout the U.S. bought several millions of dollars worth of duct tape and gas masks, puzzled over the meaning of terror alert color codes, and became extremely suspicious of men in turbans and women wearing head scarves. A few days after 9/11, Balbir Singh Sodhi, a Sikh gas station owner, was shot and killed in Phoenix by a local man who assumed Sodhi was a Muslim.

What is the nature of the fears that drive such behaviors? To what extent are the fears useful and reasonable, and to what extent are they harmful and irrational? What, if anything, should public officials do about fear? What can ordinary citizens do about it? These are the issues we take up in this paper.

1. Fear

1.1. The Anatomy of Fear

Terror is, by definition, a matter of fear: "terror" means fear in the extreme. (The word derives from the Latin verb *terrere*, to cause trembling.) The power of terrorism lies "almost exclusively in the fear it creates" [1]. Terrorists commit violent acts against noncombatant populations typically because they anticipate that the acts will strike fear in the hearts of the population. Terrorists might, of course, attack innocents purely out of hatred of them and a desire to exterminate them. But in those cases too, fear is a critical factor: even small elements of fear generated by acts of terrorism create new problems and impose further harms, above and beyond those caused by the acts themselves, and do so in both the near-term and long-term.

From the perspective of the terrorist, acts of violence are most successful when they create mass hysteria, inducing target populations to implode, to impose vastly greater harms on themselves as a consequence of their own fear than from the immediate damage associated with the initial acts. This serves, in turn, to reward the terrorist by yielding a considerably larger payoff than from the initial attack, and so it creates incentives for further acts of terrorism. This cycle can be broken either when the public sees that the acts have subsided or when prospective terrorists understand that their acts, even substantial ones, draw limited attention and have little subsequent impact on the target population. The problem is one that may lend itself to a demand reduction strategy.

To develop such a strategy, we must first understand fear more clearly. Because fear is a central aspect of terrorism, our ability to understand terrorism and deal with it effectively depends critically on our understanding the nature and sources of fear and the harms it imposes on society. Strategies for dealing with offenders and protecting targets against street crimes have been effectively complemented with strategies for managing the public's fear of crime. Because of the unique importance of fear to terrorism, it would be reasonable to expect that we might, even more fruitfully than in the case of crime, complement strategies for dealing with terrorists and targets of terrorism by finding and implementing effective strategies for managing the public's fear of terrorism and thus reduce the demand for terrorism.

1.2. Short- and Long-term Consequences of Excessive Fear

The demand side of terrorism is the product of both short-term fear and long-term fear. Just as doctors distinguish between short-term *acute pain* and long-lasting *chronic pain*, so has a distinction been made between *acute fear* - a natural, immediate response to danger that tends to subside quickly - and *chronic fear* - fear that persists after an immediate danger has passed [2, 3]. Reasonable levels of fear are helpful to generate the sort of concerns about terrorism that help us to develop coherent approaches to prevent it in the first place and deal with it effectively when it does occur.

There are ample reasons to assert, however, that the public's fears of terrorism are inflated, and that inflated fears tend to harm us both in the short term and long term. In the short term, fear diverts people from productive activities, it induces them to consume resources that may do little to protect them against harm, and it can produce severe stresses and reduce social capital and the quality of life over an extended period. It can create detachment and distrust and can harm emotional and physical health and economic well-being. In extreme cases it can produce public panics, severe social and financial disruptions, and sharp spikes in accidental deaths and injuries and suicides. Over the longer term, it can induce politicians to pander to the public's fears, reduce freedoms and invoke responses at home and abroad that may serve more to alienate prospective allies than to reduce the sources of the threats and thus enhance security. *New Yorker* essayist Adam Gopnik has put it succinctly: "Terror makes fear, and fear stops thinking." Our failure to think, by many accounts, has contributed to behaviors that have increased the demand for acts of terrorism.

1.3. Fear of Crime, Fear of Terrorism

Terror means fear in the extreme largely because terrorism is crime in the extreme. Fear of crime can impose costs on society that exceed those of crime itself, manifesting as reduced quality of life, wasteful expenditures on resources and measures that do little to prevent crime, stress-related illnesses and health costs, and related social costs [4, 5, 6]. Because the damage associated with a typical act of terrorism is so much greater than for a typical street crime, the level of fear and the associated social costs are generally much greater for terrorism than for ordinary crime. It is no coincidence that the subject of terrorism has dominated the news since September 11, 2001, while crime has moved from the front pages of most major newspapers, despite the fact that the level of crime has not declined in the years following 9/11, and has in fact begun to increase recently.

The public's fear of terrorism is very much like its fear of crime in one important respect: fear levels remain high even as most objective evidence about the threat of harm has declined. Fear of crime remained high throughout the 1990's even as crime rates plummeted: the homicide rate in the United States dropped from about 9 homicides per 100,000 residents in 1990 to about 5 per 100,000 in 2000 [7].

Similarly, the ending of the cold war brought with it a huge decline in the amount of international violence. There were 40 percent fewer conflicts throughout the world in 2003 than in 1992, and 80 percent fewer deadly conflicts involving 1,000 or more battle deaths, as well as an 80 percent decline in the number of genocides and other mass slaughters of civilians. International terrorism did increase substantially during the period, but terrorists, conventionally defined, still kill just a small fraction of the number who die in wars [8].

2. The Relationship between Fear and Risk

Fear is largely a matter of biology, a physical response to stimuli. It is in the genes. The mechanics of fear are centered in the amygdala, an almond-shaped mass of gray matter in the anterior portion of the temporal lobe. Stimulation of the amygdala generates an outpouring of stress hormones, including adrenaline, producing a state of extreme alertness, followed by secretion of a natural steroid, cortisol. While the triggers of fear vary from one species to the next, all animals with this brain architecture experience fear through this basic mechanism.

Fear is also environmentally determined. First-born children tend to be more cautious than second-born. And it is learned: most of us are inclined not to repeat behaviors when, through direct experience, we know that those behaviors threaten our safety or the safety of others. Fears are shaped as well by others: parents, neighbors, teachers, media and peers. What is learned from each of these sources may produce misperceptions of actual risks, but they are learned nonetheless, and they in turn alter fear levels, for better or worse.

But fear is also a matter of risk, both real and perceived. The misperceptions of risk that give rise to either inflated fears, as in the case of sharks and terrorism, or deflated fears, as in the case of driving and diets rich in transfats, are universal, although they vary considerably from place to place and over time. The United States has responded to the attack of 9/11 in its way, while Europeans have expressed concerns about terrorist attacks in Spain, Holland and elsewhere on the continent; they are considerably more exposed to threats of terrorist attacks than are citizens of the U.S. Traditional societies the world over had feared the corruption of their youth following years of invasive Western pop culture now broadcast through new communication and information technologies, and the 9/11 attack left Muslims everywhere feeling even more under siege than before, in fear of reprisal [9].

How do an individual's fears correspond to the actual risk levels of the threats perceived? Each person's unique combination of inherent inclinations and personal experiences shape both his or her sense of the risks associated with various threats and the fear that the person attaches to those perceptions. The lack of correspondence is based on a myriad of factors, including widespread tendencies to ignore certain types of pertinent information; people tend to give excessive weight to the worst possible outcome [10, 11]. They are based as well on misinformation obtained from parents, peers, media, and other sources, which can be significantly heightened through tipping point mechanisms such as social cascades and group polarization [12]. The influence of others serves to validate and deepen such individual inclinations toward vulnerability.

We can identify two distinct facets of an individual's tendency to over-react, or occasionally to under-react, to threats: making subjective assessments of risks that are high or low relative to the objective risk levels, and having fear levels that are high or low relative to one's subjective assessments. Rare but extreme threats tend to activate both aspects of distortion. The distortions are caused by a variety of factors, including parental influences, local folklore and media distortions.

Our sense of danger is often out of line with reality because our perceptions are often distorted by unsystematic evidence -- even when our fear level is parallel with our perception of the risk of various threats. Unsystematic evidence may be highly unrepresentative of reality because the nature of the event experienced directly is itself unrepresentative of the class of events with which we associate the experience; or because the event may occur more or less frequently than we realize; or because of physical interference or emotion. Moreover, our recollections of events change over time; and our filtering of information about events not directly experienced may distort our perceptions of the risk and typical nature of the thing feared.

Mixed messages from others can add to this confusion. Parents often condition children to err on the side of caution and overestimate threats, while peers often countervail against such messages, encouraging their friends to engage in risky behaviors. Social scientists have discovered that the net effect of this interaction of our unique innate predispositions with a vast jumble of mixed information from the environment can cause our subjective assessments of risk of a particular threat to be often at considerable variance with the actual objective risk of the threat. We tend to exaggerate some threats and underestimate others.

Virtually every day someone somewhere becomes the widely publicized victim of a tragic but rare event. Yet for each such person the quality of many thousands of other lives may be diminished substantially when they live their lives beyond reasonable precaution, in fear that they too might succumb to the unlikely tragic prospects that have befallen the few, about whom we may know more than is good for our own safety and well-being.

3. Media and Fear

We learn about serious acts of violence generally, and terrorism in particular, through the media: television, radio, newspapers, magazines, and increasingly, the Internet. In our free and open democratic society, the public is served with such information under the First Amendment to the Constitution: "Congress shall make no law ... abridging the freedom of speech, or of the press." Restrictions on such information would make it more difficult for the public to hold their elected officials accountable for failures to provide protection for which they are responsible. The public obtains useful information about terrorism principally through the media.

At the same time, however, the media serve as an essential instrument of terror: without media, terrorists would have no stage on which to perform their acts of flagrant violence against noncombatants. The fear that defines terrorism requires media broadcasting; the wider the audience reached, the greater the fear and more effective the act.

The public is especially fearful of extreme predatory acts of violence, acts against which they are powerless to defend or protect themselves. This sense of powerlessness surely contributes to the public's exaggerated fears of terrorism, crime and shark attacks. Media accounts of surprise attacks by predators against innocent victims tend to seize the public's attention more indelibly than do depictions of readily preventable fatal falls down staircases or from ladders, or of heart attacks that result from overeating and lack of exercise.

In the case of terrorism, the media have not passed up many opportunities to exploit the public's innate fear of it. What are the consequences of this fear-feeding frenzy?

Perhaps the most serious consequence is that media preoccupations with terrorism may contribute significantly to self-fulfilling cycles of fear and violence. Terrorists use the media as a tool for terror, taping videos of the beheadings of noncombatants and broadcasting warnings of further attacks by jihadist leaders. Western media outlets ordinarily edit and often censor the more gruesome of these media presentations, but there can be little doubt that the widespread airings of these events and threats in news reports feed the fires of fear and over-reaction. Media coverage shapes public opinion, and public opinion shapes public policy.

4. Exploitation of Fear by Politicians

The media have company in feeding and inflating our fears: politicians. Politicians often take the messages of the media a step further and convert the inflated fear into bad policy. Why? Because feeding the public's fear gets votes. Failure to do so can end political careers. This was done famously with crime in the presidential election of 1988, with the "Willie Hortonization" of Michael Dukakis, and it was done more recently on the terrorism issue in the presidential election of 2004, with the "Swiftboat Campaign" stigmatization of Democratic candidate John Kerry for his expression of antiwar sentiments toward the end of the Vietnam War. Politicians who avoid such exploitations can be found in both major political parties, but many other politicians across the political spectrum have shown little hesitancy to exploit public fears about threats to domestic and foreign security in order to win votes, and they have done so with impunity.

One of the characteristic strengths of an established free society is a bond of mutual trust and responsibility between the elected and the governed: government ensures that the information the public has about domestic and foreign threats is accurate and balanced, and it trusts them to handle the information responsibly. Terrorism can erode this cohesion, and politicians who use terrorism for political ends may accelerate the erosion.

This is not to suggest that political pandering in the presence of serious threats to security is inevitable and inescapable. Effective political leadership does occasionally emerge, especially in times of grave threats to national security. One has only to consider Prime Minister Winston Churchill's effective exhortations to the English public, and Londoners in particular, to be courageous in the face of brutal and incessant blitzkrieg bombings by the Germans in World War II. He led both by both word and example, holding cabinet meetings at his home office rather than in bunkers, often dangerously well into the nighttime as bombs exploded nearby. The people followed Churchill's lead, and the courage of the British helped first to enable them to survive the attacks and carry on, and eventually to contribute in significant ways to the defeat of Germany. A memorable display of fear-reduction leadership echoing Churchill's was revealed by New York Mayor Rudy Giuliani in the hours and days following the 2001 attack on the World Trade Towers.

5. Fear and Public Policy

Given the central role that fear plays in terrorism, public policy makers would do well to combine their interventions against terrorists and the protection of targets with policies for managing the public's fear of terrorism. Fear is not an immutable given, a phenomenon over which we have no control. It is manageable, both for individuals and groups, and by both public and private interveners. How can public officials work with private citizens to do this?

They can begin by considering the relevance of fear reduction programs that have proven successful in managing the fear of crime [13] to the domain of terrorism. Fear reduction strategies for conventional crime instituted as part of the 1980s community policing movement have elements that are applicable to the problem of terrorism, where the stakes may be much higher. Local authorities have every reason to regard acts of terrorism as extreme violent crimes under state law. From their perspective, fear management interventions should be highly relevant and useful.

At the same time, some fear reduction interventions for street crimes are likely to be more relevant and practical than others for the prevention of terrorism. Effective outreach programs to mosques in neighborhoods with Muslim populations, for example, are likely to be more useful to deal with fear within both the Muslim and non-Muslim communities than programs aimed at removing ordinary graffiti. Moreover, outreach programs that induce effective adaptive behaviors -- such as avoidance, professional help, insurance, pertinent information, planning, coping and protective actions -- are likely to be more effective than ones that do not [14].

It would seem useful, in any case, to consider the full range of fear reduction strategies and interventions to ensure that policies and practices that are applicable to the public's fear of terrorism are not overlooked. These programs have proven their value in neighborhoods throughout the United States, and they are likely to have parallel applicability for individuals and institutions, public and private, to reduce the destructive effects of the fear of terrorism.

Analysis may help immeasurably to understand the relationship between fear and terrorism and help to identify policies that may serve to manage fear and reduce the prospects of terrorism. Two particularly suitable frameworks for such consideration are the Routine Activities Theory and the notion of an optimal level of fear. Let us consider each of these in turn.

5.1. Modeling Fear in a Routine Activities Theory Framework

The Routine Activities Theory (RAT) of crime, proposed by Lawrence Cohen and Marcus Felson in 1979, provides a conceptual framework for terrorism within which fear and other pertinent variables can be incorporated. The RAT model holds that crime cannot occur without any of three essential components: motivated offenders, suitable targets, and the absence of capable guardians to protect the targets. The central idea is that routine patterns of work and leisure influence the convergence of these three components in time and place, and motivated, rational offenders are inclined to seize opportunities presented by such patterns. Accordingly, the theory is alternately referred to as "*opportunity theory*" [15]. Public and private resources can intervene by providing guardianship to protect the targets at these intersections of attractive targets and willing offenders.

The RAT can be expressed as a simultaneous system of equations with a supply side describing willing terrorists and a demand side describing available targets.[1] The system has four endogenous variables, each appearing as both dependent and independent variables within the system, with endogenous variables underscored when they appear as independent variables:

- Targets (demand): Attractiveness of prospective targets (P) = a + b*Social cost of a successful attack + c*Dollars spent on guardianship (G) + d*Fear level (F) + e*Other demand-side factors + residual;
- Terrorists (supply): Number of terrorist attack attempts (Q) = f + g*P+ h*G+ i*Other supply-side factors + residual;
- Guardianship: G = j + k*P+ l*Q+ m*Availability of guardianship resources + n*Effectiveness of guardianship resources + o*F + residual; and
- Fear: F = p + q*Q + r*G + s*Other fear factors + residual.

The model can apply either to a prospective target and be aggregated over all such targets or it can apply to the aggregate of targets using averages across the prospective targets. In each instance in which an endogenous variable appears as an independent variable, an instrument should be used instead of the raw data for that variable, in order to eliminate simultaneity bias. The instrument gives an unbiased estimate of that endogenous variable based on the values of all the exogenous variables in the system. The challenges of finding reliable data for each of the key variables in the model and assuring that the identification restrictions are satisfied both theoretically and empirically are considerable, but the model does provide a useful conceptual starting point for thinking about the relationships among key variables and how they must be analyzed to ensure that valid estimators of the effects of pertinent interventions in particular settings are generated.

This model helps, in particular, to clarify the central role that public policy can play in managing fear. Fear should decline both as the number of terrorist attacks decline and as the extent of guardianship increases. Increases in the extent of guardianship should reduce fear both by reducing the number of terrorist attacks and by increasing the perception of security independent of the actual effects of guardianship on the level of terrorist attacks. And, of particular importance, the reduction of fear should reduce the attractiveness of prospective terrorist targets. The reduction of fear should, moreover, increase the quality of life, independently of its terrorism effects.

5.2. Managing Fear by Balancing Its Social Costs

The total elimination of fear is neither an attainable nor a desirable goal. Just as it would not be healthy to eliminate pain altogether, so would it be unsafe to reduce it to a suboptimally low level or, worse, to work to eliminate it altogether. Some level of fear is necessary for us to feel compelled first to take ourselves out of harm's way, and then to take measures to counter the sources of the danger. The 9/11 Commission concluded that there was too little concern about terrorism prior to the 2001 attack; by many

---

[1] The prototype economic model is that of demand and supply, both functions of the price and quantity of a good or service. The challenge is to identify the system in such a way that distinguishes the positive relationship between price and quantity on the supply side from the negative relationship on the demand side [16].

accounts inflated fear of terrorism afterward has imposed vast unnecessary costs on people throughout the world [17, 18, 19].

In the case of both crime and terrorism, the goal should be twofold: 1. make accurate objective assessments of the risks of threats and then realign subjective assessments of the risks so that they correspond to the objective assessments, and 2. remove elements of fear that serve no useful purpose. In much the same way that we can consider frameworks to assist us in finding an optimal balance of security and liberty, and can assess criminal sanctions in terms of the total social costs of crimes and sanctions [20], so might we do well to consider policies that aim for optimal levels of fear for various threats. See Figure 1 for a depiction of an optimal level of fear, the level that balances the cost of fear with the cost of victimization averted by fear. Such frameworks cannot determine public policies, but they can help to identify the key factors for consideration and determine how to organize them coherently to provide a basis for assessing those policies.

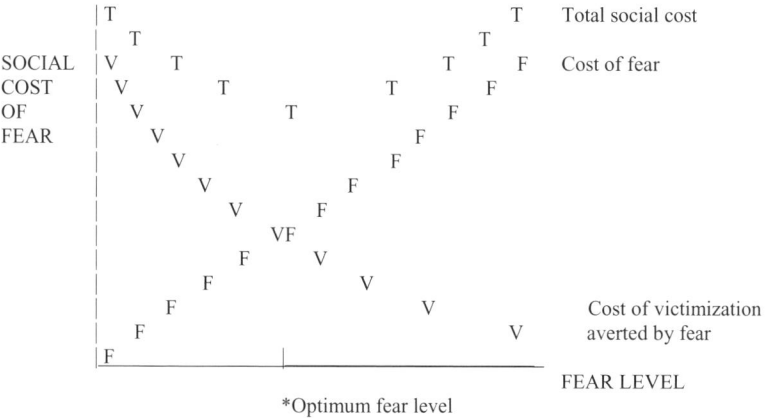

Figure 1. Optimal level of fear

6. An Agenda for Reducing the Social Costs of Fear

How might policy makers and public officials to think about the management of the public's fear? At the local level, fear reduction strategies that have been a key aspect of successful community policing programs can be tailored to deal with fear of terrorism, as we have noted above. At the federal level, just as effective energy policy cannot ignore the public's insatiable demand for and often wasteful consumption of scarce energy resources, so must an effective terrorism policy recognize the importance of interventions that deal effectively with a parallel problem on the demand side of terrorism: dysfunctional fear. Strategies for managing the public's fear of terrorism might be developed in such a way that satisfies both liberals and conservatives alike. Neither group can take comfort in the prospect that we may have actually contributed to our insecurity and misallocated resources in the process by placating exaggerated public fears - for example, by overemphasizing airport security at the expense of vulnerability at ports, nuclear and chemical facilities, and other critical, more vulnerable targets. Several authorities have argued persuasively that such misallocations have been induced by misplaced fears [21, 17]. Systems of accountability used by the office of homeland security and associated agencies can be reshaped to support fear management as a legitimate goal of those agencies.

Sunstein has proposed the strengthening of deliberative democracies to help manage fear generally; he has proposed, in particular, a federal risk assessment agency to collect data and conduct research aimed at reducing actual risks and better aligning objective and subjective risk levels [22]. He notes that a significant barrier to the adoption of such reform is that public-minded administrators who dismiss the public's irrationality are often overruled by populist politicians who respond to parochial agendas and short-term concerns, however irresponsible for the nation as a whole, and to public concerns of the moment, however irrational and short-sighted [22, 11]. He adds that education and public information can help to restore rational deliberation to the process. Tharoor has suggested along a similar line that the media, for too long a source of fear-mongering, are capable of serving no less as an instrument of education and tolerance [23].

Protection of the public is the first responsibility of government, and misplaced fears undermine public safety. The effective public management of fear is central to this responsibility of government. In cases of extreme abuse of the media's responsibility not to harm the public, the courts may be able to step in to provide protections. Justice Oliver Wendell Holmes observed in the landmark 1917 case of *Schenck* v. *United States*, "The most stringent protection of free speech would not protect a man in falsely shouting fire in a theater, and causing a panic." This could apply as well to needlessly incendiary media accounts of violence or threats of violence.

Effective, credible leadership is critical. It creates a bond of trust between the government and the governed, a social contract in which the people will follow loyally and manage their fear responsibly when they have sufficient reason to believe that the government is leveling with them without divulging information that helps terrorists needlessly, when the government attains a proper balance between liberty and security.

When a Churchill or Roosevelt-caliber leader fails to emerge, or when effective leaders get assassinated - an all-too-frequent occurrence in places most desperately in need of effective leaders - nongovernmental organizations and responsible citizens are left to find ways to fill the void. In such cases ordinary citizens must become extraordinary; to step up and become leaders. Shows of extraordinary courage in the face of extreme terror have been displayed by citizens in India, Iraq, and Israel in recent years even in the absence of a Churchill-like figure. The day after a series of bombings on commuter trains in Mumbai (formerly Bombay) killed over 200 people, Mumbai's tracks were cleared, trains resumed their routes, and the Bombay Stock Exchange's stock index rose by 3% [2] [24].

7. Conclusion

Some portion of fear is, of course, unmanageable. Fear is, after all, in our genes, a natural survival instinct. Yet when such biological instincts get out of hand and worsen the dangers we confront, it is precisely the capacity of humans to reason -- to "get a

---

[2] Prime Minister Manmohan Singh offered helpful words of inspiration to his people, but Wonacott and Bellman attribute India's strength in the face of terror to the indominatable spirit of ordinary people, a deep understanding that life must go on.

grip" on ourselves under stress - that has contributed immeasurably to the resilience of our species.

We have reason to fear terrorism, surely more so today than prior to September 11, 2001, but we will do well to keep the risks of terrorism to our national security and the security of our allies in perspective. Cataclysmic risks were more immediate in the United States in World War II and during the Cuban Missile Crisis of 1962 than today, and people in most other countries have for years been considerably more exposed to terrorism than have people in the U.S. There is no cause for alarm if we take reasonable and effective measures to neutralize persons who have demonstrated a clear intent to commit acts of terrorism, if we protect the primary targets of terrorism, and if we can manage to manage our fear. The 9/11 attack revealed that concerns of the U.S. government and its citizens about terrorism had been inadequate, that the risks exceeded our fear. Today fear is the greater problem, and it is dangerous because of the strong tendency for it to feed on itself, to make us behave badly, to allow our instincts to overrule our ability to think. Perhaps our greatest challenge is to master our capacity to "get a grip" when confronted with real danger, to find ways of strengthening our capacity to reason, to overcome our natural tendency to be more easily frightened than unfrightened[3] -- and to groom leaders who will reduce the demand for terrorism by inspiring us and calming our inflated fears.

References

[1]   D.C. Martin, J. Walcott, Best laid plans: The inside story of America's war against terrorism. New York: Harper-Collins; 1988. 392 p.
[2]   J. Hollander, Fear itself. *Social Research, 71/4* (2004), 1-23.
[3]   G.F. Mahl, Relationship between acute and chronic fear and the gastric acidity and blood sugar levels in macaca mulatta monkeys. *Psychosomatic Medicine* **14** (1952), 182-210.
[4]   M.A. Cohen, Measuring the costs and benefits of crime and justice. *Criminal Justice 2000* (Washington, DC: U.S. Department of Justice) **4** (2000), 263-315.
[5]   President's Commission on Law Enforcement and Administration of Justice, *The Challenge of Crime in a Free Society,* Washington, DC: U.S. Government Printing Office; 1967.
[6]   M. Warr, Fear of crime in the United States: Avenues for research and policy. *Criminal Justice 2000,* Washington, DC: U.S. Department of Justice; **4** (2000), 451-89.
[7]   UCR-U.S. Department of Justice, Federal Bureau of Investigation, [Online] Available from; URL: http://www.fbi.gov/ucr/05cius/data/table_01.html [2006, September].
[8]   A. Mack, Peace on earth? Increasingly, yes. *Washington Post,* 2005, December 28, p. A21.
[9]   A.S. Ahmed, *Islam under siege,* Cambridge, England: Polity Press; 2003. 224 p.
[10] D. Kahneman, A. Tversky, *Choices, values and frames.* Cambridge, England: University Press; 2000. 860 p.
[11] C.R. Sunstein, *Laws of fear: Beyond the precautionary principle.* Cambridge, England: Cambridge University Press; 2005. 246 p.
[12] F. Furedi Politics of fear. London. *Spiked;* 2004 October 28. Available from: http://www.frankfuredi.com/articles/politicsFear-20041028.shtml.
[13] W.G. Cordner, Fear of crime and the police, an evaluation of a fear-reduction strategy. *Journal of Police Administration;* **14/3** (1986 Sep.), 223-233.
[14] A. Kirschenbaum, Terror, adaptation and preparedness: A trilogy for survival. *Journal of Homeland Security and Emergency Management.* Berkeley, CA. Berkeley Electronic Press; **3/1** (2006), 3 Available from: http://www.bepress.com/jhsem/vol3/iss1/3.
[15] L.E. Cohen, M. Felson, Social change and crime rate trends: A routine activity approach. *American Sociological Review,* **44** (1979), 588-608.
[16] B.R. Chiswick, S.J. Chiswick, *Statistics and econometrics: A problem-solving text.* Baltimore:

---

[3]As psychologist Paul Slovic has observed, "It's much easier to scare than unscare." [25]

University Park Press; 1975. 261 p.

[17] A. Applebaum, Finding things to fear. *Washington Post,* 2003, September 24, p. A29.

[18] F. Furedi Politics of fear: *Beyond left and right*. London. Continuum International Publishing Group; 2006. 160 p.

[19] D. Ropeik, We're being scared to death. Los Angeles, CA. *Los Angeles Times;* 2004, September 22 [cited 2006 August 21] Available from: http://www.commondreams.org/views04/0922-12.htm

[20] B. Forst, *Errors of Justice*. Cambridge, England: Cambridge University Press; 2004. 272 p.

[21] J. Fallows, Success without victory: A 'containment' strategy for the age of terror. *Atlantic Monthly* **295/1** (2005 January/February), 80-90.

[22] C.R. Sunstein, *Risk and reason: Safety, law and the environment*. Cambridge, England: Cambridge University Press; 2002. 342 p.

[23] S. Tharoor, The role of the media in promoting tolerance. In A. Ahmed , B. Forst, editors. *After terror: Promoting dialogue among civilizations*. Cambridge: Polity Press; 2005. p 160.

[24] P. Wonacott, E. Bellman, India is resilient in wake of deadly blasts. *The Wall Street Journal,* 2006, July 13, p. A5

[25] J. Spencer, C. Crossen, Why do Americans feel that danger lurks everywhere? *The Wall Street Journal,* 2003, April 24, pp. A1, A12.

Terrorism: A Socio-Economic Analysis

Ismail OZSOY

International Black Sea University, Georgia

Abstract. The fundamental problems of the international political order currently seem mainly to be the inability of many states to provide for the welfare and security of their citizens and the demands of global governance in an anarchic world, the horrifying economic disparities between the rich north and the impoverished south, global warming, and AIDS. In addition to these, terrorism has become the number one item on the agenda of world politics since September 11. This paper tries to analyze the case of terrorism through the view of an economic historian, its relation with religions, the causes of terrorism from both sides, from attackers and those who are subject to these attacks. The paper focuses on the importance of education to eradicate it and offers to use the ability of empathy, a natural, wonderful God-given gift man is bestowed, to understand each other and act accordingly, and finally suggests a model of man, which is termed man of society, for a peaceful world community.

Keywords. Terrorism, religious terrorism, world peace, international order, man of society.

Introduction

As a human conduct and action, although it goes back deep into human history, terror has not presented itself in so bloody and so violent a way, nor occupied the world agenda such a long time, nor sneaked into our homes as it has done since World War II. Moreover, since the events of 11th September, 2001, the world has changed in that emerging global terrorism acquired the ability to mount an attack of the scale of that on 11th September. For the first time in modern international politics, a truly global terrorist network has emerged, intent on waging a global campaign against the US and its allies and unconstrained in the violence it is willing to use [1]. Terrorism's cruel and ruthless disregard of laws and ethics was shown by the attacks of September 11. In addition, now that terrorists or their organizations potentially have access to chemical, nuclear, and biological weapons, the possibility of killing large numbers of innocent people and mass destruction has increased to a frightening extent. Some suggest that there is evidence that Al-Qaeda may obtain weapons-grade nuclear materials to make nuclear bombs [2]. Now everybody is vulnerable to a terrorist attack and many live in a continual state of fear. These crimes are perpetrated across borders and cause global unrest and create anarchy, fear, and uncertainty. Much worse than this, the terrorists who have unleashed this global calamity against all humanity do not see themselves as guilty. Furthermore, their attacks on innocent people only serve to increase their internal solidarity, resistance, unity, and conviction of their own righteousness [3]. Therefore, though this new terrorist threat posed by Al Qaeda is being assertively responded to by US policies and though these policies may achieve some short run accomplishments, the extent to which the US will be successful in its attempts in the long run will be determined by how far the terrorism is understood and how successfully it is approached.

Terrorism can be prevented only if its causes are eradicated, for it is only an effect, a symptom. It is not possible to root it out without eliminating its causes. Thus, it is unreasonable to expect to solve the problem of terror through military and police precautions because military sanctions will be retaliated against with more severe violence and trigger a vicious cycle. Nor will police forces assure a stronghold against terrorism. The initial step of fighting with terrorism is to comprehend the terrorist's point of view towards the world, humanity, and their justification of their violent methods. Some people who favor a pure military solution to terrorism simply want to destroy terrorists and be done with it. At best, it's an emotional reaction to the horrors of terrorism which should have been overcome by more rational and sensible thinking. Even if terrorists don't have any legitimate grievances, they think they *do* and unless those grievances are dealt with on some level, more extremism and terrorism will keep being produced. As Betts says [4], this doesn't mean "meeting their demands," but at the very least we have to think about what the demands are and what can be done. Perhaps we'll find some legitimate arguments and will thus have to admit to having to change.

1. Understanding Terrorism

1.1. Religions and Terrorism

Before handling the problem of terrorism, particularly so-called religious terrorism, we must note first that the acts of terror that have been carried out in recent years, sometimes intended as a rebellion against modern values, sometimes in order to get opinions heard, along with individual or collective acts of suicide, are all outlawed by Islam. Whatever the reason may be, the individual has no right to act in such a manner. Some of these incidents stem from a misunderstanding or a misinterpretation of the religion, while others stem from a lack of a reliable and sound religious knowledge. Still, the fact that such acts have become more common is an issue that must be examined. Whatever the aim of such an act, the reasons that lead a person to commit terrorism must be uncovered and eradicated; this is the foremost duty of humanity. Taking this situation lightly, turning a blind eye to it for petty reasons, or supporting those who cause such acts to be repeated must also be regarded as crimes against all of humanity [5].

In fact there is no religion in the world which condones terror. Because religions aim at assuring peace, happiness, and prosperity, terror is clearly incompatible with their basic tenets. It is therefore not reasonable to attribute a terrorist act to the religion of a particular terrorist. The terrorist might be Muslim, Christian, or Jewish, but this does not mean that his or her act is an Islamic, a Christian, or a Jewish act. Thus the phrase 'Islamic terror' should be regarded as an insult to pious, sincere, and innocent Muslims all over the world; a few uneducated, discontented, misled, deceived, brain-washed fanatics should not be taken to represent countless sincere believers. Etymologically derived from the Arabic root 'silm', Islam means 'peace', 'submission', 'deliverance' and 'safety'. Thus, the association of Islam with terrorism is clearly a grievous mistake. Islam is a religion of peace and safety and 'Muslim' means a trustworthy, peaceful, and reliable person. When the Prophet Muhammed describes the Muslim he says that the people are safe from his hand and tongue. It should first be emphasized that one of the the most grievous sins in Islam is killing a person. Islam also strictly prohibits suicide because one has no right to end one's own life or damage one's body.

The Qur'an gives honour and glory equally to all mankind, and considers killing one innocent person equal to killing the whole of human kind[1]. The Qur'an places great emphasis on the virtue of peace.[2] There is no Islamic text which allows the killing of innocent civilians in war, let alone in peacetime, because they are held to be not warriors. The Qur'an states clearly 'Fight in the cause of God those who fight you (who are liable and able to fight, and who participate actively in the fight) but do not transgress the limits; for God loves not transgressors' (Baqara, 2:190). The meaning of 'transgression' here is not to kill civilians, not to torture enemy warriors, to respect the dead bodies of the enemy, to meet the basic needs of the enemy and to obey the rules of war. Islam prohibits even transgression in the form of reprisal/retaliation. For example, if the enemy's soldiers rape Muslim women, Muslim soldiers should not rape the enemy's women; this prohibition also applies to the torture of captured warriors, to attacks on civilians, and so on. If the enemy is protected by Islam, the civilian is protected even more stringently. No one may touch an innocent person; no one may be a 'suicide bomber' who rushes into crowds with bombs tied to his or her body; no one may kidnap innocent civilians and behead them, no matter what their religion. Moreover, as it bans attacking civilians in war, Islam considers attacking civilians in peace as the most grievous sin. The Qur'an equates killing innocent people with unbelief, which is the greatest sin that God does not forgive (Furqan, 25:68; An'am, 6:151). Thus those who attack the lives of innocent people in the name of religion will lose their happiness in this world and salvation in the hereafter [3].

1.2. Understanding Terrorists to Combat Terrorism

Richard K. Betts writes [4] that victories against terrorism, not final but close enough to final, usually result from a combination of forcible attrition and an evolution in the political contexts and social environments of these movements that reduces sympathy for their agendas. Effective counterterrorism thus needs to begin with an understanding of the political motives and incentives of terrorists and, where possible, with the ability to dampen them. Doing this requires trying to *understand* the terrorists - understand what motivates them, what they want, why they want it, and so forth. This isn't a very popular thing to recommend because terrorists have been portrayed as the epitome of evil, as people who are psychologically deranged and therefore unworthy of study or negotiation. Although this attitude is a mistake, according to Betts, understanding radical groups in other cultures is not easy. An insight requires a degree of empathy, and parochial observers find it hard to empathize with different worldviews, while cosmopolitan observers naturally find reactionary ideologies alien and unfathomable. To the present writer, though different worldviews combined with lack of dialogue and any interaction make it difficult to feel empathy[3] with others, it must be enough simply

---

[1] According to Quran (Mâida, 5:32), "whoever kills a soul, unless it be for manslaughter or for mischief in the land, is like one who kills the whole of mankind; and whoever saves a life, is like one who saves the lives of all mankind." The Qur'an places great emphasis on the virtue of peace (Nisa, 4:128)

[2] Quran, Nisa, 4:128.

[3] It is vital to distinguish between empathy and sympathy. Anyone who appears to sympathize with terrorists will be discredited as a source of wisdom on counterterrorism, but those who do not empathize with terrorists will not get far enough inside their heads to develop the maximum base of intelligence for counterterrorism.

to be a human being to have such a lofty feeling as empathy with other human beings. For Betts, Americans need worry much about understanding and dealing head-on with the problem of Al-Qaeda at which American counterterrorism efforts are now directed. Most normal Americans find it impossible to empathize with any movement that uses suicide bombers to kill large numbers of civilians, especially American civilians, because empathy requires admitting that intelligent people somewhere in the world regard U.S. policy as aggressive, oppressive, and murderous.

Betts [4] writes that the prevalent urges to attack the 'root causes' of terrorism are generally misguided and unconvincing, because they cite generic problems, such as poverty, religious fanaticism, or poor education that exist in far more places than the few that spawn (create and feed) terrorists. Nevertheless, these root causes are so seriously to be dealt with that, when combined with a foreign military intervention, they are ready to erupt as with the case of US military interference in the Middle East and the rise of Al-Qaeda, which is an outcome of religious fanaticism and poor and/or wrong religious education aided by the poor members whose poverty is manipulated by a rich leader of the organization. In addition, that eruption implies that the justification of US military intervention on the grounds of bringing to the region democracy, human rights and civil society has not been agreed upon by the people of the region due to continuous US support to undemocratic authoritarian governments in other countries. Still Betts does not deny the urgency of these complications and suggests that, if, however, we think of the root causes as the specific political grievances of the groups in question, the urge to focus on them is a good one. Confronting the enemy's political agenda will clarify just how much U.S. policy can or cannot do to reduce the incentives to use terror against US society, and determine whether counterterrorism has to rely on force alone to suppress the terrorist actions that flow from those incentives. He notes that this does not mean that we should meet terrorist demands, but rather that knowing the enemy better increases the odds of finding an opening in his armor, or of figuring out better ways to use propaganda to sway the populations whose allegiance is at issue. Dealing with future terrorism will require plenty of inventive intelligence activities, to be sure, but there will be no single technological or bureaucratic fix on which to pin all our hopes. Counterterrorism will require a lot of plain old politics and psychology.

It is a great mistake to compare Al-Qaeda with the KKK[4], and to imagine that Al Qaeda will become a shadow of its former self, unable to be more than the butt of jokes without finding permanent solutions to the vital causes that gave way to the rise of Al-Qaeda and/or denying them access to any support they need to continue over the long term. KKK terrorists were ultimately subverted by the government strongly backing integration even though there was no declared war, but there was a great deal of social and legal pressure placed on the KKK. Today, they aren't a threat anymore and they don't have enough broad support in the community to even have serious influence anywhere. As for Al-Qaeda, in addition to the socio-economic causes to its rise, it is first of all urged by such theories as 'Clash of Civilizations' of Samuel Huntington and the widespread Islamophobia in Western societies, which is always bolstered intentionally by mass media not only in the West but also in the countries of which the populations are Muslims.[5] Thus, that problem should be treated as delicately and subtly as possible for the sake of all mankind.

---

[4] Ku Klux Klan: a terrorist organization of white men in the southern states of the US who use violence to oppose social change and equal rights for black people.
[5] The bikini case in Turkey, which is widely debated by the Turkish mass media and then served to the Western newspapers, in the middle of August, 2006, is an epitome of that phenomenon.

1.3. Psychology of Terrorism

It is the psychology of terrorism that causes it to command so much attention compared to other threats to life[6] [2]. Terrorists have many different reasons or motives for their acts. Many politically motivated terrorists want to bring down an existing government or regime. Many religious terrorists want to attack those that they see as attacking their religion. Others want publicity for their cause. Suicide terrorists have almost always had at least one relative or close friend who has been killed, maimed or abused by an enemy [6]. There is also no single profile of terrorists. For example most, but not all, suicide terrorists are aged between 16 and 28. Most are male, but 15% are female and that proportion is rising. Most come from *poor backgounds* and have *limited education*, but some have university degrees and come from wealthy families [7].

When describing the psychology of terrorists as one of the few psychologists to interview suicide bombers, Merari says of them:

"Culture in general and religion in particular seem to be relatively unimportant in the phenomenon of terrorist suicide. Terrorist suicide, like any other suicide, is basically an individual rather than a group phenomenon: it is done by people who wish to die for personal reasons. The terrorist framework simply offers the excuse (rather than the real drive) for doing it and the legitimation for carrying it out in a violent way." [7 pg 206]

Very few terrorists feel pity or empathy for the people they kill or maim. However little they feel for the suffering of others, terrorists are usually aware that their supporters or potential supporters need to feel that the killing, injuring, or threatening of the victims of terror is justified. A common way of doing that is to equate the victims with those who are perceived to be attacking them directly. For example, Osama bin Laden, in an interview with Hamid Mir, editor of the Urdu newspaper Ausaf, is quoted as follows:

"The American people should remember that they pay taxes to their government, they elect their president, their government manufactures arms and gives them to Israel and Israel uses them to massacre Palestinians. The American Congress endorses all government measures and this proves that the entire America is responsible for the atrocities perpetrated against Muslims. The entire America because they elect Congress."[7]

Most terrorists feel that they are doing nothing wrong when they kill and injure people, or damage property. Most seem to share a feature of a psychological condition known as anti-social personality disorder or psychopathic personality disorder, which is an absence of empathy for the suffering of others - they don't feel other people's pain. However, they do not appear unstable or mentally ill[8] [2]. Silke [8] says that it is very rare to find a terrorist who suffers from a clinically defined 'personality disorder' or who could in any other way be regarded as mentally ill or psychologically deviant. Someone who is mentally ill may want to commit an act of terror, but as most terrorism requires cooperating with others, this makes it less likely that a mentally ill person will actually carry out such an act because of the difficulty they have in working with others.

In some cases, the *social environment* the individual lives in leads him/her to be a terrorist, which is called the social learning model. It is not a coincidence that many terrorists come from places where peace is not the norm, places like the Middle East or

---

[6] The death toll of the September 11th attack in the USA, the most devastating terror attack in US history, was placed at 3,016 by December 15, 2001.

[7] http://www.dawn.com/2001/11/10/top1.htm, accessed on 26th February, 2007.

[8] The behaviour of Nezar Hindawi, a freelance Jordanian terrorist is very similar to that of those diagnosed with psychopathic personality disorder. In April 1986 he sent his pregnant Irish girlfriend on an El Al flight to Israel, saying they would be married when he joined her there. She apparently was not aware that Hindawi had hidden a bomb provided by the Abu Nidal Organization in her luggage. Hindawi's willingness to sacrifice his girlfriend and unborn child displays an exceptional lack of empathy.

Northern Ireland, where all the present generation of young people have known is regular, extreme, well-publicised violence. Violence could be the norm for such young people, whether it is on a wide scale or within a smaller community or family. It may come to be considered the normal response to achieve objectives. Silke [9] exemplifies this approach when he describes the process of becoming a terrorist as being primarily an issue of socialisation. Some terrorists are following family tradition, as in the case of both Protestant and Catholic fighters in Northern Ireland or some groups of Palestinians in the Middle East, and the social learning model, with its emphasis on imitation and role models, can easily accommodate this. Forster, referring to Fields [10], in an eight-year longitudinal study, found that exposure to terrorism as a child can produce a tendency to terrorism as an adult [2].

Social networks are also important in the recruitment of new members into violent Islamic fundamentalist groups, including Al-Qaeda. Marc Sageman has studied biographical data for over 400 members of such groups [11]. He found that about 70% of terrorists had joined while they were living as expatriates in other countries, looking for jobs and education.

The solutions proposed by this approach emphasize education and the provision of peaceful role models, particularly aimed at children in their formative years. Silke [9] recommends that addressing the genuine grievances of minorities and other disaffected groups is one of the methods of preventing further atrocities. He adds that security forces should also be restrained in their use of force towards such groups. He thus predicts that military reactions to terror attacks have no deterrant effect and are more likely to lead to an escalation of violence [2].

Nationalist-separatist groups, such as ETA in the Basque region of France and Spain, the IRA in the Irish Republic and the United Kingdom, and Al-Qaeda in some countries such as Morocco, are embedded in a supportive community of family, friends, and sympathisers. However, anarchist groups such as the Bader-Meinhoff Gang and the Red Brigades are usually isolated and alienated from family, friends, and other members of society. Group dynamics are much more significant in the latter case. For these people, the group becomes the sole source of support and friendship. Their sense of belonging, sense of purpose, perhaps even their sense of identity, is derived from the relationships within the group. For such people, providing an alternative support structure may be a way of preventing involvement in a terror group.

Basing his approach on the frustration-aggression hypothesis, Margolin [12 pp 273-274] argues that "much terrorist behavior is a response to the frustration of various political, economic, and personal needs or objectives." Also complicating the issue is that terrorism often works. Yesterday's terrorist leaders can become today's statesmen, justifying their past use of terror as a paramilitary instrument to even the odds between the weak and the powerful.

The Stockholm Syndrome (SS) is an emotional attachment between captive and captor that develops 'when someone threatens your life, deliberates, and doesn't kill you' [13]. Hostages have been known to sympathize with their captors and become emotionally attached -- in one case even get married. The relief resulting from the removal of the threat of death generates intense feelings of gratitude and fear that combine to make the captive reluctant to display negative feelings toward the captor or terrorist. The present writer thinks that this is because of an empathy that may be combined with a sympathy that could be promoted by the captor with the hostage while he/she holds him/her. The SS tells us in fact the importance of developing the feelings of empathy and sympathy between individuals, communities, and nations in order to prevent future conflicts, enmities and terrorist acts.

1.4. Poverty as a Source of Terrorism: The Case of Turkey

There seems to be a striking correlation between the welfare level and the party preference of voters. Accordingly, as the income level of individuals fall, the tendency towards the marginal parties increases. Taking into account the relation between income level and average literacy level, it is possible to assert the tie between low income and tendency towards marginality. We can reflect this correlation through April 18, 1999 General Election results of Turkey as such:

- When we analyze the State Statistical Institute data, GDP per capita was 3020 dollars.
- In 2 cities where GDP is less than $1000, HADEP (Peoples' Democracy Party) which does ethnic politics, wins the first place.
- Among 17 cities where income is $1000-1500; in 7 cities HADEP, and in 5 cities FP, which is considered as the utmost right wing party, wins the first place.
- Among 12 cities where the GDP is $1500-2000; in 6 cities MHP (National Movement party), which does politics over the general concepts of nationalism, wins the first place.
- Among 17 cities where income is $2000- 2500; in 8 cities MHP, and in 4 cities DSP (Democratic Leftist Party) is in the first place.
- Among 9 cities where income is $2500- 3020; in 3 cities DSP, and in 4 cities MHP is in the first place.
- Among 16 cities where GDP is $3020- 4000; in 11 cities DSP, and in 4 cities MHP is in the first place.
- In all of the 7 cities where GDP is $4000- 7882; DSP is in the first place.

Another noticeable point is that DSP and CHP vote ratio increases in high income cities and HADEP vote ratio tends to decrease as the welfare of the city increases. MHP, on the other hand, does not have high vote ratios in prosperous and poor cities but, has high votes in average income cities.

From these statistical data we can clearly conclude that; as the income level of a community decreases, the tendency towards the parties which are out of the mainstream and are in the marginal zone, increases. There is a strong relation between these two concepts. In short, poverty leads to political marginality [14]. Poverty and poor education breed violence. There is a remarkable relation between the rampant cases of theft, purse-snatching and the income inequality in which the gap is getting wider in Turkey.

2. Economic Bases of Conflict and Terrorism

2.1. From Economic Man to 'Economic Nation' Policies

Adam Smith [15] takes 'economic man' as the base for a civilized community. In *The Wealth of Nations* (2004) (first published in 1776) he argues that, in the presence of competition among both firms and consumers, the price system guides private parties to do what is best for society. He writes that every individual necessarily labours to render the annual revenue of the society as great as he can. By pursuing his own interest he frequently promotes that of the society more effactually than when he really intends to promote it. It was this streak or aspect of human nature and behaviour, --that is, egoistic, rational/calculating, commercial/acquisitive that Smith took as a base for a civilized society and that many other economists so carefully depicted as 'economic'. The standard conception of economic man is a totally selfish and insatiable satisfaction-seeker at home, in the work and marketplace [16]. Economic man is separate and distinct from his physical world and from other humans, namely individuals, organizations, and other collective entities. Oriented to getting more things to benefit the self, he acts in a machine-like way to make decisions that lead to his maximum satisfaction. He is unaffected by culture/values, society, politics, fads, enthusiasms, and so forth unless these enter his preferences. Economic man's consciousness is dominated by his calculating, choosing, and satisfaction obtainment activity. He is not reflective regarding these activities. Economic man, as he is ordinarily understood, is not capable of empathy, significant intellectual or intuitive insight, transcendental oneness or other capabilities of a transverbal nature. Nor for that matter does economic man have personal problems; he does not have psychological hang-ups or evil intentions. As described by Tomer, economic man*, after all, is simply a machine-like version of a person who has achieved a somewhat typical level of development in a modem capitalistic country* [17]. It is widely accepted that the invisible hand hypothesized by Adam Smith has guided the self-interested actions of individuals toward a dramatic *increase* in the collective wealth and *productive capacity*. Yet, this increase has been to some extent accompanied by some serious social, economic and ethical problems on the national level.

2.2. Societies of Economic Men Facing Economic Problems and Ethical Crisis

Admittedly, Smith recognizes that self-interest in the formation of class identities effectively limits the possibilities of free trade and corrupts the institutions of democratic government. He confesses that economic growth can be impeded by individuals, classes, or *nations* that put their particular interests above the efficient workings of the market. For example, in the case of *monopolies*, self-interest leads to the formation of groups that impede the growth of all. Thus all men are not rational economic man, but some are limited by their class position, and markets are not free but subject to the manipulations of power [18]. This gives way to the impoverishment of some segments of society and/or some nations of the world population.

Just as the price system that is based on the model of economic man has certain major drawbacks despite its strengths. It works well only when markets are competitive and, even then, it fails to produce the socially optimal amount of output in the presence of *public goods* or *externalities*. It also results in a highly *unequal distribution* of income, failing to guarantee a basic standard of living for all consumers. Moreover, economies that rely on the price system are characterized by considerable economic *instabilities* [19]. All these weaknesses and limitations of the price system, we think, stem from the fact that it is based on homo economicus who is neutral in social outcomes and concerns. Though all these concepts have been widely used to justify *government* intervention, one can hardly conclude that government always leads to socially preferable outcomes for the fact that government policy is not made by a benign, all-knowing God but by politicians who can hardly be disinterested, ones who may be influenced by personal feelings and biases or by the chance of getting advantage for themselves. Moreover, if they succumb to pressures from special-interest groups, government intervention may actually harm society, even all mankind if it is a power of world proportions.

Besides economic problems, today's Western civilization is suffering from a widespread ethical crisis. The nineteenth century had seen numerous social movements and philosophies arise to contend against the inequalities, inhumanities, and socially atomizing tendencies of industrial capitalism. With the collapse of Soviet-style socialism at the end of the 1980s, the system which is based on economic man taking self-interest as given, one that had evinced as well relative hospitality towards political democracy and individual freedoms, emerged victorious, with leading public, civic, and intellectual figures throughout the world concurring in the belief that desired prosperity and liberty can best be achieved through its institutions of free exchange and private property. Yet, the viability of the prevailing order was coming increasingly into question, for the internal discontents of industrial market societies appeared to loom as large as ever. Typical listings of these problems have included high levels of crime and violence, family instability, racial tensions and xenophobia, seemingly intractable poverty and unemployment, self-destructive behaviors including substance abuse and suicide, social disintegration and depression, and widespread alienation among the young. Such problems seem to be more severe today in some global sense than was the case fifty or one hundred years ago [20]. When we extend the issue from individual/ society level to the international community level, we observe "economic nations" who try to maximize their national interests by using force at the cost of other nations. That reminds us of the bloody mercantilistic period of the 16th to late 18th centuries.

2.3. Remembering History

The economic theory and policy of the early modern period (1500-1750) is called mercantilism, an economic theory that a nation's prosperity depended upon its supply of gold and silver, that the total volume of trade was unchangeable, and that the government should play an active role in the economy by encouraging exports and discouraging imports, especially through the use of tariffs. Mercantilists believed that nations are in a direct zero-sum competition with each other for wealth; thus, what one party gains is that which the other party has to give up. In other words, a country can gain in a trade only at the expense of the other country. Mercantilism was based on bitter rivalry for trade and colonies and almost constant wars. It fueled colonialism under the belief that a large empire was the key to wealth. It also fueled the intense violence of the 17th and 18th centuries in Europe. War was almost a normal relationship among national states. From 1494 to 1559 there was fighting nearly every year in some part of Europe; the 17th century enjoyed only seven calendar years of complete peace, and England, the world power of the time, was at war during eighty-four of the 165 years between 1650 and 1815. It resulted in an outlook that regards other nations as rivals if not enemies. In the early days of mercantilism, its expression was highly chauvinistic and bellicose, and it remained self-centered to the end. In large measure, it was due to a static view of the world and its resources. International conflict was inevitable due to the conviction that the position of a particular country could change only through acquisitions from other countries. Since the level of world trade was viewed as fixed, it followed that the only way to increase a nation's trade was to take it from another. This was the tragedy of mercantilism. With its theory and practice, mercantilism left behind bitter historical lessons.[9]

The modern international system can be said to have originated from the developments in the European politics between 1618 and 1648. After the Peace of

---

[9] http://en.wikipedia.org/wiki/Mercantilism (Accessed on 23 March, 2005)

Westphalia (1648) following the Thirty Years War in Europe, the language of justification shifted away from Christian unity towards international diversity based on a secular society of sovereign states. Realism became the dominant theory of the Westphalian state-centered international system. *The essence of this system is the clash of nation states in order to maximize their interests, which is called rationalism.* Power, as an objective category which is universally valid, is the keyword to explain the international system. By accepting the power-interest link as the organizing principle of the international system, politics became an autonomous sphere of action apart from other spheres such as economics, ethics, aesthetics, or religion [as cited in 21]. As with the problems that arose in the societies based on the model of economic man due to selfish acts that don't regard others' needs, the one-sided acts of the Western countries, especially the US, that are exposed to terrorist attacks, who have been trying to maximize their interests by resorting to all kinds of means including military force without regarding the needs of the other nations, may have given way to the present worldwide terrorism.

2.4. Preferring Less to More

To put it more clearly, today the US economy has begun to slow down when compared to fast growing countries and her share in the total global GDP is lessening with the likelihood of lagging behind the international economic competition, while she is still the number one military power on the earth. China in particular is threatening US interests and Russia is rising afresh. This happening may have urged the US to reach the economic -especially energy- resources and markets as soon as possible by using her force without rival in order to regain her number one position in the economic sphere. Unfortunately, the great military power the US has misled her. Whereas, the US could achieve her aim to be leading economic power in the long run by making use of the most effective weapons she has of democracy, human rights and civil society, thanks to which she overcame another world power, the Soviet Union, who lacked them. The recent case of Iraq seems to have damaged the image of the US to be the bastion/stronghold/bulwark/citadel of these crucially important human values, the sweet fruits of the human being's common bitter experiences of centuries.[10] The US administration seems to have preferred the less short term US economic acquisitions to the more long term benefits for both the US and the world communities. Trying to maximize economic interests at all costs, neglecting the rights of the peoples of the Middle East by taking them as a secondary class, and a widespread idea of a Western double standard towards them, in short, acting as a mere "economic nation" seeking only self-interest and disregarding all others, must have provoked an anti-Americanism which has appeared as a religious terrorism. It is crucially important to note that the fact that this opposition is dressed up with a religious cloth must be a political strategy in order to get the support of the Muslims of different nations living in that geography, not that a religion like Islam allows such terrorist activities. Exploiting Islam for such illegal acts is the biggest harm that could be done to that religion.

   To sum up through the view of an economist, the US approach of maximizing self interests whatever it costs, that is, the behavior of a mere economic nation, may be said

---

[10] As Bulent Aras says the September attacks consolidated the principle of non-intervention in the international system for the sake of preserving national security at the domestic level. Such concepts as democracy, human rights and civil society have historically emerged out of the human being's common experience; yet they have reproduced after being filtered through western practices, and at times, this reproduction mechanism may fall apart from its former context and serve to achieve a completely new meaning. By virtue of becoming global norms, these concepts have begun to trigger anxiety of the authoritarian state establishments in the so-called third world countries [22].

to make the US and her allies suffer from such a threat of international terrorism. Just as some commentators have pointed to a list of political grievances as the main motivating factor for the attacks of September 11. Noam Chomsky, Aaron Lehmer, Bill Christison, a longtime CIA analyst, have spelled out four political root causes of these attacks. These are the presence of US troops in the Saudi region and possibly also the Persian Gulf region, the strong slant in American policy towards the Israeli-Palestinian conflict, the ongoing, devastating sanctions on Iraq, and the wide US support for repressive dictatorial regimes in the Muslim and non-Muslim world [23].

2.5. September 11th Attacks

Forster writes that the September 11th attacks in the USA on the World Trade Center and Pentagon were probably carried out by Osama bin Laden's organisation, al-Qaeda. In part, bin Laden is motivated by anger against the USA after the Gulf War, in which his country of origin, Saudi Arabia, provided a base for attacks by the USA and its allies against the Iraqi occupation of Kuwait. He also sees the USA as an enemy of Islam, particularly through its support of Israel and, despite having been supported by the USA during the cold war, disdains US culture and values. However, not everyone connected with al-Qaeda, which means 'the base,' have the same motives. They often recruit operatives to work for them from amongst young men at mosques who have a powerful urge to defend Islam from perceived attacks world-wide. These attacks may be by Serbs in the former Yugoslavia, by Russians in Chechnya or formerly in Afghanistan, or most often, by the USA and Israel in the Middle East. However, these passionate and emotional young men are not usually permitted into the inner organisation of al-Qaeda. Among the terrorists who carried out the bombings in Madrid and London were young men with long criminal records for such things as drug dealing and theft [2].

2.6. Jewish Killing Civilians

One of the reasons for some Muslim oriented terrorist organizations to appear might be the civilians being killed by the Jewish military force in Palestine and Lebanon and the inclination of the relatives or fellow countrymen of the victims of the Jewish attacks to take revenge in retaliation. Some writers search for the reason of killing civilians by the Jewish soldiers in the religious background. In the Old Testament, (Tasniya, 20:10), the Jews are allowed to kill, when they enter a town of the enemy, everybody, anything that breathes, including babies and women. Even though some pacifist Jews[11] of today argue that this is a historical permission not related to modern days, the fact is that the Jewish army has always been killing the civilian people in Palestine and Lebanon. The last war that took place in July and August 2006 is the epitome of that phenomenon. Since this crime is perpetrated by the Jews for decades in the region, it may have been a starting point of a religious terrorism which does not distinguish between the civilians and the armed powers of Israel and its supporters, even though, as mentioned above, it is strictly forbidden by Islam even if it is in retaliation for Israeli attacks.

---

[11] http://www.aksiyon.com.tr/detay.php?id=25032&yorum_id=12129, accessed on August 6, 2006)

3. The Model of Man of Society for a Nonviolent Society

The globalizing world requires a new man type who could balance between nationalism which corresponds to regionalism on one hand and becoming a world citizen which corresponds to globalization on the other hand. We call that type of man 'man of society'. Though that model has been developed for a socio-economic peace in a society, it also serves political peace since any political peace, on the national or international scale, can not exist, or can not be attained, without any social and economic peace, serenity, and contentment.

This model evaluates an individual person as a separate and unique 'world' regardless of his/her race, colour, gender, nationality, religion, class and social status. He is the most superior and valuable, complete and dignified being on the earth. He is more valuable than the whole universe. The coinage 'man of society' has two aspects. First is man's being an individual person, second is his being a member of society. Here society refers to a globalized world as well as the narrow social environment the individual lives in. The term 'man' in the coinage stands for his being an individual person, and 'of society' for his membership of society, in a broader sense, his connection with the outside world as a whole including human beings, animals, plants; in short, the world he lives in. Man's being an individual person which is represented by his being "man" of society, he must initially be a selfish human being, one who cares about himself rather than others and pursues his own interest, to the extent that he maintains his complete being and intactness, for society is after all composed of selves and one who is of no use/help to himself is of no use/help to others. Moreover, it is the selfish, rational and calculative behaviour of man in the marketplace that gives way to the efficient use of resources on both sides of consumers and producers. In this respect, Adam Smith had an appropriate insight into human nature and his contribution to society through the best use of resources.

As for man's being "of society", that tie relates him to the outside world. Man is a part of the whole universe to which he is connected with all his creation, emotions, needs, imaginations, hopes and fears. Therefore, he has empathy -ability to understand feelings of others- with others, making him concerned about, and responsible for, others. His connection with the outside world is at the highest level with the immediate members of the society he lives in as well as with all other living or nonliving beings; that is the natural basis of existence. So, starting from the closest family members, he has responsibilities towards his relatives, friends, neighbors, compatriots, and even towards animals, other living beings and nature. He is affected by the joys and sorrows of others besides his own. He is concerned about the distress of a human being as well as the pain of an animal in the farthest corner of the world, and tends to do what he can. Thus, man of society is concerned about all the human beings regardless of their nationality as well as his compatriots. All these apply to almost all human beings, though the degree of their concern for others differs depending on the level of their personal development, as put by Wilber [24], as well as the development level of the society they live in, just as the rate of concern for others varies from Western societies to Eastern ones and likewise ranges from one person to another within a society.

Though "of society" in the coinage "*man of society*" refers to the whole outside world of man, it first and foremost befits and pertains to the society man lives in. Humans are intrinsically social and, human nature is not geared to living alone. Hence, man lives in a society. Implicit in the meaning of society is that its members share some mutual concern or interest in a common objective. Society serves in general to aid individuals in times of crisis and emergency. Historically, when an individual in some community requires aid, for example at birth, death, sickness, or disaster, like-minded members of that community will rally to others in that society to render aid, in some form, whether the aid is symbolic, linguistic, physical, mental, emotional, financial, medical, religious, etc. Regardless of their base -subsistence or technology- all societies actually exhibit the characteristics of community action, generosity, and shared risk/reward.

Ethical values and religion encourage the attributes of *man of society*, influencing the behaviors of man in everyday life and in all decisions he makes, whether economic or non-economic. Thus, the concept of *man of society* includes both positive and normative elements. One reason that man has empathy with others, among others, is that morality requires 'moral man' to be a social being [25], meaning that he has to have social concerns. This is because, as Campbell argues, ethics correspond to the way we would like others to behave and that we accept the same strictures/restrictions for ourselves at most as a necessary cost of getting them to do so. We might accept this cost due to the fact that we prefer to think of ourselves as moral individuals insofar as we care how others regard us [20, 26]. Ben-Ner and Putterman argue that human nature is not strictly selfish but rather includes dispositions towards *altruism* and openness to moral sensibilities which are shaped over time by environmental stimuli. Institutions and organizations influence behaviors and moral sensibilities of individuals [20].

The fact that man consists of a spiritual element as well as a physical body explains any non-economic spending decisions of *man of society*. While maximizing his material profit/utility through efficient economic decisions, he does maximize his spiritual utility through so-called non-economic decisions. As a matter of fact, when *man of society* spends on others, even when he sacrifices his soul for his country, he maximizes his utility as economic man does, but this being not a physical but a spiritual one. Since *man of society* is a member, and a component of his family, his society, the whole of mankind, and even the natural environment he lives in, his spending on them provides him the same pleasure, satisfaction and utility as he receives from any spending on his own physical needs. If he makes these expenditures because of a religious belief, then his religious expectations, i.e. winning approval of God, acquiring paradise, will be his spiritual utility, as Bryant argues it in his article with the title "Cost-Benefit Accounting and the Piety Business: Is Homo Religiosus, at Bottom, a Homo Economicus?" [27], which includes a question with an implied affirmative answer. Even a non-believer who sacrifices his soul for his family or country maximizes his utility by exchanging his soul for the lives of many people from his family or his country; a simple, difficult, but profitable exchange: Many souls saved in return for one soul sacrificed. Unlike animals, human beings are equipped with exalted feelings to their fellows. Then, why shouldn't people who sacrifice their souls for their countries share some of their surpluses with people who starve? Why shouldn't they prefer high spiritual pleasures to lower physical utilities?

As for the attributes of *man of society*, he has all the positive features of homo economicus besides many pluses. The strengths of economic man are those of homo societius. But, the weaknesses of economic man are not mostly those of homo societius. He acts in the marketplace as economic man does to the extent that these actions are related to economy. He tries to maximise his utility as a consumer and his profit as an entrepreneur. Thus, he contributes to the society as much as he can. There is no reason that he will contribute to the revenue of society less than economic man will. He works in a free market, owns production of factors, builds his own business, produces and sells. He observes the rules of the game because it is in his self-interest to conform. As seen, so far the behaviours of economic man are those of *man of society* in economic life only with one exception: while economic man always cares only for his interest, even sometimes to the loss of his partner as buyer or seller, *man of society* cares about his buyer when selling and his seller when buying, having empathy with them. But from that point on, their ways distinctly separate, and while economic man is still left to take care of him, *man of society* turns his face to the society once he achieves more or less an average standard of life, or a subsistence level (when his minimal needs are satisfied), for a hungry man can rarely be concerned about other hungry people. He concerns himself with the needs of others without any discrimination. He is as individualist as economic man and as socialist as homo Sovieticus. He shares out some of his surplus with the rest of society. It is not rare that a purchaser who drives a hard bargain for lower prices in the market place donates a considerable amount of money to the needy.

In short, *man of society* is one who spends out of what he earns/owns, or of whatever he is endowed with, on the needy including relatives, neighbors, or gives charity to the organizations dealing with it, as well as spending on himself and family members. What he can do for others may range from such big expenditures as building a hospital or a school to helping an old or blind man cross the street or to relieving a distressed man of his grief with kind and calming words. That is to say everybody is potentially a *man of society*, for everyone, well-to-do or not, has something to give to others, let it be a material/financial or spiritual/moral thing; even sometimes spiritual/moral contributions might be more helpful. The motto/maxim of the model of man of society is "*live and let live*". That is what the current international political and economic order needs for world peace. What some world famous characters with so broad a horizon that embraces all mankind mean by their own terminology seems to be the same as 'man of society'. One of the best examples is Kofi Annan, Ghanaian diplomat, seventh secretary-general of the United Nations, and the winner of the 2001 Nobel Peace Prize. Annan who quotes: "A citizen of the world in the fullest sense is one whose vision and culture gave him a deep empathy with fellow human beings of every creed and color"[12] seems to mean 'the man of society' by his 'citizen of the world'.

4. Conclusion

This paper concludes that terrorism, especially the religious kind, has emerged to grow into one of the most serious problems of the contemporary world as a phenomenon originating more from social and economic reasons, as was the case in history, than from the religious factors. Rather, a religious robe is worn on the worldly interests in order to conceal them and to get widespread support of the followers of the relevant religion. Terrorism seems to be the number one problem also in the long run in the current international political and economic order, for it has other deep-rooted causes such as psychological, social, cultural, and educational reasons besides economic and religious ones. Unless all these causes are wiped out, it sounds as if it might not to be possible to eliminate terrorism from the surface of the world. Military policies or police measures may at best solve the problem for the short term if they don't delay the fundemantal solution or even worsen the problem. The September 11 attacks, which have been said to be made by al-Qaeda that is acting like a virtual world state, show

---

[12] http://en.thinkexist.com/search/searchquotation.asp?search=empathy, accessed on August 15, 2006.

that the notion of 'nation state' of the Westfalian international political system is about to be replaced by a 'virtual one'. If, for the time being, the first virtual state is a terrorist organization and if it consists of only so-called Islamist terrorists, what falls on us as the whole mankind is to form a counter-terror --we can call it a "*Peace Front*"-- against that destructive being. The biggest force of that Peace Front is to be made up of the members of all religions. It may be seen that first the Turkish Muslims then all other Muslims support forming such a Peace Front. The nationals of that pacifist, anti-terrorist virtual world state are the men of society who manage to identify and balance their own national interests with those of other nations. It can be said that the Turkish education system with its schools spread all over the world at which the students are studying in an atmosphere of peace and tranquility with all nationalities, races, colours, languages, and religions can be said to be bringing up those men of society. Last, the US had better recover its position of being the citadel of such crucially important human values as human rights, democracy and civil society, which has been damaged in recent years, for the world needs such a power who embraces it with a motherly warmth rather than acting any other way.

References

[1]   A. Cottey, September 11th 2001: A new era in world politics. In G. Baci, B. Aras, Editors. *September 11 and World Politics.* Istanbul, Turkey: Fatih University; 2004.
[2]   P.M. Forster, The psychology of terror -the mind of the terrorist" [Online], Available from; URL: http://www.blue-oceans.com/psychology/terror_psych.html, [2006, August 1].
[3]   İ. Albayrak, Islam and terror: From the perspective of Fethullah Gulen, [Online], Available from; URL: http://www.fethullahgulenconference.org/dallas/proceedings/ IAlbayrak.pdf, 12 [2006, August].
[4]   R.K. Betts, How to think about terrorism", *Wilson Quarterly*, **30/1** (2006, Winter), 44-49.
[5]   B. Karliga, Religion, terror, war, and the need for global ethics, [Online], Available from; URL: http://www.muslimway.org/en/Islam/terror_and_Islam/a.42008.html, [2006, August 25].
[6]   H. Kushner, Suicide bombers: Business as usual. *Studies in Conflict and Terrorism*. **19** (1996), 329 - 338.
[7]   A. Merari, The readiness to kill and die: Suicidal terrorism in the Middle East. In W. Reich, Editor. *Origins of terrorism: Psychologies, ideologies, theologies and states of mind*. Cambridge University Press; 1990.
[8]   A. Silke, Cheshire-cat logic: The recurring theme of terrorist abnormality in psychological research. *Psychology, Crime and Law*, **4** (1998), 51 - 69.
[9]   A. Silke, Terrorism. *The Psychologist*, **14** (2001), 580 - 581.
[10] R.M. Fields, Child Terror Victims and Adult Terrorists, *Journal of Psychohistory*, **7/1** (1979) 71-75.
[11] M. Sageman, *Understanding terror networks*. University of Pennsylvania Pres; 2004.
[12] J. Margolin, Psychological perspectives in terrorism. In Y. Alexander, S.M. Finger Editors. *Terrorism: Interdisciplinary perspectives*. New York: John Jay; 1977.
[13] M. Symonds, Victim responses to terror, Annals of the N.Y. Academy of Sciences: 1980.
[14] O. Ozsoy, Voter behavior and effective propaganda in Turkey. İstanbul: 2002.
[15] A. Smith, *An inquiry into the nature and causes of the wealth of nations: Part 10 Harvard classics.* Kessinger Publishing; 2004.
[16] T.O. Nitsch, Economic man, socio-economic man and homo-economicus humanus. International Journal of Social Economics. **9/6-7** (1982), 20-49.
[17] J.F. Tomer, Economic man vs. hetedox men: The concepts of human nature in schools of economic thought. *Journal of Socio-Economics*. 10535357. **30/4** (2001), 281-294.
[18] R. Gagnier, On the insatiability of human wants: Economic and aesthetic man. *Victorian Studies*. **36/2** (1993), 125-53.
[19] R.E. Backhouse, The ordinary business of life: A history of economics from the ancient world to the twenty-first century. Princeton and Oxford: Princeton University Pres; 2002.
[20] A. Ben-Ner, L. Putterman, Values and institutions in economic analysis 1. Version 1997, January 27, [Online], Available from; URL: http://www.brown.edu [2005, August 16].
[21] G. Bacik, The resistance of the westfalian system. In G. Baci, B. Aras, Editors. *September 11 and world politics.* Istanbul, Turkey: Fatih University; 2004.
[22] B. Aras, September 11 and world politics. In G. Baci, B. Aras, Editors. *September 11 and world*

politics. Istanbul, Turkey: Fatih University; 2004.

[23] M. Anas, Selected reflections on the muslim world in the aftermath of 9-11. In G. Baci, B. Aras, Editors. *September 11 and world politics.* Istanbul, Turkey: Fatih University; 2004.

[24] K.Wilber, *The Atman Project: A transpersonal view of human development.* Wheaton, IL: Quest Books; 1996.

[25] J.C. Dingley, Durkheim, mayo, morality and management. *Journal of Business Ethics.* **16/11** (1997 Augustos), 1117-1129.

[26] D. T. Campbell, The two distinct routes beyond kin selection to ultrasociality: Implications for the humanities and the social sciences. *The nature of prosocial development: Interdisciplinary theories and strategies.* In D. Bridgeman, Editor. New York: Academic Press; 1983.

[27] J.M. Bryant, Cost-benefit accounting and the piety business: Is homo religiosus, at bottom, a homo economicus? *Method & Theory in the Study of Religion.* 09433058. 12/4 (2000).

Part II

Suicide Attacks, Radical Terrorism and Case Studies

Suicide Attacks as a Devastating Terrorist Modus Operandi: An Updated Evaluation of Turkish Cases

Ozgur NIKBAY[a,b], Cindy J. SMITH[c], PhD. & Ekrem MUS[a,b]

[a]*Ph.D. Candidate, Virginia Commonwealth University, USA*
[b]*Superintendent, Turkish National Police*
[c]*University of Baltimore, USA*

Abstract. Suicide bombings, a subset of general terrorism, modus operandi provide an advantage to the perpetrators. A militant who intends to detonate the explosives at a particular target is the ultimate *smart bomb*, aiming to kill both him/herself and destroy the target to send the terrorist's message. This paper analyzes the uncompleted suicide attacks from the original interview statements of perpetrators along with an up-dated analysis of completed suicide attacks committed in Turkey between 1996 and 2005. This research answers questions about suicide bombings in areas where police and researchers have very limited information: What are the known characteristics of suicide bombers across time in Turkey? What additional characteristics exist for unsuccessful suicide bombers?

Keywords. Turkey, suicide attack, terrorism, PKK-KONGRA GEL, Al-Qaeda, DHKP/C, ICCB-AFID.

Introduction

Terrorism has been a major problem for many years around the world, but many countries underestimated it before the September 11 terrorist assaults. These assaults showed the world that terrorism does not differentiate between targets; whether strong or weak, Muslim, Christian or Jewish, adult or children. The only goal of terrorism is to destroy the targets and send a message to its audience. September 11 suicide attacks made the terrorism issue a global problem, which is strongly fueled by terrorist organizations in the Middle East. These assaults also pointed out how terrorists can be fatally creative for the maximization of destruction by combining high technology vehicles with one of the most devastating terrorist modus operandi, such as suicide attacks in which the perpetrators aim to kill themselves along with killing and destroying their targets.

Understanding and properly responding to terrorism requires understanding terrorists' minds, cultures, belief systems, and ways of life. Turkey has a special location in terms of presenting access for all these connections to the Middle East because it is at the cross roads of Middle East and Europe. Both culturally and geographically, it is an important bridge between cultures and communities in Europe and the Middle East due to its historical background and unique religious and political structures. Therefore, understanding the underlying factors of terrorist attacks in Turkey may be a gateway to understanding terrorism in the Middle East to some extent.

This paper aims to analyze the uncompleted suicide attacks from the original interview statements of perpetrators along with the analysis of the updated version, including 2006 of the same dataset used in an earlier study by these authors [1] that analyzed completed suicide attacks based on a dataset compiled of all cases committed in Turkey between 1996 and 2005. This research is unique in terms of uncovering the answers to questions about suicide bombings using qualitative analysis of unsuccessful suicide bombings perpetrators' statements. These statements are distinctive resources for researchers because often police and researchers have very limited information on completed suicide bombings other than characteristics of the events. Therefore, 'the impacts of suicide attacks' is a topic that is full of vague inferences and gaps in knowledge requiring further study. Additionally, there are limited studies about terrorist organizations conducting suicide attacks in Turkey. Predominantly, the terrorist organization PKK-KONGRA GEL was very active along with a few other Marxist-Leninist terrorist organizations until 2003, when Al-Qaeda began to conduct terrorist activities in Turkey in the form of suicide attacks.

1. Statement of the Problem

Suicide attacks as a terrorist modus operandi provide an advantage to the perpetrators. A militant who intends to detonate the explosives in his bag or belt when he meets with the target is the ultimate smart bomb. It is very dangerous to prevent these attacks because he or she becomes a missile arranging the time of the explosion with the ability to make last second changes. It is more risky to stop a suicide bomber intending to explode the bomb in a crowded area, such as malls or business centers, than dealing with most of the other kinds of warfare tactics. The bomber uses the advantages of getting closer to the targets, and timing the assault according to the density of population and security officials [2]. This situation also creates a dilemma for the security officers who notice a suicide bomber approaching his or her target. Interruption or any act preventing him from exploding the bomb may trigger the bomber to begin the operation, which can immediately impact the security guards and the people around him at that moment. These advantages of the bomber make suicide attacks very sensitive and important to handle the issue very carefully.

2. Research Questions

The advantages provided by suicide attacks could be better diminished if the basic characteristics are known. Therefore, this research seeks to respond to the following two questions:

RQ 1: What are the known characteristics of suicide bombers across time in Turkey?

RQ 2: What additional characteristics exist for unsuccessful suicide bombers?

This paper will first summarize the relevant data presented in 2005 and articulate any changes based on additional cases that occurred after that study [1]. This discussion will include the relevant literature and methods from that study. Next, the methods and findings from the interview statement data are reported; policy recommendations and recommendations for future research are offered to guide further studies on this topic.

3. Definition of Terms

Two terms require a brief definition to clarify the meanings. First, completed suicide attack is a case in which the offender exploded the bomb. It is irrelevant where the bomber exploded [3]. Second, uncompleted suicide attack is a case in which the offender did not explode the bomb [3].

4. Limitations

This study is limited in two ways. First, the study is limited in its generalizability to larger populations of suicide bombers because of its small sample size and the unique structure and location of Turkey. Turkey is unique because it is a predominantly Islamic democratic country and located adjacent to the Middle Eastern countries, connecting Asia and Europe. Additionally, the sample size of 36 cases is too small for sub analyses within the data, which would yield more specific information about a given subgroup (i.e., Al-Qaeda versus PKK). Second, the qualitative analysis of the statements made to the police by uncompleted suicide bombers makes assumptions that those bombers who successfully completed are similar to those who were not successful. There is no way to know, at this time, if these two groups are similar.

5. Significance of the Study

Official records offer some limited insight into the background and characteristics of the suicide bombers. This background information is important for prevention and intervention preparation. Additionally, anecdotal data and inadequate profiles limit theory development. The significance of the study is to examine the known profiles [1] and the additional profile characteristics gleaned from the more detailed reports from the uncompleted suicide bombers. This research builds on the quantitatively analyzed data, by incorporating the qualitative data for a more complete understanding of suicide bombers.

6. Review of Literature

This literature review is a summary of the more detailed review presented in previous writings [1]. First, the four terrorist organizations that conducted suicide bombings in Turkey are discussed. Understanding their goals and characteristics are key to understanding their behaviors. Second, a discussion of what is known about the characteristics of suicide bombers is discussed.

6.1. Terrorist Organizations Using Suicide Attacks in Turkey

There are several terrorist organizations using suicide attacks in the world, but this article focuses on the ones using suicide attacks in Turkey because understanding the structure and ideologies of these groups assists in understanding their operations, especially suicide operations. Four terrorist organizations employed suicide attacks in Turkey; The Kurdistan Workers Party[1] (PKK-KONGRA-GEL), Revolutionary People's Liberation Party/Front (DHKP/C), Union of Islamic Communities (also known as Anatolia Federative Islamic State) (ICCB-AFID), and Al-Qaeda. These four terrorist organizations have some fundamental similarities and differences. Al-Qaeda and ICCB-AFID purport religious motivations, while the other two organizations (PKK-KONGRA GEL and DHKP/C) have Marxist-Leninist/Maoist motives. PKK-KONGRA GEL aims to separate the Turkish land and establish a Kurdish country. On the other hand, DHKP/C pursues changing the regime of the Turkish Republic into a communist regime. Al-Qaeda and ICCB-AFID aim to start a revolution and create a country ruled by an Islamic regime.

6.1.1. The Kurdistan Workers Party (PKK/KONGRA-GEL)

The Kurdistan Workers party is a Marxist Leninist terrorist organization, founded by the Kurdish student association in the Ankara University in 1974 and has grown to almost 20,000 members during the 1990s [4]. Abdullah Ocalan is the leader of the terrorist organization and he was a student of political science in this University [5, 6]. Its central goal is to create an independent Kurdish state, Kurdistan, by separating the southeast part of Turkey and the northern part of Iraq, Syria and Iran by using guerilla warfare [7]. This terrorist organization conducts its activities against the Turkish regime and its cohorts, Turkish people, opponent Kurds and Europeans in Turkey and Europe. It employs both Maoist activities, such as killing all the people in a village who do not follow its orders, and Marxist activities, which reflects the characteristics of a nationalistic pressure group. It began using religious sayings in 1995 [8]. But according to Ergil [4], PKK/KONGRA GEL has secular rhetoric instead of religious motives.

PKK/KONGRA GEL conducted 21 suicide attacks between 1996 and 1999. While six of these attacks were prevented and the actors were captured before the assault, 15 of the suicide bombers completed the attacks. Their major targets were high level regional administrators, soldiers, police officers and their facilities. In these attacks, 15 officials and 4 civilians were killed; 75 officials and 63 civilians were injured. The organization assigned more female militants than males for these operations. They were between the ages of 17 and 27. They were the members of large families who were living in poverty [4]. Almost 65 percent of the suicide bombers were females and they specifically transported the explosives on their bodies [5, 9]. However, the organization

---

[1] The organization has changed its name for several times in the last decade. Although it is said that the organization has recently begun using the original and commonly known name 'PKK' to revive the organizational morale, we will use PKK/KONGRA GEL because even it is not much active, KONGRA GEL is still a subsection of the organization; and any activity of KONGRA GEL will be pointed to PKK by including both names.

conducted another suicide attack in 2006, which will be added to these data later in the paper.

The organization was responsible for more than 22,000 terrorist activities between 1984 and 2000 [7]. They are credited for the deaths of over 30,000 civilians and officials including, tourists, women and children [4, 10].

6.1.2. Revolutionary People's Liberation Party/Front (DHKP/C)

People's Liberation Party/Front (DHKP/C) is a terrorist organization whose goal is to destroy the constitutional regime and democracy by applying armed warfare and replacing the regime with a communist regime dependent on Marxist-Leninist ideology. The organization uses the Politicized Armed Warfare Strategy (PASS) to achieve this goal (See [11] for a discussion of the five stages of this method). This strategy suggests long term community warfare based on armed struggle. The organization pursues pulling society into the armed struggle by using guerilla tactics in urban and rural areas and creating a massive community movement against the existing governance. The militants apply armed assaults to receive attention from the community and achieve the organization's goal of communism [12]. This terrorist organization also conducted suicide attack operations in 2001. The targets of almost all these attacks were Turkish Police Forces [13]. Suicide bombings are a recent development for this group following the transfer of militants to the new F type prisons with single cell construction [12].

6.1.3. Union of Islamic Communities (ICCB) or Anatolia Federative Islamic State (AFID)

The Union of Islamic Communities (ICCB) is a terrorist organization purporting religious doctrine and it is also known as the Anatolia Federative Islamic State (AFID) [13]. The political goal of this organization is to destroy the regime of the Turkish Republic and establish a state governed by the Islamic rules. The AFID was formed from the ICCB by Cemalettin Kaplan in 1984–1985 [14]. Most of the members of this organization live in Germany. It is stated that while 200 to 300 members of this organization have been conducting activities in Turkey, 1,300 members have been involved in the organizational activities in Germany. Two AFID members attempted to commit suicide attack in Turkey. However, the Turkish National Police (TNP) prevented the suicide attack. They were planning to conduct this assault using a small plane loaded with bombs and they targeted the Ataturk Mausoleum during the ceremony when most of the leaders of government and officials attend on Republic Day. The proposed perpetrators of this attack were captured before the suicide operation was conducted in October 1998 [13]. The members of this organization have been conducting rhetoric assaults against the Turkish government.

6.1.4. Al-Qaeda

Little is known about Al-Qaeda activities in Turkey because there are a limited number of studies about the terrorist organization purporting religious motivations in Turkey [15]. Additionally, Al-Qaeda has only recently begun conducting terrorist activities in Turkey. This country never experienced a threat or attack with a major impact from an externally sourced terrorist organization until the suicide attacks of by Al-Qaeda in 2003. In 1999, the Turkish National Police detained six persons from Libya who were suspected for connection with the Al-Qaeda terrorist organization. It is believed that they were preparing an assault on the U.S. Embassy in Ankara. Following this event, intelligence reported additional members were coming into Turkey. The terrorist organizations from outside the country were also supporting the Turkish groups. Other conditions, such as the American invasion of Iraq and its strategy against Al-Qaeda, as well as the uprising of other reportedly religiously motivated terrorist organizations, have created a fertile field for Al-Qaeda to become active in Turkey [13].

Two suicide attacks were simultaneously committed against two synagogues in 2003 [16]. The trucks crashed into the synagogues and detonated the explosives killing 23 people along with themselves [13]. Five days later, two simultaneous suicide attacks were conducted against the British consulate in the Taksim district in Istanbul and the Hong Kong and Shanghai Banking Corporation (HSBC) building in the city commercial center. Two trucks loaded with the bombs exploded and killed 27 persons together with the British Consul General and injured 450 people [16]. Another report indicates that 62 people were killed and more than 650 people, including many civilians, were wounded in these attacks committed in one week [13].

6.2. Characteristics of Suicide Bombers

The literature is generally mixed for most characteristics of suicide bombers. The following discussion presents a summary of the literature and a brief presentation of the policy implications based on that summary.

6.2.1. Outstanding Warrants

Only two studies have examined whether the offenders have active warrants before the suicide bombings in Turkey [1, 3]. Both studies revealed that more than 60% of the suicide bombers had active warrants before the assaults. This would indicate that more active implementation of arresting those with outstanding warrants would reduce suicide attacks.

6.2.2. Prior Arrests

Generally, most research found that suicide bombers had no criminal records [17, 18]. In other words, there is little support for the notion that suicide bombers are "generalized criminals." However, in the case of Turkish suicide bombings, Nikbay [3] found an almost equal division between those who were criminally involved and those who were not criminally involved. This indicates that prevention methods focused on generalized criminals in Turkey will be almost as effective as focusing on those who are not otherwise criminally involved. Finally, Weinberg and his colleagues [19] found that suicide bombers had many previous experiences in armed conflict.

6.2.3. Gender

The literature is mixed on the topic of gender. Some researchers found that males comprise the majority of suicide bombers [2, 20, 21, 22, as cited in 19, 23]. However, some terrorist organizations are more likely to use female suicide bombers, such as the Liberation Tigers of Tamil Eelam-LTTE (Tamil Tigers) and Kurdistan Workers Party-PKK/KONGRA GEL [1, 3, 9]. This mixture of terrorist recruitment of both genders indicates the need to have prevention strategies for both genders.

6.2.4. Education

The literature is mixed about the education of suicide bombers. Some authors have found that the bombers are uneducated [17, 24], while others have found moderate to high levels of education [20, 5, 25]. This mixture of findings may be explained by the results of some studies that the leaders of terrorist organizations are usually well-educated, and the militants are less educated [18, 26] or it may be explained that different organizations have different levels of education [1, 9]. The differences among the studies would indicate that education level is not a good predictor without further study, which is difficult with the small sample sizes. However, it might be useful in prevention. Most of the suicide bombers have at least an elementary education. Therefore, school-based prevention techniques might be focused at children at a very young age.

6.2.5. Age

The majority of the studies indicate that suicide attacks are committed by young offenders ranging from 13 to 48, but the median and mode is in the mid 20s [5, 9, 20, 22, 27, as cited in 18, 20, 24]. The age of onset for suicide bombers is generally 18 years old. This indicates that prevention must occur early.

6.2.6. Targets of Bombing

Terrorist organizations mostly chose their targets according to "symbolic and propaganda" values. They wanted to create the maximum sensation in the public agenda and they want to spread the fear of terrorism to the heart of their audiences, thereby promoting their ideology. They want the government to lose the authority or appear to lose the authority of providing order and circumstances for daily life in the public mind by changing their targets of criminal activities. Their scope may include both official and civilian (symbolic or real) targets, such as government/party officials, tourists, foreign workers, embassies, diplomatic persons, symbolic buildings/ areas, and passenger carriers [23]. Hoffman and McCormik [25] also points out the propaganda value of impacting target audiences of the terrorist assaults, specifically the suicide attacks. They send messages by their choice of targets.

Dolnik [9] also stated that the PKK/ KONGRA GEL terrorist organization had chosen similar targets, and they committed suicide attacks against military forces and law enforcement officials. Even though they killed four and wounded 63 civilians in 15 suicide attacks between 1996 and 1999, their major targets were still military and police [9]. Similarly, Karademir [28] reported that PKK/ KONGRA GEL suicide attackers primarily targeted police and military forces, due to their position in countering terrorism and representation of authority. However, they also committed suicide attacks against protocol during ceremonies, in supermarkets and in entertainment centers, which were populated with tourists and local residents between 1996 and 1999. Additionally, Karademir [28] refers to the declaration of this terrorist organization's leader ordering the PKK/ KONGRA GEL militants to target the crowded civilian populations for suicide attacks in late 1998. PKK/ KONGRA GEL tried to choose the situations which resulted in the maximum damage while in large groups, such as protocol and officials during ceremonies attended by official personnel [28].

7. Methods

7.1. Research Design

The purpose of this study was to further the research on the characteristics of the suicide bombers and related victims of suicide attacks committed in Turkey by adding 2006 official data and data from the original interview statements of the perpetrators of uncompleted suicide attacks. Hence, this research is designed including two parts. The first part depends on quantitative analysis of updated secondary data on suicide attacks conducted from 1996 to 2006. The analyses are simply a replication of the previous study using updated data. The findings are enhanced with some aspects of suicide cases that are not included in the dataset using the statements of the perpetrators of uncompleted suicide attacks in the second part. The secondary data were re-analyzed in response to the research questions, furthering the trend analysis to identify any changes and to provide further understanding of suicide bombers using the statements made by the perpetrators of incomplete cases. Therefore, this research depends on both quantitative and qualitative analyses of completed and uncompleted suicide attacks in Turkey.

7.2. Data sources & sample

The previous study by the authors about the suicide attacks [1] revealed the basic characteristics of suicide bombers and the victims in Turkey. One of the major conclusions was the need for continuous streaming data up-dates about suicide attacks in Turkey because they are rare events and the dataset is comprised of a small sample size (n=36 cases). The probability that one or two cases can change the profiles is great. Therefore, the first part of this research reanalyzes the updated secondary data including the completed suicide attacks between 1996 and 2006 in Turkey. The second part of the data includes the statements of suicide bombers who were assigned by the terrorist organizations but were not able to complete the suicide attacks.

Data were collected from Turkish National Police records. The scope of data includes suicide attacks conducted from 1996 to 2006, which includes all the known suicide assaults in Turkey. The generalizability of this study is probably limited to Turkey, but it is possible that other countries are similar. The dataset includes all cases between 1996 and 2006. The decade of data were originally compiled through official records and interviews with officers in counter-terrorism and intelligence of the Turkish National Police (See [29] for a complete description of the data collection process).

7.3. Description of the Data

There are 38 offenders in a total of 36 suicide attack cases. The cases in this study include all the perpetrators and cases in these assaults across the decade of 1996 to 2006 in Turkey. Of the 36 cases in this time period, 23 are completed and 13 are uncompleted. There is one case in which two offenders took part in the same attack in both completed and uncompleted cases, so 24 offenders completed and 14 offenders did not complete the attacks. The second part based on the content analyses examines the statements of 13 assigned/attempted suicide bombers out of the 14 perpetrators. One case is missing due to having no statement because he was killed during his attempt to detonate the explosives.

The updated dataset presents that 22 suicide bombers were identified as the members of PKK/KONGRA GEL between 1996 and 2006. While 7 of them were incomplete, 15 were completed suicide attacks. Although there is one additional suicide attack in which the perpetrator could not be identified due to the severity of explosion, it is strongly considered to be credited to this organization by the professionals. Including this case, PKK/KONGRA GEL killed 17 officials and 6 civilians; wounded 97 officials and 74 civilians in 16 of the completed 23 suicide attacks. Although the number of murdered officials is almost threefold that of murdered civilians and the number of wounded officials and civilians are similar, there is a larger difference between the specific targets of the suicide attacks. Including the uncompleted ones, the organization had 18 official targets; such as personnel, buildings and vehicles of police, military, protocol, municipality and governors' offices. While the targets of two uncompleted suicide attacks were not determined yet, three of them targeted civilian people and buildings; such as a mall and entertainment center.

DHKP/C terrorist organization organized two completed and five uncompleted suicide attacks. While the organization targeted the police twice and the department of justice once, the target is not known in three cases and the last one targeted an entertainment center. There were 3 officials and 1 civilian murdered, along with 21 officials and 5 civilians wounded in the 2 completed attacks of DHKP/C.

Al-Qaeda conducted 5 completed suicide attacks with 6 perpetrators, killing 4 officials and 63 civilians along with wounding between 450 and 650 people, who were almost all civilians. All targets of Al-Qaeda were Western and/or Jewish civilians or their representatives. ICCB-AFID is the other terrorist organization conducting suicide attacks in Turkey. They organized a kamikaze type assault on a symbolic target during an official ceremony in which the highest protocol would attend. Since they were captured before the assault, there are no fatalities in this case.

7.4. Analysis Techniques

The first part of the data was analyzed by quantitative techniques using SPSS software. Because we sought identification of the changes in numbers of victims, both wounded and deaths across time, the trend analysis technique was used. Then, cluster analysis was used to determine how the characteristics cluster around a given concept.

The second part includes the qualitative analysis of interview statements' contents of failed/assigned suicide bombers. This part of the analyses examined the statements in terms of the following categories; recruitment, volunteerism, training, family attachment, position in the organization, waiting period before attack, and pathways of the suicide bombers during their indoctrination and transportation until the assignment or attempt of the suicide attack. The question of how common were the suicide bombers' experience in terms of these categories was explored.

8. Findings

8.1. Discussion of the Trend in Suicide Attacks Based on Quantitative Data

The previous study generally reached the conclusions of:

1. A change in the active organizations using suicide attacks in 2003
2. A change in the target and victims of suicide attacks in Turkey correlating with the change in active organizations using suicide bombings.

3.   A change in some major characteristics of suicide bombers in Turkey correlating with the change in active organizations using suicide bombings.

It was reported that while suicide attacks in Turkey were generally committed by nationalist and revolutionist (Marxist-Leninist) terrorist organizations prior to 2003, Al-Qaeda began to apply this modus operandi in Turkey beginning by 2003. Based on the entrance of the Al-Qaeda terrorist organization in this arena, a drastic change in the characteristics of suicide bombers and victims was experienced. In other words, a profile of pre-2003 attackers was reported to be dominated by PKK-KONGRA GEL, whereas a different profile of suicide bombers and victims was observed by Al-Qaeda's use of this type of attack by beginning from 2003 [1].

The analysis of updated data does make some minor change in the conclusions of the previous study. The dominancy of PKK-KONGRA GEL terrorist organization in pre-2003 cases and Al-Qaeda terrorist organization's dominancy in post-2003 cases emerge in the analysis (Figure 1). However, a single suicide attack conducted by PKK-KONGRA GEL terrorist organization in 2006 indicates the reutilization of suicide attacks by this organization, while Al-Qaeda terrorist organization have been silent in using this modus operandi for two years.

Figure 1: Changes in the suicide attacks

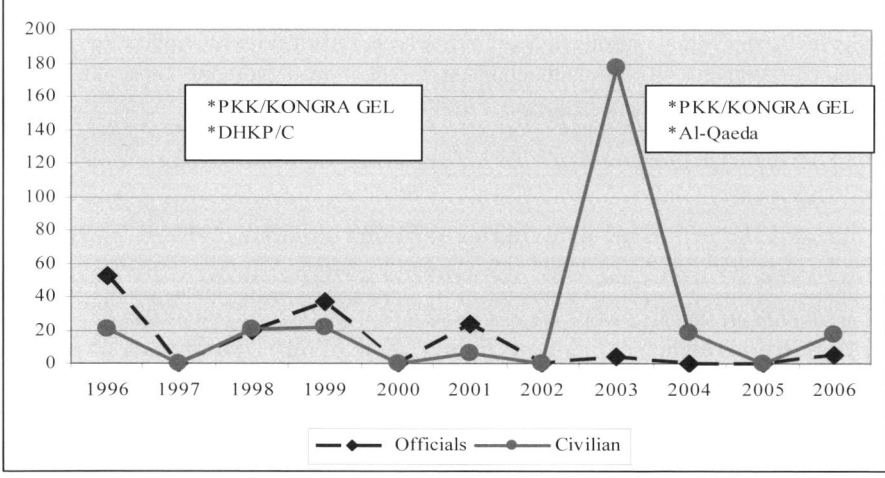

While the targets of pre-2003 suicide attacks were generally official institutions and victims were the representatives of those institutions, most of the post-2003 suicide attacks targeted civilians as indicated in the previous study. The impact of the change in member organizations resulted in a very large increase in the number of injuries and deaths, along with the change in the focus of the target from officials to civilians. Additionally, the pre-2003 suicide bombers were less educated than post-2003 perpetrators. It was also reported that two-thirds of the suicide bombers in pre-2003 cases had outstanding warrants, prior arrests and were females. On the other hand, none of the post-2003 suicide bombers had outstanding warrants, prior arrests and included females [1].

Since the single suicide attack in 2006 was conducted by a PKK-KONGRA GEL terrorist organization member, the presented target and victim profile is slightly changed but, it still supports the conclusion of previous study that the characteristics should be analyzed based on the organizations because of the variance in motivations and structures of different organization.

This study indicates also that there is an approximately even split between those who have prior arrests and those who do not. Additionally, a majority have an outstanding warrant. However, when examining those with a prior arrest and without an active warrant as compared to those with a prior arrest and an active warrant, there is no difference. This means that those who have a prior arrest are equally split between being wanted and not being wanted at the time of the suicide attack. Similarly, there is no significant difference between no prior arrest and being wanted or not wanted (Table 1).

Table 1- Completed suicide bombers

	Pre-2003 (n=17)	Post-2003 (n=7)
Outstanding warrants	60% (n=10)	0
Prior arrests	60% (n=10)	1
Female	65% (n=11)	0
High school and above education	46% (n=8)	71% (n=5)
Carrying on person	95% (n=16)	42% (n=3)
Under 25 years old	53% (n=9)	29% (n=2)
Targets (Victims)	Turkish officials (Off. 14 out of 17)	Civilians (i.e. Jewish) (Civ. 6 out of 7)
Organizations	-PKK-KONGRA GEL -DHKP/C	Al-Qaeda

8.2. Content Analysis of the Second Part of Data

The statements of 13 suicide bombers, who were assigned but not completed or captured before their attempt, were available for the qualitative examination. A review of the 13 cases identified that the perpetrators show varying degrees of common characteristics in terms of the categories of recruitment, volunteerism, training, family attachment, position in the organization, waiting period before attack, and pathways of the suicide bombers during their indoctrination and transportation until the assignment or attempt of suicide attacks.

There are three terrorist organizations represented among this part of the analysis; PKK/KONGRA GEL (7), DHKP/C (4) and ICCB-AFID (2 perpetrators in one case) terrorist organizations. Therefore, Al-Qaeda is not represented in this part of analysis.

8.2.1. Recruitment of New Members to the Terrorist Organizations

The statements reflected that Marxist-Leninist/Maoist organizations (PKK/KONGRA GEL and DHKP/C) generally use magazines and newspapers published by the legal institutions operated or supported by the terrorist organizations to ideologically attract new sympathizers. Along with the offices of these publications, youth associations and cultural clubs provide a way for the new and potential recruits to socialize, which creates peer pressure for the recruitment of new members and indoctrination. On the other hand, one of the members of ICCB-AFID terrorist organization purporting religious principles indicated that he used to live in a mosque controlled by the organization in Frankfurt/Germany for a while and the conversations that in the mosque affected and encouraged him to join the organization.

8.2.2. Volunteerism to Be a Suicide Bomber

The analysis of 13 statements indicated that most of the suicide bombers from all organizations volunteered for this modus operandi. While 10 out of 13 volunteered, one of them was assigned by a higher level militant in PKK/KONGRA GEL terrorist organization without her consent, and the others did not mention anything indicating their voluntariness. The one who was assigned without her consent indicated that she had not felt comfortable with the organization's activities and she was planning to leave the organization. However, she was afraid of being harmed if she stated her intention. When she was assigned, she thought that it might be a good chance to escape and asked her relatives to inform the Turkish National Police about the propose of her entry, place, date and time to Turkey so that she could be captured and be safe.

Although assignment regardless of voluntariness or forcing a militant by terrorist organizations to commit a suicide attack is not common in the literature for other organizations, this case is not the only case reported for PKK/KONGRA GEL terrorist organization about this issue. The organization's male leader of Adana city was captured on the 30th of October, 1996. He commented about the suicide attack committed in Adana on the 25th of October, 1996 in his statement that 'initially, a female militant was assigned for this suicide attack by her superior male militant. However, she was killed with the order of her superior male militant when she refused to be a suicide bomber and another female militant was assigned for the same mission and she committed the suicide attack on 25th of October, 1996.'[2]

8.2.3. Training

The existing information indicates that most of the suicide bombers (9 of 13) had attended at least one of the training "camps" for military tactics and ideological conversion process of the terrorist organizations. Almost half of them experienced some type of graduated tactical practice operations before being suicide bombers. In other words, 6 out of 13 developed their organizational skills by conducting some smaller activities such as plaquing, throwing Molotov cocktails, attending demonstrations, rioting, distributing fliers promoting terrorist organizations, or being involved in armed fights with law enforcement agencies.

In terms of their armed struggling experiences, the statements reflect that five of them were involved at least once in armed conflict with law enforcement, military or other groups, while five others were not involved. The other three were not involved in any armed conflict, although they had been armed militants in rural areas for a while. One of them wounded herself with a shotgun in a training camp, and she was wounded a second time in an armed conflict.

---

[2] Statement of PKK/KONGRA GEL terrorist organization member on 30th of October, 1996.

8.2.4. Family Attachment

The examination of suicide bombers' characteristics in terms of their attachment to the families showed that 5 of the 13 perpetrators of uncompleted suicide attacks had family connections where the contacts were rare, whereas 4 of them had no contacts for a long period of time. For instance, one of them had never seen his last child who was 5 years old when he was captured before the suicide attack. Another one had no contact with his family for almost 10 years; he had no knowledge whether his parents were alive or dead when he was captured.

Regardless of having family contact or not, four of them had positive family attachments, which is defined as their attachment to family promoted their involvement in the terrorist activities. For instance, one of the suicide bombers' family lost two members in armed conflict with law enforcement agencies. In another case, almost the whole family belongs to the same terrorist organization, so they encouraged the suicide bombers involvement in terrorist activities. Additionally, 4 out of the 13 perpetrators had family members who were imprisoned.

8.2.5. Positions in the Organizations

In agreement with the literature, which indicates that terrorist organizations usually do not assign their high level ranking militants for suicide assaults, almost all of the suicide bombers were at low level positions in the organizational hierarchy. They were usually soldiers, carrier/smugglers, or responsible for the organizational activities in very small areas. The examination of the number of years that the suicide bombers spent between joining the organization and becoming suicide bombers emerged as an average of approximately 7 years.

8.2.6. Waiting Period before Attack

Official investigators hold several beliefs about suicide attacks that have some support in the statements. First, the intelligence collection process about the vulnerabilities of targets is completed someone other than the person assigned as the suicide bomber. The content analysis of the statements provided supportive results; intelligence on vulnerabilities of the target is collected by another person for the suicide attacks in 8 out of 13 cases. However, the data are not sufficient to demonstrate other suspected points by official investigators such as;

- Targets are known to only on high level officials in the terrorist organization and even the suicide bombers learn immediately preceding the attack.
- Suicide bombers are isolated from all activities for a period of time before the attack so they do not draw police attention.
- Senior militants who are in prison have considerable impact on controlling and directing the organizational activities, as it is in dispatching suicide bombers. (Only one of PKK/KONGRA GEL suicide bombers indicated that he received a direct order from imprisoned seniors of the organization to commit the suicide attack; and three of them stated that senior PKK/KONGRA GEL militants in prison arranged volunteers to go to the rural area for armed conflict in the name of the organization.)

Therefore, these points are suggested for future research.

8.2.7. International Issues: Pathways

The analysis of 13 perpetrators' statements of uncompleted suicide attacks revealed an international issue. While suicide bombers were telling about their background in the terrorist organizations, they also mention how, when and where they received ideological, political and armed trainings. Since, most of the terrorist assaults of these organizations were conducted within Turkish soil and/or aim Turkish government or people; they were tolerated by governmental agencies of some other countries during their transportation and indoctrination in the camps belonging to the aforementioned terrorist organizations, which were established in soil outside of Turkey. Even some of the suicide bombers were captured numerous times by governmental agencies of these countries while they were illegally passing the borders, or they were known to be members of these terrorist organizations. The members were released in that country, handed over to the other members of their own organizations, given refugee status for a certain time, or sent back to the entering country.

For example, one of the male suicide bombers from DHKP/C terrorist organization who was previously involved in numerous political/armed training camps and involved in rural armed guerilla activities was assigned by a superior militant to go to Greece using the route from Syria to Beirut/Lebanon by car and then to Greece by sea in April 1999. While he and two other militants were being guided by a smuggler from Syria to Beirut Harbor by a car, they were arrested by Lebanon soldiers because they did not have passports. They were deported back to the Syrian Police after being detained for one week. They told the Syrian Police that they were DHKP/C militants acting under the order of a superior male militant using the alias name of X. They stated the following:

"Then, Alias X came soon; he took us from the Syrian Police, and brought us to his place in Damascus to wait for another plan. In the beginning of August 1999, Alias X brought us fake passports prepared in the names of some Turkish people and we flew from Damascus to Athens/Greece without a problem. When we landed, we were arrested by the Greek Police at the airport because our passports were counterfeited. We again told them that we were DHKP/C members, and we wanted to be refugees in Greece. They wanted to send us back to Syria, but they did not. They took our statements and brought us to a place to keep us until our demand for being refugees would be determined. After 30-35 days, we were told that our refugee status was granted for 5 years and we were given refugee IDs. Then we were brought by a DHKP/C member to a home belonging to the organization in Athens."

He also mentioned in his statement that he was together in the same house with another suicide bomber with the alias name of Y, who conducted a suicide attack on a police building in Istanbul on 3rd January, 2001, while he was living in Athens.

Another male suicide bomber from DHKP/C terrorist organization who could not complete the attack also provides very similar information about his pathway between Syria, Lebanon and Greece. He was involved in numerous political/armed guerilla training camps of the organization and armed conflicts with Turkish Armed Forces in rural areas. He made the following statement:

"While I was in Latakia/Syria, I gave ideological training to nine militants including alias name of Y, who conducted a suicide attack on a police building in Istanbul on 3rd January, 2001. Officials from the Syrian Service conducted an operation and arrested me with nine others and brought us to Damascus. They also seized the guns and bombs in the house. After three months detention, we were deported to Lebanon at the end of 1998. After a while, five of us were again arrested while we were trying to go to Syria using illegal ways. After we were kept as arrestees of the Syrian Military Intelligence for 2.5 months, they handed us over to the Syrian Police. They sent us to Greece based on our wish by airway. When we landed in Athens, we were arrested by Greek Police. We said that we were DHKP/C members and demanded to become refugees. Almost one month later our refugee status was granted and we were given IDs. We were brought to a house belonging to the organization by other militants after being released."

These are just two examples about the pathways of suicide bombers, whose terrorist organizational status was clearly known and who had been under the control of some regional states' governmental agencies. Almost all of the suicide bombers telling that they received ideological, political and/or armed conflict trainings in any camp in other countries point out the same international issue that these countries are supporting the terrorist camps or are ignorant that they exist. This clearly indicates very complicated international law issues that need to be resolved for countering terrorism. With the global risk of terrorism, no country can be safe by ignoring the issue as if it is a domestic issue.

8.2.8. A General Discussion about the Contents of Statements

This research also aimed to find out if there are specific reasons motivating the perpetrators to become suicide bombers. We noticed that some of the suicide bombers from PKK/KONGRA GEL were basically motivated by the capture of the organization's leader, Abdullah Ocalan, in February 1999. For the two suicide bombers from ICCB-AFID terrorist organization, a jihad campaign declared in 1998 is identified as the motivating factor. This campaign makes each member responsible for doing as many types of assaults that they can do with their possibilities, which would promote their organizational status.

The statements of the two ICCB-AFID suicide bombers point out that the capture of this leader could have been a signal given in 1998 for the terrorist organization's probability and/or capability to conduct suicide attacks, such as the 9/11. Both of the suicide bombers made very coordinated statements about the suicide attack plan that they would commit together. According to their statements; one of the perpetrators was assigned as a suicide bomber by the leader of ICCB-AFID terrorist organization, who is known to be in Germany. The suicide attack would be conducted by using an airplane full of explosives with the target of the Turkish Grand National Assembly or Ataturk Mausoleum on 29th October of 1998, which is the annual celebration of the foundation of the modern Turkish Republic. The bomber went to Turkey and convinced the other male suicide bomber from the same organization to join the task. One of them served his mandatory military service in one of the airbases of the Turkish Military. They together hired a small plane with the pilot and made an exploratory flight a couple days before the ceremony. They were hoping that almost all of the protocol would attend the ceremony. They arranged numerous butane gas tubes and dynamite for detonation. They would hijack the plane, load the explosives in it and fly to the Ataturk Mausoleum while all the protocol were attending the ceremony. However, they were captured before the suicide attack by Turkish National Police.

There are interesting parallels that should be highlighted in this case. First of all, one of the attempting suicide bombers served in one of the Turkish Air Force bases, which is similar to the 9/11 suicide bombers that would later be trained on U.S. soil. Additionally, the 9/11 suicide attacks were very similar, but much larger in size than what they planned to conduct in Turkey on 29th November, 1998. It is possible that the perpetrators of the 9/11 suicide bombings were inspired by this attempted attack. Third, one of the suicide bombers was questioned about whether they have any relationship with the Al Qaeda terrorist organization's leader Osama bin Laden. He responded that he knows Osama bin Laden from the TVs, but had no contact with him or his organization. He also stated:

"There was news about ICCB-AFID's help of one hundred thousand Marks (former currency of Germany before EU membership) to Laden and I just laughed at this news, because I know he is very rich and he does not need our organization's money. If there was a relationship, he would help the ICCB-AFID."

9. Summary of Conclusions and Related Policy Implications

The following conclusions and the related policy implications are a result of the literature review:

- More than 60% of the bombers have an active warrant. Increase **arrests of those with outstanding warrants.**
- The mixture of terrorist recruitment of both **genders** indicates the need to have prevention strategies for both genders.
- **Education level** is not a good predictor. However, it might be useful in prevention. Most of the suicide bombers had at least an elementary education. Therefore, school based prevention techniques should be focused at a young age.
- **Age** of onset for suicide bombers is generally 18 years old. This indicates that prevention must occur early.
- When examining those with and **without an active warrant to those with a prior arrest**, there is no difference.
- Prevention methods focused on **generalized criminals** is probably not as effective as focusing on those who are not otherwise criminally involved. However, this is a small difference (20 to 14). While this is significantly different, if we want to prevent a majority, this variable is not very informative.
- Targets for bombers are based on the organization. Intelligence on preparatory activities is the only way to identify potential targets. For example, **tracking components** for making these bombs would be beneficial. This would include tracking sources.

The following conclusion and policy implication are a result of the quantitative and qualitative data:

- Between pre-2003 and post-2003, there is an inverse change in the characteristics; outstanding warrants, prior arrests, gender, education level, age, targets and organization. However, the recent 2006 attack by PKK KONGRA GEL mirrors pre-2003 data. This highlights the **need to do sub analyses** as the sample grows.

The following conclusions and policy implications are based on the 13 interview statements of the uncompleted bombers:

- **Recruitment uses peer or principle pressure**. Early prevention efforts may teach youth to resist peer pressure.
- Most **volunteer for this task**, but there is one case indicating that a refusal is a death sentence also.

- **Training is provided** for a majority of the bombers. Prevention efforts should focus on closing training camps. However, "street training" is more difficult to address.
- The bombers had weak family ties or the family was terrorist involved. Prevention / **intervention must be at the family level**.
- The majority of the bombers are **low level ranking participants in the organization**. Prevention should target this level of involvement.
- The waiting period prior to an attack needs further investigation. The data are too scarce at this time.
- The use of international pathways highlights the **need for international cooperation** to prevent terrorism.

References

[1]   C. J. Smith, O. Nikbay, Suicide attacks in contemporary terrorism: The ultimate impacts in Turkey. Ankara, Turkey: Oncu Press; 2006. 779-789. (Paper presented at Istanbul Conference on Democracy and Global Security, 2005)

[2]   B. Hoffman, Editor, *The Logic of Suicide Terrorism. Terrorism and Counterterrorism: Understanding the New Security Environment.* Guilford: Connecticut; McGraw Hill Company; 2003.

[3]   O. Nikbay, Intihar Saldirilari ve Turkiye'deki Intihar Saldirilarinin Sosyo-Dinamik Acidan Incelenmesi. Institute of Forensic Science. Istanbul/Turkey, Istanbul University: 2002, 131.

[4]   D. Ergil, Suicide Terrorism in Turkey. *Civil Wars* **3** (2000), 37-54.

[5]   R. A. Hudson, *The Sociology and psychology of terrorism: Who becomes a terrorist and why?* Washington, D.C.: Federal Research Division of the Library of Congress; 1999.

[6]   U. Ozdag, E. Aydinli *Winning a low intensity conflict: Drawing lessons from the Turkish case.* Portland: Frank Cass Publishers; 2003.

[7]   S. Ozeren, C. V. Voorde. *Turkish Hizballah: A case study of radical terrorism.* December 01,2004.

[8]   J. R. White. *Terrorism.* Ontario, Canada: Thomson & Wadsworth Publishing; 2002.

[9]   A. Dolnik, Die and let die: Exploring links between suicide terrorism and terrorist use of chemical, biological, radiological, and nuclear weapons. *Studies in Conflict & Terrorism,* **26** (2003), 17-35.

[10] C.E. Simonsen, J. R. Spindlove *Terrorism today: The past, the players, the future.* New Jersey; Pearson Prentice Hall; 2004.

[11] S. Teymur. *An Analysis of terrorist recruitment by observing the Revolutionary People's Liberation Party/Front (DHKP/C) terrorist organization in Turkey.* Department of Criminal Justice, University of North Texas: Texas; 2003, 86.

[12] N. Alkan, *Genclik ve Terorizm.* Ankara, Turkey: Emniyet Genel Mudurlugu Basimevi; 2002.

[13] L. E. Cline, From Ocalan to Al Qaida: The continuing terrorist threat in Turkey. *Studies in Conflict & Terrorism,* **27** (2004), 321-335.

[14] R. J. Chasdi. *Tapestry of terror: A portrait of Middle East terrorism, 1994-1999.* Langham, Maryland: Lexington Books; 2002.

[15] E. Karmon, Islamic terrorist activities in Turkey in the 1990s. *Terrorism and Political Violence* **10** (1998), 101-121.

[16] A. M. Rabasa, C. Benard, et al. *The Muslim world after 9/11.* Arlington, VA,: RAND Project Air Force; 2005.

[17] J. M. Poland, *Understanding terrorism: Groups, strategies, and responses.* New Jersey; Pearson Prentice Hall; 2005.

[18] M. Soibelman, Palestinian suicide bombers. *Journal of Investigative Psychology and Offender Profiling* **1** (2004), 175-190.

[19] L. Weinberg, A. Pedahzur, et al. The social and religious characteristics of suicide bombers and their victims. *Terrorism and Political Violence* **15** (2003), 139-153.

[20] S. Atran, Genesis of suicide terrorism. *Science* **299** (2003), 1534-1539.

[21] R. D. Hecth, Deadly history, deadly actions, and deadly bodies: A response to Ivan Strenski's 'sacrifice, gift and the social logic of Muslim "human bombers". *Terrorism and Political Violence* **15** (2003), 35-47.

[22] A. Margalit, *The suicide bombers.* The New York Review of Books; 2003.

[23] G. Martin, *Understanding terrorism: Challenges, perspectives, and issues.* Thousand Oaks, CA: Sage Publications; 2003.

[24] A. Schbley, Defining religious terrorism: A causal and anthological profile. *Studies in Conflict & Terrorism* **26** (2003), 105–134.

[25] B. Hoffman, G. H. McCormick, Terrorism, signaling, and suicide attack. *Studies in Conflict & Terrorism,* **27** (2004), 243-281.

[26] C. A. Russel, H. M. Bowman. Miller. *Profile of a terrorist. Perspectives on terrorism.* In Z. F. L. and Y. A. Silke, Editors. Wilmington, DE.: 1983; 45-60.

[27] D. Burdman, Education, indoctrination, and incitement: Palestinian children on their way to martyrdom. *Terrorism and Political Violence,* **15** (2003), 96-123.

[28] K. Karademir, *Intihar Saldirilari.* Ankara, Turkey: Emniyet Genel Mudurlugu Terorle Mucadele Daire Baskanligi Yayinlari; 2003.

[29] O. Nikbay, Suicide attacks in Turkey: An analysis of trends and charcteristics. Division of Criminology, Criminal Justice and Policy. Baltimore, MD., University of Baltimore; 2005.

Understanding and Responding to the Terrorism Phenomenon
O. Nikbay and S. Hancerli (Eds.)
IOS Press, 2007

Palestinian Istishhadia Campaign:
A Dynamic and Practical Tool

Yoram SCHWEITZER

Institute for National Security Studies (INSS), Israel

Abstract. This paper examines the phenomenon of Palestinian *Istishhadia,* the term used by Palestinians to describe suicide bombings, and is based on personal interviews with imprisoned Palestinian surviving suicide bombers and their dispatchers from various organizations between 1993 and 2006. This neither linear nor static phenomenon is divisible into two main periods. The first period spans from April 1993 to March 2000 and the second from October 2000 to June 2006. In addition to examining the principal methods of both periods, this paper analyzes organizational distinctions in the planning and management of suicide bombings as well as the motives that led individuals and organizations to choose these methods. In spite of the fact that many in the Palestinian leadership realized that the suicide weapon was a double-edged sword, suicide operations are still being launched. However, their numbers have lessened greatly due to Israel's effective counter terrorism policy and Palestinian indigenous political considerations.

Keywords. Istishhadia (suicide bombings), Istishhadis (suicide bombers), terrorism, Palestinian, Israeli, tahadiya

Introduction

The paper is based on personal interviews conducted with Palestinian surviving suicide bombers and their dispatchers who were prisoners from various organizations between 1993 and 2006. Among the interviewees there were about 3 suicide bombers and 40 dispatchers. These interviews unveiled the dynamics of the suicide industry which has developed among the Palestinians since the introduction of this modus operandi in April 1993. The paper will examine the way it evolved and how it was used by the organizations to promote their political agenda.

1. Palestinian Suicide Terrorism: Two Distinct Periods

In principle, suicide terrorism has served terrorists all over the world as a weapon intended to balance (at least to some extent) the inherent asymmetry that exists in the confrontation between a weaker side - terrorist organizations - and a stronger side - the opposing government. This has been true for the Palestinian suicide terror campaign as well.

Yet one cannot consider this campaign as a linear and static phenomenon, as it has developed and changed over the years, and can be roughly divided into two main periods. Each had its unique dynamic, objectives, and characteristics, and each was highly affected by changing political circumstances. The division into two separate periods is important in order to focus more accurately on the roots of suicide terrorism, to indicate the direction of its development, and to examine its circumstances, aims, and achievements. The two phases are:

- April 1993 to March 2000,
- October 2000 to June 2006, often referred to in Israeli parlance as the "Second Intifada" or "Al-Aqsa Intifada."

All in all, the State of Israel experienced 189 suicide attacks up till August 2006; about 38 were carried out in the first period, and the remaining 151 in the second period (involving many more suicide bombers). In addition, more than two hundred suicide bombers (*Istishhadis*) were apprehended on their way to an attack or while engaged in preparations, and many more expressed a desire to do so [1].

At the beginning of the first period, the pattern of *Istishhadia* was trial and error. Initially, there were individual operatives who worked underground to carry out suicide attacks, later perfecting their procedures. In the second period, however, the terrorists relied on the precedents that had been set, and the scope of technical knowledge disseminated by veteran terrorists in preparing demolition charges grew by leaps and bounds. The number of organizations involved in dispatching *Istishhadis* also grew, as did the number of people involved in terrorist attacks. The volunteers offering themselves for *Istishhadia* increased mainly for emotional reasons: hate, anger, despair and lack of hope among widening circles of the Palestinian rank and file.

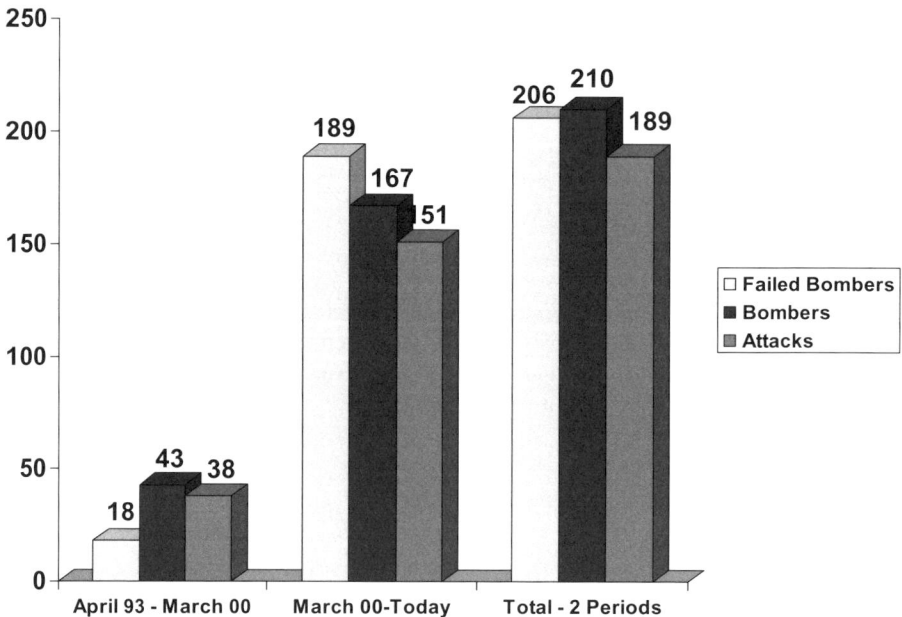

Figure 1. Suicide attacks in the two periods (Source: Yoram Schweitzer)

The major differences between the two periods can be summarized as follows:

- Quantitative differences in the number of *Istishhadis* - growth by a factor of almost four.
- Growth in the number of participating organizations. Hamas and Palestinian Islamic Jihad (PIJ) were active in the first period, and in the second were joined by additional factions, including various arms of Fatah, the Popular Front for the Liberation of Palestine (PFLP) and *ad hoc* networks.
- Involvement of women and children in the second period.
- More extensive popular Palestinian support of *Istishhadia* in the second period than in the first period, when they were still perceived by the majority of Palestinians as a potential obstacle to political or diplomatic progress.

Table 1. First vs. Second Phase

Phase 1	Phase 2
61	400 and many more volunteers
Males	Males females and children
2 orgs	4 orgs
Members and close associates	Members and non affiliated newcomers
More planning and discipline	An all out war
Almost every cell member was ready to sacrifice only few were selected	Due to almost unlimited pool of volunteers a smart use of available men power was taken
Mukawama, defiance and revenge	Retaliation revenge and defiance

2. The Dynamic of the Palestinian Suicide Attacks

In practice, the *Istishhadia* model is rooted in the significant inferiority of Palestinian military strength compared to Israel. According to the interviewees, since the Israelis suffered far fewer losses than the Palestinians in the first Intifada, when the Palestinians mostly used stones as weapons, Palestinian Islamic organizations began planning a transition to the use of light arms [2, 3]. With organizational backing and the initiative of field operators, the Palestinians attempted to prove their ability to inflict heavy losses on Israel despite their inferior capabilities. Suicide bombing was selected as the most appropriate method, as it is financially cheap, precise, and has an immensely deadly effect [4].

The use of suicide bombing led to the creation of new myths. The attackers were transformed into heroes, and the terrorist organizations were perceived as immensely powerful. The bombers expressed the desire to retaliate inside the borders of Israel. They also viewed these actions as compensation for the humiliation and powerlessness felt by Palestinians, and for their perception of ongoing victim hood. Soon Palestinians learned that the power of *Istishhadia* went far beyond the death and destruction it caused, because it had an enormous psychological effect not only in Israel, but beyond the national borders.

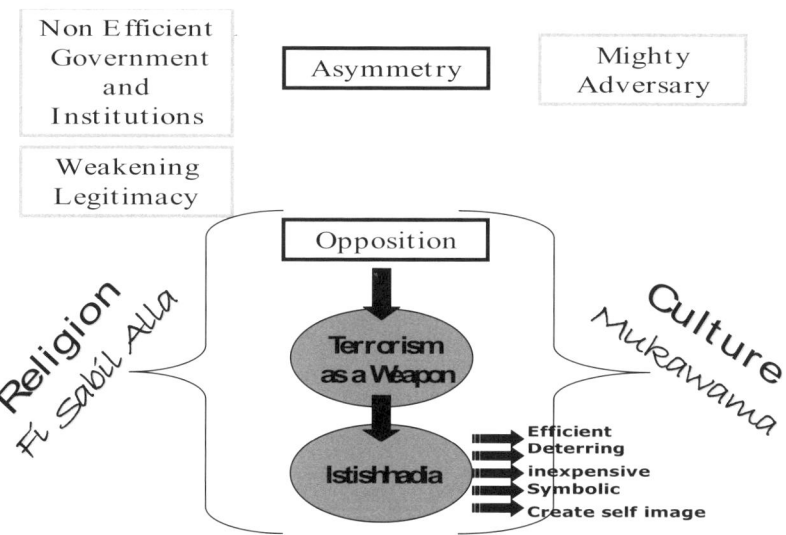

These kinds of terrorist attacks are, by their very nature, "media prone." Their perpetrators wanted to achieve international coverage and to convey the hardships of the Palestinian nation, alongside the bravery and devotion of its warriors, while making sure this would remain on the international agenda. The horrifying pictures of carnage wreaked by terrorist attacks were meant to highlight Palestinian aspirations for independence and political sovereignty. The Palestinians attempted to demonstrate the price that would be exacted on Israel and the entire Middle East in the event of a continued Israeli occupation: the lack of personal and political security, and the undermining of regional stability.

In addition to examining the principal methods common to both periods, it is important to examine the motives that led individuals and organizations to choose these methods. Despite similarities, the motives are not identical. They are influenced by the different circumstances of each period, as well as by different social situations and political changes that were evident over time in the Palestinian and Israeli milieu.

The attack-reprisal cycle led to the acceleration of suicide attacks on two levels:

- The pool of potential *Istishhadis* grew significantly, in line with the rising number of Palestinians who wished to retaliate against Israel. Their ranks expanded in response to an unfolding cycle of events: The Palestinian Authority (PA) did not fully cooperate with Israel to prevent terror in general and suicide attacks in particular. Israel therefore increased its targeted killings, causing a large number of casualties among the Palestinians. This, in turn, provided fertile ground for recruitment of new *Istishhadis* who sought to avenge these deaths.
- The wanted terrorists understood that they had nothing to lose, because they were likely to be killed by Israel. This increased their motivation to sacrifice themselves in the process of killing as many Israelis as possible through *Istishhadia* operations.

As a result of targeted killings and the arrests, the organizations made structural and personnel adjustments. They carried out their attacks via regional networks and local cells, and when members of these local units were arrested or eliminated, the new ones entering the fray were highly motivated to revenge the death of their comrades and create as much mayhem as possible. Thus, in the beginning of second period, Hamas carried out a series of attacks in retaliation for the killing of Fawaz Badran, another explosives expert, who had independently initiated the suicide attack in the Netanya Mall (January 2001), in which 35 people were wounded. The Netanya attack was planned by Badran as his "entrance ticket" to Hamas, [5, 6] and was the first of several such attacks in the ensuing months that took a large toll of Israeli lives.

The elimination of Badran led Abbas al-Sayed, the Hamas spokesman who was also the military commander of the organization's network in the West Bank town of Tul Karem, to announce that Hamas would carry out ten revenge suicide attacks. Al-Sayed himself later masterminded a series of suicide attacks, including the infamous bombing at Netanya's Park Hotel, which took the lives of 30 elderly Israelis and led Israel to initiate Operation Defensive Shield, reoccupying the major Palestinian cities, in March 2002. The series of "promised" suicide bombings - all of which were ultimately carried out - included the Dolphinarium discotheque in Tel Aviv (21 killed), the Sbarro pizza restaurant in the heart of Jerusalem (15 killed), and others. These accelerated the deterioration between the two sides.

As Palestinian public support for *Istishhadia* grew, the number of volunteers for the missions increased exponentially. During the first period and at the beginning of the second, the organizations had to expend efforts to recruit operatives. As time went on, there was such an assortment of volunteers that the terror networks could pick and choose the most appropriate candidates. In many cases, it appeared that the *Istishhadis* themselves had "recruited" their dispatchers, instead of the reverse. The easy availability of volunteers turned the method into an extremely "cheap" and accessible instrument [7].

During the second period, the lines that distinguished the various organizations - Hamas, the PIJ, Fatah and the PFLP - became blurred. Palestinian society as a whole cultivated the suicide ethos as a weapon of defiance and as its principal tool against the Israeli occupation, whereas it had previously been an option only for solitary members of the Hamas and the PIJ. Now, deep into the second period, the suicide subculture became firmly entrenched.

At times, it seemed that *Istishhadia* served mainly as a retaliatory weapon rather than furthering any clear strategic or political objective. This became particularly evident when Fatah itself began to dispatch *Istishhadis* at the beginning of 2002, in retaliation for the elimination of Riyad Karmi. Karmi was a Fatah activist who operated terror cells at the same time as serving in the PA's security apparatus, and, as a result he was targeted by Israel. From this time on, suicide bombing became an integral part of Fatah network operations and opened a new round of bloodshed endorsed by the largest Palestinian organization - and the one in government.

In addition to the social and cultural factors that reinforced the strategic rationales of the suicide bombing campaign in the second period, the Palestinians had a strong desire for a miraculous instrument to balance their profound asymmetry in the conflict. "We wanted Israel to pay part of the price of the occupation, and not only enjoy the profits." [6] The violent method they chose was intended to prove to the world that the Palestinian problem must be solved. The regional instability seeped outwards, arousing general public interest in the Islamic world and causing it to step up its support for the Palestinian struggle. The price, of course, was that after 9/11 international public opinion began to identify Palestinian terror with worldwide terror purporting Islamic principles.

3. Groups and Organizations Promoting Suicide Bombings

The first organization to carry out *Istishhadia* was Hamas. Hamas paved the way and was the most dominant and effective of all the organizations that adopted *Istishhadia*. In the first period, Hamas was joined by the PIJ. The two organizations shared a national-religious perspective that denied Israel's right to exist and aspired to establish Islamic religious law throughout "Palestine". *Istishhadia* was consistent with this worldview, which promoted the use of armed resistance by all possible means, including self-sacrifice. The PIJ, however, lacked the social and organizational infrastructure of Hamas and was therefore smaller, had a narrower support base, and wielded less influence.

Hamas and the PIJ together dispatched about eight *Istishhadis* even before the Oslo Agreement was signed and the PA arrived on the scene. Their sporadic acts of *Istishhadia* were based on trial and error; they used small amounts of explosives and were not very effective. They mainly expressed the desire to escalate the struggle and to demonstrate opposition. At the time, both organizations were on the margins of Palestinian political life. For many years, they were overshadowed by the PLO under the leadership of Arafat and his Fatah organization, and their views were not taken into account. When the PA took over control of sections of the West Bank and Gaza in 1994 under the Oslo Agreement, the opposition organizations employed *Istishhadia* to express their armed opposition to what they called "capitulation to Israeli dictates and acceptance of Israel's existence."

Other events that accelerated the dispatch of *Istishhadis* were the massacre of 29 Arabs by a Jewish settler in a Hebron mosque (February 1994), and Israel's arrests and targeted killings of high-ranking Hamas and PIJ *Istishhadi* operatives. These events escalated the confrontation between Israel and the Islamic opposition organizations, and led to mounting strife between Israel and the PA. *Istishhadia*, which started as an attempt to ratchet up the military activity of the organizations, to redress the asymmetry in the casualty equation, and to express the *mukawama* (resistance) ethos, turned into a primary instrument of revenge, destruction, and terrorization directed against Israeli citizens. The result, intentional or not, was disruption of the Oslo process, leading to a bloodbath in which *Istishhadis* played a central role.

In the second period, from October 2000, the process of disintegration of the PA mandate went into high gear. As violence between Israel and the Palestinians increased, Hamas and the PIJ continued to dispatch *Istishhadis*, and were gradually joined by Fatah, PFLP, and other organizations. Despite the fact that *Istishhadi* candidates did not particularly care which group sent them, the organizations competed among themselves to enhance their prestige by recruiting into their ranks almost all available volunteers (as long as these seemed intent on carrying out their mission). In the second period, Hamas continued to be more meticulous in its selection of volunteers, but even it enlarged its ranks and recruited *Istishhadis* from among the *Dawa* (Muslims who exhort other Muslims to deeper commitment to Islam, and who are influential in daily religious life), students in Islamic colleges and universities, and high school pupils.

Hamas was relatively more organized than the other organizations in its operations and was guided by a strategic objective. The PIJ and Fatah dispatched their attackers in accordance with their operative abilities, but with no guiding strategy beyond the desire to cause as many casualties as possible. As one of the main PIJ *Istishhadi* dispatchers admitted:

"We made a mistake in that we operated in a disorganized fashion without a set objective, beyond the [general] struggle against the occupation, and therefore we were not successful in evicting Israel from the West Bank in the first stage. If we would have operated in a strategically coordinated fashion and would have focused on striking at soldiers and settlers in the disputed territories, we could have caused the end of the occupation on the West Bank, in the first stage." [8]

A Fatah operative who commanded a cell that dispatched four *Istishhadis* (including two women) also admitted that "we had no strategy. It's impossible to operate without a plan and a political objective. Extreme violence must have an objective, and an appropriate time schedule for a specific operation and for halting the operation if there is a chance for political process." [9]

Another Fatah operative explained: "Our [terrorist] operations in general and *Istishhadia* specifically, were expressions of organized anarchy. Our organization was purely tactical - connecting a bomber with a dispatcher and with a Kalashnikov or a demolition charge." This operative was an assistant to Marwan Barghouti (the influential Fatah leader and Tanzim commander currently in prison in Israel) and was involved in terror operations and the dispatching of *Istishhadis*, particularly those without explosive belts, who carried light arms [10].

Thus it can be said that the objectives of the suicide campaign in the second period were retaliatory and vindictive, especially on the part of the field operatives. The strategy of the organizational commanders was to force Israel to change its policies. When this did not happen, they continued their attacks as a wave of action-reprisals, until circumstances allowed the Palestinians to accept a temporary *de facto* ceasefire or *tahadiya*.

4. Planning and Management of Suicide Bombings

The planning of *Istishhadia* was often shaped by constraints and circumstances in the field. The organizations acted underground and in secrecy, via networks and terror cells, because of Israel's policy of arrests and targeted killings - sometimes with the assistance of the PA, which opposed the independent policies of Hamas and the PIJ. The more pressure that was applied by Israel on the terrorist organizations, and at times in the first period also by the PA, the more these organizations functioned within secret cells and networks that were often autonomous.

In the first period, when only Hamas and the PIJ dispatched suicide bombers, they chose their targets carefully, and the network and cell leaders guided the perpetrators to their destinations. The attractiveness of the destinations was determined by the relative ease of reaching them and by their potential for producing as many fatalities as possible. When attacks were organized to avenge Israel's elimination of terror network heads, the targets, in 1995 and 1996, were bustling civilian areas such as Jerusalem's Central Bus Station and buses (by Hamas) and Tel Aviv's Dizengoff Street (by the PIJ and Hamas). In the second period as well, crowded targets were deliberately sought. Some - buses, shopping centers, restaurants, and clubs - were determined in advance and specifically marked out, while in other cases the perpetrators themselves chose particular targets.

In the second period, especially in its initial stage, Hamas continued to maintain its relatively organized administrative hierarchy compared to other organizations, especially among the young generation of commanders who remained outside prison. The various Hamas networks maintained contact and coordination, despite the fact that they operated independently, while also keeping contact with organizational command abroad (in Jordan, Syria and Lebanon). An infamous example of coordination between the networks was the series of ten suicide operations carried out by Hamas in retaliation for the killing of one of its demolition experts [11].

As Israeli pressure mounted and many commanders were arrested or killed, the operations became more decentralized under the control of regional leaders. When these leaders were arrested, they were replaced by others, these, in turn, activated cell leaders who had, for the most part, the means and connections needed to continue organizing attacks. Some of the cells were only partially guided; they chose their goals according to their understanding of the general directives and the best means of carrying them out. For example, a cell leader responsible for a large number of operations including suicide attacks, said, "They asked me to look for targets for possible attacks, like restaurants, for instance. They gave me written instructions about their preferences and about easy targets, and they told me to look for a new target or a unique attack." [12] In regard to a devastating café bombing in Jerusalem, he explained:

"They asked us to locate a target for the attack and a time when we were willing to pull it off. I went around and located the Moment Café. There were also people who gave me tips about possible places. Our preference was central Jerusalem, because the army and security service were always claiming that central Jerusalem was an area that no terrorist could enter, and we wanted to prove to them that we could get into any place [12]."

From the beginning of the second period, the PIJ, as opposed to Hamas, acted on the initiative of the field operatives, who had prepared themselves before the outbreak of the Second Intifada. The operations were centered in the West Bank city of Jenin. The group began to dispatch *Istishhadis* on its own initiative. As the conflict with Israel grew more heated and several of its leaders were killed, new members joined. Their actions were directed by a number of regional terror networks, whose coordination was based on the mutual acquaintance and trust of their leaders.

These PIJ networks were characterized by a large degree of independence. "I made the decisions myself, according to my own judgment, and if I needed assistance, I had a connection with the organization," explained one leader. "They knew they could depend on me. I prepared everything - the explosive belts, sending out people to recruit the *Istishhadis* for me, and I would check them before they went out and decide who would go and who wouldn't. It's not as hard as it seems." [13]

The leaders, however, were strict about partitioning the membership to protect identities in case of arrest, so that only a few were acquainted with most of their fellow members. Accessories were used to recruit *Istishhadis* and collect information about targets, and chose their own targets and dates of attack. They were given the necessary supplies by their commanders, to whom they reported, usually after an attack [14]. The first instances of *Istishhadia* were car bombs. Later, as the organizations obtained knowledge about explosive belts, that method was put to use. When the Israel Defense Forces entered Jenin during Operation Defensive Shield, all these networks were dealt a heavy blow, with many of their members killed or arrested.

Fatah, which began to dispatch suicide bombers only in January 2002, about 15 months after the start of the conflict, conducted its first attack in an "anarchistic-orderly" fashion [15]. Its earliest actions were sweeping acts of vengeance following the death of Raed Karmi, a key activist and a personal friend of members of Tanzim (the armed militia of Fatah) who were, at the time, also members of the Palestinian security forces and were wanted terrorists. They answered the call for vengeance, each one doing his best to recruit and dispatch *Istishhadis*, with no defined strategic aim, either political or military. Targets were chosen almost randomly, with an underlying desire to cause injury to Israel, its soldiers, and its citizens.

The initiatives were usually taken by members via a coordinator, who had the necessary means and funds. Some supplied the perpetrators, some the weapons, and some the means of transporting the perpetrators to their destinations. The desire for vengeance grew with the number of members injured, and new actions were taken by autonomous cells. According to one commander:

"I made the decisions about timing according to my strategic understanding. I had experience, and I was responsible for the group in my area. I was attentive to what people were saying in the street. I didn't blindly dispatch people. There was no orderly leadership that took charge. Every region had a task and commanders, who would analyze the situation according to their understanding and plan responses on the basis of their reasoning [9]."

Some of the cells maintained contact with drivers who held Israeli identity cards and were familiar with the country, and knew where it would be most lethal to operate. It was these drivers who chose the locations for attacks and served, to some extent, as operational contractors.

"I plan everything; the attack and how many *Istishhadis* are needed. My job is to be independent. No one tells me where to attack. I decide. I don't tell anyone where I'm planning the attack or how I plan to get there so the police won't be waiting for me and no one will inform on me [16]."

5. The Recruitment of Suicide Bombers

In the first period and the initial phase of the Second Intifada, volunteers had to be identified and recruited for suicide missions. However, as acts of terror grew more prevalent and acceptable, and the number of attacks even exceeded the ability of the organizations to provide opportunities for them, the recruitment process became easier. Dispatchers had a larger pool of candidates and could be more selective in choosing volunteers whom they considered reliable. Recruiters gained status. They were familiar and they were heroes.

A very large bank of volunteers for *Istishhadia* was created, and often it was these attackers who "recruited" the dispatchers to find ways for them to fulfill their consuming desire to commit suicide. At times, the urgent need to orchestrate attacks outweighed judgments about the most suitable candidate for the mission. As a result, the criteria for screening and selecting perpetrators became more flexible. A member of the PFLP described it thus:

"The new reality opened the door to entrepreneurs, and that's how the privatization process for the suicide industry began. The market was supply-saturated, and the means of production were available, as were human resources. This situation demanded that leadership let the field operatives initiate and operate, rather than spell out the details of whom they take and who they reject. Members of the PA mechanism who had previously intercepted organizations dispatching *Istishhadis* were now themselves wanted by Israel. The new entrepreneurs didn't need permission to act; they just acted. From an operational point of view, the activities and their timing were not tightly supervised. The use of women and children resulted from a breach in frameworks and limits. There is no more 'forbidden' and 'allowed' [17]."

During the first period, most of the *Istishhadis* recruited by Hamas and the PIJ were organizational members of cells or accessories close to them. If they were found suitably loyal to Islam and to the organization's principles, they would be evaluated in conversations with the cell leader and usually also by the network head, who would approve their "eligibility." Their close familiarity and organizational membership obviated the need for a complex "recruitment" process. They needed only to maintain their willingness and occasionally to be bolstered a bit by a religious authority. Of all the organizations, Hamas selected its *Istishhadis* with greatest precision. The recruiter had to be acquainted with the person he recruited and to recommend him as suitable for the mission. Selection was rarely *ad hoc*.

In the second period, there were nuances of selectiveness among the organizations at various times. But as long as there were plenty of volunteers, their screening was primarily technical, to ascertain seriousness of intent.

One example of how accessories became bombers was the recruitment of Saher, the first Palestinian *Istishhadi*, mentioned above. He was an occasional driver for the leader of a terrorist cell that included Yihye Ayyash as its demolition expert. Regardless of his status as an Israeli target, Saher envisaged taking his own life, and volunteered to become the first *Istishhadi*. Another bomber sent by Hamas was an accessory to a cell headed by one of Ayyash's chief assistants. The cell leader recruited him, first speaking with him at length to assess his character and learn more about him. Convinced of his suitability, the cell head instructed him about the operation. The terrorist needed no special preparation. He set out on his mission two days after his commander was arrested, and blew himself up on a bus near Tel Aviv [4, 18].

In the second period, although Hamas continued to insist on religious faith as a criterion for recruitment, neither the issue of formal affiliation with an organization, nor the circle of accessories around a candidate, presented an obstacle if the need for an operation arose. The majority of recruits emerged from religious frameworks of supporters, such as members of *Dawa* and students at religious colleges and universities, notably the El Najah University in Nablus (the site of widespread student activity and an inexhaustible source of candidates). In Tul Karem, for example, Hamas members were involved in the dispatch of several terrorists, two of whom were their classmates and fellow worshippers at a mosque. The request was made following prayers at the mosque.

One of the recruiters told how he identified a suitable candidate and knew he would get a positive response. He said it was hard to explain in words; he simply had a "gut feeling" although it was based on prior acquaintance with the candidate. He said it was instantly clear who was truly religious and willing to do anything for the religion, based on observing the person and how he behaved in the mosque and among others. "If you were to go into the room and see the boy, you would know [19]."

Once an *Istishhadi* candidate's suitability was confirmed, the process of maintaining his readiness until he was called upon to act, depended on the period in which he was recruited and the timing of the operation. The perpetrator of the Park Hotel bombing in Netanya (March 2002) for instance, in which 30 people were killed, was to have performed an earlier act of *Istishhadia* that was postponed due to focused prevention efforts by Israel. He remained with his cell and was sent on his deadly mission seven months later.

The PIJ was consistently more flexible than Hamas in recruiting *Istishhadis* from its ranks and setting criteria for recruitment. At first, the PIJ also recruited from among its own members. Later, *Istishhadis* were selected from all sectors of the population, with preference given to highly religious candidates. In the second period, in which the organization dispatched dozens of *Istishhadis*, its criteria became more flexible. Some candidates were recommended by recruiters; others volunteered on their own initiative. Some of those recruited had no organizational affiliation, but were looking for action. High motivation for *Istishhadia* was sufficient, even if the candidate was not identified with a particular organization or its goals. Candidates underwent brief interrogations to ensure they were not motivated by personal interests and that they believed in God, without having to prove they adhered strictly to religious commandments, or had a deep understanding of religious law and of the need for a national struggle. The most important criterion was that they proved "serious" in their intention to fulfill the task and would not change their mind.

On the other hand, one PIJ dispatcher admitted that if he concluded that a candidate was charismatic and highly capable, he would reject his request and ask that he be given a different, more useful role in the organization. He gave the example of such a young man whom he had dispatched, in the end, as an *Istishhadi* after keeping him on hold for five months. Frustrated, the young man threatened that if he were not given an assignment, he would attack soldiers with a knife and die for nothing, and the dispatcher said he had no choice but to meet his demand for *Istishhadia* [14].

Fatah recruited anyone willing to volunteer for a mission, as long as the dispatchers were convinced he would remain devoted to the task and to his desire to fight the enemy without second thoughts. "We were flooded with *Istishhadis*. At every demonstration, we were approached by a serious group that wanted to commit suicide. After the assassination of Raed Karmi, for example, many were aroused to volunteer for *Istishhadia*. As soon as a young man comes to us and asks to be an *Istishhadi*, he is automatically a potential for dispatch [20]."

In interviews with senior dispatchers working in the same terror network, one of them replacing the other after he was arrested, it became clear that the main criterion was, in the end, "operational need," and the primary consideration was the certainty that the mission would be accomplished. Fatah, like the PIJ, "gave in" to pressure by *Istishhadis* (females as well) who threatened to attack with a knife and die without having caused damage to the enemy if their demands for an *Istishhadia* operation were not met [14, 21]. At times, then, these organizations compromised on their choice of perpetrator.

6. Conclusion

Suicide terrorism which has been produced by the Palestinian organizations to serve multiple aims succeeded in inflicting an unprecedented number of casualties on the Israeli civil society during the thirteen years of its existence. Yet at the same time it also deepened the agony of Palestinian society, which suffered multiple casualties and was greatly impoverished by the consequences of the terror campaign. Consequently, many in the Palestinian leadership realized that the suicide weapon proved to be a double-edged sword.

The massive Israeli counter-measures, which significantly reduced the number of suicide attacks and casualties among its citizens, together with the resilience of the Israeli public, helped to convince the Palestinians that the path of *Istishhadia* would not compel Israel to capitulate. The Israeli unilateral disengagement from Gaza in August 2005 gave the Palestinians a sense of victory and helped them to declare unilateral cease fire known as the *Tahadiya*. Albeit it hasn't stopped suicide attacks on Israel it helped to reduce the number of attacks carried out by the major players in this campaign mainly from Hamas. Yet it should be remembered that the unilateral decision taken by the Palestinian organizations to suspend the *Istishhadia* campaign was conditional, and the attacks can be revived if one or more groups decide this would serve their interests. Indeed, some suicide operations have continued even during the *tahadiya* period up till today, mainly by the PIJ and splinter factions of Fatah.

References

[1]   The source of the statistical data included in this article is a database maintained by the author at the Institute for National Security Studies (INSS).
[2]   Interview with Harun, March 23, 2005.
[3]   Interview with Zaher Jabarin, June 1, 2005.
[4]   Interview with Nasser Issa, March 30, 2005.
[5]   Interview with Nihad Abu Kishak, Hamas, January 17, 2005.
[6]   Interview with Abbas Sayed, Hamas, January 10, 2005.
[7]   Interview with Nasser Abu Hmeid, Fatah, January 3, 2006.
[8]   Interview with Thabet Mardawi, PIJ, February 7, 2006.
[9]   Interview with Ahmad Mugrabi, Fatah, October 19, 2005.
[10] Interview with Ahmad Barghouti, Fatah, March 14, 2005.
[11] Interview with Abbas Sayed, Hamas, January 2004.
[12] Interview with Wael Kassaem, Hamas, December 8, 2005.
[13] Interview with Amjad Obeidi, November 2, 2005.
[14] Interview with Thabet Mardawi, PIJ, November 23, 2005.
[15] Interview with Ahmed Barghouti, March 8, 2006.
[16] Interview with Ibrahim Sarakhne, Fatah, November 14, 2005.
[17] Interview with Walid Daka, PFLP, September 27, 2004.
[18] Interview with Nassar Issa, November 23, 2005
[19] Interview with Abu Qishaq, Hamas, August, 2005.
[20] Interview with Abu Hmeid, PIJ, January 3, 2006.
[21] Interview with Amjad Obedei, November 2, 2005.

The Rise of Radical Islam[1] in Post-Soviet States: Fiction or Reality?[*]

Kamil YILMAZ

School of International and Public Affairs (SIPA),
Columbia University, USA

Abstract. In recent years, the concept of "Radical Islam" in post-Soviet states has been articulated quite frequently. This paper provides a brief historical overview of Islam in post-Soviet states, and examines whether the claims that radical Islam in post-Soviet states is growing and poses a threat to regional and global security are justified. The paper also examines the two Islamic movements that have had the greatest impact especially in Central Asia in recent years: the Islamic Movement of Uzbekistan (the IMU) and Hizb ut-Tahrir. Finally, the paper seeks answers to the following question: What should be done to eliminate at best, or reduce at least, the influence of radical Islamic movements in post-Soviet states?

The author concludes that the threat of radical Islamic movements in post-Soviet states is neither a fiction to ignore, nor a reality to fear. He opines that the existing, but exaggerated threat of radical Islamic movements is used to justify aggressive measures by the governments of post-Soviet countries, particularly Uzbekistan, Tajikistan, Kyrgyzstan and the Russian Federation. Finally, the author suggests several recommendations to external actors and the governments of post-Soviet states, particularly the government of the Russian Federation which still has the greatest impact on the region's politics, to skillfully absorb the negative influences of the relatively slowly rising trend, radical Islam; and to utilize the high values of Islam against the terrorists and separatists in the region.

Keywords. Radical Islam, post-Soviet states, Islamic Movement of Uzbekistan (the IMU), Hizb ut-Tahrir

"In the coming years, Russia will struggle with radicals fiercely, but even if the state totally eliminates [existing] Islamic extremists, the problem will not be solved, because the conditions for their proliferation will remain."

Aleksandr Iskandaryan[2]

"When Communism ends, when people are ignorant of democracy and are oppressed by local corrupt elites, they turn to the Islamic alternative."

Alexei Malashenko[3]

---

[1] In this paper, "radical Islam" is used to refer to the kind of Islam that is a danger to regional and global security. Much can be said about nomenclature that is beyond the scope of this paper, but it is important to note here that using "radical" is preferable to "militant" because the latter has negative connotations and its frequent use would contribute to the provocation of inter-civilizational tensions. Therefore, the word "militant" should be neither juxtaposed textually nor imbricated conceptually with the word "Islam." Militancy is what *people* make of it.

[*] I am grateful to Professor Alexei Malashenko, Professor Leonid Sykiainen and Emil Jeenbekov for their invaluable remarks on this article's topic during our informal talks in July 2006 in Moscow, Russia.

[2] Alexandr Iskandaryan is the head of the Moscow-based Center for Caucasian Studies.

[3] Alexei Malashenko is a Professor and Scholar-in-Residence at the Carnegie Moscow Center.

Introduction

In recent years, the concept of "Radical Islam" in Post-Soviet states has been articulated quite frequently. The opening quote to this paper accurately describes the fear that has been entrenched in people's minds in these states; whereas proceeding from the second quote, a myriad of factors can be suggested to be behind this growth and appeal of Islamic extremism in the above mentioned states, especially in Uzbekistan, Tajikistan and Kyrgyzstan. In particular, many people including scholars and politicians noted that after the collapse of the Soviet Union, the successor states have not been able to come up with constructive policies that would legitimize power in these states.

"Evidently, one of the tragedies of the recent era has been in the post-Soviet breakup. There was an Islamic revival around the world, and there were many triggers to it. There was the defeat of the Soviets in Afghanistan; there was a general revival in Islamic culture, and people wanting to know about religion. And the Gulf War, for example, in '91, was a big trigger also. But most regimes failed to understand what was going on below the surface"[1].

There seems to be a consensus, however, that the ideological vacuum left after communism, along with the underlying structural problems faced by Central Asian states, such as growing inequality and persistent poverty, account for the growing appeal of radical Islam among the region's Muslims. To be more specific, "widespread poverty, social and economic instability, corruption among government officials, and broad-based discontent among the population are also mentioned as elements contributing to the emergence of a threat of Islamic extremism" [2].

Undoubtedly, Islam has a great impact on post-Soviet politics. Unfortunately, however, beginning with the mid 1990s most of the actions of Islam have been observed in terrorist and separatist movements. That is why nowadays we observe post-Soviet States' policies towards Islam in the form of "tackling a threat," which intrinsically pushes these states towards more aggressive measures. Thus, it can be argued that there is a positive relationship between the level of measures taken and the level of radicalism in the region, i.e. increased assertion begets increased radicalism.

This paper will provide a brief historical overview of Islam in post-Soviet states, and examine whether the claims that radical Islam in post-Soviet states is growing and poses a threat to regional and global security are justified. The paper will also examine the two Islamic groups [4] that have had the greatest impact especially in Central Asia in recent years: the Islamic Movement of Uzbekistan and Hizb ut-Tahrir. Finally, the paper will seek answers to the following question: What should be done to eliminate at best, or reduce at least, the influence of radical Islamic movements in post-Soviet states?

1. The Phenomenon: Is Islam Really on the Rise?

According to a report of *Dhimmi Watch,* Russia's leading Muslim cleric has alarmed Orthodox Church leaders and nationalists by claiming that the country has 23 million Muslims, 3 million more than previously believed. The report conveyed that the mufti said: "they are indigenous residents of our country, not migrants or immigrants, and

---

[4] I avoid using the terms "radical or extremist" to name these Islamic movements, because at least one of them - that is Hizb-ut Tahrir, has not been observed as a violent organization as of yet. The purpose of this organization will be reviewed in the following sections of this paper. See especially the section entitled "Hizb-ut Tahrir."

have been living here from time immemorial. The number of people professing Islam in Russia is constantly growing" [3]. It is important to note that the latter may be due more to increasing fertility rates in regions where Muslims are densely populated, than to Russian conversions to Islam. Moreover, it should be noted that many Russians are not fearful of the increase in numbers of traditional Muslims; they simply are concerned by the radical Islamic movements.

Regarding Islam in Central Asia, one has to keep in mind that despite country-level variability, the majority within the societies of the former Soviet Central Asian republics is Muslim. Alexei Malashenko, a renowned scholar of Islam at Carnegie Moscow Center, states that:

"At the beginning of the 1990s, there was intense discussion on how to categorize the countries of Central Asia-as post-Soviet or Muslim. Gradually these discussions declined, and former Soviet Central Asian states are now considered a legitimate part of Muslim world. The overwhelming majority of the native population here identify themselves with Islam, and the processes characteristic of most Muslim countries are developing within these societies-among them the spread of political Islam and fundamentalism" [4 pg 49].

Malashenko also notes, however, that it is noticeable that the current leaders of the Central Asian states openly declare that their countries are not fully-fledged Muslim societies.

2. Background of Islam in Central Asia

Islam arrived in Central Asia at the hands of Arab invaders at the beginning of the seventh century. It was embraced only gradually and variously, however, becoming the majority religion around the ninth century. By the tenth century, Central Asia had become one of the great centers of Islamic learning and culture, particularly the great Silk Road cities of Bukhara and Samarkand [5]. The region was also home to a remarkable assortment of cultural influences, and linguistically "the vernacular tended to be a Turkic language, with the exception of the version of Persian spoken in Tajikistan, while the predominant language of literature was Persian and the language of religion was Arabic" [5 pg 3].

The majority of Central Asian Muslims, as well as Muslims living in the borders of the Russian Federation, embraced Sunni Islam, although Shia Muslims also can be found throughout the region, i.e. Tajikistan.

"Sunni Islam was first embraced by the settled populations of today's Tajikistan and Uzbekistan, while the nomadic peoples of Kazakhstan, Kyrgyzstan, and Turkmenistan maintained stronger ties to their pre-Islamic culture and beliefs. Sunni Islam eventually spread to Central Asia's nomadic populations by incorporating local traditions and aspects of Sufism-an indigenous form of Islamic mysticism. Sufism appealed to the nomadic peoples by emphasizing a direct experience with God, as well as preaching tolerance and respect for other forms of worship" [6 pg 141].

The speed and degree to which Islam was embraced by the peoples of the region varied [5]. Moreover, "early differences in how Islam was embraced in Central Asia continue to be reflected in local practices in the region. In the twenty-first century, identification with Islam remains stronger in Tajikistan and Uzbekistan than in Kazakhstan, Kyrgyzstan, and Turkmenistan" [6 pg 141].

3. The Soviet Era

"The peoples of Central Asia did not suffer repression at the hands of Soviet Communism because they were Uzbeks or Tajiks, rather, it was because they were Muslims. The Communists viewed Islam with hostility and suspicion and subjected the Muslims of the Soviet Union to countless secularization campaigns. They also tried to replace the regions' Islamic identity and loyalty, with ethnically created republics" [7].

Consequently, the great majority of mosques were destroyed, and most members of the Islamic clergy were jailed or shot. Nevertheless, World War II alleviated the campaign against organized religion. Eventually, a consensus was reached between the regime and Islam. A so-called Muslim Religious Board was established in Tashkent for Central Asia and Kazakhstan, which became the most prestigious and powerful of four such Religious Boards in the USSR [5].

Ahmed Rashid, a well-known Pakistani journalist, asserts that there were three crucial mistakes from the Soviet period, the effects of which are still seen in Central Asia today:

"The first one is that Stalin designated five ethnic groups as the five major nationalities of Central Asia. Central Asia has something like a hundred ethnic groups. And he made nations out of these ethnic groups -- so, the Uzbeks were given Uzbekistan, the Kazaks were given Kazakhstan. But, Central Asia was an amalgam of tribes, clans, ethnic groups, principalities. Stalin created these ethnic divisions, and then gave them a very falsified history, which, of course, was a Sovietized history. Their "history" had nothing to do with their own real history. Parallel to this, of course, he completely suppressed Islam. Religion was not allowed. Islam was very much part of their history and tradition and culture; by suppressing Islam, he cut them off from their past completely. Certainly, when Central Asia emerged in '91 of five independent states, the majority of the population knew very little about Islam and their history. The third important aspect was that the Soviets delayed, for as long as possible, the creation of indigenous local elite in Central Asia. So Central Asia, right up to the fifties, was, in fact, ruled by White Russia rather than the local elite. And so finally, in the fifties and sixties, you get this local elite, Uzbek Communist elite, Turkman, the Tajeks, who were extremely isolated, cut off, highly bureaucratized, and very much in debt to Moscow for just having been allowed to come up. So these elite were even, in my opinion, far more backward. And, of course, this elite is still ruling today, because there have been no leadership changes in Central Asia. These elite were far more backward than the kind of movements that were taking place in the Soviet Communist Party in Russia" [1].

"With the launching of the Gorbachev reforms [Perestroika and Glasnost] the region began to undergo an 'Islamic revival.' Such policies relaxed the Soviet Union's rigid authoritarianism and permitted a modicum of free expression to exist, thus in republics like Uzbekistan, Islamic practices and sentiments to resurface. There was a great upsurge in the study of Islam and Arabic, with many Central Asian youth studying Islamic courses abroad" [7].

Ironically, both elites and society in Central Asia remained politically conservative throughout the Gorbachev period, suspicious in general of Gorbachev's liberalizing reforms and very opposed to the breakup of the USSR. Independence for them was for the most part an unwelcome surprise. In the decade since, Central Asia's Islamic revival has continued, and the great majority of the traditionally Muslim peoples of the region today identify themselves as believers [5].

4. Influence of Radical Islamic Movements in Central Asia

So far Islamic radicalism, more often called Wahhabism,[5] has furthered the unity of the ruling elites in Central Asian states. The domestic threat to the secular regimes by Islamic radicals was revealed in Tajikistan at the end of the 1980s, but many thought

---

[5] The term "Wahhabi" (*Wahhābīya*) refers to the movement's founder Muhammad ibn Abd al Wahhab. It is rarely used by members of this group today, although the Saudis did use it in the past. The Wahhabis claim to hold to the way of the "Salaf as-Salih", the "pious predecessors" as earlier propagated mainly by Ibn Taymiyya, his students Ibn Al Qayyim, and later by Muhammad ibn Abdul Wahhab and his followers. See, http://en.wikipedia.org/wiki/Wahhabism, for more information about Wahhabism. I will also write more on Wahhabism in the following sections of this paper.

this threat was the exception rather than the rule and that it was specific to Tajikistan and would not spread to neighboring states. With the outbreak of a bloody civil war in Tajikistan, the presidents of all the Central Asian states blamed Tajikistan and pointed to the consequences of a weakening of state power and indecisive behavior when dealing with Islamists [4 pg 51].

At the beginning of the 1990s, Islamic political organizations and movements appeared in all the Central Asian states. In Uzbekistan the Islamic Party of Revival, Adolat, and the Islamic party of Turkistan were formed; in Kazakhstan the Alash Party of National Salvation; in Kyrgyzstan the Islamic Centre. Undoubtedly, the most influential political process was in Tajikistan, with the loyal party of Islamic Revival [4 pg 52].

Significant majorities in Central Asia describe themselves as believers, as Walker put it, but large majorities also feel that secular, not Islamic, law should govern and that Islamic parties should be banned. And few have even heard of the Islamic Movement of Uzbekistan (the IMU), the Islamic group that was designated a terrorist organization by the State Department last year and that President Bush mentioned in his War on Terrorism speech [5].

Similarly to Walker, Malashenko states that:

"In relations between the Central Asian states, religion does not play a significant role. While defining the nature of their relationships, the common culture and traditions are often referred to. However, emphasis tends to be put on the openness of Central Asian culture and the common characteristics of the region's people. The religious dimension-that is, Islamic solidarity-has secondary importance" [4 pg 50].

It is possible to say that all five states are formally secular, with the exception of Tajikistan which, as mentioned before, has allowed an Islamic party to participate in government. There is, however, considerable variation in the way that Islam is practiced in the five Central Asian successor states, as well as in the way that different regimes have reacted to politicized Islam [5 pg 5].

In 1996, the situation suddenly changed with the establishment of an Islamic movement in Pakistan, namely the Taliban movement. Malashenko elaborates on the influence of the establishment of this movement on Central Asian States:

It seems that Central Asian elites did not believe in the likelihood of the Taliban expanding to the North and invading Uzbekistan and Tajikistan, but rather feared that the success of radical Islam would produce a euphoria among like-minded people in Central Asia, in particular in the Ferghana Valley, where an Islamic opposition by that time had already appeared. The victory of the Taliban at least facilitated the contacts, if not the coordination, between different Islamic groups. Without doubt the authority of political Islam grew and "radical Islam" became a regional concern. As a result, elites in Central Asian states felt that a cooperation to respond these Islamic groups is needed. Turkmenistan was an exception. The president of Turkmenistan Saparmurat Niyazov tried to avoid criticizing Islamic radicalism and in 1996 declared that: "The situation in Afghanistan cannot be considered from any common platform. Each of the countries bordering Afghanistan has its own peculiarities in relations with that country" [4 pg 53].

Despite Niyazov's efforts to single his country out of the discussion on the Taliban victory, explosions in Tashkent and border incursions in the Batken region in 1999 compelled Central Asian States to revise their approaches to security cooperation. They agreed upon taking real measures against the Islamists.

On 16 February 1999 six car bombs exploded in Tashkent, outside government offices in an apparent attempt on the president's life, resulted in the killing of sixteen people; a number of radical Islamists were held in connection with the bombings [8]. According to Polat and Butkevich,

"The attack called the stability of the nation into question for the first time. Two hours after the explosions, before an investigation had been started or any arrests made, President Karimov and the heads of the Uzbek security service and police announced that Islamic militants were responsible. They soon named militant Islamic leaders in exile, including the political head of the Islamic Movement of Uzbekistan (IMU), Tohir Yoldosh, and its military commander, Juma Namangoni, as the masterminds behind the explosions. Less than two weeks later, the Uzbek authorities expanded their list of suspects to include Muhammad Solih, leader of the opposition Erk (Freedom) party, who has lived in exile since 1993. All three men were accused of conspiring to forcibly take over the government" [9].

A few months later, on May 1999, gunmen attacked border posts on both sides of the frontier between Kyrgyzstan and Tajikistan early Friday, killing five people and injuring two Kyrgyz and Tajik officials. The group then clashed with Kyrgyz border guards, killing two soldiers in the Batken region, about 450 miles southwest of the Kyrgyz capital, Bishkek. They then fled further into mountains in Kyrgyzstan [10].

"The terrorists called themselves *mujahedeen*. They were well-armed and had modern communication equipment. The overall objective of the militants, according to the politicians, was the destabilization of the situation in Uzbekistan and the creation of an Islamic state in the Ferghana Valley" [11][6].

5. The Situation in Dagestan and Chechnya

The Northern Caucasus may be characterized as having two areas differing in religiosity: the North-East Caucasus, including Dagestan, Chechnya and Ingushetia, where the population is traditionally more religious; and the North-West Caucasus, encompassing mainly Adigei and Turkic people. Islam did not take root among them as much as it did among their eastern neighbors [13].

During the mid-1990s, Dagestan became the ideological center of Islamic radicalism, and Chechnya rapidly became the proving ground. "The establishing of the Dudaev regime, which aimed at building an 'Islamic state' promoted the spread as well. Such prominent politicians as Zelimkhan Yandarbiev and Movladi Udugov are considered the protectors of the Wahhabis. The war also promoted the strengthening of the Wahhabis' positions; volunteers from many Muslim countries, including those with fundamentalist beliefs, flooded Chechnya" [13 pg 10].

As mentioned above, the Islamic radicals of the North Caucasus are mostly *Wahhabis*.

"Wahhabis do not follow any specific madhhab (method or school of jurisprudence), but claim to interpret the words of the prophet Muhammad directly, using the four madhhab for reference. However, they are often associated with the Hanbali madhhab. Wahhabi theology advocates a puritanical and legalistic stance in matters of faith and religious practice. Wahhabis see their role as a movement to restore Islam from what they perceive to be innovations, superstitions, deviances, heresies and idolatries" [14].

There are many practices that they believe are contrary to Islam, such as visiting the graves of Sufi saints or prophets, asking the dead for help, the wearing of charms, and practicing magic for healing.

---

[6] Naumkin, Vitali is the President of the International Center for Strategic and Political Studies, Moscow, the head of the Center for Middle Eastern Studies, Institute of Oriental Studies, Russian Academy of Sciences. Here I also would like to pay attention to the importance of the Ferghana Valley in Central Asia. The fertile Ferghana valley is a backward as well as the most densely populated area in all of Central Asia, home to more than ten million people, and for centuries has been a centre for Islamic traditionalism and occasional fanaticism. Since 1929 (when Tajikistan was taken out of Uzbekistan and established as a Soviet republic), the Ferghana valley has been divided among Uzbekistan, Kyrgyzstan, and Tajikistan. For details, see '*Uzbekistan and the Threat from Islamic Extremism*' [12].

The chief teachers and preachers of North Caucasian radicalism are by birth from Dagestan. There are also moderate fundamentalists in the North Caucasus. Their leader was the Avar Ahmad Hadji Akhtayev (1942-1998), a native of the village of Kudali in Dagestan. He tried to emphasize peaceful methods, preaching his views and developing a concept about the mutual supplementability of Islam and orthodoxy in Russia as a Eurasian country [15].[7]

On the other hand, the leader of Northern Caucasus radicals was the Dagestani Bagauddin Kebedov (b.1945). In 1990 together with Akhtayev he became one of the founders of the Islamic Party of Revival, which had a distinctly expressed fundamentalist orientation. In contrast to Akhtayev, Kebedov always clearly gravitated towards public activity, and quickly began to assemble the organization of radical Islamic fundamentalists called *Jamaat* (community). According to Kebedov, the post-communist government of Dagestan was in the state of *shirka* (polytheism). He summarized his *modus operandi* with the following sentence: "For us geographical and state borders do not have a value, we work and act, where this is possible." [15 pp 53-54] Kebedov also emphasized that Islam is the integral system of human life, and the consequent inevitability that Islam includes attempts at the construction of Islamic society and statehood [15].

In the first Chechen war (1994-1996) radical groups formed the military wing, the leader of which became Khattab, a native of Saudi Arabia. From August 1995 the force of Khattab was part of the Central Front of the armed forces of the Chechen republic of Ichkeria under the command of Shamil Basayev. After the end of the first Chechen war Khattab organized several military training camps in the territory of Chechnya, where, first of all Dagestanis and Chechens, but also people from other Muslim republics of Russia went through military-diversionary preparation [15].

Undoubtedly, the North Caucasus is the main southern sea gate for Russia. Yet, this region seems a potential explosive locus for ethno-political conflicts. Particularly, the Chechen question has been the center of inter-civilizational opposition in the Caucasus.

6. The Islamic Movement of Uzbekistan (IMU)

"The Islamic Movement of Uzbekistan (IMU), or *Ozbekiston Islam Harakati* as it is known locally (*Harakat ul-Islamiyyah* in Arabic), can be said to have formed part of the Arab-Afghan network and to have shared a recruiting base of primarily unemployed young men as well as attitudes toward Wahhabism, with the Taliban and the Arab Afghans, the Islamic extremists in Afghanistan. The movement relied on bases in Afghanistan (Mazar-e Sharif, Kondoz, and Taloqan) and Tajikistan (Hoit in the Karategin valley and Sangvor in the Tavildara valley)" [12 pg 3].

The groups that comprised the IMU had their origin in the public manifestation of the Islamic movement called *Adolat* Justice, which arose in the city of Namangan in the Uzbek part of the Ferghana valley in 1990 as a response to what was perceived as widespread corruption and social injustice exposed by the liberal *perestroyka* era and by the resurgence in Islamic activities which were no longer prohibited by the Soviet government. The movement, funded by sources in Saudi Arabia, was led by two young men: the passionate college drop-out and local mullah Tohir Yuldosh and the former conscript soldier Jumaboy Khojiev (later known as Juma Namangani) [12].

---

[7] Emil Jeenbekov, a PhD Candidate at the Academy of Interior Ministry in Moscow helped me with the translation of this information from Russian to English.

The purpose of the organization is to restore the Islamic caliphate in the territory of central Asia, the nucleus of which, in the opinion of the leaders of the movement, must be the Fergana valley. On the other hand, according to Ahmed Rashid, the IMU, like the Taliban and al-Qaeda, has no overarching political manifesto, being more interested in implementing shariah "not as a way of creating just society but simply as a means to regulate personal behavior and dress code for Muslims - a concept that distorts centuries of tradition, culture, history, and even the religion of Islam itself." [16] Conversely, the US Department of State reported that:

"The Islamic Movement of Uzbekistan has publicly called for the violent overthrow of the Government of Uzbekistan and has claimed responsibility for ongoing armed incursions into the territory of Uzbekistan and Kyrgyzstan. These actions have resulted in the deaths of a number of civilian Uzbek security personnel. There are indications that the Islamic Movement of Uzbekistan continues planning for additional terrorist attacks" [17].

There has also been much speculation about possible cooperation between the IMU and al-Qaeda. Vitali Naumkin states that:

"With its leaders and operatives now in hiding, it is not clear whether al-Qaeda could mount an operation in Central Asia even if it wanted to. Nor is it clear if such a dangerous alliance would benefit the IMU. However, it is clear that IMU militants who had been fighting alongside the Taliban in 2001 escaped to Pakistan together with al-Qaeda members" [11 pg 61].

It is possible to assert that IMU to some extent survived the post-911 War on Terrorism. The organization is believed to have regrouped in Tajikistan, in an effort to find safe haven during increased scrutiny [12].

It is not clear, however, that the IMU will reemerge as an active player in Central Asia to mobilize violence. What is clear is that the prospects of launching new operations in Uzbekistan are narrower now than before September 11, 2001, because of the tremendous risks of becoming associated with an organization that the international community has designated a terrorist group. As a result, there is a likelihood that political opposition will gravitate today towards other Islamic movements, such as the Hizb at-Tahrir al-Islami (HTI) and the Islamic Revival Party of Tajikistan (IRPT). Among them, the essential one that requires more attention is the nonviolent but clandestine Hizb at-Tahrir al-Islami [11].

7. Hizb ut-Tahrir

The international extremist organization Hizb-ut Tahrir was founded in 1953 by Sheikh Taqiuddin al-Nabhani, a judge (*qadi*) from Jerusalem [18]. The group's aim is to resume the Islamic way of life and to convey the Islamic da'wah[8] to the world. The ultimate goal of this secretive sectarian group is to unite the entire ummah, or Islamic world community, into a single caliphate. The aim is to bring the Muslims back to living an Islamic way of life in Dar al-Islam (the land where the rules of Islam are being implemented, as opposed to the non-Islamic world) and in an Islamic society such that all life's affairs in society are administered according to the Shariah rules [19].

---

[8] The term *da'wah* is explained in different sources as "the duty of Muslims-that is to invite humanity to the way of Allah." See, for instance http://www.islamic-world.net/dakwah/articles.htm, for more information about da'wah. Allah said in the Qur'an: *"Invite to the Way of your Lord* (i.e. Islam) *with wisdom and fair preaching, and argue with them in a way that is better. Truly, your Lord knows best who has gone astray from His Path, and He is the Best Aware of those who are guided."* [An-Nisaa'(16) :125].

Hizb ut-Tahrir now has its main base in Western Europe, but it has large followings in Uzbekistan, Tajikistan, Kyrgyzstan, and Kazakhstan, as well as in China's traditionally Muslim Xinjiang Province. It is active all over the world but there is little information on the number of its members. By one estimate there are more than 10,000 followers in Central Asia. Hizb ut-Tahrir al-Islami has been active in Central Asia since the breakup of the Soviet Union. Most of its members are believed to be ethnic Uzbeks [19].

The Foreign Ministry of Russia qualified this organization as the most radical and well-planned extremist group which is financed by foreign centers pursuing the plans of step by step Islamization of Russia and adjacent countries. As reported on December 16, 2002, in a conversation with the journalists the director of Russian Federal Security Service (FSB) N. Patrushev said that "Hizb ut-Tahrir encroaches on the constitutional system of states" and "organizes the illegal armed units, and also it participates in them" [20].

"The United States has important national security interests at stake in Central Asia, including access to the military bases used to support operations in Afghanistan, prevention of the proliferation of weapons of mass destruction and technologies used for their production, and the securing of access to natural resources, including oil and gas. The U.S. is also committed to spreading democracy, promoting market reforms, and improving human rights standards in the vast heartland of Eurasia" [21].

The United States government still continues simply to monitor Hizb ut-Tahrir. Despite the statements of governments of the region, the United States has found no clear ties between Hizb ut-Tahrir and terrorist activity. Hizb ut-Tahrir has not been proven to have involvement in or direct links to any recent acts of violence or terrorism. Nor has it been proven to give financial support to other groups engaged in terrorism. Because of this, it falls outside the definitions used by the United States and others to designate a terrorist group [19]. Since 2001, Hizb ut-Tahrir has retained its headquarters in London, while withstanding tremendous changes. Hizb ut-Tahrir's base in Europe has come under pressure. It was made illegal in Germany in 2003 and in Russia in 1999 [22]. After seven explosions in London's public transportation system on July 21, 2005, the British PM Tony Blair finally made a proposal to forbid the activity of Hizb ut-Tahrir [23].

On the other hand, it has been frequently argued that repressive measures taken against this group by either Western regimes or the post-Soviet states worsen the regional and global security. To give an example, Gulnoza Saidazimova conveys the notion that:

"The situation in which there is unjustified repression by the authorities, the fabrication of criminal charges - when people see clear injustice, they start perceiving repressed people as victims of the fight for justice. They get a sense of solidarity. Some of them start saying, 'If justice can't be achieved by peaceful means, more radical ways should be found.' In this regard, Uzbekistan is a highly illustrative example. There, repression begun by [President] Karimov in late 1990s became the main instrument of destabilization in the whole region" [24][9].

8. Conclusion

Five years after the 9/11 attacks in New York, all states have learned a great deal about how to fight a war on terror. Unfortunately, the terrorist organizations have also learned much in the new age of terror. No matter how often a top terrorist leader is captured-for example an al-Qaeda leader-a new one seems to emerge as the shadowy terror network metastasizes [25]. One significant contributor to this new trend, in my opinion, is the

---

[9] Gulnoza Saidazimova conveys from Vitaly Ponomaryov who runs a human rights monitoring program that focuses on Central Asia for the Moscow-based nonprofit group Memorial. "He says circumstantial evidence points to desperate youths who turn to Hizb ut-Tahrir out of frustration with the system -- in Uzbekistan, for instance."

repressive measures of the states which claim to be in a war against terrorism. Supporting this argument, Richard Clarke, the former counter-terror chief who served under President Bill Clinton and briefly under President Bush, states that "it is almost to the point where for everyone we kill and capture, they grow three" [25 pg 23]. Therefore, there is need for a revision of the policies implemented by the states that are fighting with radical and/or militant Islam all over the world. The first step may be to avoid juxtaposing the words "*terrorist*" and "*Islam.*"

As for Russia, Nabi Abdullaev of *The Moscow Times* states that there is no unanimity about the future of Islam in Russia. According to him, mainstream Muslim leaders downplay the tensions between Islam and the society at large. He cites Farid Asadullin, head of the Science and Public Relations Department at the Council of Muftis, who states that "for Muslims brought up in the Russian cultural and informational environment, Russians are not infidels. Moreover, Islam and Christianity have the same ethical base." [26] He notes, however, that unlike mainstream Russian Muslim clerics striving for integration into the establishment, radicals seek support on the ground.

It seems that there is a common understanding among the majority of people living in post-Soviet states that Islam as a political factor is often used for purposes of destruction rather than for social consolidation and the strengthening of state power, and that political extremism and terrorism that use Islamic slogans are extreme forms of anti-state activities. It is believed by and large that in recent years the danger against states created by them has not declined-it is mounting. That is why most regimes in the region preferred to apply assertive policies, instead of constructive ones, to eliminate this danger. For instance, Leonid Sykiainen states that:

"No wonder, in its relations with political Islam the Russian State recurs to law enforcement measures and operations involving power structures. It rarely takes positive measures to tap Islamic values for the purposes of political stabilization, social consolidation, and strengthening Russia's statehood" [27].

Contrary to intended outcome, as it was mentioned in an International Crisis Group report, some government agencies in Central Asia claim tacit or explicit Western support for policies of exclusion and suppression of Islamic elements that are likely to lead to intensified political polarization and ultimately to a severe danger of political and military clashes [28].

After reviewing related writings and conducting informal talks with ordinary Russian people, as well as with the leading scholars who specialize in Islam in Russia, I conclude that the threat of radical Islamic movements in post-Soviet states is neither a fiction to ignore, nor a reality to fear. I believe that the existing, but exaggerated threat of radical Islamic movements is used to justify aggressive measures by the governments of post-Soviet countries, particularly Uzbekistan, Tajikistan, Kyrgyzstan and the Russian Federation. One should keep in mind, however, that repressive measures do nothing but exacerbate the security situation in the region and beyond.

Listed below are my recommendations to external actors and the governments of post-Soviet states, particularly the government of the Russian Federation which still has the greatest impact on the region's politics, to skillfully absorb the negative influences of the relatively slowly rising trend, radical Islam; and to utilize the high values of Islam against the terrorists and separatists in the region.

First of all, it is essential that Russia understands that it should not oppose Islam as a foe but be convinced that Islamic resurrection is a positive factor of the country's sustainable development; and that Islam and Muslim culture (political and legal culture included) comprise an important part of life in Russia at the social and state levels.

Islamic values should not be regarded as a threat to Russia's national interests and security but as its potentially ally [27].

As far as Central Asian governments are concerned, I believe that they should reorient internal security policies to emphasize the positive values of civil society institutions, including a vigorous free press, and of religious toleration.

"Repressive religious policies promote polarization of the society and discredit its political institutions, including Islamic organizations that are in any way associated with the state. The governments should restore their credibility as protectors of the legitimate rights of all individuals, including the most observant Muslims, by clearly articulating and demonstrating their commitment to protecting these rights" [29].

For external powers and international organizations, it is crucial that they unequivocally advocate that regional security can only be assured if religious freedom is guaranteed and legitimate activities of groups and individuals are not suppressed [29]. Furthermore, the strengthening economic, social and political Western support - which should be free from opportunistic desires, such as access to oil, obtaining geographical advantages via the creation of bases in these states, etc.-to the Central Asian states is vital for the stability of the region which naturally has ramifications for the security beyond that region. It is almost certain that:

"Weak states, especially anocracies (that is, states that are neither clearly democratic nor authoritarian), are inherently unstable and highly susceptible to failure. The region's two autocracies, Turkmenistan and Uzbekistan, seem now to be politically stable, but their stability is not likely to be sustainable over the long run. The May 2005 riots in Uzbekistan and the political unrest that brought down the Askar Akaev presidency in Kyrgyzstan are recent examples of the kinds of instability that could lead to state failure" [30 pg 6].

"In the social, spiritual and cultural spheres, the authorities can no longer limit themselves to stating their respect for the positive Muslim heritage. The thesis about Islam's huge spiritual and moral potential and its clear social message stated by the Muslim leaders and accepted by the authorities should acquire real content and be substantiated with Islamic arguments applicable to a secular state. Muslims, their ideologists and centers should do this while the state can and should stimulate the process and channel it along the lines that meet the interests of Muslims and society as a whole" [29 pg 121].

In conclusion, the positive moral and intellectual aspect of Islam should be made inextricably intertwined with Russian culture. Islam's power should be used against extremists and separatists. There is a misconception that terrorists do not know about the religion of Islam. Indeed they know more than ordinary Muslims [31]. For this purpose, Russian people should be given more information about the intellectual heritage of Islam. Islam is very influential even in world politics. Therefore, Russia should cultivate good relations not only with Western countries but also with Islamic ones. Recently, Russia's relationship with Turkey, for instance, has been quite fruitful in different fields ranging from economy and tourism to security cooperation. The same relationship should be maintained with other countries in which the majority of the population is Muslim.

References

[1]   Ahmed Rashid Interview: Conversations with history: Institute of International Studies, U.C. Berkeley. [Online] Available from; URL: http://globetrotter.berkeley.edu/people2/Rashid/rashid-con3.html [2006, July].

[2]   The closing statement of a seminar titled 'Regional conflict prevention/resolution and promoting stability in Central Asia and Afghanistan" of Chatham House. [Online] Available from; URL: www.chathamhouse.org.uk/pdf/research/rep /RTashkent.doc [2006, July].

[3]   Dhimmi Watch, August 07, 2005. [Online] Available from; URL: http://www.jihadwatch.org/ dhimmiwatch/archives/007556.php

[4] A. Malashenko, Islam in Central Asia, Royal Institute of International Affairs. In R. Allison, L. Jonson. *Central Asian security: The new international context*. Washington DC: The Brookings Institution Pres; 2001. [Online] Available from; URL: http://brookings.nap.edu/books/0815701055/html/49.html [2006, July].

[5] E. Walker, Roots of rage: Militant Islam in Central Asia. Panel presentation at University of California, Berkeley, on October 29, 2001. [Online] Available from; URL: http://socrates.berkeley.edu/~bsp /caucasus/articles/walker_2001-1029.pdf [2006, July].

[6] T. Petros. Islam in Central Asia: The emergence and growth of radicalism in post-communist era, In D.L. Burghart and T. Sabonis-Helf, Editors. In *The Tracks of Tamerlane* Central Asia's path to the 21st century. National Defence University; 2004, 139-155. [Online] Available from; URL: http://www.ndu.edu/ctnsp/tamerlane/Tamerlane-Chapter7.pdf [2006, July].

[7] Anonymous, A history of Islam in Central Asia. [Online] Available from; URL: http://archive.muslimuzbekistan.com/eng/ennews/2002/07/ennews25072002.html [2006, July].

[8] Anonymous, Modern history of Uzbekistan. [Online] Available from; URL: http://columbia.thefreedictionary.com/Uzbekistan

[9] A. Polat, N. Butkevich, Unraveling the mystery of the Tashkent bombings: Theories and implications. International Eurasian Institute for Economic and Political Research. [Online] Available from; URL: http://iicas.org/english/Krsten_4_12_00.htm [2006, July].

[10] K. Toktogulov, 5 killed at Kyrgyz, Tajik border posts. The Associated Press; 2006, May 12. [Online] Available from; URL: http://ap.lancasteronline.com/4/kyrgyzstan _border_attack

[11] V.V. Naumkin, Militant Islam in Central Asia: The case of the Islamic movement of Uzbekistan, University of California, Berkeley; 2003. [Online] Available from; URL: http://socrates.berkeley.edu/ ~bsp/publications/2003_06-naum.pdf [2006, August].

[12] M. Fredholm, Uzbekistan and the threat from Islamic Extremism. Defense Academy, Conflict Studies Research Center; 2003 March, [Online] Available from; URL: http://www.defac.ac.uk/rcds/CSRC/ documents/CentralAsia/K39-MP.pdf/file_view [2006, August].

[13] A. Yarlykapov, Islamic fundamentalism in the Northern Caucasus: Towards a formulation of the problem. *Causasian Studies*, **4/1**(1999), pr 3. [Online] Available from; URL: http://poli.vub.ac.be/publi /crs/eng/0401-02.htm [2006, August].

[14] Anonymous, Wahhabism, (Beliefs). [Online] Available from; URL: http://en.wikipedia.org/wiki/ Wahhabism [2006, August].

[15] M. U. Roshin, Fundamentalism. Institute for Oriental Studies, Russian Academy of Sciences Press; 2003 (in Russian).

[16] CDI Terrorism Project. In the Spotlight: Islamic movement of Uzbekistan (IMU). [Online] Available from; URL: http://www.cdi.org/terrorism/imu.cfm [2006, August].

[17] R. Baucer, Spokesman of US Department of State, press statement. Redesignation of the Islamic movement of Uzbekistan as a foreign terrorist organization, 2002. [Online] Available from; URL: http://www.state.gov/r/pa/prs/ps/2002/13708.htm

[18] Anonymous, Hizb ut-Tahrir. [Online] Available from; URL: http://en.wikipedia. org/wiki/Hizb_ut-Tahrir

[19] Anonymous, Hızb-ut Tahrir-al Islami (Islamic Party of Liberation), [Online] Available from; URL: http://www.globalsecurity.org/military/world/para/Hizb ut-Tahrir.htm

[20] Kosicenko, Ashimbaev, Sovremenniy Terrorizm: Vglyad iz Cenralnoj Asii. Almati: Dayk- Press (2002) p-150 (Cited in Emil Jeenbekov's draft dissertation.)

[21] Cohen, Ariel, (2003). *Hizb ut-Tahrir: An Emerging Threat to U.S. Interests in Central Asia*, para-3. Retrieved on August 2006 from the World Wide Web: http://www.heritage.org/Research/ RussiaandEurasia/BG1656.cfm

[22] D.C. Isby, The Hizb ut-Tahrir: Stronger in Central Asia. *Terrorism Monitor*, Global Terrorism Analysis. **1/5** (2003, November 7), 1-10. [Online] Available from; URL: http://jamestown.org/terrorism /news/article.php?articleid=23401 [2006, August].

[23] 'V Londonistane Zapretat Hizb-ut Tahrir.' *Vecerniy, Bishkek*, 2005, 18 August. (Cited in Emil Jeenbekov's draft dissertation.)

[24] G. Saidazimova, Central Asia: Suppressing Hizb Ut-Tahrir could radicalize youths. (2006). [Online] Available from; URL: http://www.rferl.org/featuresarticle /2006/07/8B126BD9-4FD5-4D70-A42E-85E1CE7A5DE5.html [2006, August].

[25] E. Thomas, The new age of terror, *Newsweek* (Special Issue), 2006, August 21/23.

[26] N. Abdullaev, The growth of Islam in Russia. Jamestown Foundation, 7/11 (2001, December 6). [Online] Available from; URL: http://www.jamestown.org/publications_details.php?volume_id= 8&issue_id=451&article_id=3853.

[27] L. Sykiainen, Russia's Islamic Policy. *Central Asia and Caucasus*, **2/20** (2003), 118.

[28] International Crisis Group, Islam in Russia, Report No.14 for details about the influences of radical/militant Islam in Central Asia.

[29] ICG Asia Report, (No: 14) Central Asia: Islamist mobilization and regional security, Osh, Brussels: 2001, March 1 [Online] Available from; URL: http://www.untj.org/files/reports/Central%20Asia Islamist%20Mobilisation%20and%20Regional%20Security.pdf

[30] A.L. Boyer, U.S. foreign policy in Central Asia: Risks, ends and means, *Naval War College Review,* **59/1** (2006, Winter), pr 6 Accessed on August 2006: http://www.nwc.navy.mil/press/Review/2006 /winter/art4-w06.htm.

[31] Personal communication with Professor Sykiainen.

Understanding and Responding to the Terrorism Phenomenon
O. Nikbay and S. Hancerli (Eds.)
IOS Press, 2007

The Rise of the Periphery and Peripheralization of the Center: Moderation of Islamic and Kurdish Extremism in Turkey

Seda DEMIRALP
American University, Washington DC, USA

Abstract. This paper will explore how and why the anti-systemic movements in Turkey, such as the radical Islamists and the Kurdish separatists, that arose approximately in the same period of time and geographic region, almost simultaneously started to moderate their demands, gave up their utopian ethnic or religious ideals and showed interest in a pluralist solution from within the preexisting political and geographic boundaries[1]. I suggest that what define Turkish politics are the relations of power between the urban ruling elite and the isolated and agitated agrarian periphery. I find that in either movement, the "peripheral" identity was more critical than religion or ethnicity. Therefore, the changes in the center-periphery relations that took place in the late 1990s marked the beginning of a new era in Turkish politics. The decentralization of the state and its approximation to the EU created new opportunities for the periphery to enhance its condition from within the legal framework. These developments led to the moderation of previously anti-systemic Islamic and Kurdish movements, a de-emphasis on ethnic and religious elements in their discourse and the emergence of a new consensus around a cosmopolitan democratic approach.

Keywords. Extremism, radicalism, Kurdish separatism, Islamism

Introduction

Anti-systemic movements that were mobilized along ethnic or religious identities posed a major challenge to the integrity and continuity of the legal framework in Turkey as well as in other parts of the world in the Middle East, Balkans, and Africa. Kaldor called these confrontations the "new wars" since they characterized 21st century combat [1]. The goal of these new "warrior" groups was the claim to power on the basis of seemingly traditional identities such as ethnicity, religion, or sect. As these were fed by differences, they sabotaged state efforts to unify the nation and sought state collapse, social disintegration, and polarization.

In the case of the Turkish state the "attackers" were radical Islamists and Kurdish separatists. Each movement based its discourse on attacking one of the two founding

---

[1] In this paper, the concept Islamists indicates those political actors that seek to promote an Islamist political agenda and impose a theocratic regime instead of the secularist system. The Islamist movement that I refer to therefore indicates the political mobilization that seeks to reach this radical political goal. The Kurdish movement that I refer to consists of Kurdish separatists who want to establish an independent Kurdish state or Kurds or to promote a political agenda that acknowledges the distinct characteristics and needs of Kurdish citizens.

stones of the state's public discourse: secularism and unitarism, and engaged in destabilizing activities, ranging from civil initiatives such as organizing religious brotherhoods and dormitories for students (in the case of the radical Islamists) to violent attacks on civilians such as shooting school teachers (in the case of the Kurdish militants who protested the Turkish education system). The state retaliated with political repression and counter-guerilla warfare, and postponed democratic openings in the name of protecting the most fundamental principles of the Republic, secularism and national integrity. As a result, the conflict constituted a significant barrier to the country's democratic improvement.

Democracy requires the consensus of its actors on the basic rules of the game, their willingness to work together and make mutual concessions. Democratization theorists widely agree that moderation of radical opposition groups eases the fears of ruling groups who hope to survive the aftermath of political liberalization [2, 3, 4]. Abandonment, postponement or reconsideration of radical ambitions and demands, denouncement of violent means of activism, and willingness to operate within the rules of the legal framework are central to the peaceful coexistence of conflicting groups without the assurance of military forces or external guarantor states. The absence of strong anti-systemic groups is essential for the consolidation of democracy [5, 6]. Nevertheless, moderation is not always the most popular choice that movements and parties pursue.

This paper will explore how and why anti-systemic ethnic and religious movements such as the radical Islamists or the Kurdish separatists in Turkey that arose approximately in the same period of time and geographic region almost simultaneously moderated their demands, gave up their utopian ideals, and accepted a pluralist solution after 20 years. This question remains unanswered because important studies on Islamic and Kurdish movements such as those of Keyman [7], Yegen [8], Gulalp [9], or Kirisci [10] overemphasized the ethnic or religious identity of these groups and overwhelmingly focused on radicals. These studies emphasized the tension between the identity of the ruling elite and that of the ruled as the driving force of Turkish politics. The dialectics of the local and global identities that dates back to the Ottoman Empire was what produced this recent episode of identity conflict.

Outside of Turkey too, there has been a significant emphasis on cultural explanations of identity movements. In fact, some of the most popular and already discredited studies on Islamic movements argue that Islam is inherently antidemocratic and extremist [11, 12, 13]. Other cultural approaches, which are not as offensive, still suggested that cultural identities, whether religious or ethnic based, have clear boundaries that we need to understand in order to understand their holders' political behavior [14, 15]. Some nationalism studies suggest that it is a modernist fallacy to assume that ethnic or religious sentiments can be dissolved in or repressed by superior political identities [16]. According to these views, the new rise of primordial politics shows the persistence of these sentiments and signal that they will be important determinants of political behavior. Thus, Huntington claims, the new century will witness a major 'clash of civilizations.' As these "civilizational" identities are harder to be modified than ideational ones, finding solutions to recurring ethno-religious conflicts without destabilizing the religious or ethnic shape of the preexisting regime may seem difficult to the culturalist- nationalist observer.

Nevertheless, these perspectives fall short in explaining why actors decide and succeed to politicize these identities in some cases and not in others. In fact, ethnic or religious movements may not be primarily about ethnic or religious sentiments, and they are not necessarily more rigid about their demands than ideational movements are.

A comparative study of the evolution of two anti-systemic "identity movements" in Turkey, which are radical Islamism and Kurdish separatism, shows that underneath the religious or ethnic cause of some revolutionary movements there may lie a broader problem that cuts across ethnic and religious issues. The case of Turkey suggests that the radical Islamist and Kurdish separatist movements represented in fact a discontent of a rural "peripheral" population in underdeveloped regions of Turkey that has remained excluded from the political, economic and cultural resources of the urban, industrialized center. Despite its unitary discourse and its large size, the incapacity of the state in integrating the periphery, providing a fair distribution of political and economic resources between the center and the periphery, and providing a better life for the people of the latter turned the periphery to a space of contention. Religion and ethnicity were the resources available in the periphery that actors used to mobilize the contention.

1. The Periphery of Turkey

We inherited the center-periphery categorization from dependency theorists including Cardoso and Faletto [17], Prebisch [18], Frank [19] and Wallerstein [20], who introduced this perspective as the most meaningful way of understanding the economic and political problems of Latin America. The theory suggested that development in the world has been an uneven process that led to a dualism internationally and domestically, creating centers and peripheries. The early industrialized countries, states, or cities constituted the centers and the rest constituted the periphery that was dependent on the former. The two had different roles in their transactions. While the early developers played a central role in exporting expensive and developed goods and technologies, the role of the periphery was based on primary goods exports and technology. Consequently, a hierarchical and dependent relationship emerged between the two which made it incredibly difficult for the periphery to catch up with the center.

As postmodernist studies have shown, this development paradigm produced a discourse of civilized vs. uncivilized that provided intellectual justification for the hierarchy between the two and thereby strengthened the political, economic, and social privileges of the former [21, 22]. Through this discourse the center came to be the symbol of, not only the "developed," but also the "culturally and intellectually superior" that was therefore justified in controlling decision making. Yet, these centralist states' decisions and modernization projects often failed dramatically to improve the human condition in the localities [23]. Most often, these development projects further deepened the gap between political, material, and ideational resources between the center and the local.

The center-periphery perspective is helpful to understand the relationships between the elites of Turkey and the non-elites who supported radical Islamist and Kurdish separatist movements. The State Planning Institution's (SPI) records indicate a dramatic socio-economic disparity between the North-West to South-Eastern regions, as well as within the North-Western cities, between the *gecekondu* (squatter) areas where migrants live and the rest where the real "owners" of the cities reside[2]. The peripheral is the "other" in the eyes of the urban elite and is looked down upon for its "uncivilized" position. His tastes, accent, or religiosity are all clues that make his peripheral situation identifiable and therefore a reason for his exclusion from the spaces

---

[2] SPI records can be found at the official website of the institution at www.dpt.gov.tr

that traditionally belonged to the urban elite that may range from social clubs to business associations, political parties, bureaucratic positions, to teaching cadres in a university. The "rural other" of the 1950s and 1960s became the "disadvantaged other" in the 1970s, the "urban-poor other" in the 1980s, the "undeserving-rich other" and "culturally inferior other" in early 1990s, and finally the "threatening *varoslu* (shantytowner) other" in late 1990s, when they finally captured political power, but they were always the "other" [24].

2. Periphery and Extremism

Voting patterns between 1982 (the re-start of democracy after the 1980 military intervention) and 2004 suggest that the support for Islamist and Kurdish parties significantly overlap in this peripheral southeast region of Turkey.[3] With the mass migrations from the periphery to the industrializing center to supply workforce in the 1970s and 1980s, the peripheral votes for anti-systemic parties were carried over to the urban cities, along with the extension of the rural poverty to urban poverty as a result of a rapid and unhealthy urbanization process. Within this process, gecekondus, which are shanty towns and squatter areas where migrants built primitive housing that had no license, did not comply with any standard, lacked infrastructure and other urban services, and occupied the outskirts of the cities. Today, 50% to 60% of the population of the three major Turkish cities, Ankara, Istanbul and Izmir, live in gecekondus, which represent the re-constitution of the periphery in the heart of the center [25].

Election surveys demonstrate that the votes that religious and ethnic parties won in urban cities come mainly from gecekondus [26].

The electoral support that the Islamic and Kurdish parties received from rural and urban peripheral populations suggests that, in a situation where the state institution ceases to be a giver and becomes only a repressive institution, when political alternatives and a history of political participation and debate is absent, and when other political ideas increasingly lose meaning, people frequently turn to ethnic or religious symbols to avoid isolation and connect with others. At this moment political movements that emphasize religious or ethnic discourses achieve considerable success in terms of mobilizing people by speaking a language they can associate with (see Kaldor's study [1], for a similar analysis of the conflicts in Kosovo and Bosnia). This was the case in Turkey's periphery where people were alienated from the state and turned to the available alternatives that were the Islamist and Kurdish parties with the expectation of a "radical" change.

Historical examples from radical socialist parties in Latin America and Eastern Europe suggest that institutional openings and political participation lead to moderation. Once they enter the democratic framework, previously anti-democratic and anti-systemic groups quickly discover that they can actually survive and advance their situation within democracy [3, 2, 27, 28]. Similarly, cases of Islamists in Egypt (The Wasat Party) and Jordan (The Muslim Brothers) suggest that even small institutional openings can reinforce moderation [29, 30]. Yet, if states are totally exclusionary and restrictive and if effective conventional channels of participation are absent, dissidents radicalize [31, 32].

---

[3] For national election results see Turkish Grand National Assembly web page: http://www.tbmm.gov.tr/develop/owa/secim_sorgu.genel_secimler and for municipal elections see Center for Education and Research in Local Administration web page: http://www.yerelnet.org.tr/secimler.

3. Moderation of Culturalist Extremism in Turkey

The ethnic and religious dissent movements of the periphery started to soften following the advent of increasing opportunities for the marginalized populations of Turkey, also referred as the "black Turks," by political and economic decentralization that resulted from a combination of domestic and international developments. The changes in the state-society relationship and redistribution of power started via the political and economic liberalization in the 1980s, and accelerated after the 1989 municipal elections when the Islamists won control over local governments, signaling the rise of an Islamic/peripheral counter-elite in this period [33, 34]. As the Islamists gained significant power, they had to broaden their larger and increasingly urban constituencies to win re-election, and over time, they found radicalism less attractive as it limited the size of their constituencies. Therefore, the expansion of Islamism ironically led to a muting of an Islamist discourse to win more support from an urban secular audience. The more the actors approached the center, the more they moderated. Scholars often associated the 1990s with the peak of political Islam but failed to predict that this peak would also mark the end of radicalism.

Yet, the most dramatic change in the state-society relationships in Turkey and the most significant moderation in Islamist and Kurdish movements took place as a result of Turkey's relations with the EU. An invaluable opportunity for the black Turks emerged when Turkey signed the Helsinki Accession Partnership Treaty in 1999 and became an official candidate for EU membership. Sikkink et al. [35] suggest that the rise of supranational actors and international treaties created opportunities for domestic societal actors to increase their power against their target states. In the interdependent environment of the global world societal actors have more resources to mobilize against their states. When states are unresponsive to the demands of particular segments of their society, when domestic spheres are too limited, or when channels between states and certain societal groups are blocked, these groups can bypass their state and apply to international actors for support. These supranational actors can then pressure those nation states to make them respond to the demands of their people, which Sikkink called the "boomerang effect." Hence, excluded peripheral groups represented by the Islamist and Kurdish parties saw that EU membership could change the center-periphery relations in Turkey by shifting the central role away from the oversized-yet-ineffective state toward the EU parliament, which would be more accessible, effective, and accountable. As Middle East studies often suggested, the disproportion between the size and capacity of the state has been indeed a major problem in the overall region [15, 36, 37].

This situation not only created an imbalance in the relationships between the state and society and precluded the societal actors from having a fair say in decision making, but it was not economically efficient either. Yet, thanks to its military and economic resources, the Middle Eastern state could preserve this situation in the absence of effective counter-powers [38, 39, 37, 40]. As Islamic and Kurdish movements realized, this situation could change in Turkey as a result of the country's membership in the EU. Under the circumstances, leading actors both in the Islamic and the Kurdish party made a radical maneuver and changed the party discourse from emphasis on ethnic or religious differences to an embracement of universalist pluralist values [41, 42]. Here, we must once again remember the role of political parties in moderation, in terms of their capability to mediate between the ruling authority and the radicals among their supporters (see O'Donnell and Schmitter [2], and Przeworski [3]'s studies for political parties and moderation). Moderation would take longer, if both the Islamist and Kurdish party elite did not propagate it to their party base and were unable to control the radicals in the party base. The parties played an important role in explaining to the supporters not only the political advantages but also the economic benefits of EU membership, which may be more relevant to people with serious economic hardship. Indeed, potential employment/ migration opportunities that would be associated with EU membership as well as the EU's structural adjustment projects that seek the development of underdeveloped regions and areas facing structural difficulties through education, training, and employment created hopes for the populations of problem regions in Turkey [43].

Another sector that functioned as a major supporter of Turkey's EU membership has been the provincial businessmen, such as the members of Independent Businessmen Association (MUSIAD), South Eastern Industrialists and Businessmen Association GUNSIAD, or Diyarbakir Industrialists and Businessmen Association (DISIAD), who had a comparative disadvantage in the domestic market since the state traditionally favored the Turkish Industrialists and Businessmen Association (TUSIAD). Provincial businessmen, whether organized on religious or ethnic lines, saw a benefit for themselves in joining the EU as this would enable them to bypass the domestic market, where TUSIAD has traditionally more advantages, and to open up to Western markets. Under the circumstances, the Turkish elite's historic desire to unite with the West was ironically embraced by both the Islamic capitalist or religious elite who previously pushed for unification with Muslim countries, and also by Kurdish capitalists and nationalist leaders who wanted to unite with their brothers and sisters in Iran, Iraq, and Syria. In this period, both of these groups abandoned their extremist discourse and accepted the EU's democratic principles as the key elements of their discourse. Democracy had become the new consensus.

4. Conclusion

A structural approach that connects the Islamist and the Kurdish movements has critical political implications as it indicates that a solution to the conflict between the state and radical societal movements as the Islamists or the Kurds does not necessarily depend on the Islamization of the polity, or through ethnic reconfiguration of borders. Even though these solutions constitute some of the most frequently cited alternatives today in Turkish political debates against the state's 'military' solution, in fact, prospects of peace are contingent upon enhancing life in the periphery. Moderation and integration with the legal framework is possible through the establishment of a more legitimate source of authority and a more pluralist democratic approach. Such a social transformation is indeed what started to come true in Turkey in the post 1980 era, but especially after the events that took place in 1999, which explains the sudden moderation and democratization of Islamic and Kurdish separatist movements.

The Turkish lesson has particular importance in the contemporary international climate. While a new politics is being constructed in Iraq, actors from around the world are looking for political formulas to deal with two issues, Islamic fundamentalism and Kurdish separatism, which makes the Turkish lesson particularly important. Contemporary debates about constructing a democracy in Iraq revolve around two issues: creating a moderate Islam and re-configuring the ethnic borders of Iraq. While policymakers often consider top down regime imposition as a working model in these debates, this thesis will suggest a skeptical view of these policy formulas. This paper considers moderate Islam as a consequence of actual and potential changes in the relations of power that, therefore, may not be injected into a system from above. Similarly, reconfiguring Iraqi borders to create a separate space for the Kurds may not eradicate future ethnic radicalization unless it stimulates growth, and a fair distribution of newly acquired resources (economic and political) follows.

To conclude, what we must learn from the Turkish experience is that in the 21st century the periphery is not the old "disadvantaged-other" anymore, but finally it is the "threatening-other." It is the last call for states to finally worry about the conditions of their peripheries if non-violent solutions are desired.

References

[1]   M. Kaldor, *New and Old wars: Organized Violence in a Global Era.* Cambridge: Polity; 1999.
[2]   G. O'Donnell, P. Schmitter, *Transition from Authoritarian Rule.* Baltimore and London: The Johns Hopkins University Press; 1986.
[3]   A. Przeworski, *Democracy and the Market: Political and Economic Reforms in Eastern Europe and Latin America.* New York: Cambridge University Press; 1991.
[4]   N. Bermeo, Myths of Moderation: Confrontation and Conflict During Democratic Transitions, *Comparative Politics* **293/3** (1997), 305-322.
[5]   J. Linz, A. Stepan, Toward Consolidated Democracies. In L. Diamond, M.F. Plattner, Editors. *The Global Divergence of Democracies.* The Johns Hopkins University Press; 2001.
[6]   R. Gunther, N. Diamandouros, H.J. Puhle, O'Donnell's Illusions. In L. Diamond, M.F. Plattner, Editors. *The Global Divergence of Democracies.* The Johns Hopkins University Press; 2001.
[7]   F. Keyman, On the Relation between Global Modernity and Nationalism: The Crisis of Hegemony and the Rise of (Islamic) Identity in Turkey, *New Perspectives on Turkey,* **13/3** (1995) 93-120.
[8]   M. Yegen, The Turkish State and the Exclusion of Kurdish Identity, *Middle Eastern Studies.* **32/2** (1996) 216-229.
[9]   H. Gulalp, A postmodern reaction to dependent modernization: The social and historical roots of Islamic radicalism. *New Perspectives on Turkey,* **8** (1992, Fall), 15-26.
[10] K. Kirisci, G. Winrow, The Kurdish Question and Turkey, London: Frank Cass; 1997.
[11] S. Huntington, The Clash of Civilizations? *Foreign Affairs,* **72/3** (1993, Summer), 22.
[12] F. Fukuyama, *Trust: The social virtues and the creation of prosperity.* New York: Free Press; 1996.
[13] D. Pipes, There are no moderates: Dealing with Fundamentalist Islam, *The National Interest,* **41** (1995 Fall), 48-58.
[14] A. Hammodi, *Master and Disciple: The Cultural Foundations of Moroccan Authoritarianism.* Chicago and London: The University of Chicago Press; 1997.
[15] N. Ayubi, *Overstating the Arab State: Politics and Society in the Middle East.* London and New York: I B Tauris Press; 1995.
[16] A. Smith, *Nations and Nationalism in a Global Era.* Oxford: Polity Press; 1995.
[17] F.H. Cardoso, E. Faletto, *Dependency and Development in Latin America,* University of California Press; 1979.
[18] R. Prebish, International Trade and Payments in an Era of Coexistence. *American Economic Review,* XLIX (1959).
[19] A.G. Frank, *Development of Underdevelopment.* NY: Monthly Review; 1966.
[20] I. Wallerstein, *The Modern World System, II: Mercantilism and the Consolidation of the European World Economy, 1600-1750.* New York: Academic Press; 1980.
[21] E. Said, *Orientalism.* New York: Vintage; 1979.
[22] A. Escobar, *Encountering Development: The Making and Unmaking of the Third World.* Princeton: Princeton University Press; 1995.
[23] J. Scott, *Seeing Like a State: How Certain Schemes to Improve the Human condition Have Failed.* New Haven: Yale University Press; 1998.

[24] T. Erman, The Politics of Squatter (gecekondu) Studies in Turkey: The Changing Representations of Rural Migrants in the Academic Discourse. *Urban Studies.* **38/7** (2001), 983-1003.

[25] E. Ocak, Yoksulun Evi, In N. Erdoğan, Editor. *Yoksulluk Hâlleri: Türkiye'de Kent Yoksulluğunun Toplumsal Görünümleri.* Istanbul, Turkey: Deki; 2002.

[26] K.H. Karpat, The Genesis of the Gecekondu : Rural Migration and Urbanization (1976), *European Journal of Turkish Studies*, 1(2004) [Online] Available from; URL: http://www.ejts.org/document54. html [2006, May 24].

[27] G. Salame, Introduction: Where Are the Democrats? In G. Salame, Editor. *Democracy Without Democrats? The Renewal of Politics in the Muslim world.* London: I.B.Tauris; 1994.

[28] J. Waterbury, Democracy Without Democrats? The Potential for Political Liberalization in the Middle East, In G. Salame, Editor. *Democracy Without Democrats? The Renewal of Politics in the Muslim world.* London: I.B.Tauris; 1994.

[29] C. Wickham, The Path to Moderation: Strategy and Learning in the Formation of Egypt's Wasat Party. *Comparative Politics,* **36/2** (2004, January) 205-228.

[30] Q. Wictorowicz, *The Management of Islamic Activism.* NY: SUNY Press; 2001.

[31] H. Kriesie, R. Koopmans et al., New Social Movements and Political Opportunities in Western Europe. *European Journal of Political Research* **22** (1992), 219-244.

[32] M. Hafez, From Marginalization to Massacres: A Political Process Explanation of GIA Violence in Algeria, In Q. Wictorowicz, Editor. *Islamic Activism: A Social Movement Approach*, Indiana: Indiana Univeristy Press; 2004.

[33] N. Gole, *Melez Desenler (Mixed Patterns).*Istanbul, Turkey: Metis; 2000.

[34] B. Toprak, A. Carkoglu. *Turkiye'de Din, Toplum ve Siyaset (Religion,Society and State in Turkey).* Istanbul, Turkey: Tesev Yayinlari; 2000.

[35] K. Sikkink, M.E. Keck, *Activists Without Borders: Advocacy Networks in International Politics.* New York: Cornell University Press; 1998.

[36] E. Sahliyeh, The Limits of State Power in the Middle East. *Arab Studies Quarterly.* **22/4** (2000, Fall), 1-29.

[37] L. Anderson, The State in the Middle East and North Africa. *Comparative Politics.* **20/1**(1987, October) 1-18.

[38] E. Bellin, The Robustness of Authoritarianism in the Middle East: Exceptionalism in Comparative Perspective, *Comparative Politics,* **36/2** (2004) 139-157.

[39] M. Ross, Does Oil Hinder Democracy? *World Politics,* **53/3** (2001) 325-361.

[40] C. Tilly, *Coercion, Capital, and European States, AD 990-1992.* Cambridge: Blackwell; 1992.

[41] S. Taniyici, Transformation of Political Islam in Turkey: Islamist Welfare Party's U-turn, *Party Politics.* **9/4** (2003).

[42] T. Akyol, *Milliyet Newspaper,* 2005, March 23.

[43] Hurriyet Newspaper, EU Opinion Polls 2000.

Understanding and Responding to the Terrorism Phenomenon
O. Nikbay and S. Hancerli (Eds.)
IOS Press, 2007
© 2007 IOS Press. All rights reserved.

War of Paradigms:
the PKK, Europe, and Turkey

Emrullah USLU[a] and Onder AYTAC[b]

[a]*Middle-East Center, University of Utah, USA*
[b]*National Police Academy, Turkey*

Abstract. The PKK has long been able to establish associations throughout Europe. What Turkish authorities want from their European allies is to close down these associations and cut off the PKK's organizations across Europe and financial support that come through these associations. Yet, European countries are reluctant to take such measures. The schism between Turkey and European countries regarding taking effective measures against the PKK is an outcome of different paradigms. European countries and Turkey, have two different opinions on international relations. In their foreign affairs, most European countries, especially the north-western ones, see the world from the perspective of interdependency theories. However, Turkish authorities, on the other hand, see the world as an "anarchy," from the viewpoint of the realist perspective. Therefore, conflicts occur due to the different perspectives of understanding the issue of the PKK.

Keywords. Terror, PKK, Turkey, Europe, international relations, IR paradigms

Introduction

The Kurdistan Worker's Party (PKK/Kongra-Gel) (Due to its common usage in internationally recognized scholarly works, in rest of the article we will use abbreviation (PKK) for Kurdistan Workers Party, instead of the organizations' recently adopted name PKK/Kongra-Gel) is one of the long-lived terrorist organizations, having existed since 1984. A suitable sociopolitical environment, which helped the PKK to generate and recruit militants mainly from the Kurdish population of Turkey, has been the main cause for this terrorist organization's longevity, and the international environment has also been another prominent cause of its survival.

Since the first terror attack by the PKK in 1984, six significant international developments which exerted impact upon the PKK's survival ability have occurred. The first of these developments was the collapse of the Soviet Union. The second development has been the first gulf war in 1991; the third development has been the formation of a Kurdish Diaspora in Europe. The civil strife in southeastern Turkey led to a massive migration from this region into western cities of Turkey as well as Europe. The fourth factor has been the international operation led by the US against the PKK's leader, Abdullah Ocalan. At the end of this operation, Ocalan was arrested and brought to Turkey and has been imprisoned. The fifth factor was Justice and Development Party (AKP)'s rapid reformation policies toward Turkey's EU membership process. The sixth and the most important factor is the war conducted against terrorism led by the US as part of its anti-terror campaign and its intercession in Iraq. Above these developments countries foreign policy attitudes shape their understanding of the world, which, at the end affect their relationships with state and non-state actors. In this sense, the European countries' tolerance toward the PKK was the most crucial international factor for the durability of the PKK.

These national and international factors led to the creation of a suitable environment for the PKK's survival in international territories. In addition to all this, the PKK's ability to transform itself according to these developments also had an impact upon its long lasting intensive terror campaign. Moreover, the lack of an international definition of terrorism also helped PKK members to seek asylum in Europe, a situation which eventually helped the organization to collect money from the Kurdish Diaspora and recruit militants from Kurdish Europe. During this long period of time, European countries have allowed PKK members to become organized within their territories. Because of this, Turkey has always blamed European states for their "support" of the PKK.

In this study, out of above-mentioned six intertwined factors, we examine how differences of foreign policy outlooks between European countries and Turkey have helped the durability of the PKK. We organize our study to examine the following questions: Why does the European countries have tolerant attitude toward the PKK? Is it because of European hostility toward Turkey to destabilize the country or is it because of something else?

What we think is that the European tolerance toward the PKK is not because of an outcome of European hostile attitude to destabilize Turkey but because of the differences in foreign policy perspectives. Therefore, what we argue is foreign policy perspectives matter.

When blaming its allies what Turkish authorities failed to understand was the difference of perspectives between the European governments and Turkey. On this issue, the two sides, that is, European countries and Turkey, had two different opinions on international relations. In their foreign attitudes, most European countries, especially those situated in the north-west, see the world from the perspective of interdependency theories. However, Turkish authorities, on the other hand, perceive the world as an "anarchy," as the realist theory portrays it. Thus, a conflict of perspective confuses the understanding of the problem of the PKK.

In this paper, we apply Wendtzian constructivist theory to the case to understand why each side, Turkey and Europe, could not understand each other until very recently. We will examine realist and neo-liberal theories and apply them to the PKK issue. First we will summarize the constructivist theory to examine why each side has different paradigms in their foreign policy attitudes; then we will examine which side's foreign policy behaviors falls into what IR paradigm. The PKK problem between the two sides will be used as a case study to examine how differences in IR paradigms affect states' foreign policy perspectives.

1. Theoretical Paradigm

The capacity and will of individuals to take an aggressive and belligerent attitude against the world is the main conception of the theoretical approach of this paper. This approach contends not only that identities and interests of actors are socially constructed, but also that they must share the stage with a whole host of other ideational factors emanating from individuals as cultural beings [1]. Therefore, international politics are "socially constructed." In this sense, shared ideas primarily determine structures of human association, rather than material forces. Identities and interests of purposive actors are constructed by these shared ideas rather than given by nature [2]. Identities of individuals are constructed by society and how these evolve is based on the individuals' dependence on society. The primary actors in international politics are states; their foreign policy behavior, however, is often determined by domestic policies, analogous to individual personality, rather than international systems and material interests [2].

The important role played by identities, norms, and culture is one of the main assumptions of our approach to world politics. Identities and interests of states are not simply and structurally determined, but are rather produced by interactions, institutions, norms, and cultures. The process, not the structure, determines the manner in which states interact [3]. Collective identity formation, which eventually exerts a substantial impact upon foreign policy attitudes of states, is strongly related to the past. The past interactions set the precedent for future interaction. Nations, international organizations, and ethnic groups hardly forget their history. History, however, is not inescapable, something which Wendt uses to explain how nations change their interactions.

The role of ideas is more important than the role of material forces. The role of ideas makes it possible for agents to identify their starting point. In this sense, it becomes clear how actors identify their material structures. Identity constitutes interests and actions, while identities form the basis for interests. Agents and structures are mutually constituted, because structure is constructed by the way states define their identities and interests [3]. Moreover, social structure can matter by constituting identities and interests, by helping actors to find solutions to problems, by defining expectation for behavior, and by constituting threats [2].

Constructivism assumes that the "self" or identity of a state is a dependent variable determined by historical, cultural, social, and political context. States with self-interests and power-seeking characters are contingent and socially constructed. In the state-centric approach, efforts of states not only reproduce their own identity, but also the identity of the system to which they belong.

Identities evolve through two basic processes; natural and cultural selection. Natural selection is a process of differential reproduction which explains well the emergence of the Hobbesean anarchy in the international system. Natural selection plays a greater explanatory role in the world without shared ideas [2]. Cultural selection, on the other hand, consists of mechanisms of important social learning. It refers to imitation and social learning. Imitation occurs when states imitate successful former states, and these imitations promote the homogenization of the state-system and cultural change involving the emergence of new forms of collective identity. Collective identity formation is possible through interdependence, common fate, homogenization, and self-restraint.

In this sense, the content and meaning of power and interests are constituted by ideas and culture. These are important factors in international life but because of their effects, they are a culturally constituted function [2]. The function of shared ideas matter in terms of international relations, for example, material interests. Power and interests are a distinct and important set of social causes, whereas they are formed by diverse ideas. In this regard distribution of ideas or knowledge is the most fundamental fact about society.

From this perspective, states, depending on their culture, identity, and historical background, have a certain outlook in their international behaviors. As it is also accepted by the constructivist approach that the attitudes of states exhibited in their foreign policies change with great difficulties, we cannot predict how fast a foreign policy behavior can change. Therefore, in our analysis, we will treat the two different foreign policy attitudes as given attitudes of Turkey and European countries.

2. Turkish Foreign Policy Behavior

Its history, (Ottoman Empire as its descendent, traumatic end of World War I and independent war, losing 2/3 of its land in less than 10 years), culture, identity formation process and ethnic fragmentation, and being close to the troubled region of the Middle East shaped Turkey's prime foreign policy attitudes. Therefore, when we analyze her foreign policy preferences, Turkish foreign policy falls into the category of the neo-realist paradigm (see following part for the causes why Turkey adopted such paradigm).

2.1. Neo-Realist Paradigm

According to this paradigm, international relations are a struggle of power assumptions. Power is the key for states to pursue their interests in anarchy of international arena. The international system is a self-help system; anarchy is taken to mean not just the absence of government but also the presence of disorder and chaos. "International politics is then described as being flecked with particles of government and alloyed with elements of community-supranational organizations whether universal or regional, alliances, multinational corporations, networks of trade" [4 pg 114]. In any anarchy states have deep concerns for their own survival, and this anxiety determines and conditions their behavior. Due to these concerns, states come together to build alliances which provide them more security and some stability, though less independence. Furthermore, alliance between states requires a strategy with power balance as theorized by Waltz as follows: states are unitary actors who, at a minimum, seek their own preservation and, at a maximum, drive for universal domain. States use (a) internal efforts (increase in capability, military strength, clever strategies) or (b) external efforts (strengthen own alliance or weaken opposing one) to achieve their aims. Two or more states coexist in a self-help system with no one to come to their aid or deny them the use of whatever instruments may serve their purposes [4].

In realism, a) states in this system act as coherent units and they are the dominant actors; b) national security dominates foreign policy agendas; and c) military force is an effective instrument of statecraft.

2.2. Neo-Realist Paradigm and its Application on Turkish Foreign Policy

The following examples show that preferences of Turkish foreign policy makers overlap with the rationalist paradigm. The basic premise of Turkish foreign policy is built on security and regional stability concerns, according to which Turkey has shaped its IR behaviors. Alliances, trade relations, and military cooperation with different regional and global actors indicate that Turkish foreign policy is mostly shaped by security concerns. For example, Turkey was not heavily involved in Middle East politics until the end of the Cold War Era. During this time, the most influential factors for Turkey's external behavior were emerging from its geo-strategic position where it has a border with the Soviet Union. Against Soviet expansionism, Turkey was at a key position for Western allies to keep the Soviet Union out of the Eastern Mediterranean and the Middle East. Thus, during the cold war, for Europe, Turkey acted as a bulwark against Soviet expansionism into the eastern Mediterranean and the Middle East. Because of its security concerns, which are shaped by its history, identity, and culture, Turkey preferred to be one of the frontier defenders of the Western bloc against the Soviet bloc. Thus, Turkey's foreign policy horizons were very dependent on NATO and the western outlook. Therefore, the most important factor for Turkey at the beginning of 1950 was to join NATO. In order to join NATO, Turkey sent troops to the Korean War alongside of American troops. In 1952 Turkey became a NATO member and Turkey's foreign policy from then till the end of the Cold War was steadily maintained along the line of Western allies.

With the Cold War ended, under the new circumstances, as the rationalist paradigm envisions, Turkey reshaped its foreign policy behavior from being a dependent actor of the West to being an independent regional actor. By such policies, Turkey was trying to maximize its benefits, while, at the same time, trying to find a place to increase its security in this unstable region. For instance, the horizon of the Ankara government's policy has greatly expanded since 1991, and Turkey became an independent actor on the international stage. Turkey is situated at a geo-strategic position, standing at the nexus of three areas of increasing strategic importance to the US and Europe: the Balkans, the Caspian Region, and the Middle East. Having to play three different roles in three different regions with different conditions and problems, Turkey evolved to an important level of being an independent actor both towards the US and towards the EU.

This new independent international position of Turkey was mainly developed after the Cold War era, during which Turkey's actions merely depended upon US and NATO polices. In the Middle East, for example, under the rule of Ataturk and several decades after his death, Turkey eschewed involvement in the Middle East. In recent years, however, Turkey has been heavily engaged in the region. This policy shift is mainly a result of the Cold War and the Gulf War.

Turgut Ozal foresaw the new developments and has shifted Turkey's policy toward multi-dimensional engagements. One of these was a more active involvement in the Middle East. Turgut Ozal thought that at the end of the Cold War, because Turkey would no longer be a strategic security bulwark for the Western powers, since there was no more Soviet threat of expansion toward the Eastern Mediterranean and the Middle East, Turkey should be involved in multi-dimensional engagements within which it can maintain its geo-strategic importance. In this respect, during the Gulf War, by taking sides with the Western alliance led by the United States, Turkey took an active role in Middle Eastern affairs. This provided Turkey a distinctive position in the eye of the US. However, Turkey's engagement in the Middle East caused fear in some European countries because they thought that in such a situation, Turkey's EU membership would bring the EU border into the vortex of the Middle East.

Another development that brought Turkey into the international arena as an important regional actor is events in the Caucasus and Central Asia. When the Cold War era ended, new horizons opened before Turkish foreign policy. While the Caucasus and Central Asia highlighted the security concern of the EU, on one hand, on the other, they made its relations with Russia more complex. In addition to these complicated foreign policy paradigms, Turkey also acted, and still acts, in Central Asia, in alliance with the US, blockading the Russian and Iranian influence over the region. Russia has come to see that Turkey's efforts to establish a geo-strategic foothold would undermine its interest in the region. Thus, Turkey is a rival of Russia in the region, as well as an important trade partner with around $15 billion trade volume.

In addition to these two dimensions, Turkey's EU membership process, and its Balkan policies show that Turkish foreign affairs are heavily determined according to the realist paradigm. In the Balkans recently, Turkey's interests with Albania, Macedonia, and Bulgaria have visibly improved. Turkey has actively participated in peace-keeping and stabilization operations in Bosnia and Kosovo and would like to contribute to any Western peace-keeping operation in Macedonia. Turkey's sympathy for Bosnians and other Muslims elsewhere in the Balkan region worries many Europeans, especially Greeks, who fear, at some point, Turkey might attempt to play a "Muslim Card" if a nationalist government took power in Ankara. There are many examples that can be applied here, yet this is beyond the scope of this study.

2.3. The Causes and Reflections of Neo-Realist Paradigm in Turkish Foreign Policy

What we believe is that although these elements show that Turkish foreign policy behaviors overlap with the realist paradigm, we must note that the reason why Turkey follows this paradigm is not because of its nature, but because its history, culture and identity [Kemalism] shaped its foreign policy attitudes.

History in the collective memory of the Turkish people is so vivid that even decades after the collapse of the Ottoman Empire, issues related to countries which were former Ottoman territories are reported with a reference to their connection with the Ottomans. These types of media reports can be seen in the reports about Kosovo, Bosnia, Iraq (especially in the Kirkuk issue), Cyprus, and other formerly Ottoman territories. Just recently, for example, when the Turkish Parliament decided to send Turkish troops to Lebanon to join UN peace-keeping forces, Turkish media reported this decision with a reference to the Ottoman period. *Milliyet*, one of the mainstream secular newspapers, for instance, used the headline "In Lebanon 88 years later." In detail, the newspaper stated, "88 years after the last Ottoman troops left Lebanon, Turkish soldiers will again serve in Lebanon within the UN Peace Keeping forces." [5] The leading secular newspaper *Hurriyet* used exactly the same title as *Milliyet*, "In Lebanon 88 years later" in its headline, once again, with the reference to the Ottoman connection of the event [6]. Along with other reports that can be listed here, these two reports show that history in Turkish collective memory is so alive that in the media, in the national education system and in other public spheres, the *"historization"* of Turkish identity has been constantly aroused. This process had a strong impact on Turkish foreign policy attitude.

Three important historical events mark Turkish identity: the Ottoman-Russian war of the late 19th century, the Treaty of Sevres, which divided the Ottoman Empire and from its territory formed new states and colonies, and the betrayal of Arabs in World War I. When Turkey was founded, Turkish foreign policy was formalized to protect the existing borders of the new republic. Whenever a conflict occurs between Turkey and other states in the language of diplomacy, the media always refers to a historical connection(s), which relates to the conflicts. America is an exception to this because Turks had no significant historical confrontation with the United States. Because these historical reasons shaped its foreign attitude, until the 1990s we see very limited foreign relations with the Arab world and Soviet Russia. Turkey's relations with Europe have always been cautious toward Europeans' attitude. The biggest fear that Turkey has in its foreign policy is whether the European states want to bring the treaty of Sevres before Turkey once again. In this period, because of historical fears Turkish foreign policy relied on its military power and its alliance with the Unites States; because Turkey had had no historical confrontation with the US, there was no fear. This attitude reflects that Turkish foreign policy at this time falls into the category of the neo-realist paradigm.

In addition, when we analyze the Turkish school textbooks, we see that a great deal of emphasis is placed upon how Turkish people fought to gain their independence. It is not unusual to see such emphasis on "official" history writings; however, what makes the Turkish case unique is that the "history" in Turkey is treated as a life-giving element of social structure. In other words, there is too much emphasis on Turkish independence and the Western invasion of the country; people treat it as if it had happened just yesterday. In the identity formation process, values like loyalty, self-sacrifice, courage, strength and patriotism are revered at almost all levels of social life. These values are continually stressed, both within the family and in the national education curriculum [7]. In this learning process which eventually shapes Turkish people's identity, their outlook toward Europeans is also shaped. Its historic origins and patriotic features form an important part of Turkish culture [8]. Because the republican foreign policy was formulated as a "peace in the country, peace in the world" principle, the patriotic heritage of the Ottoman Empire is reshaped by putting too much emphasis on how Turks fought to tear up the treaty of Sevres[1]. With this treaty, the collapse of the Ottoman Empire was declared and the establishment of an independent Armenian state in Anatolia was envisioned and gave Kurds a chance to declare their independence [9]. In fact, it is true that it was a huge success for the early republican elites to fight back and not to accept the Treaty of Sevres. Whereas, on the other hand, putting too much emphasis on this thrashing treaty to show the bravery of early republican elites as the last brave fight of the modern Turkish military until the Cyprus operation, kept alive the trauma of the treaty of Sevres in the psychology of Turkish society. Now, especially the nationalist segments of Turkish society do have a suspicious attitude toward the intentions of the EU. They question the intentions of the EU demands, by seeing these demands under the shadow of the Sevres Treaty fear. "What if the EU has a secret agenda to bring the Treaty of Sevres back?" is the common question that is put forward, especially when EU leaders demand political/cultural rights for Kurds and when they bring the Armenian issue into the debate.

2.4. Fear of Sevres and Kurdish Question

For instance, during his visit to Turkey in 1995, when French Prime Minister commented upon the Kurdish question saying Turkey needs to solve the Kurdish question through political solutions, Turkish President Suleyman Demirel accused him by saying that this attitude of Europeans aims to separate the southeastern provinces from Turkey. This rhetoric became a permanent rhetoric of Turkish bureaucracy to resist Europe's demands related to issues like the Kurdish question [10]. In a different occasion, Demirel in early 1990s accused England of "allowing terror organization PKK to broadcast a TV channel from England." [11]

---

[1] Despite the fact that War of Independence compare to other wars in Turkish history was a relatively easy one, yet official history books portray it as if one of the biggest war of Turkish history. In terms of the consequence, the War of Independence was an important war but militaristically it was not on of the biggest wars of Turkish history.

Demirel is not the only leading figure who has questioned the EU's attitudes exhibited towards the Kurdish question. Even most liberal figures, when it comes to the matter of Kurdish broadcasting, for example, became suspicious whether the EU has a secret agenda against Turkey [12].

When we trace back the reactions toward the EU's policies on the Kurdish question, we once again find the military elites are the most skeptical republicans towards the EU's sincerity about the Kurdish question. In the year 2000, in Nice, France, a Turkish military representative stated that, by allowing and advocating Kurdish broadcasting, the EU helped the PKK to accelerate its politicization process. Thanks to the EU, Turkey's membership process allowed the PKK to increase its politicization process [13].

Recently, Military Chief of Staff, Gen. Buyukanit, in his inaugural speech which was full of criticisms against EU policies, made reference to two historical events, saying, "I recommend that my colleagues carefully study Ottoman history from 1830 to 1918." In different parts of his speech, he also referred to the Treaty of Sevres. "Within the context of security, I would like to bring to your attention a very important issue," he said. "Although it is with good faith, some argue that the Turkish Republic will have to confront the Treaty of Sevres. I would like to clearly state that, although some circles may have such an endeavor and others may have such expectations [to confront Turkey with the Treaty of Sevres], I do not think that there is any power to force Turkey to confront the Treaty of Sevres once again." [14].

Although the fear of the Treaty of Sevres is not a lively debate in some segments of Turkish society, the republican elite, especially the military elite, believe that European countries have a secret agenda to bring the treaty of Sevres before Turkey. As mentioned above, this fear became nerve-breaking, especially during talks with Europeans about the issues related to Kurdish, Armenian and Cyprus questions.

When the Swedish ambassador to Ankara, Henrik Lilyegren, made a comment on Turks' sensitivity on the Treaty of Sevres, he received an outraged response for his following comment: "On issues like education and broadcasting in Kurdish language, I see an historical fear exists. This is a Treaty of Sevres syndrome. Turks should forget the Sevres, but should remember the Helsinki summit [that Turkey's EU membership was granted] [15]. When it comes to Sevres, even liberal intellectuals, like Sedat Laciner, questioned the ambassador's intention [12].

These responses depict that actually there is a Sevres syndrome among Turkish intellectuals. Especially nationalists believe that the EU wants to implement an amended version of the Sevres Treaty and the eagerness of the EU to defend Kurdish rights is one example of this intention. Umit Ozdag, for instance, believed that MED TV, the pro-PKK Kurdish satellite TV channel, was allowed to broadcast from England as part of a big plan that will bring Turkey to its knees [16]. (a note: Due to Turkish pressure, MED TV was banned by English authorities, however, its sister channel, ROJ TV still broadcasts out of Denmark)

The whole content of Turkish bureaucracy, especially military bureaucracy that has full control over issues like the Kurdish question, is filled with nationalist bureaucrats. Turkey's nationalist behaviour, therefore, related to its preferences in foreign policy, match with the identity of Turkish bureaucrats. In other words, Turkish bureaucrats who shape Turkey's foreign policy attitudes are graduates of the nationalist education system that put too much emphasis on issues in history, such as Sevres Treaty, and spread an idea that Europeans do not have very good intentions about Turkey. According to this supposition, when suitable ground is found, they will try to implement the amended version of the Sevres Treaty. Consequently, preferences of Turkish foreign policy are defined more or less within this mentality. On key issues like the Kurdish question, it becomes easy for bureaucrats, as well as politicians, to rage against the EU demands. From the realist perspective, it seems very reasonable to think that under the anarchical international system, European countries would try to weaken Turkey by allowing PKK activities in their countries and become advocators of Kurdish rights in Turkey.

2.5. Recent Trends

Recently, however, internal social structural changes have been influencing Turkey's foreign policy. The democratization of Turkish society has created a space for a variety of new groups and forces that have challenged the power of the Kemalist state. Hence, fanatic Kemalist doctrines have been undermined. This created a tension between the Kemalist elite and peripheral communities who marched into the center of politics in recent decades. During this period, Muslim Democrats appeared and have shaped Turkey's international policy. The EU process, on the other hand, is causing the nationalist ideology to rise as well. Independent media, Islamic media, and Kurdish media also became influential factors exerting pressures upon governments' decisions related to international policies of Turkey. In addition to the media pressure, the private sector emerged as a strong power-group. For example, the Turkish Industrialists and Businessmen Association (TUSIAD) is an outspoken advocate of reforms and proposed liberal policy initiatives on Kurdish issues, the EU, the Middle East, etc. They support expansion of economic ties with Russia, Central Asia, and the Middle East.

These internal developments change, culture, perspective and the identity of Turkish society and at the end Turkey's foreign policy attitude changes toward the neo-liberal paradigm. Despite the fact that Turkey has still had security concerns and fears which from time to time are reflected in her foreign policy attitude in recent years, it is evident that Turkish foreign policy appears to be more liberal then ever. Yet when it comes to security issues, Turkey's traditional fear, or paranoia if you will, resurfaces and its foreign policy attitude became clear along the line of realist paradigm. The Kurdish issue is one of the security issues of Turkey that marks Turkey's foreign policy preferences in the realist camp.

3. The PKK in Europe

As mentioned above, regarding the PKK issue, Turkish authorities, especially the military/police authorities, have accused the West either of being passive against the PKK or of supporting the terror organizations. Except Turgut Ozal, almost all Presidents, Prime Ministers, and the Chief of Staffs, have somehow accused Turkey's allies in the West in this matter. At first glance, there seems a contradiction here; on one hand, Turkey considers the European countries and the European Union as its allies, whereas on the other hand, the Turkish authorities have lined up to accuse their allies. This fear of the west can only be explained with the realist paradigm of Turkey. Since the PKK issue is a persistent matter which lived so long with the support provided by many countries, including European countries, to the terrorist organization,

Turkish state elitists formalized this support within the realist paradigm, stating that every state tries to weaken other states whenever they have the chance to do so.

Accepting this ideology as the base of the realist paradigm of the country, we see the elements of realist paradigms in Turkish authorities' criticism of European countries. Turkish President, for instance, criticized Turkey's western allies in recent years for not helping Turkey in her battle against terrorism [17]. The Prime Minister openly criticized a European country [Norway] by saying "a political party in a Scandinavian country is financially supporting the terror organization." [18] The Military Chief of Staff's criticism was among the most forward of these criticisms. He stated:

"Some countries turn a blind eye on the activities of this terrorist organization [PKK], and allow them to organize activities freely, to collect money, and to lobby against Turkey in their territories. Beyond this, when they arrest terrorists in their territories, either they do not prosecute them [Denmark] or even if they prosecute, they fail to put them in prison by allowing them to escape while 30 or more security guards are escorting them [Belgium]. In some cases, against the court decision to deport a terrorist, what these countries conduct is, instead of deporting these terrorists to Turkey, sending them to the camps of this terrorist organization to fight against the Turkish Armed Forces. One country, unfortunately, under the cloak of freedom of speech, by allowing the broadcast of a satellite TV channel which makes propagandist programs about the terrorist organization and incites violence, does not prefer to take sides with its ally [Turkey] but prefers to take sides with the terrorists. For instance, European Court of Justice accepted a case to rule whether the PKK is a terror organization or not. Well then, where are your decisions to fight against terrorism? Where is the cooperation which was undersigned in the line of decisions taken to combat against terrorism?" [19].

In fact, it might be true that in many European countries there could be PKK affiliated "civil" organizations. For instance, the following list of PKK affiliated organizations indicates that the PKK has influential organizations throughout Europe.

According to Turkish intelligence reports, Norway allowed the PKK's political wing, Kurdistan National Independence Front (ERNK), to open offices in 1999. PKK members in this country collect money (mostly by threat) from Kurds and Turks to finance the PKK. PKK members are allowed to seek political asylum. In Finland Finn-Kurdish Friendship associations and Kurdish Information Center and other associations are still operating. PKK sympathizers are allowed to collect money under the name of "charity." In Sweden, although the PKK is recognized as a terror organization, interestingly, ERNK and other PKK affiliated associations are allowed to be active. In this country there are more than 40 associations forming a federation under the name of "Swedish Kurdish Associations Federation." [18]

In Denmark also, the ERNK was allowed to open offices. Along with other PKK affiliated associations, the pro PKK satellite TV, Roj TV and MMC TV, have been broadcasting in this country. In this country, a ROJ TV correspondent was allowed to be in a joint press conference of the Turkish Prime Minister and Danish Prime Minister [20].

In Germany, there are 189 associations, clubs or federations that are organized under the roof of German Kurdish Associations Federations. In this country, PKK affiliated organizations are publishing a newspaper, journals and magazines [21].

In Brussels, the capital of the EU, Zubeyr Aydar, the head of the PKK, arranged to organize a press conference. Although, with pressure from Turkey, Belgian authorities did not allow the press conference, the head of the PKK was not arrested even though the EU recognizes the PKK as a terrorist organization [22]. In other European countries, pro-PKK organizations are listed as follows: In Austria, 9 associations; in Belgium, under the roof of European Kurdish Association Federation (KONKURD), 9 federations, 11 Associations and 2 sport clubs; in France, 11 associations; in Holland, 11 associations, 4 unions, 1 committee, and an education center; in England, 9 associations and a committee; in Switzerland, 20 associations, 5 unions; in Italy, 3 associations and 2 offices; in Greece, 10 associations; and in Spain, 3 associations [21].

Yet these PKK proxies exist throughout Europe not because of European countries want to weaken Turkey but because of the conjunctions of domestic issues which shapes their foreign policy attitudes.

4. EU's Foreign Policy Behavior: Neo-Liberal Paradigm

Unlike Turkish foreign policy behavior that follows the realist paradigm, thanks to their geographic location, cultural differences, economic wealth and political stability, domestic institutions of many European countries formed their foreign policy behaviors within the line of neo-liberal paradigm.

Although a few European countries may have different foreign policy behaviors, the majority of European countries and the EU have a foreign policy attitude that falls into the category of neo-liberal paradigm. This paradigm focuses heavily on the role of institutions in the international system. States do not coexist in a self-help system. A complex interdependency is the key concept to understand the international system. For neo-liberalists, besides states, non-state actors also play important roles in international relations. The concept of power for neo-liberal argument is different than that of realist argument. For neo-liberal theory, two types of power exist in international relations. One is defined as *hard power,* which describes the ability to get others to do what they otherwise would not do through threats or rewards. Both by economic carrots or military sticks, the ability to coax or coerce has long been the central element of power. The other definition is *soft power,* which indicates the ability to obtain desired outcomes because others want what you want. It is the ability to achieve goals through attraction rather than coercion. It works by convincing others to follow or getting them to agree to norms and institutions that produce the desired behavior [23].

In complex interdependence, military forces may be insignificant on some issues. Moreover, neither military force as the chief source of power nor security and its relative positions are overriding goals of states. "Exercising more dominant forms of power brings higher costs. Thus relative to cost, there is no guarantee that military means will be more effective than economic ones to achieve a given purpose." [23 pp 271-272]

For the neo-liberal paradigm, non-state actors and government bureaucracies are increasingly important in international affairs. Outcomes will be shaped by the distribution of resources and vulnerabilities; international relations will become crucial factors in decision-making processes; traditional security concerns will have little effect on issues and agendas of states' power; and institutions will act for transnational coalitions [24].

Collective action, high transaction costs, and information deficits or asymmetries are the main reasons why states need to form international institutions. And states want to be connected with institutions because an unanticipated outcome is too risky for states in the international arena to act as an individual entity, and because international institutions have the ability to reduce risk of an unanticipated outcome, states are more willing to participate in international institutions. When dealing with issues that exhibit increasing returns to scale, in case of frequently occurring unpleasantness, states are still less willing to withdraw from an institution in the face of unanticipated consequences.

There can be found many examples which show that the foreign policy behavior of European countries mostly falls into the category of the neo-liberal paradigm, not to mention the EU project itself as one of the "success" stories of the neo-liberal interdependency paradigm. Since it is widely discussed in neo-liberal literature, instead of giving neo-liberal examples in foreign affairs of European countries, here, we would like to discuss how the PKK issue fits into this paradigm and the foreign policy behaviors of European countries.

4.1. Why the EU Wants to be Involved in Turkey's Kurdish Question

It is a commonly told story that during his visit to Austria, a Danish journalist asked the opinion of Turkish President Suleyman Demirel about the Kurdish question. When Demirel told the journalist, "in my country there is no Kurdish question", the journalist responded, "in my country we do have a Kurdish question, because in Denmark there are 15 thousand Kurds residing." Whether true or not, this story tells us the gist of the problem of why Europeans want to be involved in the Kurdish question in Turkey.

From the mid 1990's until today, thanks to the growing number of Kurdish refugee movements in Europe, the PKK found an opportunity to organize within the Kurdish people who are uprooted from their home country. As time elapsed, these refugees became an economically and politically powerful community within Europe to influence European governments even without help of their foreign friends such as Armenian Diaspora and Church-based organizations. As a result of these Kurdish refugee movements, many European countries recognized that the Kurdish question is no longer a problem of Turkey alone but is a problem of Europeans, too. In this regard, because of their neo-liberal policy outlooks and democratic mechanisms which influence foreign policies of the governments, European countries have always been reluctant to see that the PKK is operating in their territories. For Europeans, it is impossible to uproot PKK organizations from their countries because of the PKK's good relationships with other non-governmental organizations, such as Church-based organizations. Therefore, Europeans want Turkey to solve this problem within democratic and political solutions.

In addition, European elites think that the PKK activities in Europe could not turn into a terror threat for their countries. They think it can cause some criminal problems, such as gangs or drug smuggling, but a terror threat can not emerge from the pro-PKK activities. For instance, the French government's "white book," which assesses potential terror threats for France, does not even mention the name of the PKK [25]. The police operations against the PKK members mainly in France and other European countries in February 2007, were another indication of how the European countries perceive the PKK terror in Europe. The nature of the police operations was not anti-terrorism operations but operation against money laundering [26].

Since there is no public pressure for European governments to take effective measures to avoid worsening the problem, (Europeans are afraid of having vandalism rise in their countries if they try to stop PKK's activities), European countries tend to be reluctant to take active precautions against PKK activities in Europe. Yet, this is not because they want to weaken Turkey, but because non-state actors are influencing the foreign policy preferences of European states.

4.2. Why Europeans are So Reluctant to Act Against the PKK

It is not a secret that European countries have a reluctant attitude in acting against the PKK terror. However, unlike the Turkish claim, this is not because they want to weaken Turkey by using the PKK as a club, but because they build their international behaviors upon the neo-liberal paradigm. This paradigm gives extra credit to the roles of non-state actors in international relations as we see Europeans being reluctant to interfere with activities of the PKK in Europe.

When we examine how the PKK is mobilized to derive support from Europeans, we can obtain an answer to the question why Europeans are reluctant to see the PKK as a terrorist organization. In order to win hearts and minds of Europeans, the PKK has launched a public relations campaign within Europe. In this campaign, establishing a church-based organization was the first priority of the PKK to reach out to Christian non-governmental organizations. In its campaign, the PKK has utilized the concerns and criticisms of some Christian organizations related to Turkey's policies about the rights of the Christian minority and extended these criticisms into the rights of Kurds as well. For example, the PKK's political wing, ERNK, accused 'Turkish Troops and KDP (to) Massacre Assyrian Christians in Kurdistan [27].' PKK has been successful in its campaign to reach out to Christian organizations to derive some support. For instance, when Abdullah Ocalan was arrested, *the World Council of Churches* in Switzerland released a press release which showed how pro-PKK organizations influence church-based organizations. The Statement indicates that members of the Kurdish community in Switzerland came to the World Council of Churches at the Ecumenical Centre in Geneva and presented an appeal concerning Abdullah Ocalan. The group expressed their concern about the arrest and detention of their leader Abdullah Ocalan by the Turkish authorities and called on the WCC to intervene in this matter [28].

Because of this relationship, the World Council of Churches released a press statement saying:

"The WCC has followed the issue of the Kurdish people over the years. Given the WCC's stated commitment to human rights and self-determination, the WCC calls on its member churches in Europe to seize this opportunity and urge their respective foreign policy behaviors governments to seek a peaceful political solution to the plight of the Kurdish people. The Kurdish community has expressed concerns about the physical safety and security of Abdullah Ocalan. The WCC appeals to the Turkish government to ensure Mr. Ocalan's safety and that he can receive visits from his lawyers. The WCC further appeals to the Turkish authorities to ensure Mr. Ocalan receives a fair trial in accordance with international norms and procedures of the Rule of Law." [28]

As it is seen in this press release, the *World Council of Churches,* with 336 associated Evangelical churches in more than 100 countries, urges their governments to intervene in the Kurdish question in Turkey. Beyond Church-based organizations, pro-PKK organizations in Europe have also successfully allied themselves with existing anti-Turkish organizations and associations to also derive support from them. For instance, Turkish intelligence agencies reported that the Armenian Diaspora in Europe helped PKK organizations to be recognized internationally. Some agencies reported that the Armenian Disaspora's logistic support was another reason why pro-PKK organizations operate so freely throughout Europe [29].

According to Abdullah Ocalan, this campaign was so successful that NGO's not only provided the PKK political support, but also this terrorist organization has also received some financial support from NGO's for MED TV, the pro-PKK satellite TV channel [30].

In addition, international human rights organizations reports on Turkey's use of force, such as uprooting Kurdish villages and homes from their lands, have also influenced European governments' attitudes toward Turkey. Because of the human rights reports, European countries, until recent years, had doubts about Turkey's human rights record. Recently, however, as a result of AKP government's democratization reforms and their initiative of 'zero tolerance to torture,' European countries changed their views. For the first time in 20 years, during which Turkey has been struggling to fight against Kurdish terrorism, European Union took the side of Turkey and criticized the PKK's terror campaign in its 2005 Progress report [31].

5. Why Turkey Wants to Join the EU

As there is skepticism against the EU, one might raise the question "Why then does Turkey still want to be a member of the EU?" One answer to this question is, although some statist elitists are thinking that some European countries carry the intention of dividing Turkey, the united structure of the European Union provides strategic security opportunities that can prevent ethnic partitioning for its members. In other words, while statist elitists criticize the attitudes of European states from a realist perspective on one hand, on the other, they want to use the European Union's structure to prevent Kurds from seceding. Suleyman Demirel, during his Presidency, formalized this perspective as the following: "the relationships between Turkey and the EU, despite conjectural problems, is a priority of Turkish foreign policy. In this sense, our national interests and vision for our future require us to build and develop our relationship with the European Union. This is the Turkey's strategic vision and goal that cannot be omitted. EU membership is Turkey's strategic interest." [32]

As it is also seen here, the same Suleyman Demirel who accused Europeans of having an evil intention to divide Turkey, at the same time advocates EU membership. At first glance, it seems that accusing Europeans and demanding EU membership at the same time is a contradiction, but when analyzed, it becomes clear that the statist elites criticize the Europeans when they put their finger on Turkey's sore point; "comments or demands reminding Turkish state elites of the treaty of Sevres," whereas Turkish republican elitists want to join the EU for strategic concerns such as for security, stability and protecting the integrity of their country.

6. Conclusion

The schism between Turkey and European countries regarding taking effective measures against the PKK is an outcome of different paradigms. European countries have allowed PKK members to be organized within their territories. Because of this, Turkey always blamed European countries for their "support" for the PKK. When blaming its allies, Turkish authorities failed to understand the differences of perspectives between the European countries and Turkey. On this issue, the two sides, the European countries and Turkey, have two different opinions on international relations. In their foreign affairs, most European countries, especially the north-western ones, see the world from the perspective of interdependency theories. However, Turkish authorities, on the other hand, see the world as an "anarchy," from the viewpoint of the realist perspective. Therefore, conflicts occur due to the different perspectives of understanding the issue of the PKK.

The PKK has long been able to establish associations throughout Europe. What Turkish authorities want from their European allies is to close down these associations and cut off the PKK's financial support which comes through these associations. Yet, European countries are reluctant to take such measures. How the parties read the existence of these associations and their pro-PKK activities throughout Europe is very much shaped by their foreign policy behaviors. For instance, the Turkish side has a suspicious outlook towards the Europeans. This attitude comes from its history, cultural differences, and ethnically fragmented society that eventually shape its foreign policy behavior. European state elites, on the other hand, are doubtful about Turkey's human rights records. In addition, foreign policy behaviors of European countries are shaped by their internal society structure, in which NGOs play a significant role in influencing governmental activities. Hence, European foreign policy attitudes fall into the category of neo-liberal foreign policy paradigms. These two paradigms, realist and neo-liberal paradigms, are the reason why Turkey and European countries do not understand each other on the issue of the Kurdish question.

References

[1]   J.G. Ruggie, What makes the world hang together? Neo-utilitarianism and the social constructivist challenge", *International Organization*, **52/4** (1998) 855-885.
[2]   A. Wendt, *Social Theory of international politics,* Cambridge: Cambridge University Press; 2003, p 1.
[3]   A. Wendt, Anarchy is what states make of it, *International Organization*, **46/2** (1992) 391-425.
[4]   K.N. Waltz, *Theory of International Politics*, New York: Random House; 1979, 114.
[5]   *Milliyet*, 2006, October 21.
[6]   *Hurriyet*, 2006, October 21.
[7]   G. Jenkins, *Context and circumstance: The Turkish Military and politics*, Oxford: Oxford University Press; 2001.
[8]   W. Hale, *Türkiye'de Ordu ve Siyaset.* Ankara, Turkey: Hil Yayınları; 1998.
[9]   Treaty of Sevres, 1920, August 10.
[10] K. Kirisci, La Turquie entre évolution des mentalités et euroscepticisme, In Billion Didier, Editor. *La Turquie vers un rendez-vous décisif avec l'Union Européenne*, Paris, France: Iris/PF; 2004, pp.83-89,
[11] *Hürriyet*, 1995, July 24.
[12] S. Laçiner, Ayrilikci televizyon yayinlarinda dis destek ve nedenleri, *Avrasya Dosyası.* **8/4** (2002) 227-252.
[13] *Zaman*, 2000, December 8. 'Kürtçe TV PKK Söylemi'.
[14] General Yasar Buyukanit's Inaugural Speech, Aug 30 2006 [Online] Available at: URL: www.tsk.mil.tr
[15] *NTV/MSNBC*, 2001, January 3. 'Büyükelçiden Sevr Sendromu İddiası'.
[16] U. Ozdag, *Türkiye, Kuzey Irak ve PKK, bir gayri nizami savaş'in anatomisi*, Ankara, Turkey: ASAM; 1999, p. 145.
[17] Turkish 10th President A. Nejdet Sezer's talk which is presented at the opening session of strategic foresight: 2023 workshop, 2006, September 10; Sezer's talk at the opening of TBMM's 22nd Period Fifth Legislative Year, 2006 January 10; and the talk he presented in a conference at military academies, [Online] Available from; URL: www.chankaya.gov.tr [2006, December 4].
[18] O. Sert, A Scandinavian country supports PKK, *Hürriyet*, 2005, July 23.
[19] General Yasar Buyukanit's opening speech delivered at the War Academy. 2006, October 2. [Online] Available from; URL: www.tsk.mil.tr
[20] H. Cucuk, Danimarka'nin bitmeyen PKK aski, *Aksiyon*, No.572, 2005, November 21.
[21] *Hürriyet*, 2005, July 23.
[22] *Milliyet*, 2005, August 21. 'Aydar'a yasak Avrupa mantigi'.
[23] R. Keohane, J.S. Nye, *Power and interdependence*, New York: Longman; 2001, p. 218
[24] S.J. Nye, Neorealism and neoliberalism, *World Politics,* **40/2** (1988 January).
[25] *La France face au terrorisme* (Le livre blanc du gouvernement sur la sécurité intérieure face au terrorisme), Paris, France: La Découverte française; 2006.

[26] 'Fransa'da 14 PKK'li tutuklandi,' [Online] Available from; URL: www.cnnturk.com [2007, February 10].

[27] National Liberation Front of Kurdistan, Press Release, 1997, December 18.

[28] World Council of Churches, Office of Communication, Press Release, 1999, February 19.

[29] C. Kazdagli, 'Kanlı örgütün son umudu İslam', *Aksiyon*, No: 35, 1995, May 08.

[30] S. Laçiner, Ayrilikci televizyon yayinlarinda dis destek ve nedenleri: MED-TV Örneği,, *Avrasya Dosyası*. **8/2** (2002 Summer) 329-371.

[31] *European Commission 2005 Progress report: Turkey*.

[32] Turkish 9th President Suleyman Demirel's opening speech of the 20th Period, 4th Legislative Year of Turkish General Assembly, 1998, October 1.

Understanding and Responding to the Terrorism Phenomenon
O. Nikbay and S. Hancerli (Eds.)
IOS Press, 2007

Narcoterrorism in Turkey:
The Financing of PKK-KONGRA GEL
from Illicit Drug Business

Ahmet PEK[a] and Behsat EKICI[b]

[a]*Head of Department of Anti-Smuggling and Organized Crime, Turkish National Police*
[b]*University of Pittsburgh, USA*

Abstract. The non-state actors of security studies such as transnational organized crime and terrorism are more complicated and challenging in terms of empirical support. The comparative decrease in state sponsorship of terrorism after the end of cold war led the scholars, law enforcement agencies and intelligence organizations to investigate the financial resources of global terrorism. The nexus between terrorists and organized crime groups is based on ad hoc interdependence rather than alleged continual convergence. However, terrorist organizations are more involved into organized crime activities without cooperating with the transnational organized crime groups. This paper examines the evolution of PKK-KONGRA GEL's involvement into illicit drug business from taxing the traffickers to distribution of heroin over the Western European street markets.

Keywords. Transnational organized crimes, drugs, narcoterrorism, financing of terrorism, PKK-KONGRA-GEL, international security, intelligence

Introduction

The procurement of financial resources depends on the ideology and scale of the terrorist organization. While some of the narco-guerilla groups such as Revolutionary Armed Forces of Colombia (FARC) and Liberation Tigers of Tamil Eelam (LTTE) may predominantly finance their activities from the illicit drug business, some other terrorist groups may be dependent on state sponsorship, charities, extortion or legal companies. Much has been written by scholars about the symbiotic relationship of drugs and terrorism, but common deficiencies are dependence on secondary data analysis and lack of evidence. While law enforcement and intelligence agencies put forward allegations of narcoterrorist financing, the terrorist organizations strictly deny involvement in the narcotics business since it undermines the propaganda campaigns. Thus, narcoterrorism studies need utmost scrutiny because of the high controversy and criticality of the issue. Apart from academic research, the collaboration of law enforcement investigators and intelligence analysts is essential to accumulate substantial evidence and evaluations in narcoterrorism cases.

Recognizing the need for better analysis, the Narcoterrorism Project was launched in 2003 with the encouragement of the Head of Department of Anti-Smuggling and Organized Crime (KOM) and the Director of Central Narcotics Division. The project was run by the analysts of KOM but it was supported by National Intelligence Agency,

Intelligence and Anti-Terrorism Departments of Turkish National Police and General Command Gendarmerie. Apart from the national agencies, liaison officers from Interpol, The German Federal Criminal Police Office BKA, USA Drug Enforcement Agency (DEA) and several European law enforcement agencies sent relevant documents to the analysis center in central narcotics division. Hundreds of narcoterrorism cases were analyzed in 2 years with data from National Organized Crime and Terrorism Databases, case reports, the statements of the criminals and PKK-KONGRA GEL members, law enforcement and intelligence reports (national/international) and Interpol investigations/ reports. The purpose of the project was to find out potential evidence rather than theoretical explanations to the narcoterrorism phenomenon. This paper is a brief outline of the project report on the descriptive analysis of narcoterrorism cases in Turkey.

1. Overview of Narcoterrorism in Turkey

Operating under a code of secrecy has ever been a priority for terrorists and organized crime networks. Especially, the illicit drug business has been carried out by highly professionalized and sophisticated cell structures of terrorist organizations on a need-to-know basis. However, substantial evidence has been found in 332 cases about the involvement of Kurdistan Workers' Party (PKK-KONGRA GEL), Revolutionary People's Liberation Party/Front (DHKP/C) and The Turkish Communist Party/Marxist-Leninist (TKP/ML) terrorist organizations in the illicit drug business. The most substantial evidence was the confessions of several PKK-KONGRA GEL leaders (i.e Abdullah Ocalan and Semdin Sakik), seizures of tons of drugs in 56 shelters and residential centers of the organization, and Interpol investigations in various European countries.

The PKK-KONGRA GEL members were involved in more than 90 percent of the 332 cases starting from 1984, and the narcoterrorism connections of the DHKP/C and TKP/ML organizations remained negligible in comparison with the PKK-KONGRA GEL. While there is no recent evidence for the nexus of DHKP/C and TKP/ML members after 2000, the involvement of PKK-KONGRA GEL members is confirmed in our up-to-date operations in 2005 and 2006. However, the influence of drug-related antagonism was observed more severely among the leaders of TKP/ML, which led the organization into fragmentation by the mid 1990s. An active exclusion campaign was launched by the East Anatolian Committee (DABK) against the Conference Branch after the conviction of four leaders from the Conference Branch (OPK) for heroin trafficking in 1994. As a counter strategy, nearly 40 members of the conference group declared independence from the party under the umbrella of the Salvation Army of Turkish Workers and Peasantry (TIKKO). The counternarcotics investigations revealed that top leaders from the DHKP/C organization, including Dursun Karatas, Pasa Guven, Faruk Ereren and Semih Genc, were the organizers of several transnational heroin trafficking cases overland through Turkcy. Moreover, Adana provincial leader of the DHKP/C was arrested in 1998 with 603 kg of cocaine in Mersin Free Trade Area together with four other members of the organization. The narcoterrorist connections of PKK-KONGRA GEL, TKP/ML and DHKP/C organizations are studied comprehensively in the KOM report, but this paper will focus on the nexus of the PKK-KONGRA GEL in five different categories: taxing and extortion, cultivation and production, trafficking, street delivery and money laundering through MED TV (later changed the name to MEDYA TV).

2. Why and How PKK-KONGRA GEL is Involved in Illicit Drug Business

A decade after its inception, the PKK-KONGRA GEL became one of the most active, effective, and largest terrorist groups operating in the Middle East and Europe with active cadres of thousands of militants and several thousand active supporters [1]. This success in terms of "enlargement" and "offensive campaign" brought rigorous organizational demands and financial resources. The PKK-KONGRA GEL used the Diaspora and Turkish migrants living on the European continent as bridgeheads, with the players setting up networks to earn cash for its cause [2]. It is observed that the PKK-KONGRA GEL established symbiotic relationships with transnational organized crime groups to purchase arms/ammunition, maintain the logistics of its militant cadre, and perform propaganda activities.

A great amount of Southwest Asian heroin is transshipped over the Balkan route towards the main consumption markets in Europe and North America. According to annual United Nations Office on Drugs and Crime (UNODC) reports for the past several years; successively Iran, Pakistan, and Turkey have conducted the highest levels of opiate seizures in the world [3, 4, 5]. The importance of the route has increased during the new opium boom in Afghanistan since the overthrow of the Taliban in 2001. Opium cultivation has continued to increase since 2002 and reached a record level in 2006 by cultivation of over 165,000 hectares [6]. The Balkan route starts from Afghanistan and continues through Iran, Turkey and European countries. The southeastern provinces of Turkey on the Iranian border have been traditional transit destinations not only for the drug traffickers but also for all kinds of transnational criminal activities including terrorism. The PKK-KONGRA GEL abused the common ties of language, culture and religion among the residents of Southeastern Turkey, Northern Iraq and Northwestern Iran to propagandize its terrorist campaign and extort financial sources.

Particularly since 1984, the convergence of drug trafficking and terrorism within the same territory has been a facilitator for the cooperation of organized crime groups and the PKK-KONGRA GEL. The B1, B2, C1, C2, K1, K2, K3, A1, A2, S1 and S2 families were protected and taxed by the PKK-KONGRA GEL after the third congress which recommended extorting money from Kurdish organized crime groups, businessmen and contractors [7]. The extended network of these families in Germany, Netherlands, UK, Hungary, Belgium, Austria, Italy and Spain enabled the PKK-KONGRA GEL to contact the grey market of small arms and extort money from the street delivery of heroin. Especially, the B1 family provided weapons and ammunition for the PKK-KONGRA GEL through their well established network of connections to weapons traders in Europe. Moreover, the family covered nearly 40 percent of the expenses of MED TV until the leader of the family was arrested by a joint operation of Turkish and Dutch counternarcotics investigators [8].

The co-existence and cooperation of profit-oriented organized crime groups and ideology-oriented terrorists survived until the motivations of PKK-KONGRA GEL leaders in Europe intensified because of the high profitability of drugs. Several armed clashes and fierce assassinations of opponent groups have been reported by the law enforcement agencies of the Netherlands, Belgium and the U.K. Interpol [9] reports the assassination of active PKK-KONGRA GEL militant Huseyin Akpinar in Amsterdam by Muhittin Erik, who was working as a clandestine lab assistant for the B1 family. The motivation for the assassination was the non-delivery and non-payment of 40 kilos of heroin.

Over time, the profitability led the PKK-KONGRA GEL to eliminate the mediators who get the lion's share from the illicit drug business. By the early 1990's, while a kilo of heroin was US$ 3,000-4,000 in Southwest Asia, the price increased to US$ 45,000 in Germany, US$ 54,000 in the UK, US$ 160,000 in Spain and US$ 353,000 in Finland [5]. Moreover, the purity levels decreased from 90 percent in Southwest Asia to less than 8 percent in Western Europe, which indicates that the organization could make nearly 1000 times profit if it handles the drugs without middlemen. The wide network of the PKK-KONGRA GEL from Central Asia to Western Europe enabled the organization to take part in every phase of the illicit drug business starting from cultivation to distribution on the streets of European countries. The investigations for the KISMETIM-1 operation revealed that, during the 1990's, the PKK-KONGRA GEL was a shareholder in trafficking multiple tons of drugs from Southwest Asia to Western Europe through the Eastern Mediterranean route by Kurdish organized crime groups. The PKK-KONGRA GEL also established the networks of distribution in the illicit drug markets of Western Europe to maximize the profits from drugs. Apart from the satellite criminal networks, PKK-KONGRA GEL oriented cultural associations and Kurdish political refugees were abused for the distribution of drugs.

2.1. Taxing and Extortion of Drug Traffickers

After launching active operations in 1984, PKK-KONGRA GEL began taxing and commissioning drug traffickers and cannabis cultivators in southeastern Turkey, northern Iraq, the Bekaa valley and northwestern Iran. Their territorial control over the mountainous borders with Iran enabled the organization to establish illegal customs checkpoints for the drug traffickers who were using the same transit destinations. The PKK-KONGRA GEL helped potentially weak traffickers who were having trouble with passing the mountainous borders. The earlier commission rate was 1000 DM per kilo of heroin, which was collected by threatening, blackmailing and abduction of disobedient traffickers. The taxing and commissioning activities over the Iranian border were coordinated by Osman Ocalan (a.k.a. Ferhat). Abdullah Ocalan confessed that

"On the borders, a certain amount of money is collected from traffickers under the title of taxes…I learned that some people in the organization, in particular my brother, were trafficking drugs to Europe though Iran, Zagros and Romania… at certain points, it is obvious that I could not control the organization very well…" [10].

On October 22, 1998, 107.680 kilos of heroin were seized and 28 individuals were arrested in Hakkari/Yuksekova by local KOM officers. One of the defendants named Zikri Demir acknowledged the taxation of heroin traffickers by the PKK-KONGRA GEL;

"We have to give 1000 DM to the PKK-KONGRA GEL per kilo of heroin and I was obligated to tribute nearly 1,000,000 DM annually" [11].

Secondly, the PKK-KONGRA GEL established symbiotic relationships with organized crime groups such as the B2, C2, S2, K2 and Y families, which were operating over the same territory and trafficking heroin from Iran. On December 7, 1996, Istanbul Narcotics Police units seized 750 kg of morphine base and 2 kg of opium with 11 suspects. Hursit Han, who was identified as the organizer of the incident, stated that

"Four individuals headed by Osman Tim demanded money on behalf of the PKK-KONGRA GEL. Fearing the assassination/abduction of my relatives in Yuksekova I had to donate 1 billion Turkish Liras. As far as I know, Adnan Yildirim donated 40,000 DM and Savas Buldan donated 70,000 DM" [11].

Upon questioning by the judge during his trials in Imrali Island, Abdullah Ocalan stated that the annual turnover of the organization was around 200 million dollars and several organized crime groups transferred funds to the PKK-KONGRA GEL:

"Behçet Canturk was supporting our organization as well. The PKK-KONGRA GEL has collected money from the Cihangir family in Yüksekova, the Türk family and the Kahramanlar family in Mardin. Besides them, financial support has been provided by many businessmen, whose names I do not know…Moreover, Osman Ocalan, with the code name of Ferhat, is collecting the money from people who are trafficking drugs, arms and ammunition. In addition, there are some structures called the customs units of the organization, located along the borders. They collect the money as well from illicit transiters... [10]"

The taxing and commissioning activities of the PKK-KONGRA GEL continued in Europe. Apart from the individual sellers, the Kurdish heroin distribution networks were extorted on monthly bases depending on their capacity. The German focus magazine reported in September 7, 1999 that the nexus of the PKK-KONGRA GEL and drugs was once more revealed by the dismantling of a heroin distribution network in Hamburg and Hannover. The police authorities emphasized that the network transferred 1 Million Marks to the PKK-KONGRA GEL per month over the past 9 month period. All of the members were born in Bingol and the network made over 250 million Marks of profit annually [12].

2.2. Drug Cultivation and Production

The analysis of the investigation reports revealed that the PKK-KONGRA GEL controlled illicit cannabis cultivation fields in the mountainous parts of East and Southeast Anatolia. The PKK-KONGRA GEL not only taxed the existing cultivators but also forced pro-PKK-KONGRA GEL farmers to cultivate cannabis on behalf of the organization. Multiple tons of hashish/cannabis has been seized from the shelters of PKK-KONGRA GEL. The cannabis cultivation and hashish seizures in the PKK-KONGRA GEL shelters peaked between 1993 and 1997. More interestingly, the seizures of significant amounts of cannabis roots and seeds in the shelters indicate that the PKK-KONGRA GEL was actively involved in the cultivation of cannabis in the mountainous parts of northern Iraq, northwestern Iran and Southeastern Anatolia. As seen in Table 1, 470 kilos of hashish and 180 kilos of cannabis seeds were seized in a PKK-KONGRA GEL shelter in Beytussebap district of Sirnak province on December 16, 1994, by the local counterterrorism units.

On August 01, 1994, 13 individuals were arrested with 2 kilos of hashish and 120.000 roots of cannabis in Diyarbakir province. One of the defendants named Remzi Inceoren stated that the PKK-KONGRA GEL established sophisticated structures for cannabis cultivation within surrounding villages of Diyarbakir province. He confessed cultivating cannabis on behalf of the PKK-KONGRA GEL over 250-300 hectares in cooperation with other PKK-KONGRA GEL members. His interrogation led to the seizure of 1,150,000 additional cannabis plants on August 12-16, 1994, by the joint interdiction teams of local police and gendarmerie. Currently, 9,300,000 cannabis roots have been seized in Diyarbakir/Kulp district in July 2006 from 11 fields controlled by the PKK-KONGRA GEL militants. During the eradication efforts over three days, PKK-KONGRA GEL militants continually opened fire on Gendarmerie forces. 14 terrorists were killed in the same district in March 2006 [13].

Table 1. Some cannabis seizures in PKK-KONGRA GEL shelters

Date	Providence	Amount
31.07.1993	Hakkari	439 kg hashish
23.10.1993	Bingöl	16 sacks of hashish
18.12.1993	Van	600 kg hashish
15.01.1994	Şırnak	700 kg hashish/ 130 kg cannabis
23.03.1994	Hakkari	328 kg hashish
22.06.1994	Diyarbakır	15 sacks of hashish
15.07.1994	Bitlis	17,000 roots of cannabis
09.08.1994	Şırnak	400 kg cannabis
18.08.1994	Diyarbakır	1500 kg hashish/1,467,000 roots of cannabis
16.12.1994	Şırnak	470 kg hashish/ 180 kg cannabis seeds
15.03.1995	Şırnak	300 kg hashish
31.03.1995	Şırnak	850 kg hashish
28.04.1995	Hakkari	750 kg hashish
15.04.1995	Hakkari	500 kg hashish
25.10.1997	Şırnak	10 kg 600 gr hashish/6,4 kg cannabis seeds

According to Observatoire Geopolitique Des Drugs (OGD) [14],

"The rebel Kurdistan Workers' Party (PKK-KONGRA GEL) has set up laboratories in areas under its control and organized distribution networks in Europe. Mafias, feudal paramilitaries, and guerrillas are all in fierce competition to control the profits from the heroin trade."

By the end of the 1980's PKK-KONGRA GEL members also explored ways to produce heroin from the morphine base. The intelligence reports indicated that PKK-KONGRA GEL established mobile heroin laboratories over the mountainous borders with Iran and Iraq. The well established clandestine network of PKK-KONGRA GEL began to purchase morphine base and acetic anhydride for heroin production. Instead of purchasing heroin, producing it from the morphine base was much cheaper and secure for the organization. Moreover, they were able to obtain 1100 grams of heroin from 1000 grams of morphine base and they were able to reduce the purity levels of the heroin to increase the profitability. One of the Iranian citizens arrested for drug trafficking reported that:

"PKK-KONGRA GEL has established several drug labs in Urumiye-Aliabat District of Iran under the control of Osman Ocalan. The chemists receive 40-50,000 Toman per kg for producing heroin. After the production heroin is transferred to the Banya village (Iran) to be transferred to Yuksekova (Turkey) under the control of Osman Ocalan's militants." [11]

The official reports of KOM highlighted dismantling of two heroin laboratories which were directly run by the PKK-KONGRA GEL members. However, numerous PKK-KONGRA GEL members were arrested in Turkey, Germany and UK in 17 additional heroin laboratory cases. These 17 cases are not evaluated as PKK-KONGRA GEL activities since there was no substantial evidence that the individuals were acting on behalf of the PKK-KONGRA GEL for heroin production. The first heroin laboratory of the PKK-KONGRA GEL was dismantled in Tekirdag Province on March 7, 1995, on a farm owned by the K1 family. Together with the heroin, morphine base and acetic anhydride, numerous propaganda documents, brochures, PKK-KONGRA GEL flags, weapons and ammunition were seized at the farm. Haci Bekir Konuklu was the leader of the K1 family and an active member of the PKK-KONGRA GEL terrorist organization. The investigations revealed that K1 was transferring 10 percent of the drug revenues to the PKK-KONGRA GEL's accountants in Europe. More interestingly, K1 had established strong relationships with the A1 family based on kinship ties. Apart from participating in the terror campaign and armed encounter, several members of the A1 family were arrested in Turkey and Europe for transferring drug money to the PKK-KONGRA GEL. The second heroin laboratory was dismantled in Istanbul by the Istanbul Narcotics Division on November 12, 1998. Four PKK-KONGRA GEL members were arrested for heroin production in this laboratory, including Fethullah Dur who was the Maltepe district leader of HADEP (Political Branch of the PKK-KONGRA GEL, founded on 11th May 1994), and transferring the heroin funds for political activities of the PKK-KONGRA GEL.

2.3. Drug Trafficking

After the 1990's, the PKK-KONGRA GEL enjoyed more profits from the illicit drug business through trafficking of heroin, morphine base, opium, hashish, acetic anhydride and synthetic drugs, in addition to taxing the drug traffickers and organizing cannabis cultivation. The PKK-KONGRA GEL used its well established, trained, armed and hierarchical cadre for the clandestine drug business. Since both the drug traffickers and terrorist organizations operate on cell structures, scrupulously deployed PKK-KONGRA GEL members adopted the new illicit environment in a short time. The drug related activities were organized by top level regional coordinators and the PKK-KONGRA GEL particularly used unconvicted members for the transfer of the drugs. Although PKK-KONGRA GEL leaders handled the drug business with the utmost care, the investigations (in Germany, UK, Italy, Netherlands and Turkey), Interpol reports and statements of the convicted PKK-KONGRA GEL members and drug seizures in PKK-KONGRA GEL's residential centers revealed the active involvement of the PKK-KONGRA GEL in drug trafficking. Particularly, the project Asena/Anadolu, run by joint efforts of KOM and BKA (Germany), revealed that the PKK-KONGRA GEL was monopolizing and professionalizing drug trafficking, cooperating with Kurdish organized crime groups and forcing the political Kurdish refugees into drug trafficking. Not only was the overwhelming role of the PKK-KONGRA GEL in illicit drug trafficking reported by law enforcement agencies in Western Europe, but also the judicial authorities continuously highlighted the narcoterrorism connection of the PKK-KONGRA GEL. For example, the chief prosecutor of Frankfurt highlighted that the PKK-KONGRA GEL is affiliated with 80 percent of the drug trafficking in Europe and the organization purchased arms and ammunitions by the money generated from drug trafficking [1].

In fact, the figures given by Turkish authorities overlap with the Interpol findings. According to Interpol records the Agency investigated over 100 cases of PKK-KONGRA GEL members' involvement in drug trafficking. The Interpol report further concluded that more than 15 tons of different types of drugs, reaching a base value of millions of US dollars, were seized [9]. The Chairman of the Human Rights Commission of the Turkish Grand National Assembly (TGNA) conducted an interview with Semdin SAKIK at the Diyarbakir Prison. Sakik provided the following impressive information:

"The resource of our money was drug trafficking. The PKK-KONGRA GEL and Apo (Abdullah Ocalan) have always gotten a big share from the drug trafficking on the Turkey-Middle East Route. We bought arms with the money gained from there." [10]

Table 2. Summary of drug seizures from PKK-KONGRA GEL

	OHAL territory	Other territories	Total
Case	107	225	332
Heroine	181	3,370	3.551 kg
Hashish	7,812	15,588	23.383 kg
Cannabis	11.784.003 root		11.784.003 root
Morphine base	42	4,263	4.305 kg
Acetic anhydride		26,190	26,190 litters
Cocaine		710	710 kg
Opium gum		8	8 kg
Amphetamine		277.000 tabl	277.000 tabl
Sodium carbonade		1,080	1.080 kg
Drug lab	1	1	2 labs
Total Defendants 762 Persons			

21 kilos of heroin were seized in Duisburg, Germany on September 17, 1992, in a truck registered to the Kaya Transportation Company. Upon receiving the case report from BKA, the Mersin KOM division investigated the owners and activities of the company. The investigations revealed that Osman Kaya, who was the owner of the company, was providing weapons and ammunition to the PKK-KONGRA GEL with the illicit drug money. Further investigations led to the seizure of 18 Kalashnikovs and 4000 rounds of ammunition from the PKK-KONGRA GEL concealed in one of the trucks of the same company on April 12, 1993. Interpol [9] reported that 73.5 kilos of heroin were seized in a truck after joint investigations of the law enforcement agencies of Turkey, Germany and Austria on December 12, 1989. The German driver of the truck reported that he trafficked 110 kilos of heroin in 1999 on behalf of the PKK-KONGRA GEL and delivered the heroin to PKK-KONGRA GEL members in Amsterdam. However, the seizures in numerous residential centers of PKK-KONGRA GEL has been more convincing evidence for the involvement of the organization in drug trafficking. As seen in Table 3, the German Police seized 9,745 kg of heroin from the five PKK-KONGRA GEL members in a political refugee camp in 1993. Apart from their active terrorism records, one of the defendants had connections to the K3 family, which is one of the notorious organized crime networks financing the PKK-KONGRA GEL through drug trafficking.

Table 3. Some seizures in political refugee camps and residential centers

Date	Providence	Amount	The place
1993	Germany	9.745 kg heroin	refugee camp
01.09.1994	Hakkari	1 kg heroin	residential center
13.08.1994	Diyarbakir	60 kg heroin	residential center
13.08.1994	Hakkari	1 kg heroin	residential center
12.10.1994	Van	23 kg hashish	residential center
13.02.1996	Sirnak	37 kg hashish	residential center
14.10.1996	Diyarbakir	49.571 kg hashish	residential center

The Central Narcotics Division of KOM conducted a comprehensive investigation project under the name of MATRUSKA in collaboration with the DEA Ankara Office and Drug Enforcement Agencies of Russia. The controlled delivery operation and interdiction in Elazig province led to the seizure of 3 tons 496 liters of acetic anhydride with 14 individuals in Turkey and 4 individuals in the Russian Federation. The initial reports from the Russian law enforcement agencies revealed that the providers of Acetic Anhydride had strong relations with the PKK-KONGRA GEL's Russian Federation representative (ŞIYAR Code). In their residences several training videos, posters, books, and magazines of the PKK-KONGRA GEL were found. Moreover, their walls were decorated with Abdullah Ocalan's posters. Apart from drug trafficking, Operation MATRUSKA had implications about ongoing heroin production activities of the PKK-KONGRA GEL.

2.4. Street Delivery of Drugs

The street delivery of drugs is the last stand of the illicit drug business for terrorists and organized crime groups which require extra professionalism and a comprehensive network of distribution. The PKK-KONGRA GEL started by taxing the drug traffickers and ended up engaging in all phases of the illicit drug business including street delivery of heroin in Europe. The heroin markets in the Netherlands, Germany and some parts of the U.K were controlled by the PKK-KONGRA GEL by the mid 1990s. According to Sahin [2] the PKK-KONGRA GEL did not need an exclusive organizational structure to deal with drugs; its already existing migrant Diaspora of supporters in European countries was the necessary tool for street dealing and further, major heroin routes toward the consuming zones were passing through its area of operation. As seen in Table 4, when the activities of the PKK-KONGRA GEL culminated by the early 1990's, the organization had established 298 cultural and political associations in Europe. However, the number of associations decreased to 211 by 2004 in parallel with the waning of political and armed campaigns. The leaders of the PKK-KONGRA GEL organized drug related activities from the terrorism camps in northern Iraq, northwestern Iran and southeastern Turkey, but they coordinated heroin distribution from the cultural associations in Europe. The encrypted communication network, hierarchical structure and courier system for the terrorist campaign was used for transfer and distribution of drugs. The use of Kurdish language in communication complicated the electronic surveillance and use of undercover agents to penetrate the organization.

The PKK-KONGRA GEL particularly used unemployed refugees and Kurdish children for heroin distribution. European governments and law enforcement agencies have exercised very little control on the Kurdish political refugee camps. The atmosphere of freedom helped the PKK-KONGRA GEL organize the political refugees for heroin distribution and take control of drug markets in Europe [15]. In 1992, Hamburg local police in Germany arrested numerous Kurdish children aged between 8 and 12, (including a child of 8 carrying firearms) brought from southeastern Turkey for heroin distribution on the streets of Hamburg. During the interrogation, all these children confessed that the PKK-KONGRA GEL was forcing them to sell drugs since they did not have penal responsibility. The authorities in Hamburg estimated that the PKK-KONGRA GEL earns more than 56 million DM from the narcotics trade [16]. The Hamburg

Criminal Police arrested a Kurdish network of drug dealers on 15 September 1993. An 11-year-old child, who was also arrested with the other members of the band, later confessed that the PKK-KONGRA GEL brought them from Turkey to Germany via illegal means in order to make them sell drugs for the organization [17]. The Stuttgart Police arrested 76 Kurdish Origin Turkish citizens after six weeks of investigation and interdiction against street dealers in January 1994. Almost all the arrestees were political refugees and among them, there were 6 people who previously were convicted in Turkey in relation to PKK-KONGRA GEL terrorist organizations with charges ranging from aiding and abetting and armed strikes against Turkish military forces [18].

Table 4. Number of PKK-KONGRA GEL associations in Europe

Country	1993	2004
Germany	178	84
France	23	5
Sweden	20	20
Switzerland	13	19
Netherlands	12	11
Austria	10	7
England	10	8
Denmark	9	8
Belgium	6	10
Greece	6	10
Other	11	29
Total	298	211

Initially the Kurdish organized crime groups in Europe got on well with the PKK-KONGRA GEL by paying taxes but by the end of the 1990's, PKK-KONGRA GEL's monopolization efforts in heroin distribution irritated particularly powerful organized crime groups such as the B1 family. Apart from paying taxes, the members of A1, K3, K1, K4, S1 and S2 families helped the PKK-KONGRA GEL with heroin distribution in Europe. For example, Sertif Kitay, who is one of the members of K3, stated that he has seen and done some "street-level" drug dealing, in addition to delivery of organizational publications to a refugee camp in Germany in 1992 where he remained until his 'political refugee' status was granted by the authorities [18]. The B1 family provided financial resources for the PKK-KONGRA GEL and financed MED TV until the early 2000's, but the atmosphere has changed since Huseyin Baybasin (the leader of the organization) was arrested in 2000 by a joint operation of KOM and drug investigation units of the Dutch police. Several armed conflicts have been reported from the Netherlands and the UK since 2000. Two individuals died and 20 were wounded in an armed conflict in London between PKK-KONGRA GEL members and the Kurdish group under the name of BOMBACILAR which is working on behalf of the B1 family to suppress opponent heroin distribution networks [11]. According to Bovenkerk and Yesilgoz [8], several fierce armed conflicts and assassinations took place in the Netherlands between the members of the PKK-KONGRA GEL and the B1 family to establish a monopoly of heroin distribution networks.

3. Money Laundering and Financing MED TV

Over the years the PKK-KONGRA GEL needed sophisticated financial structures to coordinate the collection and distribution of legal/illegal funds for the needs of militant cadres, weapons and ammunition, propaganda activities and TV/broadcasting expenses. The financial branch of the Kurdish Democratic People's Unions (KDHB)[1] was responsible for the extortion of revenues from legal Kurdish companies, usurpation of money and passports from Turkish citizens, collection of donations from the cultural associations and the pooling of money gathered from the drug illicit drug business and human trafficking. The Kurdish Employers Association (KARSAZ) was founded in January 2001 in Amsterdam. The main purpose of the organization was organizing and supervising the financial initiatives of PKK-KONGRA GEL and laundering the money raised from drugs and other illicit activities. Selim Curukkaya (a.k.a. Tilki), was the chief financial executive for the PKK-KONGRA GEL who later deserted the organization and participated in the counterterrorist struggle of the Turkish and European law enforcement agencies. Curukkaya mentioned that he had made considerable amounts of money from drug deals to finance the activities of the PKK-KONGRA GEL. The statement of the members of the K3 family confirms the allegations of Curukkaya: particularly Hakki Kitay (leader of the K3 Family) admitted transferring drug money to Curukkaya several times. Curukkaya was threatened with death by the PKK-KONGRA GEL after his withdrawal from the organization.

According to Sahin [2], the PKK-KONGRA GEL always utilized modern propaganda mechanisms such as television, the Internet, and electronic magazines and newspapers. The terrorist organization founded MED TV (later changed the name to MEDYA TV) in May 1995 to be broadcast from British satellites to all the European countries. The MED TV station broadcast the propaganda of the PKK-KONGRA GEL, Abdullah Ocalan's speeches and calls for violent crimes including terrorism plots against Turks and Turkey to establish free Kurdistan. The broadcasting license of the TV station was cancelled by the British authorities on April 23, 1999, for not meeting the official procedures, instigating violence against Turkey and Turks and being financed by illicit drug money. Currently the following message appears on the website of the MED TV.

According to Interpol [9] the MED TV had a huge budget in mid-August of 1995, to cover the annual rental cost of the transponder (estimated at $ 3.2 million), considerable amount of staff and substantial broadcast expenditures. The executives of the TV Company have always stressed their financial independence pretending to have their members' volunteer contributions. The law enforcement agencies of Luxembourg, Belgium Police and Scotland Yard launched the operation "Sapoutnik" on September 18, 1996, against MED TV upon the allegations of MED TV's involvement in money laundering [11]. The investigations within the cooperation framework of the Operation Spoutnik and the seizure of 350 million Belgium Francs (equivalent of 8 million US dollars in

---

[1] The KDHB is the central body of decision making for PKK-KONGRA GEL in Europe. The former name of the organization was the European Front Center (ACM)

1998) belonging to MED TV in a Luxembourg bank, revealed that this money simply comes from drugs, arms, and human smuggling contrary to the PKK-KONGRA GEL's consistent denial [11]. This operation also revealed an extremely complicated financial construction, with branches to other European countries and Canada and that the PKK-KONGRA GEL disposed of 15 companies, used for money laundering operations [9].

4. Conclusion

The PKK-KONGRA GEL covertly financed its growing militant cadre and propaganda activities from the illicit drug business in cooperation with several Kurdish organized crime networks. The PKK-KONGRA GEL initially extorted taxes from the heroin traffickers and cannabis cultivators in northwestern Iran, northern Iraq and southeastern Turkey, but the organization later professionalized in more sophisticated forms of the illicit drug business. Particularly after the 1990s, the KOM received hundreds of case reports and evidence about the involvement of PKK-KONGRA GEL members in drug trafficking, heroin production, street delivery of drugs, money laundering and assassination of rival drug network members.

The analysis of the case reports from Turkish and International law enforcement agencies, statements of PKK-KONGRA GEL members, shelter seizures, intelligence reports and interviews with former top level PKK-KONGRA GEL executives revealed that firstly, the PKK-KONGRA GEL members under the leadership of Osman Ocalan established customs check points over the borders of Turkey with Iran and Iraq to extort the drug traffickers. Secondly, the PKK-KONGRA GEL controlled illicit cannabis cultivation fields in the mountainous parts of northwestern Iran, northern Iraq, the Bekaa Valley (for a limited time) and Southeast Anatolia. Multiple tons of hashish/cannabis and cannabis seeds have been seized from the shelters of the PKK-KONGRA GEL. Thirdly, the PKK-KONGRA GEL used its well established, trained, armed and hierarchical cadre and courier system for the transfer of heroin from Iran to Europe overland through Turkey. The PKK-KONGRA GEL was monopolizing and professionalizing the drug trafficking, cooperating with Kurdish organized crime groups and forcing the political Kurdish refugees into drug trafficking. Fourthly, the PKK-KONGRA GEL abused the Kurdish Diaspora and refugee status of the Kurdish immigrants (especially children) for the street delivery of heroin in Europe. The heroin markets in the Netherlands, Germany and some parts of the U.K were controlled by the PKK-KONGRA GEL by the mid 1990s. The leaders of the PKK-KONGRA GEL coordinated heroin distribution from the cultural associations in Europe. The encrypted communication network, hierarchical structure and courier system for terrorist campaigns was used for the transfer and distribution of drugs. The use of the Kurdish language in communication complicated the electronic surveillance and use of undercover agents to penetrate the organization. Ultimately, the PKK-KONGRA GEL established sophisticated financial structures to coordinate the collection and distribution of funds from legal or illegal resources. The drug money was laundered by chief financial executives in Europe to finance the political propaganda activities, cultural associations and MED TV.

References

[1]   M.M. Gunter, *The Kurds and the future of Turkey*. New York: St. Martin's Press; 1997.
[2]   F.S. Sahin, Case studies in terrorism-drug connection: The Kurdistan Workers' Party, The Liberation Tigers of Tamil Eelam, and the Shining Path (unpublished master thesis). University of North Texas, Robert B. Toulouse School of Graduate Studies; 2001.
[3]   UNODCCP-United Nations Office for Drug Control and Crime Prevention, *World drug report 2000*. New York: Oxford University Press; 2001.
[4]   UNODC-United Nations Office on Drugs and Crime, *The opium economy in Afghanistan.* Vienna: United Nations Publications; 2003.
[5]   UNODC-United Nations Office on Drugs and Crime, *World drug report,* Volume 1: Analysis. Vienna: United Nations Publications; 2006.
[6]   UNODC-United Nations Office on Drugs and Crime, *Afghanistan opium survey: Executive summary.* Vienna: United Nations Publications; 2006.
[7]   E. Demirel, *Terör (Terror)*. Cagaloglu/Istanbul, Turkey: IQ Kültür Sanat Yayincilik; 2001.
[8]   F. Bovenkerk, Y. Yeşilgöz, *Türkiye'nin Mafyası (Turkish Mafia)*. Cagaloglu/Istanbul, Turkey: Iletişim Yayinlari; 2004.
[9]   Interpol General Secretariat, Financing of terrorism. Paper presented at International Terrorism Symposium. Colombo, Sri Lanka: 1999.
[10] Department of Anti-Smuggling and Organized Crime-KOM, Turkish drug report 2003. (Report No: 2003/2). KOM Headquarters /Ankara, Turkey: 2003, p 44.
[11] Department of Anti-Smuggling and Organized Crime-KOM, Narco-terrorism in Turkey: The nexus of PKK, DHKP/C and TKP/ML terrorist organizations with illicit drug business (unpublished official report prepared by Behsat Ekici). KOM Headquarters /Ankara, Turkey: 2005, pp 48, 50, 67-68.
[12] Focus Magazine. Mit drogengeld den terror finanziert. Munich, Germany: 1999, September 7.
[13] Sabah Daily Newspaper, Diyarbakir'da PKK'nin esrar tarlalari (The cannabis fields of PKK in Diyarbakir). 2006, July 5. Available from; URL: http://www.sabah.com.tr/2006/07/05/gnd98.html, [2006, December 5].
[14] Observatorie Geopolitique Des Drouges. *The world geopolitics of drugs: Annual report 1998-1999.* Paris, France; (1999). [Online] Available from; URL http://www.ogd.org/2000/en/99en.html, [2005, November 29].
[15] Department of Anti-Smuggling and Organized Crime-KOM, *Turkish drug report 1995*, Ankara, Turkey: Evren Yayincilik Basim San. Tic. A.S.; 1996.
[16] VOX TV, Hamburg Police arrested Kurdish children aged between 8-12, for heroin distribution. 1993, February 12. Available from; URL: http://www.ataa.org/ataa/ref/pkk/mfa/pkk-drugs.html, [2006, December 5].
[17] Hamburg Local TV Broadcast, PKK organizes teenagers for heroin distribution in Hamburg. 1993, September 15. Available from; http://www.ataa.org/ataa/ref/pkk/mfa/pkk-drugs.html, [2006, December 5].
[18] Department of Anti-Smuggling and Organized Crime-KOM, *Turkish drug report 1997*. Ankara, Turkey: Evren Yayincilik Basim San. Tic. A.S.; 1998.

Understanding and Responding to the Terrorism Phenomenon
O. Nikbay and S. Hancerli (Eds.)
IOS Press, 2007

Spatial Pattern Analysis of PKK-KONGRA GEL Terror Incidents in Turkey: 2003-2004

Suleyman Demirci[a], ABD, I-Shian Suen[a], Ph.D.

[a]*L. Douglas Wilder School of Government and Public Affairs,*
Virginia Commonwealth University, USA

Abstract. This study attempts to explore potential spatial association among PKK-KONGRA GEL (People's Congress of Kurdistan) terror incidents rates across the cities in Turkey from 2003 to 2004. To fill the possible deficiencies for traditional statistical analyses across the geography, the current research addresses the significant role of spatial dependency before finalizing any statistical model associated with the geography. It, therefore, realizes positive spatial autocorrelation by utilizing Moran's I and LISA statistics. Accordingly, it contends that any results with these models might more reliably direct the essential policy considerations about terrorism after understanding and coping with the possible spatial dependency in the incident distribution.

Keywords. Geography of terrorism, spatial association, public policy, and PKK-KONGRA GEL.

Introduction

Terror incidents, as catastrophic events, have been frequently questioned from various aspects in recent years. The 9/11 event has already driven various policy related arguments for these incidents. That is, it has been a symbolic event to trigger new policy developments for terrorism issue in both national and international arena. Such triggering events lead to many policy issues from the perspective of law enforcement agencies as well.

Researchers essentially aim to set different frameworks to make such ambiguous topics clearer in the mind, and to obtain more effective policy alternatives. As Weimer and Vining [1] argue for a generic analytical toolkit as a problem solving method for policy analysis, spatial methodologies might provide decision makers with "advice" to initiate more timely and effective strategies and outcomes for minimizing the effects of terror incidents in urban and rural areas.

1. Purpose and Research Questions

The researchers want to examine the relative differences with the characteristics of localities where the terror events occur, and to obtain useful information to lessen the impact of terror incidents in these areas. Geographic differences have essentially been the main concern for researchers to explore the distribution of terror incidents across space. The present study, therefore, focuses on a very specific purpose and attempts to answer the following question.

Purpose: To explore the spatial dependency (pattern) in terror incidents across the cities in Turkey

Research Question: Are terror incidents rates spatially related across the cities in Turkey?

2. Related Literature

This section primarily aims to provide fundamental information for the purpose of the study, and therefore to help the readers comprehend both methodological and theoretical approaches.

2.1. Terrorism and PKK-KONGRA GEL

Interestingly enough, there is no unique definition of terrorism that has been universally accepted due to the various approaches for terrorist activities. Although the scholars have approached terrorism with very diverse definitions and characteristics, terrorism and its elements reflect some common features. For example, according to Mathewson and Steinberg [2], the major element of definitions on terrorism has not changed such as "intimidation through violence". They address continuous changes in social, economical, and political aspects over the time and with geographic composition. Commonly speaking, terrorist incidents might *intimidate* the citizenry in different locations [3]. Nevertheless, this study does not aim to address the diversity of terror definitions. Instead, it offers a location based methodology to better delineate the distribution of terrorist incidents across space. It, therefore, intends to integrate location based intelligence by various spatial analyses to support better decision-making.

Although Turkey suffers from various terrorist groups (radical leftist, ethnic separatist, and religiously inspired) [4], PKK terrorism, as an ethnic separatist, has been the most challenging one in the country [5]. The PKK terrorism with its Marxist-Leninist elements has further been diffused around Turkey since the very first foundation. In fact, the main objective of the PKK-KONGRA GEL was to be an essential step to reach communist revolution against Turkish Government [4]. Over the years, this organization has irritated the nationalist thoughts of Kurdish identity to legitimize its activities, but has still promoted its original Marxist-Leninist ideology [5]. PKK-KONGRA GEL has continued to update its tools and strategies to reach its final goal, Marxist-Leninist Kurdistan in the southeastern part of Turkey [6]. That is, it has even extensively exploited religious and traditional motives in southeastern part of Turkey although its main ideology contradicts with religious motives.

Simsek [6] further contends that the chaos in Northern Iraq has made PKK-KONGRA GEL increase their terrorist attacks in Southeastern Turkey over years. In fact, many believe that there are significant associations between the events in Northern Iraq and PKK-KONGRA GEL attacks in the region. However, it requires very complicated conceptual and methodological approaches to realize such claim, which is beyond the scope of this study.

Regarding illegal activities in Turkey, PKK-KONGRA GEL has significantly decreased its violent attacks against both Turkish Government and local people living in the region [6]. Such a decrease in the general trend has primarily been experienced since Abdullah Ocalan was arrested in 1999 although it significantly increased the number of suicide attacks and bombings in the short run afterwards. However, that is more likely to be a marginal reaction against the arrest. Dilmac [7] further addresses efficient security operations and effective state policies as he explains such significant decreases in the KONGRA-GEL activities in Turkey. Their illegal activities spread around other countries. Dilmac [7] then clearly defines the PKK issue as a global threat as he comprehends the terrorism and its impacts on Turkey. As a confirmatory element, the U.S. Department of State [8] informs that the countries surrounding Turkey have still been accommodating majority of PKK-KONGRA GEL terrorists, and they have still actively been involving in violent incidents across Turkey even they have decreased the intensity since then.

In fact, the U.S. Department of State [8] confirms the violence of PKK-KONGRA GEL by placing more attentions on killing, kidnapping, and threatening as its primary strategy over time. Simsek [6] further elaborates these points, and he focuses how these terror incidents might accelerate the regional mobility and increase the migration rates across Turkey. Koseli [9] more complicates the issue and attempts to explore the association between terrorism and some socio-economic factors such as poverty and inequality. Simsek [6] finds that terrorism positively affects migration, whereas Koseli [9] realizes some significant associations between socio-economic factors and terrorism while statistically controlling other characteristics of cities across Turkey. Accordingly, the findings of their studies become the continuum of the same terrorism issue.

Instead of repeating their studies, the present study attempts to explore possible spatial dependency across the city level terror incidents in Turkey. That is, terror incidents in one city might be spatially dependent upon one another across Turkey. For the purpose of the study, spatial methodologies might be essential when the researchers approach the terrorism issue across the geography such as county, city, region, or country. Therefore, the present study aims to demonstrate whether geographic distribution of these incidents has any pattern across Turkey by focusing on the incidents induced by PKK-KONGRA GEL terror organization in Turkey between 2003 and 2004.

2.2. Geographic Information Systems (GIS) for Terror Incidents Analyses

Geographic Information Systems are powerful technological tools for law enforcement agencies and other public agencies to prepare geographically thematic representations from one-dimensional to three-dimensional visualization of both spatial and/or temporal data [10]. GIS, undeniably, provides indispensable analytical approaches to gather, relate, analyze, and distribute information obtained from different databases [11, 12]. In the perspectives of law enforcement agencies, such technology has been primarily utilized for the street level crimes till now. However, Demirci [13] clearly suggests utilizing spatial methodologies to analyze terror incidents. In fact, GIS offers policy makers, law enforcement agencies, and intelligence agencies with new problem solving strategies such as Hotspot Policing, Information Driven Policing, etc. [10].

Additionally, GIS enables the police to better fulfill their traditional responsibilities since it can store, interrelate, analyze, and display a vast amount of spatially referenced information [14]. With the integrated capability to merge very diverse data coming from different organizations, it helps promote smoother information-sharing among the organizations [15]. Of the contributions, therefore, GIS has a great potential to foster law enforcement and provides an analytical framework as existing crime databases are integrated with GIS databases for better planning with other public agencies, such as taxation, education, and transportation [16]. Terror incident mapping should, therefore, be considered as a process of utilizing the GIS to perform spatial analyses of terror incident distributions and other policy-related issues.

In other words, the main argument should be that GIS can work for both social and crime related problems/issues that consist of location references (spatial reference) in nature. Considering terror incidents, GIS can help the analysts map these incidents across the country. With integrated geo-statistical components, GIS extensively prepares a suitable mechanism to thoroughly analyze the incidents. Mapping terror incidents can further be integrated with any other information, such as socioeconomic characteristics of geography. Such integration offers many advantages to explore, visualize, and understand the associations between these characteristics and terror incidents. All these capabilities can, therefore, enhance location-based intelligence for law enforcement agencies.

GIS realizes the significant role of location based information in public policy analysis [17]. In fact, the policies for urbanization and public management are more likely to be related to location based information [18]. Consequently, urban planners and policy makers need to deal with the characteristics of locations in order to interpret the urban and community problems, and establish the most suitable solutions [19]. The creation of a comprehensive GIS database is resource-demanding since GIS clearly requires location reference (x/y coordinates, neighborhoods, counties, cities, or regions) to integrate various databases as aforementioned. Nonetheless, this may not be so problematic as long as both law enforcement and other public agencies record their valuable information with the location references in their databases.

Taken together, GIS can be utilized for the following purposes;

- To display, analyze, and distribute spatial and non-spatial data
- To integrate various data sets
- To provide an analytical framework for problem solving
- To promote effective decision making and intelligent resource allocation and deployment
- To explore spatial dependency and pattern across the predefined contiguous city boundaries
- To promote location based intelligence

More specifically, this study posits that GIS technology with its essential components can enhance the policy analysis for local and global effects of terror incidents. That is, it pinpoints spatial pattern of terror incidents by GIS and other geo-statistical software packages. Such an approach in this study should not be considered only thematic mapping of the incidents. Rather, it statistically constructs one hypothesis and attempts to test it through advanced geo-statistical tools. Then, it ultimately determines the level of spatial pattern and dependency for the PKK KONGRA-GEL terror incidents across Turkey.

2.3. Spatial Dependency

The current study postulates that spatially integrated methodology might help the researchers construct the best fitted statistical models to understand the context of terror incidents across space. This is because the variation of incident context might be spatially correlated as taking care of the spatial variations of crime within other neighborhoods throughout the whole city [20]. Statistically speaking, the explanatory power of previous statistical models (regardless of spatial autocorrelation) has been moderate to explore the relationships between urban crime and structural characteristics of locations [21]. One reason might be the lack of consideration about spatial dependency in the previous models since traditional statistical models just assume that the error terms within the model is independent to each other [22]. This should be considered as a deficiency of the traditional statistical models since the error terms, from the social ecologists' point of view, might be spatially correlated to each other [23]. Once a study realizes the possibility of spatial autocorrelation, it should address the problem before finalizing the statistical models.

  For example, terror incidents in one city may also be dependent upon the terror incident rates observed in contiguous cities across Turkey. When such neighboring observations are dependent to each other, traditional statistical techniques might not result in consistent statistical models [24]. And, the results of traditional regression models may not be appropriately generalized since the researcher might disregard fixing possible spatial autocorrelation that might lead to some external validity issues. In geography, everything is more likely to be associated with everything else. Near subjects, however, might be more associated with one another than distant ones. Accordingly, spatial autocorrelation might be a serious problem as much as multicollinearity (high correlation among the variables as they explain the variation within dependent variable) is. For many regression models with a geography component, in fact, the independent variables may not actually be independent to one another because of the likelihood of spatial autocorrelation.

  Furthermore, spatial error terms for exogenous variables and spatial lag terms for the variation in terror incident rates might also be utilized as control variables to acknowledge the spatial dependency amongst the neighborhoods within the cities. Spatial lag model, on the other hand, adds a spatial regression coefficient for the weighted mean value of local dependent variable as taking care of the consistency within the statistical model [24]. In fact, spatial weight matrix might be calculated by either distance or contiguity as the researcher defines the distribution of neighborhoods across the cities. However, since the city geography in Turkey has various sizes, the distance criteria might not be an objective criterion to determine the spatial weight. In this study, therefore, the spatial weight matrix is expressed as first order contiguity, which defines cities as having a common border to one another [25]. According to Chainey and Ratcliffe [23], such spatial lag model might be applied for any geographic clustering of crimes within various locations.

  However, the present study only attempts to discover whether spatial dependency exists or not as it examines spatial (geographic) patterns of terror incident rates in cities across Turkey between 2003 and 2004. Constructing predictive models merged with socio-economic characteristics and impacts of policy programs across the cities requires further multivariate methods with advanced geo-statistical components.

3. Research Methodology

This study drives a quantitative research methodology. It utilizes secondary data and constructs a cross-sectional research design and compares the Moran's I statistical values to determine a possible spatial dependency among terror incidents across Turkey. Secondary data analysis requires examining major sources of data to test the hypotheses derived by the research studies [26]. Conceptually speaking, secondary data would be the only data that can possibly be used in certain research problems. Therefore, it would be a good entry point to examine social issues. Methodologically speaking, it offers some advantages, such as opportunity for replication, reliable and accurate data, availability of data at different time date scales, and the ability to improve the validity of measurement. Lastly, it is comparably inexpensive to utilize existing data than specifically collecting data. Police terror incident records and GIS layers for cities are the only necessary data sources to accomplish the objectives of this study.

Accordingly, these relative advantages initiate the use of secondary data in this research although some possible limitations exist for such data in terms of testing hypotheses, accessibility to data, and insufficient information [26]. If this study could access relevant socio-economic changes from 2003 to 2004, it would be able to construct more robust spatially regressed models to explore more reliable associations between the distributions of terror incidents rates and other policy related factors such as socio-economic factors, voting, government programs, and other specific characteristics across the cities in the country.

3.1. Research Design and Essential Elements

This section covers the type of research design, unit of analyses, measurement of variable, and hypothesis. Further, it discusses primary justifications on deciding such research elements as constructing a valid research design for the study.

Nachimias and Nachimias [26] emphasize on the cross-sectional design as one of the most predominant non-experimental research design in social sciences. Unlike experimental research design, non-experimental research primarily explores the current status of study subject without altering certain conditions impacting on such subject over time [27]. Since the present study mainly focuses on the spatial associations between terror incident rates across the cities in Turkey, the cross-sectional design allows the present study to explore the terror incident clusters and their spatial dependencies across Turkey.

The cross-sectional design, however, has its methodological limitations that might impact on internal validity of the research [26]. One limitation is that such design cannot allow the researchers to construct causality between independent and dependent variable since it cannot determine how the subject changes over relatively long time. Another limitation is that the cross-sectional design does not allow the researchers to construct pretest and posttest together. Such limitations, therefore, might be potential threats to the internal validity of the study, and obstacles against assessing causality.

To overcome some limitations of cross-sectional design, this study uses statistical analyses to approximate its applications to the experimental design. In addition, since the data set of terror incidents rates is spatially autocorrelated by spatial weights over the cities, the limitations against internal validity might be necessarily resolved by controlling the spatial dependency within cases. Finally, this study chooses to work on the entire population of the working area instead of establishing any sampling procedure. Working with the population might also reduce possible threats against internal validity in a cross-sectional research design. Accordingly, such preferences in this study are more likely to minimize the effects related to the possible methodological limitations of cross-sectional research design.

The present study utilizes cities as the unit of analysis. Cities are considered appropriate units to capture possible geographic clusters and spatial dependencies since it works across the entire Country. There are currently eighty one (81) cities in Turkey. The terror incidents are then aggregated for such administrative spatial units of observation. Terror incidents aggregated to this scale of administrative units are also convenient for policy considerations to explore geographic pattern(s) and its correlation with other factors.

This study only deals with terror incident rates as a measurement of variable. It therefore determines whether terror incident rates are spatially dependent across the cities in Turkey. Once the numbers of terror incidents are obtained from police archive, this study weights and calculates the rates as the numbers of terror incidents per 10,000 people. It therefore normalizes the values of terror incidents, and makes them comparable across the cities.

This study, accordingly, is designed to test the following hypothesis:

H_0: PKK-KONGRA GEL incident rate at city level is not spatially dependent to each other in Turkey.

3.2. Analytical Steps and Findings

The present research has performed subsequently related steps to analyze the possible spatial dependency for the distribution of terror incidents across the cities in Turkey. It has gathered the number of terror incidents per cities from Turkish National Police. Since the incidents are aggregated to the city-level, they do not threat any human subjects according to IRB (Institutional Review Board) notes in the U.S. Once the data were obtained from formal documents, they are merged with geographic data layer of cities by using their unique ID (City IDs) in ArcGIS 9.1 software. Then, terror incidents with city ID are ready to be mapped in any GIS environment. This study further utilizes GeoDa software to explore the possible spatial dependency.

Global Moran's I statistics and Local LISA statistics are the primary methods to determine the spatial autocorrelation for terror incident rates across the cities in Turkey. When the variables (such as terror incidents rates per cities) are measured at continuous level, Moran's I statistics calculates the deviation from spatial randomness, and becomes the most appropriate method for global spatial dependency [20]. In fact, positive values for Moran's I indicate positive spatial dependency, and vice versa. The geographic units with these values are termed as spatial outliers in the literature. Rather than giving more technical information on spatial autocorrelation, this study fundamentally interprets the values of Moran's I statistics for detecting spatial clusters of terror incidents across the cities in Turkey.

Figure-1: LISA Cluster Map, Moran's I, and Local Moran's I

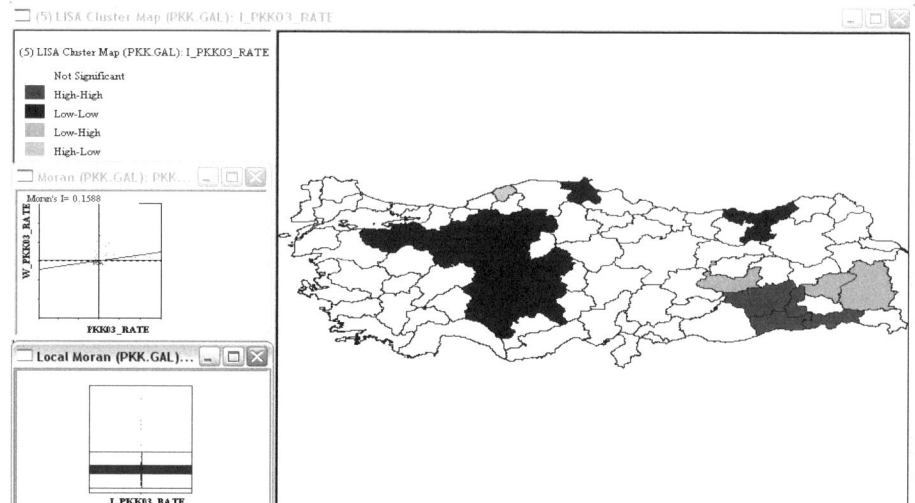

The present study further elaborates its spatial analyses to determine Local Indicators of Spatial Association (LISA statistics). Rather than examining spatial dependency in a broad view, LISA provides very specific measurements around a specific location (such as a known city). In fact, LISA statistics is utilized to determine spatial clusters of high and low values around one location [20]. That is, LISA values can be derived from either local Moran or Geary Statistics values. In this study, spatial deviations for either of them are based on the contiguity of the cities. More specifically, LISA statistics are then visualized with various combinations (low/low, high/high, high/low, and low/high) in the GIS environment (Figure-1 and 2). Figure-1 illustrates Moran's I statistics value, local Moran, and visualization of LISA clusters for the PKK terror incidents rates in 2003. Figure-2 illustrates the same values and visualization for the year 2004.

Figure-2: LISA Cluster Map, Moran's I, and Local Moran's I

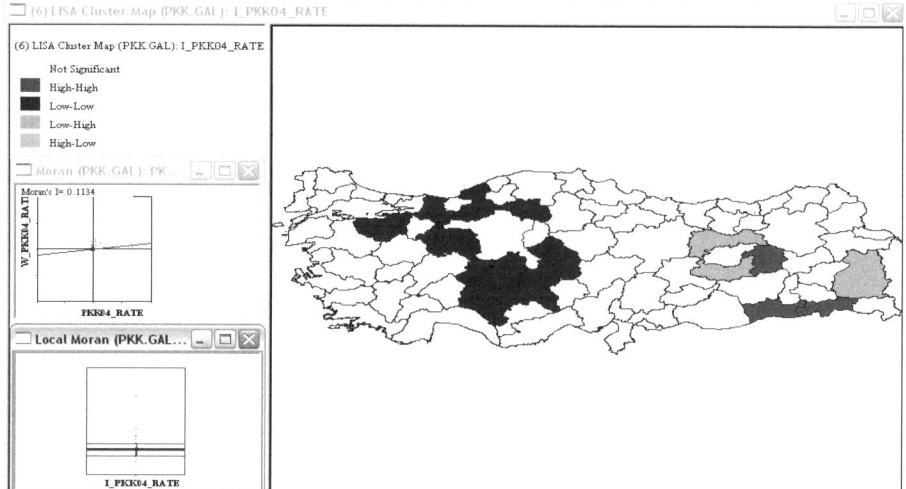

Figure-3: Thematic Mapping with Standard Deviation of Terror Incident Rates

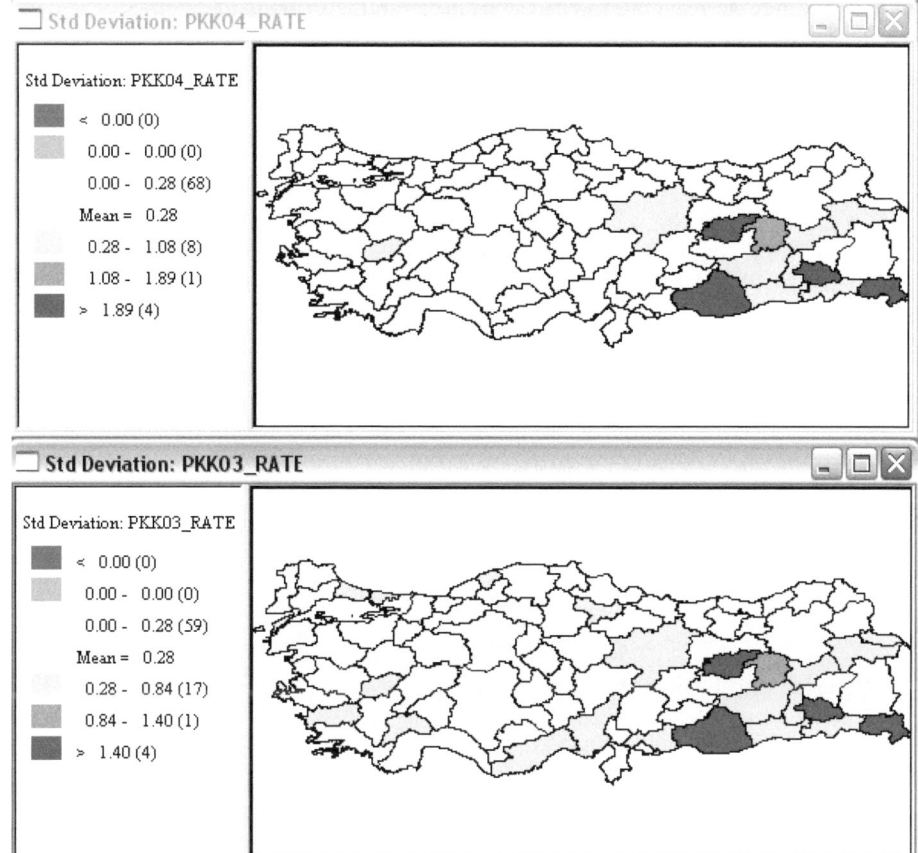

Figure-3 includes geographic distribution of standard deviations of terror incident rates to enhance the traditional thematic mappings for both 2003 and 2004. The present research, therefore, clearly identifies four (4) cities with the highest standard deviation against the mean of PKK-KONGRA GEL terror incidents rates across Turkey. There are twenty two (22) cities of eighty one (81) which have higher values than the mean. Policy makers should, therefore, pay more attention to these cities. In terms of detecting spatial outliers, four cities with the highest standard deviation should be considered the most problematic ones for the PKK terror incident rates. Interestingly, the mean values for each year remained the same although their spatial distribution changed from 2003 to 2004. Accordingly, examining only mean values (for Central Tendency) across the space may not capture all variation in the terror incidents rates such as spatial variation across the cities.

In Figure-1 and 2; LISA mapping, different than classic thematic mapping in GIS, illustrates only significant clusters across the cities in Turkey. It, therefore, provides better illustrations to realize the most problematic cities with respect to spatial distribution of terror incidents in Turkey. Red colored cities address that these have high terror incidents and are surrounded by the cities having high terror incidents in 2003 and 2004. They are significant clusters with high values. They might be called as hotspots in crime mapping literature. Blue colored ones are also considered spatial outliers, but they do have the low terror incidents in their surrounding cities. They are significant spatial clusters with low values. And, they are sometimes called as cold spots in the literature. The rest with blanked cities are not significantly clustered to each other across the country.

Accordingly, in both 2003 and 2004, the most problematic cities are clustered in southeastern side of Turkey. However, each spatial cluster may not be significant according to LISA cluster mapping above. On the other hand, the results for both years confirm the argument Simsek [6] made in his very systematic dissertation project. In fact, political and ethnic movements in Northern side of Iraq might have contributed to the increase of PKK terror incidents. The incidents have, therefore, moved from mid-eastern to southeastern region of Turkey between 2003 and 2004.

Moran's I statistics provides 0.1588, which means positive spatial autocorrelation in 2003. It further provides 0.1134, which also means positive spatial autocorrelation in 2004.

$MI_{03} = 0.1588 > 0$, Positive Spatial Association
$MI_{04} = 0.1134 > 0$, Positive Spatial Association

These results conclude that low to low values and high to high values of terror incidents rates across the cities are significantly clustered in a geographic setting.

4. Conclusion and Future Directions

This study has utilized the analytical capabilities of GIS and supplementary software (GeoDa) to examine the spatial dependency within terror incidents rates across the cities. Accordingly, by incorporating the geography component into the analysis, decision makers are more likely to be better equipped with crucial knowledge and insights to confront terrorism in a geography setting. In fact, possible findings might allow the policy makers and security forces to narrow down the possible targets so that they can deploy and allocate their resources in a more efficient and effective manner. Such awareness about the most vulnerable cities and population might provide them with strategic information for future plans to enhance the security measures in urban and rural areas. Consequently, preemptive policing and anti-terrorism strategies can be formulated to fight and dwarf domestic terrorism.

The methodology developed in this study can also be applied for all other types of crime incidents when spatial component is included in the research. The present study, therefore, expects to generalize its methodological approach to explore any crime variation across geography, and promotes spatially integrated policy analysis.

This study can be further enhanced by including more complicated spatial analyses with socio-economic and other policy oriented dimensions to explore the reasons of such spatial movement over time. The present research should be considered the first step of such more comprehensive approach to understand why terror incidents are spatially changed over time.

References

[1] D.L. Weimer, A.R. Vining, *Policy analysis: Concepts and practice.* Second Edition. New Jersey: Prentice Hall; 1992, p. 1-14.

[2] K.M. Mathewson, M.K. Steinberg, Geographic dimensions of drugs and terrorism: Contexts, cases, and connections, In S.L. Cutter, D. Richordson, T.J. Willbanks *The Geographical Dimensions of Terrorism: A Research Agenda for the Discipline*, New York: Routledge Press; 2003, p. 59-66.

[3] S.L. Cutter, D. Richordson, T.J. Willbanks, Editors. *The geographical dimensions of terrorism.* New York: Routledge Press; 2003.

[4] A.S. Yayla, S. Teymur, Turkey, terrorism and the PKK/KONGRA-GEL. *Tips Connections*, NATO & TIPS Terrorism Project Special Issue. 2006, September.

[5] T. Durna, The PKK terrorism in Turkey. *Tips Connections*, NATO & TIPS Terrorism Project Special Issue. 2006, September.

[6] Y. Simsek, Impact of terrorism on migration patterns in Turkey. PhD Dissertation, Virginia Commonwealth University, Richmond, Virginia; 2006.

[7] S. Dilmac, Global threat: Terrorism and its impact on Turkey. Istanbul Conference on Democracy & Global Security 2005, Istanbul/Turkey. Turkish National Police, Foreign Relations Department. 2005.

[8] U.S. Department of State. *Report on human rights in Turkey and situation in Cyprus.* 2001. [Online] Available from; URL: http://dosfan.lib.uic.edu/erc/bureaus/eur/releases/950601TurkeyCyprus.html [2005, September 22].

[9] M. Koseli, Poverty, inequality & terrorism relationship in Turkey. PhD Dissertation, Virginia Commonwealth University, Richmond, Virginia; 2006.

[10] R. Boba, Crime analysis and crime mapping. Thousand Oaks, California: Sage Publications, 2005.

[11] A. Getis, et al., Geographic information science and crime analysis. *URISA Journal,* **12/2** (2000): 7-14.

[12] K. Harries, Mapping crime: Principle and practice, 1999. [Online] Available from; URL: http://www.ncjrs.org/html/nij/mapping/pdf.html [2005, September 14].

[13] S. Demirci, Emniyet teskilatinda cografi bilgi sistemlerinin uygulanabilirligi: Mobese basari oykusu. First Police Information Technology Symposium, Ankara/Turkey, 2003. [Online] Available from; URL :http://www.egm.gov.tr/sempozyum2003/Bildiriler/Emniyet_Teskilatinda_Cografi_Bilgi_Sistemler.pdf

[14] T. Dunworth, Criminal justice and the IT revolution. In J. Horney, Editor., *Policies, processes, and decisions of the criminal justice system; Criminal justice 2000 ,* 2000, 371-426). [Online] Available from; URL: http://www.ncjrs.org/criminal_justice2000/vol_3/03h.pdf [2000, September 15].

[15] J.E. Innes, D.M. Simpson, Implementing GIS for planning. *Journal of the American Planning Association* 59/2 (1993), 230-237.

[16] D.G. Garson, I.B. Vann, Geographic information Systems for Small and Medium Law enforcement Jurisdictions: Strategies and Effective Practices, 2001. [Online]. Available from; URL: http://www.gcc.state.nc.us/gispage/ep1.htm [2004, September 30].

[17] R.W. Greene, *GIS in public policy: Using geographic information for more effective government.* Esri; 2000.

[18] X. Lopez, *The impact of government information policy on the dissemination of spatial data.* PhD Dissertation, University of Maine, 1996.

[19] I. Masser, *Governments and geographic information.* Taylor & Francis Ltd. 1998.

[20] L. Anselin, J. Cohen, D. Cook, W.L. Gorr, G. Tita, Spatial Analyses of Crime. *Measurement and analyses of Crime Justice,* **4** (2000), 213-243.

[21] M.E. Cahill, Geographies of urban crime: An intra-urban study of crime in Nashville, TN; Portland, or; and Tucson, AZ. 2004. [Online] Available from; URL: http://www.ncjrs.gov/pdffiles1/nij/grants/209263.pdf. [2005, Nov. 16].

[22] B.G. Tabachnick, L.S. Fidell, *Using multivariate statistics*, 4th ed., US: Ally & Bacon; 2001.

[23] S. Chainey, J. Ratcliffe, *GIS and crime mapping.* England: Wiley; 2005.

[24] L. Anselin, *Spatial econometrics: Methods and models.* Dordrecht: Kluwer Academic Press; 1988.

[25] R.J Sampson, J.D. Morenoff, Spatial (Dis)Advantage and homicide in Chicago neighborhoods. In M.F. Goodchild, D.G. Janelle, Editors. *Spatially integrated social science.* New York: Oxford University Press; 2004, p. 145-170.

[26] C. Nachmias-Frankfurt, D. Nachmias, *Research methods in the social sciences.* New York: Worth Publishers; 2000.

[27] J. McMillan, *Educational research: Fundamentals for the consumer.* Fourth ed. Boston: Pearson; 2004.

Part III

Strategies and Tactics for Dealing with Terrorist Hostage Sieges, Hijackings and Kidnappings

Local Law Enforcement Hostage/Crisis Negotiation: An Essay on Continued Viability in the Aftermath of the Attacks of 9/11

Robert J. LOUDEN, Ph.D.
Department of Sociology, Anthropology and Criminal Justice,
Georgian Court University, USA

Abstract. Hostage holding has been utilized as an instrument of politics and commerce since the beginning of recorded history. For those events that took place in public view a familiar official response was to meet force with force. Social unrest in various parts of the world during the 1960s and 1970s sometimes resulted in an assortment of domestic and international terrorist events. Time and again, hostages were held. Although official response was often predicated on a swift resolution through the application of necessary force, authorities were frequently thrust into the reluctant role of negotiator. Police Hostage Negotiation (HN) in the US began as an innovative NYPD practice more than 30 years ago largely as a result of the 1972 terrorist attack at the Munich Olympics. The vast majority of incidents were concluded without loss of life. Included in these numbers are responses to airplane hijacking events in conjunction with the Police Department of the Port Authority of New York and New Jersey and with the FBI. In the ensuing years HN practices were adapted and adopted by the majority of US police agencies. The 9-11 attacks prompted some to question the future value of HN as a police tactic. This essay discusses the issues and suggests that HN should continue as a tool in the arsenal for responding to hostage holding events.

Keywords. Hostage situation, crisis negotiation, hostage negotiation, hostage negotiator, negotiator training, NYPD, and 9-11 attacks.

Introduction

Hostage holding has been utilized as an instrument of politics and commerce since the beginning of recorded history. Dealing with these events presents dangerous and challenging dilemmas for those that must take action in response. During cycles of peace and war, through optimistic and pessimistic political and economic times, groups and individuals have chosen to take hold of people and control them as hostages. Generally, demands to be fulfilled were made in exchange for release at an appointed time or the captive was to be held for some longer term as collateral. Events would unfold as staged barricade and siege scenarios or as kidnap and extortion type situations. For those events that took place in public view a familiar official response was to meet force with force.

Social unrest in various parts of the world during the 1960's and 1970's sometimes resulted in an assortment of domestic and international terrorist events. Time and again, hostages were held. Although official response was often predicated on a swift resolution through the application of necessary force, authorities were frequently thrust into the reluctant role of negotiator. One such situation, on September 5, 1972 at the Munich Olympics, caught the eye of political and law enforcement officials in New York City.

It was presumed that it was only a matter of time before a Munich type event would be attempted in the United States and that New York City would be a logical location since NYC was the actual and symbolic focus of much that is identified as American; it is also home to the United Nations.

The ensuing research and planning yielded a hostage rescue and recovery plan for the New York Police Department. One premise was that the agency would be prepared to negotiate rather than have that role spontaneously thrust upon them. Originally designed as a mechanism for response to terrorist events, the plan was soon expanded to a range of events that were perhaps more mundane but still life threatening. Incidents that were motivated not only by cause but also for personal gain or to temporarily satisfy some internal imbalance became the mandate of the hostage recovery effort. Later, dealing with certain dangerous but non hostage holding individuals, including some contemplating suicide, became part of these newly organized efforts. Many law enforcement agencies including local departments from various parts of the US, several federal US agencies and comparable groups from different countries around the world studied and adopted or adapted the NYC plan.

From the inception of the hostage recovery team concept in 1973 until the attacks of September 11, 2001, the NYPD working alone and in conjunction with other agencies responded to several thousand situations. The vast majority of incidents were concluded without loss of life. Included in these numbers are responses to airplane hijacking events in conjunction with the Police Department of the Port Authority of New York and New Jersey and with the FBI. In the NY metropolitan area, and elsewhere, the preferred response to sky jacking was a coordinated effort that included potential for a swift tactical operation within the context on containment and negotiation. Loss of life was likewise minimized during negotiations involving planes. It must be noted that civil policing in the US does not ordinarily operate in terms of 'acceptable casualty rates' and it is the goal of hostage recovery team efforts to save all, so 'minimal' loss of life is not to be taken lightly. The belief is that if coordinated containment and negotiation efforts had not been initiated during these many disparate events, there would have been a far greater casualty rate for hostages and for rescuers.

1. Preliminary Thoughts

Hostage Negotiation (HN) began as an innovative NYPD practice more than 30 years ago. The original NYPD HN plan was developed in response to the terrorist attack against Israeli athletes at the 1972 Munich Olympic Games. The assessment at the time was that New York City was a probable terrorist target and that a hostage or siege situation was likely since there had been a number of such incidents, primarily throughout Europe and the Middle East, in the preceding years.

Actual terrorist hostage holdings in NYC have not occurred, although events inside three foreign missions to the UN closely mimicked genuine hostage situations. The nature of actions that negotiators are dispatched to has been expanded to include trapped perpetrators, emotionally disturbed persons, suicide attempts, high risk raid and warrant preparation, and kidnap and extortion investigations. Some of these incidents involved hostages while others were more akin to barricade or siege operations. NYPD negotiators have responded to probably more then 2000 events since their team was first formed. They have also shared their knowledge and experience with law enforcement agencies throughout the country and around the world. Interestingly, the original HN methodology has not changed dramatically.

The FBI became involved in HN research, response and training in 1973 and has been involved in negotiation and rescue operations throughout the US and worldwide ever since. By 1999, some derivation of the original NYPD HN policy had been adopted by most of the police departments in the country that employ at least 100 sworn officers. During the summer of 2001 the newly formed National Council of Negotiation Associations (NCNA) in conjunction with the FBI Crisis Negotiation Unit (CNU) recommended that all law enforcement agencies should maintain a negotiation capability either in-house or through mutual aid.

And then came 9/11/01!

An early reaction to the devastation by a veteran police practitioner turned academic, including the death of friends and colleagues, was that hostage negotiation might no longer have a place in our society; all bets were off. Then, the other side of the brain woke up with a realization that now, perhaps more than ever before, democratic policing must be prepared to engage in meaningful dialogues with despicable people in order to help save lives.

This paper will discuss some terrorist related aspects of hostage negotiation from the perspective of a research project: The Structure and Procedures of Hostage/Crisis Negotiation Units in U.S. Police Organizations [1].

2. Definition of Hostage/Crisis Negotiation

Negotiation is a transaction between two parties, representing themselves or others, which is designed to arrive at a mutually agreeable resolution. A dictionary definition of negotiation [2] includes, "to confer with another in order to come to terms." Negotiation does not automatically presuppose equality between parties but does recognize the relative strength or power of each side. Implied in the negotiation process is that each side has something that the other wants, that there is no better mutually acceptable solution immediately available, and that there is a willingness to communicate and to discuss compromise.

Police officers engage in the practice of negotiation throughout their daily assignments, especially in these times of community policing and collaborative approaches to problem solving. They negotiate events such as noise complaints, neighborhood disputes, situations with disorderly youth, and parking conditions. The concept of negotiation that is the subject of this paper is somewhat more complex because issues of safety, life and death, are always present, and these situations typically involve the response of a large number of law enforcement personnel, a potentially confusing command structure and adherence to special procedures. Media attention is a given at virtually every hostage/crisis negotiation scene.

According to Crelinsten and Szabo [3] "Hostage-taking is a very ancient form of criminal activity. In fact, it was even an accepted tool of diplomacy when used by legitimate authority" [3 pg ix]. Levitt [4] stated that hostage-taking is defined by the United Nations as "the seizing or detaining and threatening to kill, injure, or continue to detain another person to compel a third party to do or abstain from doing any act as a condition for the release of the hostage" [4 pg 14]. Rogan, et al reported that "hostage takers act to create an extortionate transaction with the police" [5 pg 3].

Hostage/crisis negotiation is a police strategy, which consists of responding to a situation that involves imminent danger to the life or limb of a person(s) being held against their will. There is not necessarily an immediately apparent connection between captor and victim, as Buhite noted, individuals are often "taken hostage [only] because they were available and vulnerable" [6 pg xv].

A law enforcement organization designates an individual as the negotiator to engage the hostage holder in a dialogue in an effort to find a peaceful resolution to the instant problem. The hostage holding may originally be motivated by criminal intent, emotional crisis or politics. The negotiator will attempt to persuade the holder to release the hostage(s) unharmed in return for a pledge that the captor will not be harmed and may actually be assisted in resolving problems in a legitimate way. In this way "negotiation is thought of as the process of discussion engaged in by two or more parties, each of which wants to achieve a desired aim" [7 pg xii]. For situations where negotiation does not seem to be effective, the process will attempt to facilitate the rescue of the victim and apprehension of the perpetrator by distracting or disabling the hostage holder. In a discussion on siege management, Bahn [8] observed that a common element in hostage and barricaded subject incidents is defiance by the subject to orders of the authorities to come out peacefully. He noted that "a standoff develops between the overwhelming power -- manpower, firepower and legal authority -- of the police, military or other authorities and the defiant, trapped offender" [8 pg 1].

The negotiation process which is the subject of this paper involves "law enforcement officers who are selected and trained for the task and who are acting on behalf of their employing agency" [9 pg 308]. For many years the commonly used term was "hostage negotiation" and in many jurisdictions it still is. Since approximately 1989 [10] the FBI switched to "crisis negotiation" and many agencies have followed suit. The International Association of Chiefs of Police [11] utilizes the term hostage communicator. The term hostage/crisis negotiation is utilized throughout this paper.

Police hostage/crisis negotiators view "the negotiation of substantive and non-substantive wants or demands in similar terms: agreement making through bargaining or problem solving, typically via quid pro quo" [5 pg 11]. Police hostage/crisis negotiation involves bargaining for the life of an innocent person, or may involve dealing with a non-hostage holding barricaded criminal, or dealing with individuals who may be emotionally disturbed or mentally ill. Police generally engage in hostage/crisis negotiation in order to save hostage lives, without unnecessarily endangering the lives of the helpers. Captors and other subjects engage in negotiation for these same hostages for a variety of reasons, initially defined by the original motivation for the event, whether criminal, political or emotional.

3. A Hostage Negotiation History

Two hostage events, prior to September 1972 that occurred in New York State, one in 1971 and the other in 1972 are often referred to in the literature of hostage situations but did not at the time prompt any changes in law enforcement policy. The September 1971 Attica prison riot and hostage holding in northwest New York State resulted in death for twenty-eight correction officers and ten inmates during a rescue attempt. This tragedy prompted controversy in criminal justice and social science circles over force versus restraint in approaching hostage incidents [12, 13, 14, 15, 16]. It did not, however, prompt interest by the NYPD, perhaps because it involved prisoners and was contained within the walls of a correctional facility located hundreds of miles away. Similarly, almost one year later, in August 1972, a bank robbery hostage situation in Brooklyn, New York which has been perpetuated in a fictionalized account in the popular movie *Dog Day Afternoon* [17] did not immediately result in seeing a need for change in situations involving hostages. However, Attica and Dog-Day as well as additional examples were examined later, when negotiation came to be seen as a viable strategy for dealing with hostage situations [18, 19].

Cooper [20] noted that there was a shift in official responses to hostage situations following the 1972 Munich Olympics incident, and Welch [21] included a reference to the influence of the crisis at the 1972 Munich Olympics in his historical treatment of hostage negotiations. In the Munich Olympic hostage situation two members of the Israeli Olympic team were killed in the original takeover. Additionally, one West German police officer, five PLO terrorists and eight Israeli hostages died during an attempt to free the hostages by force [22, 19, 23].

The Munich event alerted the New York City Police Department that their jurisdiction could provide a similar opportunity for some group to engage in terrorist diplomacy. The fact that the hostage holding occurred during the International Olympics, involved American allies, Israel and West Germany, and was broadcast live by the media was enough to prompt an immediate study of the issues [24, 18, 25].

The post-Munich study period resulted in promulgation of new *Recommended Guidelines; Incidents Involving Hostages*. These contingency plans stressed, "The primary consideration in such circumstances is to secure the lives and safety of the threatened hostages, the police officers, innocent bystanders, and the criminals themselves" [26 pg 1]. John A. Culley [27], a Detective Bureau lieutenant, referring to the draft document, noted that Chief Inspector Michael J. Codd had recently "reviewed and approved plans for hostage situations, plans which [Codd] had been working on with various units of the police department since September 1972" [28 pg 1]. This original plan did not specifically mention hostage negotiators.

In a then far-reaching review of hostage incident responses Gettinger noted "Shortly after the Munich incident [1972], Patrick Murphy, the New York City Police Commissioner gave the order that New York should prepare itself for terrorist hostage-taking" [25 pg 14]. His Chief of Special Operations, Simon Eisendorfer, formed a committee consisting of patrol, detective, training and psychological services representatives. Gettinger further reported that the FBI followed suit in 1973 when it initiated research and training in hostage negotiation. One of the original FBI negotiators, Conrad Hassel, noted that this specialty was not even conceived until 1972 and that it soon spread across the country [25]. Soskis, in an article which discussed behavioral scientists and law enforcement personnel working together, reviewed various possible collaborations and noted that the "new discipline of hostage negotiations . . . had its beginning in the New York City Police Department" [23 pg 49]. The first formal practice of police hostage negotiation was established in New York City during the period between September 1972 and April 1973 [29, 19, 18, 30, 31]. It was established as a direct result of an attack by terrorists against US allies.

In January 1973 a significant event in the evolution of hostage negotiation took place over a two-day period in Brooklyn, New York at a location known as John & Al's Sporting Goods Store. The local precinct police had responded to a silent alarm call of a possible robbery in progress and were met with gunfire from within the store. Reinforcements arrived, including ESU tactical officers, which is the equivalent of Special Weapons and Tactics (SWAT) Team personnel in some other jurisdictions. One ESU officer was killed and two other officers were wounded in the quickly unfolding event. One of four suspects was also wounded and eight hostages were held in the store. The new operational plan for incidents involving hostages, that Chief Eisendorfer had organized a few months earlier at Commissioner Murphy's direction, was spontaneously field-tested for the first time. Its primary concerns were with containment of the scene, control of personnel and resources and communication with the captors [32]. Forty-seven hours after the incident began, all of the hostages were safe, the four perpetrators were in custody and there was no further injury to police officers or other responders.

A comprehensive critique of the incident at John & Al's was undertaken. Although, according to Welch [21], the plan had not been eagerly received throughout the Department, its basic principles were validated by the activities surrounding the forty-seven-hour siege at John & Al's. Even though the original plan had stressed the importance of communicating with hostage holders, there had been no prior indication as to who the negotiator would be. The critique made commanders aware of "negotiation deficits" [21 pg 66]. A wide variety of police and non-police had 'negotiated' during the forty-seven hours, largely without measurable success. As a result of the incident, the idea of having specific individuals designated as hostage negotiators was introduced into the NYPD for the first time. By April 1973 a team of negotiators had been selected from the ranks of the Detective Bureau and put through a four-week training program [21 pg 66].

Police Commissioner Michael J. Codd in a report on police preparedness for terrorist events indicated that the hostage situation guide had been designed to "focus on functional team work, effective communications, and skilled coordination of tactics, under the management of a high ranking police commander" [28 pg 3]. A major change to the original draft of the plan, following John & Al's, was the establishment of "a group of specially trained negotiators responsible for communicating with barricaded suspects" in place of "the more traditional response of unconditional assault" [33 pg 64].

In 1974, the NYPD received a grant from the New York State Division of Criminal Justice Services to support the efforts which had been initiated post-Munich and revised as a result of John & Al's. A hostage confrontation response system, utilizing Detective Bureau investigators and ESU tactical specialists, was formalized. The investigators and the tactical officers were trained to "meet the problem of hostage negotiating and rescue" under the direction of an incident commander, according to a Police Department document *Terrorism Control in New York City* [34]. The recommended guidelines had evolved into a *Tactical Manual for Hostage Situations* [35].

The Emergency Service Unit of the NYPD is a highly diverse mobile force of uniformed officers with full-time citywide responsibility. The members of this all volunteer group must have extensive uniformed patrol experience before applying for a transfer into the ESU. The members are rescue oriented and perform a wide range of specialized tasks. According to their *Operational Policies and Tactics*, among other tasks, they are certified Emergency Medical Technicians, take potential jumpers off bridges and buildings, handle radiation accidents, search for and transport improvised explosive devices and operate the Emergency Rescue Vehicle (a tank). "They are the

[New York City Police] Department's Firearms Battalion. They are the only members qualified to use tear gas. They are also skilled in the use of anti-sniper rifles, carbines, machine guns, and the shotgun, their most basic weapon" [36 pg 1]. One chapter of their *Operational Policies and Tactics* manual was devoted to confrontations, which included "sniper, barricaded criminal/hostage, disorderly group/mob, civilian clothed member [and] dangerous psychotic" [36 pg 20]. The Emergency Service Unit was selected to be the tactical [SWAT] component of the new hostage confrontation program because of its involvement in closely related activities for many years.

It was an Emergency Service Police Officer, Steve Gilroy, who was killed in the early stages of the siege at John & Al's. It was not surprising that officers assigned to Emergency Service might resent, if not resist, creation of a new team of officers to perform part of their [ESU] jobs as described by Welch [21].

The newly created Detective Bureau Hostage Negotiating Team was also an all volunteer function most often performed as needed by full-time New York City Police Investigators, primarily Detectives and Sergeants.

The decision to house the negotiator component of the new program in the Detective Bureau rather than Patrol or Special Operations was based on a variety of personnel factors which Schlossberg and Freeman [30], Bard [37] and Symonds [38] had suggested as appropriate criteria for candidates to become successful hostage/crisis negotiators.

Since a range of other policing experiences had preceded assignment to the Detective Bureau, the investigator would be chronologically and experientially mature. Investigators worked in civilian clothes, which fit with the crisis intervention notion of non-hostile representation of authority. Detective assignments are normally case driven as compared to uniformed patrol officers who are often radio-run-incident driven, so investigators do not have to be readily available for the next routine radio-run. Investigators are also expected to be competent in the gathering and analysis of intelligence as well as in conducting interviews and interrogations. These skills were deemed necessary for success in hostage/crisis negotiation.

To have been accepted as a negotiator, the volunteer investigator needed a positive recommendation from his commander, participated in a paper and pencil psychological examination and a follow-up interview with a police department psychologist, and had to be favorably interviewed by the Hostage Team Coordinator. Those chosen were then assigned to a four week training program, designed specifically for the purpose and including: psychology, physical fitness, firearms, electronic equipment, and liaison [27]. Assigned full time in civilian clothes to various Detective Squads, a number of trained negotiators, based on geographic area of assignment, scheduled work time and any special qualifications were called together for an incident. After the incident, the negotiators returned to their regular investigative duties. These individuals performed the additional duties of hostage/crisis negotiator, without additional pay, although their base investigator's salary was higher than the base pay of the uniformed Emergency Service Officers.

When the hostage confrontation program was formally launched, as a result of the critique of the John & Al's siege, the newly designated Hostage Coordinator, a Lieutenant assigned to the Brooklyn Detective command, was placed in charge and transferred into the Major Crimes Section of the city-wide Special Investigation Division. He was also responsible for various aspects of kidnap and extortion investigations.

There were several changes in the organizational placement and reporting lines of the hostage negotiation program between 1973 and 1983. Most were due to resistance or a lack of acceptance on the part of some senior police commanders during a period of adjustment for a new function. The personality of the hostage team coordinator and positive media attention to early successes of the team also created resentment. The team coordinator was an extremely out going individual who was also active in many social organizations within the Department. The New York media provided extensive coverage to the highly successful operational activities of the hostage negotiators and the coordinator was often available to a variety of interviewers. This was with the approval of the press office of the Police Department but yet engendered negative reaction by other commanders. This is consistent with Welch's [21] observation about organizational resistance in his examination of hostage situations.

Another change, which took place during this same time period, was in the types of incidents to which hostage/crisis negotiators were dispatched. Originally they responded only to confirmed hostage holdings and the ESU supervisor at the scene initiated the request for hostage/crisis negotiators. Gradually, based on hostage/crisis negotiation success, and accompanying positive media attention, they were dispatched to some non-hostage crisis situation such as barricaded criminals and people threatening suicide. Both of these functions previously had been the exclusive purview of the ESU. Contemporaneous with these expanded duties hostage/crisis negotiation personnel were also being utilized in kidnap and extortion cases, and in operational planning for high risk raid and warrant execution. A significant change took place with the publication of the Police Department's *Interim Order # 51* [39] when for the first time it was mandated that negotiators be dispatched to certain situations involving non-hostage holding emotionally disturbed persons. The ESU previously handled the majority of these situations without negotiators. This last change was the direct result of a critical incident that had resulted in the death of an emotionally disturbed person.

4. Aspects of a Hostage Negotiation Research Project

During 1999 I completed a study of hostage/crisis negotiation units in US police agencies. Data was collected from departments that employed at least 100 sworn officers. Six hundred sixty one state and local law enforcement agencies had responded to the *Law Enforcement Management and Administrative Statistics: 1993* [40] (LEMAS) survey conducted by the U.S. Department of Justice, Bureau of Justice Statistics indicated that they employed at least 100 officers. Langworthy had noted, "LEMAS data is an incredibly valuable vehicle for providing information about policing" [41 pg 15]. The selection of the 661 agencies was based primarily on two factors. One factor was agency size; there are approximately 17,000 police agencies in the U.S. with department size varying from one individual to more than 35,000 sworn officers. However, Murphy & Plate [42] suggested that small agencies probably did not have the resources to have their own hostage negotiation teams. The second factor in the sample selection was geographical diversity. All fifty states and the District of Columbia, including municipal, county, sheriff, special police and state police agencies would provide the richest data. Federal law enforcement agencies and U.S. military agencies, which often have their own hostage/crisis negotiation teams, were not included.

This was a descriptive study designed to gather data about the formation and current status of hostage/crisis negotiation in U.S. policing. The study examined hostage/crisis negotiation and variables such as agency size, organizational structure, chain of command, written policy, and innovation. The opinions of respondents about satisfaction in hostage/crisis negotiation and about the effectiveness of negotiation were also examined. This study did not examine the inner workings of a hostage/crisis negotiation unit but focused on its relationship to the larger police organization.

An analysis of certain characteristics of police agencies in the United States as they pertain to hostage/crisis negotiation was the focus of the study. This questionnaire phase of the project yielded a return rate of approximately 48% (315), including 39 (6%) that were not useable because they did not contain sufficient information (16) or indicated that the agency did not have a hostage/crisis negotiation team (23). Data from 276 (42%) returned questionnaires were utilized for analysis. Two hundred seventy-five of the respondents indicated that their agency had formed a hostage/crisis negotiation team. Some of the items considered follow [1].

4.1. Direct Action Orientation vs. Negotiation

Noesner and Dolan [43], both FBI negotiators, have noted that from the first day of training and throughout their careers, police officers are taught to take the initiative to resolve situations that threaten life or property. They also cautioned that immediate, aggressive response might not be an appropriate course of action in every situation. Davis [44] believed that law enforcement officers were generally action-oriented in a hostage crisis and that negotiation was underutilized. Wargo [45] noted concern with the knowledge of the police officers on the scene about hostage/crisis policy. He was also interested in how to most effectively use personnel. Klein [46] reported that hostage/crisis technique was very successful because of the ability of the police or military to contain and negotiate, but that most experts had focused on the negotiations within such operations. Nudell and Antokol [47] noted that although hostage taking is only a small part of a greater problem it often has impact out of proportion to its actual threat. They recommended a strategy of 'firm flexibility' in dealing with such incidents. This concept, which involves communication without substantial compromise, seems to mesh with the notion of 'dynamic inactivity' introduced by Schlossberg [48]. His 'dynamic inactivity' referred to a negotiation posture in which no overt activity appears to be taking place, but in reality, in addition to preparation for physical force maneuvers, there are also planning and calculation of alternatives designed to maximize a nonviolent outcome [49].

4.2. SWAT vs. Negotiation

While always prepared and justified to use force, a hostage/crisis negotiation posture attempts resolution without unnecessarily resorting to violence. In a democracy police work often focuses a great deal of attention on means as opposed to ends, which has an important impact on how the job is to be performed [50]. For example, discussions in policing dealing with concepts such as zero tolerance, pursuit driving or handling emotionally disturbed or mentally ill people may be related to justification for the use of force in a given incident. In each of these types of incidents an officer is faced with a choice of means in order to achieve a desired end. The discussion of ends-means is a persistent dilemma in law enforcement and may be relevant to locating the hostage/crisis negotiators in an agency; should it be part of the Special Weapons and Tactics Team (SWAT) or not. The SWAT concept is action oriented, most often associated with physical activities and specialized equipment. The negotiation concept is more communication and dialogue oriented, chiefly associated with patience and persuasion. Both concepts have the same end in sight, resolution of a situation, but each emphasizes a different means. Each concept may actually be mutually dependent on its ability to perform successfully. An important consideration may be the placement of each unit in the overall departmental structure. Police chief executives and incident commanders may receive filtered information and advice when the negotiation function reports through the tactical element rather than directly to the decision maker.

4.3. Development of Written Policies

In previous research Borum and Strentz [51] emphasized that a planned and tested response was required due to the volatility and complexity of hostage incidents. While Ochberg and Soskis [52] indicated that only techniques, which have demonstrably worked in the past, should be used. MacWillson [53] stressed that incident management, response planning, and strategic and tactical decision making help to determine the effectiveness of government in crisis management, which is often the responsibility of a police department. Whittle [54] discussed issues, which must be considered in planning policies and procedures including resources, personnel and training. Friedland [55] noted the need for constituent support for policy and public confidence in the soundness of government's [the police] decisions. Public support and confidence are more likely if policies are in writing. Cooper [20] explored the feasibility of developing uniform standards for dealing with hostage situations. Policies cannot be effective over time if they are not formally written. As Severn [56] noted the most important asset for a situation commander is a clear policy or standard operating procedure manual that defines the chain of command and lays out the agency's tactical principles, mission, and philosophy.

Eighty-one percent (222) of the respondents to my study had adopted a written policy for hostage/crisis negotiation incidents; 51 (19%) had not. In addition to asking if a written policy existed, I requested a copy of the policy. Only 60 (22%) were received. There was a wide range in degree of specificity. Two agencies provided a single page policy statement. Another agency provided a comprehensive document that exceeded 60 pages. Some policy documents contained recent revision dates; one agency provided a three page item dated 1975. An undated and untitled ten-page checklist, which apparently originated with a different agency, was submitted as its own from one responding agency.

4.4 Selection and Training of Negotiators

There had been a general lack of information on the selection and preparation of negotiating unit members. This made it problematic to have in mind the implementation of a standard to assess the readiness and competence of negotiating units and personnel. Hammer, et al. [57] and Rogan, et al. [58] reported that the majority of police departments did not have written guidelines for the selection of hostage/crisis negotiators. Hammer also noted that initial hostage/crisis negotiator training consisted of up to ten days of training for 74% of the departments reporting. Culley [27] reported that the initial training for the original hostage negotiation team was one month long.

As noted above, the majority of responding agencies (81%) had developed a written policy for hostage/crisis negotiation incidents. However, 56% (150) did not have a written policy for the selection of their negotiators. Whether written or not, there was a range of selection tools utilized by the respondents. Even without a written selection policy, 99% of the responding agencies provided negotiator training to those individuals who had been selected. The range in the number of hours of initial hostage/crisis negotiation training was from a low of two hours, one agency (0.4%), to a high of 250 hours, again one agency (0.4%). The mean was 47 hours. The range of topics was as wide as the number of hours. In response to a series of questions about training topics, several respondents indicated that they were not aware of the curriculum provided to their personnel because it had been provided by another agency. Training was received from a variety of sources, including: 22% in-house; 14% by a regional academy; 13% by a state academy; 35% from the FBI; and 16% received their training from a non-law enforcement agency, usually a college or university.

Almost 75% did indicate that 'terrorism' was included in the negotiator-training program. The range was from a low of fifteen minutes for one agency to a high of fifteen hours for another agency. The mean time spent on terrorism related material was 2.23 hours.

5. Concluding Observations

Crucial to the tenets of safe hostage recovery through controlled negotiation is a fundamental question: Is this situation manageable? The responding authorities must reasonably and realistically believe that more good than harm will result from their activities. Care must be given not to be lulled into a false sense of capacity to safely manage all events; most will work out fine, not all.

I believe a crucial consideration in the minds of some officials during the early stages of the multiple coordinated sky jacking events that became 9/11; airplane hijack incidents are usually manageable events. Further, after the fact reports indicate that some of the hijackers on 9/11 sought to pacify their victims by offering the potential for safe resolution by signifying that it was 'only a hijacking' or words to that effect. Absent adequate reliable intelligence, so well documented post 9/11, were we about to be lulled into a false sense of security that these events would have been manageable?

Additionally, accounts attributed to Bin Laden indicate that not all of the hijackers were fully aware of the ultimate plan. And, examples like the sympathetic copy-cat teenage suicide event in Tampa, Florida soon after 9/11 may tend to indicate that negotiation for this type of incident may become a necessary reality. One must also consider that some terror oriented groups lack the level of preparedness and resolve observed on 9/11; others may still seek the theater of terror that hostage holding offers. The non-cause oriented criminals and emotionally disturbed persons will also continue to present their own unique brand of hostage holding life threatening behavior.

In a recent essay, this author noted that: in these times of threat and response some important factors about preparing police for role change became apparent. First, there is a need to specify the new reality and determine what is to be done about it. Next, a review of legal and administrative directives would be appropriate. These two items should identify (1) the nature of the problem, (2) the legislated parties responsible for response (3), the actual parties involved in attempts at resolution, and (4) suggested changes in mandate or practice which would provide an improved conclusion. Another basic factor for any role change in policing is to specify appropriate organizational change, if any, and delineate the nature resources needed and of training required. Adequate and appropriate funding is a must [59].

As noted, the research report cited in this paper was completed in 1999. Although additional research will be undertaken to update the data, anecdotal information based on regular contact with the law enforcement hostage /crisis negotiation community indicates that there has not been a great deal of change.

References

[1] R.J. Louden, The structure and procedures of hostage / crisis negotiation units in US police organizations: Doctoral dissertation, City University of New York; 1999.
[2] *American Heritage Dictionary,* Second College Edition. New York: Dell Publishing; 1983.
[3] R.D. Crelinsten, D. Szabo, *Hostage-Taking.* Lexington: D.C.: Heath and Company; 1979.
[4] G.M.Levitt, *Democracies against terror: The Western response to state-supported terrorism* . New York: Prager; 1988, p 14.
[5] R.G. Rogan, M.R. Hammer, C.R. Van Zandt, *Dynamic processes of crisis negotiation: Theory, research and practice.* Westport: Praeger; 1997.
[6] R.D. Buhite, *Lives at risk: hostages and victims in American foreign policy.* Wilmington: Schorlarly Resources Inc.; 1995.
[7] J. Edelman, M.B. Crain, *The Tao of negotiation.* New York: Harper Business; 1993.
[8] C. Bahn, *Sieges and their aftermaths.* New York: John Jay College of Criminal Justice; Unpublished Manuscript, 1987.
[9] M.R. Volpe, R.J. Louden, Hostage negotiations: skills and strategies for third party intervention in high stress situations. In D.M. McCabe, W. Wilkins, Editors. *Dispute resolution and democracy in the 1990's: Shaping the agenda.* Washington: Society of Professionals in Dispute Resolution; 1990.
[10] N.F. Kaiser, The tactical incident: A total police response, *FBI LawEnforcement Bulletin.* **59/8** (1990, August), 14 - 18.
[11] International Association of Chiefs of Police *Hostage/Barricaded subject incidents.* Arlington, VA: IACP National Law Enforcement Policy Center; 1992.
[12] G.D.Garson, Force versus restraint in prison riots. *Crime and Delinquency,* **18/4** (1972, October), 411 - 421.
[13] T. Wicker, *A time to die.* New York: Quandrangle; 1975.
[14] B. Useem, P. Kimball, *States of siege - U.S. prison riots 1971 - 1986.* New York: Oxford University Press; 1989.
[15] P.T. Shelton, Attica -1971- LeBastille Extraordinaire, *History of the New York State Police 1917 - 1987.* New York: Trooper Foundation of the State of New York; 1994.
[16] A.R. Strollo, D. Wills-Raftery, *Four long days: Return to Attica.* Hurley, NY: American Life Associates; 1994.
[17] *Dog day afternoon.* Burbank: Warner Brothers; 1975.
[18] F. Bolz, E. Hershey, *Hostage cop.* New York: Rawson Wade; 1979.
[19] C. Moorehead, *Hostages to fortune.* New York: Atheneum; 1980.
[20] H.H.A. Cooper, Hostage rights - law and practice in throes of evolution *Journal of International Law.* **15/1** (1985, Winter)
[21] M.F. Welch, The applied typology and victimology in the hostage negotiation process *Crime and Justice.* **7** (1984), 63-86.
[22] M. Schreiber, *After-action report of terrorist activity: 20th Olympic Games Munich, West Germany.* Quantico, VA: Unpublished FBI Manuscript; 1973.

[23] D.A. Soskis, C.R. Van Zandt, Hostage negotiation: Law enforcement's most effective non-lethal weapon, *Management Quarterly.* Washington: U.S. Department of Justice; **6/4** (1986, Autumn).

[24] B. Gelb, The cop who saves lives, *New York Times Magazine,* 1977, April 17.

[25] S. Gettinger, Hostage negotiators bring them out alive, *Police Magazine.* **6/1** (1983, January) 10 -28.

[26] Recommended guidelines: Incidents involving hostages. New York City Police Department: Unpublished, 1973.

[27] J.A. Culley, Hostage negotiations, *FBI Law Enforcement Bulletin.* **43/10** (1974, October), 10-14.

[28] M.J. Codd, *Police management of terrorist caused crises: A metropolitan perspective.* New York City Police Department: Unpublished, 1977.

[29] J.B. Bell, *A time of terror.* New York: Basic Books; 1978.

[30] H. Schlossberg, L. Freeman*, Psychologist with a Gun.* New York: Coward McCann; 1974.

[31] J. Douglas, M. Olshaker, *Mind Hunter.* New York: Simon & Schuster; 1995.

[32] D. Cawley, Anatomy of a seige. *The Police Chief.* **41/1** (1974, January), 30 – 34.

[33] R.W. Taylor, Hostage and crisis negotiation procedures: Assessing police liability *Trial.* **19/3** (1983, March), 64 – 69.

[34] *Terrorism control in New York City.* New York City Police Department: Unpublished; 1979.

[35] *Tactical manual for hostage situations.* New York City Police Department: Unpublished; 1974.

[36] *Operational policies and tactics.* New York City Police Department: Unpublished; 1977.

[37] M. Bard, Hostage negotiations; Part I, Tactical procedures, & Part II, Negotiating techniques. New York: Harper & Row Films; 1978.

[38] M. Symonds, Victim responses to terror, *Annals of the New York Academy of Sciences.* **347** (1980, June), 129-136.

[39] Interim Order No.51, Aided cases, mentally ill or emotionally disturbed persons. New York: NYCPD departmental order; 1984.

[40] U.S. Department of Justice, Bureau of Justice Statistics, Law enforcement management and administrative statistics (LEMAS), 1993. [Computer file], Conducted by U.S. Department of Commerce, Bureau of the Census. ICPSR, Editor. Ann Arbor, MI: Inter-university Consortium for Political and Social Research [producer and distributor], 1996; [paper file, 1995].

[41] T.V. Brady, *Measuring what matters.* Washington, DC: U.S. Department of Justice; 1996.

[42] P.V. Murphy, T.G. Plate, *Commissioner.* New York: Simon and Schuster; 1977.

[43] G.W. Noesner, J.T. Dolan, First responder negotiation training. *FBI Law Enforcement Bulletin,* **61/8** (1992, August), 1 – 5.

[44] R.C. Davis, Hostage negotiations: First thought or afterthought? *Law Enforcement Technology.* **20/5** (1993, May), 28 - 30 and 52 – 53.

[45] M.G. Wargo, Chief's role in a hostage/barricaded subject incident. *Police Chief.* **56/11** (1989, November), 59 - 61.

[46] G.C. Klein, Studying delta force or death squads: The politics of hostage negotiations. *Journal of Contemporary Criminal Justice.* **11/1** (1995, February), 67- 88.

[47] M. Nudell, N. Antokol, Democratic dilemma, *Security Management.* 35/3 (1991, March), 26 – 36.

[48] Law Enforcement News. Police psychologist says time is on side of police. New York: John Jay College of Criminal Justice; (1977, May), 3-7.

[49] H. Schlossberg, Psychiatric principles of negotiations, *The U.S. Negotiator.* Montgomery, AL: (1996, Spring) 5-6.

[50] J. Kuykendall, R.R. Roberg, Mapping police organizational change, *Criminology.* **20/3** (1982, August), 241 - 256.

[51] R. Borum, T. Strentz, Borderline personality: Negotiation strategies, *FBI Law Enforcement Bulletin.* **61/8** (1992, August), 6 -10.

[52] F.M. Ochberg, D.A. Soskis, *Victims of terrorism.* Boulder, CO: Westview Press; 1982.

[53] A.C. MacWilson, *Hostage-taking negotiations: Incident-response strategy.* New York: St. Martin's Press; 1992.

[54] R.A. Whittle, Hostage negotiations: A situational/motivational approach for police response, *Critical Issues in Criminal Investigations.* Cincinnati, OH: Anderson; 1988.

[55] N. Friedland, Hostage negotiations: Dilemmas about policy, In L.Z. Freedman, Y. Alexander, Editors*. Perspectives on terrorism.* Wilmington, DE: Scholarly Resources; 1983.

[56] D.H. Jr. Severn, Coaching clinic: Crisis management training for situation commanders, *Texas Police Journal.* **40/12** (1993, January), 8 – 10.

[57] M.R. Hammer, C.R. Van Zandt, R.G. Rogan, Crisis/hostage negotiation team profile, *FBI Law Enforcement Bulletin.* **63/3** (1994, March), 8 - 11.

[58] R.G. Rogan, M.R. Hammer, C.R. Van Zandt, Profiling crisis negotiation teams, *The Police Chief.* **61/11** (1994, November), 14 - 18.

[59] R.J. Louden, Policing post – 9/11 in Fordham urban, *Law Journal,* **XXXII/4** (2005, July), 757-765.

Understanding and Responding to the Terrorism Phenomenon
O. Nikbay and S. Hancerli (Eds.)
IOS Press, 2007

Probability of Hostage Fatality in Hostage-Taking Terrorism: Negotiation Option and Characteristics of Negotiators

Murat KOCAK
Kent State University, USA

Abstract. The ITERATE (International Terrorism: Attributes of Terrorist Events) data set compiled by Mickolus et al., indicates that governments basically respond to terrorist hostage incidents in three ways: negotiation, shootout, and other responses such as massive nationwide searches for terrorists, especially when kidnapping occurs. This empirical study by using logit models, tries to estimate the probability of hostages being killed because of these response options. It focuses on characteristics of negotiators and tries to estimate the probability of hostages being killed when the number of negotiators increases, controlling for: the duration and the size of the incident, the number of governments and entities involved, terrorists' demands and behaviors, and the effect of having non-governmental targets when ransom is demanded by terrorists. It offers policy implications regarding how to handle hostage-taking terrorism incidents and the appropriate number of negotiators in a negotiation process.

Keywords. Negotiation, terrorists, hostages, logit model, probability, number of negotiators, shootout, response, hostage fatality

Introduction

Use of force was the main response to hostage-taking incidents in the 1960s. Many hostages, hostage takers, and police officers were killed during these interventions until the early 1970s as a result of this way of thinking. In this context, Miller, based on figures released by RAND Corporation stated that, "more hostages die as a result of assaults than from direct killing by terrorists" [1 pg 138].

In 1971, a historical change took place in this field. Hatcher et al. [2], examining the historical development of special tactical units, report that The New York City Police Commissioner, Simon Eisendorfer, assigned Lieutenant Frank Bolz and psychologist/police officer, Harvey Schlossberg to find a solution to this problem. Therefore, in 1973, the New York City Police Department was the first to introduce the newly developed negotiation tactics, and those tactics have continued to develop with the contributions of psychologists [2]. Vecchi et al. [3] see this development as the most important one in the law enforcement field during the past few decades.

However, while this development has taken place in some parts of the world, other parts of the world did not achieve the same development, especially regarding transnational hostage-taking terrorism. The ITERATE (International Terrorism: Attributes of Terrorist Events) data set compiled by Mickolus et al., shows that approximately 14% of the transnational terrorists' hostage-taking incidents between 1978 and 1991 (including kidnappings) result in death of hostages. The data show that only 43% of these incidents are responded to with a negotiation option. It also indicates that official and unofficial individuals other than police negotiators served as negotiators. Mickolus et al[4]'s Chronology of Events shows that doctors, ambassadors, ministers, prime ministers, religious leaders, party leaders, journalists and even other extremist organizations' members served as negotiators in some incidents. It seems that because professional negotiation units were not institutionalized in some countries, they were not able to avoid mishandlings in negotiations. Furthermore, this increased the number of negotiators who had direct contact with the terrorists. These findings could make one believe that use of force and mishandling of negotiation processes, including having too many negotiators for one incident, might be the major reasons for the high number of fatalities in transnational hostage-taking terrorism.

Faure views hostage incidents as consisting of three types: hostage-barricade incidents, skyjackings, and kidnappings. He defines hostage-taking as "the detention of individuals whose release is conditional on the realization of certain conditions determined by their captures" [5 pg 470]. So the hostage is seen as a "currency of exchange," and his/her life is threatened in the illegal detention by their captures [5]. The following study includes these three types of hostage incidents considering this definition and the characteristics of the ITERATE dataset.

The ITERATE dataset shows that governments basically respond to hostage incidents in three ways: negotiation, shootout, and other responses such as, massive nationwide searches for terrorists, especially in kidnapping events. This study will be an attempt to determine the estimates of the probability of hostages being killed as a result of these options, particularly negotiation and shootout with terrorists. The shootout option might be chosen by governments either at the beginning of incidents or at the end when they find terrorists nonnegotiable after having long negotiations with them. This study will treat all of these responses as "shootout," whether this option is carried out either at the end or at the beginning. The argument of the study is that the shootout response increases the probability of hostage fatalities rather than the negotiation response. Contrary to the shootout option, negotiation should have a negative effect on this probability.

Another argument of the study is that the number of negotiators who contact terrorists in order to convince perpetrators to release hostages and surrender themselves should not exceed two. Having more than two negotiators endangers hostages' lives in a high probability. Although having one negotiator during an incident is preferable in order to build trust of terrorists and maintain the communication link with them, having two negotiators is essential. Thus, two negotiators will be able to rotate and keep their strength during an incident. Having two vigorous negotiators is essential to carrying on the negotiation process for a longer time[1] [6].

MacWillson [6] draws attention to practitioners' concerns regarding having more than one negotiator. Therefore, it is important to discover and compare the impact of having two negotiators to the impact of having one negotiator on the probability of hostage fatality. This study will be an attempt to calculate estimates of the risk probabilities of hostage fatality in hostage-taking terrorism incidents for having one negotiator and having two. In addition, the ITERATE dataset shows that there are incidents in which three or more persons served as negotiators. In fact, in over 25 % of the total number of hostage negotiation incidents, three or more negotiators participated

---

[1] The ITERATE dataset indicates that the average duration of a terrorism motivated hostage-taking incident is 38.

in the negotiations. Therefore, the impact of having high numbers of negotiators will also be investigated in terms of those prediction probabilities. In the literature review, the study will propose a proper negotiation-team structure and present a short description of the characteristics of an ideal negotiator. The intention is to provide an example of the way to handle negotiation processes correctly. Ultimately, this study might be used to avoid hostage fatalities which would be consequences of mishandlings in those processes in any future hostage situations.

1. Why Must We Negotiate?

MacWillson [6] states a couple of reasons we negotiate:

1. Principally, we place value on human life. It does not matter whose life it is: the life of hostages, security forces, or to a degree, terrorists or criminals.
2. Dialogue and conversation reduce the anxieties and tensions of the incident.
3. Hostage takers assess their own position more rationally.
4. We gain time to take control and implement measures and necessary interventions for the incident.

The author argues that from analysis of the previous hostage-taking incidents, it is understood that, "the longer the period the hostages spend with their captors, the chances of the hostages being injured or killed, unless under extreme provocations, reduces accordingly" [6 pg 40]. Gaining time is also considered to be a necessity of preparation for appropriate options. Gathering essential intelligence and information, liaison with other governments, exploitation of terrorists' weaknesses and mistakes, and preparation for a tactical assault all require gaining time [6].

Furthermore, a negotiation response is considered to be the first and sometimes (depending on the situation) the sole option for saving lives, regardless of whose lives they are. Unless, this option loses its effectiveness and usefulness and creates danger for hostages' lives, we should continue to negotiate.

2. A Proposal for the Negotiation Team Structure and the Negotiator

MacWillson [6] says that it is not uncommon that it is preferred to have one responsible man for negotiation. However, he suggests that there should be two negotiation teams which are headed by a lead negotiator in order to maintain a healthy negotiation process for an indefinite period. Rotating from one to the other periodically also reduces the stress of the job.

Birge [7] suggests that a negotiation team consists of four to six well-trained members. The author names members of a negotiation team and their duties as follows:

1. Team leader: the leader must have an equal rank with the tactical leader to allow a balance in the decision making process. He/she must be a well trained negotiator although he/she will not be physically present with the negotiation

team during the incident. The leader develops important strategies and options for the command base.

2. Assistant team leader: he/she is present with the team as the team manager during the incident. He/she directly communicates with the team leader and the command base, and ensures information and intelligence flow. He/she also maintains the brainstorming of the team for analyzing the progress and finding appropriate solutions.

3. Primary negotiator: only the primary negotiator talks to the perpetrators. He/she must have several vital skills (mentioned on the next page).

4. Coach or backup officer: he/she is present to replace the primary negotiator in the event that the primary negotiator is not available at that time. He/she monitors the conversations between the primary negotiator and perpetrators and assists by acting as the coach for the primary negotiator.

5. Team chorographer: he/she maintains a chronological log of events. It is and will be a key source for evaluating the negotiation process. He/she also records all communications during the incident.

6. Intelligence coordinator: this officer is responsible for gathering information which may be helpful for negotiation, such as personality type, phobias, hobbies, relationships, and so on.

7. We can add a psychologist to the negotiation team although Birge [7] does not include a psychologist in the negotiation team. We need to note that Hatcher et al. [2] suggest the use of psychologists as consultants but not as primary negotiators.

Another important suggestion of MacWillson [6] is that a negotiator must serve as a medium of communication. He/she should not be a decision maker in the strategy. It is the job of the Crisis Management Center. However, as it is mentioned earlier, it is possible to observe that governors, internal ministers, vice presidents, and even sometimes presidents serve as negotiators in hostage-taking terrorism incidents [4]. According to MacWillson, by doing so, they are leaving no flexibility for themselves to refer to anyone else regarding terrorists' demands and their own decisions. Terrorists usually take advantage of this situation. In addition, decision makers must be free of negotiation stress and effects of emotions [6].

MacWillson [6] summarizes characteristics of an ideal negotiator[2] as follows: (1) he/she must be recognized by terrorists as a person who is taking them seriously; (2) he/she must be able to understand the decision making machinery; (3) he/she must not be a decision maker in the incident; (4) he/she must be in the middle rank; (5) he/she must be experienced and well educated for negotiations; (6) he/she must have clarity of expression; (7) he/she must have strength enough to do his job for a long and stressful period; (8) he/she must have strength in personality, such as intelligence, resourcefulness, patience, sense of humor, loyalty, and dedication.

It follows that the choice of the primary negotiator must be made very carefully as he/she stands at a very important position in the negotiation process. On the other hand, the number of negotiators is also important. It is preferred to have only one or two negotiators who contact terrorists. Any increase in the number of negotiators may diminish the authority of the negotiator in the eyes of the terrorists. This increase in negotiators may also damage the established communication link.

---

[2] In this study, the word of negotiator refers to primary negotiators.

In this context, MacWillson [6] mentions that there is a hesitation among practitioners to have more than one primary negotiator. Although he suggests two primary negotiators, he draws attention to the terrorists' possible reaction to the change of the negotiator and suggests careful consideration of this possibility. Therefore, the effect of the number of negotiators must be investigated, and it seems that there is lack of research on this matter. This paper is an attempt to fulfill this need by analyzing empirical data.

2.1. Hypotheses

1. The ITERATE data set shows that governments basically respond to hostage incidents in three ways: negotiation, shootout, and other responses such as massive nationwide searches for terrorists especially in kidnapping events. By using logit models this study obtains estimates for the probability of hostages being killed with these three options.

The first hypothesis is that when the shootout option is carried out by authorities the probability of hostage fatalities will be much higher than the probability of fatalities estimated for other options. Contrary to the shootout option, the negotiation option should decrease this probability.

2. The other argument is that the number of negotiators who contact terrorists must be limited. Therefore, the probability of hostage fatalities should increase when the number of negotiators increases.

The study will check the significance of the effect of the number of negotiators on hostage fatality by controlling other factors such as duration and size of the incident, number of governments and entities involved in it, terrorists' demands and behaviors, and the effect of having non-governmental targets when ransom is demanded by terrorists.

2.2. Data and Methods

The data compiled in the International Terrorism: Attributes of Terrorist Events (ITERATE) Project was collected by Edward Mickolus, Todd Sandler, Jean Murdock, and Peter Flemming. The purpose of the ITERATE project is to "quantify data on the characteristics of transnational terrorist groups, their activities which have international impact, and the environment in which they operate" [8 pg 1]. The dataset consists of four parts. The data used in this paper named HOSTAGE is one of the parts of this dataset. It covers transnational terrorist hostage-taking incidents between 1978 and 1991, including aerial, land and sea hijackings, hostage-barricade incidents, and kidnappings.

The dependent variable of this analysis is "hostage killed" which is created from the "first hostage's fate" variable. It is recoded as "1" if the hostages are killed and "0" if they are not killed. In order to avoid a misleading of cross recordings, this study considered only fatalities. Wounded hostages might lose their lives in later days after an incident, and this situation might create cross recordings of killed and wounded hostages.

The independent variable, "negotiation," is created from the "response of target" variable, and recoded as "1" if the government carried out a negotiation as a response and "0" if the government chose options besides the negotiation. Similarly, the "shootout" variable is created from the same variable, and reflects shootout options only. The "other response" variable reflects options other than the negotiation and shootout options. Another independent variable this study focuses on is the "number of negotiators." It reflects the actual number of negotiators who directly contact terrorists. Table 1 displays a description of all variables which are used in logit models of the study.

Table 1. Descriptive statistics of variables in the study

Variable	Obs	Mean	Std. Dev.	Min	Max
Hostages killed	534	.1348315	.3418637	0	1
Negotiation response	472	.4258475	.4949955	0	1
Shootout response	472	.125	.3310698	0	1
Other response	472	.4491525	.4979356	0	1
# of negotiator	287	.5156794	1.164269	0	7
# of hostages	658	21.13374	62.3508	0	998
# of entities	473	1.071882	1.082953	0	7
Demand political	536	.1847015	.3884177	0	1
Demand ransom	542	.1863469	.389746	0	1
Demand prisoners	542	.2269373	.4192386	0	1
Demand safe haven	537	.1266294	.3328675	0	1
Demand safe passage	540	.1111111	.3145611	0	1
Passed dead lines	716	.0893855	.2854988	0	1
Threat carried out	716	.0321229	.1764497	0	1
Sequential release	591	.4940778	.5003884	0	1
Non-gov. target	603	.2421227	.4287238	0	1
Duration in days	503	37.91252	98.26633	0	804

At the beginning, three logit models are created to test the first hypothesis regarding the effects of the three response options (shootout, negotiation and others). Then six additional logit models (model-4 to model-9) are created to test the second hypothesis. These models include "number of negotiators" and "response negotiation" as independent variables together. Logically, a negotiation option requires negotiators, while other options may not require them. Besides, the number of negotiators must be recorded more precisely with the negotiation option rather than the other options when considering limitations of the data. There are only 287 observations of hostage incidents with known values of the number of negotiators out of 716 observations. Hence, including the number of negotiators and the negotiation response, our remaining models are going to show the effect of the number of negotiators on the probability of hostages being killed in different circumstances:

- Model-4 was created to see this effect, controlling for the effects of duration and its interaction with the number of negotiators.
- Model-5 controls for the effects of the size of an incident and its interaction with the number of negotiators in addition to the effect of duration.
- Model-6 controls for the effects of number of entities and its interaction with the number of negotiators including the effect of duration.
- Model-7 controls for the effects of terrorists' demands.

- Model-8 focuses on one of the terrorists' behaviors by controlling for the effects of ransom demand from nongovernmental targets and their interactions with the number of negotiators.[3]
- Finally, model-9 controls for the effects of terrorists' negotiation behaviors.

2.3. Results

None of these models indicates a sign of a multi-collinearity problem. All models have significant chi[2]-ratios, except the 3rd model, regarding the independent variable of other response. The first three models indicate that the shootout response is likely to produce hostage fatalities (Table 2). Furthermore, while the shootout option has a positive effect (z: 4.29) on hostages being killed, the negotiation option has a negative significant effect (z:-3.59) on the dependent variable. In other words, these models suggest that only the negotiation option may be the most likely solution to save hostages' lives, while the shootout option is estimated to be the probable cause of hostage fatalities. Therefore, these findings support the 1st hypothesis. In addition, the 3rd model indicates that the other response options, which do not include negotiation and shootout, do not have a significant effect on the hostage fatalities.

Table 2. Logit regression of hostages killed on targets' response options in terrorists' transnational hostage-taking incidents between 1978 and 1991

Regressor	Model 1 Coefficients (s.errors)	Model 2 Coefficients (s.errors)	Model 3 Coefficients (s.errors)
Shootout Response	1.77*** (.414)		
Negotiation Response		-1.70*** (.474)	
Other Response			.246 (.459)
# of Hostages	.002 (.001)	.005* (.002)	.004* (.002)
# of Entities	.012 (.157)	.351* (.152)	.162 (.168)
Duration in days	.002 (.001)	.004* (.001)	.002 (.001)
Constant	-2.54*** (.282)	-2.12*** (.26)	-2.55*** (.418)
LR chi^2	21.05	22.77	7.76
Pseudo R^2	0.0909	0.0984	0.0335
Observation	314	313	313

Notes: logit estimates. All tests two-tailed.   * p≤ 05; **p≤ 01; ***p≤ 001.

In addition to these findings, our 2nd and 3rd models indicate that the number of hostages has a positive relationship (z: 2.06 in model-2; and z: 2.17 in model-3) with

---

[3] Nongovernmental targets of hostage taking incidents might face with ransom demands, and this situation might increase the number of negotiator.

the dependent variable, controlling for other variables. If it increases, the probability of hostages being killed also increases. By checking for influential outliers before the final model, the study found that both model-2 and 3 have one influential outlier. However, omitting these two observations increases the significance level of the effect of the number of hostages and makes it significant in both models.

One of the findings of model-2 is that the duration in days variable has a positive effect (z: 2.39) on the hostages killed, controlling for the negotiation response, number of hostages and number of entities. If the duration increases, the probability of hostage fatalities also increases. It seems that there is a contradiction with the literature on this matter. As we mentioned above, time works for the advantage of hostages, unless a provocation takes place [6]. However, the data covers not only transnational hostage barricade incidents, but also kidnappings. Therefore, we need to check for the effect of kidnappings in our model. Because of the limitation of the data, this study is not able to check for this effect. However, it can be said that kidnapping incidents differ from other hostage incidents with some of their characteristics. For example, terrorists are not surrounded-as they are in hostage barricade incidents, by law enforcement forces during kidnapping incidents. In addition, Faure [5] mentions that if terrorists are in an environment friendly to them, time works to the advantage of terrorists rather than hostages.

Another finding of Model-2 is that the number of governments/entities upon whom demands were made has a significant effect (z: 2.31) on hostage fatalities. If the number of entities increases, the probability of hostages being killed also increases, controlling for the negotiation response, number of hostages, and duration in days.

The effect of the number of negotiators in different circumstances can be observed in the six remaining models. Interactions of these circumstances with the number of negotiators might have significant effects on the results. However, it is observed from the models that none of these circumstances affects the significance of the number of negotiators. Overall our models suggest that the number of negotiators has a positively correlating pattern with hostages being killed at the significance level of 0.05 (in model-8 significance level is 0.01). The probability of hostage fatalities increases when there is an increase in the number of negotiators (Table 3).

Being one of these factors, the effect of duration might increase the number of negotiators. Thus, its effect on the number of negotiators might be one of the most important factors which increases or decreases the probability of hostage fatality. Model-4 clearly shows the effect of the number of negotiators and its interaction with the duration in this circumstance. The number of negotiators is significant (z: 2.34) at 0.05 level.

Model-5 shows the effect of the other factor, the size of the event, which is represented with the number of hostages variable in the model. The model suggests that the number of negotiators is still significant (z: 2.22) at 0.05 level. Although an influential outlier can be found in the model, it does not create much problem; omitting the influential observation from the model makes the number of negotiators again statistically significant.

Controlling the effect of the number of entities variable, Model-6 indicates no change in the significance level of the number of negotiators. In other words, numbers of governments and units involved in the incidents regarding terrorists' demands do not influence the effect of the number of negotiators on the hostage fatality. The effect of number of negotiators is significant when controlling for other variables.

Table 3. Logit regression of hostages killed on negotiation response option and number of negotiator, controlling for the duration and size of the incident, and number of entities involved in the terrorists' transnational hostage-taking incidents between 1978 and 1991

Regressor	Model 4 Coefficients (s.errors)	Model 5 Coefficients (s.errors)	Model 6 Coefficients (s.errors)
Negotiation Response	-2.51* (1.05)	-2.34* (1.02)	-2.25* (1.08)
# of Hostages		.008 (.005)	
# of Entities			.132 (.243)
Duration in days	.0001 (.004)	.0009 (.004)	.003 (.004)
# of Negotiators	.548* (.234)	.650* (.292)	.926* (.448)
# of Negotiators * days	.002 (.004)	.001 (.004)	-.147 (.122)
# of Negotiators * # of Hostages		-.003 (.004)	
# of Negotiators * # of Entities			-.046 (.106)
Constant	-2.07*** (.244)	-2.37*** (.321)	-2.20*** (.294)
LR chi^2	11.66	12.78	11.93
Pseudo R^2	0.07	0.10	0.08
Observation	225	196	207

Notes: logit estimates. All tests two-tailed.   * p$\leq$ 05; **p$\leq$ 01; ***p$\leq$ 001.

Model-7 checks the effect of the number of negotiators by controlling for terrorists' demands such as demand for political change, ransom, prisoner release, safe haven, and safe passage. These demands might have affected the effect of the number of negotiators. Model-7 proved that none of these demands influenced the effect of the number of negotiators. It still continues to be significant (z: 2.35) in its relationship with the dependant variable at the level of 0.05 (Table 4).

Terrorists might kidnap people and demand ransom from their non-governmental targets, such as business corporations and families, and this situation might create additional negotiators. Therefore, model-8 tries to check the effect of the number of negotiators controlling for the effect of this possibility. As a result, the number of negotiators has still kept its significance level with the hostage fatality. Moreover, its significance level has increased. The obtained evidence (z: 2.57) suggest that when the number of negotiators increases, the probability of hostages being killed also increases at the significance level of 0.01, controlling for: response negotiation, demand for ransom, interaction of number of negotiators with ransom demand, non-governmental targets, and interaction of number of negotiators with non-governmental targets.

Similarly, model-9 indicates that terrorists' negotiation behaviors, such as allowing sequential releases of hostages, allowing deadlines to pass, and carrying out their threats after deadlines do not influence the significant effect of the number of negotiators (z: 2.17) on the hostage fatality. The other finding is that, among terrorists' negotiation behaviors, sequential release has a negative effect (z: -2.81 at level of 0.01) on hostages being killed. In other words, when terrorists allow sequential releases of hostages, it decreases the probability of the hostage fatality. Although model-9 has an influential outlier which causes the number of negotiators to lose its significance level, it does not create much of a problem. Omitting this one observation makes the number of negotiators gain its significance at the level of 0.05.

Table 4. Logit regression of hostages killed on negotiation response option and number of negotiators, controlling for terrorists' demands, their negotiation behavior, and the effect of non-governmental targets in case of ransom demanded in the transnational hostage-taking incidents between 1978 and 1991

Regressor	Model 7 Coefficients (s.errors)	Model 8 Coefficients (s.errors)	Model 9 Coefficients (s.errors)
Negotiation Response	-5.11** (1.66)	-2.93** (1.05)	-3.72* (1.45)
# of Negotiators	.783* (.332)	.869** (.339)	1.10* (.506)
Demand for Political Change	.755 (.888)		
Demand for Ransom	.242 (1.26)	.085 (1.27)	
Demand for Prisoner Release	2.34 (1.21)		
Demand for Safe Haven	-5.03 (2.83)		
Demand for Safe Passage	1.86 (1.41)		
# of Negotiators * Ransom Dem.	-.378 (.524)	-.515 (.463)	
Non-Gov. Target		-.174 (.536)	
# of Negotiators * Non-Gov.Targ		-.191 (.447)	
Sequential Releases			-2.25** (.801)
Passed Deadlines			1.62 (.888)
Threat Carried out			.605 (1.39)
# of Negotiators * Seq. Release			-.210 (.484)
Constant	-1.87*** (.228)	-1.85*** (.250)	-1.62*** (.238)
LR chi^2	24.38	14.07	30.94
Pseudo R^2	0.13	0.08	0.17
Observation	230	233	244

Notes: logit estimates. All tests two-tailed.   * p$\leq$ 05; **p$\leq$ 01; ***p$\leq$ 001.

As the focus of the study is on variables of the negotiation response and the number of negotiators, it is observed that these variables followed the same stable pattern in all nine regression models. The number of negotiators variable always keeps its significance (at levels of 0.05 and 0.01) with its negative sign, while the response negotiation variable keeps its significance (at levels of 0.05 and 0.001) on the dependent variable with a positive sign.

Furthermore, the predicted probabilities of positive outcomes for the hostage fatality variable are determined as follows by the number of negotiators and response options including shootout:

1. The probability of hostages being killed is 31% when authorities carry out shootout with terrorists, controlling for incident days and number of hostages, keeping values of these control variables at their means.

Shootout as a response	Predicted Probability
0	0.0817
1	0.3146

2. Contrary to this high risk of shootout option, the probability of hostages being killed is only 1% if the negotiation option is chosen by governments.

Negotiation as a response	Predicted Probability
0	0.1454
1	0.0136

3. The probability of hostage fatality increases when the number of negotiators increases. The probability of the risk is 34% when the number of negotiators is 7. It is 2% for one negotiator, controlling for negotiation response at the value of "1," and keeping values of other control variables at their means (incident days and interaction of incident days with the number of negotiators). The risk of lives lost increases sharply when there is a high number of negotiators. However, there is good news for negotiation teams. The probability is 3% for having 2 negotiators, and so the difference between the probability of hostage fatality for one negotiator and two negotiators is only 1%.

Number of Negotiators	Predicted Probability
1	0.0186
2	0.0318
3	0.0538
4	0.0895
5	0.1454
6	0.2273
7	0.3373

However, these numbers of predictions, especially for high numbers of negotiators, do not seem so reliable due to the limitation of the data. There were seven negotiators in only 2 cases and, similarly, other numbers of negotiators did not seem represented either. There were six negotiators in 2 cases, 5 in 2, 4 in 5, 3 in 7, 2 in 15, and 1 in 38 cases from a total of 284 observations (Table 5). In addition, this variable has a lot of missing observations (432 of 716) due to undetermined information.

Table 5. Summary of "Number of negotiators" variable

Number of negotiators	Freq.	Percent	Cum.
0	213	75.00	75.00
1	38	13.38	88.38
2	15	5.28	93.66
3	7	2.46	96.13
4	5	1.76	97.89
5	2	0.70	98.59
6	2	0.70	99.30
7	2	0.70	100.00

Therefore, after obtaining the results above, unknown values on the number of negotiators were filled with predicted values of the number of negotiators as being one of the ways of tackling a missing data problem. First, the number of negotiators variable was regressed on the other independent variables, and predicted values for the number of negotiators were calculated. Then, missing values of the number of negotiators were replaced with the newly produced predicted values. The hostage fatality variable was regressed on the variables of the newly developed number of negotiators, negotiation response, incident days, and interaction of incident days with the newly developed number of negotiators. As a result, it is observed that the number of observations of the model reached to 400 observations with an increased secure chi^2-ratio (18.96). Both z-values of the response negotiation (z: -3.88) and the number of negotiators variable (z: 2.54) also increased.

3. Conclusion

3.1. Recommendations for Future Studies

Future studies would be beneficial to confirm the effect of the negotiation option and number of negotiators on hostages being killed in order to reach more precise probability predictions. Considering the large number of missing values in many variables in this study, further research is required. Furthermore, the data subjected to the analysis only covered incidents between 1978 and 1991. Therefore, this study is unaware of any change of patterns in terrorists' hostage taking operations in the last decade. Professor Sloan [9] suggests that there is a probability of a transition in terrorists' behavioral patterns in recent years. He says that terrorists who are determined unto death for their cause may not be found as negotiable persons. Therefore, whether the negotiation option works or does not work is unclear for these incidents. Similarly, it is possible that there are considerable incidents in which terrorists kidnap people in order to interrogate and punish them. Kidnappings of Hizbullah/Ilim (it emerged in Turkey/Turkiye and does not have connections with Lebanon Hezbollah) until the year of 2000, were domestic terrorism examples of this kind of terrorist behavior [10], which do not fit Faure's [5] definition of hostage as a "currency of exchange." Those terrorists neither tried to negotiate nor accepted allegations of their involvements with the kidnappings during those incidents. Therefore, it would be beneficial to analyze recent events to discover whether there is a sign of new trends worldwide. In addition, this study strongly recommends investigating kidnapping incidents separately because terrorists may have different behavioral patterns in these incidents.

As previously mentioned, it was not possible for this study to analyze hostage taking incidents separately from kidnappings. I was not able to check the effect of kidnappings on the probability predictions of the study either. Similarly, I was not able check the effect of the negotiator on its characteristics due to the limitation of the data. Thus, other suggestions for future studies are to check the effects of: (1) decision maker- negotiators, (2) professional negotiators, and (3) other negotiators who are in direct contact with terrorists during a hostage taking incident.

3.2. Recommendations for Governments and Law Enforcement

Based on findings in the analyses of the empirical data, this study suggests that governments must continue to apply negotiation as the first resource instead of the shootout option if their priority is to save lives. However, they must try to discover the perpetrators' real intentions in order to decide the appropriate response option. Logically, if the perpetrators' intention is to kill all hostages, the negotiation option may not work to save hostages' lives without conducting a tactical assault [9].

It is also important to perform the negotiation process in the correct format. This study indicates that a high number of negotiators endangers hostages' lives and may cause a high probability of negative consequences. Any attempt to contact terrorists by a party other than the primary negotiators increases the probability of losing hostages' lives as the attempt would increase the number of negotiators. Furthermore, being a negotiator is a very hard job that requires special training, experience, skill, strength, and harmonious teamwork [6] rather than skills of psychologists [2], journalists, or political and social leaders. Moreover, negotiators must not be decision makers in order to reach healthy decisions in crisis management [6]. Therefore, governments need professional negotiation teams (of law enforcement) to serve in hostage-taking incidents.

Regression analyses of this study regarding hostage-taking terrorism incidents indicate that one negotiator is preferable. But since most of the hostage-taking incidents require long negotiations (an average of 38 days), it is not possible to avoid having two primary negotiators who are in direct contact with perpetrators. Also, our study predicts that there is a 1% difference in the probability of hostages being killed between having one negotiator and having two. Therefore, it seems that the risk of having two primary negotiators is acceptable in order to be able to continue a long duration negotiation and let negotiators rotate to keep their strength.

Additional findings of the study are as follows:

- First, as the number of hostages increases the probability of hostage fatalities also increases.
- Second, as the number of governments/entities upon whom demands are made increases, the probability of hostage fatality also increases controlling for

other factors. Therefore, those probabilities of high risks must be considered in order to take further steps in dealing with hostage situations.

- Third, allowance of hostages' sequential release decreases the probability of hostage fatality. Hence, observing sequential releases at an incident may be considered as a sign of encouragement for decision makers to continue the negotiation process.
- Fourth, although the regression analysis suggests that an increase in duration may increase the probability of hostage fatality, it depends on the type of the incident (kidnappings may require a different strategy of crisis management than hostage barricade incidents) and the environmental situation. Time usually works to the advantage of hostages unless a provocation takes place [6], or unless terrorists are in an environment friendly to them [5].

References

[1]　H.A. Miller, Hostage negotiations and the concept of transference. In Y. Alexander, D. Carlton, P. Wilkinson, Editors. *Terrorism: Theory and Practice.* Boulder, Colorado: Westview Press; 1979.

[2]　C. Hatcher, K. Mohandie, J. Turner, M.G. Gelles, The role of the psychologist in crisis/hostage negotiations. *Behavioral Sciences and the Law.* **16** (1998), 455-472.

[3]　G.M. Vecchi, V.B.V. Hasselt, S.J. Romano, Crisis (hostage) negotiation: Current strategies and issues in high-risk conflict resolution. *Aggression and Violent Behavior,* **10** (2005), 533–551.

[4]　E. F. Mickolus, T. Sandler, J.M. Murdock, *International terrorism in the 1980s: A chronology of Events.* Ames, Iowa: Iowa State University Press; 1989.

[5]　G.O. Faure, Negotiating with Terrorists: The Hostage Case. *International Negotiations.* **8** (2003), 469-494.

[6]　A.C. MacWillson, *Hostage taking terrorism: Incident response strategy.* New York: St. Martin's Press; 1992.

[7]　R. Birge, Conducting successful hostage negotiations: Balance is the key. *Criminal Justice Periodicals, Law & Order,* **50/3** (2002, March), 102.

[8]　E. F. Mickolus, T. Sandler, J.M. Murdock, P.A. Flemming, International terrorism: Attributes of terrorist events, 1968-2003. *Data code book for the data compiled for ITERATE project;* 2004.

[9]　S. Sloan, Personal communication. Advanced research workshop for NATO & TIPS terrorism project, Washington, DC, 2006, September 09.

[10]　Yilanli kuyuda sorguladik. *Hurriyet,* 2000, January 22. [Online] Available from; URL: http://arsiv.hurriyetim.com.tr/hur/turk/00/01/22/turkiye/03tur.htm. [2006, September 13]

Appendix

Correlation Matrix

Variable	Resnego	Ressho	Resoth	#nego	#host	#entit	Depolit	Derans	Depriso	Desafh	Desafp	Seqrls	Pasdea	Thrtcar	Drday	Nongo
Resnego	1.0000															
Resshoot	-0.1350	1.0000														
Resother	-0.7914	-0.4988	1.0000													
# nego	0.6072	0.2255	-0.6702	1.0000												
# host	0.1607	0.1431	-0.2289	0.3327	1.0000											
#entity	0.4633	0.3579	-0.6260	0.5071	0.5177	1.0000										
Depoli	0.4711	0.1575	-0.5092	0.3840	0.0382	0.3804	1.0000									
Derans	0.4453	0.1021	-0.4526	0.4312	0.1733	0.3033	0.2571	1.0000								
Depris	0.6292	0.1198	-0.6243	0.5604	0.2782	0.5257	0.3541	0.2619	1.0000							
Desafeh	0.2640	0.0378	-0.2543	0.2770	0.3373	0.4960	0.1976	0.0860	0.2619	1.0000						
Desafep	0.3713	0.1027	-0.3882	0.4969	0.2979	0.3761	0.2397	0.1695	0.4104	0.5697	1.0000					
Seqreleas	0.2499	0.0583	-0.2546	0.2356	0.1913	0.3378	0.1501	0.1327	0.2282	0.2385	0.0917	1.0000				
Passdead	0.3093	0.2307	-0.4129	0.4466	0.2450	0.3515	0.4950	0.2079	0.4765	0.1470	0.2496	0.2032	1.0000			
Thrtca	-0.0655	0.0902	0.0016	0.0068	0.0319	-0.0483	-0.0453	-0.0440	0.0581	-0.0440	-0.0321	0.1004	0.2053	1.0000		
Durday	-0.0710	0.0206	0.0494	-0.1437	0.0265	-0.1119	-0.0594	-0.1451	-0.0514	-0.1363	0.0010	-0.2021	-0.0045	0.0438	1.0000	
Nongovt	0.0556	0.0563	-0.0833	0.0108	0.2020	0.3677	-0.0156	0.2187	0.0305	0.2640	-0.0455	0.2237	0.0373	0.0273	-0.0420	1.0000

Successful Police Negotiation Strategies in Terrorism Motivated Hostage Situations

Suleyman HANCERLI,[a] Tuncay DURNA,[b] Ph.D.
[a]*Ph.D. Candidate, University of North Texas*
[b]*Police Training Adviser, OSCE Mission to Serbia*
[a,b]*Superintendent, Turkish National Police*

Abstract: In the last four decades, hostage situations have rapidly increased in the world due to the threat of terrorism and other social problems. The goals of hostage takers are to achieve certain political, criminal, or social benefits through hostage situations. Hostage incidents are common types of situations that police are forced to confront in the societies. Police apply either negotiation or tactical team intervention in hostage situations to recover hostages. In the past, the police most commonly used the tactical operations to end situations often resulting in the loss of lives of hostages, but in the last few decades there has been a change in favor of negotiation. The real success in this endeavor is based on effective communication strategies. The purposes of this study are to analyze the historical background of hostage situations, to identify effective negotiation strategies in a case study approach, and to provide some future recommendations for governments, police agencies, and researchers for peaceful resolutions in hostage situations.

Keywords: Terrorist hostage siege, hostage negotiation, police communication, political violence, and terrorist.

Introduction and Historical Background

The history of hostage situations was examined to better understand hostage takers' approaches and governmental agencies' applications of negotiating techniques or force against hostage takers. This helps the researcher makes useful recommendations for the future. In addition, this historical background gives broader understanding of the components and dynamics of hostage situations. In fact, the first, second, and current generations of resolutions in hostage situations have been reviewed very carefully to enhance the negotiation application of police in the future.

Historically, holding of hostages is a very old type of criminal behavior. In this century, nothing has changed with this crime. Taking of hostages is still employed by perpetrators as an effective means of gaining some benefits [1]. Hostage situations have dramatically increased in the last four decades in the U.S. [2]. As Goldaber states, a number of terrorist hostage situations have happened, especially in the 1960s and 1970s. Hostage incidents were a major threat to public safety in those years (As cited in [2]). The first tactical police team was created by the Los Angeles Police Department, LAPD, to fight against hostage takers in 1967 [3]. Using tactical police team intervention was the best and most familiar practice at that time since the negotiation process was not effectively developed until the 1970s [2, 3]. After the tactical team approach became popular with police agencies, it was known as the first generation of hostage resolution in the 1960s and 1970s [2]. Unfortunately, many people lost their lives during the tactical team interventions. For example, in the Munich Olympics Games situation in 1972, all hostages, 5 hostage takers, and 1 police officer lost their lives (As cited in [2, 3]).

According to Gettinger evaluation, roughly 80% of people killed in hostage situations lose their lives during police tactical team applications rather than negotiations (As cited in [4]). The general public, however, was not happy with the number of deaths as a result of tactical team interventions [2, 3]. As Bolz and Hershey mention, Lieutenant Frank Bolz from the New York Police Department, NYPD, suggested the verbal negotiation technique to replace tactical team intervention in 1971 (As cited in [2]). The NYPD initiated employment of the negotiation practice in 1972. After the NYPD pioneered its use, the negotiation practice was expanded by the FBI, and it is still being used today by negotiators [5]. Hatcher in addition to Doane & Hatcher mention that the New York, San Francisco and Los Angeles Police Departments made some noteworthy contributions to the negotiation doctrine in handling hostage incidents. As Bell et al., state, a similar method was launched in some European countries, such as the Netherlands and the U.K. in those years (As cited in [2]).

In sum, in the 1960s and 1970s, politically motivated hostage incidents were a major threat in communities. However, the first generation of hostage resolution focused on the tactical team intervention against hostage takers [2]. As Fuselier and Strentz state, mentally ill and domestically disturbed hostage takers, however, were more frequent than terrorist hostage takers in the 1980s. The second generation of hostage resolution focused on negotiation. As Mohandie and Albanese indicate, using communication skills was the dominant strategy in the second generation of hostage resolution (As cited in [2]). Many lives have been saved through negotiation practice [6]. In the current generation of hostage resolution, officers focused on a broad range of situations, such as barricade, hostage, suicidal, and kidnap situations. Negotiation tools and techniques of current negotiators might be required to larger or lesser degrees depending on an incident's key characteristics [3].

Police agencies today have two options to resolve hostage situations: the negotiation, and tactical police team intervention. The negotiation is the first resort; all available communication tools and a full negotiation process should be used by negotiators before using deadly force [5]. During the negotiation, negotiators endeavor to build rapport between hostage takers and themselves by using some negotiation techniques. If the negotiation does not work to free hostages without any deaths/injuries, the negotiation is abandoned, and the tactical team takes the responsibility for using deadly force against hostage takers [7].

The main purpose of this study is to make a contribution to negotiation strategies of police agencies, to make recommendations for governments, and to make recommendations to the future research studies of researchers. The researcher in this study has one central avenue to review the dynamics of the successful negotiation resolution of hostage situations: identify the successful negotiation strategies in a case study approach. In addition, the researcher discusses how to use negotiation skills, tools, and central strategies of negotiators to promote effective resolutions in hostage situations.

1. Methodology

In data collection of this study, books, articles, and police course manuals have been used by the researcher. In addition, the researcher was one of the participants in the "Hostage Negotiator Training Course" conducted by the Turkish National Police, TNP, at Turkish International Academy against Drugs and Organized Crimes, TADOC, in 2002 through instructions of Barney McNeilly, the President of Canadian Critical Incident Incorporated, CCII. Later, the researcher participated in the "Basic Tactical Orientation Course" in Toronto conducted by the Emergency Task Force of the Toronto Police Service in 2002. These courses and activities of the researcher facilitated the collecting and classification of data and the preparation of the study outline.

All of the information which was gathered here was carefully classified to prepare the outline in accordance with the research purposes. After that, all classified information was analyzed to provide a comprehensive literature review and to better understand the cases studies. Multiple sources that provide a broad range of viewpoints have been examined by the researcher to avoid biased information. Information and documents have been cross-verified through the use of multiple sources to provide a neutral and valid study.

In addition to the literature review, four case studies involving different police applications and methods were examined and compared to evaluate negotiation techniques. In each case study, facts of cases, hostage taker motivations and demands, resolutions, and evaluation and summary were examined. There is a significant point to be made that every case has its own unique dangers, difficulties, and methods. Every case was evaluated first on its own merit and then in a comparative analysis with others. Evidently, one of the additional important points is how the cases were selected from among the thousands of situations. Essentially, there are several critical points for choosing the cases. First, every case reflects different aspects of hostage situation concepts in terms of movements, effectiveness, and police applications. Second, every case has different motivations, resolutions, and notable results. These features help to better understand the major points to make valuable contributions to hostage taking literature. Finally, each case has its own outcome that points to a possible resolution even if such resolution was not achieved.

On the other hand, there are a few primary limitations to this study. First, there are very few academic studies of hostage incidents that are likely to be written by police negotiators. Second, today, there are limited databases, such as The Hostage Barricade Database System (HOBAS) and some unofficial databases developed by some individual enterprises, for researchers to use nationwide. Third, there is no objective criterion to measure the effectiveness of hostage negotiations because each hostage rescue operation has its own unique characteristics and difficulties; therefore, each one is evaluated in terms of its own conditions whether or not it had a successful outcome. Finally, dealing with hostage situations is police work; police agencies usually do not want to share their information, knowledge, and records with researchers. Some very detailed, crucial, and up-dated information, knowledge, and techniques that police agencies employ during situations might not be available in this study. All of the gathered information was derived from the available sources in the public domain.

1.1. Description and Discussion of the Case Studies

Four case studies have been evaluated to prove the importance of successful negotiation in hostage situations. The researcher focused on two significant points here. First, each case is evaluated on its own merits; second, a comparative analysis is made to show the differences between successful and unsuccessful negotiation techniques the police apply. The major aim is to prove negotiation works to resolve situations without bloodshed if it is taken seriously by the police and the government. The four cases are listed in terms of their chronologies since modification and improvement of the negotiation concept can be understood very clearly. General information on the four case studies is given in Table 1.

Table 1: Four Case Studies

Case Name	Target Country	Year	State	Police Agency
Munich Olympic Games Situation	German Government	1972	Munich	German Police
Balcombe Street Siege	British Government	1975	London	Metropolitan Police of London
Iranian Embassy Siege	British Government	1980	London	Scotland Yard Metropolitan Police
Branch Davidians Standoff	United States of America	1993	Texas	FBI and BATF

Source: Various resources cited in the case studies.

1.1.1. Munich Olympic Games Hostage Situation, 1972

After the 20th Olympic Games started in Munich on August 26, 1972 [8], 11 Israeli athletes were taken hostage by 8 terrorists of the Black September Organization (BSO) in the Olympic Village. Since the hostages resisted the hostage takers at the very beginning of the situation, 2 hostages were killed and 3 hostages were injured by the hostage takers [9]. Upon taking the hostages, the terrorists made their demands. They wanted Israel to release 200 Arab inmates from their prisons and Germany to provide a plane to go to Egypt with the hostages [10]. They set the deadline and threatened the government that if the demands were not met, they would kill the hostages [9]. Israel did not consent to the release of the inmates, and Egypt did not allow the hostage takers to come to their land [10]. Once the negotiation was started, the police followed a very flexible and conciliatory strategy to prevent loss of lives. The police never refused the demands of the terrorists; they wanted the terrorists to think that they would fly to Egypt. Meanwhile, the German authority offered to make payment in exchange for the hostages and suggested that they exchange the hostages. This was refused because the terrorists responded that money and their lives were not important to them anymore [8].

Meanwhile, the deadline was postponed by the terrorists 7 times. And, in the following days, the terrorists made some demands for food, which was provided by the police. This showed that as long as the police acceded to the demands, they would not execute the hostages. Although the inmates were not released from the Israeli prisons, safe passage from the country became the first concern for the terrorists. Despite what they said at the beginning of the negotiation, their lives were important to them [8]. Unfortunately, the Stockholm syndrome was non-existent due to the cultural antagonism between the Israeli hostages and the Arab hostage takers [9].

While the police were still negotiating with the terrorists, the government was taking into account some alternative means, such as using deadly force. However, it was unsafe for the hostages and the bystanders at the scene. They considered using chemical weapons, but it was also unsafe. Finally, the government decided to confront the terrorists at an isolated area. They gave the terrorists a helicopter to transport them to the Furstenfeldbruck NATO Airport. This isolated area was an excellent location to confront them. The terrorists asked for a bus to transport them from the scene to the helicopter in the village; it was given to them, too. Finally, they arrived at the airport with the hostages. Hence, the 14 hour bargaining phase was over; it was time to use deadly force. Although the police knew that the chance to achieve success was not high, they did use deadly force [9]. In terms of the international reputation and defense strategy, the government wanted to resolve this siege immediately [8]. After the terrorists landed at the airport, they approached the plane to check it out. In the meantime, a police sniper shot at them. The police killed 5 hostage takers, and 3 others surrendered to the police in this battle [9].

There are two significant points to evaluate this situation. As Miller stated, the police in this siege could not succeed in the release of the hostages, but they attained partial success in this siege. Their strategy caused the loss of all hostages and 1 police officer; in fact, 17 people were killed in this siege [8]. This siege was important to the police because after this case, they paid attention to the negotiation practice instead of using deadly force in hostage situations. Dr. Schlossberg from the NYPD argued that although negotiation was used in this siege, there were no specific negotiation techniques to use and apply to the situation [10]. In other words, in this siege, the negotiation was unlike what is now applied in hostage situations.

In addition, terrorist blackmail was a serious crime in the 1970s. It increased the crime rate and bolstered terrorists terrorizing governments. In those years, it seemed that the German government was more likely to make concession to terrorist hostage takers. For example, the German government released some inmates during the skyjacking at Dawson Field in 1970. They paid ransom to the terrorists in the skyjacking at Aden in 1972. They released inmates in the kidnapping of Peter Lorenz in 1975. The German government was more likely to be selected as a target in several politically motivated hostage situations. Only one month after the Munich siege, the German government was the victim in the Zagreb situation too. Terrorists were released by the German authorities in this situation [11]. Making concessions or paying ransoms to the terrorists cannot be a reliable and consistent policy on the part of a government. If it makes concessions, it probably cannot prevent being a new target for terrorists later.

1.1.2. Balcombe Street Siege, 1975

Four militants of the Irish Republican Army, IRA, assaulted Scotts Restaurant in London on December 6, 1975. Since the same men had assaulted the same place only one month earlier, the police were chasing them. After the assault on the restaurant, the hot pursuit started with the men in a stolen car. Later, they left the stolen vehicle and ran away on foot. Since they understood that there was no way to escape from the police, they randomly selected a place to hide. It was the apartment of J. and S. Mathews family on Balcombe Street. The Mathews family was taken as hostages. The terrorists barricaded themselves in this apartment. After the perimeter was evacuated by the police, negotiation started. The terrorists set their demands with a deadline. They claimed that they would let the hostages free if the demands were met [12].

The terrorist hostage takers had basically one chief demand, which was safe passage to Ireland. However, this demand was instantly refused by the police because it was unacceptable. In the following days of the siege, they demanded some hot meals and drinks. The police focused on the four significant points during the negotiation. First, to disconnect them from the world, the police cut off the availability of the phone line and the electricity and offered them a mobile phone line. There was no light, no phone line, and no heat in the building. Also, the building was covered with a huge curtain from temporary scaffolding. The terrorists could not see or hear any movement around them. The aim was to make them suffer because of separation and isolation from the outside. The police also used cutting off the utilities as negotiation tools. Since the terrorists had a radio, they probably gained some hearsay from the radio that the Special Air Service, SAS, was deployed on the scene. Their presence might have affected their decision to release the hostages and to surrender to the police [12].

Second, after the police examined the fingerprints of the terrorist hostage takers on the bag abandoned during the chase, they found that one of the terrorist hostage takers was a dangerous murderer. He had the potential to kill the hostages. The police, therefore, were getting help from a psychologist, Dr. Peter Scott, during the negotiation. Dr. Scott recommended that although the police refused the chief demand, the terrorists should believe they might get a concession from the police through the negotiation. The point was to make the terrorists believe that negotiation was the way they could get a concession [12].

Third, the terrorists noticed that the Mathews did not look like individuals who were being targeted by the IRA. They were ordinary people; Mr. Mathew was a poor worker. Also, living in a room with the Mathews for a week might have promoted the Stockholm syndrome [12].

Fourth, when the terrorists made their demand, they were faced with a counter-demand from the police. When they asked for a hot meal, the police offered them to exchange one hostage for the hot meal. They did not accept that, and they were not given hot soup. The negotiators were using even a small demand, including drinking water, as a negotiation tool. In the following days of the siege, the terrorists felt exhausted and abandoned. Their chief demand, safe exit from the country, turned into a small concession because they accepted exchanging Mrs. Mathews for a hot meal. The hostage takers had already given the most important concession to the police. They attenuated their power by releasing one hostage. There was no way to change the direction of the ongoing negotiation [12].

There are three significant points to evaluate this situation. As Moysey mentioned, the successful negotiation strategy of the police was very worthwhile because this situation was resolved without tragedy. The philosophy of the police was based on the 'wait and see' technique during the negotiation. In the meantime, the police never ignored their brutality and prior criminal records. The police would use the experience gained in the Balcombe siege in the Iranian Embassy siege. In addition, the cultural background of the actors in the siege was the same and there was no language barrier. The Stockholm syndrome might have helped to resolve the siege peacefully [12]. In sum, the Balcombe siege occurred in 1975. The negotiation concept was gradually improving on the part of the police. The spectacular outcome of the siege showed that all known and available negotiation techniques were used by the negotiators.

1.1.3. Iranian Embassy Siege, 1980

The militants of the Democratic Revolutionary Movement for the Liberation of Arabia, DRMLA, invaded to the Iranian Embassy in London on April 30, 1980. The terrorist hostage takers took 24 hostages, including Embassy employees, correspondents, and visitors, during the six days of the siege [12]. After the police initiated the negotiation with the terrorist hostage takers, they stated that if the terrorist hostage takers did not hurt any captives, they would not be hurt by the police. The terrorist hostage takers expressed that they had no problem with the British people; they took hostages so that they could demonstrate against the Khomeini regime in Iran [13].

They made their demands and set a deadline [13]. They, in fact, made four demands. First, they wanted the Iranian government to release 91 Arab inmates from Iranian prisons. Second, they wanted the British government to provide a bus to go to the airport and a plane to leave the country [12]. Third, they wanted one of the Arab ambassadors to work as a mediator between the host government and them. Fourth, they wanted to talk to the BBC executive director immediately. The aim was to ask him to broadcast their declaration on the TV. They also wanted to talk to the Iranian Foreign Minister on the phone to convey their demand, which was the release of inmates from Iranian prisons. When their demand was passed to the Iranian Foreign Minister, the Minister claimed that the hostage takers were spies of the U.S., and he also invited the Iranian hostages to sacrifice their lives for the Iran regime to show their loyalty and to protest the hostage takers [13].

Since the police did not cut off the electricity and the telephone, the terrorists made phone calls to the media. However, later the police cut the telephone as well as other communication utilities. The terrorist hostage takers accepted a mobile phone to make contact with the police. Sometimes they negotiated face-to-face instead of using the mobile phone. Meanwhile, the terrorist hostage takers released the sick captives. The negotiation in this situation was improving because they released a couple of hostages and the deadline was postponed a couple of times. The negotiators built rapport with the hostage takers [13]. However, on the sixth day of the siege, the terrorists killed one of the Iranian hostages [12], claiming that their demands were not met and the deadlines were ignored [13]. As a result, the government allowed the SAS to use the deadly force. While the negotiator was keeping Oan Ali, the leader of the terrorist hostage takers, on the phone to make him less prepared for the sudden attack, the SAS did an unexpected entry to the compound. They killed the 5 terrorist hostage takers out of 6 because some female hostages were defending one from the police raid. These hostages said that he had been gentle towards them. This was absolutely the Stockholm syndrome [12].

During the negotiation in this situation, as stated earlier, the hostage takers were more likely to focus on the two chief demands. First, they wanted the police to broadcast their message on TV, and second, they wanted to talk with an Arab ambassador to ask him to be a mediator between the British government and themselves. Meanwhile, the police asked them to release more hostages if they were to be allowed to talk to the executive director of the BBC. Then, they released a hostage and they were allowed to deliver their message. It was broadcast on the TV. For the second chief demand, Arab ambassadors were asked to mediate between the two parties. However, an agreement could not be reached. The negotiators began to stall for additional time to extend the deadline, and they blamed the politicians for failing on the second chief demand. The hostage takers complained that the police did not do anything to execute this demand. Finally, they killed one hostage on the sixth day of the siege [13]. Therefore, the British government sanctioned to use the deadly force [12].

There are three of significant points by which to evaluate this siege. First, although there was no clear evidence why the terrorists selected the British government as a target, they might have selected the Iranian Embassy as a victim because there was no capital punishment in England as a result of taking hostages [12]. After the siege started, the terrorist hostage takers asked the Pakistani correspondent hostage, if the statute in London was severe against the hostage takers [13]. It seemed that they were thinking of surrender. Second, the raid of the SAS on the terrorist hostage takers was broadcast on the TV [14]. The aim was to show to the world how the British police responded to the terrorists. They wanted to discourage terrorists from selecting the British people in the future situations as a target again. Third, according to the Geneva Convention, the British government should have asked either the Iranian government or the person in command of the Embassy of Iran in London if they could raid the compound. However, the person in command of the embassy mission was already a hostage, and the Iranian government had already said that if the hostages were killed by the terrorists, they were martyrs of the Iran revolution. And the British government did not want to make any payment or concessions to the terrorists, so they used deadly force as a last resort [12].

1.1.4. Branch Davidians Standoff in Waco, 1993

In 1981, Vernon Howell joined the Branch Davidians. In a short period of time, he became the new leader of this group. There were roughly 130 followers of the Branch Davidians in Waco. Howell changed his name in 1993 to David Koresh [10]. Koresh told the followers there would be an 'end' very soon. They should prepare [15] and protect themselves from their opponents [16]. For the approaching end, the Davidians stored guns and weapons in their compounds [10]. Officers of the Bureau of Alcohol, Tobacco and Firearms (BATF) went to the compound with a search warrant to seize unlawful weapons on February 28, 1993 [15]. But, the Davidians did not allow the officers to come into the compound and they fought with the officers. In this battle, the four officers and six Davidians were killed, and many officers and Davidians were injured [15, 17]. After the bloody gunfight, the FBI took charge to resolve this standoff [15].

There were approximately 668 FBI officers and 367 officers of other agencies on the scene. Once the negotiation was initiated, it lasted roughly 51 days [10]. Jamar, the incident commander of the standoff, allowed the agents to use some tactics, such as cutting off the electricity, using loud music and noise, and using tear gas [15]. He supposed that these tactics would work to resolve the standoff [18]. But, the standoff did not look like a typical hostage incident. As Heyman believed, the followers were staying in the compound voluntarily, unlike a typical hostage incident (as cited in [15]).

Even though a number of Davidians were released through the negotiation, the agents believed that the negotiation was getting worse in the following days [10]. Some negotiators, including Sage, the negotiation team leader, believed that if Koresh was a real psychopath, the negotiation would be fruitless and hopeless [15]. After the 51 days of negotiation, the agents became impatient [10]. Finally, the command post, FBI Director William Sessions, and General Attorney Janet Reno agreed with the use of CS gas on the Davidians [15]. They shot CS gas into the compound [10]. Since the

Davidians had procured the gas masks in advance, they used the gas masks and started to fire on the tanks in the compound [15]. Soon the entire building was in flames [10]. The fire spread very fast in the compound [17]. Roughly 75 Davidians died that day. Some Davidians died from gunfire, some of them died from the flames [15].

The investigative arson report affirmed that the fire was started by the Davidians rather than the CS gas. However, there was no evidence if starting the fire was the idea of all of the Davidians or just a few Davidians [17]. Roughly 75 Davidians died in the compound on April 19 [15]. Even though the Davidians shot at the FBI agents, the agents never shot at the Davidians on the last day of the standoff [17].

Although the Davidians stated that suicide was impermissible in their beliefs, some released Davidians mentioned about the suicide preparation. Koresh told his followers they should follow him until the end, which might mean killing themselves. The negotiators talked to the followers to convince them to capitulate. Also, the negotiators sent them the released followers' statements to convince them to capitulate [17]. During the entire negotiation, 35 Davidians were released through the negotiation [10]. The experts said that if the police had followed the recommendations of the experts, the consequences would have been better. The tragedy and failure surprised even the FBI agents [15].

In sum, there are two significant points by which to evaluate this standoff: as Ammerman stated, ignoring the religious motivations of the Davidians and the recommendations of the experts on Davidians, the police might have failed to understand the religious extremists' motivations. They were not an ordinary group of people. The situation required more than understanding an ordinary group of people [16]. Additionally, there were some other problems between the negotiation and the tactical teams [10]. Even though both teams should have shared information, the negotiation team charged that the tactical team did not provide sufficient information, and the tactical team responded with the same charge [17].

2. General Findings and Analysis

As stated earlier, every hostage taking incident is unique because of its own difficulties and characteristics [19]. Each case study has different key players, motivations, demands, and police responses. Thus, each case is evaluated under its own conditions first. However, some general aspects of the four cases are compared to see if the negotiation and other governmental applications were successful and appropriate; the aim is to aid governments, police, and future studies on hostage situations, which is the main purpose of this study.

In the Munich Olympic Games Situation, there are the two main reasons why it ended in tragedy. First, as Aston stated, even though the police employed negotiation in the situation first [9], they could not gain the release of the hostages through negotiation. The police suggested the terrorists accept payment or exchange the hostages during the negotiation [8] because the German government was likely to make concessions to the terrorist hostage takers in those years [11]. Probably it destroyed the ongoing negotiation because both making payments to the terrorists and exchanging hostages are totally against the negotiation philosophy. The negotiators should have used stalling and delaying techniques. Unlike the Balcombe Street Siege, the negotiation techniques that the police used in the Munich situation were inadequate because of the lack of successful communication strategies. After this hostage situation, as Poland and McCrystle mentioned, the police agencies started to pay attention to the importance of the negotiation in order to improve and to modify the negotiation concept [10]. Second, according to Hatcher and others, in the 1970s, politically motivated hostage situations were a major threat to governments. The best known response was using deadly force rather than the negotiation because using deadly force was the chief idea of the first generation of hostage resolution [2]. The German government probably wanted to show by using the deadly force against the terrorist hostage takers that they wouldn't make any concessions to terrorists anymore.

In the Branch Davidians Standoff, there are three significant reasons why the police failed to rescue the Davidians. First, according to Barkun, the police thought that traditional techniques would work in the standoff [18] since they believed that this standoff was a typical hostage situation. But, it did not work, and the standoff ended with bloodshed [15]. Second, the police probably were not familiar with religious extremists. Third, they might have ignored the recommendations of the experts regarding the Davidians [16]. In summary, although the negotiation lasted 51 days, this standoff showed that the negotiation was abandoned by the police earlier than it should have been. Unlike the Munich Olympic Games, the Balcombe Street, and the Iran Embassy cases, the Waco case was a religiously motivated barricade-standoff and its length was much longer than the other three cases. Meanwhile, unlike the Munich and the Iran Embassy sieges, the cultural background of the two major actors, the police and the Davidians, was the same in the Waco standoff. There was no language obstacle between the two parties in the Waco standoff, which was also true in the Balcombe Street siege.

In the Iranian Embassy Siege, there is one significant point why the siege could not be resolved peacefully. As MacWillson stated, the police initiated negotiation first [13]. When the hostage takers killed a hostage, negotiation became useless and hopeless. The police abandoned the negotiation immediately and used deadly force [12]. Even though the police did a good job during the negotiation, the negotiation became unfeasible as a result of the hostage takers' volatile behaviors. It seems that the police's decision to abandon the negotiation and the use the deadly force were correct because if they had insisted on maintaining negotiations, the terrorists would have killed more hostages. The timing of giving up the negotiation was perfectly accurate on the part of the police. In hostage situations, although the negotiation techniques are correctly used, sometimes they might not work. The point is to know when negotiation becomes hopeless and useless.

In the Balcombe Street Siege, there are three significant points revealing why the police were successful through negotiation. First, unlike the other three cases, the IRA terrorists in this case were not planning to take hostages. Since the terrorists could not escape from the police, they had to take hostages to gain safe passage to their country. Second, unlike two of the other three cases, as Moysey [12] mentioned, the cultural backgrounds of both parties, the police and the hostage takers, were the same. Therefore, there was no language barrier between the two parties. It might have helped to promote the Stockholm syndrome between the two parties as well as helped promote negotiation. Third, the police probably did not have as advanced negotiation techniques in those years as they have today, but they apparently used all available and known negotiation techniques successfully because unlike the other three cases, this case was resolved peacefully through negotiation.

There are similarities and dissimilarities in the four cases. The motivation was political objectives in three cases, whereas the motivation was religious beliefs only in the Waco standoff. The target was the British government in two cases, while the targets were the U.S. and the German governments in the other two cases. The shortest case was 17 hours (Munich Olympic Games Situation), whereas the longest case was 51 days (Branch Davidians). Three cases were resolved with tactical force, while only one case (Balcombe Street Siege) was resolved with the negotiation. The most important difference in the four cases is that, unlike the other three cases, as Edwards [15] stated, the police supposed that they faced a typical hostage situation in the Waco standoff. But, it was not a typical hostage situation because there were not any hostage takers or hostages.

3. Future Recommendations

As mentioned earlier, the purposes of this study are to make contributions to the negotiation strategies of police agencies, to make recommendations for governments, and to make recommendations for the future research studies about hostage situations.

3.1. Recommendations for Governments

Hostage takers victimize not only the hostages but also governments because every government has to protect its citizens against criminals and terrorists either in their land or abroad. During hostage situations, governments protect their citizens. However, sometimes it might be difficult because some hostage takers are professionals and have prior criminal records. In this sense, the researcher makes five recommendations for governments to protect their people in hostage situations and to prevent possible situations in the future.

First, terrorist hostage takers make demands in hostage situations to change the general belief of the public and the policies of a government by using the threat of violence [20]. They compel the government either (1) to make concessions to them or (2) to refuse to make any concessions to them. Each way has its own risks for the government. For example, if the government makes any concession, it will be criticized because it could not resolve the situation without making a concession. If the government does not make any concession, it will also be criticized because it did not take care of its citizens [21]. To protect their citizens in any circumstances, the governments rely on their well-trained police agencies while they deal with terrorist events.

Although the government may have a 'no-concession' policy, negotiators should always be allowed to negotiate with hostage takers. A government does not have to give any concessions to hostage takers. The government should not reject negotiation with hostage takers. Refusing negotiation or making payment for ransom never works to resolve situations. Terrorist hostage takers usually select targets based on their past experiences. If they have succeeded in gaining concessions from a target country in previous actions, they will probably take hostages from the same population again. Terrorist hostage takers should be led to believe that they will be able to get their demands by negotiating with the police [11]. Negotiation means the police are stalling the hostage takers. Since negotiation is delaying tactic, as long as the hostage takers do not kill or harm the hostages, negotiation should be maintained by the police.

Second, the government should never seem to be okay to agree to the hostage takers' blackmail because it encourages them to select the same government as a new target for the next hostage situation [11]. Agreeing to pay ransoms to the terrorists is not a good way to deal with their blackmail. Third, as Jenkins stated, a government should trust its own police units to take the responsibility to resolve the situation. The police are responsible for ending the situation and making any announcements to the public and media if such is required. For example, the BSO took American Embassy employees in Saudi Arabia in 1973. After President Nixon's statement about the situation was broadcast on the radio, the hostage takers killed the hostages immediately. Of course, nobody blames the President for the hostages being killed by the terrorists. However, this type of announcement by politicians might complicate the ongoing negotiation of the police. There must be a single voice speaking to the hostage takers to resolve the problem [22].

Fourth, although every government has its own policy to deal with criminal and terrorist hostage takers, unified international policies and commitments should be adopted to prevent future situations. The governments should work together for better outcomes. They might have regional and international agreements and commitments that show consensus in the way to deal with criminal and terrorist hostage takers. They should build international cooperation for reactive and proactive resolutions. Fifth, Poland & McCrystle state that hostages are the most affected actors in hostage situations. The question is how hostage takers choose hostages. What is the criterion for that? They are selected by hostage takers because of their status. The possible targets are companies, airlines, banks, passengers, rich people, politicians, and government representatives [10]. The most popular targets are American diplomats/politicians abroad [23]. The people with their lives at stake should be trained to avoid becoming hostages and taught how to survive if they are taken hostages. Personal security guidelines must be taught to them in seminars and lectures by government agencies before they go abroad.

3.2. Recommendations for Police Agencies

Inefficient police responses to hostage situations are always criticized by the general public, media, and governments because people lose their lives. Using deadly force is the last option, and negotiation is the best option in hostage situations [4]. Today, negotiation is known as the correct response to the situations. The police are aware of the negotiation's importance to end the situations without tragedy. According to this criterion, there are four recommendations for police agencies here.

First, every police agency should have a hostage negotiation unit in its organization structure. As Perkins and Mijares mention, there might be staff and monetary shortages, which makes it difficult, for small police departments to have a negotiation unit [24]. However, if they can afford it, it works very well. As Wind stated, negotiation has some difficulties and challenges and it is police work [25]. Before starting to work as a negotiator in the field, negotiation courses are definitely needed for the police [26]. In the courses, they are taught not only communication skills and the use of negotiation tools but also psychological and sociological concepts of human behavior [6]. They are trained in complex psychological characteristics and criminal characteristics by acting out real case scenarios [27].

Second, the negotiation team should be taught never to compete with the tactical team. The negotiation team is neither subordinate nor superior to the tactical team. Both teams get important information for the command post [27]. If the teams are trained within the same training program, they can be better prepared to avoid misunderstanding among the teams. Third, Ammerman states that police agencies should establish behavioral science units in their organization structures and cooperate with experts/consultants to get better results [16]. They can better understand and evaluate the behaviors of hostage takers through those consultants. Fourth, as Jenkins stated, terrorist organizations attract more attention worldwide by influencing the media. Unfortunately, some media publish the demands and declarations of the hostage takers to gain more influence in the situations. However, they might manipulate the ongoing negotiation process. It is better for the media to have a limited role for the sake of public safety and the success of the police [22].

3.3. Recommendations for Researchers

Not many scholarly research studies on hostage situations exist. The reason is that researchers would have to be involved in a number of interactions and activities with the police to learn more about hostage resolution doctrine. In many cases, their participation might be difficult due to the dangers, difficulties, and limitations of environment in hostage situations. However, there are some questions that can only be answered through empirical research studies. Unfortunately, due to the risks and dangers at the scene, researchers can answer these questions only after the hostage incidents end. The hostage incident is based on behavioral interaction that is accounted for by different actors. These parties will be available for study only after a hostage incident ends if, of course, these parties survive. One of the aims of this study is to encourage researchers to make academic contributions to the literature of hostage negotiation resolutions. There are two important recommendations for researchers to be involved in hostage situations.

First, the HOBAS is the only database in which the FBI collects data and statistics from not only the federal police responses but also the state police responses to hostage and barricade situations in the U.S. The HOBAS analyzes the information that comes from all over the country to make appropriate new guidelines and principles for policy makers and the police. In addition to the HOBAS, some individual researchers gathered and analyzed the information on hostage situations in the past [28]. For example, Mickolus created a database, titled "International Terrorism: Attributes of Terrorist Events Database (ITERATE)", which was based on 3,329 international terrorism motivated hostage incidents outside the U.S. between 1968 and 1977. Friedland and Merari created a database based on roughly 70 international and domestic political hostage incidents between 1979 and 1988. Head created the Hostage Event Analytic Database (HEAD), consisting of 3,300 hostage incidents. Feldman developed a database based on 120 domestic hostage incidents. Negotiators can learn more about the negotiation concept and better understand the behaviors of the hostage takers and assess the threat levels of the situations through the database programs [3]. The police can see and evaluate what was wrong and what was right in past situations through databases made by researchers. Looking at past situations' classifications and evaluations in database studies to create new policies to deal with hostage takers is the best practice. Negotiators are likely to understand the general characteristics of incidents through databases.

Even though some believe that the HOBAS does not characterize the American society because of its data selection and gathering strategy prejudices [28] and the individual enterprises mentioned above might be too limited to make significant contributions to police studies, it is the only option to increase the success of the police in hostage situation resolutions. Additionally, negotiation is based on the interaction between the police and the extremists, who are likely to have prior criminal records. Therefore, it requires more than the traditional approach of the police. Since the researchers' scholarly contributions enhance police activities, and also new rules and guidelines for the police are well established through the research studies, researchers are encouraged to work on more empirical research studies related to hostage situation doctrine.

Second, greater cooperation between the police and researchers will help to promote advanced resolutions to bring an end to situations without loss of life. The only way to enhance the negotiating concept is for researchers to work together with the police. Therefore, researchers must be encouraged to establish more association and cooperation with the police. To make this possible, not only national but also international training programs, conferences, and seminars for both parties should be established.

4. Conclusion

The taking of hostages is a very common type of criminal act, and today it is the same because it is still employed as an effective means for criminals and terrorists to gain some benefits. Dealing with hostage takers has become one of the major focuses of the police. In fact, a number of terrorist hostage situations happened in the 1960s and 1970s. They were a major threat to the public safety. During that time, deadly force was likely to be used by the police against the politically motivated hostage takers. However, it was not a successful means for saving lives because many people lost their lives during the tactical team interventions. Nobody was happy with the number of deaths as a result of these interventions. Today, negotiation is more likely to be used by the police. Many lives are saved through the negotiation practice. In other words, negotiation is the first strategy for the police to resolve hostage situations without bloodshed. Therefore, governments should always allow negotiators to negotiate with hostage takers because refusing negotiation or making payment for ransom is not the point. In fact, in negotiation practice, hostage takers should be led to believe the idea that they can get their demands by negotiating with the police.

In sum, the past experiences proved that the formulating of negotiation practice to deal with volatile and extreme hostage situations without bloodshed is the only means on the part of governments. Since each hostage situation is unique due to the different motivations, demands, deadlines, and key players, each situation might require a different resolution on the part of the police. However, the unified resolutions for handling the situations increase the credibility and reliability of the police. The outcomes of hostage situations are improved through the collective empirical research studies of the both parties, the police and researchers. New reliable guidelines for the police to prevent future hostage situations and to deal with hostage situations can only be established through collective research studies.

References

[1]   J.M. McMains, C.W. Mullins, Crisis negotiations: Managing critical incidents and hostage situations in law enforcement and corrections. Cincinnati, OH: Anderson Publishing; 1996.

[2]   C. Hatcher, K. Mohandie, J.Turner, G.M. Gelles, The role of the psychologist in crisis/hostage negotiations. Behavioral Sciences and the Law, **16** (1998), 455-472.
[3]   A.J. Call, Negotiation crises: The evolution of hostage/barricade crisis negotiation. Journal of Threat Assessment, **2/3** (2003), 69-94.
[4]   W. Michalowski, K.Gregory, Z. Koperczak, S. Matvin, S. Szpakowicz, M. Connolly, How to talk to a terrorist: An expert system approach. Canadian Police College Journal, **12/2** (1988), 69-85.
[5]   W.G. Noesner, Negotiation concepts for commanders. FBI Law Enforcement Bulletin, **68/1** (1998), 6-18.
[6]   C. Regini, Crisis negotiation teams: Selection and training. FBI Law Enforcement Bulletin, **71/11** (2002), 1-9.
[7]   D. Goodwin, A poison chalice: Negotiating with extremists. Royal Military Academy Sandhurst, 2004. [Online] Available from; URL: http://www.ima.org.uk/conflict/ papers/Goodwin.pdf. [2005, January]
[8]   R.R. Miller, Negotiating with terrorists: A comparative analysis of three cases. Terrorism and Political Violence, **5/3** (1993), 78-105.
[9]   C.C. Aston, A contemporary crisis: Political hostage-taking and the experience of Western Europe. London: Greenwood Press; 1982.
[10] M.J. Poland, J.M. McCrystle, Practical, tactical and legal perspectives of terrorism and hostage taking. Lewiston, NY: Edwin Mellen Press; 1999.
[11] R. Clutterbuck, Negotiating with terrorists. Terrorism and Political Violence, **4/4** (1992), 263-287.
[12] P.S. Moysey, The Balcombe street and Iranian embassy sieges: A comparative examination of two hostage negotiation events. Journal of Police Crisis Negotiations, **4/1** (2004), 67-96.
[13] C.A. MacWillson, Hostage-taking terrorism: Incident-response strategy. New York, N.Y.: St. Martin's Press; 1992.
[14] A. Billen, The day Maggie won the 1980s. New Statesman London, **15/717** (2002), 33.
[15] C.J. Edwards, Self-Fulfilling Prophecy and Escalating Commitment: Fuel for the Waco Fire. The Journal of Applied Behavioral Science, **37/3** (2001), 343-360.
[16] N.T. Ammerman, Waco, federal law enforcement, and scholars of religion. University of Chicago Press; 1995. [Online] Available from; URL: http://hirr.hartsem.edu/sociology/ articles/Waco%20Fed.%20Law%20Enf.%20&%20Scholars.pdf [2005, February].
[17] S.G.D. Edward, Evaluation of the handling of the branch Davidian Stand-off in Waco, Texas: February 28 to April 19, 1993. Washington, D.C: U.S. Department of Justice; 1993.
[18] M. Barkun, Reflections after Waco: Millennialists and the state-cover story. Christian Century. 1993. [Online] Available from; URL: http://www.findarticles.com/p/articles/ mi_m1058/is_n18_v110/ai_13884022 [2004, September].
[19] J.T. Fagan, Conflict management. Corrections Today, **62/6** (2000), 132.
[20] T. Sandler, L.J. Scott, Terrorist success in hostage-taking incidents: An empirical study. The Journal of Conflict Resolution, **31/1** (1987), 35-53.
[21] N. Friedland, A. Merari, Hostage events: Descriptive profile and analysis of outcomes. Journal of Applied Social Psychology, **22/2** (1992), 134-156.
[22] M.B. Jenkins, Effective communication in a hostage crisis. In F.M. Herz, Editor. Diplomats and terrorists: What works, what doesn't. Washington, DC: Institute for the Study of Diplomacy, Georgetown University; 1982.
[23] B. Jenkins, J. Johnson, D. Ronfeldt, Numbered lives: Some statistical observations from 77 international hostage episodes. Santa Monica, California: Rand Corporation; 1977.
[24] B.D. Perkins, C.T. Mijares, Crisis negotiation units within the small department context. Journal of Police Crisis Negotiations, **4/2** (2004), 53-57.
[25] A.B. Wind, A guide to crisis negotiations. FBI Law Enforcement Bulletin, **64/10** (1995), 7.
[26] R. Borum, T. Strentz, Borderline personality: Negotiation strategies. FBI Law Enforcement Bulletin, 1992, Aug 08, [Online] Available from; URL: http://www.fbi.gov/publications /leb/1989-1995/leb89-95.htm. [2004, December]
[27] G.R. Rogan, R.M. Hammer, R.C. Van Zandt, Editors. Dynamic processes of crisis negotiation: Theory, research and practice. Westport, CT: Praeger; 1997.
[28] A. Lipetsker, Evaluating the hostage barricade database system (HOBAS). Journal of Police Crisis Negotiations, **4/2** (2004), 3-27.

Understanding and Responding to the Terrorism Phenomenon
O. Nikbay and S. Hancerli (Eds.)
IOS Press, 2007

Negotiating the Terrorist Hostage Siege: Are Nations Prepared to Respond and Manage Effectively?

Gary W. NOESNER, M.Ed.
Senior Vice President of Control Risks, USA
Former Chief, FBI Crisis Negotiation Unit (Retired)

Abstract: Governments today must be prepared to face a wide range of possible terrorist acts. Among the likely acts of terrorism is the terrorist hostage siege incident. Experience shows that governments are not sufficiently prepared for this type of event. Many countries have trained tactical teams ready to confront terrorists with force, but these same countries do not typically have qualified negotiation teams that are able to peacefully resolve such incidents. This lack of capability greatly limits the ability of these countries to effectively manage and peacefully resolve terrorist hostage sieges. In addition, political decision makers often do not understand what their proper roles are in the effective management of such sieges. Governments require the services of trained and skilled negotiators, operating as part of a larger law enforcement response apparatus, if they wish to properly and effectively manage a terrorist hostage siege incident. In this study, the critical issues related to this need are discussed and specific future recommendations made by the researcher[1] for governments and police agencies to consider. The information in this study is based on the researcher's personal work experience. The primary aim of this article, in fact, is to make contributions to police agencies' negotiation strategies.

Keywords: political violence, terrorism, hostage situation, hijacking, suicide bombing, hostage negotiation, and police training.

Introduction

When anticipating acts of terrorism, nations must be fully prepared to deal with a wide range of incidents. A key capability required for governments is to have a robust and experienced crisis negotiation team prepared to stabilize a terrorist hostage siege event and seek a non-violent peaceful resolution. Absent this capability, governments are left with only one tool; the use of tactical law enforcement or military teams to overpower terrorists to thwart their plans. Without a well balanced and holistic capability, governments are limiting the tools available for resolving these tense and often fatal situations. Maslow said that if someone is a hammer, the world looks like a nail. Those charged with resolving terrorist hostage sieges should not limit their tools to just a

---

[1] Gary Noesner spent 30 years in the FBI, retiring in 2003 as the Chief of the FBI's Crisis Negotiation Unit, Critical Incident Response Group where he was assigned from 1993 to 2003. He has published multiple articles relating to the crisis negotiation and siege management field in various law enforcement and academic journals.

hammer. They should ensure that a skilled and professional negotiation team is prepared and immediately deployed to contain the crisis and seek a peaceful resolution. Not having this capability jeopardizes the safety of all involved and limits the resolution options available. In this article, the researcher makes some critical recommendations and policy implications for governments and police agencies. The primary aim of the researcher in this examination is to make contributions to police agencies' hostage negotiation strategies.

1. Definition of Hostage Negotiation

To give a general idea about the term of 'hostage negotiation', the researcher makes a conceptual definition of this term. The aim of this is to make clearer the general concept of the article and to make the readers understand the meanings of this term. Hostage Negotiations in this context can be defined as "the use of dialogue to resolve a conflict in which a person or persons is being held and threatened in order to force a third party to do, or abstain from doing something in exchange for the safe release of the hostage(s)."

1.1. No Negotiation Policy

Many governments have taken a strong public position that boldly declares that they will not negotiate with terrorists. Unfortunately, in this context "negotiations" have come to be viewed as synonymous with capitulation, making undesirable substantive concessions such as paying ransom, releasing prisoners, or altering foreign policy. According to Webster's dictionary, "negotiation" simply means to "discuss, confer, or bargain to reach agreement." Nothing in the definition suggests that making concessions or "giving in" is required. In reality, it would be foolish for any government to refuse to engage in dialogue with terrorists holding hostages. Such dialogue does not require that substantive concessions be made, and should not be viewed as a demonstration of governmental weakness. Authorities should always be willing to talk. Refusal to engage in dialogue may compel the terrorists to execute hostages to gain the attention they seek. Such an act could compel a lethal and undesirable tactical response from the authorities.

1.2. The Reason to Negotiate

Negotiations are undertaken for a variety of purposes, to slow the operational tempo of the incident and buy time in order to: (1) gather additional information and resources, (2) gather more accurate information from the terrorists through statements of their demands and demonstrations of their behaviors, (3) gain the release of hostages for intelligence purposes, and (4) assemble and prepare (practice) a tactical team that may be compelled by events to conduct a rescue attempt. All of these objectives require buying time, and time is best obtained by undertaking prolonged and professional negotiations. Negotiation not only supports these important objectives, it also provides an opportunity for reaching a peaceful resolution, the most desirable outcome for everyone involved. By the very nature of terrorism, peacefully resolving any siege incident with terrorists will be very challenging. Despite the significant obstacles, there is ample evidence to support the belief that negotiations should always be pursued.

While, authorities must always prepare to use force, they should never abandon negotiations. In fact, they should give the negotiation process every opportunity to succeed. In the negotiation field we call this pursuing the parallel resolution track. It would be unwise to pursue only one resolution strategy. It should be noted that any required tactical intervention can follow unsuccessful negotiations, whereas, unsuccessful tactical intervention no opportunity to re-open negotiations and achieve a peaceful settlement.

In many cases, the negotiation team can play a critically important supportive role in "setting up" terrorists, making them expose themselves, appear to make concessions, or explain or mask required tactical movements and activities. The negotiation process may itself help in lowering the terrorists guard, thereby making them more susceptible to any necessary tactical action. Countries that discount, undervalue, or fail to appreciate this vital role played by negotiations seriously limit their options for resolving siege incidents. In reality, most terrorist hostage incidents are peacefully resolved through effective negotiations. Governments need to prepare for the worst (tactical action) yet always strive for the best outcome (negotiated surrender). It is highly recommended that negotiations should always commence as early as possible in an incident, not only after tactical containment is established, as is often the protocol. Early negotiation contact provides a major benefit in siege management in that it constitutes "verbal containment." This serves to keep a tense event from exploding as containment is being initially setup and as tense personnel are responding to an unclear event. Negotiators can attempt to keep the terrorists calm while authorities are getting ready with a viable tactical rescue plan. Negotiations should properly be viewed as supporting a full range of resolution options and used as soon as possible.

2. Threat of Terrorism in the World

Since September 11, 2001, the world has directed its attention toward the issue of terrorism. We have seen a dramatic increase in focus and concern over the destabilizing impact major acts of terrorism have had on both the victim nation and larger world community. Most would agree that major acts of terrorism have had significant political, social, and economic ramifications. Many countries have embraced the concept of a worldwide war against terrorism, cooperating with other nations in trying to expel terrorists from within their borders, sharing intelligence and working to break up terrorist cells. There have been many successes in the growing war against terrorism, however, the threat remains significant and much work is left to be done.

Al-Qaeda and other Islamic extremist groups represent the most challenging worldwide terrorist threat today. Their radical ideology and demonstrated willingness to inflict large numbers of civilian casualties make them a particular concern. While the world has never had a shortage of extremists and revolutionaries, current world events seem to be polarizing east and west as never before. This growing clash of cultures, values, and religion raises grave concerns about the nature and level of future acts of terrorism.

When the planes crashed into the World Trade Centers, the world was shocked by the blatant disregard for human life and the radical ideology that fueled these acts. In response, enhanced security arrangements were implemented at airports worldwide in the hope of preventing a repeat occurrence. A host of "terrorist experts" and government representatives began to speculate about the capability and likelihood that such groups would attempt more widespread and destructive acts of terrorism. Importantly, the potential use by terrorists of weapons of mass destruction (WMDs) remains a major concern for those responsible for protecting their countries. The prospect of terrorists armed with nuclear, biological, or chemical weapons cause grave concern within the policy, intelligence, and academic communities. Most experts believe that if successful in acquiring a WMD capability, terrorist groups will not hesitate to use them. This is indeed a frightening prospect.

Today, the Middle East has become a far less stable place than before September 11, 2001. As this article was written, Israel became engaged in intense fighting with both Hezbollah in Lebanon. In addition, the United States is still attempting to bring peace and stability to Iraq, encountering significant difficulties along the way. Many now fear an inevitable descent into civil war, which will serve to further de-stabilize the region. Also, Iranian President Ahmadinejad is publicly calling for the destruction of Israel and is pushing forward with a controversial nuclear enrichment program. What new radical views and manifestations of hatred might emerge from such a volatile environment?

Diplomacy, military action, law enforcement cooperation, and other actions are being undertaken for the express purpose of countering the spreading violence and preventing future acts of terrorism. Will those efforts be successful in achieving a more stable and peaceful world? To be realistic, we should not be optimistic about near-term prospects for peace and stability in the region. Therefore, we should be prepared for the worst.

Nations tend to focus on the crisis of the moment, expending considerable time and effort, as well as human capital and material resources, to deal with the current perceived threat. The current perceived threat has largely been defined by a host of notorious terrorist bombing incidents in Kenya, Tanzania, London, Bali, Madrid, Jakarta, Amman, and elsewhere. In addition to the ever-present fear of skyjackings, these bombings constitute the most likely form of future terrorist attacks. If the best predictor of future behavior is past behavior; these are the terrorist acts we will probably see repeated. Airports, embassies, military installations, and important high profile events such as the Olympics and the G-8 Summit Conference have all worked to enhance security in recent years to prevent these types of acts. The primary objective is to try and harden the targets terrorists are thought most likely to attack.

Following September 11, airports have received the largest share of funding and public scrutiny. While airports have initiated security enhancements, we continue to struggle with the appropriate level of security required for other potential terrorism targets. What should be considered a terrorist target and who makes the decision about what should be protected pose significant challenges. There seems to be no uniform or standardized basis for these decisions. Nations continue to struggle with defining terrorist targets and knowing what needs to be protected, how this is to be done.

As a demonstration of our reactive way of doing business, most countries have yet to implement appropriate security procedures on ship or rail transportation, on highways, or at busy seaports since we've not seen significant acts of terrorism in this area. Today, one can ride an Amtrak train from Washington, D.C. to New York and never have a bag screened for bombs or weapons. This is also true in Europe. The terrorist acts in Madrid and London demonstrated that terrorists will adapt to our heightened security measures and will seek such softer targets. When they were attacked, these were not the targets we were most concerned about, leaving them vulnerable to terrorists. Is it even possible to fully protect these vulnerable targets?

How much can and should we do in a free society to enhance security? When does security infringe on basic civil rights? Is searching an elderly woman at an airport helping to fight terrorism? Is it fair to profile individuals as a screening tool? These are difficult questions for open, democratic societies to ponder, but they are questions that need to be examined and answered. Countries need to undertake thorough but realistic assessments of vulnerabilities and initiate "reasonable" measures that can have a meaningful impact. For example, most experts agree that profiling is more effective than random screening at airports, yet that is perceived by some as being politically incorrect or discriminatory. In this instance politics may outweigh efficiency.

2.1. Nations Need to Properly Plan For Terrorist Acts

There is an inherent danger in exclusively focusing our prevention activities in anticipation of only the recent types of terrorist acts alone. While terrorists may well repeat a successful operation, they might just as easily employ new methods of attack against non-traditional targets. Governments usually respond to terrorism fears by focusing resources on short-term remedies aimed at treating the symptoms rather than the sources. Expenditures are more likely to be focused on screening machines and bomb barriers than quality training to enhance analysis and decision making. Building a security wall is more easily undertaken than altering the culture of the people using the facility, even though the later may achieve a higher level of overall safety. Spending money on equipment can justify bureaucracies and provide a false sense of preparedness. Spending money on hazardous material suits for agencies in Wyoming may bring much needed money to that state government, and will truly enhance readiness there, but does it really help in fighting terrorism overall? Is the funding and training adequately focused where it needs to be? Would a terrorist really want to blow up a water tower in Kansas or a food processing plant in Missouri?

What if a group of terrorists seized a government building, a train, an aircraft or other symbolic target? In such an instance, the lack of preventative security will be faulted for having failed to stop the act from taking place. In the meantime, authorities are left with the task of safely resolving the incident, an event that should never have occurred in the first place. If one accepts that security is never perfect, then one might agree that we are likely to have terrorist hostage sieges in the future. We can all recall watching the news in horror when Chechen terrorists seized citizens in the Dubrovka Theater in Moscow in 2002 leaving 129 dead, or when Chechen terrorists seized a school in Beslan in 2004 leaving 331 killed, mostly children. The MRTA took over the Japanese Ambassadors residence in Lima in 1996, and the Abu Sayaf has traveled over the sea to grab western hostages vacationing at posh diving resorts. Is there any country that secures its hotels, schools or movie theaters against such events? What other attractive and unprotected public targets are out there?

What is the likelihood that a terrorist siege will happen? Many terrorist experts would suggest that such an event is less likely today than it was back in the 1970's and 80's. In that period, terrorists hijacked a number of commercial aircraft or engaged in other dramatic actions, such as holding hostages for prolonged periods of time in order to gain notoriety for their cause and press for their demands. Recalling such infamous names as Black September (Munich Olympics) and "Carlos the Jackal" (OPEC Oil Ministers Incident) reminds us of the powerful impact terrorist hostage takings had on the world stage. Other well known incidents, such as Entebbe, Mogadishu, Princess Gate in London, TWA Flight 847, and the Achille Lauro, all served to display the global impact of these horrific acts. Despite the extreme challenges faced when responding to these incidents, most were resolved with limited loss of life, either through negotiations or through tactical intervention. Have the terrorists learned from their past siege activities? Are they better prepared for this task? During the Beslan siege, the terrorists clearly knew what to expect from the government response and were prepared to counter that effort.

Authorities will need to determine the best way to resolve the terrorist hostage incident without reacting in a manner that further endangers the lives of the hostages, or rewards the terrorists for their behavior. Governments and their law enforcement agencies need to have a range of capabilities if they expect to be successful in their efforts when responding to this type of incident. Key personnel need to be well trained and prepared if called upon to make the required life and death decisions that will be required. These are critically important issues which should be fully examined by countries before an actual terrorist hostage incident occurs, not during one.

3. Government Decision Makers and Some Barriers to Negotiation in Managing Incidents

Sadly, there are many examples of siege incidents in which officials who made the key decisions failed to fully appreciate the unique management challenges they faced, or they lacked sufficient levels of self-control or discipline to be successful. Key decisions based on anger, frustration, or from being overwhelmed by an event are signs of poor planning and preparation. Nations need to exercise care and select only the most qualified incident commanders for these tasks.

Countries need to be prepared to effectively respond to and manage a high profile terrorist incident. The required response will not be limited to the expected and established protocols for evacuation, bomb scene investigation, witness interviews, and tactical containment, to name a few. A terrorist hostage siege also requires that the authorities have a highly trained crisis management apparatus which incorporates a wide range of capabilities and skills. Among those needed capabilities is a highly trained tactical response team that can be called upon to contain an incident and attempt to rescue hostages if necessary. Most nations have such trained forces. Less appreciated, but every bit as important, is the need for a highly trained and professional hostage negotiation team.

With the focus of today's terrorists on producing large numbers of casualties, many experts believe that the hostage siege incident is less likely today. This view is guided by the belief that the terrorists do not expect governments to make concessions and are satisfied to engage in mass murder in furtherance of their cause. Many feel that today's terrorists are more suicidal, more "willing to die" for their cause. Indeed, we have seen an alarming increase in suicide bombings and other seemingly senseless and self-destructive acts by radical terrorists. The belief is that terrorists with access to a pool of hostages on a plane or within a building would simply detonate explosives to obtain mass casualties without ever seeking to "negotiate" with authorities. It is hard to argue that this could not happen, but this is not the only potential scenario. Negotiations were conducted in both Russian situations, at the theater and the school.

Terrorists are likely to want to prolong the siege to obtain publicity for their cause or press for substantive demands. Terrorists may not fit into the expected suicide profile, or if they may have no clear cut objectives. They may not even be sure what they want to accomplish. A terrorist stating that he is "willing to die" can be quite different from one actually "wanting to die." Terrorists did in fact engage in negotiations during the Air France incident in Marseilles and when the MRTA terrorists took over the Japanese Ambassadors residence in Lima, Peru. Time and again negotiations have been conducted, yet so many countries are ill prepared to effectively negotiate. Authorities need to be fully prepared to engage in meaningful dialogue with terrorists. Experience has shown that key government decision makers often do not understand the complexities of negotiation.

Decision makers need to understand and trust in their trained and experienced negotiators. If they don't understand or appreciate negotiation capabilities, they may feel compelled to become personally involved and interfere, or make decisions they are not qualified to make. This type of behavior can be expected to lead to undesirable consequences. In addition, key decision making officials need to be open to trying to understand the behavior and intent of the terrorists as displayed, rather than relying on their preconceived notions of how they think a terrorist is supposed to behave.

It is critical that governments and their decision makers manage the incident in a logical and non-emotional way. When dealing with terrorists we should keep in mind this important principle: in order to influence the behavior of others (terrorists in this instance), we need first to have our own behavior in control. When dealing with an emotionally high or angry terrorist hostage taker it will not be helpful for key decision makers to allow their own emotions to drive their decision making. There is an old adage in law enforcement negotiations, "don't get even, rather, and get your way." Officials need to maintain an unemotional and clear perspective in order to make the best decisions during any siege. Individuals generally do not act rationally when they are emotionally aroused, whether they are terrorists, negotiators, or political decision-makers. Having a plan, a procedure, a protocol, and a highly trained negotiation team will ensure that the government response will be professional, analytical, and flexible.

3.1. The Importance of Training

Realistic training scenarios provide the best training for all authorities who respond and handle such incidents. This must start at the top of the decision-making tree and go down to the lowest ranking officer. If top officials do not take the time to train, how can they be expected to perform successfully during a pressure filled incident? There is a reason athletic teams practice before a game. Effectively managing a life threatening terrorist hostage siege requires no less. If a key decision maker plans to be involved, he or she needs to understand the challenges, decision-making process, equipment resources, and personnel capabilities of all responding elements. A coach has to know what talent rests on the team. The United States government has undertaken a series of exercises called "TOPOFF," intended to train top officials. The quality, complexity, and realism of the training, scenarios, and the commitment of involved officials has been an improvement over the past, yet leaves much to be desired.

During the infamous 1993 Branch Davidian siege in Waco, Texas, FBI Incident Commanders often responded angrily when Branch Davidian leader David Koresh broke promises or acted against their wishes. In contrast, the FBI negotiation team, experienced in dealing with manipulative individuals in crisis, was not surprised or unduly affected by Koresh's erratic and frustrating behavior. If experienced law enforcement leaders can respond in this way, what about untrained politicians or inexperienced government officials. In contrast, Koresh's erratic behavioral swings were not unexpected by the negotiation team, and were actually anticipated. This allowed the negotiation team to avoid responding in an angry and emotional manner. The negotiation team was able to readily adapt to changing events and was successful in obtaining the release of 35 individuals, despite Incident Command decisions which tended to exacerbate the situation.

3.2. Untrained and Inexperienced Politicians

Sadly, there are numerous examples of terrorist hostage sieges in which untrained or inexperienced politicians, or self-described terrorist experts, have been thrust into dialogue with terrorists by officials who pushed aside trained and talented negotiators at the scene. During the Egypt air hijacking in Malta, untrained high-level government officials went to the control tower to manage the incident and speak with the hijackers. During the Air France hijack incident in Marseilles, a provincial politician conducted negotiations rather than one of the highly skilled negotiators present. Both of these incidents ended violently. When the MRTA terrorists took over the Japanese Ambassadors residence in Lima, Peru, President Fujimori personally insisted on making daily public statements challenging the terrorists and agitating the situation. His actions were an impediment to establishing effective dialogue. That incident ultimately required a tactical rescue. These outcomes might have been different if qualified negotiators had been allowed to do their jobs without undue influence from inexperienced politicians.

3.3. The Action Imperative

When managing a terrorist hostage siege, decision makers need to avoid getting pulled into the "action imperative." The action imperative is the compelling need to be seen as doing something, anything. Politicians in particular can be expected to feel the need to be seen by the public as being in charge and doing something, anything, to resolve the incident. This often leads to inappropriate or unhelpful statements or actions that end up inflaming or complicating the management of the incident. As previously mentioned, President Fujimori did this repeatedly in Lima to the detriment of the negotiation process. Often in siege incidents, prolonged periods of time go by with seemingly little action. This is not necessarily indicative that the situation is worsening. In fact, it may constitute a positive sign that the terrorists are willing to wait longer for what they want and are purposefully avoiding violent actions which they know will trigger a tactical response from authorities. When things seem to be stuck or not moving forward quickly enough, politicians and others should be careful about what they say and how their statements and behaviors might negatively impact on the overall outcome.

3.4. Preconceived ideas

Understanding behavioral uncertainties is especially important when confronting a terrorist. While each of us may feel that we can identify an act of terrorism when we see it; that should not mean that all terrorists will think and act the same way. Our preconceived notions about the behaviors of Islamic terrorists may prevent us from keeping an open mind to a flexible approach to problem solving (negotiations). During the researcher's FBI career he was once told by a high-level government official that it was a waste of time to try to interview a captured hijacker during an actual investigation. When questioned about this statement, the official said this was because the arrested individual was a terrorist and everyone knew that terrorists would not talk. This was shocking to hear from a high-level terrorism official, and very wrong, as the researcher had at that time interviewed other terrorists and had yet to encounter an arrested terrorist that had refused to talk, or who had not ultimately provided useful information. Somehow this official's preconceived idea of what a terrorist would or would not do almost prevented a useful, and in that case rather productive, law enforcement debrief of a terrorist. His preconceived about all terrorists was entirely inaccurate and had his decision been allowed to stand, it would have resulted in the loss of valuable information.

It is unclear whether decision makers responding to and managing a terrorist siege will understand these things. What experience do they have in such matters and what training have they received? Have they participated in training exercises, spent years working terrorist investigations, traveled to the region of the world, or even attended relevant lectures? Siege decision makers are often selected because they have achieved a certain rank rather than because they have the needed experience and skills required to be effective. Hopefully, such leaders will realize that like common criminals, not all terrorists have the same background nor should they be expected to behave in the same manner. The Researcher has learned from personal experience that not every religious zealot can be expected to behave the same way every time. Authorities should not be fooled into negotiating with each one in the same way. We do not possess a foolproof formula for conversing with every religious zealot.

3.5. Misinterpreting behaviors of hostage takers

As a negotiation instructor for many years, the researcher often spoke with law enforcement personnel about mental impairment and the various types of emotionally disturbed individuals negotiators might face during a siege incident. The risk in this approach was that of "a little bit of knowledge is a dangerous thing." While it was appropriate to help students better appreciate some of the common manifestations of mental health and behaviors, there was a significant risk of students misinterpreting manifested behaviors and then wrongly labeling someone based on their preconceived notions. If a negotiator believes he/she is dealing with a certain type of person, and then proceeds to deal with the individual in a manner consistent with that perception, yet the underlying perception may be wrong.

In the medical field if a diagnosis is bad it often leads to the wrong cure being attempted. It would be a terrible mistake to treat all bi-polar and schizophrenic patients the same, or all alcoholics, or depressed individuals the same. Such individuals may often manifest similar behaviors, yet each individual can reliably be expected to act differently in a stressful situation. This is just as true for "terrorists." They are not all the same. Labels can lead to preconceived notions as to what to expect and what should be done, when in reality the individual in question will probably not follow an anticipated pattern of behaviors and actions. Effective negotiations, as well as effective incident command decision making, should be based on a realistic assessment of the demonstrated behaviors, and not simply be driven by placing someone in a category and following a "cookbook recipe" approach to dealing with them.

4. Peaceful Resolution: Negotiation

In 1999 the researcher participated in law enforcement and academic conference in Israel focused on dealing with religious fanatics during the forthcoming millennium. A hypothetical question introduced in the discussions dealt with a notional Christian fanatic threatening to kill an innocent hostage in furtherance of his belief that the world was coming to an end. Several religious scholars attended that conference. Most felt the best approach in such a case would be for one of them to engage the religious fanatic in dialogue to discuss beliefs, and ultimately convince the person that their religious interpretation was incorrect. They felt their arguments in favor of the proper interpretation of the bible would be convincing and turn the fanatic away from violence. Experienced negotiators know well the risks of attempting to turn someone away from their core beliefs.

At the conference in response, the researcher pointed out that if his own child was held at knife point by this same religious fanatic, that he would want one of the many talented Israeli police negotiators to do the negotiations rather than one of the religious scholars. In support of this argument, police negotiators have conducted such dangerous and delicate negotiations hundreds of times, convincing depressed, suicidal, radical, criminal, fanatical, and deranged individuals from becoming violent. Effective negotiations have a success rate in the 90 percentile range. Such trained negotiators have the right skills needed to defuse most volatile situations by lowering the emotional tension. Experienced negotiators have the best chance of achieving a peaceful resolution, not a religious scholar who has never been in this position before and has probably never spoken to an individual in a life threatening crisis before.

An experienced crisis negotiator will focus on creating a relationship of trust through active listening skills. The goal is to build rapport, show understanding and respect, and influence the individual away from violence. Challenging core beliefs always meets with resistance and inhibits rapport building. When put in the context of one's own child at risk, deciding who is best to negotiate for their life is an easy decision to make. Go with experience or not? This is the same reason that untrained politicians should not negotiate directly with the terrorists during a siege. This is why authorities should avoid bringing in so called "outside experts" to conduct negotiations just because they have knowledge of the terrorist's religion for example. It is far more likely that the terrorist's motivation and behavior will be the key elements in seeking a peaceful resolution, not their specific religious belief. While it is valuable to learn as much as possible about a terrorist's background and culture, it should not be assumed this will provide a clear guide for a successful negotiation strategy.

4.1. Coordinating Crisis Management

The proper management of a terrorist hostage siege requires close coordination between the principal components representing the authorities. In general, active management of any siege should not involve direct engagement of politicians; rather it should be viewed as a law enforcement function. The law enforcement incident commander should constantly consult with both the negotiation team leader and the tactical team leader. These three represent the siege management triad that allows all options to be continuously weighed and strategy modified as necessary. The incident commander will be required to brief political leadership during a siege, as these incidents have broad political and foreign policy implications. The incident commander should receive overall strategic guidance from politicians, but then should be given the action authority and latitude to make the critical on-scene decisions required to resolve the incident without undue political interference. Most experts would agree that management of a terrorist hostage siege should be undertaken by trained and experienced law enforcement personnel, not politicians.

Many nations have trained tactical teams to deploy in the event of a terrorist hostage siege. These teams are highly trained and have the special equipment and skills necessary to undertake difficult hostage rescue missions. Despite such capabilities, the use of tactical resources to resolve terrorist incidents usually leads to violence. A rescue mission undertaken with skill, and perhaps a healthy dose of luck, might result in only the terrorists losing their lives. However, reality is that there is a high probability that both hostages and tactical rescuers will suffer loses. The tragic 1985 Egypt Air hijacking in Malta underscores how good intentions can do the hostages more harm than good. The rescue attempt in Malta sadly resulted in over 60 hostages dying. In that case the cure was worse than the disease. Undertaking tactical action to resolve an incident should only be undertaken when no other option is left. Nations should not use force because they can, rather they should use tactical force only when they have no other choice.

There have been several notable successful rescues (Entebbe, Mogadishu, London, Lima) but there have also been many tragic incidents in which the tactical rescue went badly and many died (Waco, Beslan, Karachi, Moscow). The risks to the hostages in any high profile terrorist siege are great. Rescue attempts almost always incur a high level of risk to all involved. With this in mind, such a resolution strategy should only be undertaken if absolutely necessary. No one expects a nation to sit by and watch hostages be executed one after the other. On the other hand, careful thought must be given before launching a high risk rescue that may not be necessary, and that may ultimately place the hostages in great danger.

5. Conclusion

In order to be fully effective in managing terrorist hostage sieges, governments should have qualified and trained professional law enforcement personnel authorized and prepared to handle any terrorist hostage siege incident. Governments need to be flexible and creative in the management of a terrorist siege incident. Such incidents are always challenging, dangerous, and complicated by the number of involved and effected parties. It can be stated that these competing interests constitute the "crisis within the crisis." Only with well-written procedures, policies, and vigorous training exercises can a country expect to respond to such incidents in a unified and effective manner. Top law enforcement personnel, government officials, and political figures should devote time and energy to participate and train in national efforts to prepare for these events in advance. If they are not willing to devote the time and energy to train and prepare, they should stay out of the way during a real crisis event and allow the professionals to do their jobs.

In addition to a tactical team, every nation needs a robust and effective negotiation team to support this effort, because focusing solely on tactical capabilities alone limits viable options. Negotiation does not equate to capitulation and does not necessarily lead nations to make unacceptable concessions. Negotiation buys time, gathers information, and supports a broad range of resolution options, to include peaceful surrender. Effective negotiations can resolve most incidents and can help support any required tactical resolution efforts, if that becomes necessary. Therefore, every nation needs a trained and equipped professional negotiation team. Periodic training exercises should be undertaken and key personnel should be given the resources and authority to act.

Finally, politicians should avoid unhelpful public statements that may negatively impact upon the management of the incident, instead allow law enforcement professionals to help prepare or at least review all press statements. Remember that any statement made by a government can have an impact on the outcome of the incident. Nations should always remember that they will be judged on how effectively they manage a terrorist hostage siege, not how quickly.

Understanding and Responding to the Terrorism Phenomenon
O. Nikbay and S. Hancerli (Eds.)
IOS Press, 2007

Hostage Negotiation: A Systems Perspective in a Case Study Approach

Brian RICHARDSON, Ph.D.
University of North Texas, USA

Abstract. The purpose of this essay is to argue for a systems perspective of crisis negotiation. Previous research and literature has primarily focused on parts, or subunits, of the negotiation process. For example, much of the research into crisis negotiations has addressed the interaction between negotiators and hostage taker. While such research is valuable, over-emphasis on this interaction may result in the neglecting of other key components of the negotiation process. This essay will begin by introducing systems theory and arguing that a crisis negotiation is a system. A review of case studies will be used to support this claim. The paper will conclude with practical and theoretical implications of the utilizing a systems perspective.

Keywords. Systems theory, political violence, crisis negotiation, hostage negotiation, and police communication.

Introduction

The purpose of this essay is to argue for a systems perspective of crisis negotiation. Previous research and literature has primarily focused on parts, or subunits, of the negotiation process. For example, much of the research into crisis negotiations has addressed the interaction between negotiators and hostage taker. While such research is valuable, over-emphasis on this interaction may result in the neglecting of other key components of the negotiation process.

The act of taking someone hostage, whether it be in an unplanned siege or a premeditated, politically motivated act, appears to be an increasingly used criminal and terrorist tactic [1, 2]. While tactical interventions to such cases were the rule of thumb until the 1970's, law enforcement agencies have begun to rely on other methods in order to resolve crisis incidents. In the past thirty years, negotiation has become the primary method of dealing with hostage and barricade situations in many Western countries [3]. Hostage negotiations involve a number of key participants, including the hostage, hostage negotiator, hostage taker, and incident commander. Hostage is defined as "a person held by force as security that specified terms will be met" [4 pg 405]. The hostage taker is the individual or group of individuals holding the hostage. Hostage takers may be antisocial personalities who want money and transportation, terrorists, or emotionally disturbed individuals using the incident to express some negative emotion [1]. The hostage negotiator is the individual responsible for talking directly to the hostage taker, managing the negotiation, and monitoring and analyzing both the hostage taker's emotional state and communicative ability [1]. Finally, the incident, or field, commander, is the ranking law enforcement officer at the hostage incident scene.

As the frequency and profile of hostage situations increases, so too does scholarly interest in crisis negotiations. It appears that most practical advice and research into crisis negotiation has focused on the interaction between negotiators and hostage takers. While this attention is valuable for understanding the dynamic interplay between negotiator and hostage taker, others areas of the crisis negotiation process may be neglected. If crisis negotiations are viewed from a systems perspective [5], we may be able to see them from a broader point of view and locate additional areas ripe for practical advice and research. Indeed, crisis negotiations involve important interactions between hostage taker and hostages, the news media and law enforcement representatives, and members of the crisis negotiation team. Thus, the purpose of this paper is to frame crisis negotiation from a systems perspective. This paper will begin with a brief discussion of systems theory. Next, the paper will argue that crisis negotiations can be viewed from a systems perspective, and a review of case studies will be used to support this claim. The paper will conclude with practical and theoretical implications of the utilizing a systems perspective.

1. Systems Perspectives

Systems theory is an interdisciplinary field which is used as a framework for taking concepts which were previously seen as disconnected, unrelated, and disjointed, and viewing them as whole systems [6]. Systems theory has been applied in a number of disciplines, including sociology, economics, political science, information science, and organizational studies. Organizational systems perspectives evolved because of theorists growing dissatisfaction with mechanistic views of organizations. These mechanistic perspectives regarded organizations as isolated from their environments, and viewed organizational subunits in isolation from one another. Scholars such as Katz and Kahn [5] and Thompson [7] argued that organizations (and groups) should instead be viewed as complex open systems requiring interaction among component parts and with the environment in order to ensure survival. There are a number of basic systems principles useful for explaining its general premises[1]. First, a system is an assemblage of parts, components, or subunits. For example, the human body is comprised of a heart, lungs, stomach, and a host of other important organs. Similarly, an organization may be comprised of a manufacturing facility, and a number of departments including human resources, marketing, sales, and legal. A second characteristic of systems is interdependence, which suggests that the functioning of one system unit is dependent upon the functioning of other units. In the human body, the circulatory system is dependent upon the respiratory system; within organizations, the sales department is dependent upon the proper functioning of the manufacturing department. Because of their interdependence, systems are susceptible to the "ripple effect," [8 pg 40], or chain reactions. A flaw in one part of the system can cause a chain reaction and affect other parts of the system.

---

[1] This essay does not provide a comprehensive list of systems theory principles or properties. For a more thorough treatment, please see Katz and Kahn [5].

A third systems principle concerns boundaries, or permeability. Boundaries regulate interaction between the system and its environment. Living systems cannot be completely shut off from their environments; those that are will die. By opening its boundaries, a system can bring in important resources, e.g. information, or raw materials, which it can then transform into energy or other positive outputs. Interaction with the environment also informs the system about important environmental changes to which it must adapt. For example, a computer software company must interact with the environment to bring in new employees, and to discover innovations within the industry. Systems enact many types of boundaries, including those that are physical, psychological, and linguistic, as well as those built upon rules and roles [8]. Each of these types of boundaries helps identify that which is in the system, and that which is part of the environment. Finally, there are a number of systems properties, which are likewise useful in understanding systems theory. Three that are appropriate for the present essay include holism, equifinality, and requisite variety. Holism suggests that a system is more than merely the sum of its parts. Systems can produce results above and beyond (or sometimes worse) than what would be expected based upon their individual parts. When systems produce positive results greater than the sum of their parts, this is called synergy; the opposite case is called negative synergy [9]. Equifinality suggests that "a system can reach the same final state from differing initial conditions and by a variety of paths" [5 pg 30]. For example, let's suppose that a university wants to increase enrollment by five percent. There are a number of ways the system could accomplish this goal, including increasing recruitment, lowering tuition, and spending more on advertising. As systems become more complex, there may be an increasing number of ways to reach objectives. A second system property is requisite variety, which suggests that the internal components of a system must be as diverse and complicated as the environment in which it resides. An example of requisite variety involves the need of airlines and airports to become increasingly capable of handling security threats as their environments become increasingly threatening. In the next section, the researcher will argue that crisis negotiations can be viewed from a systems perspective.

2. Crisis Negotiation from a Systems Perspective

If hostage negotiations are viewed merely as a communication episode between hostage taker and negotiator, we may be missing a number of systems components and properties which could make a difference in the negotiation process. Like any system, crisis negotiations are comprised of a number of subunits all of which may have interactions with other subunits (see Appendix A). These may include the field commander, various support personnel, e.g. traffic control, negotiation supervisor, negotiation team, including primary negotiator, secondary negotiator, and intelligence, tactical supervisor, and tactical team, psychological consultant, hostage(s), and hostage taker [1]. Depending upon the scope of the situation, other subunits may include higher-ranking government officials, the chief of police, family members and associates, and almost certainly, the news media. It is important to remember that each of these subunits (or subsystems) within the larger system, is also a system within itself. For example, the tactical team is its own system, the negotiating team is a system, and the hostage taker(s) represents another system. Each of these systems is likewise embedded in a larger system, in this case the crisis negotiation scene. This hierarchical ordering of systems may be an important perspective for understanding both successful and unsuccessful crisis negotiations. Not only are these subunits operating within the negotiation context, they are also interdependent.

In other words, the functioning of one subunit within the system is dependent upon the functioning of the other units. Even the hostage taker is viewed as an important subunit within the system. If the hostage taker takes aggressive action, the other, interdependent subunits are likewise affected. The negotiation team may cease negotiation, the tactical team may initiate an assault, and the hostages may resist the hostage taker. Even those subunits not directly affected may have to adjust their behaviors; the traffic officer may have to become more vigilant in order to protect the public, and the news media may have to adjust stories being written. Thus, a change in one component may cause a ripple effect throughout the entire system. Finally, crisis negotiations are characterized by boundaries. The most obvious boundary is the physical one, which usually includes creating inner and outer perimeters which are manned by law enforcement [10]. "No one is allowed inside, on, or through the inner perimeter unless the tactical team approves" … and "only authorized personnel are permitted through the outer perimeter" [10 pg 74]. Another boundary type is roles, which represent patterns of expected behavior relevant to parts individuals play in the system [8]. Within the negotiation scene, family members are sometimes called in to speak with hostage takers. As long as they play out their assigned role, they can remain within the system. However, if they step out of that role, and escalate the situation, they will likely be expelled from the system.

By viewing crisis negotiation scenes as systems, we can begin to see a number of areas, in addition to the communication between hostage taker and negotiator, which can affect the process. Case studies of hostage negotiation situations illuminate the systems perspective. Several of these will be discussed next.

2.1. Munich Olympics Hostage Taking (1972) – Requisite Variety

This case witnessed a group of Israeli athletes and coaches taken hostage by the Palestinian terrorist group Black September during the 1972 Olympic games in Munich, Germany. On September 5, Palestinian terrorists held 9 Israeli athletes hostage and killed two others (for a complete review of the Munich Olympics terrorist act, see Reeve's study [11]). German government officials negotiated futilely with the hostage takers. After promising the hostage takers safe passage out of the country, German police agents planned to ambush the hostage takers at a German airfield. The ambush attempt resulted in a shootout; the terrorists killed eleven Israeli athletes and one German police officer. Police killed five of the eight hostage-takers. A systems theory property which seems to describe this situation is that of requisite variety. Again, requisite variety suggests that the processes and properties of a system must be as complex as the environment in which the system operates. If the environment becomes more complex, then the system must enhance its complexity. In Munich, the terrorist group consistently appeared to be in control of the situation, while German officials gave the impression of being incompetent [12]. In the comprehensive narrative *One Day in September* [12, 11], German law enforcement personnel and government bureaucrats routinely give away their strategies and their positions to the terrorists. Regardless of which move the negotiation team made, it seems the terrorists had a ready, more effective countermove. The German government did not possess the necessary requisite variety to deal with the terrorist threat. Its system complexity was no match for that of the terrorists during this era. Since this time, Germany and other European countries have developed increasingly complex strategies for dealing with such situations, and are flexible enough to use those which are most appropriate. With the increased use of technology within terrorist-related, hostage events, law enforcement systems must develop the requisite variety to match the complexity of the hostage-taking environment.

The inclusion of religious experts as crisis negotiation consultants provides an example of law enforcement agencies increasing their requisite variety. Following the Branch Davidian Compound Siege near Waco, Texas, law enforcement officials recognized their inadequacies in understanding domestic, religious, extremist groups. In response to that incident, the FBI has initiated dialogue with scholars who study extreme religious movements [13] with the hopes that it can facilitate understanding in similar situations. This response demonstrates law enforcements' ability to increase its complexity in the face of an environment which increasingly becomes more complicated.

2.2. Branch Davidian Compound Incident – Role/Boundary Violation

On February 28, 1993, the Bureau of Alcohol, Tobacco, and Firearms (BATF) conducted a military-like raid on Mount Carmel, Texas, where the Branch Davidians resided. The Davidians refused to surrender and a gunfire exchange ensued. Four agents and six Davidians were killed in the firefight. The Federal Bureau of Investigation then assumed control of the site, surrounding Mount Carmel, and demanding the surrender of the Davidians [14]. After a 51-day standoff, federal agents used flammable CS tear gas on the compound in an attempt to encourage evacuation. However, a number of fires broke out, burning the compound, and ultimately killing 80 Davidians.

This case demonstrates another critical error which occurred when FBI officials met with U.S. Attorney General Janet Reno, without the knowledge of on-site negotiators. The purpose of their meeting was to advocate the use of force in order to end the standoff. From a systems perspective, the FBI directors stepped outside of their on-scene roles and violated the boundary of the negotiation system; in effect, they eliminated the role of negotiator, much to the negotiators' dismay [15, 13]. Furthermore, the site of armored vehicles ramming the compound demonstrates how one system unit can affect other units. In this case, the aggressive tactics of the tactical squad may have resulted in aggressiveness from the Davidians who ultimately set fire to their compound [16].

2.3. Bus 174 Incident – Permeable Boundaries and Role Violation

In this situation, featured in the documentary *Bus 174*, an armed suspect ran onto a city bus while being chased by police. The gunman, Sandro do Nascimento, immediately took a hostage and the police backed off. Over the next four hours, do Nascimento held 13 passengers hostage while the scene was broadcast nationally by Brazilian news agencies. In this case, the hostage negotiation boundaries were too permeable. A perimeter was not established and both the news media and the public-at-large witnessed the event at close range [17]. Eventually, do Nascimento exited the bus, taking one hostage with him. Without warning, a single policeman rushed the hostage taker and took aim. However, he accidentally shot the hostage instead; do Nascimento instinctively fired his gun twice, hitting the hostage two more times. do Nascimento was quickly taken into custody and the hostage eventually died. Although the situation could have ended peacefully, one breakdown in the system, caused by a single police officer, resulted in a breakdown of the negotiation process. This case provides another example of one member of the system not knowing his role. By taking action into his own hands, a ripple effect occurs, and the entire system collapses.

2.4. Hierarchical Embeddedness

Both the Branch Davidian and the Bus 174 incidents introduce another systems component to crisis negotiations: that such negotiations are embedded within more powerful systems. In both cases, the actual, on-scene negotiation was impinged upon by those in higher levels of government. In the Branch Davidian case, the higher-ranking system was the U.S. Attorney General's office. In the Bus 174 standoff, the state governor ordered the police not to shoot the hostage, despite the perception by some members of Brazil's elite SWAT team that this was the best way to diffuse the situation without the loss of innocent lives [17]. Such cases indicate that solely focusing on the interaction between negotiators and hostage takers may miss greater system effects, such as the influence of high-ranking government officials and politicians. While the three case studies explored above suggest systemic failures, a number of increasingly successful hostage negotiations suggest system synergy.

2.5. Alexandria, Virginia Cash Store Pawn Shop incident – Boundary Management

In this crisis negotiation incident, all components of the system seemed to work well together, resulting in a generally positive, though not perfect, outcome. A 34-year-old man was holding seven people hostage at a pawn shop that he had attempted to rob [18]. There was no intention to take hostages but the suspect was compelled to when police descended upon the scene. As quickly as possible, the Alexandria police established two key boundaries: one was used to prevent traffic, human and otherwise, from entering the scene, while the second was used to isolate the negotiation team from unnecessary influence. However, the latter boundary was permeable. While negotiations were ongoing, other members of the crisis management team began researching the perpetrator's background and learned that he had two small children. Systems theory suggests that living systems must be open to important inputs from the environment, including human resources, material goods, and, in this case, information. Negotiators used the information about the perpetrator's children, in order to instill hope into the situation [18]. The perpetrator eventually released all of the hostages before taking his life. In this particular case, the system's components demonstrated their interdependence and seemed to work well together. However, one system component, the hostage taker, eradicated himself from the system, furthering the argument that it only takes on faulty system component to cause damage to the overall system.

2.6. Freemen's Standoff (1996) – Permeability of boundaries

The Freemen were a Christian Patriot group based at a ranch house in Montana [19]. In March, 1996, the FBI attempted to bring into custody members of the group for alleged federal law violations. For months they refused to leave the ranch, which they claimed as sovereign territory. The FBI hoped for a peaceful resolution to the standoff especially in the wake of the Branch Davidian tragedy. For this situation, the FBI invited Bo Gritz, former Army Green Beret and sympathizer to the militia movement to meet with group members and encourage their surrender. In early June, 1996, the remaining members of the Freemen surrendered to FBI officials.

The Freeman's Standoff in Montana is similar to the Alexandria, Virginia, case in at least one critical way: the permeability of system boundaries in order to allow "outside" resources or information into the system and affect the negotiation. In this case, a third-party individual, respected by the standoff group, were brought into the case in order to facilitate a settlement. This standoff lasted 81 days and served to test the FBI's new crisis negotiation strategy just three years after the Branch Davidian tragedy.

2.7. South Maluccan Independence Movement (SMIM) Train Takeover (1975)

In this frequently documented case, we see another system component, the hostage, demonstrating his influence upon the hostage negotiation system. In this incident, the SMIM assumed control of a train in the Netherlands. To demonstrate its seriousness, the group chose one passenger for immediate execution [20, 1]. Before killing him, he was allowed to speak with and give his farewells to his family via telephone. The emotional scene of the hostage saying goodbye to his family was evidently too much for the terrorists. They decided not to execute him, instead choosing another passenger who was killed on the spot. This narrative is not intended to suggest that the terrorists had a heart; indeed, an innocent person was still killed in cold blood. However, the story does highlight the role of the hostage as part of the hostage negotiation system. Again, systems are comprised of interdependent parts; hostages and hostage takers are dependent upon one another. In this particular case, the hostage demonstrated significant influence over the system and changed the course of the situation.

3. Conclusion

A number of practical implications arise when considering crisis negotiation from a systems perspective. First, a systems perspective aligns with views of crisis negotiation experts who advocate the use of simulations and role-plays [21], which consider the roles of multiple actors within negotiations. A systems perspective of simulations and role-plays might include the anticipated roles of all actors who could become involved in a hostage negotiation and how they might impinge on the negotiator-hostage taker interaction. Additionally, these role-plays would likely include key third-parties such as the news media and psychologists [22] and consider their influence on the proceedings. Second, the role of the environment would hold a prominent position within a systems perspective. Practitioners utilizing a systems perspective would constantly monitor the environment for potential threats. This monitoring might include socio-economic conditions, jobless rates, changes in immigration policies, and other factors which may cause increases or declines in hostage taking opportunities. Finally, as the principle of requisite variety suggests, law enforcement must consistently learn from the hostage takers they encounter and expand their investigation/negotiation capacity in order to match the complexity of the environment.

A systems perspective would have significant implications for the ways crisis negotiation is empirically researched. Such a perspective would call into question studies that examine a small number of variables, e.g. the relationship between negotiation tactics and outcomes, in isolation from their environment. A systems perspective would advocate consideration of all key variables and the manner in which they interact within crisis negotiation events. It is important to note that scholars have recognized that "methodological problems have prevented systems theory from not living up to its billing" [23 pg 10]. While a full test of systems theory may not be possible as it applies to crisis negotiation, research examining a small number of variables should consider the influence of those variables which are not under investigation. The purpose of this essay was to advocate for a systems theory of crisis negotiation. It is hoped that this argument will instigate a dialogue about the usefulness of systems perspectives within this context.

Appendix A: The "parts" of a hostage negotiation, all of which comprise the crisis negotiation system. The arrows represent potential interactions between the parts. The dashed line represents the larger environment.

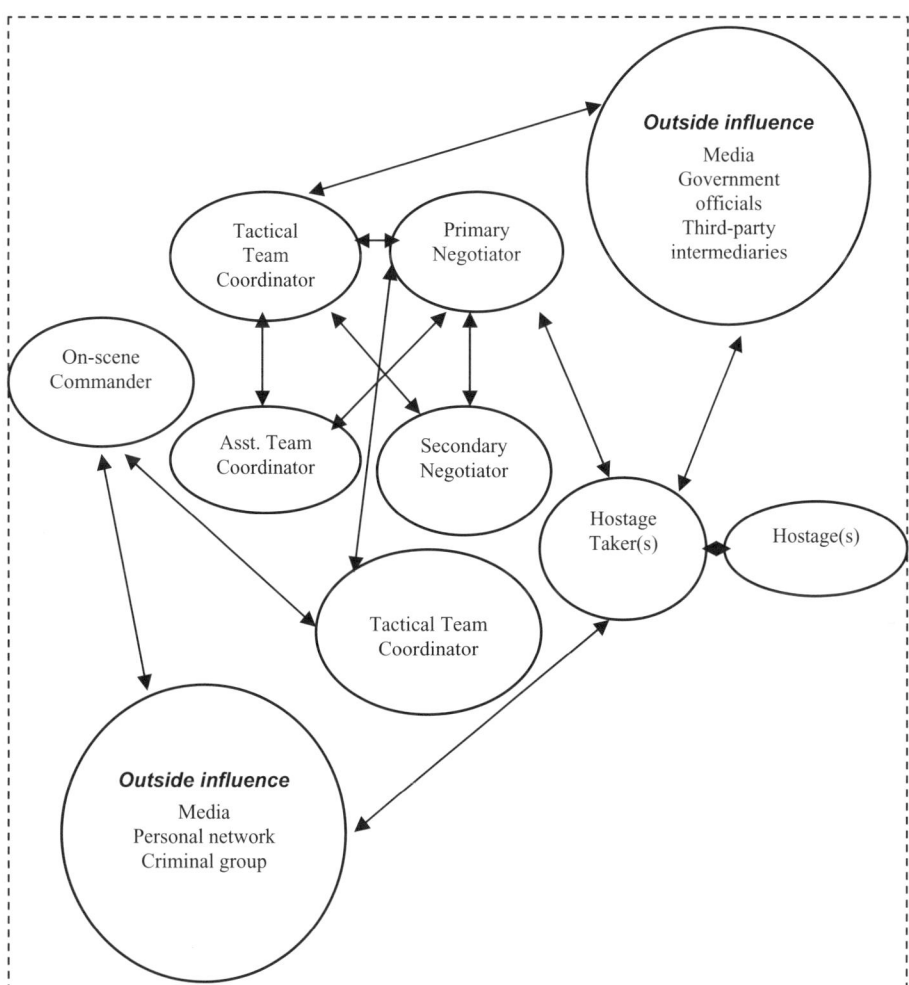

References

[1]   M.J. McMains, W.C. Mullins, Crisis negotiations: Managing critical incidents and hostage negotiations in law enforcement and corrections. Cincinnati, OH: Anderson; 1996.

[2]   J.M. Poland, M.J. McCrystle, Practical, tactical, and legal perspectives of terrorism and hostage-taking. Lewiston, NY: E. Mellon Press; 1999.

[3]   A.Dolnik, R. Pilch, The Moscow Theater hostage crisis: The perpetrators, their tactics, and the Russian response. International Negotiation, **8** (2003), 577-611.

[4]   American Heritage Dictionary New York: Houghton and Mifflin Company; 1994.

[5]   D. Katz, R.L. Kahn, The social psychology of organizations (2nd Ed.). New York: Wiley; 1978.

[6]   L. Von Bertalanffy, General systems theory. New York: Braziller; 1968.

[7]   J.D. Thompson, Organizations in action: Social science bases of Administrative Theory. New York: McGraw-Hill; 1967.

[8]   J.D. Rothwell, In mixed company: Communicating in small groups and teams. Belmont, CA: Thomson Wadsworth; 2007.

[9]   A.J. Salazar, Understanding the synergistic effects of communication in small groups. Small Group Research, **26/2** (1995), 169-200.

[10] F.J. Lanceley, On-scene guide for crisis negotiators (2nd Ed.). Boca Raton, FL: CRC Press; 2003.

[11] S. Reeve, One day in September: The full story of the 1972 Munich Olympics massacre and the Israeli revenge operation "Wrath of God." New York: Arcade Publishing; 2000.

[12] K. MacDonald, (Director), A. Cohn, (Producer), One day in September. United States: Sony Picture Classics; 2001.

[13] H.D. Motyl, (Producer), K. McClurkin, (Producer), The final report: Waco tragedy [Television series episode]. Washington, D. C.: National Geographic Television; 2004.

[14] D. Terry, Authorities plan to wait for end of cult standoff. The New York Times, 1993, March 4, p. A16.

[15] D. Goodwin, A police chalice? Negotiating with extremists, 2004. [Online] Available from; URL:http://www.ima.org.uk/conflict/papers/Goodwin.pdf#search=%22a%20police%20chalice%3F%20negotiating%20with%20extremists%20goodwin%202004%22 [2006, October 15].

[16] Judge clears government of blame in deaths at Waco. The Houston Chronicle, 2000, September 21, p. A23.

[17] A. Bellos, He will kill us all at six. The Guardian, 2004, April 16, p. 10.

[18] P. Davis, Using words, not weapons. The Washington Post, 1998, August 6, p. V01.

[19] S.J. Romano, Third-party intermediaries and crisis negotiations. FBI Law Enforcement Bulletin, (1998) 20-24.

[20] A. Dolnik, Contrasting dynamics of crisis negotiations: Barricade versus Kidnapping Incidents. International Negotiation, **8,** (2003), 495-526.

[21] V.B.Van Hasselt, S.J. Romano, A vital tool is crisis negotiation skills training: Role playing. The FBI Law Enforcement Bulletin, **73,** (2004), 12-21.

[22] C. Hatcher, K. Mohandie, J. Turner, M.G. Gelles, The role of the psychologist in crisis/hostage negotiations. Behavioral Sciences and the Law, **16,** (1998), 455-472.

[23] J.J. McMillan, N.A. Northern, Organizational codependency: The creation and maintenance of closed systems. Management Communication Quarterly, **9,** (1995), 6-45.

Kidnapping: A Brief Psychological Overview

Mike WEBSTER,[1] Ed.D.
Consulting Psychologist, Canada

Abstract. In today's world replete with conflict, national law enforcement agencies are often required to assist in negotiating the release of kidnapped countrymen. There is, however, little understanding of the bargaining process among law enforcement officials. This paper was written by the author in an effort to equip law enforcement negotiators with the skills necessary to function in this high stakes trade in human misery. The paper outlines a model of response that includes kidnapper motivation, types of kidnapping, kidnap dynamics, management strategies and tactics.

Keywords. Psychology of kidnapping, kidnap types, kidnap motives, incident dynamics, and management strategies.

Introduction

The word "kidnap" entered the English language late in the seventeenth century, to describe the practice of stealing children for the purpose of forced labor. Prior to that time, and dating back to the fourteenth century, the act of redeeming captives, whether men, women, or children, by providing valuables, or performing a service, was called "ransoming." By the eighteenth century the word "kidnap" had replaced "ransoming" in everyday parlance and has persisted to the present day.

The act of kidnapping is a weapon with a long history. It is found in myth and folklore and was described in the early writings of the Old Testament. In ancient Rome the Emperor Constantine (AD 315) was so troubled by the increasing occurrence of kidnappings, he ordered the death penalty for those convicted of the crime [1]. During the middle Ages robber-barons were fond of kidnapping merchants and holding them for ransom. Richard I — "Richard the Lionhearted" — was seized by Leopold of Austria and held for several months in a castle at a secret location. Legend has it that Richard's minstrel, Blondel, wandered Europe singing the king's favourite song under castle windows searching for his master. He was rewarded one day when he heard, to his delight, Richard sing the refrain to his favourite ballad. The king was released upon payment of the 150,000 marks demanded by Leopold. By the 1800's kidnapping had become so routine, in that part of the world that is the Philippines today, a scale for the payment of ransom had been established. A European priest, for example, could bring up to 200 pesos whereas 50 pesos was sufficient to redeem an adult male Filipino [2].

---

[1] Dr. Webster has been a consulting psychologist for approximately 30 years. His clients include the Royal Canadian Mounted Police, RCMP, the Federal Bureau of Investigation, FBI, and many overseas law enforcement agencies. He specializes in conflict management and national security issues.

On the North American continent kidnapping for political reasons was a rare occurrence. However, kidnapping for criminal purposes had become a perennial problem. The most publicized criminal kidnapping of the last century was the abduction and murder of the first transatlantic pilot Charles Lindbergh's infant son. The baby was abducted from his crib on the night of March 1, 1932, and never seen alive again.

This notorious crime leads to the passage of the Lindbergh Law in 1933. The law made kidnapping a federal offense, and provided for the death penalty in the event that the victim was injured or still missing at the time of sentencing. Prior to the passing of the law by the American Congress, kidnappings in the U.S. had climbed to an all-time high of 279 recorded cases in 1931 [3]. In 1968 the U.S. Supreme Court declared the Lindbergh Law's death penalty provision unconstitutional; but not before 22 kidnappers was executed in approximately 30 years. The drastic reduction in the number of kidnappings, from the record high of 1931, was attributed to the FBI's improved investigative techniques and closer working relationships with local law enforcement agencies.

Kidnapping, by organized criminal gangs, had become so frequent and lucrative, during the 1930's, it was dubbed "the snatch racket" by the American press. It certainly appears that the benefits of snatching for profit did not go unnoticed by politically oriented groups; as kidnapping has become one of their major sources of revenue. A government study, spanning the years from 1968 to 1982, advised that 951 hostages were abducted in 73 countries worldwide [4]. One expert stated that approximately half of all those kidnapped between 1970 and 1985 were corporate executives, or wealthy business persons, who were "bought back" by their firms at a cost of nearly $250 million in ransom [5]. More recently, at least 6500 kidnappings took place in Latin America alone in 1995. Estimates of annual kidnap totals, worldwide during the 1990's, reached as high as 30,000 according to surveys conducted by both government agencies and private sector groups. Most experts agreed, by 1997, the countries hardest hit, from most effected to least, were: Colombia, the Philippines, Brazil, Mexico, Pakistan, Guatemala, the USA, Venezuela, India, and Ecuador [6].

Caution, however, should be exercised when interpreting kidnap statistics [7]. Statistics related to international kidnapping incidents are unreliable for a multitude of reasons. The fear of retribution from kidnappers, police corruption, police incompetence, and laws prohibiting ransom payments, all provide powerful disincentives to reporting abduction. Moreover, governments themselves attempting to attract foreign investment and tourism are provided with little incentive to report a kidnapping problem. Consequently, there are large discrepancies between official statistics and informed estimates. Experts advise that the numbers are useful only in identifying high risk countries and tracking high risk trends.

Authorities are divided in their opinions as to motive. Some favour the ideological motive, as reflected in acts where kidnappers attempt to gain the release of incarcerated compatriots or discourage foreign investment exploration, or occupation, as in present day Iraq. Others favor the profit motive and use the increase in ransom incidents as proof. While still others state that it has become difficult to determine exact motives. The latter point to incidents where political groups have employed criminals to undertake kidnappings for ransom, and where criminal groups in an attempt to increase their profile, and maximize their profit, have posed as political groups. It is not uncommon for a criminal group to sell a kidnap victim to a political group who then utilize their purchase to meet political objectives or garner ransom.

Whatever the motive, or statistics, it is certain that a series of contemporary events have come together to catalyze the kidnapping phenomenon. With the end of the Cold War, cold warriors on both sides found themselves out of work. Leftist rebels around the world were no longer funded by the defunct Soviet Union — and on the right, their contra enemies were abandoned by a disinterested U.S. government. These highly skilled individuals were seduced by the "snatch racket" as an attractive alternate source of money.

With the crackdown on the Colombian drug cartels during the 1990's the sale of drugs as a method to fund military and para-military objectives was reduced in efficacy. Rebel groups throughout Latin America became more dependent upon kidnapping as a means of survival.

The dramatic increase in ransom kidnappings in many countries was a direct result of the push for globalization during the 20th century. Across the surface of the world barriers began to fall, free trade pacts were formed, markets were opened up, and foreign investment increased at a rapid pace. The result was a widening of the gap between the rich and the poor. Large amounts of money flowed from the richest nations into the poorest nations. While this influx of cash did improve the quality of living for many of the Third World's poorest inhabitants, it also lined the pockets of the Third worlds wealthiest. A United Nations study suggested that the world was becoming even more polarized economically, both between and within countries, and that economic disparities had the potential to shift from merely "inequitable to inhuman" [8]. Finding fertile ground in this gap between rich and poor, ransom kidnapping took root and began to grow.

Following the American invasion of Iraq there has been a disturbing increase in kidnapping incidents. Insurgent groups engaged in both ideological and ransom kidnappings in an effort to express their displeasure with, and to expel the foreign occupiers of their country.

In the shadow of the causes noted above one significant factor still must be noted. Kidnappers commit kidnappings because they expect to profit. Even though only a small percentage of kidnappings are reported, those that are are make big news. They usually involve big names, big money and broad media coverage. Over the last decade it became obvious that the "snatch racket" is a lucrative business for anyone willing to market in human misery. Politically oriented groups alone extorted more than $200 million worldwide in 1994, according to one government survey [9].

Kidnap victims have also contributed to the increased volume of abductions. They have presented themselves as targets in increased numbers and varieties. Kidnappers, in selecting their targets, were previously confined to diplomats, corporate executives, and wealthy business persons, but today they can select from a pool of tourists, engineers, consultants of all stripes, journalists, military personnel, aid workers and missionaries. Their target environments have been enriched through the addition of the common-person.

Kidnap targets, not unusually, have tended to change overtime. When the world was being explored and conquered the kidnapper's targets were sailors, explorers, geographers, military personnel, and the like. However, when the world was being colonized and countries were establishing embassies and consulates, diplomats and consuls became the targets of kidnappers and remained so for several hundred years. More recently, in the era of globalization with the expansion of corporations into multinationals, diplomats have lost their lustre in favor of the business executive. After all, corporations have proven themselves to be much more responsive to ransom demands than governments ever were - turning even those below the executive level into potential targets.

The act of kidnapping today appears to respect few boundaries. It crosses the lines of occupation, nationality and status. Kidnappers, whether criminally or politically oriented play a game of high stakes manipulation. Those responsible for the management of these incidents must possess the knowledge and the skills necessary to compete.

1. Defining Basic Terms

For the sakes of clarity and accuracy the present paper distinguishes between hostage taking, kidnapping, hostages, and kidnap victims. The meanings of these terms are separate and distinct and are not to be viewed as synonymous. The terms are defined as follows:

1.1. Hostage Taking

To unlawfully confine another in a known location and to threaten to do that person harm or prolong that person's confinement if certain demands, terms, or conditions are not met by a third party.

1.2. Kidnapping

To seize another, by force or fraud, and to transport that individual to, and detain that individual at, an unknown location for any reason (not necessarily for ransom).

1.3. Hostage

A person unlawfully confined at a known location by another person, or group of persons, and used as a "bargaining chip" in an attempt to satisfy certain demands, terms, or conditions.

1.4. Kidnap victim

A person seized by force or fraud, transported to, and detained at, an unknown location for any reason, including a guarantee for ransom.

2. Typology

Typologies are attempts at making order out of chaos and they do so by classifying phenomena according to patterns, themes, or similarities. Typologies have limitations but their utility as classificatory tools outweigh the risks inherent in their use. Hostage taking and kidnapping typologies [10, 11, 12, 13] provide investigators with the ability to formulate management strategies for various types of subjects and incidents. This article outlines a kidnap typology that includes kidnapper's motivations, kidnap incident types, incident dynamics, and management strategies, in an effort to similarly assist investigators.

2.1. Motivation

The first step toward choosing a management strategy is to identify the kidnapper's motivation. Motivation is concerned more with "why" the kidnapper is engaged in abduction than "what" the kidnapper is doing or asking for. A single dimension with two contrasting positions is used to identify and illustrate the kidnapper's central motive. The dimension runs from an instrumental, or goal directed, motivation at one end to an expressive, or display directed motivation at the other.

The kidnapper is instrumentally motivated when the kidnapping is being used as an instrument to attain some objective beyond the act itself. In this case the kidnapping is more a "means-to-an-end." Instrumentally motivated kidnappings include: (1) kidnapping for money or other negotiable valuables; (2) kidnapping to cause some action (e.g. payment of a debt, release of compatriots); (3) kidnapping to prevent some action (e.g. going to the police, foreign investment, exploration, or occupation); (4) kidnapping as an operational element of some larger, more complex action (e.g. overthrowing a government or a rival gang); (5) kidnapping for protective purposes (e.g. protecting the kidnappers, or the victim).

In contrast the kidnapper is expressively motivated when the kidnapping is undertaken for its own sake. The kidnapper has no greater goal beyond the kidnapping and may be driven by passion or personal belief. In this case the kidnapping is more "an-end-in-itself." Expressively motivated kidnappings include: (1) kidnapping for physical possession of a person (e.g. for intelligence purposes or parental abduction); (2) kidnapping for psychological or propaganda purposes (e.g. to demonstrate power, determination, or cunning); (3) kidnapping as a prelude to murder; (4) kidnapping for revenge; (5) kidnapping to execute a pseudo-legal sentence; (6) kidnapping for sexual purposes (e.g. assault, exploitation).

Utilizing this simple motivational continuum provides insight into kidnapping events. For example, Leopold of Austria was clearly instrumental in his motivation when he "snatched" Richard the Lionhearted. He used King Richard as a means toward the end of collecting 150,000 marks in ransom. Whereas a parent who abducts a child, from the care of the custodial parent, is more expressively motivated. The abductor is not using the child as a means toward some other end. The abduction is passionate, personal, and an end in itself. The abducting parent's objective is to possess the child.

2.2. Communication

Most kidnappings are accompanied by some form of communication, that can be used to assist in the determination of motive and the degree of danger posed for the kidnap victim. These communications whether written, spoken, or broadcast are most often described as threats. While threats can be frightening (e.g. "We have your countrymen and we are going to kill them") they are not completely so. They fail to fully complete their task, to frighten, as they reveal that the sender is more interested in communicating than murdering (at least for the time being).

Maximizing the use of these different communications hinges upon the ability to distinguish between threat and intimidation. "We have your countrymen and we are going to kill them" is truly a threat. It is a statement of the sender's intention to carry out or complete some action. It offers no terms, conditions, options, alternatives or ways out. Whereas, "we have your countrymen and we will kill them if you don't withdraw your troops from our country", is intimidation. Intimidation is a statement of a condition or conditions that, if satisfied, could avert harm. The semantics of intimidation require words like "if", "unless", "until", "or else". The statement indicates that the sender's fundamental motive is not to harm the kidnap victim, but to have the demands, terms, or conditions met. Intimidation is an attempt at a high stakes manipulation.

The threatener, on the other hand, provides no alternative as few, if any, are seen. Threats are more likely to lead to violence than intimidation is. Additionally, the timing of the threat can be informative. Threats uttered early in a conflict are probably rooted in the emotion of the moment, whereas those stated later spring from the frustration of fading options; and the fewer the options the more dangerous the threatener.

Threats are somewhat like promises in that they are meant to convince others of an intent. However, in addition to convincing others of intention, they also reflect emotion. They reflect the deep sense of frustration felt by the sender who has been unable to influence events in any other way. Now in a state of desperation the threat is all the sender has to offer. So it can be interpreted that threats come from positions of weakness. The threat's only power comes from the response it gets. It is really the receiver's response that makes or breaks a threat. (Even when a threat is determined to be serious, and precautions must be taken, receivers should be advised against showing the sender fear).

Intimidation, as a form of communication, is most often associated with instrumental motives. Those who kidnap as a means to an end are more likely to make "if", "until", "unless", "or else" statements, in an attempt to intimidate or manipulate others. Their primary motive is to obtain whatever they have demanded, not to aggress against the kidnap victim. For example, Leopold of Austria likely attempted to intimidate King Richard's family into paying the ransom by stating something like, "If you don't pay me 150,000 marks then I shall be forced to kill the king." Leopold's primary motive, as indicated by the type of communication, was not to kill the king but to obtain money for his depleted treasury. Leopold used Richard as a means to an end.

On the other hand, threat as a form of communication, is most often associated with expressive motives. Those who use kidnapping as an end in itself are more likely to utter statements of intent (including to kill) without any alternatives that could be exercised to avoid such an end. The primary motive of the more expressive kidnapper is to carry out the intent. The kidnapping is not undertaken as a means to some other end. In this case, the kidnapping is the end. So the note left for the custodial parent, by the previously mentioned abducting parent, is more likely to read "I've taken her, she's more mine than yours, I can give her a better life." The abducting parent's primary motive was the satisfaction of intent (possession of the child), not the utilization of the child as a means to some other end. The possession of the child was the end in itself.

2.3. Types of Kidnappings

With an understanding of the basic motivational concepts, instrumental and expressive, and the type of communication commonly associated with each, different types of kidnapping incidents can be identified. The first is the instrumental type where the kidnapper uses the kidnap victim as a means to an end, by providing alternatives to avert harm or prolonged confinement.

An example of this type of kidnapping might involve the members of a criminal gang abducting the parents of a rival gang member in lieu of the payment of an outstanding debt. The abductors would attempt to manipulate the rival gang member by intimidating (e.g. "We have your parents and will kill them in 48 hours if you don't pay us the money you owe"). In this case the kidnap victims are being used as a means to an end. The abductors' primary interest is the money, not murdering the victims, and they offer an alternative to murder, which is payment.

The same dynamics exist within a more "politically" oriented abduction. In January of 1996, ten former contra rebels led by Julio Cesar Vega abducted Susana Seigfried and Nicola Fleuchaus from the Laguna Del Lagarto Lodge in the spectacular Costa Rican rain forest. They demanded $1 million, an 18% pay raise for government workers, a freeze in utility rates, a price reduction in basic food items, and the release of 4 convicted kidnappers. Unless this ransom was paid, the kidnapper's advised that the women would "die of hunger." Once again the kidnap victims are being used as a means to an end. The kidnappers' primary motive is to have their demands met, not to starve the victims; and they offer alternatives to starvation.

The second type is the expressive incident where the kidnapper views the abduction as an end in itself, and perhaps utilizes threat to communicate intent. An example of this type of kidnapping is the parental abduction noted above. The abducting parent's primary motive is possession of the child. The act of kidnapping is viewed by the parent as an end in itself. The parent is not interested in offering alternatives in exchange for the child. Possession is the end in itself and this is apparent in the use of threat as the form of communication (e.g. "She's mine too, I'm taking her, you'll never find us").

An example of a more "politically" oriented expressive kidnapping took place in May of 1970 when the Montoneros, a leftist group of the Argentinean Peronist movement, kidnapped and killed former president Pedro Aramburu. This was the Montoneros debut action and they were interested in gaining attention and maximizing psychological impact. The kidnapping was viewed by the Montoneros as an end in itself consequently Sénor Aramburu was murdered almost immediately. The group was not interested in offering alternatives in exchange for Sénor Aramburu's life. Their primary motive was his abduction and murder. If any communication was made prior to the murder it would likely have threatened the Montoneros intent. "We are the Montoneros, we have Aramburu and we are going to execute him for his sins against the Argentinean people".

A further example of an expressively motivated abduction occurred in 1994. In October of that year the bodies of three young men were found in a shallow grave near a Khmer Rouge campsite. They had been dead for several weeks. No attempt had been made by the Khmer Rouge to intimidate — no demands had been made. After the discovery of the bodies was reported the rebels took credit and claimed the young men were executed as war criminals.

The Khmer Rouge then announced, in conjunction with several additional murders, that the latest tactic to be used in their struggle to defeat the Cambodian government was to hunt, abduct, and murder foreigners; with the intent of discouraging foreign investment.

Contemporary kidnappings in Iraq can be viewed as a function of the motivational continuum. They begin as instrumental (and some end there with payment or the prevention of some action) but shift to expressive (with a beheading for psychological, propaganda, or revenge purposes) when the perpetrators see that their demands will not be met.

Many expressive kidnappings involve no communication; some involve communication only after the kidnapper's intent has been carried out. This is similar to the Iraqi insurgent group taking credit for the suicide bomb only after the fact. This makes profound sense, as their primary motive was to explode the bomb, not to intimidate, or manipulate others into satisfying some demand in lieu of the explosion. If the latter was their intent they would have made contact prior to the explosion.

In the case of an absence of communication, that is, no stated intimidation or threat, a threat can be inferred. Even in silence it is impossible not to communicate. Instrumental motivation requires a statement of alternatives, silence thunders an expressive (end in itself) motivation.

As would be expected, kidnap incidents are not always easily defined. They can appear to be instrumental in nature but really be driven by expressive motives. In November of 1994, as previously mentioned, the Khmer Rouge admitted to almost immediately killing three tourists whose release the British authorities had been bargaining for since they were abducted the previous summer. In the spring of the same year the Khmer Rouge abducted 3 other foreigners and beat them to death after 4 days of captivity. No one was aware they were dead and the rebels continued to demand money long after the victims' brutal deaths.

These incidents had the appearance of instrumental motivation, but the Khmer Rouge's main intent was to frighten away foreign investors from strengthening the Cambodian government they were trying to topple. These abductions and murders were really ends in themselves designed to frighten, not means to some other end, as they appeared.

2.4. Incident Dynamics

Being armed with the ability to discern different types of kidnapping incidents allows the prediction of some dynamics associated with each. It can be said of instrumental incidents, due to the kidnapper's "means-to-an-end" motivation, that the probability of harm coming to the kidnap victim is reduced. Recall, the kidnapper's intent is not to harm the victim but to use the victim's life and/or liberty to lever the satisfaction of certain demands, terms, or conditions. The victim is the kidnapper's means to an end. So, for example, a victim kidnapped for the protection of the kidnappers (i.e. "you leave the country or else we kill your countryman") is in less danger than someone kidnapped for revenge ("you killed one of ours so we're going to kill one of yours").

It follows then that in the instrumental case the authorities have more influence over the kidnapper and/or the outcome. This follows as a consequence of the kidnapper's "means-to-an-end" motivation defining a dependent relationship with the authorities. When the kidnapper poses alternatives to harm, to the authorities, the former becomes dependent upon the latter for their satisfaction. The kidnapper needs the authorities to provide whatever was proposed. For example, if a kidnapper was attempting to intimidate authorities into releasing some of his colleagues from prison in exchange for the kidnap victim's safe release, the kidnapper is in a dependent relationship with the authorities. The abductor is dependent upon the authorities to cooperate and affect the release of prisoners, thus providing the authorities with influence over the abductor.

Finally, instrumental incidents will tolerate the adoption of a higher profile by the authorities. This type of incident requires management by negotiation, and an exercise of power is always part of the negotiation process. Therefore the instrumentally motivated kidnapping is more amenable to widely accepted negotiating tactics including advising of the consequences of no agreement, warning, and an exposure of the (authorities') best alternative to a negotiated agreement.

The likelihood of the threatened action (including harm) being carried out in an expressive kidnapping is greater. Recall, the kidnapper's motivation here is to use the kidnapping as an end in itself and not as a means to some other end. It is the possession of the victim or what can be done to the victim that is the end. So the likelihood of harm coming to a North American corporate executive kidnapped with no demands, by rebels, and charged with "capitalist crimes", against a foreign state, is greater than the abducted parents of the previously mentioned gang member.

The dependent relationship between kidnapper and authorities, inherent in the instrumental case, is missing in the expressive. The expressive kidnapper is more likely to threaten, and threats are absent alternatives, thus there is nothing that the kidnapper is depending upon authorities to provide. "We have Mr. X from company Y and will execute him for being a poor corporate citizen of our country", does not suggest any alternative to Mr. X's death, and contingently diminishes any influence the authorities may have over the kidnappers.

Finally, the expressive incident will not tolerate a higher profile on the part of the authorities, as negotiation is not the management strategy of choice, and any display of power is counter productive. While necessary in both types of incidents, the development of rapport is of utmost importance in the expressive case. The negotiator must have, given the opportunity, a working alliance with the kidnappers. If the negotiator expects to aid the kidnappers, in their crisis, the latter must come to trust the former. The kidnappers must feel comfortable enough to allow a free flow of information about the crisis in which they are presently involved. The negotiator's behaviour is central in the development of this rapport. The negotiator will be unable to convey a nonjudgmental attitude, interest, and concern to the kidnappers during a display of power. The two are inconsistent.

Imagine attempting to "negotiate" with the abductors of the above noted corporate executive. If no intimidation was attempted (i.e. no "if", "unless", "until", "or else") then negotiation would be impossible, and any attempt to impress the costs of continuing upon the group would most likely destroy any opportunity for rapport and trigger their defenses.

2.5. Management Strategies

With the abilities to assess motivation, identify incident types, and predict key dynamics associated with those incidents, the selection of an appropriate management strategy is now possible. Instrumental incidents due to the kidnapper's "means-to-an-end" motivation call for management by protracted negotiation. The negotiator (or the negotiator's constituency) has something the kidnapper wants and the kidnapper has something the negotiator wants. In a conflict of this sort the interdependent activity of bargaining (or negotiation) is indicated. The negotiation can be protracted because of the dynamics associated with the instrumental incident. That is, the victim has value to the kidnapper in terms of obtaining the latter's "end"; the kidnapper's primary interest is in obtaining the "end" not in harming the victim; the kidnapper is dependent upon the authorities to some degree; and, the authorities have some influence over the kidnapper. Therefore the incident will tolerate protraction in an effort to induce some realism and fatigue in the kidnapper, causing expectations to fall and surrender of the victim to loom as an option. (Refer to the list of potential instrumental incidents noted above, for those appropriate for negotiation).

As the expressive kidnapping is not undertaken as a means to an end but more as an "end-in-itself", negotiation is not the management strategy of choice. These incidents, given the opportunity, are more responsive to crisis intervention. Crisis theory [14] suggests that crises result when homeostasis is disrupted. That is, when the individual's mental balance is upset. The fact that many of these more expressive type abductions have their genesis in passion and personal belief seems to support this view. Crisis intervention, as a kidnapping management strategy, aims at a restoration of the pre-crisis level of functioning and a psychological resolution of the immediate problem. (Refer to the list of potential expressive incidents noted above, for those appropriate for crisis intervention). In sum, instrumentally motivated kidnappings call for management by negotiation, whereas expressively motivated incidents require crisis intervention.

3. Conclusion

This article was written to assist law enforcement authorities in their attempts to bring constructive outcomes to both domestic and foreign kidnap situations. It proposed a model that includes a discrimination of kidnap motives, an identification of different types of kidnapping, the dynamics associated with each, optimal management strategies and tactics. Law enforcement is often proficient at dealing with the practical aspects of a kidnapping. Commonly they lack psychological sophistication as these aspects are not often included in their training. The objective of this article was to present a psychological overview of this type of conflict, in an effort to avoid such a serious discussion descending into a violent strategy.

References

[1]   R.J. Gallagher, Kidnapping in the United States and the development of the Federal Kidnapping Statute. In B.M. Jenkins, Editor. *Terrorism and personal protection.* Boston, MA: Butterworth; 1985.

[2]   J.F. Warren, *The Sulu zone 1768*-1898: *The dynamics of external trade, slavery and ethnicity in the transformation of a Southeast Asian maritime state,* Quezon City: New Day Press: 1985.

[3]   R.L. Clutterbuck, Kidnap, hijack, and extortion: The response. New York: St. Martin's Press; 1987.

[4]   U.S. State Department, International terrorism: Hostage seizures. 1983, March.

[5]   C. Russell, Kidnapping as a terrorist tactic. In B.M. Jenkins, Editor. *Terrorism and personal protection.* Boston, MA: Butterworth; 1985.

[6]   A.H. Auerbach, *Ransom: The untold story of international kidnapping.* New York: Holt and Co.; 1998.

[7]   B.J. Jenkins, Kidnapping and extortion: An essay. In J. Kroll, Editor. *Risk Issues Quarterly,* New York: 1994.

[8]   J.G. Speth, Annual human development report of the United Nations development program. *New Perspectives Quarterly,* **13**/4 (1996, Fall).

[9]   U.S. State Department, Patterns in global terrorism. Washington, D.C.: 1995.

[10] I. Goldaber, A typology of hostage takers. *Police Chief.* **6** (1979), 21-22.

[11] M.S. Miron, A.P. Goldstein, *Hostage.* Kalamazoo MI: Behaviourdelia: 1978.

[12] J.G. Stratton, The terrorist act of hostage taking: A view of violence and the perpetrators. *Journal of Police Science and Administration,* **6** (1978), 1-9.

[13] M. Turner, Kidnapping and politics. *International Journal of the Sociology of Law.* 26 (1998), 145-160.

[14] A. Burgess, L. Holstrom, *Rape: Victims of crisis.* Bowie, M.D: Robert J. Brady; 1974.

Understanding and Responding to the Terrorism Phenomenon
O. Nikbay and S. Hancerli (Eds.)
IOS Press, 2007

Disrupting the Business of Kidnapping: How Kidnapping Harms the World Economy and How Governments Can Thwart Kidnapping Organizations?

John RICHARDSON[a], Christopher VOSS[b], John FLOOD[b], and Jeremy JONES[b]
[a]Boston College, Massachusetts, USA
[b]Federal Bureau of Investigation, FBI

Abstract. Kidnapping funds organized crime and terrorism, and damages developing economies by discouraging tourism and foreign investment, straining international alliances and creating human capital flight. Governments have two unattractive choices: allow payment of ransom, and thus encourage more kidnapping, or attempt to stop families and associates from paying, which, if successful, likely sacrifice the life of the hostage. This paper argues for a more vigorous and sophisticated approach: disrupting the business model of kidnapping organizations. The FBI has developed a doctrine of crisis negotiation that has proven effective at undermining the business of kidnapping while still prioritizing the life of the hostage. It steers negotiations in ways likely to produce evidence for eventual prosecution while making negotiations costly and burdensome to kidnappers without provoking an open confrontation. Our goal is to spread the use of these techniques to allied governments and law enforcement organizations.

Keywords. Kidnapping organizations, kidnap situations, business of kidnapping, and hostage negotiation.

Introduction: The Problem of Kidnapping

Economic kidnapping – that is, seizing a victim to extort ransom from his family or business associates – is a terrible burden to the developing world. It funds organized crime and terrorism, and damages developing economies by discouraging tourism and foreign investment, straining international alliances and creating human capital flight. This paper briefly describes the damage, explains the dilemma of formulating an anti-kidnapping strategy, and outlines an integrated strategy of government action and crisis negotiation techniques by law enforcement that have proven successful in combating this scourge. This paper's recommendations are based on the experience of and research by, the authors working at the Federal Bureau of Investigation's (FBI) Crisis Negotiation Unit (CNU). United States (U.S.) Government policy has designated the FBI as the lead in devising negotiation strategy in all cases of U.S. citizens kidnapped internationally. In this capacity, the CNU has collectively been engaged in over 300 extortionate kidnapping cases worldwide and the authors themselves directly involved in over 150 of those cases[1].

Direct Costs:

Some of the costs of kidnapping are obvious, though the size of the costs is often underestimated.   These direct costs include the loss of lives and freedom, the divergence of capital to pay ransoms and increased security costs.

While exact data is hard to compile, 10,000 or more people are kidnapped every year. Experts believe that the majority of kidnappings go unreported, for fear of retaliation by the kidnappers. A significant portion of victims are killed during abduction, or during imprisonment.

Some estimates of the amount of ransoms paid by families, businesses and insurers range as high as U.S. $500 million annually. This money is taken out of the pool available for investment and development in countries afflicted by kidnapping. Worse, the ransom is often used to fund organized crime and terrorism.

Massive sums are diverted to paying bodyguards, fortifying homes and businesses, and purchasing kidnapping insurance.

Indirect Costs:

As awful as the immediate toll of kidnapping is, the indirect effects are worse. Kidnapping discourages foreign investment and economic development, creates human capital flight and strains international alliances.

A recent study by the World Bank [1] investigated the underlying causes of wealth in national economies, and found that the most important predictor of wealth creation was the rule of law. Safety for people and property is what gives investors and entrepreneurs the confidence to create wealth. Because kidnapping is so visible, and so frightening, it can have a worse impact on public perceptions of lawlessness than other sorts of corruption and crime. Developing economies struggle with the problem of brain drain, as educated young people migrate to the developed world. These valuable young people are more likely to flee if they see themselves and their families in danger from kidnappers.

Good data on the direct costs are hard to come by. On the indirect costs, researchers can only guess. Each individual case generally lacks the dramatic impact of a high profile bombing. But the overall impact may be worse. Kidnapping may be analogized to boiling a frog. A frog can't be placed directly into boiling water – it would panic and jump out. But a frog can be placed in cool water and the water temperature can slowly be raised to boiling without the frog noticing. Similarly, kidnapping slowly cripples developing economies.

---

[1] Unit Chief John Flood was assigned to the CNU in January of 1998 and has been the Unit Chief since November of 2004. Supervisory Special Agent Christopher Voss was assigned to the CNU in January of 2000 and has been the lead negotiator for CNU's International Kidnapping Response program since January of 2003. John Richardson is a PhD candidate in organizational studies at Boston College's Carroll School of Management, is a graduate of Harvard Law School and has taught Negotiation and Multi-party Negotiation there. Jeremy Jones is a graduate of the University of Tennessee Law School and is a Presidential Management Fellow assigned to the FBI.

1. The Strategic Dilemma

Kidnapping presents governments and law enforcement with a terrible dilemma. Most decision-makers see only two possibilities: pay ransom, and reward the criminals, or refuse and sacrifice the hostage. Because kidnapping is such a difficult problem to deal with, and the widely understood strategies are so diametrically opposed, law enforcement and political actors will bitterly disagree on how to deal with the problem.

1.1. Failed Strategy: Stop the Payment of Ransom

Many governments and commentators take the position that paying ransom encourages more kidnapping. The more ransom is paid, and the faster it is paid, the more kidnappings will results.

A kidnapping gang that receives ransom easily learns that kidnapping is a safe and lucrative enterprise. Not only are they are immediately free to go out and kidnap again, but with every success they get more confident, and more experienced. The success of a kidnapping gang can also inspire the formation of other kidnapping gangs. Members may split off to form their own group. Other criminals may envy their success and form copycat groups.

Refusing to pay likely means accepting the death of current hostages as the necessary investment in protecting future potential hostages. A government must then estimate the number of potential future victims and compare them to the current number of victims at risk. Since the number of future victims is potentially limitless, the decision to refuse payment makes sense when the government is in unilateral control of the demanded ransom.

For example, if terrorists seize a hostage and demand the release of an imprisoned terrorist leader, the government has total control over whether the leader stays in jail. But even when the government has unilateral control, it may not be willing to face the costs of accepting the hostage's death. Family members can be expected to publicly plead for capitulation to kidnapper's demands. The sight of victims bound and threatened on television can promote a sense of chaos in the society and damage a government's standing with constituents.

When the kidnappers are demanding money governments are even more constrained. The government doesn't control the supply of ransom. If a business executive is kidnapped, there is a large group of potential payers: her company, business associates in other companies, industry organizations, insurers, her spouse, parents, children, uncles, aunts, cousins and friends. Those parties all face terrible costs if the victim is killed, and do not have responsibility for the long term costs to society of paying ransom. It is basically impossible to get them to agree to sacrifice a hostage in service of a long-term law enforcement strategy.

Another approach is to forbid anyone to pay ransom. But with so many potential payers, law enforcement will not have the resources to monitor all the actors. Freezing bank accounts has had limited success. It is easy for well-connected families to find sources of capital to be repaid once the hostage is returned and the accounts released.

Forbidding cooperation with kidnappers is not only futile: it creates another problem. It encourages families and companies to hide the case from law enforcement. Excluding law enforcement not only prevents successful management of negotiations with kidnappers, it can leave the government in ignorance about the extent of the kidnapping problem and the criminals involved.

2. Disentangling the Problems

One approach to this Hobson's choice is to square one's shoulders and take the bitter medicine: either a tough-minded agreement to let hostages die, or a tender-hearted acceptance of on-going lawless violence as the price of saving lives today. We suggest another approach.

The first thing to notice is that the two main goals of a strategy for dealing with kidnapping are very different from each other. The problem of saving a particular victim is a short term affair involving few people. The people, both hostage families and associates and kidnappers, are fearful, angry and thus prone to irrational decisions.

The problem of destroying a kidnapping industry is a long-term one involving the whole society. Moreover, in the long run even hostage takers make calculated, rational decisions about their business.

Devising a strategy to discourage kidnapping starts from the realization that a kidnapping gang is a business. Like any other organization a kidnapping gang has to meet its payroll, or lose members. It has to keep all members working toward common objectives. It has a problem of internal relationships between individuals and departments. It needs a supply of effective leadership. Start-up businesses have to do all of these things with few resources and no established procedures. All of these needs are avenues of attack for law enforcement.

3. The Theory of the Firm

A fundamental part of micro-economics is the theory of the firm, an explanation of how organizations should make decisions about doing deals and choosing lines of business. Choosing a business is based on a comparison of the money that can be made from a transaction with the costs the firm incurs. But there are two sorts of costs. Marginal cost is the cost of producing and selling one more unit of the firm's product – say, the steel and rubber and employee hours necessary to make one car. If the price the consumer pays is more than marginal cost then the firm will agree to make the transaction.

But marginal cost is not the only measure that firms apply to their business. Firms also have fixed costs – building and maintaining a place of business, paying into salaries, and so on. These don't go into the calculation of marginal cost because the firm will pay them whether or not it builds one more car. If one divides the firm's total costs, that is, fixed costs plus marginal costs, by the number of units sold, the result is the average total cost of the firm's products. In the long term, if the price a firm can get for its product is less than average total cost, then the firm is losing money by staying in that business. Thus, firms are sometimes in an uncomfortable position: the price they can get for making a deal is more than its marginal cost, but less than average total cost. If that is the case, then the firm should make that deal and sell that car, but it should also look for ways to get out of its current business and into a better line of work.

To apply the example to a kidnapping gang: the marginal cost of keeping a hostage alive one more day is the cost of salaries to gang members, food and so forth, plus the imputed cost of the risk of capture by law enforcement. If the kidnapping gang leader believes that those costs are justified by the potential for ransom, he will keep the hostage alive to trade. The fixed costs of a kidnapping operation include recruiting gang members, getting weapons, finding safe houses, scouting potential victims, and making the abduction. Each of these steps involves expense and risk of detection.

What's more, if law enforcement in the area conducts a competent program of hostage negotiation, the risk of detection and capture will increase with every job, as law enforcement gathers and analyzes more information.

Thus the question is not: pay ransom or not? Rather, it is: how much ransom to pay and how quickly? And the solution is to hold out the prospect of enough payment so that the victim isn't killed, but not enough to make kidnapping and the attendant risk of capture or death attractive compared to other possible lines of work. There are two prongs to this strategy: (1) use traditional law enforcement techniques to increase the cost of running a kidnapping gang, by raising the probability of conviction and the expected length of time served; (2) use Crisis Negotiation techniques to reduce the profits of kidnapping, and increase the risk of capture; while simultaneously using Crisis Negotiation techniques to minimize risk to the victim.

4. Raising the Costs to Kidnappers

Some governments make hostage negotiation the responsibility of their intelligence services or their diplomatic corps. There is nothing wrong with that: those negotiators are often very able. But they generally lack the expertise and institutional mandate to gather evidence for prosecution. Every hostage negotiation team should include law enforcement personnel to do the crucial work of building a case for prosecution. It is fine to make the life of the hostage the top priority. Indeed, the hostage will likely be the best witness against the kidnappers when a case has been built. But hostage negotiators must never forget the task of capturing or killing the kidnappers – to protect potential future hostages.

Law enforcement will do the work of monitoring and taping phone calls, tracing calls to locate members of the gang, marking ransom payments to track spending by gang members, and potentially setting up the gang for capture at ransom drops or in their safe houses. And if law enforcement is involved in overseeing and guiding the negotiations, then they are available themselves to provide court testimony. Diplomatic and intelligence personnel generally lack the training and experience to make good witnesses, and in some cases are even forbidden from testifying.

The effort to defeat the kidnapping epidemic in the United States in the 1930's was greatly enhanced by steep increases in penalties for convicted kidnappers [2].

Democracies face a constant problem of balancing civil liberties against effective law enforcement. An extreme emphasis on civil liberties can be self-defeating. While addressing every possible reform is beyond the scope of this paper, governments that want to defeat the plague of kidnapping should consider giving law enforcement more tools to gather evidence against kidnapping gangs.

Governments can take important steps against kidnapping by changing criminal penalties and giving law enforcement more tools. Another part of the solution is how law enforcement agents (or other experts) handle negotiations with kidnappers. The most effective methods and strategies are surprisingly counter-intuitive for both academic theorists of negotiation and traditional law enforcement personnel.

The most of the high points of these strategies can be summarized as follows: burden them with the situation, pay as little as possible, and pay as slowly as possible while prioritizing the life of the hostage.

5. Negotiating Against Kidnappers

Negotiating against kidnappers has two goals: getting the hostage back alive, and undermining the business model of the kidnapping gang. It's important to note the use of the word "against" (as opposed to "with") in the phrase "negotiating against kidnappers." Though the kidnappers will never understand the difference, this is a silently adversarial process that is in the long term dedicated to putting them out of business. They may feel they have the upper hand; however that feeling will ultimately be used to contribute to the end of their criminal enterprise.

In the short term, the life of the hostage has top priority. Discouraging the business is a long term affair. Law enforcement will get other chances to catch a repeat gang, and will have other tools to discourage would-be kidnappers. But there is no way to bring a dead hostage back to life. Moreover, cooperation from families and companies is absolutely crucial to fighting the kidnappers, and law enforcement will not get that cooperation if those people judge that the life of the victim is not the most important concern. Some of the tactics above may raise concerns with families, but they all work toward getting the hostage back alive.

It might seem that delaying the payment of ransom and release of the hostage puts the victim in danger. Surprisingly, the opposite is true. The longer the victim is held, the greater the chance of the kidnappers developing an attachment to the victim. The more time they spend eating and talking with a victim, the more reluctance kidnappers are to kill them.

What may be more important than familiarity and attachment, a long captivity tends to promote the sunk cost effect among kidnappers. The more time and effort they have poured into a project, the less likely they are to abandon it before completion. The longer kidnappers have a victim the more they need to get something to justify their work, rather than kill the victim and flee without ransom.

And the longer the kidnapping goes on, the longer law enforcement has to track the kidnappers. A long captivity develops more evidence that can lead to the capture of kidnappers, thus protecting future victims and possibly leading to the rescue of the current hostage.

Crisis negotiators usually do not deal directly with kidnappers. Rather, they help the family or business colleagues negotiate to get their loved one back. Kidnappers usually warn the family or business partners not to contact law enforcement. And they are right to do so: they're job is far more dangerous when law enforcement is collecting evidence and monitoring the negotiations. Open involvement by law enforcement puts the hostage's life in great danger.

One of the keys to kidnapping negotiation understands how a victim family or company would actually respond in a kidnapping situation and which of those responses yield advantages. For law enforcement or a government to be effective its presence needs to be hidden from the kidnappers. The law should ultimately surprise the kidnappers the way a wolf in sheep's clothing would surprise a poacher.

The countries that suffer from widespread kidnapping have big law enforcement problems. Because most hostages are eventually released unharmed, and ransoms and the cost of negotiation are chiefly born by private actors, including insurance companies, it is easy to push kidnapping down the list of priorities. We argue that the hidden economic costs of kidnapping make it a high-value area of investment. Kidnapping does such extensive damage to growth and investment that defeating it pays huge dividends to developing economies. And there is a real prospect of success.

Unlike drug trafficking, there is a clear historic record of kidnapping being eliminated in some countries by law enforcement.

Good crisis negotiation can do a lot against kidnapping. But it works far better as part of an integrated government strategy to raise the costs of kidnapping. None of the recommendations here are particularly surprising. But they are necessary for countries that want to break the stranglehold that kidnapping puts on development. Some of them require investment, but that investment can be quickly repaid by increased development and growth.

Many of the basics of effective negotiation are really the basics of effective communication, communication assessment and investigative interviewing. The more training that any law enforcement agency obtains in crisis negotiation training the more there will tend to be a positive ripple effect impacting the overall professionalism of that agency. A frequent problem in maintaining an effective cadre of negotiators in law enforcement agencies in the United States is the promotion of negotiators into the command ranks. So, a good negotiation infrastructure tends contribute to building an effective overall law enforcement infrastructure.

6. Conclusion

Using crisis negotiation can undermine the business model of kidnapping and gather evidence; solid law enforcement investigation can to raises the risks to kidnappers especially in conjunction with investment in the prosecution and long term incarceration of kidnappers. Long term strategies involving the use of effective law enforcement negotiation to counteract kidnapping can generate a virtuous spiral. Increased professionalism will enhance the ability of law enforcement to provide safety and security. Increased safety and security will help spur the nation's economic growth. Economic growth provides better employment opportunities for desperate men who might otherwise join kidnapping gangs. And the greater wealth of the country can more easily support increased professionalism in law enforcement agencies[2].

References

[1]   The World Bank, Where Is the Wealth of Nations? Measuring capital for the 21st century, Washington D.C., 2006, [Online] Available from; URL: http:// siteresources.worldbank.org/INTEEI/214578-1110886258964/20748034/All.pdf.
[2]   E.K. Alix, Ransom kidnapping in America, 1874-1974: The creation of a capital crime, Carbondale, IL: Southern Illinois University Press; 1978.

---

[2] The FBI's Crisis Negotiation Unit has developed an overall strategic framework for responding to international kidnapping. These strategies are implemented with-in an interagency response involving the U.S. Departments of Defense, State and Justice along with U.S. intelligence agencies and coordinated at Washington D.C. by the U.S. National Security Council. In the country of occurrence of the kidnapping, these efforts are coordinated by the U.S. Department of State in conjunction with, approval of and participation by the host country government. Governments wishing more information on these strategies and mechanisms, and considering training for their law enforcement personnel, please contact the Crisis Negotiation Unit at the FBI Academy, Quantico, Virginia, 22135, U.S. telephone number 703-632-4256. Information can also be obtained for the Office of the FBI Legal Attaché at most U.S. Embassies throughout the world.

Understanding and Responding to the Terrorism Phenomenon
O. Nikbay and S. Hancerli (Eds.)
IOS Press, 2007

International Kidnap Negotiations: Preparation, Response & Related Issues

Stephen J. ROMANO
President of the Stephen J. Romano & Associates, USA

Abstract. The crime of kidnapping has become a significant weapon of influence and source of funding for criminals and terrorists. Kidnapping is defined as the unlawful seizure and detention of a person usually for a ransom. Criminals view kidnapping as an effective way to get money. Terrorists may claim a political objective for taking hostages, but their ultimate goal in most instances is to obtain money. Companies that are international in scope are particularly vulnerable to having an employee kidnapped. It is a necessity to have a Kidnap Response Plan in place to provide a structured approach to successfully manage the crisis. Companies responding to international kidnappings will most likely be faced with the challenge of dealing with multiple governments and successfully interacting with law enforcement agencies, victim families and the media. The welfare of an employee may very well depend on the ability to navigate the internal and external complexities of the crisis. The primary aim of this article is to make contributions to police agencies' negotiation strategies. The information and knowledge in this study is based on the researcher's1 personal work experience.

Keywords. International kidnapping, crisis management, crisis communication, negotiator, and terrorist.

Introduction

The crime of kidnapping has become a significant weapon of influence and source of funding for criminals and terrorists organizations from South America to Southeast Asia. Kidnapping is defined as the unlawful seizure and detention of a person usually for a ransom. The latter part of this definition, "usually for a ransom," is the beacon of light that the negotiator homes in on and attempts to exploit to accomplish the mission – the safe release of the victim.

The international kidnap phenomena is a good news, bad news one. The bad news is kidnapping is a burgeoning crime and usually flourishes in countries where local law enforcement and prosecutors are unable to adequately address the problem. Consequently, the adversary perceives the commission of this crime to be low risk and high gain. So what's the good news you may ask? The good news is that the captor's motivation, in the largest majority of these kidnappings, is money. Therefore, the victim or hostage retains value alive. The captor's primary motivation is having his demands (monetary ransom) met and not harming the hostage. It is this critical

---

[1] Steve Romano spent 20 years in the FBI, retiring in 2004 as the chief negotiator in the FBI's Crisis Negotiation Unit. He has published multiple articles relating to the crisis negotiation and siege management field in various law enforcement journals.

dynamic of kidnap negotiations that provides the negotiator with the leverage and influence needed to safely liberate the hostage.

Companies that are international in scope are particularly vulnerable to having an employee kidnapped. Advances in technology and transportation have made the world a much smaller place. Citizens of the United States and other western countries are the targets of choice and they wear their ethnicity and citizenship like the clothes on their backs; it is there for all to see. Experience tells us that most kidnappings take place while the victim is in transit. Companies have a "duty of care" responsibility to their personnel to provide training and formulate procedures to minimize their potential to be victimized.

There is absolutely no substitute for planning and preparation and most companies with a significant international footprint realize that when it comes to having an employee kidnapped, it is not if, but when. Therefore, it is a necessity to have a Kidnap Response Plan in place to provide a structured approach to successfully manage the crisis and save the life of the victim.

1. Victims, Adversaries and Motivations

International kidnappings can occur at anytime and can happen to anyone. What is interesting to note is that foreign nationals account for less than 10% of victims. In countries where kidnapping has become somewhat of a cottage industry, such as Mexico and Colombia, over 90% of the victims are local nationals. However, the kidnapping of foreign nationals is a far more news worthy event as far as the media is concerned. Money is the primary goal in all but a limited number of kidnappings. Criminal gangs view kidnapping as an effective way to get money. Terrorists groups such as the FARC in Colombia and the Abu Sayyaf Group (ASG) in the Philippines may claim a political objective for taking hostages, but their ultimate goal in most instances is to obtain money.

Although money remains far and away the most common kidnapping motivation, political demands including publicity, release of prisoners and welfare items have also been used as ransom criteria. Nigerian groups have taken hostages to force oil companies to provide economic assistance to local villagers. Journalist Danny Pearl was taken to pressure the Pakistan government not to support the U.S. In all cases, the kidnapper's goal in taking a hostage is to force a third party to do something; usually pay money. Holding the hostage and threatening harm empowers the kidnapper. Nevertheless, victim companies/families have some control and influence since they control what the kidnapper wants – money. The overriding theme a negotiator wants the adversary to appreciate is, "if you harm the hostage you won't get what you want."

There are specific indicators that can assist in abductor classification. Inexperienced criminal are known to make urgent demands and violent threats and their hallmark characteristic is frequent contacts. Normally, they are operating in an urban environment with minimum infrastructure, thereby increasing their vulnerability to law enforcement intervention. Consequently, these cases are usually short in duration.

High dollar or political demands are most often related to the terrorist or experienced criminal group. The rural settings where these adversaries operate offer them a solid infrastructure that helps insulate them from police or military operations. These captors are noted for considerable patience and limited contacts to create pressure on the victim company/family. A political kidnapping will also generate intense media interest and significant government involvement since the demand in many cases is made against the government and not the family or company. These dynamics result in cases of longer duration.

2. Corporate Responsibilities

The kidnapping of an employee will have an incredible impact on a company. The severity of that impact will be directly determined by the degree of planning and preparation that was put in place for such an event. The company will be faced with a myriad of responsibilities; none greater than the timely and constant support to the victim's family. Coordination with the U.S. Government and other governmental entities involved will be challenging. Constant interaction with the news media will be required; as will the advising and shielding of the victim family from the potential media onslaught. Additionally, the welfare and safety of other employees and business continuity must also be addressed.

A Crisis Management Plan (CMP) should be a staple of every corporation. The CMP is the umbrella document that addresses, through individual annexes, the most likely crises a company may face. The annexes of the CMP are derived from a comprehensive risk assessment that also gauges the potential impact on a company. A Kidnap Response Plan should be a mandatory annex for any company with international operations. The CMP must be a living document; one that is properly disseminated, reviewed, exercised and amended on a periodic basis. The forming of a Crisis Management Team (CMT) is a critical byproduct of a CMP.

The CMT is comprised of core components (e.g. communications, general counsel, human resources, operations, security etc.) and other adhoc components that are crisis specific. Just as in athletics, we play as we practice. A good CMP assists in the successful management of a crisis by providing a structured approach while minimizing the disruption to day-to-day operations. It results in a systematic approach to confronting and managing crises and can have an invaluable inoculation effect of bringing calm to chaos.

3. Kidnap Negotiations, Strategies and Techniques

The initial stages of a kidnapping are marked by either conflicting information and/or a lack of information. Therefore, confirmation that a kidnapping has truly taken place is the number one priority at the outset. It is quite normal to have more questions than answers when an employee's whereabouts are unknown. Companies that maintain viable accountability and locator procedures enjoy a significant advantage when faced with such an event. It is always prudent to prepare for the worse case scenario so making preparations for the initial call from the abductors is highly recommended.

Once a decision is made as to where and who the initial call will be directed to the key messages must be readied. The three part message the victim company/family communicator wants to convey to the captor during the initial contact are: 1) a willingness to communicate; 2) the need for proof of possession / proof of life (POP/POL); and 3) requirement for a reasonable delay. The communicator should prepare for a high financial demand, a deadline, threats, and a warning not to involve law enforcement.

The generic negotiation strategy is to lower the expectations of the kidnappers by attempting to "shallow the pockets" of the victim family/company. The communicator will also make the connection between the payment of ransom and the welfare of the victim quite clear, and this will be an on-going theme throughout the negotiation process. The proof of life (POL) issue will also remain a critical aspect throughout the ordeal. However, the communicator should not pay to obtain it. The onus should always be put on the adversary as a requisite to achieve his goal – the ransom.

4. Financial Criteria

Ransom demands are contingent on the adversaries' expectations (going rate), and just like in the real estate arena, location is a major determinant of expectations. Intelligence regarding the captor's previous kidnap track record, including the credibility of threats and the propensity for violence, and what ransom amounts have been paid by U.S. and western victim families/companies in the abduction area, are instrumental in estimating the final amount you expect to pay the captors to secure the release of the hostage. Another key factor in deriving this figure is the ultimate amount of funds available and/or agreeable to be paid. Statistics have shown that a large majority of captors have agreed to approximately 10% of their initial ransom demand.

As a rule, the initial counteroffer to the captor's initial ransom demand should be about 2/3 of the amount you expect to pay to reach a financial agreement. In this way, a financial strategy can be employed that allows room to reach the final amount in several moves. Another general guideline is not to raise the initial counteroffer until the kidnappers have lowered their initial ransom amount, and then increases should be made in decreasing increments. Also, offering odd amounts of money is a gambit that can be used to indicate difficulty in raising funds.

Reaching a decision as to the initial counteroffer amount is truly a balancing act. It should be high enough to insure the victim's safety and not insult or anger the captors. If the captors perceive a lack of sincerity regarding the negotiation effort they may feel compelled to commit an act of violence against the victim to underscore their serious intent. Yet, the initial counteroffer must also avoid creating inflated expectations on the part of the adversaries.

Regardless of the financial resources of the victim family/company, paying too much too soon should always be avoided. This mistake can easily result in what is referred to as a "double dip." A double dip is when an apparent ransom payment agreement reached by both sides turns into a down payment, an additional demand for more money, and a failure to release the victim. A basic behavioral principle can come into play during kidnap for ransom negotiations. That is, people do not appreciate things they do not work hard to earn. If the captor obtains the ransom he asks for with little or no resistance, and in a relatively short period of time, he begins to experience buyer's remorse. In other words, the captor's perception becomes that his getting the demanded ransom was far too easy, he should have asked for a bigger ransom, and there must be a lot more money available.

The concept of prolonging a victim's captivity by hastily meeting the captor's ransom demand seems to be counterintuitive. It can be difficult to explain and convince a victim's family that it is in the best interests of the victim to extend the negotiation process. Their only goal is to get their loved one back safely and as soon as possible. It is easy to see how they could confuse the paying of ransom for the release of a victim with buying a car. If a customer agrees to pay the amount of money the dealer is asking for the car then the deal is completed. The customer gets the car and the dealer gets his asking price. Unfortunately, the bartering in human lives is fraught with critical nuances that a negotiator must be knowledgeable of in order to secure the safe and timely release of the victim.

5. The Communicator

The role of the communicator is that of a mouthpiece for the victim family/company and to act as a conduit to the adversary. The communicator has limited authority and must project subordination to the final decision makers when conversing with the captors. Following company objectives and gathering accurate information are important aspects of the communicator's duties.

The following qualities should be given serious consideration when selecting a communicator. The person must be willing to accept coaching, loyal to the company and its policies, emotionally stable and an excellent listener. Additionally, a communicator must be available and dedicated to the task, have good stamina, linguistic fluency, and patient and persuasive with good people skills. The communicator is not a debater, but more of an influencer and persuader, who conveys honesty and resolve while trying to avoid confrontation.

The ability of the communicator to maintain a low key, calm, and patient business like demeanor is imperative. One of the communicator's key tasks is to establish a window of contact with the adversary. The communicator can exert a degree of control and minimize the necessity of being continuously available by arranging a specific time frame for contacts with the captors. Once the window of contact is set it should not be deviated from. If the captor attempts to make contact outside of the arranged time, the communicator must not acknowledge the contact thereby using a classical conditioning approach to influence the adversary to abide by the agreement.

Prior to a scheduled contact the communicator will prepare and rehearse under the supervision of a trained negotiator. Objectives are set out for each contact. The communicator must be prepared to play both defense and offense during the contact. The communicator will be coached on how to respond (defense) to anticipated topics the captor may broach. At the same time the communicator will be armed with three or four key points (offense) to work into the conversation. The contact will be scripted with key words and phrases prominently posted on situation boards in the negotiation operations center (NOC).

The NOC is usually a separate room that offers the communicator and coach a private and secluded area that minimizes potential distractions and enhances the ability to fully concentrate on the contact. The room should be equipped with recording devices in order to tape record each contact for evidentiary purposes and for negotiation review and strategy formulation. The NOC will also have a number of situation boards posted so that a coach can provide real time assistance to the communicator by simply pointing to something he would like the communicator to work into the conversation. The posting of situation boards, along with the protocol of passing written notes, allows the NOC to run in a silent and efficient mode.

Two areas that a communicator needs to be properly prepared and coached to address are threats and checking on the victim's welfare or obtaining proof of life (POL). A captor will use a violent threat in an attempt to intimidate or to emphasize the consequence of non-compliance with a ransom demand. A communicator's response to a threat makes or breaks its success. If the communicator remains calm and avoids any notable reaction to the threat, the threat fails to achieve the captor's intended purpose – to intimidate. A reiteration of the communicator's desire to work out an agreement, coupled with maintaining a positive attitude while pointing out how threats can impede progress in reaching mutual goals, can be quite effective in defusing the captor's emotions and reestablishing a positive dialogue. There will be occasion when the communicator's best efforts are unsuccessful in redirecting the captor. When this occurs, the use of silence, followed by a credible excuse to break off the contact, may be the best course of action to follow.

A constant theme and key message for the communicator is to explore the victim's welfare. Initially the communicator must establish that he is in contact with those who have kidnapped the victim. A proof of possession (POP) is required before negotiations can move forward. The communicator must emphasize that he has no authority to enter into ransom discussions until it has been firmly established that the captor's are holding the victim. A simple question, "How do I know you have (name of victim) and he is alive?" This clearly puts the onus on the captor to find a way to demonstrate he has the kidnapped victim and the victim is alive. There are a number of ways to obtain POP or proof of life (POL). The best way is to speak directly with the victim. Kidnappers rarely provide this form of POP/POL since in most cases the captor's communicator is purposely geographically separated from where the victim is being held for security reasons. Many times a photo of the victim with a current newspaper, a tape recording, or the captor's correct answer to a question only the victim could know the answer to are used to convey POP/POL. A critical task for the communicator is to continuously tie the welfare of the victim to the payment of ransom.

6. The End Game

When a ransom payment agreement has been reached and a current POL has been satisfied, the communicator's next major hurdle is to iron out the details of an exchange. There are several key considerations during this phase of the negotiation. One is to ensure that the currency for the agreed upon ransom payment is available in country. Two other considerations are the selection of a courier and an exchange site that poses no safety or security concerns for the courier. Although a communicator should prod the captors for a simultaneous exchange (money or victim), it would be highly unlikely for them to agree since they fully realize they are most vulnerable to apprehension during such an exchange. Regardless, the communicator should try his best to get the captors to minimize the time between their receipt of the ransom and the release of the victim.

Lastly the victim company must make the necessary preparations to receive the victim. The victim's physical and psychological needs must be addressed. Although the physical danger to the victim may be over, in many cases the emotional dangers are only beginning. The victim will have a critical need to take back control of his own life and company personnel must respect and facilitate that need. Operational debriefings by authorities are necessary, but the reentry needs of the victim must take precedence. Whenever possible, the victim company should strive to bestow as much credit on the local authorities as possible while avoiding the media.

7. Related Issues

Potential major issues for victim companies may arise in the areas of their interaction with law enforcement, victim families, and the media. How a company plans, prepares and handles these interactions can have a direct bearing on kidnap negotiations and the ultimate outcome of the crisis.

7.1. Law Enforcement

A critical corporate decision during a kidnapping is the degree the company cooperates with local law enforcement officials. Many times law enforcement's priorities, which include the identification, apprehension and prosecution of the kidnappers, may impede effective negotiations. Law enforcement pressure can have a significant impact on the time/money correlation that is present during all kidnappings for ransom. Corporations should consider obtaining the services of a security consultancy company, such as London based Control Risks, with a proven track record in kidnap for ransom negotiations. These companies have established liaisons with law enforcement and military personnel in the countries where kidnappings are most prevalent.

The taking of a U.S. citizen hostage or a ransom demand made against the U.S. Government (USG), regardless of citizenship, is a violation of federal law. The FBI, through the Crisis Negotiation Unit, is recognized as the official negotiation arm of the USG in response to acts of terrorism. Under the direction of the US Ambassador the FBI is the lead agency for: development and implementation of negotiation strategies, conduct of investigations, and collection of evidence. The FBI will coordinate the USG's response to a kidnap but will not take over decision making. Key decisions, such as whether or not to make a ransom payment always remain the responsibility of the victim family and/or company. The FBI will not provide the funds nor make the delivery of any ransom payment overseas. Corporations still must manage the incident.

A number of countries have laws that make it mandatory to inform local authorities that a kidnapping has taken place and to request permission to enter into negotiations with the captors. A robust exchange of information with local authorities can result in permission to make a ransom payment when there is no other safe recourse to obtain the release of the victim. Additionally, a strong liaison can help authorities realize that kidnap negotiations is an investigative tool that results in excellent intelligence and creates potentially exploitable options for law enforcement. An accommodation can be reached wherein authorities agree to wait until the victim is safely recovered before pursuing the captors. In turn, a victim company may promise to turn over all available evidence and make the victim available for debriefing.

In most cases, cooperation with authorities should be the preferred option of a victim company. Cooperation is a two-way street that can build trust. A strong liaison with authorities can increase the company's ability to influence law enforcement actions. This can be most critical when seeking restraint from conducting high risk rescue attempts. Continuous contact with a high level trusted officer can reap both short and long term benefits.

7.2. Families

A company should prepare to expend a considerable amount of time and resources supporting, advising and protecting the victim family during a kidnapping. First impressions are critical, and a company should give serious consideration as to which executive level official will make the initial in person notification, and also who will be assigned as the full time family liaison for the duration of the incident. The victim's family will feel isolated, that information is being filtered, and that the company is not doing enough to obtain their loved one's release. These sentiments are quite common and understandable. It is incumbent on the company to provide the family with a realistic assessment, convince them that they will be taken care of, and attempt to form a united front with them. The victim family truly needs all the help they can get to emotionally survive their darkest hour.

Two areas that need to be addressed with the family as soon as possible are how to handle a contact by the captors and the best way to deal with media inquiries. It is not uncommon for captors to contact a victim's family. They realize the emotional impact this manipulation can cause, and know full well that it will most likely result in the family pressuring the company to quickly acquiesce to the captor's demands. A company that provides the victim family with concrete guidelines in what to expect if they are contacted by the kidnappers can minimize the emotional impact of this orchestrated manipulation. In addition, the family's confidence in the company's knowledge and competence for handling the incident increases because they anticipated the adversaries' strategy.

The family will also need media guidance and someone to act as a buffer during the kidnapping. The mantra, "if it bleeds, it leads" continues to be an accurate description of the kind of news the media relentlessly pursues. The family must be educated on the potential damage a spontaneous statement to the media can have on the negotiation process. It might be necessary to relocate the family during the duration of the incident to isolate them from the media.

7.3. Media

A Crisis Communication Plan is another recommended annex of a CMP. The three basic questions the media will ask are: What happened? How did it happen? What are you going to do about it? If the media becomes aware of a crisis at your company, it is in the company's best interest to respond. Failure to respond or delaying a response makes the company look irresponsible, unconcerned, or incompetent. An acceptable statement in the event of a kidnap might be:

"We cannot comment in detail at the present time, except to say that we are doing everything within our ability to ensure Mr. X's safe return. This is our first and foremost priority. As you are sure to understand, we do not want to influence the outcome of this situation by talking in any greater detail at this time. Our thoughts and prayers are with Mr. X and his family."

It is highly recommended for a company's communication department to craft holding statements for various crises that could arise in advance. Innocuous holding statements can help a company buy time to gather critical information during a crisis. During a kidnapping a company should not discuss financial details, their policy with regard to negotiations, nor the topic of kidnap insurance. It is also good policy not to publicly criticize any government's response efforts.

During a crisis, it is important to remember that information is provided to the family before the media. There should be only one authorized spokesperson and statements should be cleared before release. Track and monitor print, television, and internet reporting, and keep a log of all contacts from the media. Present facts you are able to share. It is acceptable to say "company policy prohibits me from commenting about that at this time." In conclusion, it is not recommended to stonewall or engage in an adversarial relationship with the media. Gather all relevant information, take control, and be seen to be in control. Do not let outside parties drive the "story." Anticipate events; do not just react to them.

8. Conclusion

Risks and crises are inherent aspects of international business operations. Although risks and crises can't be eliminated, they can be minimized, mitigated and managed. The advantage goes to those companies who take a proactive/preventative approach to crisis management. Companies responding to an international kidnapping incident will most likely be faced with the challenge of dealing with multiple governments and successfully interacting with law enforcement agencies, victim families and the media. The welfare of your employee may very well depend on your ability to navigate the internal and external complexities of the crisis. Will you be ready? There is absolutely no substitute for preparation. Prepare your company today for what may come tomorrow.

Understanding and Responding to the Terrorism Phenomenon
O. Nikbay and S. Hancerli (Eds.)
IOS Press, 2007

Hijackings and Aviation Security

Ramazan YALCINKAYA[a] and Aziz OZMEN[b]
[a]*University of North Texas, USA*
[b]*Sam Houston State University, USA*

Abstract. Including many airplanes, airports, aircrew, and employees, aviation industry is a large sector that is very vulnerable to attacks, whether it is from terrorists or criminals. Unfortunately, there are many examples of airport bombings, hijackings, and sabotage terrorist attacks in aviation history. The most destructive of which is the tragedy of September 11, 2001, the cornerstone of today's aviation security policies. This study describes the dimensions of danger and threats against the aviation industry and addresses how vulnerable the aviation sector is. After vulnerabilities and threats are examined, possible impacts of attacks against the aviation security are discussed.

Keywords. Aviation security, hijackings, sabotage, terrorism, terrorist attacks.

Introduction

In an era in which people live a fast-paced life and technological advances occur at a rapid rate, it cannot be denied that aviation is one of the most important industries in the world. It has changed the way we live drastically by carrying millions of people and millions of tons of cargo long distances in a relatively short amount of time. Airplanes have always been considered the showcases and representatives of the nations whose flags they fly [1].

Because of the numerous vulnerabilities of aviation systems and the harmful impact of attacks on it, the aviation industry has continued to be a preferred target for terrorists [2]. Almost all plane crashes result in many fatalities and draw maximum media attention, which they can use to further express their ideologies. Terrorist attacks appear in the forms of bombing airports and airplanes, hijacking, sabotaging, and issuing bomb threats. Since terrorism involves using violence, many people have suffered greatly from terrorist attacks, and these attacks on the aviation industry always result in catastrophes [3]. For these reasons, aviation security, which is attributable to techniques and security measures to protect airplanes and airports from criminals and terrorists to ensure traveling safety, is strongly required for the aviation industry. It also concerns all illegal activities related to air transportation as well as the high-risk environment of this sector [4].

In particular, the devastating events of September 11, 2001, showed how vulnerable the aviation industry was to terrorists. The tragedy of this event has heightened people's awareness for the need to consider security risks in the course of analyzing the overall system. Many governmental and commercial organizations in different countries are now taking steps to explicitly model each other's security measures. Before September 11, because both government and commercial airlines had been unsuccessful in taking sufficient security measures, terrorists were able to identify the vulnerabilities in the aviation systems easily and develop new strategies for attacking a country through aviation, which had a greater impact than any other methods that they had used [5]. In fact, before 9/11 al-Qaeda had attacked American interests several times in different countries. In 1993, they attacked the World Trade Center using a truck bomb, but its consequences were not as significant as those of September 11. Although the aim was the same, changing the means and attacking via aviation caused more damage and drew more media attention. Just this example can explain how dangerous the attacks by means of aviation can be [6]. Interestingly, the events of 9/11 destroyed people's confidence in the United States, which had been perceived as one of the most secure places against terrorism in the world.

Typically, terrorists constitute a bigger threat to aviation security. They are more diverse, more organized, more willing to take risks, and more professional than criminals. Moreover, terrorism has become a huge economic sector that has its own political and ideological objectives. Terrorists have supporters, charities, banks, specific incomes, and financial networks. They have the ability to perform sophisticated and complex operations that may affect different countries significantly [7].

The vulnerability of the aviation industry always compels many terrorist groups to use it as a tool in their propaganda. Terrorists often try to obtain maximum psycho-political influence all over the world, and attacking airports and airplanes usually enables them to accomplish this goal.

According to Wilkinson and Jenkins [8], terrorists changed their tactics after the Post-Cold War era. They began to kill innocent people and exact maximum destruction on the country that they hated and wanted to terrorize. Moreover, terrorists also started trying to kill the maximum number of people, including themselves, since the sensational nature of such killing causes more media attention.

Terrorists' motivation and perspectives of life are also important reasons why they choose the aviation industry as targets. Generally, terrorists focus more on attacking the political, military and economic infrastructures in a country. The motives of these attacks may be punitive, symbolic, religious, idealistic, ethnic, political, social or economic. From such varying motivations, we can see that terrorists and criminals will perform virtually any attack on people [9]. These attacks usually result in large civilian casualties, long-lasting economic damage, and sometimes electoral changes; for instance, Spain experienced a devastating train attack in which more than 182 people were killed and 900 wounded. This attack affected the result of its presidential election in 2004 and resulted in changing the politicians who supported the war in Iraq [7].

The other motivation is obtaining enough money from their supporters and countries sympathetic to their causes so that they can manage their long term goals, such as going to aviation schools and gaining information about airports and their systems [8]. From the terrorist's point of view, by attacking highly valued and hard targets, such as the Pentagon and World Trade Center, they believe that they can gain a significant victory against a country that they perceive as an enemy. Another indirect result of such an attack is causing people in that country to lose faith in their government's ability to protect them. In such a case, terrorists would accomplish their goal of revenge against that government because fear among people and political pressure on that particular government would increase [9].

In addition, some terrorist organizations and criminals may want to provide clues to the media and law enforcement agencies so that they can be recognized after an attack and their message can be broadcast clearly. In doing so, they can promote their strength and demonstrate how much further they are willing to go [10]. By the same token, most terrorist attacks contain implied messages for a target country. In the case of September 11, it was very meaningful that they attacked highly symbolic places for economic and military targets. If the fourth plane had not crashed in Pennsylvania, the target would have been the White House, which would have sent a clear political warning [6].

The Department of Homeland Security (DHS) indicated that terrorists are still seeking ways to attack the United States via aviation, such as attacking chemical plants, petroleum, and petrochemical facilities, transportation systems and facilities, and electric power grids. According to intelligence sources, their aim is using commercial airplanes to perform these attacks [11].

To illustrate, on September 11, one of the hijacked airplanes turned south near Albany, followed the Hudson River down to New York City and reached its target, the north tower of the World Trade Center. On its route, it passed directly over the Indian Point Nuclear Power Plant, which is located 30 miles north of Manhattan. It is not difficult to imagine that had terrorists chosen this nuclear plant instead of the World Trade Center, the effects of this attack would have been more devastating and disturbing on that day [3].

To eliminate all these vulnerabilities addressed in this paper, aviation security should be checked and undergo risk assessments regularly to prevent any future possible attacks. The purpose of this paper is to depict a general outlook of aviation industry by indicating the weaker points of its security chain. Possible solutions to deal with these terrorist attacks can be developed based on these assessments. This paper can also be evaluated as a warning regarding whether existing security measures and safeguards are adequate or need improvement.

1. Vulnerabilities of Aviation Security

Vulnerability is a measure of the likelihood that precautions against various problems or damages will fail [12]. Aviation security also has numerous vulnerabilities, including inherent risks of aviation. The vulnerabilities of aviation security are:

1.1. Insufficient Security Systems in Aviation

Insufficient security systems in the aviation industry and the sensitivity of aircraft to attacks are the other important factors that make aviation a good target. According to Wilkinson and Jenkins [8], terrorists have been successful 85% of the time when they tried to hijack an airplane in the last decades. Similarly, according to the statistics, terrorists have achieved their goals 76% of the time when they attack airplanes and airports.

Today, 2 million passengers travel by airplanes everyday using both domestic and international airways and 450,000 millions of tons of cargo are carried by aviation companies in the world annually. There are 25,000 commercial airlines and 1,500 commercial airports around the world [13]. These numbers reveal the fact that protection of aviation facilities is inherently very difficult and complex; on the other hand, attacking these targets is a relatively uncomplicated task facing terrorists and criminals. Terrorists and criminals, generally, perceive aviation facilities as areas where they can find large numbers of people and insufficient security [8]. Therefore, when terrorists and criminals make rational cost-benefit analysis, they do not hesitate to choose these places because they can kill the maximum number people and damage a large amount of infrastructure by using a small number of explosives with relatively little effort [13]. On September 11, 2001, more than 3,000 people were killed; similarly, 1,732 people were killed in 70 bomb attacks by means of aviation from 1969 to 1989. The potential for huge casualties in any attack on the aviation industry causes this industry to be a preferred target for terrorists and criminals.

After the September 11 attack, it became clear that hijackers could learn the defects in the aviation security systems from publicly available materials. Generally, by learning the weaknesses of any system of a target country, terrorists can develop strategies and methods for defeating them. Particularly, the question of why al-Qaeda chose the aviation industry as a means of attacking the United States in spite of the fact that they had not ever used the method before should be reevaluated [14].

Moreover, security measures are not limited only to the inside of the airports and airplanes. The perimeter security systems, hangars, office buildings, gas stations near airports, and accessibility of the airports may also increase the risk of the aviation industry. For instance, Dempsey [1] stated that the Department of Transportation (DOT) Inspector General found that illegal access to secured areas of the airports happened 68% of the time in 1998-99, and 30% of the time in 1999-2000 in the United States.

The aviation industry carries billions of tons of cargo each year by means of passenger and cargo airplanes [4]. Moreover, it is estimated that air cargo shipments will continue to grow substantially within the next ten years. For instance, in the United States, it is expected that air cargo shipments will increase by 49% domestically and by 86 % internationally. Air cargo constitutes 29.7 % of the value of international trade. These large volumes of cargo bring their own vulnerabilities at the time of transportation. TSA assesses that the likelihood of a possible bombing attack against a passenger or cargo aircraft is around 35%-65% and thinks that cargo is one of the main targets for terrorists according to the intelligence it has obtained [15].

The likelihood that a cargo may be tampered with while it is being transferred from its original truck, held for screening in the airport sorting centers, loaded onto an airplane, or unloaded from an airplane is very high. Passenger airplanes, in general, have been the main concern for air cargo security during the reorganization process after September 11. However, there is also potential risk for all-cargo operators' aircraft, such as UPS™[1], DHL™[2], and FedEx®[3] Airways [15].

1.2. Lack of International Security Standards

A lack of standardization in terms of responding to and suppressing the risks also causes the level of the risk to increase. Notably, with respect to managing the risk for aviation security, it is crucial not to leave any gaps within the system while securing the airports and airplanes.

Aviation security should be handled cooperatively by every country, not just an individual country. Growing globalization and increasing competition for tourism among countries have improved and increased international flights [16]. The volume of import and export among countries via aviation cargo systems has become a crucial part of the global economy. Although many international conventions dealing with aviation security

---

[1] United Parcel Service of America, Inc., www.ups.com
[2] DHL International GmbH., www.dhl.com
[3] FedEx Cooperation, www.fedex.com

have been organized and many regulations have been made, there is no comprehensive and sufficient international aviation security system in the world today. Moreover, the "it can not happen to me" syndrome is prevalent all over the globe. These situations and lack of prosecution standards among countries allow criminals and terrorists to attack by crossing international borders and choosing the aviation industry as a target. In addition, in today's global society, they can easily change their locations from one country to another because of this deficiency in security on the international level [5].

A terrorist may mislead the security guards and penetrate an airport in a country that lacks security. An armed terrorist may get into an airplane that is going to another country with a secured airport. After that specific airplane's pilots talk to the air traffic controller, the terrorist may hijack the airplane with his weapon, or after seizing control of the cockpit, he may change the direction of the airplane as it is being landed. This hypothetical scenario indicates that even if a country takes all precautions in their airports and airplanes, such as hiring air marshals or installing the latest technological equipment and screening devices in the airports, the security flaws in the systems in other countries may result in tragedies. In response, the U.S. has developed the CAPPS II program to collect information on passengers on airplanes from foreign countries. However, it is not feasible for such a program to solve the problem completely because there is no organization in the world that knows all the names and features of all the terrorists [13]. This case shows how at risk the aviation sector is without international standards.

Except for some countries that have made agreements to cooperate, most of the countries in the world have their own rules and security procedures. In addition, international terrorist organizations and organized crime groups have established networks around the globe, and today's communication systems allow them to quickly communicate and develop new strategies and actions in response to changing situations [17].

In addition, a standard and universal law enforcement system around the globe has not been established up to now. Although the International Civil Aviation Association (ICAO) attempted to resolve the conflicts between countries over the problem of jurisdiction and to settle upon a system internationally, there are not any binding and effective regulations in the world as yet. As a result, without standardized regulations around the globe, law enforcement loses its deterrent effect on criminals [1].

1.3. Vulnerabilities in General Aviation

Many people around the world including the U.S.A. have their own private airplanes, some of which are designed and manufactured by their owners. Crop dusters, along with private airplanes, number 200,000 in the United States, and they are another strong vulnerability for the aviation industry. Although the airplanes in general aviation are relatively small compared to commercial aircrafts, they may also cause substantial damage if they are misused by criminals or terrorists [18].

Typically, most of the planes in general aviation are stored in hangars near the airports, but some of them may be located on private land and fields. Wherever they are located, there is a high potential for theft of these airplanes. It is so open to threats that even a teenage flight student can steal a single engine airplane as seen in Tampa, Florida, in 2002. Moreover, these kinds of airplanes are also hardly recognizable by radar due to their ability to fly at low altitude. Due to a lack of sufficient security systems, these airplanes create vulnerability in the aviation sector [19].

If they are rented by a terrorist or criminal who is intent on attacking some important target, then nothing can be done to stop him. Background checks are not part of the requirements made on people who want to rent them [18]. Interestingly, the September 11 terrorist, Atta, was interested in crop dusters and tried to learn how to use them before the attack. His motivation for studying crop dusters was to learn the vulnerabilities in general aviation. Some experts claim that his plan was to use a crop duster to carry gasoline, which releases 15 times more energy when mixed with air than TNT, and attack the same targets in the United States [13].

1.4. Lack of Intelligence Sharing and Cooperation

Intelligence has always been an important and enduring part of governments. Operationally, it has two important roles. One is gathering information and then converting it into meaningful and useful data, and the other is implementation of this data where national security is concerned. However, it is also related to international security when governments combat terrorists or organized crime groups that have connections among different countries.

A lack of sufficient intelligence, not sharing existing intelligence among agencies and a lack of cooperation among agencies which handle aviation security are the other factors that increase the vulnerability of the aviation sector. In order to identify the potential threats, protect aviation facilities from terrorists and criminals, and respond to emergencies in a timely manner, the need for intelligence is vital for any country in the world. In terms of intelligence, one of the weakest security factors on September 11 was a lack of a system that allowed the FBI and other agencies to share their collective knowledge [14].

Thus, due to the effects of globalization, many mutual or multilateral intelligence-sharing agreements have been made, both formally and informally. For these reasons, the U.S. government has made an agreement to cooperate with 400 different foreign intelligence services and security and law enforcement agencies. While the government has increased its cooperation with other countries, it has neglected to create an intelligence sharing system at home. For instance, the case of September 11 is commonly exemplified as a failure of the U.S. intelligence community to share its data [20].

Therefore, the intelligence community has been under observation in the United States since September 11. By and large, the criticisms were related to not collecting enough information before that tragic event. However, some people stress that even if the necessary intelligence had been collected, this event would have happened anyway due to the fact that the agencies were not sharing information among themselves. For instance, although two of the terrorists in the 9/11 attacks were on the Central Intelligence Agency's (CIA) watch list, they were allowed to board the airplane because the Federal Aviation Administration (FAA) could not access the CIA's watch list. Before September 11, there was no sharing of intelligence among the airport and airline security officials and the Central Intelligence Agency (CIA), Federal Bureau of Investigation (FBI), FAA, and Immigration and Naturalization Service (INS). To rectify this problem, the Office of Homeland Security was established in the United States in 2002, but this highly authoritative department needs time to work effectively to organize all these intelligence departments in the U.S.

Generally, the response to threats to the aviation industry has been reactive and defensive in nature due to there not being a common security strategy and cooperation among agencies. As an example of lack of cooperation between agencies, The Federal Aviation Administration (FAA) and North American Aerospace Defense Command could not develop a preventive strategy on 9/11 because their individual protocols did not cover this kind of attack [14].

1.5. Easy Target for MANPADS

Shoulder-launched surface-to-air missiles, the Man-Portable Anti-aircraft Defense Systems (MANPADS), are recognized as a serious threat to aviation security systems. Predictably, there are 500,000 MANPADS in the world today, many thousands of which are thought to be on the black market and therefore accessible to terrorists and criminals. Their portability and concealable features make MANPADS dangerous and hard to detect. These weapons have a four- mile range and 15,000 feet capacity, so they may be used to attack airplanes easily [19].

Typically, they are fairly inexpensive, but extremely lethal. In addition, if trained properly, a user can use it well. Because their features enable them to be launched far from airplanes, they may be used to attack airplanes without any warning. Since 1970, 42 aircraft have been attacked and 29 aircraft have been damaged by this weapon. Furthermore, terrorists have begun to use this weapon to attack commercial airplanes in non-combat zones around the world. For instance, in 2002, terrorists attacked a commercial airplane in Kenya using this weapon [19].

If trained terrorists use this weapon against unprotected airplanes, the result of this kind of attack, without doubt, is tragedy. Moreover, countermeasures to this weapon which can be installed on airplanes are very expensive and time consuming. Thus, MANPADS form a considerable risk to civil aviation [18].

In terms of access assessment, when compared to other highly visible targets such as nuclear plants and high profile government installations, airports are public spaces and easily accessible to everyone. Terrorists can even attack the airports from nearby highways, which also increase the vulnerabilities of airports. History is fraught with examples of people who entered an airport from its weak perimeters and later fled to another country [21].

Moreover, terrorists can gain a large amount of information, including maps and scaled drawings of airports, newly regulated aviation security systems, and the features of avionics and computer systems in the airplanes from the media and the Internet [22]. Besides their current political agenda, terrorists can also use the Internet to post information on how to make bombs, biological, chemical, or other unconventional agents. Moreover, some documents that show the vulnerabilities of the aviation security systems, such as GAO Reports, are open to the public. Any terrorist can learn these deficiencies in the aviation security system and can take advantage by paying close attention to publicized details [17].

1.6. Vulnerabilities in Aviation Computer Systems

The vulnerabilities of computer systems in aviation are also important factors for terrorists and criminals when considering airplanes and airport facilities as targets. As stated at the International Conference on Aviation Safety and Security (1997), most computer programs and operating systems have authentication problems and can readily be misused by others [23].

Aviation security highly depends on computer and infrastructure networks, such as electric power, air traffic control, and telecommunications. Computers are used to store vital information, such as watch lists, passenger information, flight information, and personnel information. Vulnerabilities of the computer stem from various factors including software problems, accidents, troubles in data processing, and deliberate attacks [24].

In the world of computer hackers, attacking computer programs is relatively cheap, not very dangerous, and easy to accomplish. Any mistakes in software programs, such as inaccurate configuration or incorrect use of a function or command, can result in security problems. If any misuse happens, many inevitable and fatal results may appear in aviation. These include loss of confidentiality, pauses in air traffic control services, closing of airports, loss of airplanes, refusal to accept services, and loss of data integrity.

Typically, cyber attacks are difficult to resolve and the attackers are rarely captured. Currently, there is no firewall that can safeguard the systems from all cyber attacks completely [24]. Moreover, it is also hard to recognize whether problems are caused as a result of an attack or not. To determine what causes the problem, many alternatives should be checked. If a cyber attack targets aviation security, it may also be difficult to resolve because investigators have to work a lot to identify all the parts of a physical attack, such as the sabotage against Pan Am Flight 103 [25].

The air traffic control system, including computers, communications, and radars are one of the most vulnerable targets in the aviation industry. Every flight depends on these systems and any attack against them can cause uncontrollable damage [23]. The General Accounting Office (GAO) [26] stated that most aviation facilities had not prepared risk and threat assessment analysis for 5 years prior to review. With respect to software security, there are some claims that the FAA did not regularly conduct background checks for employees who repair and inspect high security computer systems. If any information leaked out from them to any terrorist hackers, the damage would be more devastating than September 11. Unfortunately, the threats still exist because of the vulnerability of these systems [27].

In addition, electronic and electromagnetic protection measures should also be considered in the screening areas of the airports because the detection devices for screening may be damaged or disabled remotely by terrorists. Electronic deception, which deliberately makes radiation, alteration, or reflection of electromagnetic energy to give misleading information or deny valid information, and electromagnetic interference are some techniques that terrorists and criminals use in their attacks. Therefore, electronic security is also part of the risks of aviation security [23].

2. The Impact of Terrorists' Attacks against Aviation

After considering vulnerabilities in aviation sector, the impacts of such attacks are discussed. These impacts allow us to comprehend the dimensions of these attacks and how much effort should be made to provide security in aviation sector. In this paper, the impact of attacks are explained in three basic and important areas, the effects of the media, the psychological impact on victims, and the economic impact on both governments and private companies:

2.1. Psychological Impact

Attacks against the aviation industry also have a psychological impact that increases its vulnerabilities. Although terrorist attacks are evaluated by the number of deaths, the psychological effect on people should also be taken into account [9]. Einav [5] claimed that terrorism is psychological warfare that increases people's anxiety, fear, mistrust, resentment and reactions in degrees inversely proportional to reality. Their ultimate goals are that these emotions paralyze the community in their daily routine and increase the pressure on the government to consent to the terrorists' claims.

Particularly, children are deeply affected by such incidents. For instance, a high level of distress was found in students in the United States immediately after the September 11 attack [28]. One of the most common psychological problems after terrorist attacks is posttraumatic stress disorder (PTSD), which can be defined as long-term anxiety responses to a traumatic event that damages people's normal defense mechanisms. In the case of 9/11, many people watched this tragic event on live television, and the symptoms of PTSD have been observed in many children in the United States [28]. With respect to adults, Eidelson R., D'allesion, and Eidelson J. [29] stated that in addition to PTSD, adjustment disorders, major depression, anxiety disorders, and negative feelings about work emerged in the days following the September 11 attack.

Moreover, increased tobacco and substance use, family violence, poor school performance, increased risk taking, and other behavioral problems can be observed in the people who were exposed to serious terrorist attacks [30]. Traumatizing and re-traumatizing effects can be seen in people who watched this incident on television again and again, listened to stories from survivors and rescue workers, or saw this tragic event first hand while it was happening [29].

Generally, people affected by such events have fear about their lives, their future, and wish such attacks would not happen anymore. The only thing that they want is for precautions to be taken immediately [31]. After the American Airlines crash on November 12, just two months after September 11, people were worried that another terrorist attack would happen again. These kinds of feelings cause people to show abnormal reactions. Peace and security, the roots of a healthy community, suffer seriously as a result. People in the U.S. had not been affected substantially till the tragedy of September 11 since World War II [32]. Interestingly, some people may desire the dark and uncertain atmosphere following events like these because they evaluate this as a marketing opportunity. In this period, these kinds of people always try to sell some devices and software to panicked people [33].

2.2. Economic Impact

The aviation industry is one of the most important industries in the world and a market whose costs are extremely high. In the United States, which provides 40% of all flights in the world, there are 5,000 airports, 55,000 pilots, 200,000 private airplanes, 475 commercial airport supervisors, and 7,000 air traffic controllers [13, 18]. These numbers indicate that not only do aviation facilities have symbolic importance, but they also have huge economic significance. In the United States, the aviation industry manages 11 million jobs and constitutes 6%-7% of the nation's gross domestic product (GDP) [18]. Basically, transportation has always been an inseparable part of the U.S. economy. The United States has a service economy equipped with movable brainpower to serve business immediately wherever it needs. Therefore, air transportation is one of the vital points of the U.S. economy. Even though flights were canceled for only three days immediately after September 11, the economy really suffered during this short period of time [1].

The aviation industry is very sensitive to any changes in economic cycles in the business world. Along with maintaining security, trying to reduce congestion and delays in the airports and deliver items on time for customers has major financial implications and causes problems for most aviation companies [34]. Ghobrial and Irvin [4] claimed that the aviation industry is usually the first to suffer the bad effects of a weak economy and the last to benefit from a strong economy. In addition, the competition between airlines also reduces the benefits of a good economy. Therefore, any negative intervention in this susceptible business may cause extreme damage.

After September 11, many aviation companies had to be closed down and a lot of people became unemployed. It has been appraised that September 11 caused economic losses of more than $70 billion [34, 35]. Unsurprisingly, one of the first groups that experienced the negative impact of September 11 was the owners and residents of the Towers and the surrounding buildings [36]. Kim and Gu [37] stated that worldwide commercial passenger traffic decreased approximately 18% in the year following the attack. As for the United States, commercial passenger traffic fell 40% in the same year. Campbell [38] stated that entire aviation industry in the U.S. lost $7.7 billion, even after they received $5 billion in grants. By the same token, the Gross Domestic Product (GDP) declined 0.5% in 2001. The U.S. government spent $7.9 billion to cover the damages and other related costs [39]. Airlines were severely affected due to economic waves in business markets and were on the verge of bankruptcy because booking rates declined by 70% [4].

It is clear that there was both direct and indirect significance for terrorists when choosing the World Trade Center, which was the economic symbol of the United States. They showed their success by directly striking a status symbol of a superpower. Indirectly, they accomplished their goals because increasing insurance costs, high fuel prices, and the costs of security systems have pushed the aviation industry into a troubled condition. There are several factors causing loss of revenue for airline companies:

First, one of the major economic impacts of the attack of September 11 was the profound damage to the insurance market. As a result of this impact, policyholders have faced higher costs and additional fees [40]. Liability insurance has increased from $2 million to $150 million annually. Today, approximately one fourth of an airline ticket price is tax, and it is likely to increase in the future. As a result of the tax increases, the demand for travel by airplanes has decreased. Thus, many airline companies have economic problems due to this high capacity but low demand environment [4].

Second, security expenses are also a burden on the aviation industry's shoulders. So far, $1.5 billion has been spent to increase security at the airports [27]. Airport funds, typically, come from the federal government's allowance and airline charges. Post-September 11, along with the increase in security measures, the expense of airlines also rose.

Third, federal marshals, who are assigned to protect airplanes against possible threats in the air, constitute another expense for the airline companies. They are usually placed in the first class section of the airplanes, but the federal government pays only a discounted price for them. Increasing the number of air marshals in accordance with the Air Transportation Safety and System Stabilization Act (ATSA) means increasing a lost source of income for aviation companies. Fourth, before September 11, businessmen could carry their sensitive cargo onto the same plane. However, post-9/11, the amount of this cargo has been limited by the FAA. This regulation reduced 50% of demand in this area, which means another loss of revenue for airline companies.

For those reasons, dismissing workers has been perceived as the only method to reduce the operating costs of airlines. Companies have lost millions of dollars due to negative perceptions stemming from fear of air travel and increased ticket taxes. Long lines and severe security measures that use up valuable time have resulted in switching preference to other transportation systems or canceling travel plans [4].

In the aviation industry, reducing the economic harm of terrorist and criminal attacks is really difficult and hard to accomplish. People in the aviation industry should consider various factors and endeavor to obtain economic success. For instance, to regain passenger confidence after an attack is an important factor that the people in the aviation industry should consider. Because of the fact that fears of transportation via aviation cause significant damage economically to the aviation industry, new provisions should be developed in terms of commerce. For instance, some provisions may be provided by airline companies to constitute a reasonable and fetching transportation means [41].

3. Conclusion

In conclusion, as a result of risk assessment of aviation security, it can be claimed clearly that aviation industry is high in risks and aviation security should be designed in accordance with these risks in mind because there seems to be various vulnerabilities and threats in different areas of aviation sector. In aviation security, vulnerabilities can be observed in various areas; excessive target options in terms of numbers, lack of international security standards, insufficient security systems in the aviation, vulnerabilities in cargo, airplanes, and general aviation, lack of intelligence sharing and cooperation, forgery and deception problems, being easy target for attacks, vulnerability in computer systems in aviation, unintended consequences of measures, and the dangers stem from new forms of crimes. All these vulnerabilities are threatened by two groups, terrorists and criminals. The impacts of these attacks have always been distressing for people and governments. These impacts, especially, have been observed in the media, the economy, the political arena, and the psyche of people.

Utilizing these vulnerabilities, terrorists and criminals have attacked many times in various ways to aviation sector since its inception. Particularly, the most destructive terrorist attack by means of aviation is the tragedy of September 11, which is also the cornerstone of today's aviation security policies. Before this event, the concerns were generally directed at increasing the quality of service of the aviation industry and trying to solve economic problems from which the aviation industry really suffered. After going through the shock of September 11, new legislations and agencies were established. All security precautions were reconsidered and reassessed.

As long as civil aviation has a large air traffic network, it seems that the aviation sector will never be completely secure. By accepting this undeniable truth, some countermeasures should be developed accordingly to reduce the risks. Possible remedies of these vulnerabilities are using and tracking high technology which has always been on the agenda of aviation and government executives, training all the personnel from screening officers to highest executives in the airports to deal with huge numbers of air clients by serving effective and fast service, and public education. Acquainting people on how to behave during an emergency situation in crowded places can be a solution to minimize the risks. This education can be supplied by utilizing the media including the Internet or providing necessary education programs in schools or other educational places. Similarly, if people were not trained and educated properly about how to react during attacks and in what ways they can help officers, the damage would be bigger.

Like all security organization, aviation security is composed of two important components that strongly related each other. These components are human being and hardware including technological detection devices, metal detectors, and x-ray machines. Successful aviation security can not be obtained unless both factors work together properly. Typically, hardware is related to money and technology. Today, any country can purchase the latest technological devices to protect their airports and airplanes on the condition of paying their costs. However, human factor is more complicated than hardware. It consists of people from the personnel who operate the machines at the gates to highest manager of aviation security. Training is always perceived as the best solution for the employee in security, but other factors, such as motivation, integrity, and diligence, should not be underestimated. While training personnel, other education methods, such as Neuro-Linguistic Programming (NLP) can be used for security employee to provide motivation continuously. In addition, because of the fact that they always confront with huge number people at the airports, they can be trained about human behaviors and physiology. The courses that the security personnel are trained may also include both physical, such as self-defense and situation awareness courses, and technical programs.

Both successful airport management and technological devices can provide systematic order at the airports. Not only does this situation prevent airports from becoming chaotic and disorderly, which the terrorist highly desire, but also it creates effectiveness for this service by reducing long lines that cause delays at the airports. However, while minimizing the risk, effectiveness should be taken into account. In today's world, where rapid commerce has become the norm, these systems should be effective in addition to being secure. Businessmen, especially, do not want to wait at the airports for hours. For this reason, both government and private aviation companies should work together against terrorists to take necessary precautions in both airplanes and airports.

References

[1]   P.S. Dempsey, Aviation security: The role of law in the war against terrorism. *Columbia Journal of Transnational Law,* **41** (2003), 649.
[2]   J.F. Garvey, The airline industry: Post September 11th. *Vital Speeches of the Day,* **68/9** (2002), 277-281.
[3]   K.M. Sweet, *Aviation and airport security: Terrorism and safety concerns.* New Jersey: Pearson Publication; 2004.
[4]   A. Ghobrial, W.A. Irvin, Combating air terrorism: Some implications to the aviation industry. *Journal of Air Transportation,* **9/3** (2004), 67-87.
[5]   O. Einav, Understanding aviation terrorism. *Interavia,* **58** (2003), 670-704.
[6]   J.W. Stamper, Looking at the events of September 11: Some effects and implications. *Defense Counsel Journal,* **69/2** (2002), 152-169.
[7]   J. Skinner, An American civil law responds to international terror. *Journal of Air Law and Commerce,* **69** (2004), 545.
[8]   P. Wilkinson, B. Jenkins, Introduction. *Terrorism & Political Violence,* **10** (1998).
[9]   P. Buttler, Forward: terrorism and utilitarianism: Lessons from, and for, criminal law. *Journal of Criminal Law & Criminology,* **93** (2002).
[10] J.F. Coates, R&D leaders face a post-9/11 world. *Research Technology Management,* **45/3** (2002), 7-9.
[11] DHS raises concern about attacks on chemical plants. *Chemical Week,* **165,** (2003), 31.
[12] H. Conrow, *Effective risk management: some keys to success.* VA: American Institute of Aeronautics and Astronautics, (2003), 50-58.
[13] A.R. Thomas, *Aviation insecurity,* New York: Prometheus Books; 2003.
[14] The 9/11 commission report of the national commission on terrorist attacks upon the United States; 2004. [Online] Available from; URL: http://www.gpoaccess. gov/911/ [2005, March 15]

[15] B. Elias, Air cargo security. *Congressional research service;* 2003. [Online] Available from; URL: from http://www.loc.gov/crsinfo/. [2005, January 27]

[16] J. T. Coshall, The threat of terrorism as an intervention on international travel flows. *Journal of Travel Research,* **42** (2003), 4-12.

[17] P. R. Pillar, Terrorism goes global: extremist groups extend their reach worldwide. *The Brookings Review,* **19** (2001), 34-38.

[18] J. Szyliowicz, Aviation security: Promise or reality? *Studies in Conflict & Terrorism,* **27/1** (2004) 47–63.

[19] General Accounting Office. *Aviation security: Improvement still needed in federal aviation security efforts;* 2004, 04-385.

[20] M. Herman, 11 September: Legitimizing intelligence? *International Relations,* **16/2** (2002), 227-241.

[21] E.E. Bailey, Aviation policy: Past and present. *Southern Economic Journal,* **69** (2002), 12-21.

[22] M. Greenberg, The limits of branding: The world trade center, fiscal crisis and the marketing of recovery. *International Journal of Urban and Regional Research,* **272** (2003), 386-416.

[23] P.G. Neumann, Computer security in aviation: vulnerabilities, threats, and risks. International Conference on Aviation Safety and Security Reports. Washington D.C.: 1997.

[24] B. D. Nordwall, Cyber threats place infrastructure at risk. *Aviation Week & Space Technology,* **146/27** (1997), 51.

[25] P. Mann, Cyber security `missing' from travel defenses. *Aviation Week & Space Technology,* **157/2,** (2002), 41.

[26] General Accounting Office. *Vulnerabilities and potential improvements for the air cargo system;* 2002, 03-344.

[27] C.C. Coughlin, J. P. Cohen, S.R. Khan, Aviation security and terrorism: A review of the economic issues. *The Federal Reserve Bank of St. Louis,* **84/5** (2002), 9-24.

[28] R.W. Auger, J.W. Seymour, W. Jr. Roberts, Responding to terror: The impact of September 11 on K-12 schools and schools' responses. *Professional School Counseling,* **7** (2004).

[29] R.J. Eidelson, G.R. D'Alessio, J.L. Eidelson, The impact of September 11 on psychologists. *Professional Psychology,* **34/ 2** (2003).

[30] A.M. Miller, M. Heldring, Mental health and primary care in a time of terrorism: Psychological impact of terrorist attacks. *Families, Systems, & Health,* **22/1** (2004), 7-31.

[31] J. N. Kondrasuk, The effects of 9/11 and terrorism on human resource management: recovery, reconsideration, and renewal, *Employee Responsibilities and Rights Journal,* **16/1** (2004), 25.

[32] W.L. Carol, The clash between security and liberty in the U.S. response to terror. *Public Administration Review,* **65/1** (2005), 18-31.

[33] A must-do list for commercial aviation. *Aviation Week & Space Technology,* **155/21** (2001), 110.

[34] D. Hale, A September 11th reflection. *The International Economy,* **16/4** (2002), 34-37.

[35] A.D. Balahadia, Preparations for a storm: A proposal for managing the litigation stemming from September 11th, 2001. *Pepperdine Dispute Resolution Law Journal,* **4/61** (2003).

[36] G.S. Staring, Admiralty law institute: Confused seas: Admiralty law in the wake of terrorism: Insurance and reinsurance of marine interests in the new age of terrorism. *Tulane Law Review,* **77** (2003), 1371.

[37] H. Kim, Z. Gu, Impact of the 9/11 terrorist attacks on the return and risk of airline stocks. *Tourism and Hospitality Research,* **5/2** (2004), 150-164.

[38] R.P. Campbell, America acts: Swift legislative responses to the September 11 attacks. *Defense Counsel Journal,* **69/2** (2002), 139-152.

[39] P. Looney, Security, aerospace top legislative agendas. *Aerospace America,* **40/1** (2002), 10.

[40] J.L. Rhee, Rational and constitutional approaches to airline safety in the face of terrorist threats. *DePaul Law Review,* **49** (2000), 847.

[41] R. Abeyratne, Crisis management toward restoring confidence in air transport-legal and commercial issues. *Journal of Air Law and Commerce,* **67** (2002), 595.

Understanding and Responding to the Terrorism Phenomenon
O. Nikbay and S. Hancerli (Eds.)
IOS Press, 2007

Learning from the "Lesser" Acts: Suggestions for Improving Responses to Critical Incidents

Tomas C. MIJARES, Ph.D.
Texas State University, San Marcos, USA

Abstract: This paper examines how terrorist activity produces effects upon public safety agencies that are very similar to those produced by other critical incidents normally considered to be of less importance than terrorism. Through a review of the literature and integration with current terrorist activity, observations are made showing commonalities with other forms of criminal behavior. Recommendations for ameliorative action are made using resources that are currently available to the law enforcement establishment.

Key words: Critical incidents, legal requirements, initial response, standardized procedures, common terminology, civil litigation, criminal procedures, and transfer of technology.

Introduction to the Problem

The tactics of terrorism have been used by a wide range of groups with an equally wide range of motivations, organizational skills, and combat experience [1]. These same tactics have also been used by mentally and emotionally disturbed persons such as Charles Whitman during the Texas Tower Incident in 1966, religious zealots such as David Koresh during the Branch Davidian Incident in 1993, and by common criminals such as Lawrence Phillips and Emil Matasareanu in 1997 during an aborted robbery at the North Hollywood Branch of the Bank of America [2]. Irrespective of their announced purposes, material assets, training and skill levels, these criminal perpetrators care nothing about innocent bystanders, and tend to take a polarized position of the world whereby their perspective is at one end and all other viewpoints are at the other end of a continuum. With no ability to accommodate compromise, the users of these tactics also recognize no national boundaries, respect no philosophies or opinions different from their own, and as self-proclaimed "liberators" from some sort of perceived oppression, they expect complete and undivided loyalty from their followers. Their common characteristic is their inability to recognize that their efforts are actually counter-productive to their causes and generally tend to unite the neutral and uncommitted against them. Through their own self-imposed gullibility they can at best claim a temporary disruption in the routines of the targeted population, a destruction of replaceable property, and the deaths of people who had committed no act of oppression beyond being born outside the terrorist group. However, whether intentional or inadvertent, the actions of these groups have resulted in several very inconvenient, albeit temporary, interruptions to an otherwise desired and comfortable lifestyle.

Terrorist groups may differ greatly more than in terms of philosophy and political issues. Smith and Damphousse [3] suggest that they also differ in terms of geographical location (rural versus urban), organizational structure (cellular versus confederation), symbolic targets (capitalist corporations and governmental entities) and composition (inclusive versus exclusive). Despite a normative and often emotional reaction that terrorist groups deserve immediate punitive sanctions for their actions and particularly that any foreign sponsors warrant a military response, the political and criminal justice systems dictate that such actions must be construed as criminal behavior subject to the application of the rule of law. Furthermore, since terrorist actions are criminal in nature, elevating the perpetrators to a classification beyond that of a common criminal often may afford them an undeserved hero status and produce additional followers.

Almost by an operational definition within a democratic republic the elements of the criminal justice system strive to maintain the *status quo*. In its most effective and long lasting form, societal change is evolutionary, not revolutionary. A truly free society takes pride in its tolerance and actually encourages political and philosophical discussion and courteous dissent. Much of the success, growth, and maturity of the American system of politics, economics, and criminal justice can trace their roots to various instances where the unquestioned acceptance of the *status quo* was clearly inadequate and inappropriate. But, while domestic dissent taking place during most of the twentieth century may have been relatively spontaneous and loosely knit, it has become progressively more organized, disciplined, regimented, and violent.

Nor is change forced if it is to be successful. Both the means and the end in a forced societal change in a revolutionary form is violence. Whether it is economically, politically, or religiously driven, forced change and the violent tools used to initiate such change tend to result in a continuously widening circle of destructive confrontations and disruptive behavior that are outside the routine of an evolutionary society. These disruptions are included in a generic classification known as critical incidents.

The concept of "critical incidents" is difficult to define with any degree of precision. In the law enforcement context critical incidents are those events which are immediately life-threatening and beyond the normal preparation and capability of standard patrol procedures and resources. These incidents include, but are not limited to, sniper incidents, barricaded suspects, hostage seizures, and dignitary protection situations. They also include natural and manmade disasters (hurricanes, floods, blizzards, aircraft crashes, and fires) where contingency plans may be in place, but procedures and drills are not regularly practiced [4]. Although not every incident has been as newsworthy as the shootout between two armed robbers and the Los Angles S.W.A.T. Team at a North Hollywood branch of Bank of America, the increasing frequency and the relative magnitude of these events are realities that must be faced by the professional police administrator and the elected officials to whom he must report.

Traditionally, the personnel selected for these circumstances were usually chosen on the basis of immediate availability instead of their training, experience, and demonstrated ability. Normally they received only an *ad hoc* status for a specific incident. As a result, the ranks and response time of the remaining patrol forces were depleted, and the more routine tasks of police work received a secondary priority or were ignored altogether. Members of these temporary task forces lacked the cohesiveness and coordination necessary to function properly as a unit and instead tended to operate groups of individuals.

As police administrators recognized the need to maintain unit integrity for these incidents, special units were developed. These units initially operated on a part-time basis, whereby the officers assigned were mobilized and united only on an as-needed basis and returned to their regularly scheduled duties upon completion of the event. Despite the assumption of elitism, the following shortcomings were identified by the *National Commission on Law Observation and Enforcement*[1]:

1. The selection process for most police appointments and assignments was often based on nepotism and favoritism.
2. Training was irregular, inconsistent and incomplete.
3. No continuous and concerted effort was made in large departments to integrate these units with other sections of the law enforcement agency.
4. Little research was conducted to find improvements to existing tactics, techniques and technology.
5. Specific department orders were not developed to define the deployment procedures to be followed by these specialized units.

The huge operating budgets enjoyed by organized crime, particularly the elements involved in illegal drug traffic and international terrorist operations, have produced a new breed of criminal whose weapons are equal to and usually surpass those of modern military and law enforcement forces. Their ruthless nature indicates that they have no reluctance to employ such weapons indiscriminately. Often purchased through legitimate sources, their armories include fully automatic rifles, rocket launchers, sub-machine guns, fragmentation grenades and a myriad of explosives and detonating devices.

1. Purpose and Methodology

Accordingly, the purpose of this presentation is three-fold: First, to describe how the initial response is the most critical phase of any response in the realm of law enforcement; second, to describe the legal requirements within the American legal system that guide both the initial and follow-up responses; third, to describe a current training paradigm that has been developed to cope with the problem. To accomplish this purpose substantive material was obtained through a review of relevant historical literature and legal commentary and integrated with current trends in terrorist activity and the efforts to control them.

---

[1]In 1931 the National Commission on Law Observation and Enforcement, commonly referred to as the Wickersham Commission, was charged with the responsibility of reporting on the enforcement of the Eighteenth Amendment (Prohibition). Its overall conclusion was that Prohibition was not being enforced because it was an unenforceable task placed on American law enforcement agencies. The Commission's 14 volume series of reports probed deeply into the American criminal justice system to offer the causes and effects of the situation and to suggest possible ameliorative efforts [5].

2. Observations

Since each of the following observations is extremely important to the response, it is pointless to present them in any particular rank order. Since these phenomena tend to occur simultaneously, it is meaningless to make any attempt to present them chronologically.

2.1. Observation 1:

The first few minutes of a response to a critical incident, whether driven by a terrorist motive or not, are the most critical aspect of the reaction by law enforcement personnel. The response to terrorism is usually addressed from the perspective of a national defense posture [6]. In a free society it is normally local law enforcement agencies that are required to assume the initial responsibility for responding to a terrorist action within national borders, regardless of the perpetrators' identity or country of origin. In the absence of a formal declaration of war the initial terrorist acts must be considered criminal in nature and subject to the established guidelines of criminal procedure even if an action can later be linked to an international conspiracy or to a foreign government. Although cases may ultimately be turned over to a national defense agency for subsequent investigation and action, the unmistakable fact remains that local police officers will have immediate jurisdiction and responsibility at the initial and most critical stages of the incident. Accordingly, in most instances the acts of the responding officers during the first ten minutes determine the course of the next 24 hours. This importance is obvious from an examination of the concurrent multiple tasks placed on the response personnel.

The most important task for the first responding officer is to proceed to the scene promptly but safely. This task requires the officer to regard each call for service as important and never as routine. It also requires the responder to exercise caution in terms of driving to the scene and in situational awareness. An officer becomes a liability to the organization if injured during the response and assets must be diverted from the original call for service to attend to his newly developed needs. When an officer is dispatched to a scene there is rarely even a suggestion that the incident is based on terrorism in its source, nature, or purpose. Only during the subsequent investigation does this information become known. Initially the officer can only approach the situation and accept at face value; i.e. as a traffic accident, as an industrial accident, as a natural disaster, as a crime in progress or whatever else the call for service may have indicated.

Upon arrival the author must authenticate the call for service and determine if a crisis beyond immediate resolution actually exists. If so the dispatcher must be notified. The information that is conveyed within the first few moments of arrival will provide the basis of whether a crisis is in fact taking place. This information will determine the need for additional response assets such as more police personnel, emergency medical technicians, the local fire department, or other trained specialists such as the explosive ordnance disposal unit. The information must also reflect if there is any need for a continuing or follow-up form of investigation. For example, if the incident involves any form of unnatural death, a homicide investigation must be initiated.

At this particular time the responding officer often has little indication whether the event is natural or man-made, intentional or unintentional, and, if intentional, what the motive may be. The symptoms of the event, which must be treated immediately, can be common to a very wide range of causal factors and the officer may not have even a suggestion that the incident is of a terrorist nature. While performing these many facets of a preliminary investigation, the officer is responsible for performing first-aid on the injured, directing pedestrian and vehicular traffic safely around the scene, securing the crime scene to prevent evidentiary contamination, protecting bystanders and other potential victims from further injury, and arresting the perpetrator. In short, the initial responder is instantly required to care for the direct effects of the event more than to ponder its long-range implications as the work of a terrorist.

2.2. Observation 2:

Training for critical incidents is both inconsistent and incomplete. In the United States alone there are over 75,000 different law enforcement agencies each with its own agenda, delivery system, perceived need and budgetary constraints for training its personnel. The fragmented approach to critical incident training could be seen during two significant historical events in American law enforcement. In both incidents it was primarily the courage and determination that kept a very bad situation from getting much worse.

In 1993 four federal agents were killed in Waco, Texas during a high-risk warrant service to a religious cult for a violation of the Federal Firearms Law. In this incident there were dozens of armed subjects, some of whom were equipped with fully automatic weapons and improvised explosive devices, occupying a large two story structure. Officers from over one hundred miles away responded to the call for assistance. Most of these officers were off duty and had not worked together as a unit. Through the efforts and organizational skills of the supervisory personnel from the initial responders the perimeter was secured, wounded were evacuated and treated, and the condition was stabilized until the arrival of federal reinforcements.

In 1999 a similar set of circumstances took place in Littleton Colorado at Columbine High School where two emotionally disturbed teen-aged gunmen went on a premeditated rampage and killed several classmates and a teacher. Several police officers responded to the scene. Again many of these officers were from different law enforcement agencies and many were off duty at the time. Although the responding officers have received considerable criticism for their perceived slow and deliberate approach, their efforts were consistent with the training of that particular time and the communications equipment available to them.

A major problem in both instances was a lack of standardized procedures and common terminology. This problem has been addressed by various professional associations such as the Texas Tactical Police Officers Association (TTPOA). Without assistance or guidance from any form of governmental entity this group of tactical officers from dozens of different police departments has developed training programs for all levels of responders to critical incidents throughout the state. Equally important the association has conducted research on tactics, techniques, and technology to improve responses to critical incidents. It has also made policy recommendations to the appropriate legislative and executive branches of government to guide these responses. A similar approach to training has been followed by the Texas Association of Hostage Negotiators (TAHN).

However, a significant training dilemma still exists for public administrators. Beyond the initial recruit level of instruction received by new employees, very little attention is directed to the needs of incumbent police personnel. Unlike the military law enforcement does not possess sufficient numbers of personnel to allow the release time from duty to devote to training. Unless engaged in combat duties, military personnel spend most of their time in training and equipment maintenance to reinforce and hone their knowledge bases, skills, and abilities.

Pursuant to the guidelines established by the respective state law enforcement training councils, local law enforcement agencies tend to do an adequate job of providing entry level instruction to new recruits. However, in most instances the maximum level of training for experienced police officers required by the employing law enforcement agency is the minimum required by state law. Law enforcement personnel are in a incessant response mode as they react to calls for service. When not responding to calls for service police officers are expected to be visible as a deterrent, present on the street to apprehend criminal offenders, and available as a witness for any work already completed [7].

Even the most basic of skills require continuous practice, scrutiny, and reinforcement for skill proficiency, streamlined and efficient performance, muscle memory, and endurance. The efficacy of continuous supervised training can be seen through a comparison with the most advanced of physical performers, professional athletes. Michael Jordan, John Unitas, Gordie Howe, Hank Aaron and Pele may be considered at the top of their respective sports, but each practiced his craft with unrelenting zeal[2] under the watchful scrutiny of a coach. Through supervised training constructive criticism can be offered by past performances, suggestions can be made about present operations, and instruction can be made about future applications of the performer's skills. Team sports such as football, basketball, and soccer are analogous to military and public safety operations as a collection of individuals are molded by the coach into a coordinated and cohesive unit for maximum performance.

The adage that "practice makes perfect" has a direct application to counter-terrorist operations. Not every incident allows sufficient opportunity for a rehearsal and not every rehearsal can replicate situational conditions exactly. Viewed as the logical extension of training, there are several benefits to repeated practice as often as possible especially when the practice is content valid and based on a review of past case histories.

First, practice allows a supervisory officer to observe a simulated performance, thereby identifying any need for further police assets, either in the form of personnel or equipment. Reinforcements and extra equipment are easier to find and put into operation during an organized dry run than after a crisis has escalated uncontrollably.

Second, a training session can identify potential problems, particularly if the physical conditions can be closely replicated. While a schematic description is very helpful, "hands-on" experience on a practical problem such as how a door opens is priceless. Experiential familiarity with its physical characteristics such as friction resistance and noise can be directly applied to the resolution of the problem.

Third, supervised rehearsal provides information about the anticipated chronology and amount of time between the events of a crisis. This information is critical when the actions of one aspect of the operation are dependent on the amount of time needed to

---

[2] Arnold Palmer, one of the greatest golfers ever was once confronted by a news reporter who claimed that he was a lucky golfer. Mr. Palmer admitted that indeed he was a lucky golfer and that the more he trained and practiced, the luckier he became.

complete a subsequent aspect. For example, a distraction device may be employed during a hostage rescue operation and followed at a designated time by an entry from a different location.

Finally, just as an athletic team becomes more efficient and proficient as it repeatedly runs a play during a practice session before a game, a counter-terrorist or SWAT team removes superfluous movements with a rehearsal. Excessive movements, both individual and collective, can easily alert the criminal or terrorist suspect to the approach of rescue forces and thereby jeopardize the safety of any hostages and compromise the completion of the mission.

In most instances law enforcement and other public safety personnel around the world are in a continuous response mode as they respond to calls for service. When not reacting directly to public demand they are expected to be visible as deterrents, present for immediate apprehension of offenders, and available as witnesses in court for any work already completed. Most of the moments spent in practice, preparation, or conditioning are done on the officer's off-duty time. Often at the expense of the time normally allocated to family activities in most households. Usually claiming a lack of financial resources, most public safety agencies rarely provide the opportunity, supervision, facilities, or the release-time to be excused from duty for skill maintenance once an officer receives initial training. Advanced individual training, even for specialized assignments such as a tactical unit or hostage negotiations unit, is frequently limited to the "on the job" format. This form of instructional delivery may be cost-effective, but it is limited in its ability to establish and achieve specific learning objectives, to provide constructive criticism, and to provide the documentation suggested by *Langford v. Gates* [8].

A further managerial training dilemma stems from the common perspective that responses to terrorist incidents are exclusively within the duties and jurisdiction of highly specialized and often elite national and provincial (state) counter-terrorist units. This perspective, which is fostered by the news and entertainment media and held by the public, may be valid in terms of the final resolution to a given situation. However, it is the action taken by the first responders that become the greatest single factor contributing to a successful outcome. These responding officers are often untrained, unequipped, and unprepared for this task. Regardless of the nature of any large-scale incident, the common thread is the composition of the initial responders; i.e. they are usually local public safety personnel, (police officers, fire fighters and EMS technicians) who have neither trained nor operated as a coordinated and cohesive unit and who must deal with the crisis at hand without depleting from the ability to provide a normal response to the public for routine calls for service.

2.3. Observation 3:

Any response to an act of terrorism must be conducted in accordance with the legislation and litigation of the established criminal justice system. The American criminal justice system has endured for over two hundred years. Whether the issue addresses the substance of a criminal proceeding or the process of civil litigation, the system has been successful, though not always perfect, because it outlasts and supercedes the mortals who raise the legal questions. It is always successful because the principles decided on one case can be applied to the conditions, of several other factual scenarios. The following case-studies provide a glimpse into some of the legal issues that must be addressed by a responding law enforcement agency long before the terrorist even begins to conceptualize a plan of action. While none of these cases are fact-specific, in a terrorist scenario, the ramifications of each are obvious.

The case of *Downs v. United States* [9] provides the initial backdrop for a discussion of some of the organizational issues related to the field of critical incident management. In 1971 two criminals hijacked a charter aircraft and held the crew of two persons as hostages. The wife of one of the perpetrators was also forcibly abducted and placed on the aircraft. The hijackers directed the crew to fly from Nashville, Tennessee to the Jacksonville, Florida International Airport. The criminals notified the personnel from the Jacksonville control tower to provide fuel and charts for a flight to Cuba where the hijackers presumably sought to seek asylum. The Special Agent in Charge of the Jacksonville office of the Federal Bureau of Investigation hurriedly assembled a response team to deal the incident. Despite the gravity of this type of situation, few members of the hostage rescue unit had received specific hostage rescue training. Nor were the responders equipped with any sort of tactical equipment (automatic weapons, ballistic shielding, fire-retardant uniforms, etc.).

The stolen aircraft landed at approximately 5:00 a.m. and a brief attempt to negotiate was made when one of the perpetrators and the co-pilot exited the aircraft. However, the tactical conditions quickly degenerated for the law enforcement agents and a shoot-out ensued. In the course of the incident the perpetrator and his wife as well as the remaining crew member were killed. Consequently the family of the dead pilot, Brenton Q. Downs, filed suit against the FBI for wrongful death. Although the civil action was ultimately dismissed on procedural and jurisdictional grounds, the court took judicial notice that special events require special responses by law enforcement. Although the incident may not fall within the guidelines and operational definition of being a terrorist act, the implication is clear that the law enforcement agency should be organized with its personnel trained to deal with critical incidents. While not necessarily legally binding, the case forced police administrators to re-evaluate their policies and procedures and to develop effective means to respond without depleting the ability to respond to the routine calls for police service.

The case of *City of Winter Haven v. Allen* [10] was even more explicit about the organization of a response to a critical incident. In this incident a county narcotics investigation resulted in a search and arrest warrant. Two officers from the Winter Haven Police Department were summoned to assist in the service of the warrant. Because the personnel had not trained, practiced and worked together, a series of mishaps led to the death of one of the county deputies. When his family sued the police department for wrongful death, the court ruled that any critical incident met with an *ad hoc* (makeshift or temporary) response is inappropriate. This ruling reinforces the judicial notice taken in the *Downs* case that special situations mandate special responses. Although the case does not necessarily order the creation of police counter-terrorist units, the implication is obvious that a provisional response is ineffective and unsuitable for the circumstances.

Once the decision to establish a counter-terrorist unit, or any other specialized police unit, has been made, the issue of personnel selection arises. Although the case of *Moon v. Winfield* [11] addressed the specific areas of recruiting and position assignment, it continues to have relevance to other areas of public personnel management. In this particular case the chief of police ignored the advice of his own recruiting investigators who stated that an applicant for police service was unfit for employment and that some of the applicant's comments could easily be construed as an unwarranted bias against members of minority groups. For reasons that were not fully explained during the subsequent court proceedings, the chief directed that the applicant be hired and trained. Subsequent to his training period, he was assigned to an area inhabited primarily by a population of minority group members.

After a series of complaints against the officer alleging an excessive and unwarranted use of force, a civil action was filed. The court ruled that the chief had been negligent in ignoring the recruit investigator's warnings and found the chief to be guilty of negligence in the selection of the applicant as fit for employment. The court also stated that the chief was guilty of negligence in assignment by placing the officer in an assignment where the officer's prejudices would be exercised most inappropriately.

In its application this ruling has been expanded and interpreted by many law enforcement agencies to say that it is the responsibility of the law enforcement agency to identify those who are unfit for duty and consequently to reject their applications for employment. It is further necessary for the agency to assign personnel in accordance with their demonstrable abilities and to refrain from placing individuals into specialized assignments for which they are not psychologically, intellectually, physically, or emotional suitable. This principle is particularly true in any specialized assignment, such as a counter-terrorist role where an employee does not function as an individual but as a member of a coordinated and cohesive unit.

Whether an individual has been selected for general employment as a police officer or for a specialized assignment as a counter-terrorist operative, it is essential for the organization to instruct the individual in the knowledge, skills, and abilities necessary to perform the job [12]. This particular case involved the assignment of police officers to a jail facility. After a prisoner became ill while in custody and received inadequate medical treatment, an investigation revealed that the officers had not been trained in symptom recognition and proper first aid procedures. Her family sued and the court held the city liable for negligence in training. This case has also been expanded to include many other specialized areas of assignment in law enforcement with the judicial admonition that it is legally required for the management of a police agency to ensure that its personnel receive adequate training in the knowledge bases, skills, and abilities that they are expected to possess in the normal performance of their duties. The importance of staying within the legal parameters of the criminal justice system is three-fold: (1) It provides guidelines for effective law enforcement; (2) It serves as prevention against civil liability; (3) To do otherwise would serve the interests of a terrorist group by allowing them to be given special status and the possibility of serving in a messianic fashion against an oppressive government.

3. Concluding Remarks

In many respects the response to terrorism is very similar to responding to any other life-threatening call for police service. In all cases the first few minutes of the response are the most important phase and dictate the next several hours of the response and its outcome. In addition, the social, political, moral, and practical environments of today's world require that the response fall within the existing legal structure. The law enforcement community has always been forced to deal with and learn from the ever-changing tactics, techniques, and technology of the criminal world. The counter-terrorist is now in a similar position where it is forced to learn not only from the tactics, techniques, and technology of terrorism, but also from the problems faced by the police responding to non-terrorist and supposedly routine calls for service.

Responding to acts of terrorism requires much more than intellectual resolve and lip-service to the issues. The response also requires commitment in terms of action to develop effective measures to prevent and counter terrorism. Until the present time this commitment has been less than total in terms of organizational direction to prepare the first responders and the financial and logistical support to train them.

Taking appropriate organizational management action on these observations can be enhanced by employing various currently available resources. For example, professional organizations such as the National Tactical Officers Association, the Texas Tactical Police Officers Association, the Texas Association of Hostage Negotiators, and several other national and state associations of police specialists provide research, training, organizational assessment, and technology evaluation not only for their members but also for any other legitimate full-time police agencies. These associations conduct annual conferences where the most recent research findings are disseminated to the membership. They also conduct classes on demand for the members. They publish quarterly journals for those who are unable to attend their conferences and where vendors may advertise and sell equipment relevant to the mission of these police specialists. Most importantly, these associations provide a networking system whereby information can be exchanged on an informal basis regarding recent case histories, common criminal foes, successes to follow and pitfalls to avoid.

A second method is through the transfer of already existing technology. For example, the communications system developed for space travel is the basis for portable police radios. Battle dress utility uniforms designed for combat soldiers have been modified with newly developed weather resistant and fire-retardant fabrics for use in drug raids where extremely volatile and caustic chemicals area constant hazard. Kevlar™ with its pound for pound strength exceeding that of steel was originally developed as a construction material. Through a series of series of extrusions, cross-weaves, and laminates Richard Davis transferred the technology into ballistic-resistant protective devices for police officers and military personnel. The transfer of technology is limited only by the human capacity for imagination and creativity.

Finally, counter-terrorist units can improve their capabilities by establishing partnerships. In addition to the expected intergovernmental mutual assistance pacts allowed by state laws [13], some partnerships involve collaborators not usually expected with the law enforcement establishment but whose participation is the result of mutual interests. For example, the Advanced Law Enforcement Rapid Response Training Center (A.L.E.R.R.T.) was established as a partnership among the Texas Tactical Police Officers Association, Hays County Sheriff's Office, and Texas State University. This partnership was funded through an appropriation from the United States Senate to conduct research and provide training specifically for the phenomenon of active shooters. The operation has been expanded to include several corporations who have developed various forms of technology that is transferable and applicable to the needs of national defense and criminal justice.

Appendices: Contact information for cited training sources

A.L.E.R.R.T.: Texas State University, San Marcos, TX   78666, 512/245-1744, http://www.alerrt.com

National Tactical Officers Association, P.O. Box 797, Doylestown, PA　18901, 800/279-9127, http://www.ntoa.org
Texas Association of Hostage Negotiators: P.O. Box 175321, Arlington, TX　76003, 817/419-7414, http://www.tahn.org
Texas Tactical Police Officers Association: P.O. Box 1819, Abilene, TX　79604-1819, http://www.ttpoa.org

References

[1]　F.J. Hacker, Crusaders, criminals, and crazies: Terror and terrorism in our time, New York: Norton; 1976.

[2]　T.M. Mijares, R.M. McCarthy, D.B. Perkins, *The management of police specialized tactical units,* Springfield, IL: Charles C. Thomas; 2000.

[3]　B. Smith, K. Damphouse, Two decades of terror: Characteristics, trends, and prospects for the future of terrorism in America, In H. Kushner, Editor. *The Future of terrorism: Violence in the new Millennium,* Thousand Oaks, CA: Sage Publications; 1998.

[4]　M.J. McMains, W.C. Mullins, Crisis negotiations: Managing critical incidents and hostage situations in law enforcement and corrections, (Third Edition). Cincinnati, OH: Anderson Publishing; 2006.

[5]　W.J. Bopp, D.O. Schultz, *A short history of American law enforcement,* Springfield, IL: Charles, C. Thomas; 1972.

[6]　S.F. Tomajczyk, *US elite counter-terrorist forces,* Osceola, WI: MBI Publishing; 1997.

[7]　T.C. Mijares, Beyond Canton versus Harris: Further mandates for continued crisis negotiations training, *Journal of Police Crisis Negotiations,* 6/2 (2006).

[8]　*Langford v. Gates,* 610 F.Supp 120 (D.C. Cal. 1985) and 279 P2d. 822 (Cal. 1987).

[9]　*Downs v. United States,* 522　F.2d 990 (6th Cir. 1975).

[10]　*City of Winter Haven v. Allen,* 541 So.2d 128 (Fla. App. Dist. 1991) and 689 So. 2d 968 (Fla. App. Dist. 1991).

[11]　*Moon V. Winfield* 383 F.Supp. 31 (1974).

[12]　*City of Canton v. Harris,* 489 U.S. 109 S. Ct. 1197 (1989)

[13]　D. Perkins, T. Mijares, Police liability issues associated with interagency mutual assistance pacts, *Police Liability Review,* 8/1 (1996).

Part IV

Counter Terrorism Policies: Lessons for the Future

Understanding and Responding to the Terrorism Phenomenon
O. Nikbay and S. Hancerli (Eds.)
IOS Press, 2007

Situational Crime Prevention and the Control of Terrorism

Ronald V. CLARKE[a] and Graeme R. NEWMAN[b]

[a]*Rutgers, The State University of New Jersey, USA*
[b]*The University at Albany, USA*

Abstract. There is no fundamental difference between crime and terrorism and situational crime prevention – the science of reducing opportunities for crime – has many lessons for preventing terrorism. In particular, the rationality of terrorist decision making must be recognized and the opportunity structures for each different form of attack must be separately analyzed. This will assist in protecting the most vulnerable targets, controlling the tools and weapons used in each form of attack, and eliminating some of the "facilitating conditions" that make the attacks possible. Failing to eliminate the easiest and most rewarding opportunities for terrorism could invite further attacks.

Keywords. Situational crime prevention; opportunity structure; rational choice; displacement; aircraft hijacking.

Introduction

Situational prevention seeks to reduce the opportunities, temptations and provocations to offend by altering the immediate environment in which offending occurs. The approach is heavily influenced by routine activity and rational choice theories and was developed more than 30 years ago at the British Home Office. Some 150 documented successes of situational prevention have now accumulated showing often dramatic reductions in specific forms of crime. At first, the crimes addressed were ordinary "street" crimes of car theft, vandalism, burglary and robbery. More recently situational prevention has proved effective in dealing with a wide variety of frauds and assaults and has even reduced problems of drive-by shootings. Other applications include the prevention of child sexual abuse, internet crime and specific forms of suicide [1]. This paper draws out the main lessons of situational crime prevention and considers their relevance for the prevention of terrorism. By this we mean reducing opportunities to commit acts of terrorism by protecting vulnerable targets, by controlling the tools and weapons used by terrorists and by altering some of the "facilitating conditions" for terrorist acts, such as the ability to transfer money and purchase weapons around the globe. We do not deal with other forms of prevention such as "taking out" terrorists (or suspected terrorists) or social programs to win the "hearts and minds" of populations supportive of terrorism. Nor do we discuss diplomatic or military "solutions" to the problem.

Before proceeding, we should deal with the objection that crime and terrorism are so different that the lessons of preventing crime can have little relevance to preventing terrorism. Is it not true that terrorists are better organized, more determined and more ruthless than ordinary criminals? Are they not also motivated by a "higher cause" than most criminals who are usually seeking to benefit only themselves? Finally, is it not the case that acts of terrorism are better planned and larger scale than most acts of crime? Even if these points were, the differences are merely ones of degree. Many of the acts of "organized crime" are also well planned, large scale and ruthless and many terrorist operatives are as much motivated by commonplace ambitions (e.g. gaining respect, earning a living and enjoying a life of excitement) as by the political ideals of their leaders. In any case, crime has very varied motives. Much of it is driven by greed, but other motives drive rape, homicide, vandalism and assaults to name but a few examples. In fact, the most basic motivator of crime – to achieve a benefit – is also shared by terrorism. For all these reasons, we reject a hard and fast division between crime and terrorism and prefer to regard the latter as "crime with a political motive."

We should also explain why we think that situational prevention can be effective against terrorism. Briefly, the reason is that there are already examples of its effectiveness, including that (1) the "ring of steel" consisting of fences and barriers substantially reduced IRA bombings in Belfast city center, (2) the US embassy protections introduced in the 1980s have greatly reduced embassy takeovers, and (3) the Israelis are reducing suicide bombings through intelligence work and physical protections [2]. The best documented example, however, concerns airliner hijackings, which had skyrocketed at the end of the 1960s, particularly between the US and Cuba. These were almost entirely eliminated by two situational controls, both introduced in 1973: the first was the screening of all embarking airline passengers and their luggage, and the second was the agreement reached between Cuba and the US that hijackers would no longer be treated as political refugees and heroes, but would be arrested and treated as criminals.

Table 1 shows the dramatic effect of these measures. In the five years (1968-72) before the introduction of the measures, there were 135 hijackings of U.S. airliners; in the five years after the measures were introduced, from 1973 to 1977, there were 28 hijackings of U.S airliners, a reduction of nearly 80%. Of the 135 airliners hijacked in the five years before the measures, 92 were destined to reach Cuba; in the five years after the measures only three of the 28 hijackings were destined for Cuba.

Table 1. Airliner Hijackings[1] and Sabotage Bombings[2] (Attempts and Completed), 1961-2005

Period	Number of years	Mean hijackings per year		Mean sabotage bombings per year
		U.S.	Foreign	Worldwide
1961-1967	7	1.6	3.0	1.0
1968	1	20.0	15.0	1.0
1969-1970	2	30.5	58.0	4.5
1971-1972	2	27.0	33.0	4.5
1973-1985	13	9.4	22.7	2.2
1986-1989	4	2.8	9.0	2.0
1990-2000	11	0.3	18.5	0.3
2001-2003	3	1.3	5.7	0.0
1961-2003	43	6.7	17.9	1.6

[1] Source: Dugan, LaFree and Piquero [3]. (We are indebted to the authors for supplying the data used in their article)
[2] Source: (1) The President's Commission on Aviation Security and Terrorism (1990) Report to the President, May 15, 1990; (2) U.S. Federal Aviation Administration. (1994-1996); (3) U.S. Federal Aviation Administration (1996-1999); (4) U.S. Department of State (2005).

Table 1 also shows that, despite the huge growth in air travel, the number of hijackings has been greatly reduced worldwide since the early 1970s. It shows, further, that hijackings were not displaced to other countries that were slower to introduce security than the US; and that there was no substantial displacement to bombings of airliners. It is true that the 9/11 hijackers found ways round the security that had been put into place but that is another story, to which we return below. At this point, we simply wish to note that situational measures introduced to increase the risks of hijacking (baggage and passenger screening) and to reduce its rewards (the Cuba-US pact) were highly successful for many years in combating terrorism.

With this background, we proceed in the remainder of this paper to draw out some of the lessons of situational crime prevention with the greatest relevance for terrorism prevention. We begin with the fundamental assumption of situational prevention, already alluded to above, that criminals are mostly rational.

1. Terrorists are Rational

Because their acts can be so callous and cruel, it is tempting to dismiss terrorists as "animals", as bestial or as "inhuman fanatics". In other cases, we might endow them with superhuman powers of cunning and determination. Excusable as this may be, it is a mistake to characterize terrorists in either of these ways because it places them beyond the pale of ordinary human understanding. If we are to defeat them, it is much more helpful to see them as they really are: ordinary individuals who for political reasons have decided that it is legitimate to destroy their enemies. This is not much different from soldiers at war – and of course terrorists regard themselves as being engaged in a war. If we see them as ordinary human beings, albeit with motives and rationalizations that are twisted and hateful, we are halfway to understanding them and therefore to defeating them. There are several corollaries of this position. First, we should not expend too much effort in understanding *why* terrorists harbor their hatreds and ambitions since it is unlikely we could do much to change these. Second, we should focus our research on understanding *how* they select the kinds of terrorist acts they choose to commit and *how* they go about planning and executing them. A detailed understanding of such matters usually brings a wealth of preventive insights. Acquiring this understanding involves a step-by-step analysis of each stage of the act, from conception through the various stages of its planning and execution to escape and the subsequent management of the related publicity. Third, we will be greatly aided in this process if we consistently and systematically try to "think terrorist", that is to say, put ourselves in their shoes and attempt to mimic their decision making.

2. Opportunity is Critical

If terrorists are rational, is it not strange to suggest that opportunity is key? Surely a rational actor optimizes his or her chances of success by making careful choices about how, when and where to act? This is true, but every human action is heavily determined by situational circumstances, even homicide and suicide, two acts that would seem to owe little to opportunity. Thus, the fact that the US homicide rate is six times greater than that of the UK, even though the UK has higher rates of many other crimes, is explained by the much wider availability of guns, particularly handguns, in the US. The 35% decline in the number of suicides in England and Wales in the 1970s was the result of the removal of carbon monoxide from the domestic gas supply. About 50% of the people who killed themselves in England and Wales before detoxification used domestic gas. By the end of the 1970s hardly anyone died by this method and there seems to have been limited displacement to other methods when domestic gas was no longer available for suicide [4].

If homicide and suicide are so heavily dependent on opportunity, there is no reason to doubt that terrorism is similarly dependent. This fact has important implications. It means that we must carefully study the opportunities provided by environment and the social and technological arrangements of society to see if we can find ways of blocking or removing the opportunities. And because each kind of terrorism – aircraft hijackings, suicide bombings, truck bombings, assassinations, hostage takings, etc – is made possible by a different constellation of opportunities, we must do this systematically and carefully for each of these different forms. Thus, it would serve little purpose to understand the details of the baggage and passenger screening used to prevent aircraft hijackings if the intention is to prevent truck bombings of police stations or government buildings. Indeed, even closely similar forms of terrorism, say suicide bombings in Israel and those on the London Underground, depend on opportunity structures that differ in key respects. Unlike the situation in Israel, the suicide attacks on the London Underground have not become routine and might not do so because the conditions for routine terrorism in London do not exist. There are no "occupied" adjacent ethnic/nationalist territories; there is little support for terrorism in immigrant communities; and there is no evidence of a sustained supply line of effective explosives or willing suicides for terrorist attacks [2].

3. Targets are not Randomly Selected

Thieves are very picky about what they steal and studies have shown that they strongly prefer a small range of goods, such as cash, jewelry, small electronic items, liquor and tobacco. These items are CRAVED by thieves because they are Concealable, Removable, Available, Valuable, Enjoyable and Disposable [5]. We can expect terrorists to be even more careful in the targets they select because so much more is at stake. When a small plane slammed into a Manhattan apartment block in October 2006, that was a random accident. When the 9/11 hijackers rammed their planes into the World Trade Center, that was a carefully calculated choice designed to maximize the impact of their attack. The WTC was in the headquarters of capitalism and it was an icon of America.

While it is theoretically possible that terrorists might strike anywhere at any time, this is extremely unlikely and if taken seriously could lead us to squander resources protecting targets that are in no real danger of attack. The Department of Homeland Security seems to have made this mistake in assembling the National Asset Database which in 2006 listed 77,069 critical sites. These were nominated by each state and included many bizarre listings such as Old Macdonald's Petting Zoo, the Mule Day Parade, the Mall at Sears, and Nix's Cash Checking. Indiana's list contained 50% more sites than New York State's, swelled by listings such as "Amish Country Popcorn". When questioned by reporters about its inclusion, the owner of this 5-employee business seemed as puzzled as everybody else and said "Only Amish buggies and tractors here…Maybe because popcorn explodes?" (*New York Times*, July 12, 2006).

Clearly, a more valid method is needed for determining critical sites and this should be an urgent topic for research. We offer as a starting point for such research the acronym EVIL DONE (the outcome of attempting to "think terrorist") to summarize the target attributes that terrorists are likely to seek [2]. The elements of the acronym are as follows:

- *Exposed*. A target might stick out on a city sky line, for example, the Twin Towers, or the Statue of Liberty, or it might stand out in some way – the only multi-storey building in a small town (perhaps a federal government building); or a large shopping complex; or a nuclear power plant surrounded by suburbs.
- *Vital*. Water supply, electricity, food supply chains, transportation systems are all vital to any town, small or large. If terrorists determine that their destruction will wreak havoc they may choose these targets.
- *Iconic*. Targets that have high symbolic value for a perceived enemy may attract terrorists. The Statue of Liberty for example, is a true icon of New York City, and the US in general. In contrast, Timothy McVeigh chose to bomb the Federal Building in Oklahoma City in 1995, because it stood for the federal government which he abhorred. Such a building is not quite iconic as is the Statue of Liberty, but it does stand for something abstract and important, the Federal Government.
- *Legitimate*. Terrorists debate among themselves concerning which target to hit, and an important factor in this decision is how the attack will be viewed by their sympathizers or would-be sympathizers. If the attack is viewed as illegitimate, such as for example the killing of Lord Mountbatten in 1979 by the IRA, the terrorist group may lose considerable public support. Hamas in Palestine has conducted frequent public opinion polls to find out whether or not their targets were seen as legitimate by their supporters.
- *Destructible*. For a terrorist attack to succeed, it must destroy its target. A target that is "indestructible" may therefore not be chosen. The Twin Towers were considered as such, until Al Qaeda devised a way to destroy them in its second attack.
- *Occupied*. With few exceptions, terrorists seek to kill as many people as possible, because it is this that frightens their enemies most.
- *Near*. Terrorists prefer to attack targets that are close to their home base of operations because the logistics are easier. Indeed, getting to the target is one of the major challenges for terrorists.
- *Easy*. How easy is it to access the target? For McVeigh, it was too easy: he was able to park the truck bomb just eight feet from the federal building. How easy was it for Al Qaeda to get at the World Trade Center? For the first attack in 1993, it was relatively easy since there was poor parking security in the parking garage. But for the second attack on 9/11, it was truly complicated and difficult, involving the training of pilots to fly commercial airliners into the towers.

In a simulated exercise, Table 2 applies EVIL DONE to some landmarks in Washington D.C., viewed from the perspective of foreign terrorists planning an attack by truck bomb or by plane. It would be easy to argue with the ratings in the table and we do not claim that all terrorist groups would share the same priorities. The purpose of the table is to show that in principle it would not be difficult to develop a catalog of targets within each major city, and to get them ranked by experts according to EVIL DONE criteria. It would be necessary to develop objective rating scales for each of the EVIL DONE criteria, just as similar rating scales have been developed in other fields in assessing the security levels of parking lots, or the criminogenic attributes of products. The ratings must also be made separately for different forms of attack, not just truck and airliner attacks, but also the kind of coordinated bomb attacks as occurred on public transport in London and Madrid. Then the next step would be to examine the kinds of targets within each city highly rated as vulnerable (e.g. train stations) to determine the kinds of protection that may be needed. In doing so it might be necessary to repeat EVIL DONE simply for that class of targets.

Table 2. Target Attractiveness Scale for a 9/11-Style Attack, Washington, D.C.
(1=Low attractiveness; 5=High attractiveness)

Target Characteristic	White House	Congress	Pentagon	Washing. Monument	Union Station	Washing. Cathedral	Old Post Office	Georgetown University	Washing. Zoo
Exposed	4	5	5	5	3	4	0	2	1
Vital	3	3	4	0	4	0	0	1	0
Iconic	5	5	5	2	0	1	0	0	0
Legitimate	5	5	5	5	3	1	2	1	0
Destructible	4	3	2	4	4	4	4	1	1
Occupied	4	4	3	2	4	1	2	3	3
Near	1	1	1	1	1	1	1	1	1
Easy	2	3	3	2	5	5	4	4	4
TOTAL SCORE	32	29	28	26	24	17	13	13	10

4. Proximity Simplifies Terrorism

In Table 2, "near" played no role in the choice because it was assumed that the attackers would be overseas terrorists and therefore each landmark would be equally far from their base of operations. In fact, "near" is of vital importance in understanding terrorism, just as it has been found to be in explaining crime. Study upon study has shown that offenders typically travel very short distances to commit their crimes and often prey upon their own neighborhoods and communities. Similarly, if the terrorists live cheek-by-jowl with those whom they hate, their task of mounting attacks is greatly simplified. The logistics of undertaking attacks are much easier and the scope for escape is also much greater as the terrorists can melt away into the surrounding community. The example of the IRA makes the point: from 1970-94 the IRA mounted tens of thousands of attacks in Northern Ireland, but only a handful in England [6][3].

---

[3] A more systematic demonstration of the importance of proximity is found in Townsley et al.'s (In Press) analysis of insurgent incidents in Iraq [6]. On the basis of the least effort principle [7] they hypothesized that attacks would need to occur near enough to each other to minimise the effort expended by operatives in travelling to new locations, but not so close as to make the risk of capture more than trivial. Their analysis of attacks confirmed this pattern.

In our book, *Outsmarting the Terrorists* [2], we devote three chapters to analyzing the importance of proximity and here we can only summarize the three main conclusions. First, routine terrorism, with repeated attacks, is only possible when the terrorists and those attacked live in close proximity. Foreign terrorists are only able to mount one-off attacks: this means that they will strive to make these attacks of shocking dimensions. Second, countries such as the US, without a significant domestic terrorism problem, expose themselves to the greatest risks of attack when they place themselves in close proximity to the terrorists – as in the case of US soldiers in Iraq. Third, it is vital not to confuse national policies for preventing near and far attacks since the nature and frequency of these two kinds of attack differ so greatly.

5. Tools Play a Vital Role

The burglar and the safe-cracker need the tools of their trade, the robber and hit-man need guns or other weapons, and the child pornographer needs a digital camera, Internet access and the ability to accept credit card payments. The terrorist is also dependent on tools and weapons to make his attacks, which will vary with the nature of the attacks he plans to undertake. For many of the commonest attacks, such as car or truck bombings, drive-by shootings and targeted assassinations, the terrorists are likely to need all or some of the following: cell phones or other means of communication; cars or trucks to transport themselves and weapons; cash or (false) credit cards; false documents – for example, drivers' licenses, passports or visas, and vehicle registration documents; and, finally, maps, plans, addresses, photographs and other information about the target. Many of these objects are so commonplace and widely available in everyday life that it can be difficult to see how to control their use by terrorists. In fact, there are three general approaches to tightening up controls on tools: (1) we can modify them so as to make them more difficult to convert to terrorist use; (2) we can tighten up their supply or reduce their accessibility to terrorists; and (3) we can track their distribution so we know who has acquired them.

Once again, situational crime prevention can assist in exploring these options through experience gained in "designing out crime from products" [1]. We have already mentioned the many modifications made over the years to prevent cars from being stolen from their owners. But there are many more examples of industry and business modifying products to protect not the public, but themselves from fraudsters, video pirates, hackers, vandals, counterfeiters and thieves. Similarly, governments are continually improving banknotes, passports and other documents to prevent counterfeiting. In fact, many of these measures serve the dual benefit of preventing both crime and terrorism. Improvements made to credit card authentication and delivery [9] and to cell phone subscriber authentication [10] substantially reduced fraud, but would also have made life more difficult for terrorists seeking to use these objects illegally. Indeed, the hook of dual benefits could be vital in enlisting the support of business and industry to change their products in the interests of defeating terrorism.

6. Weapons Must Be Suitable

Many in the West live in dread that terrorists might attack with biological, chemical or nuclear weapons, i.e. weapons of mass destruction (WMD). To date there have been very few attempts by terrorists to use such weapons for reasons that are not entirely clear, though these probably include the facts that they are difficult to obtain or manufacture, they require specialist knowledge, and are hazardous and unpredictable in their use. Nor does every terrorist group want to wreak destruction on such a wide scale. Thus, it suits the purposes of some groups to undertake small but carefully targeted attacks, while other groups may prefer to extort concessions through hostage takings or occupying embassies and other official buildings.

In fact, there has been little use of unconventional weapons that are relatively easy to obtain, such as ground-to-air missiles to bring down airliners or relatively easy to deploy such as "suitcase bombs", small devices that disperse radiological material by means of a conventional explosive [2]. This could be because terrorists, like criminals, prefer to stick with what they know and what they can readily obtain, i.e., guns and explosives, which have been used in the vast majority of terrorist attacks. But there are many subtle differences among different kinds of guns and different kinds of explosives that make them more or less suitable use for terrorist use. It is important to learn more about the features of weapons that make them attractive to terrorists if we are to target our efforts to control weapons. To assist this process we offer an acronym – MURDEROUS – once again resulting from our attempt to "think terrorist". The components of MURDEROUS are Multipurpose, Undetectable, Removable, Destructive, Enjoyable, Reliable, Obtainable, Uncomplicated and Safe and we explain them further below:

Multi-purpose. Some weapons have a specific use, such as a high powered rifle, while explosives have a much wider application from assassinations to conflagrations, but they cannot be reused, so their supply must be replenished. However, bullets must also be replaced, and there are ways to achieve the destructive effects of explosives, by using dum-dum bullets and such weapons as rocket propelled grenades.

Undetectable. Because of the security procedures in place in many parts of the world, especially at airports, the weapons of choice often have to be concealable or undetectable. This helps explain the popularity of Semtex among terrorists, which is small, lightweight and largely undetectable. It took only 11 ounces of Semtex packed in an 11 inch Toshiba tape recorder to bring down Pan Am 103 over Lockerbie. Because it is relatively easily concealed, it serves as an ideal weapon for suicide bombers who must penetrate layers of security in order to reach their target.

Removable. The weapons of terrorism must be portable, which means that they must be relatively light and reasonably small so they can be carried by one or two people, or at least lifted onto the back of a pick-up truck. Their portability and size also makes them very "stealable", because we know from studies of "hot products" that portable, high value objects are often targeted by thieves. Thus, when high quality stereo equipment was very expensive it was a favourite target of burglars for many years. Of course, the value they saw in these products was in their disposal for cash. To a terrorist, the value he sees in the weapon is in its utility for his terrorist mission.

Destructive. Guns may be a more efficient way to kill targeted individuals, but the weapon of choice by many terrorist groups is an explosive device that wreaks as much damage as possible. The insurgents in Iraq have killed many American soldiers using improvised explosive devices (IEDs).

Enjoyable. Terrorists are clearly attracted to their weapons, seeming to get much excitement and pleasure out of their use. In fact, it is not just terrorists who enjoy weapons. Many ordinary people do too.

Reliable. A weapon must be highly reliable, which is the reason why new military recruits require thorough training in caring for the weapons that they might have to depend on in extremely dangerous situations. Users of a weapon find out whether or not it is reliable by gaining familiarity with it. If they have used the weapon, or one like it, many times before, they are likely to favour that weapon over another. This means that unconventional weapons, of unknown reliability, will be shunned unless the mission cannot be accomplished in any other way. It is also very likely that in situations of routine terrorism, unconventional weapons or weapons with which the terrorists have little experience will be rejected in favour of those that are routinely used.

Obtainable. This is, perhaps the most important of all characteristics. How easy is it to get the weapon? Can it be bought easily? Can it be stolen easily? Or can it even be manufactured in-house? The world is awash in small arms, which are the most widely used weapons of terrorists. And because there are so many of them, there are plenty of places from which to steal them – probably the most common way in which terrorists obtain their weapons.

Uncomplicated. A weapon's user-friendliness determines how much training is needed for terrorists to operate it successfully. Even seemingly simple weapons such as a handgun require practice and training to use properly. A complicated weapon or one that demands considerable skill to use effectively, such as a free-flight armor-piercing missile, will rarely be used. In fact when these have been used by terrorist groups, they have often proved unsuccessful because of incorrect use. The attempt to bring down an El Al airliner by the Black September movement missed and brought down a Yugoslav airlines plane instead, because of improper use of the RPG-7 grenade launcher. There are other examples [11, 12].

Safe. The use of bombs as weapons is inherently more dangerous than the use of other weapons. It is claimed that during the period 1969-93 one third of PIRA members were blown up by explosives that detonated prematurely [13].

While this list of attributes might be modified by empirical research, such research is unlikely to overturn the principle that terrorists favor weapons with specific characteristics that are closely suited to the kind of attacks they want to make. Understanding the nature of these characteristics should help us find ways of controlling the weapons they favor.

7. There are Five Principal Ways to Reduce Terrorist Opportunities

Research in situational crime prevention has revealed five effective ways to reduce or prevent crime by focusing on making it harder for the offender to carry out his crime [14]. These are:

1. Increase the effort of offending
2. Increase the risks of offending
3. Reduce the rewards of offending
4. Reduce provocations to offend

5.   Remove excuses for offending

These are equally applicable to terrorist offending.

- *Increase the effort for terrorists.* The more difficult we can make it for terrorists to reach their targets, obtain their weapons, use their tools, exploit facilitating conditions and maintain their organization, the more effort they must make to succeed. If we can raise the level of effort high enough for some of their tasks, we may see them either give up on a particular target, or take much longer to execute their terrorist missions. Thus, barriers, walls, tough ID authentication, and extensive ID requirements for opening bank accounts in immigrant communities, all raise the difficulties for terrorists.
- *Increase the risks for terrorists.* By far the most important group of techniques to increase risk for the terrorists are the new tracking technologies that become cheaper and more effective every year. The miniaturization and mass production of RFID (remote frequency ID) chips coupled with GIS technology now makes it possible to track just about anything with considerable accuracy, from products and parcels, to pets, cattle and humans [15]. Thus, the tracking of electronic products that terrorists use as tools shows considerable promise for prevention. In the case of attacks from afar, it is clear that, apart from increasing the effort through tightened border controls, tracking technologies and systems are needed for individuals once they get through the border. Smart cards, national ID cards and other means of ID verification and authentication are just a few of the possibilities. Tightening up procedures for issuing documents such as drivers' licenses, health cards, birth/death certificates increases the effort needed to obtain a false ID, but also increases the risks of getting caught.
- *Reduce the rewards for terrorists.* The most effective and feasible way to reduce the rewards of terrorists is to implement as many protective measures as possible in order to make terrorist attacks unsuccessful. Not only can these techniques prevent attacks from happening but they can also mitigate their effects later, by using publicity that emphasizes the futility of the attacks and highlights their extremist, hypocritical nature [2]. Part of the reward for terrorists is the destruction of buildings and injury of people. Making buildings bombproof and indestructible, and designing public places to minimize injury from bombs therefore reduces those rewards. Immediate retaliation against successful attacks may also reduce rewards, though at least one study in Israel suggests that it may also provoke [16]. An attraction to would-be recruits to a terrorist group is the idealistic mythology that surrounds it. Highlighting incidents where terrorists either kill each other because of internal disagreements, or accidentally kill themselves such as occurs in bomb preparation may help demythologize the terrorist group, making it look less attractive.
- *Reduce the provocations for terrorists.* Convincing terrorists that the barriers to their success are considerable without at the same time provoking them into making greater efforts can be difficult. For example, touting the great advances in screening technology may also challenge some terrorists into proving that the technology can be overcome; or claiming a building to be indestructible may challenge terrorists to prove otherwise. In this sense, every

innovation we introduce to prevent terrorist attacks also invites the dedicated terrorist to overcome it. This is why we must constantly anticipate what they will do in response to our interventions. Nothing can be done, of course, about the greatest provocation of all to such terrorist groups as Al Qaeda – the very existence of the United States. The U.S. (whether government or corporate) is subject to many more attacks abroad than it is at home, for the simple reason that its facilities are much more exposed in foreign countries. However, efforts should be made to make overseas facilities and personnel blend more into the local surroundings.

- *Remove the excuses for terrorism.* Using violence in response to terrorist attacks is not only a provocation to terrorists to respond in kind, but also offers them an excuse for using violence as their central method of achieving success. "If the enemy does it, why can't we?" There is also the very strong enticement for the terrorists to provoke the enemy, when it is a government, into overreacting to their terrorist acts, resulting in deprivations of freedoms for ordinary people. This feeds the terrorists' underlying justification that the government's dependence on violence is far greater than their own. Similarly, the slightest heavy-handed treatment of terrorists in prison provides sufficient provocation and thus, in the terrorists' eyes, justification, for their violent behavior, and provides substance for powerful propaganda. Finally, refusing to talk or negotiate with terrorists also supports their basic justification for violence as a means to achieve change. We should note, however, that talking and negotiating with terrorists does not mean that one should give in to them, since that would increase their rewards. Rather, the aim of such talks should be to clearly differentiate legitimate complaints from terrorist means, offering non-terrorist alternatives to solving those complaints.

8. Displacement is not Inevitable

If we harden only the most vulnerable targets, won't the terrorists simply shift their attacks to the targets we have not hardened? In other words will not the sole result of target hardening be to displace attacks to as yet unprotected targets? We know from studies in situational crime prevention that displacement is not a foregone conclusion. It certainly does happen, but in a majority of cases it does not. Offenders who are put off by security procedures and installations mostly do not work hard to find other ways to commit their proposed crime [17, 14]. We have already noted that terrorists strongly prefer certain targets over others and that they are unlikely to invest enormous effort in attacking ones that do not produce the rewards they seek. We have also noted that the anti-hijacking measure introduced in 1973 in the US did not displace hijackings to other parts of the world. Nor was there any apparent displacement to sabotage of airliners by smuggling bombs on board.

We should not be too surprised by these facts. Most of those who hijacked planes to Cuba were Cuban nationals who had grown dissatisfied with their lives in the US or who hoped to gain political kudos in Cuba. They would have had very little interest in hijacking planes elsewhere. They are also unlikely to have been interested in sabotaging airliners instead. Sabotaging an airliner would not get them back to Cuba to a hero's welcome and it might not even have earned them much admiration. In any case, the deliberate murder of dozens of innocent passengers requires a much greater commitment to a political cause than the temporary hijacking and subsequent release of passengers.

Having said that, we must accept that, over time, the populations of terrorists (and criminals) do adjust their behavior according to the security interventions introduced. This is not so much displacement because it refers to a much longer process of change and does not involve the individuals whose actions led to the introduction of the interventions. We have seen this process in car theft. Steering column locks were shown to be very effective in reducing car theft in the 1970s in Europe and elsewhere. However, as thieves learned how to overcome these locks, new technologies were introduced such as special alarms, tracking devices and recently immobilizers that immobilize the car if it is started by anyone but the owner. It is likely that car thieves will turn to other ways to steal cars that get around these technologies, such as stealing the identities of cars, or targeting rental cars (i.e. renting them with false IDs). This lengthy process, a kind of arms race between them and us, is called adaptation. The fact that the 9/11 hijackers identified loopholes in the baggage and passenger screening methods in place, which permitted them to smuggle weapons on board is a clear example of adaptation and another is the plot uncovered in London in September 2006 to use liquid explosives on US bound airplanes. In the latter case, the terrorists figured out that despite the heightened security since 9/11 there was no ban on liquids that could be carried on board.

In response to this new threat, the authorities were forced to introduce new restrictions on carrying on liquids. As soon as a dangerous security loophole is discovered it must be closed. In a way, this renders the displacement criticism moot even if were supported by empirical evidence – which, as we have said, it is largely not.

9. Conclusion

We have argued that there is no fundamental difference between crime and terrorism and that situational crime prevention – the science of reducing opportunities for crime – has many lessons for the prevention of terrorism. In particular, it is important to recognize the rationality of the terrorists' decision making and to analyze separately the opportunity structures for each different form of attack. In each case, this will lead us to protect the most vulnerable targets, to control the tools and weapons used in each kind of attack, and to alter some of the "facilitating conditions" that make the attacks possible. To those who claim that our approach of reducing opportunities discounts the need to reduce the motivation for terrorism, we would respond that reducing motivation is extremely difficult and, if it can ever be achieved, could only have preventive benefits in the long term. On the other hand, leaving opportunities open for attack helps creates the motive for attack; indeed, we believe that it *invites* attack. If instead we work relentlessly as a society to close the easiest and most rewarding opportunities we can discourage terrorists from even thinking about attacking. Even if a small proportion of the most committed individuals continue to search for new loopholes, we can be confident that our actions will deter a much larger number of others looking for "quick wins" or easy routes to glory.

References

[1]   R.V. Clarke, G.R. Newman, editors, *Designing out crime from products and systems.* Crime Prevention Studies. Vol. 18. Monsey, NY: Criminal Justice Press; 2005.

[2]   R.V. Clarke, G.R. Newman, *Outsmarting the terrorists.* Oxford, UK: Praeger Security International; 2006.

[3]   L. Dugan, G. LaFree, A. Piquero, Testing a rational choice model of airline hijackings. *Criminology, 43/4* (2005), 1031-1066.

[4]   R.V. Clarke, P. Mayhew, The British gas suicide story and its criminological implications. In M. Tonry, N. Morris, editors, *Crime and justice: A review of research*, Vol. 10. Chicago: University of Chicago Press; 1988, p.79-116.

[5]   R.V. Clarke, *Hot products: Understanding, anticipating and reducing demand for stolen goods.* Police Research Series, Paper 112. London: Home Office; 1999. Available from: URL: www.homeoffice.gov.uk/prgpubs.htm

[6]   M. Townsley, S.D. Johnson, J.H. Ratcliffe, Space time dynamics of insurgent activity in Iraq. *Security Journal* (In Press).

[7]   G.K. Zipf, *Human behaviour and the principle of least effort: An introduction to human ecology*, Cambridge, MA: Addison-Wesley Press Inc; 1949.

[8]   Y. Alexander, editor, *Combating terrorism: Strategies of ten countries.* Ann Arbor, MI: University of Michigan Press; 2002.

[9]   M.L. Levi, J. Handley, *The prevention of plastic and cheque fraud revisited.* Home Office Research Study No 182. London: Home Office; 1998.

[10] R.V. Clarke, R. Kemper, L. Wyckoff, Controlling cell phone fraud in the US – lessons for the UK 'foresight' prevention initiative. *Security Journal* **14/1** (2001): 7-22.

[11] R. Clutterbuck, *Terrorism in an unstable world.* London; New York: Routledge; 1994.

[12] B.A. Jackson, Technology acquisition by terrorist groups. In J. Prados, editor. *America confronts terrorism*. Chicago: Ivan R. Dee; 2002, p. 216-243.

[13] C.J.S. Drake, *Terrorists' target selection.* New York: St. Martin's Press; 1998. [14] R.V. Clarke, Seven misconceptions of situational crime prevention. In N. Tilley, editor. *Handbook of crime prevention and community safety.* Cullompton, UK: Willan; 2005, chapter 3.

[15] G.R. Newman, R.V. Clarke, *Superhighway robbery: Preventing e-commerce crime.* Cullompton, UK: Willan; 2003.

[16] E.H. Kaplan, A. Mintz, M. Shaul, C. Samban, What happened to suicide bombings in Israel? Insights from a terror stock model. *Studies in Conflict and Terrorism*, **28/3** (2005), 225-235.

[17] R.B.P. Hesseling,. Displacement: A review of the empirical literature. In R.V. Clarke, editor, *Crime Prevention Studies*, Vol. 3. Monsey, NY: Criminal Justice Press; 1994, p.197-230.

Understanding and Responding to the Terrorism Phenomenon
O. Nikbay and S. Hancerli (Eds.)
IOS Press, 2007

Preventing Terrorist Attacks to Critical Infrastructure(s) by Use of Crime Prevention through Environmental Design (CPTED)

Morton GULAK[a,1,] Ulvi KUN[a], Zeki KODAY[b], Saliha KODAY[b]

[a]*Virginia Commonwealth University; US*
[b]*Ataturk University, Turkey*

Abstract. This paper mainly aims to answer "How can potential critical infrastructures be protected from possible terrorist attacks?" In this framework, probable answers may also provide bases to minimize the impact of similar future attacks. The proposition is simple but needs engagement to achieve the desired goals. Critical infrastructures should be built or reinforced considering crime prevention through environmental design (CPTED) strategies. This idea means to apply primary strategies of CPTED as the references. The use of CPTED concept is essential for any critical infrastructure because this application can become a primary base for supplementary security technologies. It is also proposed that complimentary security approaches, like Neighborhood Watch be implemented to strengthen the security subject and to advance needs.

Keywords. CPTED, crime prevention, critical infrastructure, neighborhood watch.

Introduction

The phrase, to be architecturally vulnerable, took vast attention when Timothy Mc Viegh, who was charged with blowing up the Oklahoma City Courthouse, explained his opinions in an interview after his capture. He briefly stated that the courthouse was picked because 'it was more architecturally vulnerable" [1]. A Pennsylvania Terrorism Awareness and Prevention (TAP) presentation indicates that terrorists also have some weaknesses while pursuing their goals. Spending time in the area they plan to attack is needed for logistical support and needed for gathering information to identify their targets being one of them. This indicates that terrorists may have encounters with unrelated people or may somewhat expose themselves to surveillance during these susceptible times.

The 9/11 Commission report is one of the most comprehensive documents addressing the current terrorism problem from the U.S. point of view. There are three main parts in the final commission report, including 9 main titles and 41 subtitles, each section having been awarded with a grade at F scale [2]. The first main part in this report is "Emergency

---

[1] Gulak, and Kun presented the study at NATO workshop in Washington, DC in 2006.

Preparedness and Response" and there are five subtitles in the section. Critical infrastructure is the core element of three out of five of these titles. This intensive focus is one of the clearest indicators of how important it is to take necessary steps to secure critical infrastructure in a timely manner for the future potential terrorist considerations [2].

Each infrastructure is unique and has distinctive features which require painstaking care to be followed for a desired secure position. This study proposes that CPTED strategies may be very effective for critical infrastructure protection if required steps are taken; nevertheless, they may not be as useful for all type of terrorist attacks. Atlas[2], an expert in security, advises that "Architects and security professionals should avoid worry over events that they have no control over". Instead, they are supposed to concentrate on rationally manipulating what they have. He also addresses the idea that focused areas should be "good design, integrated security systems, competent training, -qualified staff-, and keeping watchful eyes on your workplaces, living environments and residences". [3]

General recommendations of this study rely on the use of CPTED strategies compromising at three main levels. These levels cover individual, group structures and surrounding territories. These propositions are suggested for existing, ongoing and projected critical structures. It is proposed that existing critical structures be redesigned to at least a minimum applicable degree of CPTED principals. These structures also should be reinforced with secondary CPTED concepts such as: organized and mechanical strategies. Ongoing constructions should be supported via grants to implement as much as possible the primary CPTED design concepts. Finally, future plans should be required to have CPTED based blueprints in order to construct critical infrastructures. Considering more effective results, security agencies should also be advised to promote community based complimentary programs such as Neighborhood Watch (NW) in their areas.

1. Literature Review

The Great Wall of China was constructed before 200 BC with the intention of protecting Chinese[3] society from raids by the Mongols and Turkic tribes. Hun Empire[4] was in control at the time in the north side of China. Although wall constructions have different goals, the general approach was to deter undesired subjects from entering protected areas. This approach can be understood as macro level classic governmental preventive method or more specifically access control strategy for countries and regions. These types of big prohibitive walls have been used by other countries such as Germany and Israel throughout the centuries. In this section, essential key terms and underlying approaches are identified to provide a general framework for a better understanding of the CPTED concept.

---

[2] Randy Atlas Ph.D., AIA, C.P.P. Atlas Safety & Security Design Inc
[3] http://www.crystalinks.com/chinawall.html
[4] http://www.ulkuocaklari.org.tr/trktrh/1/hunlar.htm

1.1 Terrorism

Terrorism is identified in various ways in numerous sources. The term is defined as "the unlawful use of -- or threatened use of -- force or violence against individuals or property to coerce or intimidate governments or societies, often to achieve political, religious, or ideological objectives." by the US Department of Defense. For convenience, this paper use the terrorism definition as FBI cites[5] in the Code of Federal Regulations as "...the unlawful use of force and violence against persons or property to intimidate or coerce a government, the civilian population, or any segment thereof, in furtherance of political or social objectives[6]." In this context, bombings and arson may be identified as moderate level terrorist activities because these terrorist methods are in use after they had been explored. The FBI announces[7] the list of terrorist actions on the website by events between 1980 and 2001, and these are displayed below [4].

Table 1: Type Terrorist Action Taking Place between 1980 And 2001

Type of Terrorist Actions	Number
Bombings	324
Arson	33
Other	22
Assassinations	21
Shootings	19
Sabotage/Malicious Destruction	19
Robberies	19
Hostile Takeovers	19
Assaults	6
WMD	6
Hijackings/Aircraft Attacks	3
Kidnappings	2
Rocket Attacks	2

As it can be seen clearly from the distribution of events from the chart, bombings and arson are the most commonly preferred methods which may cause a lot of damage. These similar terrorist actions can be easily seen worldwide such as, suburb arson in France and multiple simultaneous forest arsons in Turkey ignited by terrorist organizations. The

---

[5] http://www.fbi.gov/publications/terror/terror2000_2001.htm
[6] (28 C.F.R. Section 0.85)
[7] (28 C.F.R. Section 0.85)

question emerges here: How can we deter strikes such as bombings and arson from critical infrastructures?

Terrorism is shown as one of the forces for change by Atlas[8]. This change may take place both in society and at institutional levels. From the institutional point of view, all federal facilities were required to be equipped against illegal activities via use of fundamental standard of security by the Department of Justice in 1995. Similar to this approach in 2001, a bill was passed to empower law enforcement and military to promote preventive actions [3].The reason for change in our physical environment done in order to decrease crime stems mostly via the media because terrorism is simply more marketable to public, so the public is informed about the fear of crime by the media. This opportunity enables politicians to form change in the security and develop essential new standards. In contrast, terrorism causes immense fear of crime in public mindsets [3].

Crime horror and fear of crime impact public opinion differently. Crime is a daily matter, and most people are used to living with it. Conversely, terrorism is a very rare act compared to crime in strong countries but more destructive than crime in people's perceptions. This means fear of terrorism may be perceived as more important than the ordinary crime cases, while it still has a considerably high effect on property and life compared to terrorist attacks. Atlas says that "The societal damage from guns and drugs far exceeds the damage from any bomb. But the perceived threat is much greater from terrorism than say getting robbed" [3].

Regulating public fear of crime is argued in different means because this need stems from the high impact of fear of crime over the people. The fear of crime has a lot of affects on public policy production specifically. [5] Findings from the former studies also supports that "the public is likely to exaggerate the frequency of rare, serious crimes and underestimate the frequency of more common, less serious ones" [5]

1.2. Critical Infrastructure

The term critical infrastructure protection was not distinctly seen in print until 1997. Critical infrastructures are defined[9] as systems whose incapacity or destruction would have a debilitating impact on the defense or economic security of the nation. They are identified by Lewis generally as telecommunications, electrical power systems, gas and oil, banking and finance, transportation, water supply systems, government services, and emergency services. In Lewis' book, critical key assets are also listed as: national monuments and Icons, Nuclear power plants, Dams, Government facilities, and commercial Key assets. This paper utilizes mentioned 'key assets' mainly as critical infrastructures. Lewis also expresses that before the 9/11 attacks "the security of infrastructure was taken for granted" and asserts that the optimal policy to secure the critical infrastructure is to identify and protect a handful of critical assets in the U.S. [6]

Assassination of important political leaders has been one of the most commonly used methods of terrorism in the past decades. This technique is still preferred in some

---

[8] President of Counter Terror Design Inc., and vice-president of Atlas Safety & Security Design Inc., in Miami, Florida.
[9] National Strategy for Homeland Security

situations, but it is not as frequent as it was before. There may be various reasons to this acquired appraisable situation, but it can be presumed that leaders have been carefully guarded more recently than before. Increasingly, political leaders have been protected by the public, governmental institutions and finally by the guardians who also use various types of mechanical physical tools to ensure the safety of very important persons. Can this position, being important, be the attracting point for the twin towers or other critical structures? The simple reason may be the inadequate ownership of these critical infrastructures. If a big house were blown up, it will not be as powerful in the public mind as an FBI structure's demolition. These exceptional structures should be treated carefully in particular because their missions and meanings are different from the others.

Here are some anecdotes related to attacks on critical structures from the 9/11 report which we prefer not to paraphrase in order to keep the actual meanings intact. Total incidents or planned acts between 1980 and 2001 are shown as 482 in number in FBI reports [4]. Some of these are also mentioned in the commission report as below.

"In February 1993, a group led by Ramzi Yousef tried to bring down the World Trade Center with a truck bomb. They killed six and wounded a thousand.

In November 1995, a car bomb exploded outside the office of the U.S. program manager for the Saudi National Guard in Riyadh, killing five Americans and two others.

In June 1996, a truck bomb demolished the Khobar Towers apartment complex in Dhahran, Saudi Arabia, killing 19 U.S. servicemen and wounding hundreds.

In August 1998, Bin Ladin's group, al Qaeda, carried out near-simultaneous truck bomb attacks on the U.S. embassies in Nairobi, Kenya, and Dar es Salaam, Tanzania. The attacks killed 224 people, including 12 Americans, and wounded thousands more [7]."

Following these actions the commission announces that: "The 9/11 attacks were a shock, but they should not have come as a surprise." And consequently the high impact of this damage is mentioned in the final report as: "The 9/11 attacks on the World Trade Center and the Pentagon were far more elaborate, precise, and destructive than any of these earlier assaults." [7].

To standardize security requirements at a basic level for critical structures is a crucial need. It was accomplished for the first time at Federal buildings after U.S Marshal Service had applied its 52 standards [3].This security standardization roughly consisted of "security, entry security, interior security, and security technology planning phases." Federal buildings were protected based on their referenced critical level that was defined based on a five scale level [3].Certainly there are other proceeding preparedness examples, like the subway system in New York. Al Baker says in his article in The New York Times that authorities are taking essential steps to secure the system considering a possible sabotage and similar attacks on the subway system as a critical infrastructure of New York. He also emphasizes for all potential targets that "to make such targets less attractive to terrorists" is another perspective to be considered. [8]

This study attempts to enlighten the reader as to what the critical targets are. As an example, the intelligence need was severely felt after the 9/11 case; however, we focus on targets' features such as the Twin Towers, the Oklahoma buildings and other former similar type of targets. It is unlikely that terrorists will use the same method as 9/11 to attack again;

nonetheless, they are most likely to prefer an analogous target, which will probably be an important structure.

1.3. Language of the Structures

Crowe has published his well-known book of CPTED[10] based on "understanding the direct relationship of the design to human behavior and crime" in 2000. Perception of the immediate physical environment is supposed to be the initiating force to maintain safety and desired behaviors in CPTED applied areas in this chief publication [9]. Implicit language of physical environment is emphasized as "expression of society's aims" by Noguchi, as Invisible Language as cited by Katyal [10]. Nonverbal messages are naturally sent via architectural design and decoded by observers, like as in the case of Berlin, where one cannot understand the Berlin Wall unless he feels expressive force of it as mentioned by Katyal [10]. Likewise, dilapidated buildings, which imply that crime is humdrum, and places that are not well kept express an attitude of negligence.

Safety by use of architectural design is not one of the primary prevention methods for deterring and reducing illegal activities among contemporary police services. Conversely, it is one of the least known and rarely used techniques. One main method in policing may be stated as to control criminals and focus on potential deviant people. This main focus, magnifying criminals, also may be the one reason for ongoing human violence cases in courts against some police forces. On the other hand, environmental design may not entirely eradicate illegal activities by itself, but, instead, it may be a more effective method by composing other complementary policing tactics.

Deterrence may be one of the most expected outputs from urban design based prevention approaches. Encouraging positive activities on streets by use of architectural means, such as illumination, is quite satisfactory in reducing fear of crime. Additionally, designing our environment affects our lives deeply as shown by Churchill's saying:[11] "We shape our buildings, and afterwards our buildings shape us." as cited by Katyal, [10].

1.4. Neighborhood Watch

Complimentary policing methods also can strengthen the use of CPTED although we don't have adequate empirical findings to support this approach. This is not only because the composed use of CPTED concept is very new, but also due to the fact that measuring the impact of all dimensions of CPTED usage with complimentary methods seems overwhelming. Various policing methods may be used or integrated with CPTED, and we propose utilizing Neighborhood Watch (NW) programs, which can be originally identified as a community based policing program. Gottfredson and Hirschi say that "A residence that appears to be observed by neighbors will be less vulnerable than a residence that cannot be seen by people living in the area" [10].

---

[10] Crime Prevention Through environmental design: Applications of Architectural design and space management concepts. Second edition
[11] Winston Churchill, in defense of rebuilding the House of Commons after the Germans bombed it

In 2002, the Attorney General of Virginia declared the development of a Neighborhood Watch supporting program to enhance local homeland security efforts   and make preparedness a part of people's daily lives. In this context, he proclaims that the more people participation in community policing programs, the safer the community people will have [11]. This program roughly suggests a community-based crime prevention program where citizens, in concert with law enforcement, work to reduce the opportunity for crime in their neighborhoods. One of the three main principals of this program requires applying CPTED strategies via neighbors' support. For evolutional purposes, the Virginia Crime Prevention Center (VCPC) applied a survey. "Survey[12] questions were produced to assess the proposition that NW should play a role in the fight against terrorism". [11]

In this report it was found that "81% (96) of the agency contact persons expressed a willingness to support and promote a homeland security role for their NW groups and 69% of the contact persons who supported a homeland security mission said that to implement such a mission, they would first need training for their agency staff and local NW leaders, or new training materials that could be distributed to NW participants." [11 pg 4]

This report concludes that NW is still a major instrument of Virginia's crime prevention initiatives. At this point, "given the concern with Homeland Security, it may be foreseen that NW will play an even more important role in the post-9/11 era." [11]

1.5. Crime Prevention

"Successful disaster recovery depends on preventing or limiting the impact of disasters before they occur" says Marty Watts[13]. In this framework perhaps, terrorist attacks may be considered as unnatural disasters. He asserts that "Disaster recovery plans are more likely to succeed if a pre-disaster program of physical security is in place prior to the advent of hurricanes, earthquakes, accidental and intentional explosions, and other potentially life- and business-threatening events" [12]. Likewise, producing effective, sustainable, and comprehensive structural crime prevention methods may be the most important policy to be considered, since there may not be a full remedy to heal the all wounds of terrorism cases, like 9/11.

Crime is defined as "a violation of a local, state, or federal law" and crime prevention is identified as "actions to reduce crime risks and build individual and community safety" by National Crime Prevention Council[14]. There is also a need for a common definition of both crime and terrorism as one. Both crime and terrorism may be joined briefly as "illegal actions" excluding their motivation sources which are as different as their natures. There were 34 known crime prevention tactics mentioned in Basic Crime Prevention Courses in Virginia Crime Prevention Association courses in 1995. Basically, mostly of these methods are in effect as one or few as combined versions against the crime by security organizations.

---

[12] The primary law enforcement agencies of all Virginia cities and counties were surveyed via mainly phone as well as the police departments of towns whose 2000 Census populations were over 2000.
[13] Marty Watts is president and CEO of V-Kool Inc
[14] http://www.ncpc.org/programs/tcc/

Neighborhood Watch is a community policing based concept and mainly relies on the public observations, including their cooperation with police. Katyal cites that different types of crime occurrences lessen considerably in different areas when crime prevention methods were used [10]. Crime prevention, specifically, CPTED may be the solution at this juncture as a sustainable terrorism prevention because we are defending structures against illegal activities. In other words, an orderly designed environment can signal people opportunity to feel any unusual action which thereafter will be reported to police. Inhabitants of the area are also more likely to actively report unusual actions, which will most likely dissuade the potential offenders from their actions.

1.6. Crime Prevention through Environmental Design

This section attempts to enlighten the reader on the roots of CPTED based on its chronology. The purpose of detailed exploration is to provide a firm base for future applicable complimentary crime prevention methods. Pre-studies, interrelated concepts, and critiques are also presented to keep holistic theoretical formation. Measurement of overall CPTED concept practice doesn't seem easily applicable, while, empirical studies were held to check its impact. CPTED strategies can be applicable separately depending on actual needs; however, they are able to form strengthened synergy if they are used concurrently. It may halt the overall system to ignore any of the strategies entirely for desired ends. CPTED concept may produce satisfactory results if it is appropriately applied to any structure; besides it can also produce more promising results as long as it is used with Neighborhood Watch based programs.

2. Theoretical Background

In the 1960s, Jacob discovered during her work in New York's Greenwich Village that placing eyes on the street can reduce the crime occurrence [13]. "Placing eyes on a street", or capable guardians, can help to make a place unattractive for offenders, thus preventing it from becoming a preference for them to commit crime. This can be accomplished in various ways, such as by the proper placement of windows, adequate lighting, and removing unsightly obstructions.

In 1972s, Oscar Newman, a consulting architect, introduced a new perspective on creating viable change in problematic public and private communities [14]. Newman examined and mentioned three different areas in his famous book 'Defensible Spaces'. These are keeping the residents by applying crime reducing amendments on their same places, scattering a public housing community through a small city and reorganization of a neighborhood into mini neighborhoods. His experiences also initiated new approaches in crime prevention methods. The Five Oaks Community in Dayton, The Clason Point Project in New York and Dispersing public housing in Yonkers are some of those cases applied by Newman. After his declaration of famed Defensible Space book, various similar and parallel studies and articles were produced.

Repetto, author of numerous books on crime, gave very wise advice for crime prevention studies in interrelated sciences even though his article is dated as 1976. In his study, Repetto reveals gaps among the Criminologists and Urban Designers. This article is a comprehensive study in terms of crime prevention through environmental design policy because most initiative debates occurred in these years. He indicates that there are integration problems in this area by claiming: "Criminological community has tended to reject or ignore design theory." He also emphasizes the presence of an inclusive explanation of the relationship between urban design and human behavior, particularly as it relates to crime [14, 15]. Particularly, he alleges "the fact that criminology is skeptical of crime prevention via urban design" [15]. After his determinations, Repetto presents, 'incorrect perceptions', and practical problems of implementation in crime prevention. Then, he encourages both urban designers and criminologists to share their evaluations on the potential of urban design theory for contributing crime prevention improvement [15].

One of the other influential articles, published in March 1982, can be mentioned as the 'Broken Windows' which involves the police and neighborhood scale safety issues [16]. This concept used a car as a tool for examination of the livable areas. They tried to learn what makes a place more livable or not. First, they placed a luxury one, Jaguar, on a street and left the vehicle unattended. They found that the car didn't provoke any attack or abuse during this time. The next time, they broke a small window on one side of the car and went back to observe. When they monitored the car along four hours time interval, results were astonishing. The car was turned, inverted, torched, and stolen. They did more studies on this issue and developed so called "Broken Windows Theory." This theory concisely means; if a window is broken in an apartment and no one fixes it, it enables more decay in the surrounding area concurrently. If the decay is a crime, consequently, its followers most likely occupy the area [16].

Although 'The Broken Windows Theory' seems to be a unique theory by itself, it has combined its way with CPTED applications to some degree. The definition of CPTED as the "The proper design and effective use of the built environment that can lead to a reduction in the fear and incidence of crime with an improvement of the quality of life" became a general accepted definition at National Crime Prevention Institution (NCPI). NCPI referenced the definition after Crowe had published the explanation in his CPTED book [9]. Broken Window's approach is very close to one of the rising additive implementation strategies of CPTED that is 'maintenance'. Crowe doesn't include the 'maintaining the structures' as one of the strategies for CPTED, but it is a most common and actual used reality in today's applications. As a present example; Henrico CPTED planning office has been a clear supporter of the maintenance strategy since the county started to apply CPTED [17].

Crowe is a criminologist specializing in consulting and training services in law enforcement, crime prevention and various similar services at the University of Louisville. CPTED phrase originally coined by Dr. C. Ray Jeffrey in 1971 have been studied and developed by Crowe since then in different formats such as books, articles, etc. He prepared CPTED training programs for the national crime prevention institute as the director of this institute as well. Explicit instructions and designations were created under his studies and collected in his book, Crime Prevention through Environmental Design in 1991. CPTED strategies were defined clearly in this book and the behavioral nature of the person in perceiving the security issues were told under different examples. It can be said that his definitions and strategies have constituted mostly today's CPTED strategies and concept nationwide. This paper intentionally addresses Crowe's ideas and approaches while using the CPTED terminology [18].

Gulak examined homicide and the physical environment assessing the CPTED approach in Richmond between 1989 and 1991 [19]. His exploratory research investigates the physical environments of homicides to explore whether -first generation- CPTED strategies are applicable in examining these crime scenes. In this study, sixteen separate homicide cases were examined occurring in Richmond, Virginia. These cases were specifically chosen by a project, VEAT15. Each case's crime scene was analyzed according to four major factors which are derived from CPTED main concept. For every case, site visits, review of the police report, review of the photos including videos taken at the time of incident, and a discussion on related issues with VEAT members took place [19].

Mainly two levels of analysis, 'immediate and surrounding areas' were examined through the study and findings suggest that there appears to be a significant relationship between the physical environment and homicide. Inadequate pedestrian lighting, lack of family defined territoriality and science's lack of visibility are some of the other merging details of findings [19].

3. Studies and Practices

To make empirical research or to measure the component part of the strategies in terms of their effectiveness of CPTED is defined as fraught with difficulty in this study [20]. Although reporting of empirical findings of CPTED is limited, the Hartford Study was conducted over three years as the first at the neighborhood level of planning study by US Department of Justice in order to analyze crime opportunities and urban structure relations in a neighborhood of Connecticut (1978). In the Harford Study it was determined that "a direct relationship between crime and the structure of neighborhood design, and that properly designed urban form can help mitigate crime opportunities [21]". The impact of this study prompted a nationwide federal program to implement and analyze CPTED strategies at numerous cities across the U.S. [20]

CPTED projects have resulted in growing property values considerably in Harbor dale, Florida as well as a significant decline in crime rates. Portland County became another successful case which testified to the effectiveness of CPTED strategies on reduction of burglaries and "stabilization of the neighborhood's quality of life" in Oregon [22]. Schneider claims that implementing CPTED strategies is the most successful when inhabitants of the area are educated and aware of the benefits of the use of design strategies [20].

The Washington DC Metro system is the other distinctive example of the CPTED implementation in crime prevention studies and its success and outcomes can be easily examined and comparable with the similar metro systems. Poyner reviewed 45 environmental design applications as crime prevention projects and found that 53.3% of

---

[15] VEAT :Richmond Violent Event Action Team

these applications show firm evidence and 27% of the projects indicated limited evidence as to crime reduction. Overall, 80% of the all cases showed fairly positive relation between environmental design and crime reduction [as cited in 20]. Altering the physical environment instead of dealing with the criminals directly can also lessen the level of human rights violence during the policing process in safety institutions [20].

There are also critiques of the CPTED base applications. The first one is support for the effectiveness of comprehensive CPTED programs has not been unequivocally demonstrated by the public. The second one is that socio economic status of the community can support or reduce the efficiency of the CPTED strategies. This critique also provoked second generation CPTED initiatives that identified "undefended space" "where cultural and social factors influence the propensity for resident action and self-policing" in late 1990s by Seville and Cleveland [as cited in 20]. Displacement has been proposed as the other critique for CPTED based studies claiming that existing crime may change its formation in five different ways. These are location, time, tactics, targets and type of crime.

3.1. CPTED and Its Strategies

CPTED is an experienced method that was justified both in increasing a sense of security and reduction in crime frequency in applied areas. To courage the communities for positive activity and to discourage offenders from getting involved in criminal activities are the main ideas of CPTED planning. The proposed idea, physical design can be manipulated to produce behavioral effects for reducing the crime incidence, is the skeleton of the concept. CPTED concept is applied based on three functions of human space according to Crowe [18]. These key issues are pointed out as consequence of human behaviors that people design environments for either a purpose, or a support to control desired behaviors. Additionally, all human spaces are accepted as having social, cultural, legal or physical definitions that express the desired and acceptable activities. These three behavioral dimensions, named Three-D concept including designation, definition and, design, take place as the primary CPTED design concept in shorter names in Crowe's. Three common strategies of the CPTED concept are 'Natural Access Control', 'Natural Surveillance', and 'Territorial Enforcement'. All these strategies are set up based on natural ways. Actually, there are various ways to deter the crime by use of CPTED based concepts but the focus of CPTED in this paper mainly addresses these three natural means. Some mechanical and organized steps are presented as the secondary concept in Crowe's book as well.

3.1.1. Natural Access Control

People's space should show some natural indications for defining where people are allowed to come and go for a building environment. This strategy desires to make a clear way to be seen for the circulation of visitors within structures. Other usage of the space for guests is not accepted as usual. In short, general application of this strategy is seen as defining a natural visible way for access of the structure by differentiating the way with stone, asphalt and etc. This lane also may be strengthened via additional fences and lighting fixtures for night vision.

3.1.2. Natural Surveillance

This strategy can be seen as a traditional one which is based on Jacob's idea of placing legitimate eyes on the street. Locating windows on the base floors and blind points are the most common method for natural surveillance. Of course improving lighting is another important dimension to be considered [21]. To raise the positive pedestrian activity on the streets via locating new shops which enable dense customer circulation in problematic streets is a new rising method related to this strategy.

3.1.3. Territorial Enforcement

Enhancement of ownership and proprietary behaviors is the main point of this strategy. Any indicators showing the possession of the structure is the expression of it. Flags, emblems, landscaping fencing and similar indications are some of the examples for this approach. Maintenance and Target Hardening are the afterward approaches for CPTED in later years. Both of these are crucial applications for providing more secure areas. But, this study restricts main propositions with three natural CPTED strategies.

3.2. Why CPTED Is a Solution?

First of all, traditional law enforcement methods against terrorism have not stopped the latest horrific cases, and governments need to develop innovative, successful cures to stop attacks and their damage. In brief, former safety methods were set up to manipulate criminal activities and generally ignored the physical environment where people found opportunities to commit crimes. Secondly, CPTED has become a dynamic ground concept which relies on urban design theory and opens to multi dimensional approaches as a fundamental platform. The Sydney Olympics in 2000, strictly considered CPTED strategies to provide safer places for participants and "CPTED principles have to be part of the initial brief to all parties concerned in design, construction and provision of services [22]."

CPTED planning is a process compared to secondary technological reinforcement efforts. For effective endings, there is a preliminary need to assess targeted structures. Next, evaluated and categorized critical structures are recommended to either be redesigned or reinforced by CPTED experts. For example, closed circuit systems are mostly used as supplementary remedies for unplanned and unaccounted for blind areas. However, these kinds of undue hardships would be eliminated or minimized in the CPTED planning phase. CPTED can easily be implemented in most of the critical infrastructures because this study also proposes recommendations for individual, group and large level locations.

3.2.1. CPTED in Individual Buildings

a. Mark the boundaries of private building space to clearly separate it from public space (sidewalks and the street)
b. Make it clear from the street where to enter private building space
c. Orient windows to the street and to view activities within the boundaries and at entrance points

d.   Locate outside private activities in areas where they can be observed from inside the building.

Figure1: Individual Building's Situation

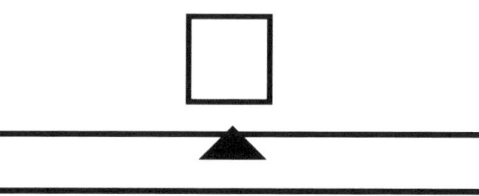

Individual Building

3.2.2. CPTED in Group of Buildings

a.   Design the entrance to the street to indicate entering a special territory
b.   Provide a sense of design coherence within the street special lights, paving, and crosswalks or furniture
c.   Identify parking spaces, entrances to lots, and pick-up locations so they are observable from individual buildings
d.   Monitor the condition of trees, vegetation, lights, sidewalks, and trash to maintain a   caring environment

Figure2: Group Building's Situation

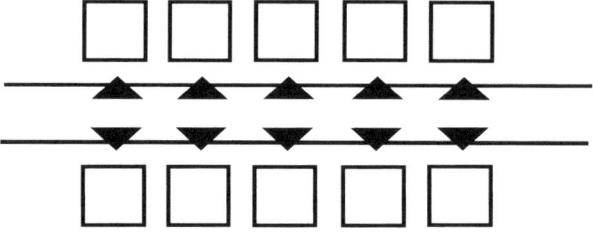

Group of Buildings

3.2.3. CPTED Application in Street and Surrounding Areas

a.   CPTED should be used as a first means of providing safety and protection from terrorist
b.   CPTED can be used for new construction and retro fitting older urban buildings and streets
c.   CPTED requires awareness by architects, landscape architects, other designers and law enforcement officials to be effective

Figure3: Overall Surrounding Area

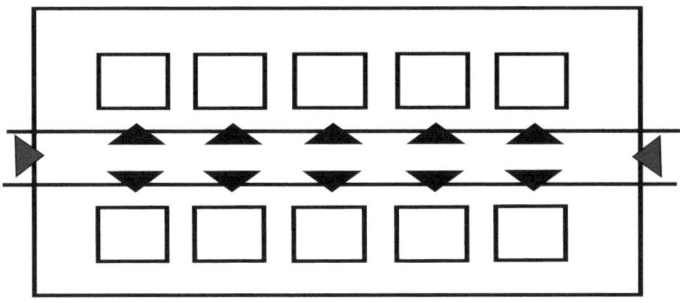

Street and Building Territorial Reinforcement

4. Conclusion

Interaction of Urban Design based theories with security sciences yielded beneficial outputs. CPTED is one of the productions of this interplay. This probable benefit can be maximized if this approach may be combined with existing compatible security techniques. This is why we additionally suggest merging Neighborhood Watch with CPTED. This newly increasing combination concept naturally should be applied differently to diverse level buildings such as individual, group and surrounding level structures. More efficiency, assessments of targeted critical structures should be prepared by authorized trained personnel for CPTED planning phase. Recommendations of these CPTED assessment reports should be implemented considering critical levels of structures. As Watts mentioned above, the cost will not be more than existing ones; only, expenditures will be used differently. There are also other reinforcing actions for this proposal to be addressed which are touched on below.

CPTED training and security awareness among critical structure managers should be nurtured. Government can promote architectural answers to crime but there must also be basic requirements for the private sector which owns and manages critical structures in energy, chemistry etc.

Instead of mandating essential amendments or redesigns, encouraging adequate effective grants and funds should be released at local, state and federal levels. Each level of governmental organization should prepare the minimum, moderate and complete CPTED application guidelines in order to provide a clear legal area for implementation. Core structures should be directly constructed or supervised by governmental authorities. Policy production should account for all related areas, not only security organizations.

Local authorities can be encouraged to redesign city streets to reduce illegal activities in a variety of ways. Public spaces' design for streets parking and common structures should be accounted for as well. Using compatible physical barriers with public fabric between pedestrian traffic and critical infrastructures as a differentiating tool ought to be considered a temporary solution but seems a necessary action for these years.

Consequently, we must make places and structures convenient, viable and sustainable for public usage. These critical and densely populated public areas should be designed via CPTED concept because we, simply, cannot afford to deploy police or law enforcement staff everywhere. A complimentary thought should be considered that neighborhood watch can be an enforcing method against terrorist activities. The idea of locating CPTED based convenient places can be more effective if mentioned statements can be smoothly decorated in these structures. This approach may be very beneficial for critical structure's protection; however it may have some side effects for public and individual interactions as well.

References:

[1]   P. Belluck, McVeigh is reported to claim responsibility for the bombing. New York Times, 1995, May 17.
[2]   9/11 Public discourse project. 9/11 Commission Recommendations. Final Report: 2005, pp 7.
[3]   R. Atlas, Designing against terror, violence and crime. Atlas Safety & Security Design Inc., [Online] Available from; URL: http://www.cpted-security.com/cpted17.htm [2006, December 15]
[4]   Federal Bureau of Investigation. Terrorism 2000/2001. U.S. Government printing office; 2004, pp 50.
[5]   M. Warr, Fear of crime in the United States: Avenues for research and policy, Criminal Justice 2000. 4 (2000) 451- 489. [Online] Available from; URL: http://www.ncjrs.gov/criminaljustice2000/vol 4/04i.pdf
[6]   T.G. Lewis, Critical infrastructure protection in homeland security: Defending a networked nation. Monterey, California: Wiley-Inter science; 2004.
[7]   The 9/11 Commission. Final report of the national commission on terrorist attacks upon the United States, Executive Summary, 2004, pp 34.
[8]   A. Baker, With terrorism concerns in mind, police prepare to guard a shuttered system. The New York times, 2005.   [Online]   Available   from;   URL: http://www.nytimes.com/2005/12/20/nyregion /nyregionspecial3/20security.html?ex=1168750800&en=a02071e145a0f496&ei=5070
[9]   T.D. Crowe, Crime prevention through environmental design, 2000.
[10]   N.K. Katyal, Architecture as crime control, Yale Law Journal. 111/5 (2002), 1039-1140.
[11]   Virginia Department of Criminal Justice Services Crime Prevention Center, Report of the Department of Criminal Justice Services: The status of Richmond, Virginia Crime Prevention Center, 2003, pp 28.
[12]   M. Watts, Before disaster strikes. Security products: The integrated product newsmagazine for security, fire & safety professionals, (2005), 32-34. [Online] Available from; URL: http://www.stevenspublishing. com/Stevens/SecProdPub.nsf/frame?open&redirect=http://www.stevenspublishing.com/stevens/secprodpub. nsf/PubArchive?openView
[13]   J. Jacobs, The death and life of great American cities. New York: Vintage; 1961.
[14]   O. Newman, Creating defensible space, New York: Henson Ville; 1996.
[15]   T.A. Repetto, Crime prevention and the displacement phenomenon, Crime and Delinquency, 22 (1976), 166–177.
[16]   J.Q. Wilson, G.L. Kelling, Broken Windows: The police and neighborhood safety, The Atlantic Monthly; 249/3 (1982), 29-38. [Online] Available from; URL: http://www.theatlantic.com/politics/crime/ windows.htm
[17]   K. Vann, VAPA Newsbrief, The newsletter of the Virginia Chapter of the American Planning Association. 18/2 (1997 May-June).
[18]   T.D. Crowe, Crime prevention through environmental design, 1991.
[19]   M. Gulak, Homicide and the physical environment: Assessing the CPTED approach. CPTED Journal, 3/1 (1995).
[20]   P.M. Cozens, G. Saville, D. Hillier, Crime prevention through environmental design (CPTED): A review and modern bibliography, Property Management. 23/5 (2005), 328-356. [Online] Available from; URL: http://www.emeraldinsight.com/Insight/ViewContentServlet?Filename=Published/EmeraldFullTextArticle/A rticles/1130230502.html
[21]   J. Brown, Editor. Basic crime prevention. Richmond, Virginia: Virginia Crime Prevention Association V.C.P.A. 2006.
[22]   P.M. Kinnon, Olympics 2000, Presented at the conference of safer communities: Strategic directions in urban. Melbourne: Olympic Security Command Centre, NSW Police Service; 1998, pp. 7.

Understanding and Responding to the Terrorism Phenomenon
O. Nikbay and S. Hancerli (Eds.)
IOS Press, 2007

A Community Based Multi-Faceted Response to the Terrorist Threat in Canada

Wayne HANNIMAN[1], Inspector
National Security Criminal Operations Support Branch,
Royal Canadian Mounted Police, Canada

Abstract. The Canadian response to the current terrorist threat was a multi-faceted one, involving Federal Government legislative, organizational and policy changes, suppress terrorist financing, provide additional resources for security agencies and law enforcement agencies, enhanced investigational and analytical support such as threat assessment tools, Intelligence-led policing, Internet Data Mining and human source recruiting, increased partnerships and cooperation including information sharing between security agencies and law enforcement agencies, and soliciting the public's help in preventing terrorism through Community Outreach to all minority communities of Canada. It is recommended that other countries study Canada's multi-faceted approach to preventing terrorism as there are valuable lessons to be learned about protecting national security while also respecting human rights and civil liberties and maintaining respectful and cooperative relations with a nation's minority communities.

Keywords. Political violence, terrorism, anti-terrorism legislation, anti-terrorism policies, policing terrorism, and community outreach.

Introduction

After 9/11, governments around the world were faced with the problem of how to respond to the changed terrorist threat. This problem was complicated by the lack of international consensus on what the threat was [1]. Even the definition of terrorism caused widespread debate. Canada's Anti-terrorism Act defined a terrorist act as: an act or omission, in or outside Canada: (i) that is committed (A) in whole or in part for a political, religious or ideological purpose, objective or cause[2], and (B) in whole or in part with the intention of intimidating the public, or a segment of the public, with regard to its security, including its economic security, or compelling a person, a government or a domestic or an international organization to do or to refrain from

---

[1] Inspector Wayne HANNIMAN is the RCMP's Officer in Charge of the National Security Community Outreach Program and liaison to the Cross Cultural Roundtable on Security. He is posted to RCMP Headquarters in Canada's capital, Ottawa. He has 28 years service in the RCMP. Insp. HANNIMAN has performed various duties in his career such as uniform patrol, Crime Readers, Community Policing/Crime Prevention, plainclothes detective, Court Liaison, Child Abuse Investigations, Fraud investigator, Major Crime investigator and the manager of an integrated Criminal Intelligence Section. Through part-time study, Insp. HANNIMAN obtained a Bachelor of Arts degree majoring in Criminology from Simon Fraser University in Canada in 1986 and a Masters degree in Criminology at the University of Ottawa in 2003. He received an RCMP Commissioner's Commendation for Bravery in 1981.

[2] This subsection was declared unconstitutional and invalid by a Canadian court in 2006, see Khawaja v. Attorney General of Canada, [2006], Ontario Superior Court of Justice.

doing any act, whether the public or the person, government or organization is inside or outside Canada, and (ii) that intentionally (A) causes death or serious bodily harm to a person by the use of violence, (B) endangers a person's life, (C) causes a serious risk to the health or safety of the public or any segment of the public, (D) causes substantial property damage, whether to public or private property, if causing such damage is likely to result in the conduct or harm referred to in any of clauses (A) to (C), or (E) causes serious interference with or serious disruption of an essential service, facility or system, whether public or private, other than as a result of advocacy, protest, dissent or stoppage of work that is not intended to result in the conduct or harm referred to in any of clauses (A) to (C), and includes a conspiracy, attempt or threat to commit any such act or omission, or being an accessory after the fact or counseling in relation to any such act or omission,

The length of this definition illustrates the complexity of defining terrorism. There are many different definitions and while some commentators view people who resort to violence to achieve political ends as "terrorists", others may define them as "freedom fighters" [2].

The Canadian approach to national security reflects the belief that law enforcement target hardening and increased security measures alone are not sufficient to deal with the terrorist threat [3]. The cooperation of Government ministries, law enforcement and security agencies and the public is needed to prevent terrorism [4]. This paper will analyze the various means of terrorism prevention that Canada adopted after the attacks on New York and Washington in 2001. This case study of governmental-wide response to threat was done through an in-depth, longitudinal examination of official policies, practices and reforms after 9/11. The information and knowledge in this study is based on the researcher's own work experience. The aim of this study is to contribute to the effectiveness of anti-terrorism measures of both governments and police agencies. In fact, the researcher will make recommendations for governments and police agencies to deal with terrorist threats.

Strategic Government policies, such as Canada's "Securing an Open Society: Canada's National Security Policy" and legislation such as the Anti-terrorism Act of Dec., 2002 formed the Government of Canada framework to counter the terrorism threat. These policies and legislation also served to clarify the mandate and strategic priorities of the agencies responsible for protecting Canada's National Security, such as the Royal Canadian Mounted Police (RCMP), Canada's national police service. Additional investigative capacity and enforcement resources along with investigational and analytical support, Internet data mining skills and capabilities and sufficient and skilled source recruiting capabilities in the form of full-time Source Development Units, further enhance the nation's capability to prevent and disrupt terrorist plots. Partnerships such as Integrated National Security Enforcement Teams (INSETs), cooperation including information sharing between law enforcement and security agencies such as the Canadian Security Intelligence Service (CSIS), and in-debt analysis by the Integrated Threat Assessment Centre (ITAC), are vital in the struggle. Intelligence-led Policing with threat prioritization tools such as SLEIPNIR also play an indispensable role. Finally but by no means of lesser importance is the public's help in preventing terrorism, through meaningful Community Outreach to all communities of Canada and ease of reporting suspicions and information about terrorism via a dedicated 1-800 number.

The information in this study was compiled from open source Government of Canada documents and other journals and studies as noted. None of the information contained herein is classified. The source materials were compiled by the author in the course of coordinating the tri-annual review of the Anti-terrorism Act in the Canadian Parliament from November, 2004 to June, 2005.

1. Government of Canada Policy

This study of Canada's response to terrorism begins with a National Terrorism prevention policy [4]. This Policy is a strategic framework and action plan designed to ensure that Canada is prepared for and can respond to current and future threats. The focus is on events and circumstances that generally require a national response as they are beyond the capacity of individuals, communities or provinces to address alone.

The National Security Policy focuses on addressing three core national security interests: protecting Canada and Canadians at home and abroad; ensuring Canada is not a base for threats to its allies; and contributing to international security [4]. It contained many measures to help build a more integrated security system in a way that is consistent with the goals of the policy, for example an Integrated Threat Assessment Centre was established to ensure that all threat-related information is brought together, assessed and reaches all who need it in a timely and effective manner. A National Security Advisory Council, made up of security experts external to government, and an advisory Cross-Cultural Roundtable on Security, composed of members of Canada's ethno-cultural and religious communities, provided public input on the goals and impacts of the anti-terrorism measures. A consolidated Ministry of Public Safety and Emergency Preparedness (similar to the U.S. Dept. of Homeland Security) was designated as the body responsible for the overseeing and coordinating federal agencies that have the key enforcement and security responsibilities and activities[3].

The National Security Policy also set out six key strategic areas for response: Intelligence, Emergency Planning and Management, Public Health, Transport Security, Border Security and International Security [4]. An enhancement of Canada's intelligence collection capacity, with a focus on Security Intelligence, was another aspect of the Policy. The Emergency Preparedness Act created a seamless national emergency management system and a Government Operations Centre provides stable, round-the-clock co-ordination and support across government. The Critical Infrastructure Protection Strategy for Canada and a National Cyber-security Strategy with increased capacity to predict and prevent cyber-security attacks against its networks were also added.

The Transport Security portion of the policy clarified responsibilities and strengthened co-ordination of marine security efforts; established networked marine security operations centres; increased the Canadian Forces, RCMP, and Canadian Coast Guard (CCG) on-water presence along with Department of Fisheries and Oceans (DFO) aerial surveillance; enhanced secure fleet communications; promoted greater

---

[3] Members of Canada's security and intelligence community are the Ministry of Public Safety and Emergency Preparedness Canada (PSEPC) which includes the Royal Canadian Mounted Police (RCMP), Canadian Security Intelligence Service (CSIS), and Canada Border Services Agency (CBSA); Department of National Defence (DND), the Communications Security Establishment (CSE), Justice Canada, Transport Canada, Citizenship and Immigration Canada (CIC), Foreign Affairs and International Trade Canada (FAITC), Financial Transactions and Reports Analysis Centre (FINTRAC) and the Privy Council Office (PCO). No single Cabinet minister is responsible for Canada's security and intelligence community. Instead, a number of ministers are accountable for the activities of the organizations that report to each of them.

marine security co-operation with the United States; and strengthened the security of marine facilities. It also included strategies to enhance Canada's aviation security, including air cargo, and expanded security background check requirements for transportation workers [5].

Two Border Security projects in particular, a facial recognition biometric technology on the Canadian passport and the RCMP Real Time Identification Project- an automated and modern fingerprint system- were funded and fast-tracked. Efforts were taken to streamline the refugee determination process. The next-generation smart borders agenda with Mexico and the United States was pursued [6]. An impetus was created to work with Canada's international partners and in international forums, such as the G8 to enhance all nations' security.

In the area of International Security, the Canadian Armed Forces were made more flexible, responsive and combat-capable for a wide range of operations, able to work with Canada's allies. This was for the purpose of building peace, order and good government by helping to develop failed and failing states, preventing the proliferation of weapons of mass destruction, and defusing key intra- and interstate conflicts.

2. Legislation

In addition to the National Security policy initiative, the Government of Canada enacted three pieces of legislation to facilitate the fight against terrorism: the Anti-Terrorism Act, the Public Safety Act, and the Immigration and Refugee Protection Act. The legislative response highlighted in this paper is the passage of the Anti-terrorism Act (ATA), which defines terrorist activity and specifies Criminal Code offences related to terrorist activity such as participation, facilitation, using or possessing property for terrorist purposes, harbouring/concealing, providing/making available property or services for terrorist purposes, etc. while safeguarding human rights and civil liberties [7]. Prior to the passage of this legislation, there were no terrorism-specific offenses or sections of the Criminal Code. Terrorism would have to be investigated and prosecuted using regular criminal offenses and powers. The ATA provided all Canadian police agencies with additional investigative tools such as Investigative Hearings, Preventative Detention (Recognizance with Conditions)[4], longer interception of private communications authorization, the ability to list organizations and individuals as a terrorist entity, and Authority for Freezing/Restraint of assets

2.1. Anti-terrorist Financing

The Anti-Terrorism Act (ATA) amended the Proceeds of Crime (Money Laundering) Act (PCTFMLA) to expand the mandate of the Financial Transactions and Reports Analysis Centre (FINTRAC), Canada's financial intelligence unit, to include the detection and deterrence of terrorist financing. An important strategy of the Government's counter terrorism plan is to deprive terrorists of the funds needed to finance their activities. Accordingly, the ATA established new criminal offences related to the financing of terrorism. As well, it implemented other measures to deter,

---

[4] Note that the Investigative Hearing and Recognizance with Conditions clauses of the Anti-terrorism Act "sunsetted", that is, expired on March 1, 2007 without ever having been used.

detect, investigate and prosecute these terrorist financing offences. The ATA made changes to Canada's existing anti-money laundering regime to both guard against the abuse of the financial system by terrorist groups and to provide law enforcement authorities and the Canadian Security Intelligence Service (CSIS) with information about suspected terrorist financing activities. The core elements of Canada's anti-money laundering regime were originally set out in the Proceeds of Crime (Money Laundering) Act (PCMLA). Among other things, the PCMLA required financial intermediaries to meet customer identification and record keeping standards and to report suspicious and prescribed transactions relevant to the identification of money laundering. The PCMLA also provided for the establishment of FINTRAC in July, 2000. FINTRAC became operational on October 28, 2001 and its primary functions were to receive reports made under the PCMLA, to analyze those reports for information relevant to money laundering, and to provide key identifying information (e.g. account holder, transaction amount and date, etc.) to Canadian law enforcement agencies.

In December 2001, following the passage of the ATA, FINTRAC's mandate was expanded to include terrorist activity financing and the PCMLA was renamed the Proceeds of Crime (Money Laundering) and Terrorist Financing Act (PCMLTFA). Associated regulations were brought into force on June 12, 2002 to require financial institutions and other financial intermediaries to report suspicions of terrorist financing and terrorist property.

2.2. Other Legislative Tools

Another significant change made to the security and law-enforcement powers by the 2001 legislative amendments was to ensure that the pre-existing Organized Crime powers and authorities were extended to include terrorist activities and the new offences established by the Anti-terrorism Act. The Anti-Terrorism Act authorized the use of existing investigative tools such as the interception of private communications for use in terrorist investigations, and made minor amendments to these powers, similar to what was already available in the organized crime context. This included eliminating the need to demonstrate that electronic surveillance is a last resort in the investigation of terrorists. The period of validity of a wiretap authorization was extended from 60 days to up to one year when police are investigating a terrorist group offence (A Superior Court judge still has to approve the use of electronic surveillance to ensure that these powers are used appropriately). Further, the requirement to notify a target after electronic surveillance has taken place can be delayed for up to three years. These changes mirror those in the electronic surveillance regime applicable to criminal organizations. It should be noted that Canadian police agencies cannot use these additional powers unless approved by the Attorney General of Canada (Minister of Justice).

The general search and seizure powers of the Canadian Criminal Code apply automatically to all criminal offences, including the new terrorism-related offences established by the Act, but a series of amendments was needed to link the new offences to other powers. For example, Clause 17 of the Act amended Criminal Code section 487.04 to include the new terrorism offences within the existing power to obtain a warrant to seize DNA samples.

2.3. Cross-Cultural Roundtable on Security

The Cross-Cultural Roundtable on Security (CCRS) was created in 2004 under Canada's National Security Policy to engage the public and the Canadian Government in a long-term dialogue on matters related to national security [8]. The Roundtable is composed of 15 members of Canada's ethno-cultural and religious communities. It aims to facilitate a broad exchange of information between the federal government and Canada's minority communities on the impact of anti-terrorism measures. The Roundtable also serves to better inform policy makers by providing insights on how national security measures may impact Canada's minority communities and by promoting the protection of civil order, mutual respect and common understanding [8].

2.4. Additional Resources

The additional policies, laws and agencies were not sufficient in themselves to protect Canadians from terrorism. Additional funding and resources were critical to making all the other changes take effect. In the 2001 Federal Budget, the Government of Canada allocated $7.7 billion in new funds to be spent over the next five years on the Public Safety and Anti-terrorism initiative to enhance security for all Canadians [9]. Canada Customs and Revenue Agency (CCRA)[5], Citizenship and Immigration Canada, Transport Canada and the RCMP received $30 million among them to provide immediate, permanent staff increases for National Security functions. An additional $250 million was set aside for immediate security initiatives-largely largely capital expenditures and equipment. The RCMP and CCRA received $71.5 million in urgent funding to offset unforeseen costs such as overtime.

3. The Royal Canadian Mounted Police Response to Terrorism

The Royal Canadian Mounted Police is Canada's national police force, created in 1873. The RCMP's policing responsibilities include Federal Policing in all provinces and territories of Canada, such as Drug Enforcement, Customs & Excise enforcement, Immigration and Passport investigations, Commercial Crimes, Proceeds of Crime, War Crimes, Serious and Organized Crimes, and National Security. The RCMP also conducts "Contract Policing" in all provinces except Ontario & Quebec, contract with provinces and municipalities to be the local police service of criminal jurisdiction, which includes enforcement of the Criminal Code, federal and provincial laws, and municipal by-laws in hundreds of large and small cities, towns, villages and rural areas. International policing and peacekeeping e.g. Bosnia, Kosovo, and Haiti is another major responsibility. Protective duties such as guarding embassies, consulates, government facilities, and Internationally Protected Persons (IPPs) and managing the Canadian law enforcement infrastructure such as the Canadian Police Information Computer (CPIC), the Criminal Records and DNA data banks, the Violent Crime Link Analysis System (VICLAS), the Canadian Police College, etc. complete the many and varied policing responsibilities of the RCMP.

One of the RCMP's Federal responsibilities is National Security, which involves prevention of terrorism and enforcement of the Anti-terrorism Act [10]. The ATA

---

[5] Now renamed the Canada Border Services Agency.

consolidated & clarified RCMP role in national security and has facilitated the investigation and prosecution of terrorist activities by precisely stating the types of activity that fall within the purview of the RCMP and other police forces in Canada. This did not change the RCMP's role in national security criminal investigations however. The RCMP's primary role in national security matters was defined under Section 6 of the Security Offences Act in 1984. The RCMP has primary responsibility to prevent and investigate offences that constitute a threat to the security of Canada (as defined by Sec. 2 in the Canadian Security Intelligence Service Act) and offences against internationally protected persons (as defined in the Criminal Code). The investigation of terrorist support activities (as defined in Anti-terrorism Act) has been added to these responsibilities.

Section 2 of the CSIS Act defines "threats to the security of Canada" as: espionage or sabotage; foreign influenced activities within or relating to Canada; acts of vandalism or violence for the purpose of achieving a religious, ideological or political objective within Canada; and activities intended to undermine the sovereignty of the government in Canada. Note that "terrorism" is defined separately in section 83.01(1) of the Criminal Code, and the threats under the CSIS act do not necessarily constitute a definition of terrorism.

While all RCMP officers are responsible for protecting Canada's national security, some RCMP members are assigned full-time to anti-terrorism duties. These investigators have extensive experience in regular policing before being considered for National Security duties. Some of the dedicated RCMP National Security Criminal investigators work in Integrated National Security Enforcement Teams (INSET's) in larger cities, i.e. Ottawa, Montreal, Toronto, which are combined teams with investigators from municipal and provincial police agencies, other law Enforcement agencies such as the Canada Border Services Agency, and Security and Intelligence agencies such as the Canadian Security Intelligence Service. Integration facilitates cooperation and information sharing, which is the life blood of law enforcement [11]. Other officers work in National Security Investigations Sections (NSIS) which are RCMP-only investigative units in the smaller Canadian cities, i.e. Halifax, Winnipeg, etc. The RCMP Headquarters National Security Criminal Investigations Directorate is responsible to assess and monitor all criminal investigations relating to national security, including overseeing the NSIS and INSETs.

When it is determined that activity either falls within the definition of threat to the security of Canada as contained in Section 2 of the CSIS Act, involves a threat to an Internationally Protected Person or falls within the definition of terrorist activity as articulated in Section 83.01 of the Criminal Code, an RCMP National Security Criminal Investigative unit will either take the primary investigative role or provide assistance to the primary enforcement. Violent crime committed by groups, in isolation of other factors, would not necessarily fit within the definition of "terrorist activity" as described in Section 83.01 of the Criminal Code and as such would not be within the mandate of RCMP National Security Criminal investigative units. The RCMP would analyze the information and ensure that these groups are attempting to achieve a political or ideological objective through the commission of acts of serious violence before investigating complaints against them. A political activist would not fall within the mandate of an RCMP National Security Criminal Investigation if that individual was engaging in legitimate protest or dissent, as this is lawful activity. Also, if a criminal act was committed during a political protest, this would not necessarily indicate that the individuals pose a national security threat. Principally, the RCMP commander must satisfy him- or herself that based on the information available, there is reason to believe that individuals are planning or have committed violent acts to achieve their political objectives.

In keeping with the Government of Canada policy on National Security, the RCMP National Strategic Priorities were amended to include terrorism with the other priorities such as organized crime, international policing, Aboriginal communities and youth. To fulfill its National Security protection responsibilities, the RCMP moved to investigations that are integrated and Intelligence-led, focusing on national strategic priorities. The RCMP has a dual role in countering threats to Canada's national security. It is the national law enforcement agency with the primary responsibility for investigating crimes which threaten Canada's national security. Also, it has a criminal intelligence role which supports both those investigations and its protective policing mandate. Accordingly, the RCMP adapted Intelligence-Led Policing for use in anti-terrorism investigation.

Strategic intelligence provides a comprehensive and current picture of the scope and direction of criminal activity. Generally a management support tool, strategic intelligence assists decision-making and the determination of future action. It is tied to organizational objectives rather than investigative necessity. Tactical intelligence affords immediate and timely support to ongoing investigations by identifying criminals and by providing advance information on their activities. It leads to specific law enforcement action, including arrests, further investigation and prosecution. Threat assessments are strategic intelligence products that provide expert understanding of, and insights into, the capabilities, intentions, vulnerabilities and limitations of groups posing a national security threat to Canada. Their outlook is generally long term and future-oriented.

3.1. Sleipnir

To make sense of the multitude of information that is generated about terrorism, the RCMP uses Sleipnir6, an important tool in the fight against terrorism. Sleipnir is an analytical threat-measurement technique for strategic intelligence analysis. It was initially developed to assess the relative threat posed by organized criminal groups to Canadian society. Sleipnir uses a rank-ordered set of 19 attributes to compare terrorist groups. Comparing the attributes of a number of terrorist groups helps assess the relative level of threat from each group. Some examples of the 19 attributes used to compare groups include: corruption, violence, subversion, mobility, and stability. Each attribute has five possible values: High, Medium, Low, Nil, or Unknown. This technique produces a framework for setting enforcement priorities by comparing the groups' capabilities, limitations and vulnerabilities. The matrix is the basis for systematically comparing the groups in order to present and explain the relative threat they pose. The matrix also effectively highlights research and intelligence gaps.

---

[6] Why is it called Sleipnir? Each RCMP project has a randomly selected name, those conducted at Headquarters start with the letter 'S'. In Old Norse mythology, Sleipnir is the name of the eight-legged horse belonging to Odin.

3.2. National Security Community Outreach

The Canadian response to terrorism was not without its unintended, negative consequences [12]. The RCMP's National Security Community Outreach Program was created to respond to issues raised by the minority communities of Canada during the Anti-terrorism Act (ATA) Tri-annual Parliamentary Review, as well as community consultations conducted since the passage of the ATA[7].

The concerns raised by minority communities members in these fora were feelings of being marginalized, ostracized, blamed or under suspicion of being terrorists or terrorist supporters or sympathizers because of their race/ethnicity etc., being treated disrespectfully because of a lack of knowledge or understanding of their cultures, fears of being a victim of terrorism, victim of a backlash against Visible Minorities because of a terrorist incident in Canada, or being an innocent victim of anti-terrorist measures. In keeping with the philosophy of Community Policing [13, 14], the RCMP realizes that it cannot protect Canadians from terrorism by itself. It requires the assistance and support of all Canadians to do so. The National Security Community Outreach Program is intended to engage all communities including the diverse ethnic, cultural and religious communities across Canada in the protection of Canada's national security; to increase the understanding of mutual goals and concerns, to ensure appropriate and informed communication should a crisis arise; and to identify/address local concerns.

Although the RCMP has the benefit of advice from a high-level citizen engagement program for national security through the Government of Canada's Cross Cultural Roundtable on Security, community outreach initiatives in each of the RCMP's Integrated National Security Enforcement Teams (INSET) and National Security Investigation Sections (NSIS) which identify local concerns are essential to the success of the National Security Program.

To achieve the goal of meaningful community outreach in the National Security Program, National Security Community Advisory Committees were created, similar to the Community Advisory committees in place at RCMP Contract Policing detachments across Canada. It must be emphasized that this is an enhancement of existing community engagement work, as the RCMP has been doing National Security Community Outreach with minority communities pre- and post-9/11, but these efforts were sporadic, uncoordinated and unfocused.

The prototype National Security Community Advisory Committee set up initially in the National Capital Region (Ottawa) to assist both the National Headquarters Policy Centre for National Security and the "A" Division Integrated National Security Enforcement Team (A INSET) serves as the model for the other INSETs/NSIS units. The NCR National Security Community Advisory Committee has completed several initiatives to assist the RCMP in its work, including development of protocol/guidelines for National Security Criminal investigators; a review of National Security training to include Community Outreach and Cultural Competency

---

[7] Such as a report of a focus group on Minority Views on the Canadian Anti-Terrorism Act prepared for Department of Justice Canada in March, 2003, the Public Safety and Emergency Preparedness Canada/Justice Canada public consultation with ethnic minority leaders on the impact of the Anti-terrorism Act on their communities in Nov., 2004, the report of a study done for the Canadian Research Institute for the Advancement of Women (CRIAW) and the National Organization of Immigrant and Visible Minority Women of Canada (NOIVMWC) on "The Impact Of The National Security Agenda On Racialized Women" dated Sept., 2004 and the Canadian Council on American-Islamic Relations (CAIR-CAN) 2004 survey "Presumption of Guilt: A National Survey on Security Visitations of Canadian Muslims"

components designed and delivered by representatives of minority communities; a community review of National Security policies and manuals, and organizing community outreach and education opportunities for RCMP National Security Criminal investigators to speak to the public on the National Security role, policies and practices of the RCMP. Canada's ethno-cultural communities are integral to its social and economic fabric and their efforts in speaking out to promote a peaceful and safe society are critical.

3.3. Project OSAGE Community Outreach

In June, 2006, the RCMP and its partner agencies in the Greater Toronto Area (GTA) arrested seventeen Canadians and charged them with terrorism offenses. This investigation and operation was code-named Project OSAGE. As part of the conclusion and take-down of Project OSAGE, it was stipulated in the Operational Plan that Muslim/ Arab community representatives and leaders in the four cities with the largest Muslim/Arab populations would be invited to meetings with representatives of the RCMP, CSIS and local Police Agency representatives. The objectives of these meetings were to address anxiety level of the communities, to ensure accurate/complete information on the charges was being disseminated, to respond to/discuss community concerns about backlash/hate crimes, and seek the help of the community to identify future terrorist conspiracies so they too could be intercepted before anyone was hurt.

3.4. Radicalization Prevention

The National Security Community Outreach program was developed in part as a response to the threat of youth political violence. It was first necessary to establish trust with the minority communities to gain their assistance and co-operation in protecting Canada's National Security, before addressing the risk of youth involvement in terrorist activities. The RCMP has been aware of the "Second Generation" phenomenon: the involvement of native-born youth in terrorist activities in Europe for some time [15], and has been particularly concerned about this occurring in Canada since the arrest of Momin Khawaja in March, 2004 [16, 17]. A number of recent domestic and international cases, including Project O-SAGE, the London bombings of July 7, 2005 and the arrests of 7 American youth in Florida in June, 2006 have demonstrated that the terrorist threat is not always an external one.

There is no single group that seeks out vulnerable and impressionable young people. Violent groups of all political ideologies employ similar recruiting strategies to target vulnerable young people and have done so throughout history. Canada has experienced this with the Front de Liberation du Quebec in the 1960s and Direct Action (the Squamish Five) in the 1980s. Neither profound religious faith nor deeply held political convictions are alien to the Canadian tradition. Nor do they necessarily manifest themselves in violence or extremism. For this reason, the RCMP is also engaged in initiatives understanding the process of radicalization and is working closely with its domestic and international partners, with academia and with minority communities to jointly develop strategies to identify, prevent and mitigate the threat posed by radicalization.

3.5. National Security Youth Outreach

In October 2005, the RCMP's National Security Youth Outreach Program (NSYOP) was implemented as part of the RCMP National Security Program. Its main goals are: (a) to engage youth on National Security issues; and, (b) to prevent youth extremism. Some of the initiatives undertaken to date include classroom presentations for university students; workshops and focus group discussions with high school students from across Canada; presentations at youth conferences; and, outreach to local community groups involved with youth.

A steering committee has being set up in Canada's National Capital Region to assist in the development of the RCMP National Security Youth Outreach Program. It is comprised of a group of young adults who provide input and guidance on initiatives for the RCMP National Security Youth Outreach program; assist in planning and organizing youth outreach activities; assist on sub-projects or sub-committees that address specific issues; and suggest how to effectively reach out to youth to get them engaged in national security issues.

The success of the RCMP's National Security Community Outreach Program demonstrates that a robust terrorism prevention program need not be pursued at the expense of human rights and civil liberties or the trust and respect of minority groups.

The policy implications for these responses to terrorism are as follows. The public including minority communities will support comprehensive terrorism prevention programs that are based on the rule of law and adhere to human rights protocols. All citizens fear being victims of terrorism. As well minority groups fear being victims of a backlash against their communities if there is a terrorist incident and also fear being an innocent victim of anti-terrorism measures. It is important that any terrorism response or preventive measure be scrutinized for the consequences it may have, unintended or not, on any part of a society.

4. Future Recommendations

As previously stated, the purpose of this study is to make a contribution to the effort against terrorism, specifically by making recommendations for governments, law enforcement agencies and for the future research on prevention and response strategies.

4.1. Recommendations for Governments

Governments should examine the multi-faceted responses that the Government of Canada used after the 9/11 attacks to prevent such occurrences here. Comprehensive anti-terrorism laws which provided tangible tools to law enforcement and security agencies while respecting human rights and civil liberties are essential to the struggle. In addition to laws, a comprehensive National policy on terrorism is needed to ensure the response is given the priority it needs to be successful. Additional resources must be made available for security agencies and law enforcement agencies, both for frontline duties and for investigational and analytical support, and human source recruiting. The Canadian experience provides valuable lessons learned and best practices for governmental response to the terrorism threat.

4.2. Recommendations for Law Enforcement Agencies

Increasing partnerships and cooperation including information sharing between and among security agencies and law enforcement agencies is another must, as incomplete information sharing can cause a great vulnerability in anti-terrorism defenses. Similarly, accuracy in reporting, sharing only on a need-to-know, right-to-know basis and respect for privacy go hand in hand with any information sharing. Law enforcement agencies also have to be aware that they will not be successful in protecting their citizens without the support and assistance of the public, including groups within society that are most likely to be impacted by anti-terrorism measures and who are most likely to withdraw from interaction and engagement with the law enforcement agencies who are trying to protect them. Law enforcement agencies should take notice of the success of the RCMP's National Security community outreach efforts with minority communities in Canada and adapt such measures to their own circumstances, in order to meet their own needs. While there is a tendency to devote as many resources as possible to frontline investigative, protective and intelligence functions in law enforcement agencies, resources devoted to developing and maintaining the public's trust and support is money well spent. As in the philosophy of Community Policing, the RCMP realizes that it cannot protect Canadians from terrorism by itself.

4.3. Recommendations for Future Research

The success or effectiveness of anti-terrorism measures is difficult to measure. Nonetheless they must be evaluated to ensure tax dollars are being spent where they will obtain the best results and to ensure both duplication and gaps in coverage are minimized. The public's support of anti-terrorism measures is also critically important and public opinion research can be invaluable in identifying shifts in opinion, confusion or a lack of understanding of anti-terrorism measures and the need for public education. The reasons native-born or long-time citizens of a country will resort to violence to achieve political goals is still not understood and must be studied empirically to minimize it as much as possible.

5. Conclusion

This study discussed the Government of Canada multi-faceted response to terrorism, which included Canada-wide government policy on National Security, legislative changes and how they facilitated terrorism investigations; specific law enforcement tools, resources and tactics; a strategic focus to investigations, integration and partnerships, cooperation and information sharing amongst the many law enforcement, security and government agencies that have a role to play in protecting National Security, Intelligence-led policing and an enhancement of the public's role in National Security, including that of the minority communities of Canada. The goal is to identify those best practices and innovations that other countries and law enforcement agencies should emulate.

Prevention of terrorism is a multi-dimensional challenge for law enforcement agencies as well and the RCMP is also addressing this on different levels. Integration facilitates cooperation and information sharing, which is the life blood of law enforcement. Enhancing investigative and analytical capacity for National Security Criminal Investigations, improving human source development techniques and training, increasing the cultural sensitivity of investigators, initiating community outreach programs, seeking the support of ethno-cultural community leaders in preventing radicalization of youth, and searching for opportunities to reach out to youth and normalize relations with them are essential to the success of the endeavor.

The main recommendation of this analysis is that no one aspect of the responses to terrorism can be successful on its own in protecting a nation's national security. The response must be multi-faceted but coordinated amongst all the government actors with roles to play in terrorism prevention and include the assistance and support of the public. This offers the best solution to the dilemma of balancing the need for national security while respecting human rights and civil liberties. It is recommended that the Canadian model for response to terrorism be considered for use by other countries seeking this proportional response to the threat.

References

[1]   M.E. Beare, *Policing with a National Security Agenda*, Nathanson Centre for the Study of Organized Crime and Corruption. Commissioned by the Department of Canadian Heritage for the National Forum on Policing in a Multicultural Society; 2003.

[2]   R.A. Hudson, *The sociology and psychology of terrorism: Who becomes a terrorist and why?* A report prepared under an interagency agreement by the Federal Research Division, U.S. Library of Congress; 1999.

[3]   A. Silke, Fire of Iolaus: The role of state countermeasures in causing terrorism and what needs to be done. In T. Borgo, Editor. *Root Causes of Terrorism: Myths, reality and ways for war,* London: Routledge; 2005, 241-255.

[4]   Securing an Open Society: Canada's National Security Policy. 2004.

[5]   *Canadian Security Guide Book*, Senate of Canada. 2005.

[6]   Canada Customs and Revenue Agency. *Fact sheet: The Smart Border Declaration.* 2002.

[7]   D. Jenkins, In support of Canada's Anti-Terrorism Act: A comparison of Canadian, British, and American Anti-Terrorism Law. *Saskatchewan Law Review*, **66** (2003), 419-454.

[8]   Public Safety and Emergency Preparedness Canada, *Cross Cultural Roundtable on Security Information Sheet*, 2005.

[9]   Report of the Auditor General of Canada to the House of Commons. Canada, 2004.

[10] S. Cohen, Policing security: The divide between crime and terror. *National Journal of Constitutional Law*, (2004).

[11] O'Connor, Commission of inquiry into the actions of Canadian officials in relation to Maher Arar. Analysis and Recommendations. Canada, 2006.

[12] I. Almeida, M. Porret, *Canadian democracy at a crossroads: The need for coherence and accountability in counter-terrorism policy and practice, rights & democracy*, International Centre for Human Rights and Democratic Development, 2004.

[13] R. Roberg, J. Kuykendall, K. Novak, *Police Management*, 3rd Ed., Los Angeles, CA: Roxbury Publishing Company; 2002.

[14] I. Waller, *Less law, more order: The truth about reducing crime*, Westport, Con: Praeger; 2006.

[15] P. Nesser, Profiles of jihadist terrorists in Europe, In C. Bernard. Editor. *A future for the young, options for helping Middle Eastern youth escape the trap of radicalization*, Washington DC: RAND; 2006.

[16] R.S. Leiken, *Europe's mujahideen: Where mass immigration meets global terrorism*, Washington, DC: Center for Immigration Studies; 2005.

[17] A. Gendron, Militant jihadism: Radicalization, conversion, recruitment. *ITAC Presents Trends in Terrorism Series*, **4** (2006).

Understanding and Responding to the Terrorism Phenomenon
O. Nikbay and S. Hancerli (Eds.)
IOS Press, 2007

Implementing Democratic Policing in the PKK Terrorism Torn Areas of Turkey

Tuncay DURNA[a], Ph.D., Suleyman HANCERLI[b]
[a]*Police Training Adviser, OSCE Mission to Serbia*
[b]*Ph.D. Candidate, University of North Texas*
[a,b]*Superintendent, Turkish National Police*

Abstract. One important goal of terrorist organizations is to provoke the governments to respond to them harshly and in an indiscriminate way in which the civilians would also suffer. Then terrorists would use that counter productive strategy of governments to gain support from the public. In this regard, Turkey's struggle against the PKK terrorism has created some indirect consequences, such as the damage in the social fabric, lack of trust of the governmental institutions, and the tension between the public and law enforcement agencies. This paper discusses implementing democratic policing principles in terrorism torn areas to alleviate the tension between the public and law enforcement agencies and to restore the public trust in the police which has been damaged during the struggle against the PKK terrorism. Moreover, it is believed that such an improvement will reinforce the development of democracy in the country.

Keywords. Terrorism, PKK-Kongra Gel, political violence, counter-terrorism, democratic policing, Turkish National Police, and Turkey

Introduction

Terrorist organizations usually desire a conflict within the society and between the society and the governments. They desire that the fear and panic they are spreading will eventually galvanize the governments to go after them very harshly, which may lead to a conflict in the society between the governmental forces and the people. They also attempt to provoke the masses into a conflict with the governmental forces, or to provoke the government against the civilians. Eventually, this conflict might be used for terrorists' own grounds to overthrow the governments or to have the governments turn against their own population for security reasons. Thus, the severity of security measures can weaken public confidence in the government and may lead to the legitimacy of the government's actions being undermined [1, 2].

Terrorism achieves its goals not solely through its acts, but also through the responses to its acts. When provocation by terrorists leads to an overreaction by the government, it makes governments appear repressive, which is, in turn, used by terrorist organizations for propaganda to undermine the governments' authority. Fromkin points to such a strategy of terrorism in the mid 1970s, stating that "…terror can accomplish nothing in terms of political goals; it can only aim at obtaining a response that will achieve those goals for it" [1 pg 689]. Finding evidence from the French government's policies in 1950s towards Algerian National Liberation Front

(NLF), he discusses how brutality –as an induced governmental response– can boomerang.

Similarly, Spain's response to ETA (Euskadi Ta Askatasuna or "Basque Homeland and Freedom") or Peruvian response to Sendero Luminoso (Shining Path) shows how terrorist organizations benefited from indiscriminate and harsh governmental response. Moreover, these cases present how democracy is damaged and terrorism makes gains when democratic rules are broken to fight terrorism [3]. In the Peruvian case, the brutal and indiscriminate response of the military in the forms of torture, disappearances, and illegal killings alienated the peasantry and created waves of internally displaced. Ron [4] notes that as a result of Peruvian response in the first five years of Sendero's insurgency, Sendero's popular appeal was broadened, and its reach spread throughout the country.

In any democratic country where public life and order are threatened by terrorism, however, it is inevitable that the government will take security measures that can constrain civil liberties. It is important that the security measures take place within the rule of law in order to avoid public grievances and dissatisfaction with law enforcement agencies.

For Turkey, terrorism has been an important problem for the last three decades with its different forms, including Marxist-Leninist, religiously inspired, and ethnic separatist ones in nature. Intensifying its activities in the southeastern part of the country, where the majority of the population is Kurdish, ethnic separatist terrorism of the PKK (Kurdistan Workers Party or "Partiya Karkerên Kurdistan") has been the most challenging one. PKK terrorism has claimed more than thirty thousand lives including civilians and the security forces over the last 25 years with an approximate cost of more than 100 billion in US dollars to the country [5].

Turkey's response to PKK terrorism varied from ignoring the PKK as a serious threat in the mid-1980s to considering it the most important problem threatening the unity of the nation state. The PKK problem has been treated mainly as a security issue rather than a broader problem with social, economic, and cultural dimensions. Such a definition and acceptance of the problem brought its own solutions in forms of tight security measures. The severity of some of those measures handed propaganda material to the terrorist organization to undermine the Turkish government's authority in the southeastern part of the country. However, although the PKK gained substantial support from the region through either propaganda or imposing fear, it could never acquire the support and acceptance of the majority to reach its goals.

Along with the casualties and its enormous cost, Turkey's struggle against PKK terrorism also caused immigration of thousands of families to safer metropolitan cities, which increased the poverty level and street crime. Beyond these "direct" consequences, however, PKK terrorism brought about some "indirect" consequences, which have not been fully addressed yet. The dominant perception of the issue as a security problem shadowed those "indirect" consequences, such as the damage in the social fabric in the region, lack of trust in the governmental institutions, and the tension between the public and the law enforcement agencies.

This paper discusses implementing democratic policing principles, especially in southeastern Turkey, where the effects of PKK terrorism have been more visible, to relieve the tension between the public and the security forces and to restore the public order. It is believed that citizen participation and contribution to community safety problems will increase their satisfaction of law enforcement services, will reduce complaints, will thwart terrorist recruitment, and will restore trust in governmental institutions.

1. History and Nature of the PKK Terrorism in Turkey

The Worker's Party of Kurdistan was formally established on November 27, 1978 in the village of Fis in Diyarbakir by Abdullah Öcalan and his friends. The PKK has its roots in the leftist movements of the1970s, and the nucleus of the organization can be dated back to 1974 [6].

The PKK was founded to stage a communist revolution through armed struggle against the Turkish government and establish a separate Kurdish state based on Marxist-Leninist ideology. However, promoting a Marxist-Leninist ideology was not an easy task in the southeastern region of the country, where people were largely religious, traditional, undereducated and still tribal in nature [7]. Terrorism, therefore, was seen as the best strategy to recruit new members to the organization. In this regard, Bruinessen [8] states that Öcalan's group was the only Kurdish organization whose members were drawn almost exclusively from the lowest social classes, half-educated village and small-town youths who wanted action rather than ideological sophistication.

Starting in 1984, the PKK started to attack Kurdish villages killing civilians including women and children. The message was that any family who dealt with the Turkish state would be destroyed. In fact, the PKK had generally lacked the support of a large proportion of the people and relied on a small minority, many of whom were forced to support the terrorist organization.

By 1987, the PKK had managed to recruit thousands of sympathizers and develop its organization. Until 1990, the terrorist organization attacked many Kurdish villages claiming thousands of innocent lives and explaining those attacks as offensive against village guards who are declared to be "state collaborators" [7]. Many Kurdish people under PKK attacks have then sought assistance from the Turkish government and joined the counterinsurgency campaign.

In the early 1990s, however, the PKK began to change the balance in regard to its own support. As the terrorist attacks forced the security forces to take a tougher stance, the local people were forced to take a neutral position. In time, this neutrality, stemming from self-survival amounted to tacit support [9]. Other factors such as the power vacuum in northern Iraq following the Gulf War, the escalating risk environment around Turkey's borders, and propaganda against Turkey playing on the human rights issues also contributed to the growth of the terrorist organization. The no-fly zone created in Northern Iraq by the Allies became the PKK's new training grounds and the most appropriate territory to organize its attacks against Turkey [10, 11]. Consequently, in the post Gulf War era, the number of attacks conducted by the PKK rose rapidly and, during the following years of active combat, on average, over a thousand people lost their lives each year.

Pressure from Turkey on the Syrian government to release Öcalan and not to harbor PKK terrorists in its territories yielded results in 1998. Feeling international pressure and fearing Turkish military action, Syria forced Öcalan to leave the country. Öcalan then unsuccessfully sought asylum in some European countries, including Russia and Italy until February 1999, when he was captured by Turkish Special Forces in Kenya where he was taking refuge in the Greek Embassy.

Abdullah Öcalan's capture marked the most important cornerstone in the terrorist organization's history. Radu [11] defines Turkey's campaign against the PKK terrorist organization as one of the few recent examples of clear victory by the state, mentioning that only Peruvian success against the Shining Path and Tupac Amaru Revolutionary Movement was similarly decisive. Following his capture, Öcalan declared that the war was over and that the Kurds should focus on political struggle rather than warfare. A Turkish court sentenced Öcalan to death; however, the sentence has never been carried out. Instead, the Turkish government commuted it to life in prison in 2002.

Captured, Öcalan's call for refraining from violence and declaration of a unilateral cease fire found support from the terrorist organization. Although there were some groups challenging the central leadership, many groups of PKK members gave up armed struggle and the rest moved to camps in Northern Iraq. Despite some internal challenges, however, Öcalan has remained the sole leader of the terrorist organization even in prison. In 2002, the PKK eventually disbanded, renaming itself KADEK (Kurdistan Freedom and Democracy Congress). The group claimed that the reason for the name change was to emphasize its renunciation of violence and commitment to democratic change. Cline [12], however, holds that, although unstated, the real reason was the fact that in the aftermath of the September 11 attacks, an increasing number of countries were including the PKK on the roster of terrorist organizations. The name change was simply a cheap deception to escape the legal results of being listed among terrorist organizations.

Despite the new title, KADEK was practically indistinguishable from its predecessor [6, 12]. The organization's armed wing, The People's Defense Force (HPG), would never disband or surrender its weapons. Evidently the name change did not serve its intended political purpose. Then, PKK/KADEK went through another political face-lift, renaming the group KONGRA-GEL (Kurdistan People's Congress) in late 2003. PKK/KONGRA-GEL ended its unilateral ceasefire in August 2004 and restarted carrying out terrorist attacks on military, civilians, police and governmental targets. Recently, there has been an increase in the number of terrorist attacks in southeastern Turkey especially in the form of roadside bombings.

In 2003 the organization went through a massive change, dissolving itself to re-form as a new, more democratic organizational structure that allows broader participation. The main objective of that reorganization was, as mentioned earlier, to escape the consequences of being listed as a terrorist organization in the post 9/11 period [12]. The "new" organization naming itself the Kurdistan People's Congress (KONGRA-GEL), however, could not escape being listed on terrorist organization rosters in many countries including the U.S. and the E.U. member states.

1.1. Ideology, Structure, and Strategy

It can be said that ideologically, the PKK has evolved through several stages, revolving around Kurdish separatism. Özcan [13] maintains that the PKK's ideology was shaped by its perception of imperialism, Cold War circumstances, socialism, and ethnic considerations. Some researchers identify three main stages: the early stage prior to 1978, the second stage between 1978 and 1989, and the third stage from 1989 onwards [7]. In the first two stages, ideology of the PKK can be characterized as Marxist-Leninist, separatist, anti-religious and anti-traditionalist and seeking an independent Kurdistan through violence [14]. Since the overwhelming majority of the population in southeastern Turkey has been traditionalist, religious, and -to some extent- tribal, the

PKK faced considerable resistance from the people in that region with its Marxist-Leninist ideology. In order to win the support of the larger religious community, religious themes were incorporated into the PKK's ideology in time, which characterizes the third stage. In addition, starting in the early 2000s arguments of Kurdish nationalism were also added to the ideology of the organization.

Radu [11], on the other hand, considers the ideology of the PKK to be coherent and notes that since the beginning, the PKK has been Marxist-Leninist in its ideology, Stalinist in its leadership style, and Maoist in its strategy for the conquest of power. Furthermore, he argues that Marxism, not Kurdish nationalism, has always defined the PKK since the founders of the PKK included ethnic Turks as well as Kurds. Radu also combines the ideology and the structure of the terrorist organization with the leadership style of Öcalan. Öcalan's willingness to ruthlessly eliminate any internal challenges led to his undisputed command of the organization and absolute authority with a cult of personality surrounding him [11, 12]. In addition, the fact that PKK attacks resulted in thousands of Kurdish civilian casualties suggests that absolute power matters far more to Öcalan than the welfare of the people he claims to lead. Over the years, the PKK killed innocent Kurdish people for collaboration with the Turkish government and for not supporting the terrorist organization. Öcalan's desire for power has continued during his time in jail; he is still the absolute leader of the PKK, and the main goal of the organization has become freeing Öcalan from the imprisonment.

The PKK terrorist organization used coercive and indiscriminate violence to establish a Marxist-Leninist Kurdish state. Based on the organization's resolutions in the fifth congress in 1995, Radu [11], however, claims that the foundation of a Kurdish state was never an ultimate goal itself, but rather a means to spread socialism. According to the same author, the PKK's strategy resembles Mao's theory of people's war, which attempts to reach its goals in three stages: gaining support of the population by attacking its rivals and government machinery, intensified terrorist attacks to break the government's authority, and conventional warfare to seize cities.

Another researcher compares PKK's overall strategy to that of Shining Path in Peru, which consists of three phases: strategic defense, strategic balance, and strategic offense [15]. The first phase would garner new recruits and would force local people to support armed struggle, while the second phase would seek to develop its authority in the region to launch a large-scale guerilla war. Finally, the third stage would be the conventional warfare with total support of the population. Apparently, the PKK was unable to progress beyond the first phase of that strategy. Extensive and indiscriminate use of terrorism resulted in lack of popular support for the PKK, which, in turn, did not allow the organization to establish safe areas and bases in the region from which to launch guerilla warfare to diminish government authority and to claim more legitimacy, thereby leading to conventional warfare [7].

Most of the PKK terrorist attacks focused on the security forces; however, the terrorist organization also attacked civilians, mostly of Kurdish origin, who would not cooperate with the group. Those indiscriminate attacks resulted in thousands of civilian casualties, sometimes eradication of entire families including infants, women, and the elderly. The terrorist organization also killed dissidents within the organization's ranks. Although the majority of the attacks were carried out in southeastern Turkey, the PKK also attacked government and civilian targets in metropolitan cities and tourist areas. Tactics of the terrorist organization included ambush, sabotage, bomb attacks, kidnapping, assassination, suicide bombings, riots, and protests. In order to undermine the Turkish government's authority, the terrorist organization attacked and killed civilian officials, like school teachers and workers, torched buildings and machinery, set up wildfires to destroy the forests and natural resources. Government officials and Kurdish tribe leaders were kidnapped or assassinated. The PKK also participated in kidnapping western tourists, primarily in Istanbul, but also at different resorts. Turkish diplomatic and commercial facilities across Western Europe also became targets for terrorist attacks.

Suicide bombing is another tactic employed by the PKK. Between 1996 and 1999 the terrorist organization managed to carry out 15 suicide attacks, while six others were aborted due to the apprehension of the perpetrators in preparation [6]. Although the targets of those attacks were high-level provincial officers, police, or military personnel and installations, innocent bystanders also suffered equally. Ergil [16] reports that those suicide attacks claimed the lives of 16 police officers and military personnel and 4 civilians, wounding around 140 people, the majority of whom were civilians. Women were used as the suicide bombers in 14 of these attacks. There are several accounts that Öcalan himself endorsed and encouraged suicide bombings [6].

2. Turkey's Counter-Terrorism Strategies

Although there have been many attacks in other parts of the country, PKK terrorism has focused on the southeastern part of the country. While the rugged mountains provided safe grounds for the terrorists, the scarce density of population in the area, which is mostly rural, challenged the security forces to provide security for the citizens. Those challenges lead the governments to take some contentious security measures, such as recruiting village guards and relocating people from remote villages to safer urban areas.

The authors of Ankara Papers [7] divide Turkish government policies for combating terrorism into three categories: proactive measures, reactive measures, and the democratization project.

2.1. Proactive Measures

The proactive measures against terrorism include socio-economic policies, health and education programs, and government subsidies for agriculture and small businesses. In the mid-1980s, the government realized the crucial role of economic development in combating terrorism. Since the unemployed, undereducated and hopeless youth have been the main target of the PKK's recruitment campaigns, through economic investment to create jobs and a better life, the government aimed to win the support of the regional people and to undermine support for the terrorist organization. Among those policies, the "Southeastern Anatolia Project", also known as GAP (Güneydoğu Anadolu Projesi), is the most significant one as being the biggest economic investment in Turkey's history. The Southeastern Anatolia Project is an integrated regional development effort, which consists of such sectors as irrigation, hydraulic energy, agriculture, rural and urban infrastructure, forestry, education and health. The project covers nine provinces in the southeastern region and comprises a network of hydroelectric power plants and irrigation canals taking advantage of the Euphrates and the Tigris rivers. Its basic objectives include the improvement of living standards and income levels of people to eliminate regional development disparities and to contribute to such national goals as social stability and economic growth by enhancing productivity and employment opportunities in the rural sector [17]. Through policies to curb the social and economic problems, the government sought to undermine the claims of the PKK and its propaganda.

2.2. Reactive Measures

The reactive policies consist of the security measures developed in the course of struggle against PKK terrorism over the last two decades. The government used the law enforcement agencies –the police and the gendarmerie forces–, military forces, temporary village guards, and special anti-terrorist units and declared states of emergency in eastern and southeastern Turkey to combat the terrorist organization. When the terrorist attacks began to increase, however, security measures stepped up and the military took over the decision-making role [7].

2.3. The Democratization Project

The democratization project mainly revolves around Turkey's accession efforts to the European Union. Several amendments to the constitution, adoption of a new penal code and a criminal procedures law, modifications in the civil law, and removal of State Security Courts (Devlet Güvenlik Mahkemeleri) are worth mentioning among those policies that form the democratization project. There are also indications that the Turkish government's approach to PKK terrorism has evolved from accepting the issue as merely a security problem to a broader perspective with socio-economic and cultural attributes. In this regard, resolutions to allow broadcasting in Kurdish language and opening language courses to teach Kurdish were enacted by the Turkish National Assembly.

Among those policies, adoption and implementation of various security measures was the most contentious. Measures like declaration of state of emergency in southeast provinces, establishment of temporary village guards, and relocation of people from remote and insecure villages or hamlets to urban areas have been the most significant ones. Those measures provided the security forces for the necessary grounds to develop effective combat strategies and contributed to Turkey's success in curbing PKK terrorism. Nevertheless, those policies account for the majority of grievances from the public.

In 1985, the Turkish government established the "temporary village guards" in areas where activities of violence required a state of emergency in order to prevent aggression against the property or lives of the villagers. Temporary village guards were drafted mainly from the local Kurdish population, a vast majority of whom were almost completely integrated into the rest of the country. This move was a vital threat to the PKK since the organization had declared itself as the representative of Kurdish nationalism. The large attendance in the temporary village guards directed the PKK's full attention on them; they became one of the major targets of terrorist attacks. In time, however, many of those village guards are reported to have become involved in arms and drug smuggling, extortion, and killings, which in turn caused complaints from the public [18].

Establishment of state of emergency inevitably imposed some constraints on the daily lives of people in the region and became a major source of public grievances. Migration from insecure villages and hamlets to urban areas resulted in a significant increase in the unemployment rate, poverty level, organized crime, and street crime over the years.

The operations of security forces were carried out under special amendments to the Prevention of Terrorism Act. In any democratic country where the public order is threatened by large-scale terrorism, enactment of legislation that puts constraints on civil liberties becomes necessary. Ünal [19] notes that many advanced western democracies enacted similar legislation. The U.S. and the U.K., for example, have taken similar measures after September 11th and the London bombings.

As mentioned earlier, in many cases, terrorist organizations attempt to achieve their goals through the response by the government to their actions. Severe measures and their indiscriminate implementation by the security forces hand over propaganda material to the terrorist organizations and undermine the authority of government. Therefore, policies to combat terrorism must aim to minimize the negative effects on the general public. Moreover, those policies must consider the delicate balance between security measures and civil liberties and all must be implemented in rule of law.

In the case of the PKK, it is often argued that the reactive actions taken by the Turkish governments often exacerbated matters and even inflamed the situation although they were necessary steps to curb terrorism [7]. The PKK took advantage of the public frustration created by those security measures and exploited the public sensitivity, frequently exaggerating every single incident. Moreover, the PKK played the ethnic identity card successfully, claiming that the Turkish government had been ignoring the Kurdish citizens and depriving them of their rights and freedoms. Coupled with the PKK's propaganda, public grievances about the constraints of the security measures on daily life and complaints of the attitudes of the security forces towards people accumulated, resulting in a lack of trust toward governmental institutions and a tension between law enforcement agencies and the public.

The dominant perception of identifying the problem as merely a security issue in which lives of the innocent citizens and security forces and the integrity of the state is at stake pushed the public grievances and their effects on public trust down in the agenda. More emphasis has been placed on providing security and hunting down terrorists than wining local support from the entire society and repairing the bonds between the public and the security forces. Capture of Öcalan in 1999 and the break of terrorist attacks afterwards brought to the surface the damage in the social fabric and the tension between the public and law enforcement agencies. The diminishing support for the PKK and protests against the terrorist organization when it restarted armed struggle in 2004 show signs of recovery; however, those indirect effects of terrorism have not been fully addressed through a comprehensive project yet.

3. Implementing Democratic Policing as a Remedy

Criminal justice is a highly sensitive and crucial point of entry where citizens are most likely to experience government in their daily lives. As Karstedt and LaFree [20] point out, encounters with criminal justice agents, especially the police, are a crucial part of the living experience of democracy. The role of the police becomes more significant where security is the most important concern in people's daily lives. If the bonds of trust between the public and the law enforcement are broken or even weakened, democracy –along with the public order and the governmental authority– begins to erode. Therefore, restoring the trust between the public and the police not only improves people's sense of security and the quality of life, but also contributes to development and sustainability of democracy. We suggest that the way to restore that trust and improve the police-public relationship is to systematically promote democratic policing principles and practices in law enforcement.

Although there are commonly agreed on definitions for democracy in general, when it comes to democratic policing, the conceptions center on a set of core values and norms which are expressed and detailed in slightly different ways and levels of complexity. For Skolnick [21], openness and accountability are the two fundamental principles for democratic policing. Stone and Ward [22] note that accountability to multiple structures, at multiple levels of control, distinguishes democratic police from police governed by other regimes. In a more detailed account, Bruce and Neild [23] point out five areas of concern in relation to democratic policing: protecting democratic political life; governance, accountability and transparency; service delivery for safety, justice and security; proper police conduct; and police as citizens.

In terms of defining the elements of democratic policing, Bayley [24, 25] sets out and elaborates four norms, which correspond to the others mentioned above. According to Bayley [25 pg 13], democratic police forces must act in accordance with the following norms:

1.   Police must give top priority to servicing needs of individual citizens and private groups.
2.   Police must be accountable to the law rather than to the government.
3.   Police must protect human rights, especially those that are required for the sort of unfettered political activity that is the hallmark of democracy.
4.   Police should be transparent in their activities.

Jones, Newburn, and Smith [26] also clearly identify a set of values that include participation, responsiveness, sharing of information, distribution of power, the notion of address, effective delivery of services, and equity. In addition to those, Marenin [27] mentions the representativeness of personnel as measured by the distribution of salient identities in society, integrity management as a central function of police administration, and a semi-autonomous status of the police organization and system as other characteristics of democratic policing.

In summary, in a free and democratic society, the police must balance demands for the maintenance of order with respect for the law and the rights of individuals. In such an environment, in which law-abiding citizens have nothing to fear from the police, the police serving the public good, are accountable for their actions, and are transparent in their activities. Moreover, the police address the concerns and the needs of the people, not necessarily the state. In this sense, democratic policing embodies the core principles of community oriented policing.

3.1. Policing in Turkey and Recommendations

It should be noted that the notion of democratic policing has mostly been emphasized to reform or establish policing systems through international assistance and advice in transitional or post-authoritarian states, which experienced recent political changes or rigorous civil unrest. In the case of Turkey, however, implementing democratic policing implies reinvigoration of the policing system to nurture the public trust, which is weakened due to the lengthy period of struggle with ethnic separatist terrorism. It can be argued that the term "community policing" could be preferred over "democratic policing" in this context. However, the authors of this paper acknowledge that democratic policing has a broader meaning, which also indicates and corresponds to the overall democratization process within Turkey's bid to be a part of the EU. Moreover, a police force carrying out its duties under principles of democratic policing can reinforce and contribute to the democratic political development and the very name democratic policing helps to cause.

During the course of Turkey's fight against PKK terrorism, in which providing security and protecting the unity of state have become the primary concern, the police have been under the total control of the state and responsive to the state identified problems. Most of the police duties were reactive in nature and an inordinate amount of time was spent on gathering intelligence and conducting covert operations. Thus, the police committed itself to the status quo and remained aloof from the community. In time, the public started to perceive the police as adversaries and as an instrument to deliver oppressive governmental policies for the sake of protecting the regime and the state even at the expense of civil liberties. Along with these duty characteristics, with its highly centralized structure and a strict hierarchical chain of command, the Turkish National Police (TNP) reflected the features of a non-democratic police organization. To restore the trust of the society, the TNP must embrace the principles of democratic policing.

It should be noted that, starting in 2000, the TNP has passed through an incredibly fast self-renovation. Corresponding to the country's bid to enter the European Union; the TNP has improved the quality of its equipment, infrastructure, and most importantly its recruitment and training procedures. The number of TNP members with advance degrees has increased along with the quality and time of the in service training, which in turn, has contributed to provision of better police services. Moreover, strict enforcement of "zero tolerance" to human rights violations within the organization created a sheer consciousness among TNP members and promoted a comprehensive and solid understanding of rule of law and respect for civil liberties.

The major difference between non-democratic and democratic policing is that in the latter, police work is in response to citizen identified problems as opposed to those identified primarily by the state. It is apparent that the needs and the problems of the citizens differ from the priorities of the state. Although security and ethnic separatism are still major concerns in some cities of southeastern Turkey, the real problems for the people stem from the rapid urban growth due to the migration from insecure villages or hamlets. Unemployed and undereducated crowds began to be involved in street crimes, gang activities, and drugs related organized crime, which dramatically increased fear of crime and decreased the quality of life, however, providing an invaluable opportunity for the police to reconstruct its ties with the communities they serve.

In the relative absence of the threat of terrorism, the TNP should reorient its forces to address citizen generated or identified problems. This strategy requires community involvement as partners in the process of identifying, prioritizing, and solving problems including crime, fear of crime, and social and physical disorder. Acquiring such a partnership in an environment in which public trust in the police has been impaired is not an easy task. Considering the strength of tribal connections in the southeast, Turkish police forces should identify and initiate contact with key community leaders to encourage citizens to participate in regular police-community meetings where local problems will be addressed. Successful police intervention to problems identified by the community will reinforce the participation process and build up mutual trust while the public experiences that their demands are being considered and their needs are being served.

Furthermore, such a move by the police will support democratization initiatives. Police are not freestanding bureaucratic actors, but their activities are matters of government or at least require governmental approval. Therefore, delivering police services in accordance with the needs of the public will enhance the legitimacy and authority of the government by demonstrating that the authority and resources of the state are being used in the interests of the people [25]. Once the trust between the public and the police is established, the perception of the police as the guarantor of civil liberties will prevail.

As Marenin [27] emphasizes, the police, however, should not be overly responsive to the demands of the civic society or local communities in order not to be slaves to the changing shifts of power and opinions in the society. Furthermore, he notes that the police have to be detached enough from external pressures to be able to do their job in accordance with legal and professional norms, whereas they have to be attached enough to societal expectations about what their job is and how it should be done to remain accountable.

In an attempt to implement democratic policing, the TNP should also put more emphasis on overt law enforcement and criminal investigations rather than conducting covert operations. This strategy supports democratic policing in two ways. First, with more visibility of the police on the street, the public will develop a sense of security and both the police and the people will benefit from having the time and opportunity to develop partnerships. Second, it serves to create a transparent police force since the public will mostly be aware of the police operations. It is apparently not enough to ensure transparency and should be supported by procedures that allow citizens to obtain information about conduct of individual police officers as well as the operations of the police forces.

As a part of the EU harmonization process, the TNP launched a community policing project in 2006 [28]. The project has been initiated in 10 pilot provinces including the southeastern city of Diyarbakir, where the majority of the citizens are of Kurdish origin. The goal of the project is to achieve the police force's cooperation with all levels of the public. Although a systematic evaluation of the project has yet to be done, our interviews with community police officers in Diyarbakir yielded promising indications; they all pointed out the citizens' satisfaction of police officers' focus on their problems.

Implementing democratic policing and adhering to its principles, however, does not necessarily mean abandoning traditional police functions but enhancing them with broader community involvement to restore public trust to the police. This is particularly important for the TNP, especially in the southeastern part of the country where security still remains as a major concern and terrorist activities and propaganda still continue.

4. Conclusion

Although Turkey's reactive policies against PKK terrorism have proved to be successful, they also resulted in frustration in the public, especially in those living in the southeast. Some security measures have been contentious and have lent themselves to fruitful propaganda material for the terrorist organization. Together with the propaganda of the terrorist organization, the security measures brought about a lack of trust in governmental institutions, a tension between the public and the security forces including the police. The steep decrease in the number of terrorist incidents after Öcalan's capture and normalization of the daily life in southeastern Turkey provide an important opportunity for the police to restore mutual trust with the community which has been constantly intimidated by the PKK.

The authors of this paper believe that the Turkish police can achieve this goal by implementing a comprehensive democratic policing program which primarily addresses the problems of the communities, provides more transparency of police operations, respects civil liberties, and operates within the rule of law. Priority should be given to addressing the public needs and problems which require active participation form the community. Initial police-community partnerships to identify and solve public problems will reinforce the practice by creating a snowball effect and providing more citizen input.

It should be noted that improving democratic policing should be considered not as an independent prospect by itself, but as one of the components of a broader policy to restore state-public relations in the region. Therefore, initiatives of the police must be supplemented and supported by other programs to address social and economic problems. Restoring the public trust through practicing democratic policing will eventually strengthen the authority of the government by showing that the state resources are being used to address community problems.

Taking advantage of some contentious security measures, the PKK has been intimidating the public to gain moral, human, and material support for their terrorist organization. Active participation of the public to address their needs and close relationships with the police to solve problems will increase satisfaction of citizens, reduce their grievances, thwart terrorist recruitment, and increase public tolerance of counter-terrorism policies. It is essential that further security measures should not be counter-productive; that is, those policies must not allow the terrorist organization to make use of them against the government. To maintain public support, possible effects of security measures on civil liberties and local sensitivities should be considered when developing counter-terrorism policies.

Turkish National Police has the manpower and experience to put democratic policing principles into practice. By doing so, it will not only restore mutual trust with the public but also will contribute to development and sustainability of democracy in Turkey.

References

[1]   D. Fromkin, The strategy of terrorism, *Foreign Affairs*. **53/4** (1975), 683–698.
[2]   I.J. Ross, R.R. Miller, The effects of oppositional political terrorism, five actors based model. *Low Intensity Conflict & Law Enforcement*. **6/3** (1997), 76-107.
[3]   P. Woodworth, The war against terrorism: The Spanish experience from ETA to Al-Qaeda. *International Journal of Iberian Studies*. **17/3** (2004), 169-182.
[4]   J. Ron, Ideology in context: Explaining Sendero Luminoso's tactical escalation. *Journal of Peace Research*. **38/5** (2001), 569-592.
[5]   İ. Cerrah, PKK terörünün sosyoekonomik ve kültürel nedenleri, *Milletlerarası Doğu ve Güneydoğu Anadolu Güvenlik ve Huzur Sempozyumu Bildirileri*. Elazığ: Fırat Üniversitesi Yayınları; 2000.
[6]   İEM (İstanbul Emniyet Müdürlüğü, Terörle Mücadele Şube Müdürlüğü) [Istanbul Police Department, Counter-Terrorism Division], *PKK/KONGRA-GEL*. Eğitim Serisi, No: 6 2004.
[7]   Ankara Papers, The case of the PKK: History, ideology, methodology, and structure (1978–99). **9/1** (2004), 1-83.

[8]   M.V. Bruinessen, Between guerrilla war and political murder: The Worker's Party of Kurdistan. *Middle East Report.* 1988, July-August, 40-46.

[9]   N.B. Criss, The nature of PKK terrorism in Turkey. *Studies in Conflict and Terrorism.* **8** (1995), 17-37.

[10] S.J. Blank, S.C. Pelletier, W.T. Johnsen, *Turkey's strategic position at the crossroads of world affairs.* (Report to Strategic Studies Institute, U.S. Army War College), 1993.

[11] M. Radu, The rise and fall of the PKK, *Orbis.* **45/1** (2001), 47-64.

[12] L.E. Cline, From Öcalan to Al Qaida: The continuing terrorist threat in Turkey. *Studies in Conflict and Terrorism.* **27**(2004), 321-335.

[13] N.A. Özcan, *PKK (Kürdistan İşçi Partisi) tarihi, ideolojisi ve yönetimi* [*PKK, its history, ideology and methods*]. Ankara: ASAM; 1999.

[14] I.G. İmset, *PKK: Ayrilikçi şiddetin 20 yili (1973-1992)* [*The PKK: Report on separatist violence in Turkey, 1973–1992.*] Ankara: Turkish Daily News Publications; 1992.

[15] T. Marks, Making revolution with shining path. In D.S. Palmer, Editor. *Shining path of Peru.* London: Hurst and Company; 1992.

[16] D. Ergil, Suicide terrorism in Turkey. *Civil Wars.* **3/1** (2000), 37-54.

[17] Southeastern Anatolia Project Regional Development Administration, 2007. [Online] Available from; URL: http://www.gap.gov.tr/gapeng.html [2007, March 04].

[18] E. Beşe, Temporary village guards. In Ü. Cizre, Editor. *Almanac Turkey 2005: Security sector and democratic oversight.* Istanbul: TESEV Publications; 2006.

[19] Ş. Ünal, Milletlerarası hukuk açisindan Güneydoğu sorunu ve terörle mücadele. Ankara: TBMM Yayınları; 1997.

[20] S. Karstedt, G. Lafree, Democracy, crime, and justice. *The Annals of the American Academy of Political and Social Science.* **605/1** (2006), 6-23.

[21] J.H. Skolnick, On democratic policing. *Ideas in American policing.* Washington, D.C.: Police Foundation; 1999.

[22] C. E. Stone, H.H. Ward, Democratic policing: A framework for action, *Policing and Society.* **10** (2000), 11-45.

[23] D. Bruce, R. Neid, *The police that we want: A handbook for oversight of the police in South Africa.* Open Society Justice Initiative; 2005.

[24] D.H. Bayley, A foreign policy for democratic policing. *Policing and Society.* **5/2** (1995), 79-94.

[25] D.H. Bayley, *Democratizing the police abroad: What to do and how to do it.* Washington, D.C.: National Institute of Justice; 2001.

[26] T. Jones, T. Newburn, D.J. Smith, Policing and the idea of democracy. *British Journal of Criminology.* **36** (1996), 182-198.

[27] O. Marenin, *Restoring policing systems in conflict torn nations: Process, problems, prospects.* Geneva: Geneva Centre for the Democratic Control of Armed Forces (DCAF); 2005.

[28] Asayiş Daire Başkanlığı, 2007. [Online] Available from; URL: http://www.egm.gov.tr/ asayis/tdpdefault1.asp [2007, March 11].

Turkish Government Policies and the Rise of the PKK/KONGRA-GEL

Niyazi EKICI, Murat OZKAN, and Oguzhan Omer DEMIR
Rutgers University, USA

Abstract. This study discusses some of the main arguments of the PKK/KONGRA-GEL terrorist organization and counterarguments of the Turkish government. It mentions how historical grievances and state repressions against the ethnically distinct groups may constitute one of the most important causes of the ethnic terrorism by examining the case of the PKK/KONGRA-GEL in Turkey. Contributions of the social context to the rise of the PKK/KONGRA-GEL during the 1960s and Turkey's response to the phenomenon are examined. In addition, the Turkish government's efforts for the conflict resolution will be briefly discussed. This study concludes that although some of the Turkish government's policies might have contributed to the rise of the PKK, it can never legitimize the activities of terrorist activities of the PKK/KONGRA-GEL.

Keywords. PKK/KONGRA-GEL, Kurds, ethnic identity, Kurdish Nationalism, Turkishness.

Introduction

Ethnic terrorism is a form of violence which purport the dominance or superiority of one ethnic group over another ethnic group specifically for the goal of political advancement. This type of terrorism based upon distinct groups within a single country or jurisdiction have caused the deaths of thousands of people. Countries such as Sri Lanka, the Sudan, Rwanda, India, the Philippines and Turkey have, for years, if not decades, suffered from the large-group conflicts. It is in this sense, that it becomes critically important to understand the underlying social factors and motivations which deplete the community of interdependence and rather produces a climate of hostility that leads to open violence [1].

Ethnic terrorism creates a serious problem for the state that attempts to retain control over their populations by using violence or coercion to quell the desire for independence. As Byman [2] mentions 'conventional countermeasures may engender broader support for an insurgency or a separatist movement even when they hamstring or defeat a specific terrorist group'. When such terrorist activities emerge, states mostly follow 'in group' policing or encourage them through carrot and stick motivations which often backfire.

The case of Turkey and the Kurdish Workers Party (PKK) is a modern day example of one ethnic group's attempt to gain political autonomy from the national government by employing animosity against the empowered ethnicity. The ultimate aim of the PKK/KONGRA-GEL's Kurdish separatist movement is to create a separate

Kurdish state in the southeastern region of Turkey. As this study will show, one of the main arguments of the PKK/KONGRA-GEL while legitimizing its activities is the historical grievances in the last century under the rule of Ottoman Empire and the Turkish Republic. Kurdish rebellions during the Ottoman Empire administration and Turkish government helped Kurds to create their own ethnic identity which has been mobilized after 1960s. What has been done for repressing the Kurdish rebellions in the past was used as an argument for the creation of the PKK/KONGRA-GEL The current study will present evidence that the PKK/KONGRA-GEL is neither a freedom fighter group, nor an armed conflict group, but a terrorist group. This study will also present the arguments of the PKK/KONGRA-GEL on behalf of the Kurds, the counter arguments of the Turkish government and Turkey's response to the PKK/KONGRA-GEL.

1. Ethnic Origins of the Kurds

As it can be easily expected, the PKK/KONGRA-GEL has many arguments on behalf of the Kurdish population in Turkey. Therefore, it will be necessary to briefly state the origins of the Kurds for the following discussions. However, before mentioning the research about Kurdish people, it should be admitted that accuracy of the very large number of existing studies are problematic since they are believed to have signs of racial or cultural biases for or against the Kurdish ethnic group [3] Many scholars mention that there is no definitive answer to the ethnic origins of the Kurds [4, cited in 3, 5, 6].

White [5] has three different theories regarding the origins of the Kurds. According to him, Kurds were the people of 'Gutium' in the ancient Sumeria. However, Johon and Harwey [4] state that Kurdish people have inhabited the mountainous region of the north of Mesopotamia for nearly two or four thousand years and they are the fathers of 'Xenophno's *Anabasis*'. They support their allegations in accordance with the ancient Greek epics which connect the *Carduchis* of 24 centuries ago to the today's Kurds. But it should be mentioned that this is not a powerful evidence to establish the actual origins of the Kurds. For example, Turkish scholar Hakan Ozoglu alleges that the origins of the Kurds and Kurdistan go to the 5th century B.C. Ozoglu refers to 'Serefname', the 16th-century-book which narrates a dynastic history of the Kurds, for his allegations [6].

Another controversy about the Kurds is their language; which is still obscure whether it is a language or not. The language which is spoken by the Kurds and called 'Kurdish' has a lot of dialects and sub-dialects which makes it difficult to define a generally accepted language explanation for it[1]. The most common dialects *Kurmanji* is spoken in Turkey as well as in former Soviet Union countries such as Azerbaijan and Armenia. *Sorani* (which is mostly spoken in Iraqi Kurdistan) and *Zaza* (which is also spoken in central Turkish Kurdistan) are the other common dialects. These are also the main dialects. Each of these dialects has different sub-dialects. For instance, Sorani has *Gurani, Kirmanshahi* and *Leki* as sub-dialects [5, 6].

---

[1] The current alphabet for the Kurdish language was created in the last two decades. It does not represent the majority of dialects. Moreover, some voices are missed even in this artificial alphabet.

2. Historical Grievances of the Kurds: The Major Argument of the PKK/KONGRA-GEL and the State Repression

2.1. Ethno-Kurdish Rebels during the Ottoman Empire

It is believed that the major impact on the emergence of the Kurdish identity took its source from the newly established Turkish Republic's policies. There were some anti-centralization revolts during the falling of the Ottoman Empire which can be accepted as an accelerator factor for the Kurdish nationalist movements [7].

In the period of the Ottoman Empire, ethnic identity was not politically important since the Ottomans embraced many different ethnic groups in their territories. Cultural diversities and religion were shaping the political loyalty [8]. It was when the Ottoman Empire tried to centralize its administration when Kurdish tribals started to revolt[2]. Because centralization efforts politicized peripheral ethnic and religious identities. Since Kurds are mostly a combination of tribes, they reacted to the centralization initiations. The administration of tribes depends extremely on '*aga*' or '*seyyid*' who is the unique leader in that society. So, centralization means any restriction in their powers and end of their 'feudal tyranny over the local people'. Since centralization was an attempt of destroying tribal ties and coalitions, this, in turn, empowered and reactivated religious and ethnic tribes such as '*Naksibendies*' and '*Kadiries*' in the region [9].

The rebellions against the centralization policy of Ottoman Empire did make little impact on the Kurdish Identity creation. Yavuz notes that geographically Kurds live on the crossroads of the Persian, Arab and Turkish worlds which gives them a high degree of tribal autonomy due to rugged, mountainous terrain. It is geographical conditions that create diverse dialects of Kurdish language and make sub-ethnic identity of Kurdish tribes more powerful than Kurdish consciousness. Therefore, all Kurdish movements in the history suffer from collectivity [9, 10].

2.2. The Establishment of Turkish Republic: The Absolute Secular and Nation State

As Posen mentions [cited in 11], after the collapse of the empires, ethnic groups are tend to mobilize. The Ottoman Empire succeeded the unification of ethnic groups inside its territories by tolerating religious and cultural diversities. When the Empire started to loose the diversity of ethnic groups by either loosing its territories or following central administration policies, political mobilization of the Kurds emerged.

After the First World War, Ottoman Empire collapsed by leaving many problems for her successor, Turkey. During the World War I. the Ottomans had to sign '*Sevres Treaty*' which were giving 'local autonomy for the land where the Kurd elements predominates' (article 62-64). Meanwhile, some Kurdish intellectuals such as Serif Pasa presented the 'Kurdish issue' in the international conferences by relying upon the British support. Even though the *Sevres Treaty* never put into practice, it is one of the main arguments of Kurdish nationalists while justifying their violent actions [9]. Fawcett mentions that these intonations and *Sevres Treaty* remained in the minds and it

---

[2] Being one of the religious leaders in the region, Seyh Ubeydullah revolted in 1880 because of the centralization efforts of the Sultan Abdulhamid II. The nature of this rebellion was religio-ethnic since Kurds had close ties with Islam. After putting down the rebellion, Sultan Abdulhamid II, the Ottoman king during that time, created Hamidiye Regiments for these rebellions and combated with 'Russian-backed Armenian nationalism' in the eastern Anatolia. These Regiments than defended the Anatolia (land of modern Turkey) during the First World War [9].

was the proclaimed goal of the PKK/KONGRA-GEL for a long time [7]. However, according to Ergil [12], it is still impossible to mention a strong Kurdish nationalism. Even though *Sevres Treaty* provisioned the construction of an independent Kurdish state, majority of Kurds struggled against the invaders of Anatolia after this Treaty. This obviously shows that religion was still the primary defining factor of Kurdish identity.

Experiencing these issues during the collapse of the Empire and having many ethnic groups in her territories, the newly established Turkish Republic (October 29, 1923) followed a 'nation-state principle' in order to protect her unification. The new policy accepted the Turkish language as the official language and those who live on the Turkish Republic's territories as 'Turks' regardless of their ethnicities[3]. The Republic also declared herself as an *absolute secular state*. These policies obviously shifted the multi-ethnic and multi-cultural realities of the Ottoman Empire by destroying the ruling effects of Islam and caliphate. As a result, they deeply affected the ethnic diversities in the country which is believed to constitute the roots of the Kurdish nationalism [3, 9, 7, 10].

The new order of the Turkish Republic was basically forceful in terms of homogenizing nationalism. According to Hakan Yavuz, homogenizing nationalism is one of the major reasons of the PKK/KONGRA-GEL which can be also defined as Kurdish conflict. Yavuz mentions that the current conflict of identity claims are 'the reflection of a deeper search for legitimacy and meaning in the post-Ottoman system' [9 pg. 1]. When the Ottoman Empire started to *govern* not to *rule* after 19th century, the politicization of ethnic identity took place. This was a result of failing in administering and regularizing the rural areas. The Empire was so weak that it was merely able to rule some urban centers throughout its territories. The efforts of centralization brought the issue of governance and this, in turn, created a conflict between local power structures and the state [9, 13].

It was the founder of Republic of Turkey, Mustafa Kemal Ataturk, who successfully led the modernization and formation of the new state. He created a new system in terms of education, urbanization, and communication which not only caused regional differences, but helped to cause 'conscious Kurdish ethnic elite'. In one of his famous declarations he says that "Happy is the man who calls himself a Turk" [14 pg.106]. The Kemalist reforms of civilizing the people of Turkey into a secular nation-state resulted Kurdish ethno-nationalism in the long run. Because Kurds were religious, living as tribes, and demanding the maintenance of their autonomous structure, the new system was perceived to be reactionary by them. The formation process and regional differences mobilized Kurdish nationalism. In other words, 'the overlap between the regional economic disparity and particular ethnic (Kurdish) identity is translated into Kurdish nationalism' [9].

Contrary to the Yavuz's allegations, Murat Somer strongly claim that identity formation can not be the major cause or argument of the PKK/KONGRA-GEL. He argues that if the definition of Turkishness in the 1924 Constitution had been the main source of the problem, it would have affected all non-Turkish Muslim ethnic groups such as Lazs, Bosnians, Chechens, and Arabs inside the country [15].

Another important argument of Somer is the inconsistency of Turkishness, which is named identity formation. He basically states that Turkishness acquired a new and more comprehensive meaning after the foundation of the Republic. Since it was a period of transition and identity flux for the elites, it may be futile to look for consistency within the official definitions. Even though the meaning of Turkishness shifts from a narrow

---

[3] 1924 Turkish Constitution: Without religious and ethnic difference, every person of the people of Turkey, who is a citizen, is regarded as Turk.

ethnic group category, it still can be more inclusive both culturally and territorially. However, the negative effects of the certain time periods such as military coups and rebels in the history which accelerates the ethnic-civic distinctions can not be underestimated. On the other hand, he asks whether a civic definition can help to resolve the Kurdish definition or not. Similarly, ethnic definition of Turkishness did not prevent Turkish policy-makers from being more generous towards the Iraqi Kurdish refugees in 1991 when Saddam Huseyin, the former leader of Iraq, forced them to migrate and used chemical weapons against them [16]. In addition to these arguments, ethnic definition is not necessary for, and does not ensure inter-ethnic harmony. For instance, Germany, France, and Britain are relatively successful in managing and accommodating their ethnic-cultural diversity on the basis of national identities that widely diverges on the ethnic-civic scale [15].

2.3. Kurdish Rebels after the Establishment of Turkey

After the establishment of Turkey, one of the bloodiest Kurdish rebels, Sheik Said, occurred in 1925 during the reform process of the Turkish Republic. The main reason of this rebel was the Mustafa Kemal Ataturk's national and secular based state-construction process. As it was mentioned before, the Ottoman Empire's multi-cultural and multi-national structure was destroyed by the new Republic. Caliphate (leadership of all Muslims in the world), which was one of the major symbols of the Islamic-sanctioned union of multi-ethnic groups, was abolished. Sheik Said, who is religious and Kurdish, started a rebellion which spread in a very short time in the east part of modern Turkey. In order to stop this rebellion, the Turkish military made operations in the region which caused a lot of casualties who were predominantly *Kurds* [17, 18].

After the first ethno-religious uprising, Sheik Said rebellion, two major rebellions occurred in the region. Because of the first rebel in the region, Turkish Republic became very suspicious about any form of Kurdish activities. After Sheik Said rebellion, a group of Kurdish tribal leaders established 'Kurdish National League' which later organized the revolt of Agri in 1930-31. Having had difficulty in putting it down, Turkey experienced the second revolt in 1937-38, known as Dersim (a Kurds living province). Dersim was led by mostly the Alevi Kurds, who are known as Zaza (these kinds of Kurds are more nationalist rather than religious) as a reaction to the Turkish Republic policies. The Turkish military hardly suppressed the rebel and erased the 'Dersim' province from the map and renamed it as 'Tunceli'. These three rebellions against the newly established state "created a cumulative image of the people of the region as socially tribal, religiously fanatic, economically backward, and most important, a threat to the national integrity of the Republic of Turkey" [9 pg.7-8, 10].

On the other hand, Somer alleges that these rebellions in the history can not demonstrate the link between Kurdish counter-nationalism and Turkishness. He mentions that "unless dispassionate historical research demonstrates that this was the case, it is more adequate to examine the Turkish and Kurdish nationalisms in a two-way relationship, whereby Turkish nationalism was hardened by the rise of Kurdish nationalism, and vice versa" [15 pg. 241-242].

2.4. Social Movements of 1960s and Mobilization of Kurdish Nationalism in Turkey

It was the consequence of Soviet Russia's challenge of importing her ideology and being one of her neighbor that deeply influenced Turkey with the leftist movements during the 1960s. As a result of interaction with the socialist ideology and a socio-political liberalization innovations made by the Constitution of 1961 in Turkey, the intellectual Kurds started to shape Kurdish identity and expressed their views on the self-determination of the Kurds. By publishing magazines and political initiations of recognition by the Turkish government, the Turkish left played a critical role in putting the Kurdish question into agenda [10].

In July 1965, one of the first Kurdish organizations, Kurdistan Democratic Party of Turkey (KDPT) was established in Diyarbakir (a city in the southeast of Turkey). The party's program mentioned 'Kurdish' as one of the official languages and demanded proportional Kurdish representation in Turkey's parliament. In addition, proportional economic investments should be done to the region. No sooner than, many party leaders and members were imprisoned or exiled by 1968 [19].

Another Kurdish political activism took part in the late 1960s by the leftist worker's party (Turkiye Isci Partisi (TIP) is its Turkish acronym). Even though the party had a negative stand about the Kurdish question in the beginning, it has changed its political view when many positions of the party were taken by Kurds. For instance, in 1969, the party's secretary-general and the president were both Kurds (Mehemt Ali Aslan). The party sponsored for a bilingual (Turkish-Kurdish) journal called *Yeni Akis (New Current)* which was purposing to raise the Kurdish question in the political agenda. But it should be mentioned that the journal was suspended after the first four issues [19].

Apart from these political engagements, Revolutionary Cultural Society of the East (Devrimci Dogu Kultur Ocaklari (DDKO) is its Turkish acronym) was one of the Kurdish organizations tried to raise Kurdish consciousness in 1969. Uneven economic distribution of the southeast Anatolia was one of the main arguments of the leftist movements at that time. So, Marxism and Kurdish nationalism constituted the central view of the DDKO's political activism [20]. It is not surprising that the founder of the PKK/KONGRA-GEL, Abdullah Ocalan, was one of the members of this organization. Mobilizing the Kurdish youth in the name of social justice and identity, many members of the DDKO became the members of the Turkish Labour party. However, this party and DDKO were outlawed during the 1971 military coup [9]. Meanwhile, another group of the Kurdish nationalists published the journal *Rizgari (Liberation)* in the early 1970s and supported the leftist Republican People's Party (RPP). Both DDKO's members and those who were publishing *Rizgari* perceived Turkish state as 'imperialist' and 'fascist.' Rizgari also declared that:

"The Kurds had nothing good to expect from the Kemalists; as colonized people, they should be more concerned with their own liberation than with the political problems of the colonized nation. This liberation will be achieved through a socialist revolution under the leadership of the Kurdish proletariat" [21 pg. 23].

The Turkish Labor Party and Revolutionary Cultural Society of the East were the most important challengers of raising the Kurdish consciousness throughout the country. One of the initiations of a parliament member named Serafettin Elci caused a serious scandal when he openly declared that he is a 'Kurd' in the parliament. At that time, the Turkish Military perceived that such kinds of political activities will lead chaos inside the country. Thus, a military coup, which identified Kurdish nationalism as a divisive force, banned all forms of cultural expression including all radical Islamist and leftists movements, occurred in 1980 [22, 9].

As a result of 1980 military coup, which used oppressive measures and destroyed the organizational power of Kurdish networks, many Kurdish nationalists took refuge or were jailed. Thus, while aiming to secure the integrity of Turkey, this military coup led these refugees to fragment in Europe and neighboring countries of Turkey which, then, created an opposite impact on the Kurdish identity. So, it is not wrong to say that this military coup, in turn, prepared the creation of the PKK/KONGRA-GEL.

Consequently, the political instability and turmoil between 1960s and 1980s in Turkey have helped the creation and the rise of the PKK/KONGRA-GEL. The political circumstances such as instable coalition governments and ascent of military regimes (1960, 1971 and 1980 military coups) nurtured political extremism of the Kurds. Especially after the 1980 military coup, the Turkish government followed strict policies in favor of creating order inside the country but it was not successful in deterring the raise of the radical Kurdish nationalism [10].

3. The PKK/KONGRA-GEL

There is no doubt that the PKK/KONGRA-GEL is a terrorist organization. The campaign that Abdullah Ocalan created was formed to destabilize Turkey and establish an independent Kurdish state that not only targeted the educational infrastructure in the southeastern and eastern part of Turkey, but also public schools which he believes they are intuitions of assimilation policy of Turkey and economic facilities which were created to serve the people of the region such as Southeastern Anatolian Project (GAP is its Turkish acronym). He and his dirty organization destroyed numerous schools and killed hundreds of teachers, and he even killed Kurds if he believed that they were pro-state or assimilated [23, 13].

Although the PKK/KONGRA-GEL claims to be a Marxist organization, its struggle is based on ethnic conflict to gain some territory and a national identity. It is also one of the few surviving revolutionary Marxist groups. One of the common characteristics of terror activities of PKK/KONGRA-GEL is the refusal of a 'national identity' which is called *'Turkishness'* throughout the country. The PKK/KONGRA-GEL argues that the Kurds have an independent national identity and opposes the Turkish national identity. Its real aim is to dismember the Turkish State in order to establish an independent, "Kurdish-Marxist-Leninist State" [16].

After committing its first heinous attack in 1984, Turkey witnessed the sharp rise of the PKK/KONGRA-GEL which has occurred in many ways. For instance, the active European diaspora and intense propaganda of the PKK/KONGRA-GEL has gained much support outside Turkey. Since Turkey is surrounded by countries such as Syria, which has provided shelter for the PKK/KONGRA-GEL for a long time, and Iraq, which has experienced Kurdish movements in the north part of the country especially after the Iran-Iraq and Gulf Wars, it is not surprising that the PKK/KONGRA-GEL became more effective and powerful. In addition, efforts of democratization and handling Islamic issue inside the country during the Presidency of Turgut Ozal[4] has raised not only the appreciations of the Country's Western allies, but also increased the

---

[4] 8th President of Turkey. He died in April 1993.

anxieties about creating a positive image of the country. This, in turn, caused delays in handling and taking the issue more serious in the country's agenda [7]. Meanwhile, Randal alleges that [cited in 7] the government policy followed by Turgut Ozal was focused on economic factors rather than political and cultural accommodation. Even though Ozal was partly willing for dialogue and granting for cultural rights, his successor Suleyman Demirel did not hesitate to follow a 'hard-line policy' by using army in dealing with the problem. According to Randal, the government followed a policy of repression and assimilation of 'Turkishness', which is strongly denied by too many Turkish scholars one of whom is Ismet Imset.

Contrary to the claims of the PKK/KONGRA-GEL regarding so-called Turkish assimilation and discrimination, Turkish scholar Ismet Imset revealed that at least one fourth of the 450-seat Turkish parliament is made up "Turks of Kurdish origin." His study states that the PKK/KONGRA-GEL used violence against "civilian targets" consisting of kidnapping tourists and journalists, attacking village guard's villages as well as off-duty soldiers, advocating, threatening and carrying out attacks on terrorism facilities and extra judicial killings of alleged "state collaborator". The author concluded that the PKK/KONGRA-GEL is neither a terrorist organization nor a national liberation movement, but rather an "Armed Conflict Group". He claimed that the PKK/KONGRA-GEL is a far more complicated phenomenon than a terrorist organization [24].

Meanwhile, the Turkish government mentions that citizens of Kurdish ethnic heritage fully enjoy all democratic rights as Turkish citizens do. So, it is not true to talk about any Kurdish problem in turkey but a terror problem. Gunter [25] mentions that after the increasing demands of the Turkey's Kurds in terms of cultural, linguistic and political rights was 'ruthlessly suppressed' by the officials due to the fear of break-up of the state. It was this suppression which caused extremism and more than 30.000 deaths (Gunter notes 31.000 deaths, as many as 3000 villages destroyed). Furthermore, three million people were displaced [26].

3.1. Does the PKK/KONGRA-GEL Represent Kurds?

Identifying the PKK/KONGRA-GEL has been one of the vital problems in explaining the very existence of the organization. Is it really a national freedom movement? There are some factors influencing the original identity of the PKK/KONGRA-GEL. As it was mentioned in the beginning of this study, there are many controversies in defining not only the Kurds, but also the land they live. Imset [27] mentions that the PKK/KONGRA-GEL is actively supported by the Kurdish population living in Turkey and Iraq. In addition, Kurdish political groups (except for the groups in Turkey and Iraq) have some considerable support for the PKK/KONGRA-GEL but their representation of the Kurdish population is questionable. Thus, the allegation that the PKK/KONGRA-GEL represents all of the Kurds is controversial. But the question is how far the PKK/KONGRA-GEL represents Turkey's Kurds. It is believed that only half of the Kurdish population lives in the southeast part of Turkey; the remaining part is spread out among the Turks in different regions of the country. In fact, there are hundreds of thousands of Kurds living in Europe. So, by looking to those who provide the essential manpower for the struggle one can see the controversy again (Table 1).

Table 1. The estimates of the Kurdish population [5 pg. 17].

Country	The Estimated Kurdish Population by		
	Chailand	McDowall	Le Monde Diplomatique
Turkey	7,557,000	8,455,000	10,000,000
Iran	5,190,400	3,105,000	6,000,000
Iraq	2,800,000	3,701,000	3,000,000
Syria	825,000	734,000	800,000
Ex-USSR	278,463	265,00	350,000
Total	**16,650,863**	**16,320,000**	**20,150,000**

On the other hand, as it was mentioned in the body of this study, Turkey's own history of repression over identities and official declaration of *Turkishness* 'serves to prove that the PKK/KONGRA-GEL has a dominant role in the current conflict and is the only single party, which is an essential part of it. It is, in effect, fighting against a systematic, state-sponsored racism. It is also fighting against attempts to kill the Kurdish identity altogether. Whatever its methods, it claims to be fighting for the Kurdish rights to self determination' [27].

However, if one argue that the PKK/KONGRA-GEL can no longer be identified as a terrorist organization alone because of the various arguments such as the Kurdish population distribution in Turkey and the region, the existence of other dominant Kurdish political entities in the area, it can not be viewed as a freedom fighter for the Kurdish majority either. Because the organization affirms its purposes to expand its influence throughout the region. Starting from rural based violent activities, it turned into a major ethnic insurgency movement in the region which is challenging all other regional powers [27].

In sum, it is true that the PKK/KONGRA-GEL is not representing majority of the Kurds in the region (Syria, Turkey, Iraq, Iran), but partly represents the Kurds in Turkey. Although Imset tries to name the organization as an *Armed Conflict Group*, when one considers the structure, policies and mass support to the organization it becomes evident that it as a terrorist group.

3.2. Turkey's Response to the PKK/KONGRA-GEL

State response to the ethnic terrorism is critical for the degree of violence and its continuation. Use of force against the ethnic group's violent activities is an issue for the states. States have to rethink before responding them in such ways. In this sense, Turkey's first response to the PKK/KONGRA-GEL was cautious. When the first attack of the PKK/KONGRA-GEL occurred, the government dismissed developments and labeled it as 'minor and isolated incidents of bandits'. Not taking it seriously, the officials defined it as a *low level terrorist action* and did not use sufficient resources for any kinds of prevention since it would require a great amount of resources and money [28].

Completing its organization and sub-structure in the Syrian controlled Beka Valley, the PKK/KONGRA-GEL militants killed more than thirty innocent villagers in the southeastern Turkey in its first attack [12]. No sooner than this first attack, the government tried to identify the type of insurgency and the organization. After examining the PKK/KONGRA-GEL documents and actions, it was concluded that this was a *'secessionist'* insurgency which clearly threatens its territorial integrity. Here, it should be noted that Turkish government does not have a policy of negotiating with terrorists. So, the government was at a point of either negotiating with the terrorist group or struggling with it.

In fighting with the PKK/KONGRA-GEL terrorism, the Turkish government decided to use several forces. Regular army was the most important force which deployed 145.000 troops in the southeast region in the early 1990s. The army engaged in several duties such as making counterinsurgency operations, conducting routine patrols, and providing convoy protection etc. Apart from the regular army, two 'elite units' of commando brigades were created specifically to deal with the PKK/KONGRA-GEL. Gendarmerie and its subset '*Ozel Timler (Special Teams)*' were also engaged in the operations since rural areas are in their responsibility in terms of providing security and handling criminal investigations. Police forces and their subset "*Ozel Hareket Timleri (Special Operation Teams)*' showed a significant success in the urban areas and attended some operations with the other forces. In addition, Turkish air forces, using F-16 and F-104 type of aircrafts and helicopters, attacked the PKK/KONGRA-GEL positions in southeastern Turkey, northern Iraq and Iran [28].

In fact, one of the most important responses of the government was '*village guard*' system. Organizing and arming those defenseless villagers who are living in the region and exposed to the PKK/KONGRA-GEL's attacks, the government tasked them to assist Turkish forces in countering the PKK/KONGRA-GEL. After the establishment of village guard system, the PKK/KONGRA-GEL turned its full attention to these 'Para-military Forces' by aiming to prevent participation in them. In 1985, the PKK/KONGRA-GEL attacks against 'civilians' increased as a response of the government's preemptive action of creating village guards. The PKK/KONGRA-GEL's policy in that time was to destroy anybody who was likely to deal with the village guards. The attacks were so brutal that many infants and women were killed during the PKK/KONGRA-GEL attacks. The PKK/KONGRA-GEL also threatened those who were likely to deal with the village guards as '*state collaborators*' and will be killed sooner or later. In 1987, the PKK/KONGRA-GEL both increased the number of its recruits and created new units of fighters called '*mountain units*' who were trained to fight full-time. As a reaction to the PKK/KONGRA-GEL's activities, the Turkish government increased the number of gendarmeries [29].

The government also declared 'Regional State of Emergency Governorate' (OHAL is its Turkish acronym) in the Kurdish-inhibited zone of Southeastern Turkey after the first series of attacks. This governorate included Bingol, Diyarbakir, Elazig, Hakkari, Mardin, Siirt, Tunceli and Van provinces. No sooner than declaring 'state of emergency' in these provinces, the government expanded the state of emergency governorate by adding more provinces which continued for almost 20 years [9]. The creation of the village guards system and OHAL were merely the first series of decisions which would turn the Kurdish problem into a major conflict [29].

Trying to legitimate its activities Abdullah Ocalan later claimed that the people who killed during their attacks 'were not killed on purpose'. They were either the families of para-military village guards or locals identified as 'state collaborators' [24]. The villages targeted in the campaigns were chosen ones and were always located in areas where the PKK/KONGRA-GEL needed to expand mass support. As ironic as it may sound, by determining the targets for such acts of terrorism in a selective way, the PKK/KONGRA-GEL was basically maintaining its effectiveness and gaining popular support. It was showing to the local Kurds what happened to 'traitors' or 'state collaborators'. The messages which PKK/KONGRA-GEL wanted to give the Kurdish people were clear: it is your best interest to give your support to this organization rather than to Turkey [24]. In response to the PKK/KONGRA-GEL, Turkish officials were so determined in fighting with terrorism that the Turkish Chief of Staff General, Necip Torumtay, stated that "We will fight against the guns with guns; we are obliged to do this." He also added that the five-year-old insurgency in southeastern Anatolia was aiming to disrupt national solidarity and territorial integrity with a wave of terrorism. In the same day of 'special warfare' decision, Prime Minister Turgut Ozal declared that there would be no political measures to diffuse the crisis, pointing out on behalf of his government, 'we will reinforce the existing measures,' meaning an increase in military activities. This turned the conflict into a real 'dirty war' [24].

The intense terror activities of the PKK/KONGRA-GEL continued until 1998, even though the Turkish military and police forces strengthened the security in the region and combat with the terrorists by hot pursuits both inside the Turkish borders and Northern Iraq until the capture of Abdullah Ocalan.

4. Turkey's Counterarguments and Discussion

The Turkey's PKK/KONGRA-GEL experience in the last few decades illustrates a dramatic flow of ethnic violence caused by extremist Kurds in Turkey. The violent campaign of the separatist PKK/KONGRA-GEL militants continued for years for the sake of an independent Kurdish state. It is very important to know that majority of terrorist actions of the PKK/KONGRA-GEL militants occurred between the *'Kurdish'* people of the southeastern Turkey, Turkish military and police forces and the PKK/KONGRA-GEL militants. Unlike the case of LTTE in Sri Lanka, the PKK/KONGRA-GEL terrorism is not a kind of violence between the two ethnic groups such as Turks and Kurds, but PKK/KONGRA-GEL terrorist and Turkish military and police forces. As it can be seen from the examples in this study, ethnic terrorism cases vary in many ways. In this regard, the PKK/KONGRA-GEL has its own characteristics.

While examining the process of Kurdish ethnic mobilization, this study focused on the historical grievances and the state repression. But it should be kept in mind that there are some other factors such as economical and geographical reasons of the problem that were not mentioned in this study. While more cultural rights and decentralization of the state are the kinds of solutions that are claimed by those who are looking for the sources of the problem in political factors [9], those who see the roots of conflict in the economic factors, such as unemployment, strongly focus on the Turkish government's projects in the region in order to stop terrorism. The GAP project is the world's second largest project which is basically purposing to serve the people of the region (the Kurds) and to accelerate the economic development. The Project is under construction for nearly 40 years. The GAP project includes 18 dams and several irrigation channels on the Euphrates and Tigris River. Turkey will complete the project by 2010 [13].

Since the Turkish government is mostly trying to solve the conflict by economic solutions, the government authorities denies the political causes by alleging that nothing is clear about the Kurds in terms of their ethnic background, language and etc. Kurds are divided tribally, geographically, politically, linguistically, and ideologically. It is obscure whether they are a nation or not. If one, nevertheless, define the Kurds geographically and linguistically, it will be true that they are the largest nation in the world without their own state. This vagueness, of course, complicates stunted sense of nationalism, and allows the existing countries, such as Turkey, to rule the Kurds in the whole region of Kurds-living geography (Iran, Syria, and Iraq). On the other hand, it is obvious that the region is blessed with ample amounts of water [13] and oil which encourages the existing states to deny any aspiration of cultural and political minority rights, autonomy etc. fearing that they would challenge with their own territorial integrity [5].

Another argument of the Turkish side is that the Kurds are not minority in Turkey. Nor are they discriminated politically or culturally. The assumption is that there would be more reaction when the government removed any restriction about the Kurdish language or any other ethnic-based languages in 2003. Currently, government's official television makes broadcasts in different Kurdish dialects; the government also gave an opportunity of Kurdish language courses and education in Kurdish language. However, among millions of the Kurdish-speaking people, a very limited number (less than thousands) of people volunteered to register for such an education. On the other hand, it should be noted that these initiatives of government were not the consequences of the political challenges of the Kurds, but the results of attempts to be a member of European Union [3].

Turkey does not accept any self-determination allegations of the Kurds which is the most critical argument of the PKK/KONGRA-GEL. The Turkey's argument against self-determination allegations is that, similar to the Kurds, there are several ethnically different groups in Turkey which is an outcome of multi-cultural background of the country. If self-determination would be the issue for the Kurds, there would be no Turkish Republic in the history. Nor any of these ethnic groups would have their own republic or state because of their weaknesses and unwillingness of such an aim. As Michael Gunter raises the issue for the Kurdish Question, self-determination (the purpose of creating an independent Kurdish state) has a problem of defining "people" and "self." Since self-determination refers to the right of a "people" living in any given territory to determine their political and legal status, then the question arises: who and where? United Nations has several resolutions concerning this issue, but it is still obscure in terms of who and where [25]. Similarly Usherwood mentions that right of self-determination is highly idealistic and controversial. When the principle first mentioned in the international arena, it was only applied to territories, not people. "it meant that self-determination called for the right of colonies to be independent, not that all 'people' had the right to self-determination, which is critical to defining this principle. The lack of emphasis on 'people' suddenly gives new meaning to the principle. No longer can subject nations, those people living with a sovereign state, claim self-determination" [30 pg. 96].

Apart from the causes of the PKK/KONGRA-GEL terrorism, the Turkish officials note that 25% of the Turkish Grand National Assembly is 'Kurd' in terms of their ethnic background. The 8th president of Turkey, Turgut Ozal, who died in 1993, and the current interior minister of Turkey are also originally Kurd. These examples challenge with the PKK/KONGRA-GEL's allegations of ethnic discrimination [3].

On the other hand, Muftuler-Bac [14] presented an empirical study made on the Kurdish Question by the Turkish Union of Chambers of Commerce (TOBB is its Turkish acronym). It is an important research because the organization is completely civil and the Chairman (Yalim Erez) of the organization is a Kurd. Involving 1500 formal interviews among randomly assigned samples in a nine months time period in 1995, the study focused on the Kurdish population living in the southeastern Turkey. The samples were including individuals from different social status such as trade union leaders, local governors, mayors, police chiefs, religious leaders, sect leaders, teachers etc. The Kurdish community was asked whether they would like to live in a separate

Kurdish state or to be a part of Turkish state. Only 13 percent of the respondents favored an independent Kurdish state. More interestingly, among those who favored an independent Kurdish state, only 9.4 percent of them supported talks between the Turkish state and the PKK/KONGRA-GEL.

As it was mentioned in the literature, one of the most important factors in ethnic identity allegations is language. In the study of TOBB, 91 percent of the respondent mentioned that they describe themselves as 'Kurd' and 65 percent of them mentioned that they only use Kurdish as language. It is also mentioned that language recognition is the key element in the conflict. Finally, it is claimed that the Kurdish problem is not one of terrorism but internal social and cultural issues. Because 35 percent of the respondents reported that they have relatives in the PKK/KONGRA-GEL where 40 percent of them viewed PKK/KONGRA-GEL as challenging for the cultural and political rights. Only 16.8 percent felt the PKK/KONGRA-GEL's aim is to establish an independent Kurdish state.

5. Conclusion

Ethnicity or ethnic identity has various roots such as language, religion, education etc. However, it should be noted that the operational dimension of ethnicity are determined to a very large extent. The socio-political system and the ideology are one of the predominant determinants of ethnic identity [8]. The ethnic formation process involves several sets of struggles such as control over its material and symbolic resources which is defining the group boundaries and its rules for inclusion or exclusion, competition for rights, privileges etc., and finally, control over local territories and populations to administer its institutions and implement its own policies [31]. This process is mentioned as identity creation and mobilization of ethnic groups. If the group fails to follow this process due to a large identity or the state repression, tension between the state or the large identity is inevitable. Even though it depends on the ethnic group's level of reaction, ethnic violence is one of the worst things that a state may experience. In this sense, case studies of ethnic terrorism may reflect significant clues for the pattern of violence and policy implications.

Terrorism, based on ethnic differences or state discriminations, may cost hundreds of thousands of lives. Once ethnic identity is created and mobilized, emergence of terrorist groups becomes highly probable. Many ethnic terror cases around the world such as the ETA in Spain, LTTE in Sri Lanka and the PKK/KONGRA-GEL in Turkey show that ethnically distinct groups are prone to violence when their identity, cultural and political rights are not recognized by the state or the rival group. Although it is not possible to show the exact pattern of the ethnic violence, this study attempted to review the case of PKK/KONGRA-GEL based on the theoretical explanation that, more or less, ethnic violence is mostly a product of state or rival group's repression. Meanwhile, the role of historical grievances and political discriminations in creation of identity and its mobilization is highly important.

There are many factors contributing to the causes of ethnic terrorism other than political repression and discrimination. It is not possible to explain the whole ethnic terror cases with one single reason. The role of the leader, the level of discrimination, the content of historical grievances, international support etc. can be a contributing factor to ethnic terrorism. In this regard, the case of PKK/KONGRA-GEL is a complex issue that needs to be explained in a very broad context. Because there are a lot of ambiguities about the Kurdish question in terms of Kurds' ethnic background, language, culture etc. which increases the possibility of biased explanations. In addition, these ambiguities make any empirical study more difficult.

The case of PKK/KONGRA-GEL showed that historical grievances during the creation of ethnic identity are not always the cause of terrorism but they are the means for terrorist groups. The political climate of the 1960s and social movements in Turkey were determinative in emergence of the PKK/KONGRA-GEL. Although these movements are ostensible reasons, there can be other factors contributing to the violence such as economic, geographic, international, and leadership factors. As it was mentioned in the study, majority of the Kurdish people live in poor socio-economic conditions in the southeast region of Turkey. In fact, one of the reasons of creating village guard system against the PKK/KONGRA-GEL was to partly improve the poor socio-economic conditions. Moreover, the region is highly mountainous and draws the border of Iran, Iraq and Syria. It is well known that the leader of the PKK/KONGRA-GEL lived in Syria for years and caught in Greek embassy. As of the leader of the PKK/KONGRA-GEL, his family structure, education and criminal career are major contributors to the emergence and the ideology of the terrorist organization.

As this study partly tried to explain, the PKK/KONGRA-GEL is far more complicated phenomenon than a terrorist organization. Although Turkish government policies might have contributed to the PKK/KONGRA-GEL's rise in the course of the time, this can never legitimize the terrorist activities.

References

[1]   V. D. Vamik, *Bloodlines: From ethnic pride to ethnic terrorism.* New York: Farrar, Straus and Giroux; 1997.
[2]   D. Byman, The logic of ethnic terrorism. *Studies in Conflict and Terrorism.* **21/2** (1998), 149-167.
[3]   S. Laciner, I. Bal, The ideological and historical roots of Kurdist movements in Turkey: Ethnicity demography, and politics. *Nationalism and Ethnic Politics.* **10** (2004), 473-504.
[4]   J. Bulloch, H. Morris, No friends but mountains: The tragic history of Kurds. *Middle East Journal,* **47/4** (1993), 55.
[5]   P. White, *Primitive rebels or revolutionary modernizers? The Kurdish national movement in Turkey*: London/New York: Zed Books; 2000.
[6]   H. Ozoglu, *Kurdish notables and the Ottoman State: Evolving identities, competing loyalties, and shifting boundaries:* SUNY press; 2004.
[7]   L. Fawcett, Down but not out? The Kurds in international politics. *Review of International Studies,* **27** (2001), 109-118.
[8]   H.K. Karpat, The ethnicity problem in a multi-ethnic national Islamic state: Continuity and recasting of ethnic identity in the Ottoman State. In P. Brass, Editor. *Ethnic groups and the state.* New Jersey: Barnes and Noble books; 1985.
[9]   H. Yavuz, Five stages of the construction of Kurdish nationalism in Turkey. *Nationalism and Ethnic Politics,* **7/3** (2001), 1-24.
[10] N.I. Grigoriadis, Turkey's political culture and minorities. Student paper submitted at the conference of 'Nationalism, society and Culture in post-Ottoman south east Europe' at St. Peter's College, Oxford; 2004.
[11] M.J. Cotter, Societal insecurity and the reaction of extremist groups in Northern Ireland, Great Britain and the USA. Doctoral dissertation submitted at the University of Kentucky; 2002.
[12] D. Ergil, The Kurdish question in Turkey. *Journal of Democracy.* **11/3** (2000), 122-135.
[13] N. Ekici, Water issue in Turkey's relations with Syria. Master Thesis submitted at Yildiz Technical University: Istanbul; 2003.
[14] M. Muftuler-Bac, Addressing Kurdish separatism in Turkey. In R.H. Marc, J. Rothman, Editors. *Theory and practice in ethnic conflict management:* New York: St. Martin's Press; 1999.
[15] M. Somer, Turkey's Kurdish conflict: Changing context, and domestic and regional implications. *The Middle East Journal,* **58/2** (2004, Spring), 235-253.

[16] U. Ozdag, *Turkiye Kuzey Irak ve PKK: Bir gayri nizami savasin anatomisi (Turkey Northern Iraq and PKK: An anatomy of a disorderly war*. Ankara, Turkey: Asam Yayinlari; 1999.

[17] R. Olson, *The emergence of Kurdish Nationalism and the Sheikh Said rebellion, 1880-1925*. Austin, Texas: University of Texas Press; 2004. [Online] Available from; URL: http://www.xs4all.nl/~tank /kurdish/htdocs/his/said.html. [2006, January 28].

[18] J.H. Barkey, F.E. Graham, *Turkey's Kurdish question*. New York: Rowman and Littlefield Publishers; 1998.

[19] C. Kutschera, *Mad dreams of independence: The Kurds of Turkey and the PKK*. Middle East report; 1994, July.

[20] C.B. Nur, The nature of PKK terrorism in Turkey. *Studies in Conflict and Terrorism*, **18** (1995), 17-37.

[21] Ankara Papers, The case of the PKK: History, ideology, methodology and structure (1978-99). **9/1** (2004), 21-59.

[22] H. Bozarslan, Why the Armed Struggle?, In F. Ibrahim, G. Gurbey, Editors. *The Kurdish conflict in Turkey: Obstacles and changes for peace and democracy*, New York: St. Martin's Press; 2000.

[23] Western Point of view on the PKK III. The Anatolian Movement for Peace and Unity Press; (1996).

[24] I.G. Imset, PKK: Ayrilikci siddetin 20 yili (1973-1992). Ankara: Turkish Daily News Press; 1993.

[25] M.M. Gunter, The Kurdish question and international law. In F. Ibrahim, G. Gurbey, Editors. *The Kurdish conflict in Turkey: Obstacles and changes for peace and democracy*, New York: St. Martin's Press; 2000.

[26] M. Kocher, The decline of PKK and the viability of a one-state solution in Turkey. *International Journal on Multicultural Societies*. **4/1** (2002), 1-20.

[27] I.G. Imset, The PKK: Freedom fighters or terrorists? 1995. [Online], Available from; URL: http://www.kurdistan.org/Articles/ismet.html. [2006, April 17].

[28] O.F. Otucu, Severe ethnic violence: An integrated explanation of the Turkish-Kurdish Case. Doctoral dissertation submitted at the University of Kentucky; 2004.

[29] Y. Simsek, The impact of terrorism on migration patterns in Turkey. Dissertation submitted at Virginia Commonwealth University for the degree of doctor of philosophy; 2006, July.

[30] M.R. Usherwood, World War I and the principle of national self-determination: A closer look at Kurdistan. Master thesis submitted at Georgia State University; 2005.

[31] P. Brass, Editor. *Ethnic Groups and the State*. New Jersey: Barnes and Noble Books; 1985.

Expansion of the Executive Power by the Patriot Act

Ali OZDOGAN
American University, Washington DC, USA

Abstract. Approach to terrorism has significantly been changed in the post 9/11 era. The new legislation, The Patriot Act, designed by the US to counter terrorism has raised concerns regarding its effect on the expansion of executive power, and the delicate balance set by the principle of "Separation of Powers". The designers of the Act take the risk of affecting this delicate balance, by relying on the support of their constituents. Therefore, the Patriot Act is a product of politicians' rational preferences shaped by their constituents' opinions

Keywords: Wiretapping, executive branch, patriot act, civil liberties, public opinion.

Introduction

After the 9/11, the comments on the media outlets started to claim that "everything has changed" without describing what "everything" refer to. What really changed? Both Al-Qaeda and terrorism were not new phenomena before 9/11. The thing changed was the lens through which terrorism is seen [1]. Before 9/11, terrorism was a crime that was handled within the conventional criminal justice system, and investigated by conventional techniques within the norms of the democratic government. On the other hand, in the post 9/11 era, terrorism was seen as "war" that was handled by military forces on the basis of exceptional rules restricting the fundamental rights [1].

Shortly after the 9/11 attack, American leaders reacted to prevent similar attacks and to capture the perpetrators, planners and supporters of the attack. Part of the reaction was to draft legislation such as the Uniting and Strengthening America by Providing Tools Required to Intercept and Obstruct Terrorism Act, shortly named as the Patriot Act [i]. This legislation grants new discretionary powers to the executive authority. These new powers were designed to immobilize the future terrorist attacks as well as to expedite the investigation of the September 11th incident. In addition, the new powers expand the power of executive branch by giving them legislative and judicial authority.

Proponents of the US Patriot Act basically argue that expanding the executive power at the expense of the civil liberties is justifiable, as exceptional incidents demand exceptional measures. However, as Al-Ghazali suggested 900 years ago: "Everything that exceeds its limit changes into its opposite." In other words, the measures exceeding the limits are relatively more subject to abuse.

The next part of this study presents a brief overview and analysis of the Patriot Act. Then the positions of the President and Congress are elaborated. The last section concludes.

1. Expansion of the Executive Power

One of the major purposes of law making is to ensure that the executive branch does not act without legislative standards and judicial overview. Unilateral executive power increases risk of abuses, such as the Watergate scandal and the wiretapping of civil rights leader Dr. Martin Luther King, Jr., among others.

The executive branch expanded its power through the Patriot Act. However, this expansion is not a new phenomenon born by 9/11. In fact, the executive branch (e.g. the President, law enforcement community, etc.) has been attempting to increase its power since the 1960s. For example, the American presidency has gained increasing control over foreign-relations, especially war-making in the last 50 years; while Congress decided to declare war against foreign nations before the Korean War, social and political norms have increasingly seen the president as the sole organ of the US in foreign relations and war-making decisions [2]. Similarly, the law enforcement community, an executive branch has increased its discretion in wiretapping since the initial Supreme Court decisions which produce the legal frame of wiretapping in 1967, and enactment of the first wiretapping law in 1968[ii]. In fact, the Electronic Communications Privacy Act of 1986, the Foreign Surveillance Intelligence Act of 1978 (FISA), and the Communication Assistance for Law Enforcement Act of 1994 (CALEA) -as well as many Supreme Court cases- have been the result of the efforts of law enforcement community to expand the power of the executive branch in the area of wiretapping[iii].

The evolution of legislation surrounding FISA reveals another example of the expansion of executive power and the role of Congress in this expansion. FISA was enacted to provide legislative standards and judicial checks for executive power in gathering information about foreign powers and "agents" of foreign powers. In its original form, FISA, which does not require "probable cause", did not authorize the executive branch for the physical searches of suspects. In 1995, and 1998 Congress amended FISA to authorize the executive branch to conduct physical searches, to use pen registers to capture the signaling information on telephone lines and to access business records under the FISA, in order to expedite the investigation of the Oklahoma City bombing and first World Trade Center bombings [3].

As it is presented here, the expansion of executive power is a trend started in the pre 9/11 era[iv]. However, 9/11 has produced a jump start effect on the expansion.

2. The Patriot Act Case

The terrorist attacks on September 11, 2001 threw the entire country into fear, sadness, and anger [4]. The Bush administration surrounded by the atmosphere of fear, sadness and anger, quickly reacted to the attack by declaring a state of emergency on September 14th, and passed the Patriot Act on October 26th, 2001[v]. The Patriot Act which originally had 342 pages passed the House by a vote of 356 to 66 and the Senate by 98 to 1. It was passed virtually without any hearing and debate, and it was not accompanied any committee report.

The Patriot Act makes changes to more than 15 existing federal statutes, broadens the definition of terrorism, increases penalties for terrorists, expands the government power on wiretapping and using pen registers, increases scope of search warrants and subpoenas by lowering the standards of probable cause, facilitates information sharing among the law enforcement agencies, expands surveillance authority under the Foreign Intelligence Surveillance Act (FISA), and restricts the rights of citizens and non-citizens [5].[vi]

Although the Patriot Act has many provisions enhancing counter-terrorism efforts, it has been criticized for indiscriminate restriction of civil rights that reach far beyond terrorists, through expansion of executive power[vii]. To Chang [6], the primary problem with the Patriot Act is that it expands the executive power while limiting the judicial review and Congressional oversight of the exercise of these powers.

In the following parts of this study, I will criticize and analyze several provisions of the Patriot Act in order to conceptualize problem of executive power expansion in the Act. I categorize my critiques in four parts: First, broad definition of domestic terrorism; second, the provisions of the Act threatening the privacy right; third, the provisions about destroying the wall between the criminal and national security investigations; finally the provisions restricting the rights of non-citizens are explored and analyzed.

2.1. Definition of the Domestic Terrorism

§ 802 of the Patriot Act extends the definition of "domestic terrorism" which was previously defined in § 2331 of the Title 18. By § 802, the new definition of domestic terrorism is extended to

"… involve acts dangerous to human life that are a violation of the criminal laws of the United States or of any State;
appear to be intended –
(i)   to intimidate or coerce a civilian population;
(ii)   to influence the policy of government by intimidation or coercion; ..." (§ 802(a)(5))

The definition above has expansive terms. For example, the activities of environmentalists, anti-globalists and anti-abortionists can be investigated and prosecuted as "terrorists", as their protests could be construed as "dangerous to human life" and "violation of criminal laws" in order to "influence the policy of government". Similarly, many other crimes that categorized as "civil disobedience" before 9/11 can be called "terrorism" in the post-9/11 era by law enforcement officials who want to overcome bureaucratic and judicial procedures of the investigation of this civil disobedience.

Briefly, § 802 expands executive power by giving law enforcement broad discretion to classify disobediences as "terrorism" of which the executive branch has relatively less Constitutional limits in an investigation[viii].

2.2. Privacy Invasions

The Patriot Act changes the standards of privacy right (i.e. The Fourth Amendment right) in the investigations. First, it authorizes the indefinite delay of notifying a person whose belongings are subject to search conducted within the protection of the Fourth Amendment. In addition, the Act grants the executive branch expansive surveillance powers including internet tracking and e-mail interceptions, obtaining sensitive personal records, by relying on subpoena (not court order), and by ignoring the "particularity" requirement of the Fourth Amendment.

2.2.1. Delay of the Notice (Sneak and Peak Searches)

§ 213 authorizes the federal agents to delay notice of the execution of a warrant, if the court finds a reasonable cause to believe that the notice produces an "adverse result", or if the warrant prohibits seizing any tangible property, communication or data (§ 213(b)). The delay of the notice is not specified in the Act. Therefore, it can be interpreted in such a way that delaying the notice indefinitely.

§ 213 is not limited to terrorism investigations but for all investigations of any crime. Moreover, § 213 is not a sunset provision. As a result notifying the target for the searches is eroded by the Patriot Act. This is a clear violation of the "knock and announce" principle of common law and the "equality of arms" principle stated in the Article 6 of the European Human Rights Convention[ix]. Furthermore, the Act leads to unfair trials if the defendant is indicted in court on the basis of information obtained during the searches. In other words, if the defendant is not given notice, and he/she is indicted, he/she does not know what the prosecution has against him/her. Consequently, he/she does not have an opportunity to defend him/herself accordingly.

§ 213 provides opportunity for covert searches and erodes one of the checks over the executive power.

2.2.2. Intercepting Internet Communications without Warrant

§ 216(c)(2) and (3) amended the §§ 3127(2) and §§ 3127(3) of title 18, so that the new provisions authorize the executive branch to intercept "signaling" information of electronic communications based on subpoena, not court warrant. This provision threatens on individual privacy because of the broad interpretation of "signaling." Before elaborating about the privacy issue, I will present some technical information.

Any electronic communications has two parts: content and signaling[x]. In telephone communication, voice constitutes the content, while dialed numbers, busy tone, ringing, duration of the talk, geographical cell information in case of cell phones, etc. constitute the signaling. Intercepting the voice content requires a warrant under both the Title III of the Omnibus Crime Control and Safety Streets Act of 1968, and Foreign Intelligence Surveillance Act of 1978[xi]. However, intercepting the signaling information calls for only subpoena which requires lower standards of the "probable cause" [7].

In case of landline telephone communications, the content and signaling can easily be separated; and pen registers and trap and trace devices are used to intercept signaling. On the other hand, digital and optic communications, such as cellular and internet, separation of the content and signaling is so complex that usually the tapping point for signal interception contains both content and signaling together[xii]. Subsequently, law enforcement personnel can easily access the content while intercepting the signaling. This is a potential threat to an individual's privacy. Indeed, the real threat to privacy is more than that. The FBI on behalf of the law enforcement community has asserted that e-mails, URL addresses, e-messages over cellular phones, etc. are not "content" but they are the part of "signaling" information. This come about during the debates and meetings between representatives of the communication sector and law enforcement over the implementation of § 103(a) and other provisions of the Communication Assistance for Law Enforcement Act of 1994 (CALEA) [8, 9, 10][xiii]. The Patriot Act was enacted before the end of the debates over the meaning of "signaling". I believe that "signaling" was inserted by the law enforcement community to obtain internet communications including e-mails, the name of the web sites any person visits, and probably other information based on the subpoena which does not require probable cause within the standards of the Fourth Amendment.

In sum, § 216(c)(2) and (3) expands the executive power by providing the lower legal requirements for interception of some private communications than the traditional legal requirements based on the Fourth Amendment.

2.2.3. Facilitating the Sharing of Private Information

§ 203 of the Patriot Act authorizes the disclosure of intercepted information and foreign intelligence information "to assist the official receiving that information in the performance of his official duties." Notwithstanding the benefits of this provision in facilitating the inter- & intra-agency information sharing, the way of information sharing defined in § 203 has the following problems. First, it does not adequately set the limits of that information sharing. For example, § 203 grants all federal law enforcement agencies and protection services broad access to financial, medical, educational, library, credit card, and other private records and communications intercepted through lawful electronic surveillance; without a court order (i.e. probable cause)[xiv].

Because of its broad language, § 203 violates the *minimization* principle which is necessary to meet the *particularity* requirement of the Fourth Amendment.[xv] Second, it does not require "probable cause" for information sharing; therefore, it circumvents judicial review of that information sharing.

§ 203 defines information sharing in three areas: grand jury information, intercepted communications, and foreign intelligence information. The information sharing provision regarding the latter two areas are sunset provisions while the first one is a permanent provision.

Because of the fact that increasing information results in increased power, § 203 expands the power of the executive branch by enhancing its authority to access the information under relatively less judicial review and legislative oversight.

2.3. Erosion of the Wall between the Criminal and Terrorism Investigations

§ 215 of the Patriot Act opens a gate of investigation between terrorism and other crimes by paving the way for the criminal investigations to obtain warrants under the FISA.

Before the Patriot Act, FISA provisions were applied only to offenses related to national security and included "foreign agent" associations. § 215 of the Patriot Act amended the FISA in such a way that the FISA court could give warrants for criminal investigations expected to produce information that may be relevant to terrorism in *general.* § 215, by its broad language, opens a gate for the crimes being investigated under the FISA which originally were enacted to regulate the foreign intelligence and provided minimal Constitutional protection. For example, FISA, after the US Patriot Act, does not require probable cause, or notice for searches and seizures. Investigations under the FISA Court order are immune from oversight of the Senate Judiciary Committee; they are subject to oversight of the Intelligence Committee which has greater secrecy than the Judiciary Committee. In addition, FISA warrants do not require the address of a person subject to search; hence, it authorizes law enforcement officials to search any place associated with the target person; and it authorizes interception of communications of all telephones of a person (not a specific telephone as it is required by the *particularity* principle). Furthermore, a communication-interception warrant approved by the FISA Court is valid for 120 days (rather than 30 days authorized by Title III).

In sum, § 215 expands the executive power in conducting criminal investigations by providing them an option for conducting the criminal investigations under the standards of terrorism investigations which requires less judicial and legislative scrutiny

2.4. Restriction of the Basic Rights of Non-Citizens

§ 411 in the "Enhanced Immigration Provisions" part of the Patriot Act defines the phrase "engage in terrorist activity" as follows: " ... the term 'engage in terrorist activity' means, in an individual capacity or as a member of an organization – I) to commit or to incite to commit, under circumstances indicating and intention to cause death or serious bodily injury, a terrorist activity. II) ... "

§ 412(a)(1) authorizes the Attorney General to detain immigrants when the Attorney General has "reasonable grounds" that the alien is "certified" to become a terrorist under the provisions mentioned in § 412(a). The Attorney General can delegate this authority only to the Deputy Attorney General who cannot delegate that authority (§ 412(a)(4)). The detention duration is seven days. If the Attorney General has reasonable ground, the detention period can be indefinitely extended by 6-month periods. The detainee may request in writing at the end of each 6 months that the Attorney General reconsider his/her "certification" to be a terrorist (§ 412(a)(7)). The Attorney General reviews the certification and makes a decision in his/her discretion to revoke or not to revoke the certification. § 412 does not give direction about any responsibility of the Attorney General in informing the detainee about the reason for the detention. The detainee can only seek review of the certification to a habeas corpus proceeding in the Court of Appeals for the District of Columbia. In such case, the government has no obligation under the Sixth Amendment to offer free counsel in such proceedings, as the habeas corpus proceedings are civil rather than criminal proceedings.

§ 412 expands the executive power in such a way that the Attorney General (*executive branch*), not a judge (*judicial branch*), has authority to deprive a person from one of basic liberties (i.e. *freedom*) in an indefinite time based on his/her subjective assessment of having a "reasonable ground". § 412 has several disputable concerns in terms of civil rights. First, the executive power has become too broad to have the sole discretion of indefinitely depriving a person of his/her freedom without judicial review. Related to this expansion of power, the "due process" of law is not implemented for the non-citizens detained under § 412[xvi]. Second, under the mode of the Patriot Act, it becomes the detainee's duty, but not government's duty, to prove he/she is not guilty. In other words, this mode violates the "presumably innocent" principle, which is one of the fundamental rights defined in the European Human Right Convention.

3. The Positions of the President and the Congress in the Expansion of the Executive Power

The expansion of power of the executive branch by reducing the legislative and judicial oversight has negative connotation [1, 2, 3, 11]. In light of this, the permission of the President and Congress for the expansion is questionable. The explanation on this questionable issue is complex as each circumstance, which provides opportunity for the expansion, has its own unique context. However, I will examine this complex issue within the scope of this study: expansion of the executive power. In my explanations, I will argue that rationalities of the President and legislators, and public opinion are two intertwined factors contributing the tolerance of the atmosphere where the expansion has been taking place.

The rational choices of the President and the legislators are different. First of all, the institutional and individual interests of the Presidents are coincidental as the Presidency has evolved to become an institution built up around one person, the President. On the other hand, individual and institutional interests of the members of the Congress are not coincidental. For example, a Congressional success may not be appreciated by the local constituents of a member of Congress. Even if the constituents appreciate the success of the Congress, they may not connect this success directly to their representative in the Congress [2]. Such situations make the Congress members being free rider in considering the institutional interests [2]. Subsequently, the Congress did not have enough motivation to prepare legislation immediately after the 9/11 attack. Instead, the Patriot Act was prepared by the executive branch headed by the President[xvii]. Partly because of this, the Patriot Act has provisions expanding the executive power.

Second, reelection is almost always a goal of rational legislators. Yet, there is no reelection possibility for Presidents elected second time. For Presidents, being victorious by winning a war after leading the nation to the war is a rational motivation. Furthermore, President's using war power meet the masculine expectations of the public; therefore, it usually increases the public popularity of the President. A member of the Congress, on the other hand, is more likely get no individual reward if the decision of the Congress about using war-like power is appropriate. Subsequently, the Congress members (i.e. legislators) do not want to be an initiating force on using war-like power unless making sure that they have overwhelming support of the constituencies in initiating the war.

In post 9/11 case, the Bush administration has been a moving force in initiating a "war" against terrorism. Congress supported the President (i.e. head of the executive power) in the war (against terrorism) initiative as they were sure that their constituents whose civil right concerns were far behind their security concerns want them to act so [2].

The Patriot Act was passed in the Senate and Congress with overwhelming majority (i.e. 356 to 66, and 98 to 1). Despite the severe provisions of the Act, the overwhelming majority indicates that legislators (i.e. the Congress and Senate), like the President, consider the public opinion and public emotion in their decisions.[xviii]

On the other hand, Congress was not completely passive in passing the Patriot Act; it played important role on moderating some severe provisions of the Act. For example, Congress eliminated the provision permitting use of information obtained from wiretapping against the American citizens by foreign governments, even if the wiretap is unlawful. In addition, Congress schedule some severe provisions sunset in December 2005[xix]. Through the sunset provisions, Congress embraced a politically popular (i.e. rational measure) measure by acknowledging the civil liberties. If the public support for the Act deteriorated, the sunset provisions will not be approved.

4. Conclusion

Expansion of the executive power has been a continuous trend at least in the last several decades. The Patriot Act produced in the post 9/11 era produced a step up effect on this trend. The act has serious restrictions in terms of the civil rights. In fact, Lewis [12] cited from the "Economist" reports that "Too many freedoms have been eroded in America since September 11th, [xx] This statement summarizes what happened in terms of civil rights in the post 9/11 era. In this era, security is upheld at the expense of the civil rights; and executive power is expanded. To the current government, the expansion is necessary in the current circumstances where terrorism is a serious threat to national security. To the American society, the civil right restrictions resulted from the executive power expansion was acceptable in the polls conducted in 2002[xxi]. On the other hand, to many scholars and civil right activists, the expansion is negative. To Benjamin Franklin, "They that can give up essential liberty to obtain a little temporary safety deserve neither liberty nor safety." [11].

Arguing terrorism is a problem that cannot be eradicated in short period of time, I argue counterterrorism policies should be made in such a way that their implications should be acceptable for long period of time. The better way of making long term policies is adherence the fundamental principles of law framed in the Constitution.

The Patriot Act changes the delicate balance between the liberties and security. The new balance established immediately after 9/11, may not be adequate for the current circumstances. Therefore it should be reviewed and changed to re-establish the delicate balance in accordance with the current circumstances of the country. Otherwise, the country (i.e. US) may no longer be a place where the people enjoy the liberties.

Congress is unwilling to use its oversight power to challenge the expansion of the executive power, without having the public support. Public opinion , providing checks to expansion of executive power has important role in influencing the legislations and policies, because both Presidents and Congress pay attention to the opinions of their constituents.

Endnotes:

[i] Pub. L. No. 107-56, 115 Stat. 272 (2001): Available at http://news.findlaw.com/cnn/docs/terrorism/hr3162.pdf

[ii] The first case related wiretapping is the Pavesich v. New England Life Insurance Co. in 1905 in the Georgia Supreme Court. The first federal Supreme Court case is the Olmstead v. US case in 1928. The first federal law having provisions about wiretapping is the Federal Communications Act of 1934.

The first Supreme Court decisions clarifying and setting the Constitutional limits of wiretapping are the Berger v. NY and Katz v. US cases in 1967. The NY Supreme Court in Berger case held that "conversation" fell within the Fourth Amendment's protection, and electronic surveillance of such conversations constituted a "search" within the meaning of the Fourth Amendment. Therefore, the Justices held that the court order had to comply with the requirements of a traditional search [5, 14, 13]. In Katz case, Justice Harlan in his concurrent opinion outlined a two-prong requirement for the constitutional (i.e. the Fourth Amendment) protection of conversations. First, "a person must have exhibited an actual subjective expectation of privacy" and, second, that "the expectation be one that society recognizes as reasonable".

The first statute regulating the electronic surveillance by considering all aspects of the surveillance is the Title III of the Omnibus Crime Control and Safe Streets Act of 1968.

[iii] Some examples of those Supreme Court cases are US v. NY Telephone Co. (1970), US v. Hall (1973), Us v. Kahn (1974), US v. Miller (1976), US v. Donovan (1977), Scott v. US (1978), Smith v. Maryland (1979), US v. Knotts (1983), State v. Delaurier (1985), Edwards v. Bardwell (1986)   are primarily the results of efforts of the law enforcement community in incorporating the use of technology in the investigations. Summary of those decisions are found at Albanese[14], Hull [13], Goldstein [15].

[iv] Lobel [16] reports that Congress passed about 470 statutes expanding the executive power from 1950s to 1970s. To Lobel [16], emergency has been the major motivation of the power expansion.

The acceleration in the expansion of law enforcement power was started after the Warren Court era, partly as a reaction of the law enforcement community to the restrictions set by the Supreme Court. Then, the innovations in communication and other technologies have fed the trend for the expansion as the new technologies (i.e. data storage, telecommunication, etc.) provided the law enforcement community for the expansion to access the information provided by these technologies.

[v] The emergency declaration is: Proclamation No. 7463, 66 Fed. Reg. 48,199 (Sept. 14, 2001).

As part of 9/11 reactions before the enactment of the Patriot Act, President Bush created the Office of Homeland Security by executive order on October 8 (Exec. Order No. 13,228, 66 Fed. Reg. 51,812), and prepared and executive order to declare that non-citizens detained in the War on Terrorism would be tried by military tribunal [17].

[vi] FISA (Pub. L. No. 95-511, 101-11, 92 Stat. 1783, 1783-96 (1978) (codified as amended at 50 U.S.C. 1801-11 (2000)) was enacted in 1978 by the Carter administration. The original form of FISA does not require the probable cause within the definition/interpretation frame of the 4th Amendment of the Constitution.

Followings are some notes about the Patriot Act [18]:

Wiretaps
- It allows wiretap order to be issued for terrorism and felony computer frauds.
- It allows accessing stored wired communications as well as e-mails by only a search warrant (not an interception warrant).

Search Warrants
- Terrorism investigations are subjected to "single-jurisdiction search warrants." : A warrant executed to search any person or property regardless of location
- It allows seizing unopened e-mail less than 180 days.
- "Sneak and peek": The notice of the target person can be delayed.

Pen/Trap Orders
- It expands the overage of pen/trap orders by including dialing, outing, signaling, and addressing information relevant to an ongoing investigation.

Subpoenas
- It amends the Electronic Privacy Act (EPA) to allow subpoenas for stored information in Internet Service Providers (ISP) to obtain records of a customer's name, address, network addresses, connecting records, types of services utilized, means and sources of payment.

- It allows ISP to "voluntarily" disclosure information if there is immediate danger.

FISA

- It allows disclosure of information obtained under FISA order to let information sharing among investigatory entities.
- "Roving wiretap": The warrant may not include particulars of target. One warrant for all!
- It expands time period of FISA search warrant.
- FISA Court cannot deny a request for subpoena when § 215 is met.

Computer Trespasses

- "Unauthorized" access to "protected" computer is subject to search.

Amendments to Computer Fraud and Abuse Act

- It contributes to the definition of terrorism: An act to influence government by intimidation or coercion, or retaliate against government conduct is a terrorist act provided that the act involves access to classified information on protected computers.

Providing Material Support for Terrorism

- It contributes to the definition of "domestic terrorism": Domestic terrorism includes criminal activities that are dangerous to human life and are intended to intimidate civilians, influence government policy by intimidation of coercion.
- Harboring or concealing of terrorists and providing material support, advice as well as training them is subject to severe penalties.

[vii] According to conventional democratic norms, any Constitutional right cannot be abridged by the executive branch of the government without a legislative support and judicial decision. In other words, any Constitutional right can only be restricted after the three major branches of the government have consensus upon that restriction. The critiques about the Patriot Act argue that it violates this principle. It grants executive branch intrudes the Constitutional rights without asking the approval of judicial branch.

[viii] As well as expansion of executive power, § 802 has another drawback: it provides an obstacle for exercising the free expression right granted by the First Amendment. Free expression provides a safety valve for the tensions, which frequently accompanies with controversies[*]. The Framers realized that the order cannot be maintained merely through punishment. They realized that discouraging thought menaces stability of the state through a breeding chain of: discouraging thought-fear-repression-hate-insurgence-unstability[**].

    [*] Linn v. United Plant Guard Workers of American Local 114, 383 US 53, 73 (1966) (Fortas, J., dissenting)

    [**]Whitney v. CA, 74 US 375-76. (Brandeis, J., concurring)

[ix] This is also known as the 1957 Rome Convention. Despite the fact that the US is not a signatory of that Convention, "equality of arms" is almost recognized as one of the universal fundamental rights.

[x] In the law, the exact phrase is "dialing, routing, addressing or signaling information". However, in this text, I simply use "signaling" as the dialing, routing and addressing information is signal in broad terms.

[xi] Hereafter, the Title III of the Omnibus Crime Control and Safety Streets Act of 1968 is simply named as Title III.

[xii] The examples of the advanced communications are ISDN, ADSL, cable internet, VoIP, GSM, and so forth. In those communications, usually the signaling and content are carried by the same physical structure such as cable.

[xiii] CALEA, enacted in 1994, has almost not been implemented since its enactment because of many disputable provisions of it.

[xiv] "… may disclose such content to Federal law enforcement, intelligence, protective, immigration, national defense or national security official…". In this sentence, I am assuming that the word "Federal" is not only describes "law enforcement", but also "intelligence", "protective", "immigration", "national defense", and "national security".

    In this clause, the word "protective" is so broad that it includes many agencies.

[xv] The minimization principle aims minimizing privacy invasion to the intercepted subject. According to § 2518 (5) of CALEA, electronic surveillance must be conducted in such a way as to minimize the privacy invasion. This requires that the private information is accessed by minimum number of people who needs that information in performance of his/her duties.

[xvi] The due process right is for all persons within the US whether they are citizen or not, lawful or not, permanent or not. (Reference: Zadvydas v. Davis, 121 S. Ct. 2491, 2500 (2001))

[xvii] Most of the provisions in the Patriot Act existed at the previous legislations brought to the Congress by the law enforcement (i.e. executive) community. After 9/11, the provisions not previously passed in the Congress were placed in the Patriot Act. For example, most of the content of the §§ 203, 215, and 216 had been debated between the FBI and telecommunication carriers [19].

[xviii] Note that, I also believe that emotions and patriotism of the members of the legislative community must also play an important role in the decisions of the legislators.
[xix] If the Congress does not re-approve the sunset provisions, they are terminated.
[xx] Lewis cited the origin of the excerpt as: "Civil Liberties in America: A Needless Victory for Terror", Economist, Aug. 31-Sept. 6, 2002, at 12.
[xxi] A poll conducted in April 2002 results that over 70 % of those polled agree that Americans have to sacrifice some liberties in order to have more security. Another poll conducted in September 2002 shows that 80 % of those polled thinks that the counterterrorist activities of the federal government are acceptable [2].

References

[1]   K.L. Scheppele, 22nd annual Edward v. Sparer symposium: Terrorism and the Constitution. *University of Pennsylvania Journal of Constitutional Law,* **6** (2004, May), 1001-1083. [Online] Available from; URL: http://www.lexis-nexis.com [2005, April 9].
[2]   N. Devins, Congress, civil liberties, and the war on terrorism. *William & Mary Bill of Rights Journal*, **11** (2003, April), 1139-1154. [Online] Available from; URL: http://www.lexis-nexis.com [2005, April 9].
[3]   P.P. Swire, The future of internet surveillance law. *George Washington Law Review*, **72** (2004, August), 1306-1371. [Online] Available from; URL: http://www.lexis-nexis.com [2005, April 9].
[4]   J.S. Lerner, M.R. Gonzalez, D.A. Small, B. Fischhoff, Effects of fear and anger on perceived risks of terrorism: A national field experiment. *Psychological Science,* **14/2** (2003), 144-150.
[5]   J.W. Whitehead, S.H. Aden, Forfeiting 'enduring freedom' for 'homeland security': A Constitutional analysis of the USA PATRIOT ACT and the Justice Department's anti-terrorism initiatives. *American University Law Review*, **51** (2002), 1081- 1088.
[6]   N. Chang, *The USA Patriot Act: What's so patriotic about trampling on the Bill of Rights?* Center for Constitutional Rights; 2001. [Online] Available from; URL: http://www.ratical.org/ratville/CAH/USAPAanalyze.html [April 07, 2005].
[7]   S. Freiwald, Uncertain privacy: Communication attributes after the digital telephony act. *California Law Review.* **69** (1996) 949 [Online] Available from; URL: http://www.lexis-nexis.com [2005, April 10].
[8]   Center for Democracy and Technology. *CDT Policy Post.* **6/15** (2000, August 15). [Online] Available from; URL: http://www.cdt.org/publications/pp_6.15.shtml [2005, February 8].
[9]   J.J. Nylund, Fire with fire: How the FBI set technical standards for the telecommunications industry under CALEA. *Commlaw Conspectus*, **8** (2000), 329. [Online] Available from; URL: http://www.lexis-nexis.com [2005, April 9].
[10] U. S. Telecom Association, et al., Petitioners v. Federal Communications Commission and U. S. of America, Respondents; Airtouch Communications, Inc., et al., Intervenors. 227 F. 3d 450 (D.C. Ct. App. 2000). [Online] Available from; URL: http://supct.law.cornell.edu/supct/cases/topic.htm [2005, February 4].
[11] W.E. Turner, New post 9/11 America or the making of King George. *West Virginia Law Review,* **106** (2004, Winter) 445-493. [Online] Available from; URL: http://www.lexis-nexis.com [2005, April 9].
[12] A. Lewis, Civil liberties in a time of terror. *Wisconsin Law Review,* (2003) 257-272. [Online] Available from; URL: http://www.lexis-nexis.com [2005, April 9].
[13] A.R. Hull, The digital dilemma: Requiring private carrier assistance to reach out and tap someone in the information age – an analysis of the digital telephony act. *Santa Clara Law Review.* **37/** (1996), 117. [Online] Available from; URL: http://www. lexis-nexis.com [2005, April 10].
[14] J.S. Albanese, *Justice, privacy, and crime control.* Lanham: University Press of America, Inc.; 1984.
[15] S. Goldstein, Twenty-eighth annual review of criminal procedure: Electronic surveillance. *Georgetown Law Journal.* **87** (1999) 1201. [Online] Available from; URL: Available: http://www.lexis-nexis.com [2005, April 10].
[16] J. Lobel, Emergency power and the decline of liberalism. *Yale Law Journal,* **98** (1989), 1385-1401.
[17] W.S. Morrow, National security & individual rights: Striking the right balance in the rules governing military tribunals. *Administrative & Regulatory Law News*, **8/8** (2002).
[18] J.E. Kirtley, The USA patriot act: Louis Freeh gets his wish. In M. Schachter, *Law of Internet Speech,* Second edition. Carolina Academic Press; 2001, pp 197-200.
[19] Federal Communications Commission. *Third Report and Order* (FCC 99-230), (1999). [Online] Available from; URL: http://www.fcc.gov/Bureaus/Wireless /Orders/1998/fcc99230.txt [2005, March 14].

Proper Proactive Training to Terrorist Presence and Operations in Friendly Urban Environments

Maria (Maki) HABERFELD[a] and Agostino von HASSELL[b]
[a]*John Jay College of Criminal Justice, New York City, USA*
[b]*The Repton Group LLC, New York City, USA*

Abstract. This paper addresses the state of police training in the area of counter-terrorism response. An overview of the responses developed by selected police forces around the world is compared and contrasted against what is needed and desired. A proactive training response to the terrorist presence and operations in friendly urban environments is presented by the authors. The approach advocates for inclusion of proactive counter-terrorism training modules in basic police academies, geared towards patrol officers who are the true first responders and intelligence gathering force on the streets of any urban environment, regardless of its geographic location. The detailed topics of such training are discussed and provide some insight into what is needed to secure the world's cities from the imminent terrorist threats.

Keywords. Counter-terrorism training, proactive modules, reactive approaches, comprehensive training, terrorist groups, community-oriented policing, urban threats, standardized solutions, home-grown threat, programmatic/strategic approach, operational/tactical approach.

Introduction

As police organizations in democratic countries struggle to mount a proper reactive and proactive approach to the internal and external terrorist threats, the variety of responses in counter-terrorism (C-T) range from innovative to inadequate or simply misguided.

This paper examines various attempts of law enforcement agencies around the world to rapidly reorganize their infrastructure to provide, at minimum, a feeling of safety and security to the public, which does not always translate into effective tactics and strategies. Suggestions for change of directions and new training modules together with reorganization of certain field units will constitute the backbone of a proper proactive response in the friendly urban environments

1. Reacting to Terrorism

Only four major countries' police forces in democratic society have had in place a sustained package of training, awareness and investigative actions vis-à-vis terrorist activities prior to September 11, 2001.

Spain (democratic only since the death of El Caudillo General Francisco Franco in November 1975) had been faced with sustained attacks in urban centers (mostly Madrid) of the Basques (*Euskadi Ta Askatasuna* or ETA). When ETA declared a cease fire in the Spring of 2006, 31 years of law enforcement response came to an end only to be replaced with strong law enforcement responses needed against Islamic Fundamentalist terrorists that killed over 200 people in simultaneous commuter train bombings in 2004. However, based on the information gathered during the field research trip to Spain in 2005, the local law enforcement will concentrate on more of a militaristic - storm the building approach to training, rather than the much broader in scope proactive training that will be introduced and discussed further down in this paper. In addition the response will differ based on the specific force as standardized training for police forces in Spain in nonexistent, and is basically regional and force specific therefore, by default, it hampers the effectiveness of a unified response, so much needed in the case of an effective and comprehensive C-T training [1].

Italy faced during the 1970-1985 period the violence and murderous spree of the Maoist-inspired Red Brigades (*Brigate Rosse)*. The Red Brigades were credited with 14,000 acts of violence in the 1970s alone and in 1978 kidnapped and murdered former Italian Prime Minister Aldo Moro. In addition, Italy's highly diverse police forces faced the actions of the various organized crime gangs (*Cosa Nostra* and others) who fought against prosecution with terror-like killings of police officers, politicians and prosecutor. Same as in Spain, the C-T response is the hands of multiple forces that are not subjected to any uniformed standard of training [1].

Germany - which has a form of democracy that can only be defined as imposed from the outside and followed as a dictate (in the writers' view democracy is not truly inherent to the Germans) - faced a wave of terrorism in the 1970s that started with the extremely violent Bader-Meinhoff Gang. In addition, Germany's police forces have attempted to combat the latent terror tendencies of the extreme right wing or Neo-Nazis as well as imported terrorism from Armenians, Turks, and gangsters from countries of the former Yugoslavia. Same as Spain and Italy, police forces are trained in sixteen federal training center that do not have a uniformed module for the C-T training [1].

The United Kingdom had a highly refined terror response, honed in over 50 years of combat against the Irish Republic Army (IRA) and its various off-shoots. Lately, the police forces of Her Majesty have tried to apply those lessons to the present terror threat of primarily home-grown Islamic fundamentalism. The situation in the United Kingdom is much better than in Spain, Italy and Germany since its 43 police forces are exposed to national standards - with exception for C-T training, where regional constraints, chief among them the budgetary considerations, do not allow for uniformity of training in this area therefore, again, hampering the effective and proactive response. Recent report published by the British authorities identified such weaknesses and recommend consolidation of the forces, especially the smaller forces and putting the total number of police forces in Britain at twelve however, nothing final has been decided in this regard and the deliberations will, probably, continue into the more distant future. In addition, British C-T efforts have almost always been in close coordination between regular police and military forces [1].

Other nations have faced terrorism and evolved their own unique counter-terrorism stance. One is the State of Israel which has confronted terrorism in some form or other since 1948. Yet for the purposes of this paper, Israel's experience - while ultra useful for other police forces - must be seen in the stark light that Israel has almost been permanently at war since 1948. It is this "war stance" that has shaped Israel's counter-terrorism response. In addition, Israel has adapted the somewhat questionable British methods (such as the destruction of houses of actual and suspected terrorists) that would not work in North America or Europe. Day-to-day tactics learned from Israel do, however, have a major lesson value, particularly with the United States now essentially on a war footing (which when observing shoppers at Bloomingdales in New York City is hard to believe).

We also have to distinguish between the ways Israelis deal with the C-T training in the occupied territories versus the response in Israel itself, which differs in a significant way from the one used in the occupied territories. The issues related to the friction between the ideas of democratic policing vis-à-vis effective C-T training can be easily demonstrated while observing the two, distinctively different, approaches.

Japan has been faced with a few incidents of terrorism. Most notable is the 1995 Sarin gas attack by Aum Shinrikyo, a religious cult. Beyond that Japan has been relatively free of terrorism. The well known Japanese Red Army has operated almost exclusively outside of the borders of this island nation. As a highly homogenous population, subject to extreme traditional discipline, few proactive steps by the well trained Japanese police forces are required. Nonetheless, the revelations of North Korean kidnappings of Japanese from Japanese shores over many decades and North Korean missile firings has had yet to be fully understood effects on the Japanese views of terrorism and national defense.

However, Japan has a strong history of modeling its police forces after certain European countries and it is only a matter of time before they can be expected to adopt one of the C-T modules of the European forces and, again, the thin line between democracy and effective policing will be put to a test.

In terms of counter-terrorism actions in democratic societies, the recent experiences in Russia cannot be included here. That country operates on a level of democracy that is not recognizable by "western standards" and is slipping back into a dictatorship-like climate.

2. Proactive Law Enforcement Response

One of the most complex problems in developing proper counter-terrorism stances in democratic police forces is the traditional police mindset. Police forces are - by training and culture - more inclined to react to a crime rather than take proactive steps to prevent a crime.

On a micro level, the typical police force will respond to reports of a crime. For instance, in the case of a burglary, the police will respond and then investigate. Only if there are multiple burglaries in a certain neighborhood and a pattern emerges will police forces attempt to take proactive steps to prevent future burglaries and get to the root cause of the societal problem.

Initiatives such as various forms of community policing and extensive data tracking as evolved by New York City Police Commissioner William Bratton - COMPSTAT (Computer Comparison Statistics) - were supposed to "fix" some of these problems. In some cities this has worked. For instance, the "impact squads" of the New York Police Department which target specific high-crime incidents, are such a positive development. Yet is this all applicable to terrorism and is this the proper response?

We must not ignore the fact that aggressive street policing is always a threat to democratic values, especially in countries where one person's problem is another person's constitutional right.

Definition is one root cause of the lack of effective response to terrorism. The general public as well as most democratic police forces see terrorism as a phenomenon *sui generis*. However, treating terrorism as a crime would and should help rapidly reshape the law enforcement response.

For instance, the at time high-intensity war against narcotics in major urban centers such as Amsterdam, London, Paris, Rome, New York, Los Angeles and Atlanta (among others) is a an action quite similar to the stance, we believe, law enforcement should take vis-à-vis terrorism. The actions of drug dealers - operating often in highly trained, well financed and quite sophisticated gangs - do parallel actions by terrorists. Additionally two other factors could help guide police response:

- Narcotics are probably the second largest source of funding for Islamic fundamentalists, apart from the various "charities." The poppy cultivation in Afghanistan, as one example, means that the drug consumer on Manhattan's Upper West Side or in the elegant streets of Paris essentially makes a "donation" to various Islamic extremists. Note further that in the United States the bulk of the true successes against terrorism came from the U.S. Drug Enforcement Agency which managed to interdict numerous times since September 11, 2001 the flow of drugs and money that would have been of benefit to terror groups.
- Traditional terror groups such as Columbia's FARC (Fuerzas Armadas Revolucionarias de Colombia) have emerged as major drug dealers on the own. With estimated annual sales just below US$1 billion, FARC does rely on the drug trade to sustain traditional terrorist operations [2].

2.1. Responses That Fail

Using the old military maxim that superior firepower will defeat the enemy, democratic police forces have resorted to response mechanisms that do little in terms of actual counter-terrorism and are, at times, downright ridiculous.

It has become the almost automatic reaction of big-city and small town police forces to react to terror incidents as follows: flood the streets with police officers, often heavily armed with submachine guns or military-quality carbines; police officers in heavy armor patrol airports, bridges, public spaces, transportation systems (such as subways and commuter rails), inspect bags at random and create a very visible presence on urban streets. This reaction is common now: in Europe and in the United States.

While this *may* help reassure the public - and a study on this would be a worthwhile academic undertaking - such efforts do next to nothing in reducing terror threats. They are costly - NYPD's Hercules and Atlas units consume substantial portions of limited budgets - and are often put in place for just a few days or maybe weeks. Possibly the most extreme (and patently ridiculous) such deployment was the multi-year stationing of heavily armored military vehicles equipped with .50-caliber machine guns on the major highways leading towards the Pentagon in Washington, D.C. Apart from utterly demoralizing the soldiers assigned to this meaningless boring duty, it would have had - even in extreme cases - no real impact on any terrorist attack planning.

Similarly the annual security effort that surround the United Nationals General Session opening session in September in New York has evolved into a extremely expensive and highly questionable form of use of law enforcement power to protect against terrorism. It would be highly unlikely that the New York - headquarters of the United Nations (an unlikely target to begin with) would be attacked during this time period when world leaders, including representative from nations who are well known sponsors of state-terrorism (i.e. Iran) assemble in New York. Yet still, over 10,000 law enforcement officers blockade the streets.

2.2. Why?

Terrorists have no known record of attacking into an alert. Counter-measures are analyzed by terrorists and their tactics will be adjusted. For instance, the first attempt at New York City's World Trade Center in 1993 used a car bomb in a garage below the center. Since that attack, the trade center incorporated sophisticated counter-measures against future bomb-laden track entering the garage. Yet the terrorists, fully aware of this, worked around this and developed a new method: using airplanes as giant bombs.

In some countries - mostly Saudi Arabia - Al-Qaeda and related groups will issue warnings of impending attacks. Typically and inside of two weeks such a warning of followed by an actual attack. Yet the warnings are sufficiently vague to prevent any effective counter-measures in terms of physical security. Globally, terrorist groups that misrepresent Islamic principles to justify their violent actions will issue routine threats, often highly vague. The only result of such threats is to instill a "feeling of terror" in the general populace and a scurrying about by intelligence services and law enforcement looking for what this vague threat could mean. Alert levels are routinely increased (and then lowered a few weeks later).

3. Suggested Mechanism for Effective Law Enforcement Counter-Terrorism

A careful study of counter-terrorism programs in England, Northern Ireland, Spain, Ireland, Sweden, Turkey, Poland and the Netherlands, as well as actual work with the New York City Police Department suggests a series of measures that may help in this current time of crisis [1].

Do note that the pro-active stance of the London Metropolitan Police that led of to the arrest of two dozen suspected bombers this past August was based in part on this approach.

- Police officers require solid training
    - o History of terrorism and terrorists groups: Just like cops study the background and Modus Operandi (M.O.) of criminals, terror groups must be subjected to the same analysis. This requires training or more adequately college level educational modules, with all the nuances and biases carefully examined and surgically addressed.
    - o Exposure to how past terrorist attacks evolved and what their root causes are will help develop a deeper understanding that can, if done right, translate into improved day-to-day policing.
    - o Simulation: We believe police officers should boost training levels by a) simulating possible attacks and b) learn to get into the mindset of the "terrorist criminal" by studying a group and then planning an attack themselves.

  o   However, training cannot be overdone: An excessively intensive exposure to terror issue will translate into mental overload.
  o   Training on how terrorists operate will help street cops in community policing to spot developments that could assist in the overall intelligence gathering effort.
- Intelligence gathering is critical yet not emphasized enough
  o   Few police departments do a good job in collecting intelligence. Major exemptions are both the London Metropolitan Police and the New York Police Department. The latter has a multi-lingual and well trained intelligence unit in place that works these issued and present a "must follow" example for other urban centers. However, New York's intelligence unit is hampered by lack of proper coordination with federal sources as well as the lack of sufficient police officers with high-enough security clearances to actually see the stream of information collected.
- Inter-agency cooperation must finally reach the levels mandated by the U.S. Congress as well as by the appalling lack of such cooperation prior to the September 11, 2001 attacks.
  o   The culture war between the various law enforcement agencies and intelligence gathering units in the United States continues. None of the Congressional mandates have been able to overcome decades of resentment. This problem has been identified some time ago with regard to non-terrorist related activities, just the "plain" 101 traditional crime activities and is referred to in the police literature as "linkage blindness". We simply became blind to the importance of cooperation and sharing that is the vital and most essential link to effective enforcement.
  o   For instance, computer systems between the FBI and the CIA are virtually incompatible. Free exchange of information between the FBI and CIA remains an occasional activity.
  o   Key units in the frontlines in the Global War on Terror - such as the U.S. Drug Enforcement Administration - are not even included in the national intelligence sharing network.

4. Definitions

It is very hard to create any type of effective C-T training or any other training for that matter without having a clearly defined and operationalized target, against which we want to train our forces.

With regard to various C-T definitions it is impossible to adopt one or even a few of the myriad of the definitions existing out there and customize any effective training module/s that will address all the complexities involved in multiple definitions and approaches.

After scanning and surveying the infinite number of such definitions the authors opt to propose one of their own - a definition that is broad enough in its scope and overreaches other definitions. This definition will enable us to create a training response that is not myopic and skewed towards particular political goal or orientation. It will allow for a much more comprehensive approach to C-T training.

The concept of ***Haves versus Have Nots*** has been popularized in social sciences for many, many decades. It goes back to the Marxists theories of power and control that led to defining and labeling certain groups and individuals and their behaviors as criminals and crimes. The "Haves" were the ones with the means and the power and the "Have Nots" the ones without.

Borrowing from this concept but reversing its order, we propose to define the terrorist phenomenon as a struggle between the Have Nots against the Haves. The Have Nots will encompass a very broad number of individuals of various ethnic, racial, religious backgrounds who harbor various grievances against the Haves.

There are two recent examples that support the validity of this definition:

- Northern Ireland has started to boom economically in the past decade: this removed one key element from the traditional war between the IRA and London, a war that was often based on claims of economic discrimination. The improvements in the economy of Northern Ireland (in part a spillover of the economic miracle of the Irish Republic) had, in the authors' view, much to do with the cease fire declared by the IRA. In a sense the IRA as a fighter for economic justice became irrelevant and lost its popular support.
- Similarly, in Spain the massive economic buildup in the Basque region - paid for in part with generous grants of the European Union - robbed the ETA of its *raison d'être* and led to the cease fire in 2006.

There is always something that one of the Have Nots is missing from his/her life that the Haves possess - be it a separatist movement that wants its own piece of land, separate from the mainland, a religious fanatic who wants his/her religion to be the one that guides and restricts the behaviors and freedoms of the Haves or the cause oriented mercenary who will perform any heinous act for the cause - and this cause will be to get the money that he himself does not have - but the Haves definitely do.

Borrowing another concept from the social sciences - "the paradox of the dispossession" - which basically spells out that the less one has to lose the less one is threatened by the authority. If you feel that you have nothing to lose - nothing will deter you - not your own death and certainly not the death of the others [3].

It would be opportune for C-T police officers to fully understand Mao Tse Tung's concept of insurgent warfare - which is based on more than 3,000 years of military thinking in China. Mao basically said that guerillas (or in modern parlance insurgents or terrorists) must swim like fish in the sea: they must be embraces by the general (impoverished) population - and use that as a place to hide and sustain themselves [4]. The economic booms in Northern Ireland and in the Basque regions essentially led to "the sea" (i.e. the aggrieved population) to reject "the fish" (i.e. the insurgents or terrorists). This, in all likelihood, may be one useful concept for the situation in Iraq: note here that the economically sound Kurdish region has little or no problems with insurgency.

In other words - we need to look for those many different individuals and groups whose claim to fail is some real or perceived injury caused by the Haves or those who the Haves represent. Such an approach will allow us to step back and away from the misguided preoccupation with one religion and one or two groups who are defined as the major threat to any given law enforcement agency. This broadening of the scope of our academic inquiries into a somewhat amorphous and esoteric definition of the phenomenon of terrorism will allow the practitioners to focus on the following - very pragmatic approach to C-T training.

5. What Can We Do? A Two-Prong Approach

The authors' propose - based on having studied C-T efforts of police forces around the globe and trained between them well over 1,500 police officers in C-T tactics - a two-prong approach to C-T training.

The first "prong" is ***Programmatic/Strategic***:

- What is the next stage in training- "the paradox of the dispossession" and
- What are the new criteria for deployment?

The second "prong" is ***Operational/Tactical***: This involves multiple steps:

- Who are the new partners? (i.e. local law enforcement coordinates efforts with national assets and the military as well as the national intelligence community).
- Who will continue with the traditional law enforcement? Care must be taken that standard police work does not suffer from the additional burden of C-T efforts.
- Who will gather and disseminate the information? This is probably the most sensitive and complex issue: who controls intelligence and who is allowed to gather it.

To lead police forces in C-T - without degrading standard police work - police leaders must proactively engage in increasing C-T awareness (i.e. communicate); decrease overreaction (i.e. extreme "flooding" of the streets with cops) and to customize a police department's response to local needs, risks and capabilities.

The final or maybe the opening statements that epitomize the importance of proper proactive training will have to deal with the implementation of an effective C-T training in a country that refers to its form of government as a democratic one. Police scholars have argued over the years that policing is hard on democracy or in reverse - democracy is hard on policing. Police after all is about use of force - and the basic principles of a democratic government are not grounded in coercion. C-T training, by default, connotes the ideas of use of force - by the police (the arm of the Haves) against certain minority members (the Have Nots) who reside amongst larger communities (of the Haves).

There is a very thin line and a very delicate balance that needs to be maintained in order to prevent the larger passive sympathizers of the Have Nots from crossing the line of passive into active. The more civilized we become as a society the more we resent the idea of use of force against us - even and when such use of force is authorized by the legitimately elected governments.

C-T training must balance the softer - more academic approach with the best of the police street operational work. In order to achieve this mix we must carefully design the training modules, the ones created for the generalists and the ones for the specialized unit. This careful design cannot be properly achieved without cross-pollination between the academics and practitioners. This approach has been already utilized in a number of countries but the key to a successful training scenario is not just the amalgamation of the academics with the practitioners but the proper blend of the right academics with the right practitioners. As enigmatic as this last statement might sound it has a very simple translation - not everybody who is a member of a give profession knows what he/she is doing.

Being a college professor who specializes in a given field does not, automatically makes one a good match with any practitioner whose major qualifications are the number of years spent on the force. Without getting into any specific details - we have seen this happen, both in the United States and in other countries. Matching the two right individuals - the academic and the practitioner - is a science in itself.

6. Proper Proactive Training to Terrorist Presence and Operations in Friendly Urban Environments

This could and should be addressed as a two-prong approach:

1. A proactive training devised for each and every law enforcement officers as they are not only the first respondents but the true eyes and ears of any police organization.
2. Focus on devising proper proactive training for specialized units that deal with counter-terrorism and Intel gathering as their primary specialization.

What we are seeing around the world is a strong focus on the training of the specialized units with almost peripheral or non-existent allocation of resources to the street officers or all the other officers in a given department.

Why is this preoccupation with the specialized units and the allocation of the majority of resources towards their training priorities? To understand this misguided approach (at least in the eyes of the authors of this paper) one needs to understand that our response to the terrorism phenomenon is grounded in the history of training and organizational structures of police departments.

O.W. Wilson studied the relationship between effective organizational structure of police agency and specialization. While he did not find much of a benefit in specialized units for smaller police departments, since their patrol officers appear to be jacks of all trades, he identified a number of advantages for large police agencies:

- placement of responsibility
- development of expertise
- promotion of group esprit de corps
- increased efficiency and effectiveness [5].

However, most police departments in the United States are small, and these are the ones who according to the above would not benefit from a specialized training. In addition, the idea of a generalist training, one that will create a well -rounded officer who is equally knowledgeable in Community Oriented Policing, Conflict Resolution, Parking Ordinances, Protection of Wild Animals and the local terrorist cells, gained a lot of popularity in the local law enforcement.

Proponents of the idea of generalist point to a number of problems associated with specialization, it appears to:

- create increased friction and conflict between the units
- create loyalty to the specialized unit instead of the department
- contribute to a decrease in overall job performance due to job factionalism
- hamper the development of a well-rounded police program [6].

Based on the above history of two extreme approaches to police training, we continue to follow the controversy by either creating only specialized C-T units and providing training modules that are very narrowly defined or will go with the generalist approach and create modules that are so general and reactive in nature that will render most, if not all, of this training as a liability insurance concept rather than something truly proactive and effective.

Unfortunately, if on one end, the idea of a "generalist" approach to C-T training will prevail in American policing and furthermore, gain some momentum, especially for the small departments, and on the other hand the idea of specialized units will take over the role of fighting the phenomenon of terrorism in urban environments, and only left-over resources will be allocated to the generalists we predict a very troublesome future.

Not only we do not give our officers the necessary tools to perform their profession, as the basic academy training can not and will not offer them these tools, (if it continues to offer modules of training that are inadequate both in length and content) the so called specialized and developmental training creates an impression, in many instances, of a further deterioration of the idea of professionalism for law enforcement.

The length of the training, in itself, is seldom a fully inclusive indicator of the quality of a given training module. However, coupled with the six answers to the following questions the picture is quite clear.

The basic questions to be answered about the quality of specialized, counter-terrorist training are:

1. what
2. when
3. where
4. who
5. by whom
6. how much

The multitude of topics and themes that needs to be covered during truly proactive counter-terrorism training points to the complexity of a proper police response. This complexity necessitates a serious and structured approach. An old and well known adage says: with force you can be successful against a specific terrorist but you will not win the war against terrorism.

On of the more prominent events that highlighted the need for specialized training can be traced to the early 1960's. In August of 1966, an incident occurred in Austin, Texas, that contrary to other incidents, pushed law enforcement towards assessment of their capabilities in handling high-risk situations. After killing his wife and mother, Charles Whitman went to the roof-top of the University of Texas and began a shooting spree, killing fifteen people and wounding thirty others. This event contributed to the establishment of special police teams to handle high risk situations [7].

9/11 was a similar catalyst in the area of counter-terrorist/intelligence training. However, when one analyzes the themes of police specialized training in the above areas it appears that the inter-relations between history, religion, social justice and real or perceived injustice, economic trends, migration trends paired with the increase in violent crimes, high-technology crimes, the increased number of high-risk repeat offenders (an outcome of prison overcrowding), the overall sophistication of criminal element, diversity related issues and a host of additional problems which create the need for a very carefully designed specialized and developmental training approach, generate, at best, what these authors would call a "post-hoc training" approach.

Police scholars, when describing police sub cultures refer to the concept of "post-hoc morality" when dealing with explanations for unethical or questionable behaviors. The post-hoc morality provides an alibi, explanation or/ and a justification for officer's behavior, after the fact [8].

The quality and quantity of various approaches to C-T and intelligence training, both during the academy and later on in-service in the form of specialized and developmental training courses seem to be providing the similar outlet for police agency as the adoption of post-hoc morality. There is, indeed, an element of alibi, explanation, and justification, in the various specialized and developmental courses offered to law enforcement officer, there is, however, no trace of an element of a true expertise.

Any of the three two day courses, "dealing with the history of terrorism," "the phenomenon of suicide bombers" or "the more "in-depth" approach to the study of Islam" certainly serves as an alibi for a department that needs to enhance its officers' people skills, or prepare for accusations of indifference toward the Islamic victims. The focus on Islam in this circumstance may be misconstrued as profiling of certain communities. However, the training will not provide the adequate tools to deal with these problems, even in a semi-effective manner.

The authors of this paper (both college professors) realize quite too well that after 15 weeks of instruction, with two and half hours a week, which amounts to about 38 hours (38-to 40 hours of instructions are considered to be an average length of a course in any college environment) the knowledge of counter-terrorism response and policies for law enforcement is, at best, comparable to scratching a tip of an ice-berg. However, 40 hours of instructions allocated to C-T training for the generalists in the field is rarely in existence in police departments around the country or the world for that matter.

But, any and all that is delivered to police officers in these areas provides an alibi for a given police organization and a false sense of security for the officers in the field. We must and actually have an obligation to look at the history of specialized training in this country and learn form our mistakes. Gould (1997) conducted a research study to evaluate the experiences of police officers exposed to a specialized Community Oriented Training offered in-service to officers with some level of seniority in the field. The experienced officers felt that the course was a waste of time, and their criticism was summarized in five points:

1. a feeling that the community did not understand or appreciate what the officers were trying to accomplish;
2. a feeling that most police administrators and many supervisors had lost touch with the reality of policing as the officers face it today;

3. a feeling that many police administrators and community politicians were looking for a quick-and-dirty scapegoat, therefore often blaming police officers for things over which they have no control;
4. that the "rules of the street" far too often weighted against the police;
5. that there is a divergence between what is being taught in the course and what society actually asks a police officer to do [9].

Gould's finding could be probably directly replicated if somebody had surveyed the C-T training offered to l/e officers today in the America and around the world. Gould suggested some policies to be considered, based on the findings of his study. Some of his suggestions about the venues to improve community oriented training were customized by these authors for the benefit of improvement of the C-T training. Following are the points that should be taken into profound consideration when a given agency puts together C-T modules that will be looked upon as proactive and not post-hoc:

1. It should be remembered that teaching C-T concepts also means the "un-teaching" of some already existing culturally intensive attitudes, prejudice, biases and behaviors.
2. A change in behavior of a given police officer will not generally result from sitting through one C-T course, no matter how extensive in scope and intensity.
3. For the training to have its greatest effect, it should be tailored to meet the needs of the officers as well as the community. In other words, it is not enough to train officers in understanding the problems, grievances, and other issues related to a particular community that might be perceived as "the assailant community" without having a real input from this community. For example, the authors spoke to a number of a minority members in England. Some of them expressed a certain degree of satisfaction with the way police treated them, the others were vocally militant in their hatred towards the police.
4. The training of experienced officers should include the training of administrators in the same classroom setting. Decision making still takes place on the top and the decision makers who do not walk the streets not always understand what is happening on the streets and how the realities of life changed since they stood in the rain. For example, of officer in Madrid told one of the authors that his bosses have no clue with regard to what is happening in this area in terms of possible counter- terrorism threat and that only those who patrol this neighborhoods realize win what direction things are deteriorating however, they are not the ones who have any influence over training or policy making of the department.
5. C-T training should begin early in an officer's career, during the basic academy and should include basic modules on intelligence gathering. When the authors spoke to police officers in England and asked them how come they had no clue about the July (2005) bombers and their activities in the respective communities, they were told that this is not the police business but rather the Security Service's. The authors cannot disagree more.
6. The training should be reinforced throughout the officer's career and especially given the almost daily developments in the C-T area - it is almost mandatory to bring it above the level of the roll-call FYI routine into a more specialized and periodically offered in-service modules.

American society is still preoccupied with race, ethnicity and diverse cultural orientations. The 9/11 events and the explosion of the C-T militaristic orientation within the local law enforcement will continue to divide and define our society. Law enforcement, in its essence, can be complex, painful and problematic regardless of the multicultural dimensions. The goal of the C-T training modules should be to analyze the concepts of racial, ethnic and cultural stereotypes, and evaluate the impact of prejudice on police professionalism.

7. Conclusion

As we continue to struggle with the proper counter-terrorism response to a threat of a myriad of terrorist activities that preoccupy the minds of policy makers and law enforcement practitioners, it is inevitable that we need and must look at the lessons learned by countries that experience the same phenomenon for quite some time. Looking at responses of law enforcement agencies and various legal systems around the world can and will provide us with some contours of the proper actions. There is no doubt that such a response needs and must be customized for the local realities of life, however there is also no doubt that the proper proactive response has to include training modules offered at the basic police academy and to all patrol officers on the streets, as they represent the first and most important line of defense against the terrorist threat that breeds on the streets of the urban environments and enjoys the support of some of its inhabitants.

References

[1] M.R. Haberfeld. Field notes. Germany, Ireland, Northern Ireland Spain, Italy, Turkey, United Kingdom; 2004-2006.
[2] A. von Hassell, M. Haberfeld. Personal communication, New York City; 2005-2006.
[3] W.K. Muir. *Police streetcorner politicians.* Chicago, IL: University of Chicago Press; 1977.
[4] Z. Mao. *Selected military writings of Mao Tse-tung .* Foreign Language Press; 1963.
[5] O.W. Wilson, R.C. McLaren. *Police administration.* New York, NY: McGraw-Hill Book Company; 1972.
[6] C.R. Swanson, L. Territo, R.W. Taylor. *Police administration: Structures, processes, and behavior* (5th ed.). Upper Saddle River, NJ: Prentice Hall; 2001.
[7] M.R. Haberfeld. *Critical issues in police training.* Upper Saddle River, NJ: Prentice Hall; 2002.
[8] J. P. Crank. *Understanding police culture.* Cincinnati, OH: Anderson; 1998.
[9] L.A. Gould. Can an old dog be taught new tricks? Teaching cultural diversity to police officers. *Policing,* **20** (1997), 339-356.

Understanding and Responding to the Terrorism Phenomenon
O. Nikbay and S. Hancerli (Eds.)
IOS Press, 2007

Comparative Analysis of the Role of Intelligence in Counterterrorism in Turkey and in the United States

Ferhat GOKTEPE[a] and Serhan ERCIKTI[b]
[a]*Spalding University, USA*
[b]*University of Louisville, USA*

Abstract. Terrorism has become one of the most pervasive and single largest problem of the decade. Terrorist organizations have become more dangerous with availability of new destructive weapons. September 11 attacks on the World Trade Center demonstrated that the nature of the terrorism problem could not be localized to respondents within a particular region. Therefore, through their analysis of the views of experts and the developments that have been taking place in the field of terrorism and intelligence, the researchers hope to gain an insight into the specific role of intelligence as a tool in counterterrorism measures. In order to narrow down the issues related to the wide-ranging issue of terrorism, it is proposed to confine this study specifically to the United States and Turkey, and the analysis of intelligence that will be undertaken will be restricted to these two countries, which may be classified as two of the salient players in the war on terrorism.

Keywords. Terrorism, counter-terrorism, intelligence, technical intelligence, and human intelligence.

Introduction

Terrorism has become one of the most pervasive and complex policy issues that confront the world in present times. It is no longer restricted to threats of destruction that are made with the objective of securing political ends and has ceased to be limited to violent acts. Defining the range and scope of terrorism has itself become a difficult issue since it involves elements from various countries and various nationalities who may band together for a common cause, which is generally political. The most difficult aspect of terrorism, however, is the ambiguity and lack of clarity associated with identifying and isolating the elements responsible for terrorism and its proliferation across the globe. Enders and Sandler [1] associate terrorism with the threat of the use of violence, which in turn is directed towards the achievement of political ends.

According to Jessica Stern [2], terrorism is not the kind of enemy that can be fought on an all out in the open combat basis. Over the years, the face of terrorism has changed; it is no longer restricted to state sponsored terrorism but has evolved into specialized local cells with individual terrorist elements spreading threat in order to achieve their own selfish political or other ends. Stern clarifies that the inability to engage terrorists out in the open arises due to that reason. She equates terrorism to a virus for which the causal factors could range from global to national or personal reasons. In some instances, the governments of certain countries could themselves function as terrorists when law enforcement power remains unrestricted [3]. Thus, the response to terrorism could itself create controversy in its manner of implementation, as highlighted by Warlaw, who states that once the objective of either defeating or weakening the terrorists is achieved, further violence by the State will only contravene democracy.[4]

While the face of terrorism itself is difficult to define, more agreement is emerging on its underlying causes, which have now deviated from purely political causes into issues that are based on religion. For example, the Turkish Chief of General Staff has identified the major causes of terrorist activity in Turkey as being centered on religious fundamentalism and Kurdish separatism [5]. Within the United States as well, there is increasing awareness of militancy purporting Islam as the unseen enemy that is at the root of terrorist activity [6]. This has highlighted the difficulties that are faced in effective counterterrorism, wherein a distinction has to be made between fundamentalist militants purporting Islam and the substantial peace loving Muslim population over the globe. It is impossible to compartmentalize the problem of terrorism to a particular country or group of people since there is also secret and unidentified support that is being provided to terrorist groups from elements that are sympathetic to their causes.

The attack on the Twin Towers on September 11, 2001 was a milestone in the sphere of terrorism because it has changed the way people use the term [7], has resulted in a global world coalition against terrorism, and was the spur for the emergence of the counterterrorism movement. Turkish Armed Forces (TAF) Chief of Staff General Hilmi Özkök said that the 9/11 terrorist attacks have brought the concept of the "asymmetric threat" into the world. Political equations in the Middle East have been changing, especially for Turkey, who plays a pivotal role in the region through its growing alliance with Israel and India. These three countries are forming a tripartite alliance in order to counter the threat posed by some nations in the region, leading to a natural alliance of pro-Western, stable and democratic nations [8]. Turkey has begun to play a more active role in initiating counterterrorism activity in the region of the Black Sea, which is known as Turkey's "Black Sea Harmony" Operation, which may also include Russian participation [9]. On November 4, 2004, Russian military intelligence GRU Head General Valentin Korabelnikov and head of General Staff Intelligence General Arslan Guner held top-secret meetings, in which they embarked on a new era of intelligence cooperation between Turkey and Russia [10]. Turkey has also been active in reestablishing diplomatic ties with countries in the Middle East previously perceived as unfriendly, and its defense budget has been increased to $8 billion, which represents an increase of 9.6% as compared to the allocation in the previous year [5].

1. Purpose of the Study

A great deal of importance has been accorded to terrorism in recent years because it has emerged as the single largest problem of the decade. Terrorist organizations have become more dangerous with availability of new and more highly destructive weapons. It is vital that law enforcement officials acquire an understanding of the nature of the problem because it has become so widespread and disjointed that it has slipped out of the areas within local jurisdictions. The problem of terrorism cannot be localized within the traditional hierarchical frameworks that have existed thus far and with which law enforcement agencies are familiar. Although terrorism, in many forms, has existed in many nations for decades, with the September 11th attacks, the United States feeling the direct effects of it, has taken the initiative in the war on terror and has played a major role in the response of the world to terrorist activity. Equations in the Middle East have changed with the defeats suffered by Iraq and Afghanistan, and the face of terrorism has become more ambiguous, retiring into the shadow and anonymity of the electronic medium, where it still poses a potent threat to world peace and stability. Within the Middle East, Turkey is emerging as one of the most important countries, together with Israel, that is allied with the pro democratic force represented by the United States.

Methods that may be identified as ways of dealing with terrorism can no longer be confined to direct straightforward attacks. Intelligence activity has come to play a vital role in dealing with the problem of terrorism. For example, immediately after the United States faced 9/11, attentions became strictly focused on national intelligence. Many criticisms, such as "Why didn't the intelligence services forewarn?", "The CIA was asleep at the wheel!", "The intelligence system isn't working!", and "The biggest intelligence system in the world, spending up to $30 billion a year, could not prevent a group of fanatics from carrying out devastating terrorist attacks!" were written by the national media [11]. Most of the criticism and questions have focused on changes the United States intelligence services should implement in order to be successful in the war against terrorism.

The undefined face of the enemy needs to be spotlighted through intelligence measures undertaken by a coalition of global forces, and responsibility for countering terrorism can no longer be restricted to the domain of a particular country. As opposed to traditional law enforcement and direct military action, covert intelligence activity is more effective in identifying and targeting the enemy.

Therefore, this study aims to undertake a detailed examination into the issue of terrorism and its ramifications, in special reference to the United States and Turkey, and to explore the role of intelligence in responding to it. Response models will be examined and an analysis will be undertaken of the manner in which the two countries have responded to and dealt with terrorism.

2. Definition of Terrorism

The Turkish Anti-Terror Law defines terrorism as the following: "Terrorism is any kind of act done by one or more persons belonging to an organization with the aim of changing the characteristics of the Republic as specified in the Constitution, its political, legal, social, secular and economic system, damaging the indivisible unity of the State with its territory and nation, endangering the existence of the Turkish State and Republic, weakening or destroying or seizing the authority of the State, eliminating fundamental rights and freedoms, or damaging the internal and external security of the State, public order or general health by means of pressure, force and violence, terror, intimidation, oppression or threat." [12].

The transnational nature of terrorism has been pointed out by Sandler, Tschirhart and Cauley who state that terrorist violence is largely pre-planned and carried out with the objectives of attaining political goals by terrorizing innocent victims [13]. Enders and Sandler [14] have highlighted the premeditated threat of use of force on large groups of people who are not involved in politics, while Jenkins [15] points out that the intent behind terrorist acts is not so much the threat of infliction of physical damage but the psychological impact of such threats. Lila Perl [16] also states that it is the illegal and intimidating aspect of terrorism which poses the greatest dangers to citizens by creating doubts in their minds that their government can protect them, thereby creating fear and unease as future attacks are anticipated, especially because terrorism may be classified as a form of warfare that is planned in advance. The fear aspect is the root of the terrorist philosophy as evidenced in a Chinese proverb that states "Kill one, frighten 10,000". When eleven Israeli athletes taking part in the Olympic Games in Munich, Germany in 1972 were killed, the success of the mission did not lie in the killing of the eight athletes, per se, but in the fear, it created among the Israelis and their supporters. Crelisten [17] equated terrorism to criminal activity because it is executed without warning and targets the civilian section of the public, while Stern [2] has identified the religious base of terrorist activity as being geared towards the achievement of political ends through the threat of use of force.

International terrorism has been defined by the United States Department of State as "a crime involving citizens or the territory of more than one country" [18]. Jenkins [15] identifies an international terrorist incident as being one that obviously involves more than one country and has worldwide results. Warlaw [19] states that any universal definition of terrorism cannot be restricted to behavioral descriptions but must also take into account individual motivation, social milieu and political purpose. For instance, while provoking a cataclysmic world revolution is a motivation for a member of Red Army, for a Palestinian Liberation Organization member, the incentive is to accomplish their national destiny and get their homeland back [20].

According to Paul Pillar [21] the former deputy chief of the Central Intelligence Agency's Counterterrorist Center, there are four elements to terrorism:

1. It is pre-meditated
2. It is political (not criminal)
3. It is targeted at civilians
4. It is carried out by sub-national groups that may or may not operate within a country or internationally but not by a country.

According to Velter and Perlstein [22], one man's terrorist may be another man's freedom fighter, which only heightens the dilemma in developing and implementing a universal definition and policy on terrorism. However, the salient factor that most of these definitions highlight is the threat of use of force that is geared towards the achievement of political ends.

3. The Role of Intelligence in Preventing Terrorism

Terrorism can be seen as a virus which directly affects individuals' lives by adversely impacting their freedom [23] by means of both victimization and fear [24]. According to Turk [25], today, terrorism is more complex because it involves today's sophisticated technology in electronic communications, international transportation networks and high explosives. Thus, there is practically no terrorism-safe place in the world. Since consciousness of terrorism has grown, especially after the 9/11 attacks, it is important to analyze the terrorist activities that have occurred in the past to discover what courses of action should be taken. Although terrorists have been carrying out their activities for a long time, the September 11 Al Qaeda attacks brought terrorism into people's view as the most significant peril that every person and state faces in various forms.

Terrorism is not conventional warfare. The fight against terrorism does not involve one clearly defined enemy but a spread out enemy base that may consist of several independent units that are constantly forming and re-organizing themselves and are difficult to pin down. Moreover, the motive of terrorists is primarily to create an atmosphere of fear and terror through implied threat, and it is difficult for intelligence agencies to pin down the sources and methods of future attacks precisely. According to Velter and Perlstein [22], most nations are unable to anticipate a terrorist attack until it actually occurs due to their inability to interpret the signs of subversion and unrest effectively. It is only by undertaking extensive surveillance and infiltrating into terrorist units that attacks can be preempted since a policy against terrorists is likely to be effective only when law enforcement is able to identify the enemy and evaluate exactly where he is likely to strike next [26]. According to Kendall [27], the strategic intelligence focuses on possible new threats by providing the identification of changing situations rather than identifying particular operational targets. For instance, in the last decades, Western governments reacted against terrorist activities by producing swifter and more effective response methods. Use of both military and spy satellites with the purpose of tracking down the terrorists has improved this approach [20]. Since terrorist attacks also target innocent sections of the public, there is also the question of loss of many lives though identifying likely victims of an oncoming attack is difficult without the gathering of proper intelligence information.

Most terrorist activity is covert but there are many sources of information available in the public domain as well since most terrorists are anxious to propagate their agenda to the public and seek support for their political causes. For example, according to the National Commission on Terrorism [28], terrorist organizations increasingly use the internet as an effective means of communications and as a path for cyber attacks. Therefore, the mining of intelligence can play a vital role in preventing terrorist attacks. Karmon [29] points out that several terrorist attacks in the last decade have caught the intelligence community by surprise. The perpetrators of several attacks, such as the bombings of Khobar Towers in Saudi Arabia in 1982 and the American Embassy in Beirut in 1983, are still unknown and unpunished while Osama Bin Laden still goes scot-free. Karmon [29] also highlights the fact that most analysts and researchers are of the view that terrorism will continue to be a threat during the next decade, fuelled by the political instability in the international environment, which has produced struggles for power and attendant difficulties in attaining equilibrium. There is also an increasing trend towards ethnic conflicts although some of them, such as the PKK in Turkey, have stabilized.

The proliferation of such ethnic groups has resulted in the search for neutral territory, such as countries where support is available for terrorist activities and which are emerging as safe havens for terrorists. In view of the political and logistical difficulties presented in dealing with terrorists in neutral states and those who enjoy state support for terrorist activities, the scope for identification and straightforward war and/or capture of terrorists becomes impossible without the aid of intelligence. Trends in globalization have also reduced territorial disputes among major nations of the world, fostering a spirit of international peace with a thrust on diplomacy, which does not support the use of overt methods to deal with terrorists but is more suitable for covert activities, such as intelligence.

The fact that terrorists often operate in small, independent, leaderless groups also makes intelligence activity even more vital. Additionally, the proliferation in Weapons of Mass Destruction (WMD), the use of the internet and the creation of faceless enemies with an enormous potential for destruction by the simple hitting of a switch or access to information, further accentuates the role of intelligence in preempting such destructive activity [29]. Terrorists are also resorting to the use of chemical and biological weapons fuelled by fanaticism and esoteric goals that are devoid of reason. Therefore, conventional methods are never enough in the fight against terrorism. Countries can only operate from a position of strength through extensive use of intelligence to gather information about terrorist groups and even infiltrate them where possible in order to gain knowledge about the terrorist groups and to deal with them in the most effective manner on a preventive basis to forestall attacks.

4. Brief History of Terrorism in the United States

The 9/11 attack is not the first time that the United States has been the target of terrorism. Terrorist attacks in the United States have occurred since the Second World War, and the Vietnam War highlighted the fact that the heartland of capitalism was vulnerable [30]. Terrorist incidents were not as common in the United States as in Russia and Europe, and terrorist incidents within the United States were limited and confined to attacks on the capitalist machine. For example, a terrorist group calling themselves the Anarchists were against any form of organized government, and one of their men shot at President McKinley one hundred years ago [31]. Ronald Reagan was one of the first American presidents to recognize the threat of terrorism [29]; however, this was mostly in relation to developments during the Cold War, which were confined to those that originated in ideological political differences.

Earlier terrorist attacks against the United States were mostly restricted to attacks abroad on the United States embassies, and the causal factor propelling these attacks was politically motivated. However, the recent spates of terrorist attacks that have erupted since the late 1980's are motivated by religious and/or ethnic reasons. As stated by David Rapaport, a professor at UCLA, in the Canada and the World Report [30], two primary events may be deemed to be the causal factors:

- The 1979 Islamic revolution in Iran
- The collapse of the Soviet Union in Afghanistan in 1989

Between 1980 and 2001, local groups perpetrated domestic terrorism within the United States, with the most notable example being the 1995 bombing of the Alfred P. Murray Federal Building in Oklahoma City, which killed 168 people and injured more than 500 [32]. Although the 9/11 attack was the biggest and the most destructive terrorist attack ever carried out by foreigners in the United States, domestic terrorism was responsible for about three-quarters of the 335 incidents between 1980 and 2000 [33]. International terrorism fuelled by militant Islamic groups in the Arab countries has, however, been growing and culminated in the single, enormously successful attack led by Osama bin Laden on the Twin Towers on September 11th. This was later found to be linked to a series of global terrorist attacks that had been planned by bin Laden's group, which were foiled through vigilant intelligence efforts [34]. With the changing global equations in the world and the collapse of Communism, a spate of international fundamentalism has been unleashed, resulting in an increase of terrorist attacks on the United States' interests across the globe.

As pointed out in the Report of the National Commission on terrorism [28] by Schelling, terrorist organizations, like the IRA and the PLO, carried out terrorist attacks in the 1970's and 1980's with purely political objectives; however, the face of international terrorism is changing and assuming a more radical, fundamentalist character, propelled by religious and/or ethnic causes. There is a growing trend of hatred towards America, which led to attempted attacks on the World Trade Center in 1993 and the Lincoln and Holland tunnels in New York. Since the 9/11 attacks, there is open and growing resentment of American hegemony, and the face of terrorism is changing as the focus changes towards attacking and killing as many people as possible. These terrorists lack a specific objective but are fuelled by racial and/or ethnic hatred against the United States and its growing role as the dominant power in the world. Recent terrorist activity has concentrated not only on the use of conventional and biological weapons but also on Cyber terrorism, so the disjointed nature of the current terrorist problem has made it more difficult to handle.

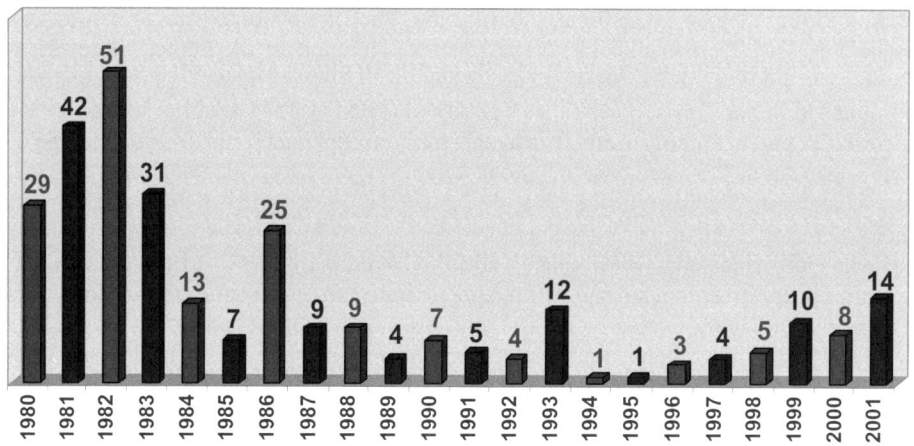

Figure 1. Terror incidents in the United States between 1980-2001
(Source: Counter-terrorism Division at Federal Bureau of Investigation [35])

5. Brief History of Terrorism in Turkey

Although Turkey became a democracy during the 1950's, not being able to fulfill public aspirations caused public disorder and strikes. After the Turkish Armed Forces seized control of the government to prevent chaos in Turkey in 1960, civil rule was effectuated after 18 months military rule, in 1961 [36]. Internal immigration to industrialized cities, extension of educational opportunity and the growth of mass communication systems not only increased economic and social expectations of people but also instigated the socialist movements, particularly among university students, who were willing to use force and/or violence to achieve their goals [36].

Terrorism in Turkey had its origins in student movements that began in the 1960's and evolved into separatist movements, especially among ethnic groups, such as the PKK, which was established in the early 1970's in search of a separate Marxist Kurdish state. These terrorists initiated violent incidents all over the country, which weakened social, political and economic conditions within the country. Because of those conditions, General Kenan Evren introduced military rule in Turkey in 1980, and the nation, again, remained under military rule until 1983. During this period, there was a crackdown on terrorists, because of which many escaped to Syria, which became a haven for the terrorists, together with Germany, Iran, Iraq and Greece. Since 1984, terrorist attacks have been dealt with through the deployment of Turkey army units and special police forces.

Left wing terrorist groups have origins in the Turkish People's Liberation Army. Leftist terrorist groups, who aspire to promote a revolt or popular national rebellion among the social classes in Turkey, have fervidly been anti-NATO as well as anti-United States. They have provided their funds mainly by committing crimes in Turkey, including armed robberies and extortion from businesses [20].

The PKK is also represented in Turkey, and specifically has received help from Syria, Iran and Armenian groups who are also pressing for separation from Turkey. PKK's ideology has been predominantly leftist and, therefore, aligned with the cause of Armenian separatists. The PKK, led by Abdullah Ocalan, who founded the organization with the specific aim of freeing the southeast part of Turkey from the control of Turkey for establishing a new Marxist Kurdish State, is also part of the international terror network and works in cooperation with other terrorist groups, such as the Hezbollah. PKK is also known as controlling drug trafficking in Europe to a substantial extent and using monies gained through these sources for its terror campaigns and activities [37].

Although Syria gave refugee status to Abdullah Ocalan in 1980's, he was extradited from Syria after international political pressure and the threat of a war with Turkey mandated action from the Syrian Government. Ocalan escaped to Russia, found no sanctuary there, and was also denied entry into Italy. He finally landed in Nairobi, Kenya, where he was captured by the Turkish Government and sentenced to the death penalty. Ocalan's case was tried by the European Court (Ocalan v Turkey (2003) 37 EHHR 10), and the Court held that death would constitute cruel and degrading treatment, which would violate the provisions of Article 3 of the European Convention of Human Rights. Thus, his sentence was commuted to life imprisonment. However, the PKK has not ended with the capture and trial of Ocalan but continued under the name of KADEK (Kurdistan Freedom and Democracy Congress). A flood of terrorist attacks were unleashed in Turkey after Ocalan's capture, and the PKK has continued to function from outside Turkey as the KONGRA-GEL (Kurdistan People's Congress) since November 1, 2003, and continues to pose a threat to Turkey's territorial integrity [38].

Additionally, Turkey also faces terrorist threats from Hezbollah and Al Qaeda, and it is gearing up to tackle this asymmetrical threat by organizing its special force and defense units to improve their defensive capabilities. Turkey has also contributed to the United States led war on terrorism through its leadership of the International Security and Assistance Force in Kabul since June 2002, while it plays a strategically important role in the war with terror by allowing the use of its Incirlik airbase for the United States and United Kingdom aircraft. It has also been strengthening its military base and is acquiring satellites, missile systems and AEW&C aircraft to enhance its surveillance and early warning capabilities.

Turkey is also willing to join the European Union and had commenced the talks as of 2005. However, Turkey still values its territorial integrity and working towards the reestablishment of severed ties with its neighbors in order to increase its influence as a strategic player in the Middle East [5]. It has also begun to establish strong and close ties with Israel and India, fuelled by an expanding agenda of common interests into a new Eurasian alliance [8]. Surrounded by Islamic interests, such as Iran with its threatening noises about WMD, a growing alliance between Pakistan and China, and Iranian and Syrian sponsorship of terrorism, the three democratic countries are moving closer together in the formulation of strategic alliances in the region to develop missile systems for defense and to combat the growing threat of terrorism.

Retired USA General Edward C. Meyer believes that Turkey's problems as a NATO ally need to be understood within the context of its location in the midst of terrorist sponsoring nations.[39]

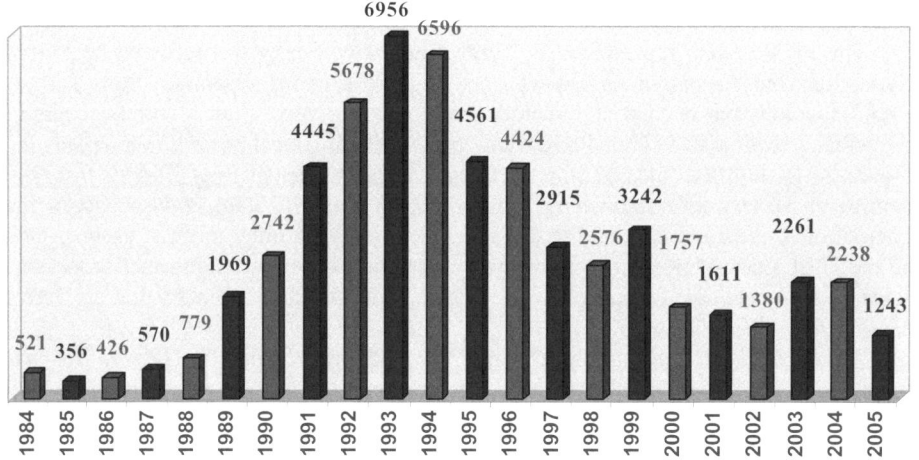

Figure 2. Terror incidents in Turkey Between 1984-2005.
(Source: Istanbul Conference on Democracy and Global Security, 2005 [40])

6. Comparative Analysis of Intelligence Systems in Turkey and in the United States

At the outset, it must be stated that both the United States and Turkey appear to be making some significant progress in their respective wars on terrorism waged within their own national territories. Turkey's centralized system is primarily comprised of police officers who are trained and equipped to handle the job of intelligence at their own local levels. There is only one National Intelligence Agency, which coordinates the reports arriving from the local intelligence and anti-terrorism units. The major problem that the Turkish intelligence system has been coping with in terms of terrorism is the activities of the PKK-KONGRA GEL led by Abdullah Ocalan, and his recent capture is, therefore, a feather in the cap of the Turkish intelligence service and a definite set back to the PKK-KONGRA GEL. Terrorist attacks increased within Turkey after the capture of Ocalan, but it may be noted that through the vigilance of the Turkish National Police, terrorist activities are being more strictly monitored and cracked down upon.

Turkey has been emerging as a crucial nodal point for control of terrorist activity in the Middle East. In a diplomatic sense, Turkey is realigning its relations with its neighbors. The new diplomatic ties that it has established with Israel and India reflect the new equations developing in the region. Israel, India and Turkey are the three nations committed to the political system of democracy. Turkey's old relationships with its Muslim neighbors are also being redefined, and all this may be seen to be the direct consequence of terrorist activity within the region and the defining of policy in accordance with the intelligence on terrorism, which is being made available to the central government. Recently, Turkey almost came to war with Syria, a long time diplomatic ally and neighbor - over the issue of Abdullah Ocalan, who was taking refuge in Syria. Turkey is also strengthening its navy and military forces and preparing itself to emerge as a major global player in the region through its strategic location in the Middle East. All these have developed as a result of the relative success of the workings of the intelligence system within the country. The fact that the PKK-KONGRA GEL range of activity has also been brought under control is largely a reflection of the success of the intelligence community within Turkey.

While there is no separate organization that is responsible for international intelligence activity, it is the National Intelligence Organization itself, which controls intelligence activity of its agents abroad. The specific demarcation of intelligence activity along regional and local levels has proved to be the strength of the intelligence gathering mechanism within Turkey, especially since all this information is contained within a centralized database, which makes it much easier for the Turkish Government to make the relevant policy decisions in this regard.

Although, traditionally, foreign and domestic intelligence were separate in the United States' system, cooperation was increased after September 11. The United States has also carried out some successful anti-terrorist activity after the 9/11 attacks. Several potential worldwide attacks that were planned by Al Qaeda on American interests abroad have been forestalled before they could be completed. Moreover, the United States has also been cracking down on the Taliban in Afghanistan and Saddam Hussein in Iraq and has entered into collaborative arrangements with several countries in the field of intelligence activity in order to aid its anti-terrorism efforts. The introduction of the Patriot Act, with its expanded provisions for surveillance, etc have provided additional ground for law enforcement authorities to go after and trap suspected terrorists, while intelligence training has been stepped up with several universities now offering courses in the subject in order to recruit more intelligence officers.

However, some differences may be observed in the intelligence community within the two countries. Firstly, the United States has a separate intelligence agency dealing with domestic terrorism - the FBI and another for international intelligence activity - the CIA, apart from the central defense intelligence agency - the National Security Agency. Therefore, the intelligence activity is not available in a centralized database as is the case with Turkey although the United States now has a new branch - Director of National Intelligence (DNI), which aims to coordinate the intelligence activity of all organizations in order to derive an integrated, overall picture of intelligence activity within the Country. Therefore, intelligence reports which are prepared are derived from a variety of sources and from the different departments such as the State Department, Law enforcement, etc., all of which must be taken into account in preparing reports and briefings for the benefit of the officials concerned with policy decisions.

The United States' intelligence is more decentralized in comparison with the Turkish intelligence system. Moreover, it is not comprised entirely of police officers. Intelligence officers are selected from candidates who possess a wide and different background in relation to skills, qualifications and profession, and several of them are covert agents. The United States also employs intelligence officers from foreign countries.

In a technological sense, the intelligence gathering system within the United States is on a much more sophisticated scale as compared to that of Turkey. Developments in Internet technology, data mining and analysis are much more highly evolved in the United States, and the country is often in a superior position in terms of availability of knowledge from technological sources. However, it may be noted that in spite of this superiority in availability of technological information, the United States is not in as good a position as Turkey as far as human intelligence is concerned. In Turkey, most of the intelligence is derived from officers who are on the ground, collecting the information from first hand sources. However, in the United States, the fact that very few Americans possess bilingual skills in Middle Eastern languages, added to the fact that they are not able to infiltrate terrorist groups successfully because of their lack of knowledge and sensitivity to Islamic traditions and sentiments is a serious drawback in the collection of intelligence.

Most of the terrorists are well aware of the levels of sophistication of technological devices used by the United States and have already learned how to circumvent many of these measures. For example, they do not use cell phones anymore because cell phones can be easily tapped and records of conversations accessed. On the contrary, they now prefer to use fiber optic technology available for wireless devices. Since most terrorist groups also do not operate from a centralized framework but function as independent units, it is even more difficult for America to successfully masquerade as terrorists to gain entry into the organization to provide first hand intelligence reports.

In the manner of operation of intelligence systems in the United States and in Turkey, a similarity arises out of the same type of political system in the countries. Both Turkey and the United States are democracies, and the Constitutions of both countries provide for freedom and privacy for their citizens. Therefore, many of the initiatives that may be taken by the police and the intelligence communities to crack down on terrorists and/or suspects of terrorist activities are often opposed by civil rights groups and by ordinary citizens. There are certain rights available to citizens of the two countries, such as the need for a search warrant before organizing a search of premises, the need to warn before documents are subpoenaed, and other such measures that are enforced to ensure that the privacy and freedom of the citizens are not encroached at any cost.

This rigid enforcement of individual freedoms often functions to handicap law enforcement authorities. The benefits that are extended to ordinary citizens are also available to terrorists, who operate within the United States and Turkey, who are able to evoke the same protection of the law in order to carry on their subversive activities. It becomes difficult to catch terrorists without them having prior knowledge that they are under suspicion and could be implicated, thereby giving such suspects adequate time to escape. Although the expanded provisions of the intelligence acts and regulations in both countries have been introduced precisely to take care of such eventualities, some citizens and civil rights groups fiercely oppose them because they violate individual privacy and freedoms guaranteed by the Constitutions. The protection of individual rights has led courts to rule against the States on many occasions both in Turkey and in the United States.

On the other hand, ever since the 9/11 attacks against the United States, the country has been functioning more or less under a system of rigid controls and security measures where the authority of the State is unquestioned and supreme, and individual rights can be limited. It is, therefore, easier for the United States Government and intelligence agencies to move against suspected individuals and crack down on terrorism as compared to Turkey.

7. Policy Implications

From the above comparisons, it may be noted that there are some policy implications that arise in the case of both Turkey and the United States. For example, intelligence efforts must be coordinated with those of other nations if they are to be truly effective. The availability of complete sources of information, or information that can be independently corroborated is likely to provide better grounds for making policy decisions. Since terrorism is no longer a local phenomenon, it is necessary to deal with other nations in arriving at solutions to the terrorist problem. Such cooperation is required not only at the initial stage of developing strategies but also in capturing terrorists, tracking terrorist activity in various nations and to ensure that the terrorists are brought to justice.

The United States and Turkey may need to work on a cooperative basis in the intelligence arena with intelligence units in other countries in order to be able to pre-empt terrorist attacks effectively. The United States has emerged as a leader in the global arena and Turkey in the Middle East, and close and effective intelligence collaboration between the two countries, as well as other willing nations, is likely to be helpful in transcending the problems that arise with criminal law in international jurisdictions through the requirements of the Geneva Convention.

In the wake of increased terrorist incidents throughout the globe, there is a need for enhanced use of both overt and covert intelligence to gather all the relevant information before policy decisions are undertaken. Decisions can no longer be taken based on overt information and in the making of such decisions; the international framework must be taken into consideration. Therefore, the issue of state sponsored terrorism assumes great importance since the seven known state sponsors of state terrorism provide safe havens where terrorists can retreat and plan their strategies and elude capture, in addition to receiving financial help and arms support from their sympathizers across the globe. Thus, it is necessary for countries, such as the United States and Turkey, to coordinate their efforts and their intelligence, in order to demand that terrorists be remanded to the custody of the world courts, so that they can receive just punishment for their crimes.

The new transnational face of terrorism has necessitated a more cooperative global, intergovernmental policy on terrorism, becoming one that can be applied worldwide. There is a special need for policy decisions to focus on the development of viable human intelligence sources in order to tackle the complex nature of terrorist problems that exist in the Middle East. There is a noticeable lack in these areas since terrorist groups are small, exclusive fundamentalist groups functioning in independent units that are difficult to penetrate effectively. The reasons for this lie in the fact that there are only a few American agents with the bilingual skills and knowledge of Islamic fundamentalism who are able to pass off as members of a terrorist group effectively so that they can collect direct, first hand information from the organization. Therefore, there is an acute need to recruit and train more agents in functioning as effective agents in the Middle East.

In this area, Turkey and the United States can cooperate and coordinate their efforts. The lack of human intelligence in the United States can be counterbalanced by the strength of the same intelligence in Turkey, and the high level of technical intelligence in the United States can increase the effectiveness of the same intelligence in Turkey. Therefore, the effective development of human intelligence that can effectively infiltrate terrorist groups is mandated, and policy makers need to take into account the importance of development of human intelligence in tackling the problem of terrorism so that adequate funds are allocated for recruitment and training.

The best way to indicate changes in policy that are caused by the changing nature of hostile threats is by examining the failure of existing intelligence analysis during the Pearl Harbor attacks and the 9/11 terrorist attack, both of which caught the United States by surprise and caused unprecedented damage because the available intelligence was not properly utilized. The United States followed an isolationist-driven downsizing in intelligence that resulted in a reduction in and failure of intelligence capability during the period of the Second World War, resulting in the inability to foresee the Pearl Harbor attack for which intelligence indications were available [41].

Such an isolationist policy followed in the present day and age could result in a similar failure to process intelligence information that is available. The 9/11 attack was also caused due to the failure to appropriately analyze and make use of available intelligence information. Therefore, this provides an indication that any future policies must focus on improving the intelligence gathering and analysis mechanism within the country. One of the salient reasons for the two attacks outlined above was also the lack of human intelligence that was available, so all-current policy decisions must focus upon strengthening human intelligence, which can be one of the most valuable sources of relevant and useful information.

Existing legislation within the United States that restricts the use of agents abroad is one area where significant policy changes are required. These restrictions make it difficult to use agents abroad and has been identified as one of the most important factors leading to the 9/11 attacks. Moreover, the CIA is not permitted to recruit agents with a criminal or questionable background due to embarrassment that may be caused to the agency [42], and this further restricts the recruitment of agents who may be effective in intelligence gathering and analysis. Since most individuals who are involved in or conversant with terrorist activities are likely to have such questionable backgrounds, yet at the same time are likely to be the best sources for reliable and relevant information, policy changes must include the removal of such restrictions as those mentioned above.

The Patriot Act and similar legislation has faced strong opposition from civil rights activists who contend that the rights to privacy of American citizens is negatively impacted because human intelligence activity within the domestic arena is akin to prying into the private lives of individual citizens. The United States intelligence has been accused of illegally investigating domestic individuals and groups [43]. The demand for secure communications availability to the public has also meant that terrorist groups within domestic territory enjoy the same advantages as private citizens to confidentiality of private information, which can be misused by these terrorists [44]. Therefore, effective policies will have to be taken up to develop a strategy that can permit wider collection of intelligence on individuals when terrorist connections are suspected.

8. Conclusion

From the above analysis, it can be seen that the face of terrorism has changed. It is not local anymore, but it has become global; it is not limited to specific large groups with specific political objectives, but it has become an uncontinuous system with no clearly identifiable leadership nodes. It is no longer confined to sporadic attacks that are unleashed with a specific political objective in mind where the extent of harm is only to the level required to secure the attention of the appropriate authorities, such as was the case with the IRA and PLO. The face of terrorism has changed and is no longer restricted to local groups with distinct leaders and command centers but into transnational units that operate in the form of independent cells and are intent upon wreaking the greatest extent of havoc that they can.

Therefore, the intelligence strategies deployed to cope with modern day terrorism must also change. In view of the fact that terrorism has become a cross border, transnational enterprise, it is necessary to focus on human intelligence, by recruiting and training multi skilled, multi lingual individuals who are also computer savvy so that the process of collection and analysis of intelligence can be carried out with the requisite degree of skill. While there is no doubt that information gathered from sophisticated technological devices is useful, they are no substitute for human intelligence; however, in the new global perspective that exists today, agents who can adapt within a global context will also have to be recruited and trained in order to effectively provide valuable human intelligence.

As pointed out by Ely Karmon [45], successful penetration into enemy territory required skilled humans. It is necessary to recruit and train intelligence agents who can effectively function in the capacity of intelligence gatherers by infiltrating terrorist organizations in order to obtain first hand information. While the use of technical intelligence is indispensable and must be coordinated with human intelligence, it cannot provide the benefit of analysis that is possible from human sources, which are able to pick up many subtle signs and indications that cannot be accessed through technical sources. Intelligence effort must also be geared towards comprehensive analysis of open source information that is available over the Internet. Since most terrorists make use of the Internet to communicate their aims and objectives to sympathizers and supporters and to pull in more supporters for their cause, intelligence available through these sources will often be a valuable source of information and may also serve as a warning of potential terrorist attacks. Although terrorists use ciphering to transfer their information over the Net, it is possible to crack such codes using intelligence resources, and such data mining on the Net can therefore be an extremely valuable source of information. Moreover, the future challenges to intelligence activity will also include data collection and analysis of non-conventional terrorist armory and weapons, such as weapons of mass destruction and biological warfare.

Also, intelligence cannot be restricted within national boundaries anymore. Terrorism has become a global problem, and unless there is a high level of cooperation existing between intelligence gathering organizations across national boundaries, no effective intelligence can be gathered about terrorist activities. Therefore, a high level of cooperation among various nations appears to be necessary for all future intelligence efforts. Especially in view of state sponsored terrorism, it is difficult for one nation working alone to get a handle on the terrorist members and effectively deal with them, leading to their capture so that they do not find sanctuary in certain states that sympathize with terrorists. Any policy against such states cannot be implemented without global support and an international cooperative effort.

References

[1]   W. Enders, T. Sandler. *What do we know about the substitution effect in transnational terrorism?* 2002 [Online] Available from; URL: http://www-rcf.usc.edu/~tsandler/substitution2ms.pdf. [2006, April 23].

[2]   J. Stern, *Terror in the name of god: Why religious militants kill.* New York: Ecco, Harper Collins Publishers; 2003.

[3]   P. Chalk, Threats to liberal democracy: the response to terrorism as a threat to liberal democracy. *Australian Journal of Politics and History ,* **44/3** (1998), 373-388.

[4]   G. Warlaw, The democratic framework. In Charters, editor. *The deadly sin of terrorism: Its effect on democracy in six countries.* CT: Greenwood Publishing Group, Inc.; 1994.

[5]   L. Sariibrahimoglu, Country briefing: Turkey - at the crossroads. *Jane's Defence Weekly,* 2005, May 25.

[6]   D. Pipes, Advancing U.S. national interests through effective counter terrorism testimony presented to secretary's open forum, Department of State. 2002. [Online] Available from; URL: http://www.danielpipes.org/ article/428 [2006, May 24].

[7]   J.R. White, *Terrorism and homeland security: An introduction (5th ed).* CA: Wadsworth Publishing; 2005.

[8]   I. Berman, Israel, India and Turkey: Triple entente? *The Middle East Quarterly, .9/4* (2002). [Online] Available from; URL: http://www.meforum.org/article/504.[2006, May, 21]

[9]   L. Sariibrahimoglu, Russia's Black Sea fleet visits Turkey. *Jane's Navy International.* 2006, *April 1.*

[10] M. Yetkin, Intelligence cooperation with Russia. 2005. [Online] Available from; URL: from http://www.byegm.gov.tr/YAYINLARIMIZ/CHR/ING2005/07/05x07x21.HTM#%207. [2006, April 21]

[11] R.K. Betts, Fixing intelligence. Foreign Affairs, 2002, January/February. [Online] Available from; URL: http://www.foreignaffairs.org/ 20020101faessay6556/richard-k-betts/fixing-intelligence.html. [2006, April 21]

[12] The Turkish Anti-Terror Law. Resmi Gazete. 1991. [Online] Available from; URL: http://www.law.qub.ac.uk/humanrts/emergency/turkey/ tur2.htm. [2006, May 14]

[13] T. Sandler, J.T. Tschirhart, J. Cauley, Atheoretical analysis of transnational terrorism. *American Political Science Review.***77/1** (1983), 36-54.

[14] W. Enders, T. Sandler, The Effectiveness of antiterrorism policies: A vector-autoregression-intervention analysis. *American Political Science Review,* **87/4** (1993), 828-844.

[15] B.M. Jenkins, Defense against terrorism. *Political Science Quarterly,* **101/5** (1986), 773-786.

[16] L. Perl, *Open for debate: Terrorism.* New York: Benchmark Books; 2004.

[17] R.D. Crelisten, The discourse and practice of counter-terrorism in liberal democracies. *Australian Journal of Politics and History,* **44/3** (1998), 389-413.

[18] U.S. Department of State. *Patterns of global terrorism.* 2000. Available from; URL: http://www.state.gov/ s/ct/rls/pgtrpt/2000/. [2006, April 14].

[19] G. Warlaw, *Political terrorism.* New York: Cambridge University Press; 1989.

[20] C.E. Simonsen, J.R. Spindlove, *Terrorism Today: The past, the players, the future.* New Jersey: Prentice; 2000.

[21] P.R. Pillar, *Terrorism and U.S. foreign policy.* Washington: Brookings Institution Press; 2001.

[22] H.J. Velter, G.R. Perlstein, *Perspective on terrorism.* California: Wardsworth Inc.; 1991.

[23] W. Laqueur, *A history of terrorism.* New York: Transaction Publishers; 2002.

[24] D.E. Long, *The anatomy of terrorism.* New York: The Free Press; 1990.

[25] A.T. Turk, Sociology of terrorism. *Annual Review of Sociology,* **30/1.** (2004), 271-286.

[26] B.M. Jenkins, *Terrorism and beyond: An international conference on terrorism and low-level conflict.* California: Rand; 1982.

[27] W. Kendall, *The function of intelligence.* 1949. Available from; URL http://www.jstor.org/view/ 00438871/di971095/97p0044t/0. [2006, April 14].

[28] National Commission on Terrorism. Countering the changing threat of international terrorism. 2000. Available from; URL: http://www.fas.org/irp/threat/commission.html. [2006, May 15].

[29] E. Karmon, *The role of intelligence in counter terrorism.* 2001. Available from; URL: http://www.ict.org.il/articles/articledet.cfm?articleid=152. [2006, May 14].

[30] Canada and the World Report, Wave upon wave: The story of terrorism is 2000 years old but its plot has scarcely changed. *Canada and the World Backgrounder,* 67/4 (2002). Available from; URL: from http://sas.epnet.com. [2006, April 14].

[31] H. Trickey, *Historical view: America has dealt with terror before CNN.com.* 2001. Available from; URL: http:// cnnstudentnews.cnn.com/2001/ fyi/news/ 09/18/history.terrorism/index.html [2006, May 14].

[32] U.S. Senate Select Committee on Intelligence. *Testimony of Robert S. Mueller, III, Director, Federal Bureau of Investigation before the Select Committee on Intelligence of the United States Senate.* 2003. Available from; URL: from http://intelligence.senate.gov/ 0302hrg/030211/mueller.pdf. [2006, May 14].

[33] Council on Foreign Relations. 2006. Available from; URL: http://www.cfr.org [2006, May 14].

[34] D. McKeeby, Seven U.S. terror suspects seeking Al-Qaeda support arrested. *The Washington File*, 2006. Available from; URL: from http://london.usembassy.gov/terror676.html

[35] Counter-terrorism Division at Federal Bureau of Investigation. Terrorism 2000-2001. Available from; URL: http://www.fbi.gov/publications/terror/terror2000_2001.pdf [2006, May 14].

[36] I. Bal, S. Laciner, Challenge of revolutionary terrorism to Turkish democracy, 1960-80. *Terrorism and Political Violence,* **13** (2001), 23-36.

[37] Assembly of Turkish American Associations (ATAA*). Report on the PKK and terrorism.* Available from; URL: http://www.ataa.org/ ataa/ref/pkk/ mfa/report-pkk-terrorism.html. [2006, April 23].

[38] L. Sariibrahimoglu, Interview: General Hilmi Ozkok: Chief of the Turkish General Staff. *Jane's Defence Weekly,* 2003, January 22.

[39] O. Karaspan, Turkey and U.S. strategy in the age of glasnost. *Middle East Report,* **160** (1989), 4-10.

[40] Istanbul Conference on Democracy and Global Security, 2005. Available from; URL: from, http://www.istanbulconference.info/Conference_documents/Proceeding.pdf?PHPSESSID=b166f2c2e3a 27b83da68a14c3e8792d0 at p.135.

[41] R. Wohlstetter, *Pearl Harbor: Warning and decision.* California: Stanford University Press; 1962.

[42] A. McLaughlin, A matter of ethics for cloak-and-dagger set. *The Christian Science Monitor,* (93) 2001, October 05. Available from; URL: http://www.csmonitor.com/2001/1005/p2s1-usju.htm. [2006, May 05].

[43] W.R. Wannall,. Undermining counterintelligence capability. *International Journal of Intelligence and Counterintelligence,* **15/3** (2002) 321-329.

[44] A.A. Pappas, J.M. Simon, The Intelligence community: 2001-2015, *Studies in Intelligence,* **46/1** (2002) 45. Available from; URL: http://www.odci.gov/ csi/studies/vol46no1/index.html [2006, May 05].

[45] E. Karmon, Intelligence and the challenge of terrorism in the 21st century. 1998. Available from; URL: http://www.ict.org.il/articles/articledet.cfm?articleid=54 [2006, April 14].

Understanding and Responding to the Terrorism Phenomenon
O. Nikbay and S. Hancerli (Eds.)
IOS Press, 2007

The Counter-Terrorism Issue
in the U.S. and Turkey's Policies

Murat GUNBEYI[a] and Tarkan GUNDOGDU[b]
[a]*Justice Administration, University of Louisville, USA*
[b]*Turkish National Police*

Abstract. Why is the attack on the Twin Towers called terrorism, while the killing of thousands people by invading Iraq for the purpose of bringing democracy to the Middle East is not? Indeed, international lawyers, experts, and authorities have struggled to define terrorism for nearly a century, largely without success. In the words of the old cliché, One man's terrorist is another man's freedom fighter. There is no single, universally accepted definition of terrorism in the literature. Because of the power of individual perspective, it is difficult to define terrorism easily and accurately. Terrorism may be motivated by political, religious, or ideological objectives, and it is the unfortunate reality that terrorists recognize no rules. This paper examines the counter-terrorism policies of the U.S. and Turkey. Throughout the study, the researchers will not only use the second hand data, but also they will profit from his ten-year experience at Counter-Terrorism Department of Turkey.

Keywords. Terrorism, counter-terrorism, torture, military tribunals, the media, intelligence.

Introduction

Why is the attack on the Twin Towers called terrorism, while the killing of thousands of people by invading Iraq for the purpose of bringing democracy to the Middle East is not? Indeed, international lawyers, experts, and authorities have struggled to define terrorism for nearly a century, largely without success. In the words of the old cliché, "One man's terrorist is another man's freedom fighter" [1]. There is no single, universally accepted definition of terrorism in the literature. Because of the power of individual perspective, it is difficult to define terrorism easily and accurately. However, according to the Federal Bureau of Investigation, it can be defined as "the unlawful use of force or violence against persons or property to intimidate or coerce a government, the civilian population, or any segment thereof, in furtherance of political or social objectives" [2]. Moreover, according to other definitions, it is a special type of violence. It is a tactic used in peace, conflict, and war. The threat of terrorism is ever present, and an attack is likely to occur when least expected. Terrorism may be motivated by political, religious, or ideological objectives, and it is the unfortunate reality that terrorists recognize no rules.

Terrorism, as the term is used today, entered to the literature after the French Revolution, leading to the period of political dominance called the Reign of Terror, in

1792-1794. In the early revolutionary years, it was largely by violence that governments in Paris tried to impose their radical new order on a reluctant citizenry [3].

The history of terrorism extends much further back than the Reign of Terror and the Revolutionary Tribunals during the French revolution. It even precedes the ancient and medieval Jewish rebellion against Roman occupation (A.D.66-73) in the Middle East. The earliest known organization that exhibited aspects of a modern terrorist organization was the Zealots of Judea [4].

The twentieth century witnessed great changes in the use and practice of terrorism. By the 1960s, the killing of civilians to instill fear and secure political gains was rampant, even in developed nations - from the Weather Underground in the U.S. to the Marxist Baader-Meinhoff Gang in West Germany to the Red Brigades in Italy [4]. Since 1970s, some countries such as Northern Ireland, Uruguay, and Turkey suffered from terrorism. During the 1980s, terror received an international dimension, and in the 1990s, it rapidly changed its situation and became more violent and fatal.

In order to understand the seriousness of the terrorism problem today, it is enough to remember the costs of the September 11, 2001 attacks on the World Trade Center. According to a study by the Milken Institute, because of the September 11 attacks, property damage was nearly $15 billion and human capital losses on the order of $40 billion [5]. The World Trade Center attacks not only caused monetary losses but also social and psychological costs. For instance, data show that at least 125,000 workers were laid off for 30 days or longer because of the September 11 attacks [6]. And also, after a major stressful event like the September 11 attacks, surviving victims might suffer post traumatic stress for the rest of their lives. Post traumatic stress mainly involves intrusive thoughts, sleeping difficulties and isolation from people. After the World Trade Center attacks, although some victims survived only with the support of their family members and their friends, many other people had to take some professional help to be rid of post traumatic stress [7].

Today, terrorism is a worldwide problem that leaves its mark on most democratic Western nations. The fight against terrorism, therefore, is an important and universal pursuit of all countries; cooperation in counter-terrorism struggles is thus a necessity. Nevertheless, some Western countries have not yet learned that they need to join their forces against terrorism with each other. Many of them see terrorism as just their internal problem. The severity of terrorism, however, proves that it is not only an internal problem but an international issue.

This paper examines the counter-terrorism policies of the U.S. and Turkey. Although both countries are democratic, secularly governed by the rule of law, and also respect human rights, they differ in combating terrorism. Turkey has been suffering from national and international terrorism for thirty-five years. The United States, on the other hand, has also been familiar with terrorist attacks on its soil since World War II. Germans landed eight men to sabotage aircraft plants and railway hubs in the US, but they could not succeed [8]. *Terrorism* is, therefore, not a new issue for not only Turkey but also the United States and their citizens.

Throughout the paper, first the literature covering this problem will be examined; second, a comparative analysis between the Turkey's and the U.S.'s counter-terrorism policies; third, the area of intelligence and terror will be explored; fourth, the importance and impact of the media on terror policies; fifth, military tribunals; sixth, torture issues and lastly policy dissimilarities will be discussed and some implications will be offered.

1. Literature Review

What actions should be defined as terrorism? What is the difference between "a terrorist" and "a freedom fighter?" In order to coordinate international efforts in counter-terrorism, it is necessary to answer these questions for the international community. It is important to define and distinguish between dissimilar forms of terrorism, and to distinguish terrorism from national liberation struggles. As long as terrorists can hide behind the term *freedom fighter*, it will be difficult to assess the necessary steps to combat terrorism efficiently because "freedom fighters use legitimate military methods to attack legitimate political targets. Freedom fighters become terrorists when they abandon military methods and military targets, or when they fight with no chance of winning" (White, 2006, p.5). William J. Crotty's *"The politics of terror: the U.S. response to 9/11"* (2003) presents an excellent argument that unclear definitions of terrorism impair any attempts to compete with terrorism. Crotty (2003) advocates an impartial and symmetrical approach to the problem of definition. This means that what counts as a terrorist act should not be predicated upon a person's or a group's opposition to the West, to capitalism, or to secularism, and that actions performed by modern states, such as the U.S., can also constitute terrorism.

Terrorism and counter-terrorism: criminological perspective is a collection of writings which was edited by Mathieu Deflem. In this book's first chapter, Donald Black [11] defines the act of terrorism as a form of unilateral self-help and describes terrorism as well-organized, mass violence, and quasi-warfare. Black utters that the key obstacle, unfortunately, in counter-terrorism activities is the absence of an agreed upon and binding definition of the term terrorism. What this means is that sincere efforts must be made to reach consensus on an objective and universal definition of *terrorism* that is acceptable to all the countries of the Western world. If Western countries were to decide to put an end to terrorism, they would take cooperative and decisive action against any country that assists or supports a terrorist organization, as well as against the organizations themselves. This cooperation would lead to the destruction of these organizations around the world, and to the prevention of many terrorist attacks.

Philip Jenkins [12], in his work *"Images of terror: what we can and can't know about terrorism,"* examines issues relating to terrorism from the perspective that political problems are socially constructed. In his study, he says terrorism in the United States is not a recent development, and he provides a chart listing more than forty-nine major acts of terrorism in the United States between 1939 and 2001. He argues that intelligence agencies and government departments change the way terrorism is understood, prompted by changing diplomatic and political realities. He claims terrorism is a real and serious problem demanding decisive action.

Philip B. Heymann [13], in his concise and crisply written work, *Terrorism, freedom, and security: winning without war* dismisses the usefulness of war as a metaphor to fight terrorism, due to the lack of a clearly defined enemy and the non-temporary nature of the terrorist threat. He argues that *war* as a means to fight terrorism is not only problematic in the light of important civil and human rights concerns, it is also misguided in failing to take into account the diverse nature of terrorism. According to Heymann [13], terrorism should be approached from a much broader strategy that should involve diplomacy, law enforcement, intelligence, and international legal arrangements, besides limited and well-targeted military interventions.

In the academic milieu, there is an important discussion about whether national security or democratic values are more important. Many experts are currently arguing how to achieve a balance between national security and civil liberties. Crotty, after discussing this issue, concludes by saying that "the hope is that the resilience of the nation's bedrock values and its historic democratic commitments will prove to be the ultimate triumph of post-9/11 period" [10 pg 300].

Another important work is *September 11 in history: a watershed moment,* edited by Dutziak. The essays in this book mainly focus on "whether the assumption that September 11 changed everything holds up under closer scrutiny" [14 pg 3]. Each essay addresses the central questions: Did the events of September 11, 2001 truly mark a "watershed moment" in both the U.S. and world experience? The authors mainly discuss the following question: Are we far enough removed from the events of that day two years ago to make a rational judgment as to its character? They conclude that everything did not change on September 11, but some bases of democratic legitimacy have been significantly eroded. Dutziak, the editor, says the results are most likely impossible to measure for now, but one change is certain: perpetual construction and reconstruction of memories of September 11th.

Even though there is not any specific study to compare and contrast Turkish and American policies used against terrorism, there are many different studies and research in the literature in order to understand both countries' combating methods in terms of law, politics, civil liberties, religion, and citizenship.

2. Comparative Analysis

The twenty-first century has begun in a most discouraging way. The problem does not only lie in September 11th and the subsequent wars in Afghanistan and Iraq. Today, nearly one-fifth of the world's borders are disputed. At this very moment, there are more than 40 international conflicts raging, and two-thirds of all the world's governments are authoritarian. Already, in terms of terrorist activities and extreme violence, the twenty-first century is significantly different from the twentieth [15]. There is no doubt that this century will witness more violence than former ones since today's terrorist organizations and states which support terrorist activities have more powerful and destructive weapons than before, such as nuclear, chemical, and biological weapons.

Following the tragic events of September 11th, departments and agencies from across the federal government took steps to strengthen the safety and security of the American people. For instance, the Homeland Security Advisory System (HSAS) was established, which is designed to be the foundation for building a comprehensive and effective communications structure for the dissemination of information regarding the risk of attacks to all levels of government and the American people. Almost one month after the 9/11 attacks, the U.S. House of Representatives passed the final USA Patriot Act (2001). The Patriot Act has produced greater collection and sharing of information within the law enforcement and intelligence communities to deter and punish terrorist acts in the United States and around the world [16]. After a short time, in the wake of the September 11th attacks, vast organizational and political changes mandated by the USA Patriot and Homeland Security Acts. The creation of the Department of Homeland Security, in George W. Bush's words, was "the most extensive reorganization of the federal government in the past fifty years" [10 pg 204]. More than 500 agents are set to be transferred from criminal investigations to terrorism prevention, 900 new agents are set to be hired by September 2002, with many in the anti-terrorism field and also a new terrorism squad within FBI headquarters is set to oversee terrorism investigations [17].

In the U.S., another effort for fighting against terrorism efficiently was the redirection of the FBI. It made terrorism its top priority and after the September 11th attacks, it began to shift nearly 500 agents from drug and other criminal investigations to the counterterrorism department and shift focus mainly from investigating crimes to preventing acts of terrorism. Congress approved a $4.6 billion budget for the FBI that provides $513 million in new money to combat terrorism in the fiscal year that started October 2003 [2]. It means that the FBI budget has doubled in three years.

One of the greatest obstacles for the Turkish government, which makes countering terrorism more difficult, is facing demands for the release of incarcerated terrorists. It is not an acceptable demand because the release itself carries the danger that such release will increase terrorism, both by the released terrorists and as a reaction of the terrorist organizations to the success of their strategy. It is important to be aware that the release of terrorists is likely to lead to further detrimental attacks, and the released terrorists are quite prone to take part in the initiation, planning, and perpetration of more deadly operations, and in the training of new terrorists. All of this is liable to cause a very large number of fatalities. There are many harmful examples concerning this issue in Turkey's counter-terrorism history, but releasing terrorists, unfortunately, is still deemed as a method to combat terrorism by some politicians. Although the Turkish government has been aware that releasing incarcerated terrorist prisoners brings nothing other than pleasing the international communities, it sometimes, unfortunately, allows the release of prisoners because of pressures exerted by some national and international politicians and terrorist groups. This idea is quite dangerous because the thought that a terrorist caught perpetrating a fatal attack will sooner or later be released leads many people to believe that it would have been preferable to kill the terrorist on the spot, even before bringing him to trial. Of course, this method of thinking is absolutely contrary to the basic values of any democratic country operating under the rule of law. The frequent release of convicted terrorists harms the counter-terrorism policies of law enforcement and military personnel. Without any exception, all terrorists must, by any criteria, serve out their sentences. Other terrorists must know that there is no excuse for terrorist attacks, and are thus deterred from perpetrating similar acts.

Turkey has much experience in the field of counter-terrorism and has acquired considerable skill and experience in dealing with terror problems, with some great success. Despite the fact that Turkey has been facing terrorist incidents for decades, the assassination of some high-level officials and highly detrimental bombing events seem to be a turning point in the way the Turkish government, security forces and public, have viewed the problem of terrorism since the early 1990s.

The Turkish National Police have been successful in their efforts to capture the members of leftist terror groups. The national protest created by the increasing extremely damaging terror events led both the public and members of the government to demand more radical and impressive steps in countering the terrorists. At the strategic and operational levels, the government decided to make some legal and practical innovations. The Turkish National Police organization and other Turkish Intelligence Services [National Intelligence Organization (MIT) and Turkish Armed Forces (TSK)] made a decision to cooperate with each other and use their experience in combating terrorism, and so a strong cooperation was rapidly established.

On February 19, 1999, the arrest of the Kurdistan Worker's Party (PKK-KONGRA GEL)'s leader Abdullah Ocalan represented a huge victory for the Turkish government.

It was clearly an achievement with psychological, moral, and political aspects. The PKK-KONGRA GEL is a highly centralized organization on the Marxist-Leninist model. Its leader's trial and its use as a political tool influenced the terror groups, Turkish community, and European countries. This international attention was attracted in favor of the Turkish government. In addition, the Turkish-Syrian agreement on terrorism, especially about Ocalan's expulsion from Syria, represented a victory in the fight against terrorism, not only for Turkey, but also for the entire international community. In this victory, the Turkish strategy was clearly influenced by the United States' policy of pursuing terrorists everywhere in the world, and its determination after the attacks to immediately respond against the responsible terrorist organization. Therefore, it is necessary for all governments to share their knowledge, experience, and intelligence to be able to achieve something positive in countering terrorism.

In order to comprehend the major policy differences between the U.S. and Turkey in terms of combating terrorism, one must examine a number of factors. These include issues like intelligence, media, trials, and human rights. Without the support of the citizens and other effective non-governmental organization, such as media and human rights organizations, it is not feasible to succeed in fighting terrorism efficiently.

2.1. Intelligence for Counter-Terror Activities

During the counter-terrorism process, intelligence is not only useful to thwart attacks but also necessary as evidence against terrorists who are put on trial. Allies of both Turkey and the U.S. provide much-needed intelligence on terrorist groups in their regions. Countries generally trade information with friendly governments through formerly defined relationships between intelligence services.

Most information on terrorist movements is obtained in the terrorists' home countries or in the countries where they live. The main difficulty with gathering such information for the Turkish intelligence departments such as MIT and TNP is that the most dangerous terrorist groups, both left and right, understand Turkey's information-gathering capabilities. Their familiarity has come about the last 30 years. As a result, terrorists have modified how they communicate and where they reside. These counter measures make intelligence collecting more difficult.

Proactive counter-terrorism policy requires understanding and predicting the would-be attacks rather than waiting to respond to them after they happen. Terrorist groups aim to destroy the vital organs of freedom and to cover the international body with a deadly network. There should be several different methods and means to fight terrorism because terrorist activities include diverse fields. Counter-terrorist forces are mostly pressed into the pattern of reaction because nobody wants to spend time to assess the situation and figure out the best way to respond to terrorists. This is the reason why patience is a virtue required of all counter-terrorist experts. One of the important aims of terrorism is to turn the tables and to confuse the audience about who is the victim and who is the criminal, for instance, the Iraq War. As of today, at least 30,000 Iraqi civilian people have been killed in Iraq because of war; on the other hand, due to September 11th attacks, 3,000 innocent American citizens in New York and more than 2,000 military personnel in Iraq were killed because of bad guys. Now here, who is the criminal and who is the real victim; this confused state is the goal of terrorism.

How should the intelligence agencies prepare in order to foil or at least minimize the future terrorist threats? The estimation of most of the analysts, researchers, and of the main intelligence services is that, in the next decade, terrorism will continue to be a serious threat on both the strategic and tactical level [18]. There is no doubt that intelligence is essential in countering terrorism, in diminishing its tactical effects and its strategic importance.

2.2. The Media in Counter-Terrorism Policy

How can a state go about combating terrorism without risking or endangering its democratic structure? Almost all nations base their policy of combating terrorism on the right of self-defense. However, this right should be explained accurately to both a country's citizens and to other countries. Hence, an effective counter-terrorism policy must include the effective and responsible role of the media. This policy must consider and deal with difficult issues like freedom of the press, information control, and the right of citizens to know what their government is doing.

Some of the main goals of terrorists are winning popular support, provoking the attacked country to act rashly, attracting recruits, and demonstrating their ability to cause pain. Terror groups are aware of the fact that any publicity is good publicity; even if they are unsuccessful in their terror attacks, they know that a failed attack can also raise awareness about their cause. Additionally, media coverage can shape the outcome of a terrorist incident in various ways; for instance, it can tell terrorists how their attack is proceeding and even provide them intelligence about a counter operation attempt. Hence, media coverage can disrupt or prevent counterterrorist operations. Conversely, despite such negative effects of the media regarding counter-terrorism efforts, it can and should be used as a means to struggle with terrorism. For example, the media can show the community how terrorist groups recruit individuals, especially young people, how they polarize public opinions, and what kind of ability they have to cause a disturbance in society. Moreover, the media can help governments to identify and capture the terrorists by sharing their records and advanced technology. If the media informs the government and the community without any biased coverage while being aware of its responsibility, the balance between the state's security concerns and the right of the citizens to the freedom of speech can be preserved without any crisis [19].

Some democratic countries which do not regulate press coverage of terrorism sometimes ask media organizations to voluntarily hold back. Following the September 11th attacks, for example, the Bush administration asked U.S. networks not to air videos of Osama bin Laden because the government said they might contain coded messages with instructions for future attacks [20]. Although some Web sites and international TV channels, such as Al Jazeera continued to show some videos of Osama bin Laden, U.S. networks generally have been careful with their coverage.

There are a number of ways for media in a democratic country to support the government in fighting against terrorism. For instance, terrorists like to show themselves as heroes who fight against government on behalf of innocent and powerless people and they look to make the public believe that they have to use violence, murder people and damage the country. A responsible media can show the savage cruelty of terrorists' brutality to society by covering news stories and photographic evidence and in doing so disrupt terrorists' plans. Second, the formulation of a successful counter-terrorism strategy requires acknowledgment of the morale element in the battle between law enforcement and terrorists. This understanding must include educating the public to be familiar with the terrorists' strategy and policy, so media can create vigilance among the public to observe suspicious persons, neighbors and unusual events and to inform the police straightaway. The other positive way for media to aid in the struggle against terrorism is to remind the governments of their responsibilities to ensure that all strategies and tactics used against terrorism are consistent with the rules, human rights, and justice.

2.3. Military Tribunals

After the September 11th attacks, the U.S. government thought that it was necessary to use some unusual and practical methods to combat terrorism more efficiently. One of them was the special court named the Military Tribunal, which is conducted by military instead of civilian judges. Tribunal courts were authorized by the government to charge the foreigners who engaged in terrorist activities. The important difference between military tribunals and civilian courts is that Military Tribunals are not bound by procedures followed in civilian courts. The government officials believe that military tribunals will help to deal with the cases quickly, efficiently, and without putting at risk the safety of the public, information methods, and operations. Also, the military tribunals are believed to protect the jurors, judges and witnesses from the potential dangers of accused terrorists [21].

It is believed that combating terrorism requires strict secrecy because of classified information and jurors' identities, so this is only possible in military tribunals. Although some believe that military tribunals are effective, appropriate, and essential for terrorism cases [22], they are not. Past terrorism trials in federal criminal courts have never caused any trouble with protection of jurors' identities or disclosing classified information. For example, not only Timothy McVeigh but also the 1993 World Trade Center bombers were convicted in the civilian courts, but some difficulties with protecting classified sources had been experienced and nobody discussed the necessity of a different judicial response. In those days, civilian courts were effective for terrorism cases; why are they not today? [23]

Another difficulty with military tribunals is their target area. Military tribunals are just for non-citizen individuals, any American citizens cannot be tried by these tribunals. It is difficult to understand the government's policy in this issue dividing people as citizens and non-citizens in terms of countering-terrorism. What are the moral and rational reasons for assuming that non-citizens have less value than American citizens to be treated with a lower standard of justice?

Even though they are called military tribunals, they are not real courts; they are just *military commissions*. That means defendants are not guaranteed the right to appeal convictions by military tribunals. Moreover, defendants do not have a right to represent themselves, they must accept a military lawyer assigned to them, or defendants can have a civilian lawyer, but he/she must be an American citizen [24]. They can not have a civilian judge, an open trial, and a right of appeal to an independent judge outside the military chain of command. Notwithstanding, defendants and the public are assumed to trust military tribunals as they are effective, unbiased and fair. However, it is quite difficult to consider that proceedings are fair in military tribunals because of secret testimony, secret witnesses, and no appeals. Besides, it is not realistic to assume that military tribunals would be fair when they are dealing with suspects whom they believe to be their enemy.

According to an Amnesty International report [25], approximately 500 al-Qaeda and Taliban suspects are at the military prison at Guantanamo Bay, Cuba. Although no charges have been filed, President George W. Bush has named six candidates for a tribunal. However, there is a controversy about military tribunals as a method to combat terrorism.

The question, "Should military actions be taken against terrorists, or is it merely law enforcement's responsibility?" may come to mind. It is difficult to answer this question with "Yes, it completely should be," but it can be said "mostly." Until the 1980s, the U.S government, like the Turkish government, considered terrorism to be primarily a police matter. There are several reasons why the military should mostly be used against terrorist activities. First, many international terrorist incidents demand a response for which law enforcement does not have the training, resources, or the personnel. Therefore, in these cases, military forces might be the only adequate response. Second, some countries, such as Iraq and Iran, support terrorist campaigns as actual instruments of their foreign policy. The United States has maintained an official list of state sponsors of terrorism since 1979 [26] and this list includes Iraq and Iran. If this support results in harm to citizens, then the supporting country has executed an act of war against the related country (e.g. the U.S. and Turkey). In these instances, a military response is the most effective and appropriate way. "The policy of the United States in the use of the military in responding to terrorist incidents has remained fairly consistent in recent years" [27].

2.4. Torture

Throughout history, torture has often been used as a method of effecting religious, political or cultural alterations; for example, as Native-American genocide, slavery and totalitarianism [28]. Like some current governments have today, the policy of torturing prisoners, in Western history, was condoned and coordinated at the highest levels of government [29].

Not only in this century but also during the last two centuries torture was a tool in political struggles. While today some U.S. politicians, such as Donald H. Rumsfeld, Secretary of Defense, sees torture as an effective method against terrorism [30], the French government, in the 1950s, used torture as an instrument in the war with Algeria [31]. The right to be free of torture is one of the most fundamental human rights recognized by the global community today. Torture, unfortunately, has become the leading moral and political question of this century [32].

In Turkey, prisoners, without exception, are taken to the hospital for examination as required by law. All detainees can have access to a lawyer without difficulties and can easily obtain their medical records, regardless of the crime they are charged with. Minors are immediately referred to the prosecutor or released if it is not necessary to hold them any longer, and their parents are informed of their whereabouts. Since 1999, Turkish governors have a duty to supervise all places of detention in their province. It means that all Police Headquarters should be regularly inspected by the governor and prosecutor because any kind of abuses have terrible long-term consequences, and all of them are absolutely prohibited by universally agreed-upon standards.

On the American side, on October 6th 2005, the Senate voted 90 to 9 to define and limit the types of interrogation techniques used against detainees and to ban the use of "cruel, inhuman or degrading treatment" of any detainee held by the U.S. government. Since torture is defined and prohibited in many international laws such as the Universal

Declaration of Human Rights (1948), the Geneva Conventions (1949), and the UN Convention Against Torture or Other Cruel, Degrading or Inhuman Treatment or Punishment (1984). However, some authors, such as Charles Krauthammer, who is widely admired in conservative circles, claims that all Americans should be prepared to *torture* to save their lives [33]. Furthermore, though the right not to be tortured is one of the main human rights and no one has a right to torture, Dershowitz [34] sees torture as tolerable and even wishes to legalize it. According to Dershowitz, the real question is not whether torture would be used or not. The question is whether it would be used outside of the law or within the law.

The United States is currently holding nearly 500 detainees at Guantanamo; however, some prisoners have been held for almost four years without any charge, and over 100 of them have been on a hunger strike protesting their conditions at the prison and their indefinite detentions. Some, such as Taylor [35] believe that prisoners held at Guantanamo and Abu Ghraib prisons cannot be named as *prisoners of war* because they do not carry arms openly and do not conduct their operations in accordance with the laws and customs. This assumption might be acceptable for Taliban or al-Qaeda members; however, the captured members of the Iraqi armed forces should be entitled to prisoner of war status [36].

Shortly after the Iraqi invasion, the media began to report allegations concerning the mistreatment of Iraqi detainees by American military personnel at Abu Ghraib and other prisons [37]. In February 2004, the International Committee of the Red Cross (ICRC) issued a report regarding the conditions of arrest and detention of Iraqis [38]. After this media coverage and human rights organizations' reports, the U.S. government appointed a general, General Antonio Taguba, to conduct an investigation at Abu Ghraib prison. According to General Taguba's report, offenses committed at the Abu Ghraib prison were "sadistic, blatant and systematic." He described the offenses as "detainees are forced to remove their clothing and remain naked for several days at a time, a male MP guard having sex with a female detainee and using military working dogs, without muzzles, to intimidate and frighten detainees" [39]. Some offending military guards, such as Charles A. Graner Jr. were tried and convicted by court-martial for assault, maltreatment and beating and humiliation of Iraqi detainees in January 2005. However, no one higher in the chain of command has faced criminal charges up to now [40].

There was probably some kind of inhuman treatment towards inmates in the history of the U.S. prisons, especially on international bases [41]; however, state-directed torture had a high profile after 9/11, so it is necessary today to consider interrogation techniques in a new light. Namely, this is not the 1960s or 1970s; we are living in the 21st century. Having a handbook on coercive interrogation methods as a *training manual*, produced during the Vietnam War, does not give the CIA the right to use the same coercive interrogation techniques today [41]. In the TV program "Democracy Now Today", Dr. Michael Wilks [30] argues:

"People who are detained at Guantanamo and Abu Ghraib, many of these people, are not actually being charged with anything. They are being held outside the Geneva Conventions, according to president's [G.Bush] dictum. Then they have limited access to lawyers. We know that health professionals have been engaged, probably not systematically, but certainly engaged in abuse and probably, if not in torture, at least ignoring torture and in handing over medical records to engage with interrogators."

In the same program another expert, Dr. Robert Lifton, thinks similarly:

"American physicians and psychologists have been active in interrogation processes at the edge of torture, and I think we have these facts from very reputable international human rights organizations, including the Red Cross."

The reason why CIA officers think they can use coercive interrogation techniques on foreign detainees is because of the *extraordinary rendition* concept. According to this concept, the CIA, to be able to avoid due process, sends suspected terrorists or supporters of terrorist groups to other countries for imprisonment and interrogation. Using countries such as Egypt, Jordan and Morocco provides interrogators and jails for the suspected terrorists without giving any worry about human rights issues. In the words of former CIA agent Bob Baer, "If you want a serious interrogation, you send a prisoner to Jordan. If you want them to be tortured, you send them to Syria. If you want someone to disappear - never to see them again - you send them to Egypt" [42].

Janis Karpinski was the highest-ranking officer in the corrections area in Iraq, and she states:

"We were directed on several occasions, and directed through the CJTF-7, through General Fast or General Sanchez, by - the instructions were originating at the Pentagon, from Secretary Rumsfeld, and we were instructed to hold prisoners without putting their - giving - assigning a prisoner number or putting them on the database and that is contrary to the Geneva Conventions. We all knew it was contrary to the Geneva Conventions. And we were told that this - these instructions were being given by Secretary Rumsfeld" [30].

She adds that:

"General Geoffrey Miller said; -You have to treat them (detainees in prison) like dogs!" and continues, "I do know that the Secretary of Defense (Donald Rumsfeld) signed a very lengthy memorandum authorizing harsher techniques to be used in Afghanistan and specifically at Guantanamo Bay. This was the global war on terrorism" [30].

According to the Human Rights Watch [43], "the U.S. has become the only government in the world to claim a legal justification for mistreating prisoners during interrogations." There are some more important questions which the U.S. decision makers and authorities leading the counter-terrorism activities should answer openly and honestly such as: 1) Why does the CIA need an exemption to a proposed ban on the torture of terror suspects in U.S. custody that would govern the conduct of the U.S. military in interrogation practices? [44], 2) What kinds of moral cause does the American military have to fight for if they do not hesitate to violate the Geneva Convention and behave in an inhuman way in abroad prisons towards some detainees, for instance in Guantanamo and Abu Ghraib thinking they are foreigners?, 3) Why do some high-ranking officials instruct military staff to hold prisoners without putting them on the database despite the Geneva Convention? [30], 4) What is the sincere/ genuine official policy of the current U.S. government regarding the counter-terrorism issue?

The U.S. government should answer these kinds of questions truthfully and should examine its current policy against terrorism. Since the policy decided to carry on may stop (at least minimize) the future terror activities or may make potential terrorists think that rather than being concerned with democracy the United States is more concerned with oil. As it is known, even though the current U.S. administration has declared many times that the real reason for the invasion of Iraq is to bring democracy to Iraq and Middle East, not only some western scholars, such as Chomsky [45] and Mandle [46] but today's religiously motivated terrorists also believe that the U.S government is actually more concerned with the petroleum issue than democratization of the Middle East.

3. Discussion

There is no question that terrorists threaten the freedom and security of all nations. At the present time, terrorists have become a major force on the international scene. Terrorism has the potential to become a serious strategic threat to each and every nation. Many terrorist events which occurred during the past three decades proved that the terrorist organizations have been in cooperation with each other and have been supported by some states at various levels [47]. It is unlikely to end the activities of a terror organization without cutting off its international support. In this context, there must be an international cooperation against terrorism because the independent counter-terrorist efforts use huge amounts of money, and achieve little impact; hence, international cooperation and harmony are essential issues in terms of counter-terrorism. In order to cope with new forms of terrorism the defense attitude, training, equipment and tactical structure of the military, intelligence, security and law enforcement communities has to be redirected and refocused into a international rather than a national format. The United States must continue to build a "culture of cooperation" if it is to develop effective anti-terrorism strategies for the future [48]. Because of its importance, Turkey signed and ratifted security and cooperation treaties with 62 countries and took an active part in 17 bilateral agreements. Turkey is one of the leading countries to sign and ratify 12 United Nations' resolutions [49].

International cooperation is necessary not only for operational success but also for universally accepted definitions. If some basic concepts are being defined unanimously, those who use terrorism to attack civilians cannot define themselves as *freedom fighters* anywhere on the earth. If terrorism is an international issue (certainly it is), counter-terrorism must also be an international issue. Moreover, among the other important benefits of international consent, cooperation in counter-terrorist policies would be the ability to set up an International Counter-Terrorist Unit. Establishing an international unit for combating terrorism will certainly have many advantages; for instance, because of the existence of an International Counter-Terrorist Unit, any terrorist action would be met by the full force of all the world's resources, instead of just by one nation alone. Today, there is no universally agreed strategy for countering the terrorism threats because the challenge is so complex and the potential anti-terrorism methods so diverse. However, many politicians and experts, in the international arena, agree that the success of any strategy depends on bilateral, multilateral, or international cooperation with each other.

A responsible and helpful media is certainly an advantage for governments which fight with terrorism; over and above, governments should determine counter-terrorism policies and some basic principles such as; 1)All strategies and tactics must be legal, humanistic, and reasonable, 2)Diplomacy should be the first option in combating terrorism, not military power and war, 3)Castigation should be used only against terrorists themselves, not their family, relatives and children, 4)Force, if it is necessary, should be just used to stop terrorist activities and future attacks, not to punish individuals as in the war (overwhelming force and civilian immunity), 5)Counterterrorism policies should be based on seeking long-term solutions, not taking revenge and meaningless hostility, 6)The main motivation for countering terrorism should be derived from wishes for living in democratic, independent and nonviolent societies, not religious, cultural, and ethnic differences, 7)Counter-terrorism efforts should stop/minimize terrorism in the short and long run, not enhance terrorist activities or create new terrorists, 8)Each kind of terrorism, without looking at its type and source (leftists, rightists and religious), should definitely be condemned and every possible way to impede it be shared with other nations.

It would be a tragic mistake for any government to think that *if the terror attacks are not in my country, it is not my problem, it is others'*. This mistake would create a negative impact on the tendency for nations to engage in international cooperation to fight terrorism.

4. Policy Dissimilarities

It is obvious that every nation has its own way and policy to combat terrorism although countering terrorism needs international cooperation and harmony. Turkey has dealt with many treacheries and terrorist attacks in the past and still faces the same things. İn world history, Turkey is one of the most affected countries by terrorism because of her geopolitical and geostrategical position. It has the 16th biggest population in the world and is the biggest country of Europe. Turkey had always been in danger because of its natural energy resources, such as gas and oil. Sometimes religious, ideological, or ethnic fights caused terrorism and destructive actions in this country. In Turkey, terrorist events that have lasted for years have caused an unstable situation. For this reason, Turkey has allocated a major part of her budget for terrorism prevention for the last three decades.

In terms of fighting against terrorism, the United States has used military power in its struggle with terrorism, but Turkey rarely favors military force against terrorists. Although Turkey has been going through the pain and devastation of terrorism from 1970 to 2005, it never declared a war against terrorism because of several reasons. First, the Turkish government considers that war can encourage a cycle of attacks and reactions that might be difficult to control later as is currently being experienced in the Iraq war. The invasion of Iraq has caused more dramatic and harmful events and the long term danger of terrorism in Iraq is growing [50]. Second, declaring war on terrorism gives a status and dignity to terrorists which they actually wish to gain. To declare war on terrorists means to confer on them a kind of legitimacy [51]. Third, the campaign against terrorism can not generate a certain military victory since terrorists can not be defeated decisively. They are irregular enemies and it is not possible to destroy them totally or remove them from the field [52]. Finally, war results not only in the loss of military lives but also in the loss of civilian life. It causes many innocent people to be killed and suffer severely. However, according to the modern judiciary perspective of today, crimes are personal; no one can be accused for some other person's crimes. In the same way punishment also cannot be collective and each criminal can be punished only for their own crime. Therefore, it is difficult to understand the mentality that accepts punishing civilian people in order to catch terrorist leaders and fight against terrorism. Any kind of war never helps to make the conditions better or humanity improve. This "truth" is very simple, but unfortunately it is easily forgotten.

Additionally, the U.S. policy of combating terrorism differs from Turkey's policy in some ways. Currently, the U.S. government's main method to combat terrorism is *war against terrorism.* However, those who oppose terrorism, if they want to be coherent, should also oppose all types of violence. Those who oppose the killing of civilians for political ends should oppose not only terrorism but also war, because in almost all modern wars, the number of civilian casualties exceeds that of the military casualties. In order to succeed in the struggle against terrorism, the state should not act like a terrorist itself, and the measures taken should be in line with international Human Rights Law and the principles of the rule of law. After the September 11th attacks, the U.S. government maintained that those who were captured and detained at the Guantanamo military base had no right to trial in U.S. courts. The discussion of whether the President has the authority to legally use military tribunals to try detainees is still continuing and the U.S. Supreme Court has not yet ruled on the issue. However, some lower courts ruled that military commissions are unlawful. For instance, on 1/31/2005 District Judge Joyce Hens Green ruled that the military tribunals created in Guantanamo were unconstitutional because they deny the detainees' due process right for detainees [53]. The first and most important stance against terrorism is the issue of ethics. Everyone regardless of religion, philosophy and political preference should, as an ethical principle, deplore every act of terrorism. It is an ethical responsibility to stand up against injustice even if it is inflicted upon the enemy. This principle eliminates such discrimination as *my terrorist and your terrorist*.

5. Conclusion

If there are no magic formulas for ending terrorism, then there are various measures that can be taken to help reduce the threat. How to combat terrorism will remain the central problem for the United States and Turkey in the coming years. The experience of the U.S. with terrorism holds some lessons as to what works- and does not work- in the battle against this violent form of international behavior [18]. The complete prevention of terror or isolation of a society from terror is almost impossible, because the terror is mainly encouraged by external forces. Therefore, there can be no easy policy recommendation that would guarantee American and Turkish immunity from future terror attacks.

The United States will certainly remain one of the favorite targets of terrorists worldwide by virtue of its power, prestige, and influential role in many regions. The official U.S. policy on terrorism, as set forth in government reports and statements over the past two decades, has been that the U.S. does not make concessions to terrorists, that it forces state-sponsors of terrorism to pay a price for their actions, and that it pursues all measures to bring terrorists to justice and destroy their operations and networks [18].

Although the United States has taken many effective steps against terrorism, many experts believe that the U.S. is still vulnerable to terrorism and the consequences of a successful future attack would be massive. The government has tightened airport security, increased scrutiny of foreign travelers, and improved protection of American diplomats. For the last three decades, Washington has pursued a tough policy of no release of prisoners in return for hostages.

The goal of counter-terrorism cannot simply be to end terrorism; therefore, alternative counter-terrorism tactics should be developed and implemented decisively. Not only military but also political solutions can also be used effectively against terrorism. It should not be forgotten that there should be a balance in political and military approaches and both approaches should be involved in the fight against terrorism. In the fight against terrorism, there should be short and long-term solutions. Security measures should be intensified in order to frustrate terrorism, and laws should be applied to eliminate terrorism and the activities supporting terrorism.

In terms of fighting terrorism, ending torture is a necessary precondition to developing an effective strategy that will actually protect rather than endanger Americans [28]. If applying inhuman treatment is not an *official -governmental- policy* for the U.S. government, a special prosecutor should be appointed, with guarantees of full independence, to determine whether there is any criminal liability under any applicable criminal statutes. Moreover, all detainees at prisons abroad must be put on the database in a timely manner. This must be mandatory, not optional. Keeping detainees in prisons or camps without putting them on the database means officials are violating the Geneva Convention.

Despite all its faults, the U.S. is still one of the nations where the principle of the supremacy of law is applied successfully. As a leader of freedom, the United States bears a special responsibility for world citizens. Even security, which humanity needs as much as water and air, cannot be a reason to use "violence" to fight against terrorism and bring democracy and peace to the world. Hence, in any case, counter-terrorist measures must not violate the accepted laws of the state. The states and institutions should approach the issue honestly and realistically. Instead of denying everything, they should be honest in determining and admitting the mistakes they have made and should try to correct them.

References

[1]   P. Weiss, Terrorism, counterterrorism and international law. *Arab Studies Quarterly,* **24** (2002).
[2]   Federal Bureau of Investigation. What we investigate- Counterterrorism, *2005.*
[3]   A. Roberts, The changing faces of Terrorism. BBC Online from URL:www.bbc.co.uk./history/war /sept_11 [2002 August 27]
[4]   D. Greenberg, Is terrorism new? [Online] Available from: URL: www.slate.com [2001, September 21].
[5]   P. Navarro, A. Spencer, September 11, 2001: Assessing the costs of terrorism. *The Milken institute review, **fourth quarter**,* (2001), 19-20
[6]   R. Keleher, The economic costs of terrorism, [Online] Available from: URL: www.house.gov [2002, May].
[7]   P.M. Forster, The psychology of terror- the mind of the terrorist, [Online] Available from: URL: www.blue-oceans.com [2006, June 26]
[8]   P. O'Donnell, *In time of war: Hitler's terrorist attack on America.* New York: The New press; 2005.
[9]   J.R. White, *Terrorism and Homeland Security.* Fifth edition, Thomson- Wadsworth; 2006.
[10]   W.J. Crotty, Editor. *The politics of terror: The U.U. response to 9/11.* Boston: Northeastern University Press; 2003.
[11]   M.Deflem, Introduction: Towards a Criminological Sociology of Terrorism and Counter-Terrorism, 2004, Pp.1-6 in *Terrorism and Counter-Terrorism: Criminological Perspectives.* Amsterdam: Elsevier.
[12]   P. Jenkins, Images of terror: What we can and can't know about terrorism. New York: Aldine de Gruyter; 2003.
[13]   P.B. Heymann, Terrorism, freedom, and security: Winning without war. Cambridge, MA: The MIT Press; 2003.
[14]   M.L. Dutziak, Editor. *September 11 in history: A watershed moment?* Durham: Duke University Press; 2003.
[15]   T. Neumann, Israel, India, and the United States. *Vital Speeches of the Day,* **69** (2003), 759-765.
[16]   R. Mueller, On the record. *Government Executive,* **35** (2003), 18-25.
[17]   CNN, FBI unveils reorganization to focus on terror. [Online] Available from: URL; www.CNN.com [2002, May 29].
[18]   J.D. Simon, *The terrorist trap: America's experience with terrorism.* Bloomington: Indiana University Press; 2001.
[19]   A. Yakovenko, Can the media help to fight terrorism? *International Affairs,* Moscow: 51(2005).
[20]   A.D. Sultanbayev, New challenges for the media in times of anti-terrorist conflict, 2002.
[21]   E.J. Klaris, Justice can't be done in secret. *The Nation,* **274** (2002) 16.
[22]   D.W. Kmiec, Military Tribunals are necessary in times of war, *Wall street journal,* 2001, November 15.
[23]   P. Knox, Just say no to military tribunals. *Toronto Globe & Mail,* 2001.

[24] R. Axelrod, Policy and Management: Military Tribunals, *The Heinz School Review, 1.* (2004). [Online] Available from; URL: www.journal.heinz.cmu.edu. [2006, May 22].

[25] Amnesty International report-2006. [Online] Available from; URL: www.web.amnesty.org [2006, February 6].

[26] R.H. Dekmejian, Deadly connections: States that sponsor terrorism. *Choice. Middletown,* 43 (2006).

[27] T. Hunter, The use of force in response to terrorism, 2002. [Online] Available from: URL; www.terrorism.com.

[28] F. Branfman, On torture and being good Americans, *Tikkun,* **21** (2006) 34.

[29] J. Ashbee, Torture at the tower. *History Today,* **53,** (2003) 10.

[30] Democracy Now Today, (2005, October 26), [Online] Available from: URL; www.democrascynow.org.

[31] J.E. McCarroll, Treating Torture Victims and Enhancing Human Rights, 2003 Pp.65-88

[32] J. Mayer, Outsourcing torture, *The New Yorker,* [Online] Available from: URL; www.newyorker.com [2005, February 14].

[33] C. Krauthammer, The truth about torture, *The weekly standard, 11,(2005, December 5).*

[34] A. Dershowitz, Let America take its cues from Israel regarding torture, *Jewish World Review,* 2002, January 30.

[35] R.S. Taylor, Models for justice in Iraq, 2003. [Online] Available from: URL; *www.worldpress.org* [2006, May 29].

[36] F.L. Kirgis, Distinctions between International and U.S. Foreign Relations Law Issues Regarding Treatment of Suspected Terrorists, *ASIL Insights, 2004, June.*

[37] CNN Headline, *8 Iraqi police killed in Kirkuk bombing,* (2004, Feb. 23). [Online] Available from: URL; www.CNN.com

[38] ICRC, The treatment by the coalition forces of prisoners of war and other protected persons by the Geneva conventions in Iraq during arrest, internment and interrogation, 2004, February, [Online] Available from: URL; www.cbsnews.com.

[39] A. Taguba, Taguba Report, part one, Findings of Fact, [Online] Available from: URL; http://www.asil.org/pdfs/news.pdf [2004].

[40] T.R. Reid, Guard convicted in the first trial from Abu Ghraib, *Washington Post,* 2005.

[41] W. Pincus, Iraq tactics have long history with U.S. interrogators, *Washington Post* 2004.

[42] K. Hawkins, Torturous passage, The American Prospect. [Online] Available from: URL; prospect.org [2004].

[43] Human Rights Watch. [Online] Available from: URL; www.hrw.org [2005, October 26].

[44] J.P.Pfiffner, Torture and Public Management: The Ethics of Interrogation, [2005, June 2]

[45] N. Chomsky, Beyond the ballot, [Online] Available from: URL; www.saaye.com/forum [2006, June 26].

[46] J.R. Mandle, Why Iraq? (2002, December 8) [Online] Available from: URL; www.democracymatters.org [2006, June 26].

[47] O. Alper, *Teror agi,* Istanbul,Turkey: Yuce press; 1981.

[48] J. Conaway, Uniting against terrorism. *Americas,* **57** (2005), 56.

[49] N. Alkan, Financial sources of terrorists organization, *Police Review,* **40** (2004).

[50] K. Katzman, Terrorism: Near Eastern group and state sponsor, Congressional Research Service Report for Congress, 2002, February 13.

[51] L. Howard, A tussle over who can legally declare war, *The Christian Science Monitor;* 2002.

[52] J. Record, Bounding the global war on terrorism (2003), [Online] Available from: URL; www.globalsecurity.org.

[53] J.B. Anderson, Hamdi v. Rumsfeld: Judicious balancing at the intersection of the executive's power to detain and the citizen-detainee's right to the due process, *Journal of Criminal Law & Criminology,* **95** (2005), 689.

Understanding and Responding to the Terrorism Phenomenon
O. Nikbay and S. Hancerli (Eds.)
IOS Press, 2007

Role of Islamic Political and Legal Thought for Responding to Terrorism

Leonid SYKIAINEN, PhD.

State University-Higher School of Economics, Moscow, Russia

Abstract. Today, the Muslim world is torn between two contradictory trends: advancing along the road toward democratization and upsurges of Islamic radicalism. How does Islamic political and legal thought - both traditional and modern – respond to international terror and estimate its ideological background? There is no doubt about the fact that the ties between Islam and extremism are very ambiguous. Islamic conceptions are often used to substantiate the goals and methods of terrorist activity. At the same time, Islamic principles and values may help to effectively oppose this global threat. To maintain this goal it is necessary to cooperate closely with the moderate Islamic regimes and authoritative centers of enlightened Islamic political and legal thought.

Keywords. Islamic radicalism – Islamic traditional and modern political and legal thought – Islamic Ideological sources of international terror – Islamic thought against extremism – International alliance for combating Islamic extremism.

Introduction

Much is being said and written about Islam in the contemporary world yet attention is mainly focused on certain sides only. "Islamic extremism" is the pet subject understood as political extremism that uses Islam as a banner and an ideological basis. "Fundamentalism," "Wahhabism," "Islamism," "political Islam," and certain other concepts are viewed as close or even identical ones. Those who try to assess the place of Islam in today's world mostly look at it as a factor of danger that threatens national security of a large number of states and the interests of their citizens. The events of 11 September, 2001 in the USA as well as terrorist attacks which occurred in Beslan in Russia and some other regions strengthened this opinion.

1. On the Islamic Ideological Sources of International Terror

The terrorist acts of 11 September, 2001 pushed political Islam back to the center of attention of scholars, journalists, national state structures and international organizations. People are inclined to think that it is Islam that is mainly responsible for the spread of terrorism and political extremism worldwide.

I should say that the leaders of the international anti-terrorist coalition, including the Russian and the American presidents, never tire of repeating that they are fighting terrorists, not the Muslims or Islam. Such statements are easy to make—it is much harder to apply them in practice. Those of the Islamic leaders who say that Islam has nothing to do with terrorism indulge themselves in wishful thinking. In fact there is an ideological link between them.

To justify terrorism Islamic extremists quote the Qur'an that says, in particular: "Fight and slay the Pagans wherever you find them... O Prophet, strive hard against the Unbelievers and the Hypocrites, and be firm against them."[1] Those who support the idea of an uncompromising struggle for Islamic consolidation at all costs like to quote from the Prophet Muhammad who allegedly permitted to use violence against unbelievers: "I was sent to fight people until they testify that there is no god but the God, and Muhammad is His Apostle, until they start praying and pay "zakat." If they do all this I shall protect their lives and property. Otherwise they should be treated according to the laws of Islam, and they will be judged by Supreme Allah."[1]

There is a popular conception based on several verses from the Qur'an used to justify violence over all those who refuse to obey the will of Allah. According to it the Muslim should encourage everybody to obey the Shari'a (Islamic law) and prevent violations of its rules: "Let there arise out of you a band of people inviting to all that is good, enjoining what is right, and forbidding what is wrong."[2] The following words of the Prophet are taken for an instruction: "If anybody of you see anything that the Shari'a forbids he should alter it by his own hand. If he is unable to do this with his hand let him stop it with his tongue. If he cannot do this either—let him do this with his heart and this will be the weakest manifestation of his faith."[2] The terrorists prefer to concentrate on the first part that instructs to use hand, that is, violence, to prevent any digressions from the Shari'a.

Finally, the central plank in the terrorist platform is rejection of any form of power that parts way with the Shari'a. The terrorists use the following Qur'anic proposition: "O you who believe, obey Allah, and obey the Apostle, and those charged with authority among you"[3] as their main argument. The Islamic radicals translate this as a categorical rejection of any "unfaithful" power. They also quote other verses: "And never will Allah grant to the Unbelievers a way (to triumphs) over the Believers"[4] and "Therefore listen not to the Unbelievers, but strive against them with the utmost strenuousness, with the Qur'an."[5]

Significantly, the terrorists refuse to recognize power not only of the unbelievers but also of those Islamic rulers who have abandoned the Shari'a. To justify their position they quote the Prophet Muhammad: "Obedience and submission to the ruler belongs to him by right if he does not order his subjects to sin. If he orders them to sin there is no duty of obedience."[3] The Islamic radicals believe that in this latter case any Muslim has the right to stop the ruler "by hand," that is, to use force. What is more, they liken the apostatic ruler to the unbelievers whose lives are not inviolable; any actions against him are considered as jihad. It is believed that this treatment is based on a fatwa of the outstanding Muslim theologian and legal scholar Ibn Taymiyyah (1263-1327) who treated the Mongolian conquerors who had adopted Islam but ignored the Shari'a as infidels. For this reason he permitted to murder negligent Muslims and their relatives.

---

[1] The Qur'an. Al-Tawba Sura (9), verses: 5, 3.
[2] The Qur'an. Al-i-'Imran Sura (3), verse: 104.
[3] The Qur'an. An-Nisa Sura (4), verse: 59.
[4] The Qur'an. An-Nisa Sura (4), verse: 141.
[5] The Qur'an. Al-Furqan Sura (25), verse: 52.

2. Islamic Thought Opposes Extremism

The above postulates that serve the terrorists as an ideological Islamic shield contradict quite a different interpretation of the Shari'a that concentrates on its major aims rather than on blind obedience to its words. It stresses the need to compare possible losses and gains of the practical implementation of the Shari'a. This is mainly related to the jihad.

Contrary to what the terrorists are saying jihad is much more than a war against the unbelievers. Precisely speaking it is not war in proper by its genuine nature and main goals. Prominent Muslim jurists say that jihad is, first and foremost, a call to follow the road of Allah; it is an effort to achieve self-perfection and to create a genuinely Islamic society based not so much on literal obedience to the Shari'a but mainly on a creative application of its guiding principles, values, and aims. The call to the non-Muslims to follow the will of Allah excludes violence. The Qur'an says about this: "Let there be no compulsion in religion"[6], "Invite (all) to the Way of your Lord with wisdom and beautiful preaching and argue with them in ways that are best and most gracious."[7]

Armed struggle as one of the forms of jihad is allowed for defense only. In other words, a war against the non-Muslims is not a means of uprooting the tack of faith but a means necessary to fight an aggression. In addition, the word jihad can be applied only to armed struggle waged to protect the Islamic values and to strengthen them [1]. Obviously the acts of the terrorists who claim that their interpretation of the Shari'a is the only correct one do not fit the above criterion.

Their positions have nothing in common with the ideas of the most respected Islamic thinkers (including those whom the Islamic extremists regard as their teachers) as far as many other points of radical ideology are concerned. This includes the key thesis of the terrorists who treat the contemporary state (in the Muslim countries as well) as imposing lack of faith on the Muslims; the radicals refuse to cooperate with the state and even call on people to fight it with arms in hand.

Formally, at first glance this corresponds to the Shari'a and is even confirmed by what the Prophet said: "The subjects should not obey their ruler who sins."[4] But a closer look, in fact, reveals that the greatest Muslim lawyers are not equally straightforward: they go deep into the Shari'a taking into account its entire range of values and priorities. Put in a nutshell their ideas say that even an unfaithful ruler is a boon for the Muslims because the Prophet said: "It is only the imam that can give a better life to people, no matter whether the ruler is faithful or unfaithful. If he is unfaithful his faithful subjects will venerate the Creator until the unfaithful ruler has lived his life."[5] By way of explanation Ibn Taymiyyah said that if the ruler did not follow the Qur'an and the Sunnah the Muslims had to obey those of his orders that are in line with the will of Allah and quoted from the Qur'an: "Help you one another in righteousness and piety, but help you not one another in sin and rancor."[8] He further wrote that experience had confirmed the truth "Sixty years with a despotic imam is a greater boon than one night without a ruler."[4]

How should Muslims treat those actions of the authorities that digress from the Shari'a? How can they "disobey the sinning ruler"? The answer is simple and clear: such rulers should be admonished, people should consistently insist that they should retract. This position is based on the words of the Prophet that Allah wished that the

---

[6] The Qur'an. Al-Baqara Sura (2), verse: 256.

[7] The Qur'an. An-Nahl Sura (16), verse: 125.

[8] The Qur'an. Al-Ma'idah Sura (5), verse: 2.

Muslims "should advice those whom He charged with settling their affairs." This should be done in good faith without rudeness. There are numerous hadiths about this. This is one of them: "Truly, Allah is kind and prefers softness; He returns softness in the way He never responds to rudeness."[2]

I should like to stress here that this pronouncement is quoted in connection with the way people should treat the unjust power. As for cutting short "unfaithful" policies with open attacks this is dismissed with the following words of the Prophet: "Those who will see in the actions of their emir something revolting should remain patient and continue obeying him."[3] One of the greatest Muslim legal scholars Ibn Qayyim al-Jawziyyah (1292-1350) commented on this hadith:

"If the effort to cut short the prohibited inevitably causes grave sins and even greater displeasure of Allah and His Apostle then it cannot be tolerated... In this way cutting short the authorities' unjust actions by acting against them leads to all sorts of evil and troubles for all times... Those who will give thought to the causes behind the great and small troubles' pestering Islam will see that they are a result of the total oblivion of this principle, an unwillingness to tolerate the prohibited that should be uprooted. This leads to even greater harm."[6]

This warning is directly related to the position taken by the Muslim jurisprudence in relation to terrorism. It points out that Allah treats man as a creature superior to all other creatures of the Creator in a special way: "We have honored the sons of Adam."[9] The Qur'an openly prefers peace to a war against the unfaithful: "But if the enemy inclines toward peace, you (also) incline toward peace."[10] Allah is always prepared to severely punish robbery and all other actions that spread evil and mischief: "The punishment of those who wage war against Allah and His Apostle, and strive with might and main for mischief through the land is execution, or crucifixion, or the cutting off of hands and feet from opposite sides, or exile from the land."[11]

Finally, the Muslim lawyers point out that religious fanatics and terrorists sow havoc in Muslim souls that does them harm contrary to the Shari'a. The Qur'an says: "And those who annoy believing men and women undeservedly, bear (on themselves) a calumny and a glaring sin."[12]

There is another much-quoted pronouncement of the Prophet who said: "For each Muslim blood, honor, and property of another Muslim are forbidden."[7] Muhammad also said: "It is forbidden to a Muslim to sow fear among the faithful."[7] The Prophet said the following: "None of you should take up arms against your brother because none of you can know whether his hand is guided by Satan."[7] What was more the Apostle condemned even those whose glances might spread fear: "Those who cast a frightening glance at a Muslim without a reason will be frightened by Allah on the Day of Judgment."[7]

Here is one of the examples of the fundamental difference between the extremist and moderate trends in Islamic thought and political practice that approach the same phenomena from opposite positions.

Abd al-Rahman bin Abd al-Khalek, an ideologist of radical Islam well known in the Gulf countries, in his book about Ibn Taymiyyah pointed to the above-mentioned fatwa on the Tartars (by the Tartars the Mongols who conquered Syria in the early 14th

---

[9] The Qur'an. Al-Isra Sura (17), verse: 70.

[10] The Qur'an. Al-Anfal Sura (8), verse: 61.

[11] The Qur'an. Al-Ma'idah Sura (5), verse: 33.

[12] The Qur'an. Al-Ahzab Sura (33), verse: 58.

century are meant) that called the occupants who had formally embraced Islam infidels. The author described the scholar's personal participation in burning the shops of wine traders and the vessels the Tartars used to drink wine from as an example of "cutting short practices forbidden by the Shari'a."[8]

Another well-known Islamic thinker of today Yousuf al-Qaradawi pointed to a different fact that had taken place during the same events. In one of his articles he recounted a story by al-Jawziyyah about his teacher Ibn Taymiyyah. The latter, together with friends and students, passed a group of Tartars who were drinking wine. His friends wanted to stop those who violated the Shari'a but Ibn Taymiyyah said: "Let them drink and be merry: Allah prohibited wine because it interfered with remembering Him and with prayers. These drunkards are kept away from bloodshed and plunder by wine."[9] In other words, the scholar believed that by allowing the Tartars to violate the Shari'a he prevented an even graver sin. He was convinced that the meaning of the Shari'a was not in following blindly all detailed norms but in comprehending their meaning and realizing their general aims.

This example proves that out of the vast Islamic heritage, including the part that belongs to Ibn Taymiyyah Muslim radicals select those ideas that confirm what they think of Islam and the Shari'a. But it is very significant that even their ideological leaders sharply criticize such theoretical narrow-mindedness and aggressive practices. For instance, Ibn Qayyim al-Jawziyyah wrote: "As for the fanatics, they can place any problem upside down. When they turn to the Sunnah they borrow only what corresponds to their pronouncements and contrive tricks to push away evidence that does not suit them. If they come across a similarly convincing or even less convincing evidence that supports their positions they immediately accept it and use it as an argument against their opponents."[6] This can hardly be better said. Here is what Muhammad ibn Abd al-Wahhab (1703-1792) thought: "Some of the religious minded people stop the   banned practices and they are right doing this. But in their zeal to do this they drive brothers to quarrels— and this is wrong."[5]

3. There are Allies not only in the West

Those lawyers who support this approach agree that the Shari'a condemns terrorism [10]. Legislation of many Islamic countries is based on this principle. This is true even of those countries that are frequently reproached of supporting international terrorists especially Saudi Arabia.

There are two opposite approaches to the Shari'a in Saudi Arabia (like in any other Muslim country): a dogmatic one oriented toward a limited interpretation of the hadiths and the traditions of the righteous ancestors (ahl ai-hadith) and a rational one concentrating on a creative approach to the Shari'a meanings and aims (ahl al-ray.) The orthodox thinkers emphasize an aggressive interpretation of jihad; the moderate thinkers lean toward ijtihad (a rational quest for answers to the questions to which the Qur'an, Sunnah or the practice of the righteous ancestors provide no answers). Typically enough that the Islamic Jurisprudence Academy of the Muslim World League confirmed that the "gates of ijtihad are open" and emphasized that the contemporary problems should be addressed in the context of contemporary conditions and the Shari'a general aims [11].

The rivalry of these two interpretations of the Shari'a and the traditions of the righteous ancestors is directly related to the global problem that lately acquired special urgency. I have in mind international terrorism that presents real danger to mankind.

The Saudi Arabia has lived through several terrorist acts perpetrated by extremists that appealed to Islam. Its official position on this issue is quite clear. The country guides itself not only by the interests of its own security but also by the legal Islamic principles. It was in 1999 that the Collegium of the Senior Ulema passed a decision about punishments for terrorist activities. It is interesting to note that this was a response to terrorist attacks of Islamic extremists because the document directly points to terrorism of those who have lost values and have no strong faith. The Collegium introduced death penalty for terrorism by analogy with the punishment the Shari'a envisages for plunder (spreading mischief in the land as is said in the Qur'an), and rioting. It is especially interesting to note that the document underlies the fact that terrorists aim at the values protected by the Shari'a: religion, life, reason, dignity, and property.

In the wake of the events of 11 September Saudi Arabia severed relations with the Taliban because it was discrediting Islam in the eyes of the world community. In other words, what the Taliban was doing aimed against religion as the main value protected by the Shari'a.

The Grand Mufti of the Kingdom of Saudi Arabia was guided by the same considerations when he called the terrorist acts in the United States actions that contradicted the Shari'a and had nothing in common with Islam. He has pointed out that the Islamic principles do not allow anybody to cause injustice and violate laws in relation to others even if there are reasons for enmity and hatred.

The Al-Azhar Academy of Islamic Research supported this position by stating that Islam proceeded from the principle of plurality of cultures, civilizations, legal systems and nations, as well as of their cooperation. It also said that jihad in Islam aims at the triumph of law, at cutting short evil and establishing justice and security. Armed struggle and violence are allowed in exceptional cases such as defense of the land of fathers, stopping strife among the Muslims and protect their faith. Even under these circumstances the Shari'a categorically forbids encroachments on the lives of old people, children, and women and all those who have not taken up arms against Muslims.

4. Conclusion

These examples provide convincing evidence that the Islamic ideological heritage contains opposite trends: some of them justify extremism and terrorism under Islamic banners while others stake on moderation, caution and realization of the Shari'a's major aims. The trends have been competing among themselves for a long time: the events of 11 September added intensity to their rivalry. Unfortunately the measures undertaken after these terrorist acts   have not succeeded to stop the international terror activities linked with Islamic extremism. Contrary to this the positions of the most radical and uncompromising interpretation of the Shari'a have become even more strong in some regions of the Muslim world. We shall live and see whether the humanitarian and moderate interpretation of Islam is able to take the initiative. The outcome of this opposition depends to a great degree on whether the so-called civilized world is able to approach Islam in a civilized way that will help separate Islamic radicalism from the genuine Islamic and Shari'a values.

This opens up wider horizons for the whole world of wide international cooperation aimed against terrorism. It should be fought not only in the Western coalitions but also side-by-side with those Islamic states that have already been victims of terrorists. It is hardly enough to fight together against something—there should be joint efforts for positive prospects. Here I have in mind the future of today's Western world cooperation with Muslim states in an effort to strengthen the genuine Islamic values as an alternative to extremism and terrorism under the banner of Islam. These are evils that threaten not only the West but also the Islamic, or to borrow a contemporary term, civilized Islamic world. The United States and the other Western countries together with Russia are allies where military, financial, organizational and information levels are concerned. But in their ideological and theoretical opposition to Islamic terrorism they should join forces with the moderate Islamic regimes and the authoritative centers of enlightened Islamic thought. The Islamic factor should become an important part of their relationships with the Muslim countries designed to strengthen their security and protect their national interests. In other words, the West including Russia and the Islamic states can, and should, ideologically disarm the Muslim radicals. The remedy for extremism and terrorism under the Islamic banners should be sought for in Islam.

References

[1]   M.S. Ramadan al-Bouti, *Jihad in islam: How do we understand and carry it out?* : Damascus, Beirut; 1993 (in Arabic).
[2]   Imam Abu Zakariyah Yahya bin Sharaf al-Nawawi, *Gardens of the righteous.* Beirut: 1996, p. 125 (in Arabic).
[3]   *Sahih al-Bukhari in concise exposition*: Riyadh; 1992, p. 322 (in Arabic).
[4]   Ibn Taymiyyah, The shari'a policy as an instruction for the shepherd and his flock, Beirut, 1988, p. 8 (in Arabic).
[5]   Muhammad ibn Abd al-Wahhab, Important advice about three problems; p. 48.
[6]   Ibn Qayyim al-Jawziyyah, Instruction for those who speak in the name of the Lord of the worlds: Beirut; Vol.1, p. 76 (in Arabic).
[7]   Qahtan Abd al-Rahman al-Douri, "Islam and Terrorism," *The State and Terrorism:* Baghdad; 1988, p. 11 (in Arabic).
[8]   Abd al-Rahman bin Abd al-Khalek, *Sheikh of Islam Ibn Taymiyyah and Activities of the Muslim Community;* 1990, p. 13 (in Arabic).
[9]   Yousuf al-Qaradawi, "The Muslim Jurist and Challenges of Contemporary Life," *Papers of the Cultural Season of 1408-1409:* Riyadh; 1997, p. 22 (in Arabic).
[10]   Jumaa Amin, *The problem of terrorism; Analysis and solution:* Cairo; 1998 (in Arabic).
[11]   Islamic Jurisprudence Academy of the Muslim World League, *Journal of Contemporary Research of Fiqh*: Riyadh; 1/3 (1985), pp. 208-210 (in Arabic).

Understanding and Responding to the Terrorism Phenomenon
O. Nikbay and S. Hancerli (Eds.)
IOS Press, 2007
© *2007 IOS Press. All rights reserved.*

Globalizing Security, Securing Globalization? Privatization, Commodification and the 'New' Terrorist Threat

Keith SPENCE, PhD.
University of Leicester, Department of Criminology, UK

Abstract. This discussion considers aspects of globalization in the construction and interpretation of terrorism, and in the exponential growth of private security and military companies (PMCs) engaged in counter-terrorism and counter-insurgency operations in Iraq and elsewhere. The nature of this development illustrates how globalization simultaneously transforms the exposure and vulnerability of nation-states to politically motivated violence, and limits their capacity to respond to this exposure. The paradoxical outcome of this development is that the globalization of security, rather than securing globalization and its prospective benefits, instead places in question both the concept of security as conventionally understood in military terms, and the wider security of globalization itself. In responding to this predicament the concept of Human Security offers a framework for the development and application of multidimensional responses to both the causes and effects of terrorism.

Keywords: Security, globalization, human security, terrorism, privatization.

Introduction

The aims and methods of groups associated with the 'new' terrorism of 9/11 and after exhibit many similarities with as well as differences from their predecessors. What is genuinely novel is to be found in the globalized environment within which both terrorist acts, and the responses they elicit, take place. This paper considers aspects of globalization in relation to the construction and interpretation of terrorism, and the reaction to that presented by the growth of private security and military subcontractors (PMCs), the number of whom operating in Iraq alone at present is conservatively estimated at thirty thousand.

Commentators [1] have noted a number of issues occasioned by this growth involving the command, control, accountability and transparency of PMCs. These issues do not arise solely because PMCs are contracted to provide counter-terrorist services, but also because the requirement to deploy them in these roles reveals the extent to which globalization simultaneously transforms the exposure and vulnerability of conventional nation-states to politically motivated violence, whilst limiting their capacity to respond to this exposure *as* nation-states.

Globalization does not involve the demise of either nations or states. Rather, the dense set of related economic, technological, political and social processes constituting globalization produce a transformation and de-coupling of nation from state. Nations and the populations that compose them are distributed across traditional territorial boundaries, and in many cases (whether voluntary or otherwise) this distribution is global. In a parallel manner, security activities of states are neither bounded within, nor necessarily defined in protection of, established borders and the territorial interests that they represent.

Flourishing late-modern states are therefore global endeavors. The threats that they encounter and engender are, however, equally global. Awareness of the character of the predicament posed by terrorism in the wake of 9/11 was signaled by the explicit declaration of 'global war against terror', but the form taken by that campaign – both bureaucratically and militarily – was, and significantly remains, patterned on the territorial assumptions and strategic norms of the established National Security State, rather than the actuality in transformation presented by globalization that has been exploited to considerable effect (especially in the use of media and communication technologies) by the ambiguous, diffuse and decentralized network denoted by the label Al-Qaeda.

The growth of PMCs within a global market for counter-terrorism and counter-insurgency services exemplifies the uneven and unequal outcomes of globalization processes. Outsourcing of tasks previously regarded as the sole responsibility of states demonstrates the erosion of both sovereignty and the monopoly of legitimate violence, defining features of the nation-state. The outcome is an entrepreneurial marketplace of violence and protection structured in such a way that it adopts, and commodifies, roles and functions that become self-sustaining and self-sufficient. The simultaneous expansion of private security and rapid increase in cases of abduction by insurgent and terrorist groups is not coincidental, as the limits of the national security model interact with the limits of the global market, representing and compounding terror and insurgency as enduring conditions rather than specific, episodic and bounded situations. This predicament can be formulated as a paradox – that the globalization of security, rather than securing globalization and its prospective benefits, instead places in question both the concept of security as conventionally understood, and the security of globalization itself.

The critical analysis of globalization generates more questions than it provides answers. At least in part, however, it illuminates aspects of contemporary terror and terrorism, and some of the limitations of reactions invoking a conception of security predicated upon territorial sovereignty and physical force. Rather than offering a defined alternative course, it instead clarifies the imperative for rethinking security and its meanings, both politically and institutionally, in accordance with emergent effects and outcomes of globalization. The paper closes with a preliminary assessment of the significance of Human Security (HS). Grounded in the practices and politics of international development, HS is an evolving paradigm that is methodologically distinguished by its individualistic focus and universality of application.

If the incidence of terrorism indicates a breakdown of politics, the development of global terrorism testifies to a comparable weakness of global governance. Securing globalization – if such an ambition is to be achieved – enjoins a movement away from nationally focused responses. In order to be clearly developed as a mode of response to terrorism, Human Security requires robust articulation as a distinct body of ideas resistant to assimilation or subsumption within conventional discourses and practices. Although no single theory or approach is adequate to a problem as complex and contested as terrorism in its contemporary forms, the HS model contributes to the evolution of a multidimensional response that recasts security interests as collectively encountered, globally distributed risks. Co-operative initiatives within counter-terrorism and law enforcement demonstrate the logic and necessity of the HS agenda. The corollary requirement to extend, embed and consolidate these developments institutionally remains, of course, to be fully achieved.

1. Globalizing Security: The Growth of the PMC Sector

The announcement in October 2006 that British armed forces personnel located in areas identified as hazardous operational areas – initially defined as Iraq, Afghanistan and the Balkans – are to receive a bonus across the ranks of UKP 2,240 (USD 4,150) for every six month of service [2] within these zones of conflict came as no surprise. As well as acknowledging the nature of the conditions within these theatres of engagement, and addressing the long-standing grievance that UK forces are required, unlike many other forces, to pay tax on their income when on operational duties overseas, the bonus scheme is also designed to address the growing problem of recruitment and retention within the UK armed services. The problem of retention is not caused by a lack of potential personnel or by concerns over the nature of the operations in themselves. It is rather an outcome of the operation of the global marketplace in security and military services that has developed in order to meet the requirements generated by the unfolding global war against terrorism declared in the aftermath of the September 11, 2001 attacks on Washington and New York, and intensified by the 2003 overthrow of Saddam Hussein and subsequent occupation of Iraq. By late 2004, for example, the issue of retention within the UK elite SAS force had reached the point where letters were written to servicemen urging them to 'consider their loyalty to the regiment and the kudos of being in the SAS' when presented with the option of earning several multiples of their present wage by moving to the private sector. In addition, rather than lose personnel to the private sector leaves of absence, during which individuals can temporarily enter the lucrative private sector, was reported as being granted to members of the SAS Territorial Army (TA) regiments. Despite this unprecedented development, however, one former soldier reported that the armed forces 'cannot stop people from leaving. The SAS lifestyle is extremely demanding...On the security circuit you have the potential to earn very high wages combined with an attractive working rotation' [3]. This issue is of course not limited to UK forces. If anything the pressures encountered by US recruiters have been even more severe, as the military struggles to meet ambitious targets of 80,000 new recruits and more per annum by, amongst other methods, reducing the standards required for eligible new candidates [4] and offering serving special forces members long term incentives worth up to USD 150,000 over a number of years [3].

The development of the global private military sector is attributable to a range of overlapping factors, the most prominent, but not of necessity the most important, being the requirements generated by the response to the 9/11 attacks. Prior to those events, plans for the modernization of US forces towards a more flexible, rapid, technologically sophisticated and numerically reduced model of provision had been gradually planned and implemented, albeit not without controversy, over a period extending back to debates surrounding a revolution in military affairs (RMA) resulting from assessments of the first Gulf War in 1991[5]. The use of subcontractors and private organizations to meet logistical, support and other non-military requirements was in consequence well-established prior to the escalations occasioned by the Department of Homeland Security and Global War Against Terror. The introduction of the former as a USD 40bn Federal Department, and the latter as the dominating objective within the USD 400bn Department of Defense, accelerated the development of a set of markets for security and risk provision that were primed for development in an era of military battlespace and organizational transformation. As with so many other parts of the military-industrial complex, however, these were untested developments.

The escalation of private provision within, and in support of, the armed services was therefore implicitly anticipated in planning, although not in scale or practice, before the launch on March 19, 2003 of Operation Iraqi Freedom. Moreover, the initial twenty-six day campaign appeared to demonstrate the effectiveness – measured against the military objective of overthrowing the incumbent regime – of military doctrines characterized by buzzwords of speed, precision, shock, awe, and minimum personnel commitments. Pre-war concerns regarding the undue reliance upon airpower over ground forces, the insufficient provision of support services and supply chain logistics, and the adequacy of post-occupation reconstruction plans [6] were, however, rapidly vindicated on the ground in Iraq. The conditions for the expansion of, and ultimately the reliance upon, PMCs in Iraq and elsewhere were established almost as rapidly as the initial declaration that the original mission in Iraq had been accomplished by the US-led coalition forces.

The number of private military and security company personnel active in Iraq, and beyond its borders within the wider campaign against terrorism and insurgency in the region, is impossible to gauge with precision. It is generally accepted, however [7,8] that PMCs constitute, with numbers in 2006 exceeding 30,000 and possibly extending to twice that number, the second largest contingent of personnel in Iraq after the US, with the 7000-strong contribution of the UK to total forces representing a somewhat distant third largest contingent. The PMC complement cannot, of course, be treated as a unit or singular form. Outside principal combat operations, which presently lie outside the acknowledged remit, roles allocated to PMCs through the Coalition Provisional Authority (CPA) include: close protection for senior and executive civilian officials; site security, logistics and convoy security; IT, infrastructure and related support services to military units; provision of training, consultancy and advice; and support for prison interrogations (including, notoriously, Abu Ghraib).

The extent of the revenues generated by these activities is as difficult to judge as the personnel numbers involved, but an indication of their scale can be gleaned from the USD 293m contract awarded to the Aegis group by the US Department of Defence. Aegis Defence Services. Aegis, a British-based and globally active company founded by the Lt. Col. Tim Spicer, whose progress was preceded, but evidently not obstructed, by previous association with Sandline, a company notoriously associated with misadventures in Papua New Guinea and Sierra Leone [9]. It is perhaps the best known of the expanding group (currently nearing 50 in number) comprising the Private Security Companies Association Iraq (PSCIA). Many of these companies - including other well known corporate brands such as Control Risks, Blackwater, Armor Group and Triple Canopy - operate on a comparable scale within an economically significant marketplace estimated in 2004 at up to USD 4.6bn [10], some 25% of the total allocated budget for reconstruction. In context, during the same period total contracts outstanding to Halliburton, Inc., the largest provider and contractor of services including but not limited to those concerning security, have been reported [11] as totaling USD 11.4bn.

In response to opportunities created by the post-conflict situation in Iraq, and the availability of capital necessary for the creation of a sustainable supply and demand in services, PMCs inevitably evolved and expanded to occupy the security vacuum. In meeting these requirements the long-established and largely reputable marketplace in private security services was joined (and challenged) by a private military counterpart. Given that commodification is a process that is difficult, if not impossible, to reverse it is appropriate to acknowledge that although regularly questioned, the contribution of PMCs to operations in Iraq has significantly legitimated their activities and established the marketplace in which they operate for the foreseeable future. The significance of that growth extends beyond particular operational and practical questions pertinent to Iraq. In the broader schema of globalization, their development calls into question both the future roles of nation-state and international community in the provision and maintenance of security, and, more radically, the nature and interpretation of the model of security itself.

2. Globalization, Security and the Nation-State

The growth rush of the PMC sector seamlessly established the label 'Private Military Company' within the security and military lexicon. It is, however, a linguistic innovation that is more telling than it first appears. In even the recent past, PMCs would be uncontroversially referred to as mercenary forces, invoking negative connotations regarding the illegitimate, unaccountable and transient loyalty of covert forces available to any and all with the ability and willingness to pay the demanded rate for services provided without guarantee and with few, if any, questions asked as to means and standards adopted in pursuit of contracted ends. Until as recently as 2001, for example, Lt. Col. Spicer had happily accepted the label 'mercenary'. In his new role, however, it is regarded as a 'pejorative term' which makes him 'uncomfortable' [9]. Contemporary PMCs instead present themselves, often with justification, as responsible partners in the pursuit of security, supportive of the coalition in Iraq and significant contributors to it. Breaking with the tradition of mercenary violence, they offer themselves as both an extension of and complement to conventional military forces – and possess the contracts, papers of incorporation, institutional investment and public relations machinery to demonstrate their *bona fides*.

The issues of command, control, accountability and liability noted in the preceding section are undoubtedly of pressing importance with regard to PMCs. They are also part of a larger space of thematic questions concerning the relationships between, and effects of, the interpenetrating triumvirate of security, sovereignty and globalization that brings into view a defining hallmark of modern statehood that is presently confronted by a challenge that is unavoidable and irrevocable. For Max Weber, the development of the modern state begins with the dispossession by the sovereign of powers and means of war, administration and related political goods held by independent, autonomous or private agents. As formulated in his 1919 lecture *Politics as a Vocation,* '[t]he entire process provides the perfect analogy to the development of a capitalist enterprise', culminating in the classical definition of the modern state, 'an institutional form of rule that has successfully fought to create a monopoly of legitimate physical force as a means of government within a particular territory' [12 pp 37-38]. This formulation was presented by Weber as a conceptual or general rule, rather than an iron law, but for almost a century offered the most useful normative encapsulation of the powers of security reserved by the ascendant nation-state. Within the present analysis the criterion of monopoly provides a standard with which some of the effects of globalization upon the meaning and role of both security and the nation-state can be assessed.

To claim that globalization entails the end or death of the nation is to fall into overstatement. Traditional ideas of the geographical nation as the purpose and centre of the state inevitably persist, but increasingly represent a shifting reality that no longer functions as the bounded container of an imagined homogeneous unity. The globalizing state is instead host to an overlapping diversity of identities, forms of association and ways of belonging, for which the nation is partial or contingent rather than essential and defining. Moreover, as the state becomes increasingly incorporated within transnational institutions it too is transformed. Concerns that were routinely divisible into national and international categories become blurred within global processes of interdependence and exchange, and the nation as sovereign territory becomes progressively less determinant of its activities and preoccupations. Relationships between states continue to be constructed in vocabularies of boundaries and limits that become points of instability and contingency rather than permanence and certainty, however, marking the nation-state as an entity in transition. Nation and state co-exist in increasingly de-coupled modes and the latter, which remains a primary site of power, is active transnationally and, in the formation of knowledge and interests, constituted fluidly.

This de-coupling of nation and state suggests a parallel reconsideration of the 'trumping' political primacy of sovereignty claims. In particular, attempts to grasp the territorially unbounded character of the threat posed by terrorism within the assumptions of the established international system are compromised from the outset. As the sociologist Ulrich Beck noted in the years prior to September 11, 2001, under conditions of globalization the challenge posed by terrorism 'loses its spatio-temporal limits and becomes global and lasting' [13 pg 36]. As such, global terrorism challenges the monopoly of violence, as does the production of the global PMC market in response. To pursue Weber's 'perfect analogy' beyond the nation-state, within a global environment no viable – that is, broadly liberal, democratic and capitalist in orientation – state, however powerful or hegemonic, can expect or desire to establish such a monopoly. But globalization and its multiplying complexities simultaneously imposes burdens upon nation -states, and generates calls upon established security mechanisms that can easily and unpredictably exceed its practical capacities, political will, and economic and human resources at any given point in time. In such a situation, the US, as the exemplary market-state [14] turns inevitably to the market. In consequence the commodification and privatisation of violence – the outsourcing of war – increasingly becomes the rule rather than the exception.

The market solution to the pressures of globalization is, arguably, in many respects an attractive one for a number of reasons. Most notably, as the innovators and entrepreneurs within the PMC market demonstrated, the private sector is able to respond more rapidly and imaginatively to unfolding situations than traditional state bureaucracies. In addition, the outsourcing of activities that might be considered either ethically or legally questionable creates a measure of distance and plausible deniability that permits states to establish a measure of distance from (some of) the means adopted in pursuit of their policies, especially those undertaken in controversial or politically inconvenient locations, whilst reaping the benefit of any positive outcomes. Perhaps most significantly, the extension of private enterprise and market mechanisms in this manner is of a piece with the ethos of liberal capitalism in general, and the neoconservative preferences of the incumbent US regime in particular, and so the policy fits neatly within the dominating ideas of the present. The coincidence of ideology, ends and means is therefore far from accidental.

The commodification of security, and the distancing through contract of the responsibilities of the commissioning bodies, thereby becomes a mechanism of disavowal inverting the Weberian monopoly that, in the modern era, defined and underwrote the legitimacy and self-sufficiency of the state in both external and (in, for example, the extent of private provision within Homeland Security in the US) ultimately domestic affairs. The effect of globalization upon security as revealed by the growth of the PMC sector is therefore the effacement of the boundaries, conceptual *and* territorial, of the nation-state. As the scale and scope of military activity increases, its control over and accountability for that activity diminishes, and the state can no longer act without contradiction in the guise and following the conventions of the Westphalian era.

Both the bare facts surrounding the unfolding events in Iraq, as well as the detailed interpretation of operations there and in the wider global campaign against terrorism will undoubtedly remain a staple of vexatious debate for the foreseeable future. Even if the civilian mortality estimate that 650,000 (one in four civilian Iraqis) have died since the invasion [15] is ultimately judged incorrect it is, however, beyond question that the outcome of operations undertaken to date has been one of tragically significant deterioration. Following the discussions of globalization and the nation-state, this unavoidably negative assessment invites consideration of the third – and thus far relatively unexamined concept – of security itself.

Pre-emptive regime change in Iraq has, regardless of long-term outcomes, provoked regional disturbance on a massive scale. It is not yet possible to assess Egyptian President Hosni Mubarak's prediction that 'instead of having one bin Laden, we will have 100' as a consequence of Operation Iraqi Freedom [16] but it unquestionable that, as presently constituted, the campaign in Iraq functions as a mechanism that generates and perpetuates its own basis, as surely as supply in any market produces demand for the goods and services that it provides. That this is the case is not directly or simply attributable either to globalization, or to the role taken up by PMCs in response to its security demands. The questions begged instead concern the adequacy of the martial and nationally grounded model of security that remains predominant, how security might be alternatively interpreted and pursued under conditions of globalization, and what form the requirements and characteristics of such a development might assume. The *prima facie* evidence noted in the brief course of this discussion is sufficient, for the present purposes, to establish the plausibility of the first contention concerning the inadequacy of prevailing security doctrines. The suggestion of the closing sections of the discussion is that the outlines of an alternative post-national conception of security and securitization interests is already available in the form of 'Human Security', a subject of extended debate within areas of international and development studies that has yet to be fully developed and applied to the problem of terror and terrorism. Moreover, subject to appropriate supplementation, reform and with the requisite political will, the fundamental framework of institutions and practices required for its further development and application is already, to a significant extent, in place within existing arrangements.

3. The Human Security Paradigm

The term 'Human Security' cannot be traced back to a single point of origin [17, 18], but its contemporary significance was announced in the form of policy orientations announced in the 1994 United Nations Development Program (UNDP) Human Development Report [19].

Within the practical shift initiated by the UNDP, Human Security invokes a transition in the interpretation of security from the politics of state, sovereignty, and military power towards a subjectively focused understanding of 'legitimate concerns of ordinary people…symbolized [by] protection from the threat of disease, hunger, unemployment, crime, social conflict, political repression, and environmental hazards' [19 pg 22]. A decade later the report of the UN High-level Panel on Threats, Challenges and Change identified 'harm to State or human security' as a 'basic criteria of legitimacy' in the justification of military intervention [20 pp 57; 85, italics added]. This individuation and reframing of security and its objectives was further endorsed in reform proposals advanced by the Secretary-General, ambitiously echoing the preamble to the 1946 charter document, under the title 'In Larger Freedom' [21 pg 35]. The conjunction of the formative objective of the UN – collective security – with individual freedom and non-territorialized development indicates the significant extension of the security remit that the HS initiative involves. The UN's variable fortunes in achieving its originally chartered mission also indicates the highly exacting nature of the challenge that reconciling individualism and globalization through Human Security poses. As such, HS is bound up with the emergence of a political accommodation that replaces the national security model with alternative transnational and multilateral norms, laws, treaties and institutions that are – in prospect if not yet fully in practice – individual in focus, universal in justification and global in application.

In keeping with the rapid unfolding of this global resecuritization, the scope and meanings of Human Security are as debated as they are diverse. This uncertainty has not, however, inhibited the progress of the term, which is variously conjoined with overlapping concerns including identity and migration, energy, health, welfare, environment, economics, food, water, and non-proliferation, to name but a few of the applications established in the course of UN deliberations and consolidated, in a recent survey of the field, under the subtitle 'an agenda for change' [22]. Setting the unquestioned interest and value of the individual contributions to this collection aside, amongst its most remarkable features is the silence of its authors on the location of HS in relation to established theories and modes of international relations, politics and economics.

The development of Human Security has, however, also generated a significant critical dialogue within security studies, and is by now established as a source of animated debate amongst analysts [23]. Whether it is welcomed as a pragmatically expansive container for responses to the burgeoning set of risks and threats that are now classified as security issues, or rejected as a vague and potentially damaging source of confusion, the impact of the concept in encouraging policy innovation and development is firmly established. The restaging of security entailed by the HS agenda remains in its early stages. Significantly, the relationships between HS established theories and concepts of international relations and politics in both theory and practice require development and clarification. If it is to be rendered distinct from, and avoid subsumption within, conventional models of security, HS must be firmly located within contexts of globalization and proliferating risk associated with the present terrorist threat. This emphasis counters the tendency towards the monolithic reproduction of conventional approaches demonstrated thus far in the prosecution of war against terror. Furthermore, maintaining this distinctiveness simultaneously creates a space of concept formation and action for Human Security that is, insofar as is practicable, independent of established conventions associated with security and securitization.

Human Security does not simply displace or substitute for its military counterpart, and there is no suggestion that a replacement for the provision of basic physical safety and the maintenance of order is envisaged. The HS challenge instead extends and complements extant understandings of security in a manner according priority to the protection, welfare, development, and fundamental interests of persons through their elementary human status, rather than through traditional enframing devices such as national, sovereign and territorial interests, or particularistic ascriptions of national, ethnic, religious or regional identities. Globalization exposes the fictitious and untenable character of such distinctions, and questions the legitimacy of interventions undertaken in their name. The requirement for justifications grounded in Human Security therefore constitutes an important, and more than symbolic, requirement that imposes equally significant obligations of conduct upon security operations, moving – albeit in an often uncertain and piecemeal manner – beyond the assumptions and interests of national security.

To reiterate, it is far from the case that globalization involves the redundancy of either nations or states, but the de-coupling and transformation of the concepts, combined with the increasingly transnational activities of the state and the institutions in which it is embedded, makes the evolution of security as indicated by Human Security as inevitable as it is desirable. Uncomfortable as it may at times be for advocates of tradition and *realpolitik,* the emergent trajectory of a range of security-related institutions is already established, if not always recognized, in the direction of Human Security. The detail and machinations surrounding these developments is beyond the scope of this discussion, but their significance and post-national credentials can nevertheless be readily conveyed in the activities of just three obvious multinational cases: the United Nations; NATO; and the European Union.

As the initiating force behind much of the Human Security agenda, the United Nations is an obvious point of focus. In addition to its Human Development initiatives, its commissions and offices in areas of Human Rights, Health, Migration and Refugee issues have raised awareness and undertaken significant emergency and remedial operations across the Human Security remit. The UN is of course a much-criticized institution, especially in respect of its arcane structure and the conduct of the Security Council, a governing body that is an artifact of the cold war and which, perversely but not unsurprisingly, deforms the foremost global institution with the perceived interests and *amour-propre* of nation-states that are as resistant to reform as they are reluctant to acknowledge the passing of the era of great powers acting autonomously. Undeniably, the UN – as with all institutions – is marked by failure. In addition to Iraq, recent failures of intervention in Rwanda (1994), Bosnia (1995) and, since 2003, in Darfur offer grounds for a pointed indictment of the institution [24]. The case made by criticism of the UN and its satellite bodies even – perhaps especially – in its most vituperative modes is, however, paradoxically positive. Quixotic calls for the abolition of the UN merely invite speculation on the consequences, certain to be disastrous, of its abandonment. In so doing the case for appropriate reform of its mechanisms and processes, an acknowledged necessity [19], is only strengthened. The process of negotiation and reform is undeniably difficult and ineluctably slow. These factors do not, however, undermine the claims of HS – instead they serve to underline its importance to its future development.

NATO, like the UN, was founded (1949) in a period dominated by the Cold War, and in its predominantly West European mission was the successful guarantor of security in the period of relatively stable hostility, preceding the fall of the Berlin Wall, towards which nostalgics increasingly look back with warmth. Since then, however, NATO has increasingly taken on roles across the globe, most recently with the ISAF force active in Afghanistan, but also in Iraq, Darfur and on more 'natural' territory in the KFOR mission in Bosnia. In addition, however, NATO forces have made major contributions to disaster relief in Indonesia, Houston and Pakistan, evolving from its military origins towards a revised identity as a risk community [25] with a global as well as regional basis through increasing projected partnership and co-operation agreements, notably within Oceania [26], that promise to extend its mission globally. Humanitarian assistance in these cases may initially appear at some remove from the response to terrorism, but as part of an integrated conception of human security they prospectively address the conditions and difficulties that become proving and recruiting grounds for terror and terrorists. In this way the indirect route of humanitarian action can, by helping to establish and maintain human security, constitute an earlier, more efficient and more effective pre-emptive intervention against terrorism than subsequent military-oriented action.

In a related manner, the European Union (EU) can be viewed from the perspective of human security as an unlikely but highly significant institution. Although made up of nation-states (some of whom, such as the United Kingdom, maintain a measure of skeptical ambivalence towards membership) the European Union is, in embryo at least, a truly post-national institution in that its constituents cede a portion of their sovereign jurisdiction to its legal and democratic institutions, and participate collectively in its various bodies, including a parliament democratically elected (albeit often with limited enthusiasm) by its entire citizenry. Despite well-founded concerns regarding bureaucracy and inefficiency, the halting attempt to secure support for a proposed constitution, and even fundamental divisions over its purpose and future expansion, the EU as an institution has arguably done more to promote security in Europe since its inception than any other institutional form. Because it involves a pooling of sovereignty, and focuses upon diplomatic, economic and developmental issues within targeted regions as well as national territories, EU membership and the benefits that it secures has helped to steer nations through periods of instability and insecurity. In many respects it can in fact be interpreted as acting, in all but name, as a guarantor of human security within an expanding territorial zone many years before the UNDP specified the term in its 1994 report.

As a putative 'postmodern state' [27] the EU is also increasingly adopting the self-image of a Security Community embracing the HS agenda in a thoroughgoing manner, as evidenced by the recent policy doctrine [28] presented to Javier Solana, the EU High Representative for Common Foreign and Security Policy. This document projects a future orientation for the EU that is explicitly predicated on the protection of human rights and the extension of the HS agenda throughout its activities. Such proposals are, at the time of writing, subject to debate and development, but indicate a clear direction that promises to consolidate the already significant security achievements of the EU.

The UN, NATO and the EU do not of course stand alone. Their activities overlap and interact, and a more comprehensive institutional review would conspicuously include – amongst other bodies – the global jurisprudence being pioneered by the International Criminal Court, and the wealth of non-governmental organizations that contribute to an increasingly integrated and effective global civil society which also, consciously or otherwise, promotes and provides goods that coincide with the Human Security agenda. Emphasis is required upon the harsh reality that HS, no more than any other programme or concept, cannot offer a panacea or simple ideal sufficient to secure globalization and its potential benefits against terrorism or any other threat. The development of increasingly post-national, post-sovereign institutions characterized by binding processes of negotiation and conciliation does, however, enable the prospective extension of co-operative rather than competitive conceptions of securitization interests and of the strategies suited to their mitigation and management.

Although the obstacles of petty nationalism and entrenched interests will inevitably persist, if Human Security is pursued, resourced, and politically supported in a sustained and consistently manner – for which there is already persuasive evidence – then development, protection and security can combine in order to promote and enhance mechanisms of postnational co-operation and governance on a potentially global scale. With regard to the question of terror, Human Security incorporates a range of domains and functions that exceed conventional definitions, but which are central to the development of an effective multilateral response to terrorism, and to the environments within which it has historically prospered.

4. Concluding Remarks

In October 2006 General Sir Richard Dannat, as chief of the general staff the UK armed forces' highest-ranking officer, candidly acknowledged that British forces should 'get themselves out sometime soon because our presence exacerbates security problems', and noted that although 'the difficulties we are experiencing around the world' are not directly caused by the presence of foreign forces in Iraq, 'undoubtedly our presence in Iraq exacerbates them' [29]. The brief political furore generated by these observations largely obscured their underlying force, which engages not only the consequences incumbent on any operation that is unable to solicit or maintain the consent, however, grudging, of the host population. At a deeper level General Dannat was acknowledging the limits of physical and force-based models of security in an era of globalization, and the consequences of those limits outwith territorial markers that no longer function as boundaries to focus and contain violence, yet continue to generate and motivate it. Furthermore, the dilemma of global security cannot be adequately addressed by the conjunction of private interests competing in a global marketplace. As recent experience demonstrates, doing so, even with the best intentions and clearest objectives, contributes to global cycles of violence and resentment even in situations where immediate local objectives are achieved. PMCs are not the cause of proliferating violence and insecurity, but their role and growth is symptomatic of the impact of globalization and its attendant commodification upon functions conventionally arrogated exclusively to the modern state. As such it is indicative of the requirement for a more expansive and appropriately deterritorialized interpretation of security and securitization interests for a progressively post-sovereign geopolitical climate.

Under conditions of globalization responses to terrorism require inter- and intra-national formulation, in a coordinated manner, by agencies acting in concert on a series of political, economic, diplomatic and military levels with the shared objective of managing collectively experienced risk. Such an approach aims to pre-emptively address the potential as well as actual exposure to acts of terror and random violence rather than persisting with policies predicated upon on a model of the modern sovereign nation-state that has proved elusive from the time of its inception in the 1648 Peace of Wesphalia, and is increasingly as obstructive as it is irrelevant to the creation and maintenance of the conditions and requirements that are condensed within the exacting and challenging, but nonetheless practically-oriented, concept of Human Security.

The outsourcing of both terrorism and of counter-terrorism in the opening years of the 21st century is a telling development, but represents only one mode of globalization and need not be its dominant form. Security is no longer a problem that can be contained, resolved or even managed by nation-states following conventional military doctrines. Nor, however, can it be addressed by the extension of these doctrines to a global marketplace, which merely relocates and reproduces dilemmas posed by globalization. The Human Security agenda does not offer a ready-made programme for securing globalization, or a panacea for the security problems that it generates. It does, however, elucidate issues and processes with the potential to address, at least provisionally, sources of instability contributing to the production of terror, and to develop mechanisms that are innovative and, most significantly, grounded in post-national presuppositions regarding the location of human interests and the concomitant objectives of appropriately determined security policies. In this way (and, perhaps, this way alone) paradoxical consequences of the globalization of terror can be addressed, and global security and the security of globalization reconciled, through a developing framework of appropriately global and interdependent concepts and institutions.

References

[1]   P.W. Singer, Corporate warriors, *International Security* **26**/3 (2001), 186-220.
[2]   C. Brown, Front-line troops to get £2,240 bonus, *The Independent*. London: 2006, Oct 11, p.19.
[3]   T. Harding, Crisis as SAS men quit for lucrative Iraq jobs, *The Daily Telegraph*. London: 2005, Feb 14, p. 1.
[4]   J. Wilson, US lowers standards in army numbers crisis, *The Guardian*. London: 2005, June 4, p. 14.
[5]   T.W. Galdi, *Revolution in military affairs? Competing concepts, organizational responses, outstanding issues*. Washington DC: Congressional Research Service Report CRS 95-1170F. 1995.
[6]   S.M. Hersh, *Chain of command*. London: Penguin; 2005.
[7]   S. Makki, Business of war, *Le Monde Diplomatique*, 2004. [Online] Available from; URL: http://mondediplo.com/2004/11/08iraq [2005, February 20].
[8]   D. Isenberg, A fistful of contractors: The case for a pragmatic assessment of private military companies in Iraq. BASIC Research Report 2004, London: British-American Security Information Council; 2004.
[9]   S. Armstrong, The enforcer, *The Guardian*. London; 2006, May 20, p. 12.
[10] J. Dao, Private US Guards take big risk for right price, *The New York Times*, 2004, April 2, p. 1.
[11] J. Didion, Cheney: The fatal touch, *The New York Review of Books*, **53**/15 (2006). [Online] Available from; URL: http://www.nyrb.com/ [2002, October 12].
[12] M. Weber, *The vocation lectures*, In D. Owen, T.B. Strong, Editors. (Translator, R. Livingstone), Indianapolis, IN: Hackett; 2004.
[13] U. Beck, *World risk society*. Cambridge: Polity Press; 1999.
[14] P. Bobbitt, *The shield of Achilles: War, peace and the course of history*. London: Penguin Books; 2002.
[15] G. Burnham, R. Lafta, S. Doocy, L. Roberts, Mortality after the 2003 invasion of Iraq: A cross-sectional cluster sample survey, *The Lancet*. London; 2006, September 12. [Online] Available from; URL: http://www.thelancet.com [2006, October 12].
[16] I. Black, C. McGreal, Conflict will create 100 bin Ladens, warns Egyptian president, *The Guardian*. London; 2003, April 1.

[17] D. Henk, Human security: Relevance and implications, *Parameters,* **XXXV/2** (2005), 91-106.

[18] E. Newman, Human security and constructivism. *International Studies Perspectives* **2** (2001), 239-251.

[19] UNDP, *Human development report.* New York: Oxford University Press; 1994.

[20] UN, *A more secure world: our shared responsibility.* Report of the Secretary General's high-level panel on threats, challenges and change. A/59/565, United Nations, New York; 2004.

[21] UN, *In larger freedom: Towards development, security and human rights for all.* Report of the Secretary General. A/59/2005. United Nations, New York; 2005.

[22] F. Dodds, T. Pippard, Editors. *Human and environmental security: An agenda for change.* London: Earthscan; 2005.

[23] T. Owen, Human security – conflict, critique and consensus: Colloquium remarks and a proposal for a threshold-based definition. *Security Dialogue* **35/3** (2004), 373-387.

[24] A. LeBor, *Complicity with evil: The United Nations in the age of modern genocide.* New Haven: Yale University Press; 2006.

[25] C. Coker, *Globalization and insecurity in the twenty-first century: NATO and the management of risk.* Adelphi Paper 345. London: International Institute for Strategic Studies; 2002.

[26] I. Daalder, J. Goldgeiger, Global NATO, *Foreign Affairs,* 2006, September. [Online] Available from; URL: http://www.foreignaffairs.org/ [2006, October 12].

[27] R. Cooper, *The breaking of nations: Order and chaos in the twenty-first century.* London: Atlantic Books; 2003.

[28] U. Albrecht, et. al. *A human security doctrine for Europe: The Barcelona report of the study group on Europe's security capabilities.* Barcelona: Caixa Catalunya; 2004.

[29] C. Brown, T. Judd, A. Buncome, Blair devastated as Army chief savages his approach to Iraq, *The Independent.* London; 2006, October 14, p. 2.

Author Index